Published by
Legends Publishing

E-mail david@legendspublishing.net
Website www.legendspublishing.net

A note on the text:
Throughout this book we have omitted Women's or Ladies wherever possible since it seems superfluous. It is only used where there could be confusion with the men's game and to distinguish Cardiff City Ladies (who compete in English football) from Cardiff City Women (who compete in Welsh football), Leicester City Ladies from Leicester City Women and to give a clearer distinction between Southampton Saints and Southampton Women.

Photo credits:
Front cover photos – courtesy of Colorsport
Arsenal's Jordan Nobbs – courtesy of The FA/Robin Parker
Birmingham City's Aoife Mannion –
courtesy of Birmingham City Women FC
Brighton & Hove Albion's Kirsty Barton – courtesy of The FA
Bristol City's Carla Humphrey – courtesy of Bristol City Women FC
Chelsea's Fran Kirby – courtesy of Chelsea FC
Everton's Faye Bryson – courtesy of The FA/Paul Greenwood
Liverpool's Neil Redfearn – courtesy of Liverpool FC/Nick Taylor
Manchester City's Nikita Parris –
courtesy of Tom Flathers/Manchester City FC
Reading's Jade Moore – courtesy of the FA/Kieran McManus
Yeovil Town's Megan Walsh – courtesy of Yeovil Town Ladies FC

Gilly Flaherty of West Ham United – courtesy of WHU FC Women
Aston Villa's Gemma Davies – courtesy of Aston Villa Ladies FC
Manchester United's Casey Stoney– courtesy of The FA/Lynne Cameron
Actonians photo – courtesy of @sniperpose
Bradford City photo – courtesy of Paul2Paul Photography
Coventry United photo – courtesy of Jeff Bennett
Enfield Town photo – courtesy of @MikeyTheTowner
Nottingham Forest photo – courtesy of Lee Samcro
Poole Town photo – courtesy of Nadia Lonnen
Swindon Town photo – courtesy of @SwindonTownLFC
Watford photo – courtesy of AW Images
Wolverhampton Wanderers photo – courtesy of Simon Faulkner

WOMEN'S FOOTBALL
YEARBOOK
2018-19

CONTENTS

2018/19 (Tier 1)

Arsenal **46**
Birmingham City **51**
Brighton & Hove Albion   **56**
Bristol City   **61**
Chelsea   **66**
Everton   **73**
Liverpool   **77**
Manchester City   **82**
Reading   **88**
West Ham United   **93**
Yeovil Town   **99**

2018/19 (Tier 2)

Aston Villa   **106**
Charlton Athletic   **110**
Crystal Palace   **116**
Durham   **121**
Leicester City Women   **125**
Lewes   **130**
London Bees   **135**
Manchester United   **139**
Millwall Lionesses   **141**
Sheffield United   **145**
Tottenham Hotspur   **150**

2018/19 (Tiers 3-4)
(includes teams relegated from Tier 4 at end of 2017/18)

Actonians   **166**
AFC Wimbledon   **169**
Barnsley   **172**
Basingstoke Town   **175**
Bedworth United   **177**
Billericay Town   **180**
Birmingham & West Midlands   **182**
Blackburn Rovers   **184**
Bolton Wanderers   **187**
Bradford City   **190**
Brighouse Town   **193**
Brislington   **196**
Buckland Athletic   **199**
Burnley   **201**
Burton Albion   **205**
C&K Basildon   **207**
Cambridge United   **210**
Cardiff City Ladies   **212**
Cheltenham Town   **214**
Chesham United   **216**
Chester-le-Street Town   **218**
Chichester City   **220**
Chorley   **222**
Coventry United   **225**
Crawley Wasps   **228**
Crewe Alexandra   **231**
Denham United   **234**
Derby County   **236**
Doncaster Rovers Belles   **239**
Enfield Town   **242**
Fylde   **244**
Gillingham   **247**

AUTHOR'S NOTE

I had the idea for the book in 2017 and immediately asked Tom Garry to work on it with me, given his comprehensive knowledge of women's football. We had a publisher and a sponsor lined up for 'The First Ever Women's Football Yearbook 2017/18' but unfortunately they pulled out when the majority of our work had been done. We decided to push ahead and self-publish at considerable cost to ourselves. We just about managed to cover those costs. The book gained many positive reviews and was included in the Guardian's Best Sports Books of 2017 article. We were delighted when David Lane at Legends Publishing agreed to take on the book for 2018/19.

While putting together the book I have learnt so much about life at all levels of the game. Outside of the very top clubs women's football is held together by the extraordinary work of volunteers. Players pay to play, coaches give up their time to coach and so many others do so much to keep their clubs going. I have decided to donate 50% of any royalties I receive from the Women's Football Yearbook 2018/19 to player sponsorship. Every copy sold will therefore play a part in growing the women's game. I really hope you enjoy the book.

Chris Slegg

FOREWORD

The 2018/19 season has the capacity to be the most exciting since the launch of the WSL era. Next summer the World Cup takes place. We have top players from across the world performing week in and week out in our domestic League and many of them will be playing for their place on the plane to France.

Among them of course our very own England players, and, for the first time ever, players from Scotland too. Every time you pull on your national shirt it is a memory to treasure. I went to two World Cups and I will never forget those experiences. England are now established as one of the strongest teams on the world stage, having finished third at the last World Cup and reached the semi-finals of Euro 2017. Hopefully now the younger players in the squad will go on to experience playing in major tournaments on a regular basis. There's simply nothing like representing your country in a World Cup.

In the FA Women's Super League it's going to be a massive year. The division is a fully professional set-up for the very first time. The impact that could have on young girls, knowing that a career as a professional footballer is a possibility, will be huge. I almost wish I could be a kid once more and start out all over again. When I was younger all your role models were male players. You almost felt like you didn't know if this was a sport for you, and you didn't know if you should be playing because there were no women to look up to. I would love to know what it is like to be a youngster now and have the feeling that football is just as much a sport for you as it is for the boys. There were of course women doing amazing things in football, women who were great pioneers. But their work wasn't visible to the mainstream. You had to know where to look, and even when you knew where to look you had to look hard to find them.

Not everyone who aspires to be a professional player will make it, but perhaps some will be inspired to get into coaching, refereeing, the medical staff or the media. Sport and football in particular, can open up a whole range of possibilities regarding careers. It's great to see so many young boys following the sport too. They know the names of the top women players now, just like they do with the top men's players. I'm sure there will be great interest from young boys and girls in the World Cup next summer. When that generation grows up, and when all they have ever known is that it is just as normal for women to play football as it is for men, then we will really start to reap the rewards.

The possibilities are endless. We are slowly getting there on the media side of things now with more games being shown on television and big events like Euro 2017, World Cup qualifiers and the FA Cup final attracting huge audiences. Outside of the WSL we have new names in the FA Women's Championship too. Perhaps unsurprisingly, much of the media attention has been on Manchester United. Having one of the biggest clubs in the world now operating a women's

FAYE WHITE PROUDLY HOLDING THE FA CUP HER ARSENAL TEAM WON IN 2008

team can only help grow the sport. Other newcomers to the second tier like Charlton, Crystal Palace, Leicester and Lewes have all been doing amazing work to take the game to a higher level. Below the Championship we also have an army of great clubs in the FA Women's National League where volunteers do an incredible job to give young players their first opportunities and provide a pathway into the sport.

It's wonderful to see that we now have our very own 'Women's Football Yearbook' too, something the men's game has benefited from since the 1970s. I am sure it will help give many people a greater understanding of the many clubs operating at all different levels in England and that it will play its own small role in the revolution women's football is undergoing.

Whichever team you follow, have a wonderful 2018/19 season.

Faye White MBE
Former England and Arsenal Captain

A TRIBUTE TO NETTIE J

The glitz and glamour of the WSL; crowds of 45,000-plus at Wembley for the FA Cup final; England's semi-final appearances at the 2015 World Cup and Euro 2017; television audiences of more than four million viewers. Would any of this have been possible without Nettie J. Honeyball, founder of the British Ladies' Football Club in 1894?

Fearing the consequences of revealing her true identity, due to the anger directed, by some, at women playing football, Nettie J. Honeyball was a pseudonym. Many believe her to have been Dublin-born London resident Mary Hutson. The Women's Football Yearbook is dedicated to the sport's greatest pioneer. Thank you Nettie J. Honeyball.

LADY FOOTBALLERS AT PLAY

The first match of the British Ladies' Football Club was played on Saturday at Hornsey, but cannot be pronounced a success either from an athletic or a spectacular point of view. Miss Nettie J Honeyball is the moving spirit of the lady footballers. The players belong mainly to London and the suburbs, but a few hail from the country. They are described as chiefly young ladies of independant means, whose parents can afford to keep them without work, though a few are married women. Saturday's match was played at Crouch End Athletic Ground, Hornsey, before a gathering numbering over ten thousand people, about a quarter of whom were female.

March 30, 1895

ACKNOWLEDGEMENTS

'The First Ever Women's Football Yearbook' was published in October 2017 after it occurred to us that men's football had had a yearbook since 1970/71 but that women's football in England had never had one. We are delighted to be back with a second edition for 2018/19, and there are so many people to thank.

Thanks to all the WSL, Championship and WNL clubs for their co-operation. We made efforts to contact every club to verify information and we are extremely grateful to those who responded. If our voicemails and emails did not find the appropriate people who are currently at some of the clubs, then we do apologise. We made our very best attempts to track people down.

Thanks also to Emily Liles, Nick Frith, Nick Smith, David Gerty, and Greg Demetriou at the FA. A huge thanks to WSL players and managers Aoife Mannion, Kirsty Barton, Carla Humphrey, Fran Kirby, Faye Bryson, Jasmine Matthews, Nikita Parris, Jade Moore, Gilly Flaherty and Megan Walsh for taking the time to speak to us. It was an honour and a privilege that former England and Arsenal captain Faye White – one of our country's most decorated players – agreed to write the foreword.

There are many more people, clubs and organisations to thank than those who appear on this list, but we are particularly grateful to: Actonians (Daniel Chitty and Linda Fox); AFC Wimbledon (John Ivers); Barnsley (Stephen Gates, Rachel Jardine and Duncan Ward); Basingstoke Town (Annaliese Watson); Berks & Bucks FA (Chris Cole); Birmingham City (Zoe Jones); Birmingham & West Midlands (Helen Carver); Brislington Town (Sharon Whelan); Bristol City (Jack Pitt); Buckland Athletic (Grant Fisher); Burnley (Matthew Bee, Sinead Kennedy-Peers and Martin Smith); C&K Basildon (Peter King); Cambridgeshire FA; Cardiff City Ladies (Karen Jones); Charlton Athletic (Stephen King); Cheltenham Town (Ian Purvis); Chesham United (Lisa Welling and Sian Williams); Chichester City (Caroline Henry-Evans and Hayley Newman); Chorley (Geoff Dawson and James Dawson); Crawley Wasps (Andrew Raeburn); Crewe Alexandra (Katie Nuttall); Crystal Palace (Dean Davenport and Richard Spokes); Denham United (Joanne Currivan); Derby County (Andy Moore); East Riding FA (Liz Shipp); Enfield Town (Michael Bunyan); Everton (Aaron Little); Fylde (Ailsa Cowen); Gillingham (Julian Hart); Guiseley Vixens (Glen Pearson); Huddersfield Town (David Mallin); Hull City (Rachel Gay); Ipswich Town (Ralph Pruden); Leicester City Ladies (Sue Foulkes); Leicester City Women (Dan Smith); Lewes (Ash Head); Leyton Orient (Chris Brayford); London Bees (Luke Swindlehurst); London FA (Dwayne Ellis and Calum Opere-Hoyal); Long Eaton United (Katherine Clarke); Loughborough Foxes (Steve Wilkinson); Liverpool Marshall Feds (Chantelle Thompson); Luton Town (David Baker); Manchester City (Mercedes Antrobus); Manchester FA (Paul Roots); Middlesbrough (Amy Cowan); Milton Keynes Dons (Karen Dean and Owen Evans); Millwall Lionesses (Dan Logue); Morecambe (Nick Barrett); Newcastle United (Lisa Bell); Norton (Victoria Burton); Norwich City (Mel Swift); Portsmouth (Bill Griffiths); QPR (Andy Watkins); Radcliffe Olympic (Alex Saulter); Reading (Russ Fraser); Rotherham United (Simon Darke); Sheffield United (Lee Walshaw); Solihull Moors (Sarah Westwood); Southampton Saints (Tracey Wheeler); Southampton Women (Amanda Burroughs); St Nicholas (Iain Prior and John Seymour); Stevenage (Reece Buck and Dave Potter); Stoke City (James Knowles); The New Saints (Andy Williams); Watford (Ed Henderson); West Bromwich Albion (Dale Brookes); Wolverhampton Wanderers (Jenny Wilkes) and many, many more.

A BRIEF HISTORY

1881: The first recorded women's international takes place in Edinburgh, in May, with Scotland beating England 3-0. Lily St Clair scores the opening goal. Four days later, in Glasgow, another match between the teams is abandoned when hundreds of male spectators run on to the pitch and fighting breaks out. Some reports suggest the majority of those fans did not approve of women playing.

1894: Nettie J. Honeyball and Florence Dixie place newspaper adverts for players, which leads to the foundation of the British Ladies' Football Club (BLFC) the following year. Its primary aim is to provide football-playing opportunities for girls and women, but it also aspires to make money from the game. Nettie J. Honeyball was a pseudonym and her true identity is still not certain though many believe her real name to have been Mary Hutson.

1895: The first official women's football match takes place under the auspices of the BLFC with North (red) beating South (light and dark blue) 7-1 in front of an estimated crowd of 10,000 at Crouch End in London on 23 March. Reports differ as to whether the teams represented the North and South of England, or of London.

1917: A Preston-based munitions factory called Dick, Kerr and Co. (named after William Dick and John Kerr), sets up a women's team called Dick, Kerr's Ladies.

1920: Dick, Kerr's Ladies (representing England) beat a France XI 2-0. A crowd of 25,000 watches on at Deepdale, the home of Preston FC men's side. The two teams meet three more times in quick succession with Dick, Kerr's again winning, 5-2 at Stockport, before a 1-1 draw in Manchester. The final match is played at Stamford Bridge with France winning 2-1. Later in the year Dick, Kerr's play a four-match series against a France XI. The first three matches in Paris, Roubaix and Le Havre finish in draws with Dick, Kerr's winning the final match in Rouen. The tours generate huge interest and on Boxing Day 1920, a crowd of 53,000 comes to Goodison Park – home of men's team Everton – to witness Dick, Kerr's Ladies beat St Helen's 4-0. To this day the attendance is still a record for a domestic women's match in England. There are reports that a further 14,000 fans have been locked out due to overcrowding. More than £3,000 (well in excess of £100,000 in today's money) is believed to have been raised for charity.

1921: The FA bans associated clubs from allowing women to play matches on their grounds. Their edict reads: 'The game of football is quite unsuitable for females and ought not to be encouraged.'

1922: With women's teams continuing to play wherever they can, Dick, Kerr's take a tour to Canada. On arrival the Dominion Football Association tells them they will not be allowed to play anywhere because it objects to women's football. The team instead heads to the US and

PORTSMOUTH LADIES PLAY A BENEFIT MATCH DURING WORLD WAR ONE

takes on nine US men's teams. They lose to Paterson FC in the first match with US goalkeeper Peter Renzulli recalling in an interview given years later: 'We were national champions and we had a hell of a job beating them.'

1926: The name of Dick, Kerr's Ladies is changed to Preston Ladies following a disagreement between the team's manager Alfred Frankland and the owners.

1937: Preston Ladies beat the best team in Scotland, Edinburgh Ladies, 5-1 to earn the title of the first unofficial World Champions. Preston Ladies are believed to have continued to attract crowds of 5,000 throughout the 1930s despite having to play their matches away from Football League grounds because of the FA ban.

1965: Preston Ladies fold due to a lack of players. The difficult decision is taken by Kath Latham who has served as the club's first female manager since the death of Alfred Frankland in 1957. She had previously been helping Frankland with the secretarial duties.

1969: The Women's Football Association (WFA), a separate entity from the FA, is founded with 44 member clubs. An unofficial European Championship – known as the European Competition for Women's Football – takes place for the first time. The tournament features four teams with all the matches played in Italy. The hosts beat France 1-0 in their semi-final in Novara with England losing the other semi-final 4-3 to Denmark in Aosta. In the third-place match England beat France 2-0 in Turin. Italy take the title as they defeat Denmark 3-1 in the final which is also played in Turin.

1971: The FA lifts the ban on women playing on Football League grounds, 50 years after it was enforced. The first Women's FA Cup final takes place that same year with Southampton beating Scottish side Stewarton and Thistle 4-1 at the Crystal Palace National Sports Centre in South London. At the time the competition is known as the Mitre Challenge Trophy.
1972: The first official women's international in Great Britain takes place with England beating Scotland 3-2 at Greenock.

1979: A second, still unofficial, European Competition for Women's Football is held a decade after the first. Italy are again hosts, but this time 12 teams take part. The winners of each of four groups of three contest the semi-finals. Italy beat England 3-1 in the last four and Denmark are 1-0 victors against Sweden. England finish fourth, losing the third-place match on penalties to Sweden after a goalless draw. Just as they did in 1969 Italy and Denmark meet in the final, but this time the Danes are 2-0 winners.

1983: The FA forms links with the WFA, inviting it to affiliate on the same basis as County Football Associations.

1984: The first official European Championship takes place. It is still known as the European Competition for Women's Football, but the 1984 edition is played under UEFA auspices. There is no single host nation. England reach the final against Sweden which is played over two legs. The Three Lionesses lose 1-0 in Gothenburg but win by the same score-line at Kenilworth Road in Luton only to lose 4-3 on penalties.

1987: Hosts Norway win the second official UEFA European Competition for Women's Football beating Sweden 2-1 in the final. England lose the third-place match 2-1 to Italy.

1988: FIFA stages a test event to help gauge whether an international tournament for women is viable. The 1988 FIFA Women's Invitational Tournament takes place in China from 1–12 June. The 12 teams compete in three groups of four prior to quarter-finals, semi-finals, a third-place match and the final. Norway beat Sweden 1-0 in the final in Guangzhou.

1989: Hosts West Germany win the third official UEFA European Competition for Women's Football thanks to a 4-1 win over Norway in the final.

1991: The FA launches its first National League with 24 clubs involved. The first FIFA Women's World Cup takes place in China. The format is the same as the 1988 test event with 12 teams competing in three groups of four prior to quarter-finals, semi-finals, a third-place match and the final. USA become the first world champions, beating Norway 2-1 in the final in Guangzhou. The competition is regarded as the first official FIFA Women's World Cup and is known as the 1st FIFA World Championship for Women's Football for the M&M's Cup. Earlier in the year Denmark host the fourth official European Championship, and the first to be known by that name. Germany beat Norway 3-1 after extra-time in the final.

1993: The FA takes over the running of the main national cup competition for women and rebrands it as the Women's FA Challenge Cup. A Women's Football Committee, and the post of women's football coordinator are also introduced at the FA. Italy host Euro 1993 and lose the final 1-0 to Norway in Cesena.

1994: The Women's National League is also brought under the control of the FA and is known as the FA Women's Premier League (FAWPL).

1995: The second official World Cup, and the first to be known as the FIFA Women's World Cup, takes place in Sweden. England are present for the first time and reach the quarter-finals where they lose 3-0 to Germany. Norway beat Germany 2-0 in the final. Earlier in the year England reach the semi-finals of Euro 1995. With no single host nation for the competition, the Three Lionesses lose a two-leg semi-final 6-2 on aggregate to Germany who go on to beat Sweden 3-2 in the final in Kaiserslautern.

1996: Women's football is introduced to the Olympic programme for the first time for Atlanta 1996. Hosts USA beat China in the final.

1997: Norway and Sweden co-host Euro 1997 with Germany beating Italy 2-0 in the final in Oslo.

1998: The FA appoints its first full-time coach for the England women's international team – Hope Powell. The FA also sets up the first 20 centres of excellence for girls and attains sponsors for the League and Cup competitions.

1999: USA hosts the World Cup which is expanded to 16 teams and draws huge crowds. A world record crowd for a women's match of 90,185 attends the final at the Rose Bowl in Pasadena, California, where the hosts beat China 5-4 on penalties following a goalless draw. Brandi Chastain converts the winning penalty kick. What becomes an iconic celebration follows as she spontaneously takes off her jersey, clenches her fists and drops to her knees in her black sports bra.

2000: Norway beat defending champions USA 3-2 with a golden goal in the Olympic final in Sydney.

2001: Germany host Euro 2001 and beat Sweden 1-0 with an extra-time golden goal scored by Claudia Muller in the final.

2002: The FA celebrates football becoming the top participation sport for girls and women in England three years ahead of schedule. The first women's Champions League final, at the time bearing the name the UEFA Cup, sees German side Frankfurt beat Umea of Sweden 2-0.

2003: USA stands in to host the World Cup for the second finals in succession. China had been due to stage the tournament, but a switch is required after the outbreak of the SARS virus. The hosts finish third with Germany beating Sweden 2-1 with an extra-time golden goal in the final.

2004: USA regain their Olympic title by beating Brazil after extra-time in the final in Sydney. The golden goal has been replaced by the silver goal in all FIFA competitions whereby if the teams are separated after 15 minutes of extra-time then no second period of extra-time is played. However Abby Wambach's winner comes seven minutes into the second period of extra-time.

2005: England host the European Championship. A television audience of 2.9 million watches the hosts' opening match against Finland live on BBC Two. A crowd of 29,092 is also present at the City of Manchester Stadium for a thrilling match. England let a 2-0 lead slip and appear to have thrown away the win when Sweden's Laura Kalmari makes it 2-2 with two minutes to play. But 17-year-old Karen Carney hits a dramatic injury-time winner. Unfortunately England fail to make it to the knockout stages as they lose their next two group games to Denmark and Sweden. Germany eventually beat Norway 3-1 in the final in front of 21,105 people at Blackburn's Ewood Park.

2007: Arsenal become the first English team to win Europe's most prestigious prize as they beat Swedish side Umea 1-0 on aggregate over two legs in the UEFA Cup final (later to become the UEFA Women's Champions League). China host the World Cup. England – who have qualified for the first time since 1995 – reach the quarter-finals where they are beaten 3-0 by USA who eventually finish third. Germany are 2-0 victors against Brazil in the final in Shanghai.

2008: Arsenal suffer their first defeat in more than 50 games as Everton pull off a huge shock in the FA Women's Premier League Cup final with a 1-0 win at Brisbane Road. The Gunners do complete the League and FA Cup double though. A then-record FA Cup final crowd of 24,582 watches the match at Nottingham Forest's City Ground where Arsenal beat Leeds 4-1. On the international front USA make it three gold medals from the four Olympic football tournaments played to date. They beat Brazil 1-0 after extra-time in the final in Beijing. The first Cyprus Cup – a global invitational tournament – is held. Canada beat USA 3-2 in the final in Nicosia.

2009: Arsenal continue their dominance of English football by winning the Treble of League, FA Cup and Premier League Cup. It's their sixth consecutive League title. England enter the Cyprus Cup for the first time and win it, beating Canada 3-1 in the final. Finland host Euro 2009 where England reach the final only to lose 6-2 to Germany. The Germans have now won seven of the last eight European Championships. The UEFA Cup is rebranded the UEFA Women's Champions League from the start of the 2009/10 season.

2010: It's a seventh straight League title for Arsenal, but there are different winners of the Cup competitions with Everton claiming the FA Cup and Leeds (then known as Leeds Carnegie) lifting the Premier League Cup. The FA announces that a new competition for the top sides in English football will launch next spring. It will be known as the Women's Super League and will run throughout the summer.

2011: The first Women's Super League contains just eight teams. Arsenal beat Chelsea 1-0 in the first ever match which is played in Tooting and eventually go on to be the inaugural WSL champions. Having also won the 2010/11 FA Cup, the Gunners make it three domestic trophies in a calendar year by winning the first WSL Continental Cup. Germany stage the World Cup where England reach the quarter-finals but they lose on penalties to France after a 1-1 draw. Japan win the tournament for the first time as they beat USA on penalty kicks following a 2-2 draw in the final.

2012: Team GB reach the quarter-finals of the Olympics where they are beaten by Canada. A crowd of 80,203 – a record for a women's Olympic football match – watches the final at Wembley where USA beat Japan 2-1. It's a successful year for England as they qualify unbeaten for Euro 2013. On the domestic front Arsenal retain their WSL title, Birmingham City win the FA Cup for the first time as they beat Chelsea on penalties following a 2-2 draw. Arsenal and Birmingham contest the WSL Continental Cup final with the Gunners prevailing 1-0.

2013: England win the Cyprus Cup for a second time beating Canada 1-0 in the final. Optimism ahead of Euro 2013 in Sweden soon dissipates as the team finishes bottom of the group. After the tournament Hope Powell – who has overseen 162 matches during her 15 years as manager – leaves her post and is replaced by Bristol Academy manager Mark Sampson. Germany claim their eighth continental title with a 1-0 win over Norway in the final. On the domestic front there are new winners of the WSL as Liverpool are crowned champions. Arsenal beat Bristol Academy 3-0 in the FA Cup final and complete a Cup double thanks to a 2-0 success over Lincoln in the WSL Continental Cup final. The FA, Sport England, the Premier League and the Football League Trust launch their first national participation programme for girls' football.

2014: Liverpool midfielder Fara Williams claims a record-breaking 130th cap for England when she starts a 4-0 friendly win over Sweden in Hartlepool on 3 August. A few months later, on a rainy afternoon in November, a record crowd for an England women's international turns up as the team plays at Wembley for the first time. The home fans among the 45,619 are left disappointed as the hosts lose a friendly 3-0 to two-time World champions Germany. Karen Carney wins her 100th cap on the night. The WSL ends in thrilling fashion with three teams still in with a chance of the title going into the final game. Liverpool, who start the day in third place, ultimately defend their title on goal difference with a 3-0 win over Bristol City. Chelsea are in the driving seat ahead of the final match but lose 2-1 at Manchester City to finish second. Birmingham City, who are two points behind Chelsea at kick-off, draw 2-2 with Notts County to finish third. Arsenal beat Everton 2-0 in the FA Cup final but lose the WSL Continental Cup final 1-0 to Manchester City. The year 2014 also sees the introduction of a second division in the WSL: WSL 2 contains 10 teams with Sunderland becoming its first ever champions.

2015: England win the Cyprus Cup for the third time beating Canada 1-0 in the final. They then enjoy their best World Cup performance as they finish as the top European nation. In a tournament which is expanded to 24 teams for the first time, the Three Lionesses finish second in their group behind France before beating Norway 2-1 in the Round of 16. A 2-1 win over hosts Canada follows in the quarter-finals before the heartbreak of an injury-time own goal by Laura Bassett sees them lose the semi-final 2-1 to Japan. In the third-place match Mark Sampson's side beat Germany for the very first time with Fara Williams' extra-time penalty giving them a 1-0 win and the bronze medal. USA win their third World Cup with a 5-2 triumph over Japan in the final. The FA Women's Cup is renamed the Women's FA Cup with the final held at Wembley for the first time. A then-record FA Cup final crowd of 30,710 watches Chelsea claim their first trophy of any sort by beating Notts County 1-0. The Blues complete the Double by winning the WSL 1 title. Arsenal are 3-0 winners over Notts County in the WSL Continental Cup final. Reading are champions of WSL 2.

2016: MBEs are awarded to England captain Steph Houghton and most-capped player Fara Williams in the New Year's Honours list. Baroness Sue Campbell is named as the FA's new Head of Women's Football. Manchester City dominate the League as they win their first trophy by claiming the WSL 1 title in September. May's FA Cup final between Arsenal and Chelsea at Wembley draws a new record crowd of 32,912 as the Gunners beat the holders 1-0. In October, Manchester City also collect the WSL Continental Cup courtesy of a 1-0 extra-time win over Birmingham City. Yeovil Town win WSL 2 on goal difference ahead of runners-up Bristol City. The FA announces that from next season WSL 1 and WSL 2 will revert to a winter calendar being played from autumn 2017 to spring 2018. To fill the void a Spring Series will be held in 2017 when the teams will play the other sides in their division just once. There will be no promotion or relegation at the end of the Spring Series. At the Olympics in Rio, hosts Brazil are under huge pressure to win a first Olympic football gold medal. While the men prevail, the women miss out on a place on the podium. They are beaten on penalties by Sweden in the semi-finals and then lose the bronze medal match 2-1 to Canada. Germany are crowned Olympic champions for the first time as they beat Sweden 2-1 in the final. For the first time in the six Olympic women's competitions played to date USA fail to reach the final, losing on penalties to Sweden in the quarter-finals.

2017: Manchester City make it three domestic trophies in a row as they beat Birmingham City 4-1 in the FA Cup final. A new FA Cup record crowd of 35,271 is present at Wembley. The WSL 1 Spring Series is won by Chelsea on goal difference ahead of Manchester City on the final day of the season. The WSL 2 Spring Series, which concludes a few weeks earlier, sees Everton beat runners-up Doncaster to the title. A record television audience for a women's football match, which peaks at more than four million, watches Channel 4's coverage of England's Euro 2017 semi-final against the Netherlands. The Dutch win 3-0 and go on to claim the title three days later when they beat Denmark 4-2 in a thrilling final.

After the tournament the FA becomes embroiled in a long-running controversy as questions are asked as to how the organisation came to clear England manager Mark Sampson of any wrongdoing following allegations of bullying and harassment by striker Eniola Aluko whose evidence included a claim that he made a discriminatory comment to an unnamed player. As the FA continues to stand by Sampson, the government orders a parliamentary hearing. However, Sampson is removed before it takes place; sacked one day after his team begin their 2019 World Cup qualifying campaign with a 6-0 win over Russia. The FA says Sampson has been removed from his post because of "inappropriate and unacceptable behaviour" with female players in a previous role.

At the end of September the FA announce the women's club game will undergo a major upheaval ahead of the 2018/19 season. Teams will have to be full-time to compete in the top division, while Tier 2 will be a part-time League. All existing WSL 1 and WSL 2 teams will have to reapply for their licences with a decision on who has been successful to be made before Christmas. At that point the application process will be opened up to clubs outside the existing top two divisions.

2018: In January the FA installs former England and Manchester United player Phil Neville as the new England women's manager.

The FA Cup final attendance record is again broken as 45,423 people are at Wembley to see Chelsea beat Arsenal 3-1. The Blues go on to complete the Double by finishing top of WSL 1 ahead of Manchester City.

At the end of May the FA confirms the full line-up for its new full-time top division, the FA Women's Super League, and its new part-time second division the FA Women's Championship. The WSL will consist of 11 teams, namely the existing WSL 1 teams Arsenal, Bristol City, Birmingham City, Chelsea Everton, Liverpool, Manchester City, Reading and Yeovil Town along with Brighton & Hove Albion (who have come up from Tier 2) and West Ham United (who have come up from Tier 3). Sunderland's bid for a Tier 1 or Tier 2 licence has been rejected. In Tier 2 Manchester United have been included. It's a controversial decision given that the club has not had a senior women's team since 2005. Other newcomers to the division include Charlton Athletic, Lewes and Leicester City Women (who have all come up from Tier 3) and Sheffield United (who have come up from Tier 4). The following existing WSL 2 sides are also initially included: Aston Villa; Doncaster Rovers Belles; Durham; London Bees; Millwall Lionesses; Sheffield FC and Tottenham Hotspur. Later in the summer Sheffield FC and Doncaster Rovers Belles withdraw from the division saying they cannot cope with the new financial demands. Tier 3 Crystal Palace are awarded one of the vacancies.

THE NEWS 2017/18

Wed 16 Aug: The FA faces intense media scrutiny as it emerges that an internal enquiry cleared England manager Mark Sampson of any wrongdoing after a bullying complaint by former international striker Eniola Aluko. The complaint contained an allegation that he had made a highly inappropriate remark with "racial and prejudicial connotations to another (unnamed) player."

Sat 2 Sep: Manchester City duo Izzy Christiansen and Jill Scott sign new contracts with the club.

Thu 7 Sep: The BBC reports that the FA is considering turning the WSL into a one-tier League from 2017/18, consisting only of clubs that can sustain full-time players. It emerges that a consultation is under way between the FA and the 20 WSL clubs. Under the proposals, part-time clubs currently in WSL 1 could be moved into Tier 2 irrespective of their 2017/18 results.

WSL 1 side Yeovil Town sign 26-year-old Wales international goalkeeper Laura O'Sullivan, formerly of Cardiff City Ladies. Her Welsh international team-mate Hannah Miles, 19, who plays at full-back, also joins the Lady Glovers.

Fri 8 Sep: Euro 2017 Golden Boot winner Jodie Taylor is named England Player of the Year at the Women's Football Awards. The Arsenal forward scored five goals in her four appearances at the finals in the Netherlands earlier this summer. Gunners team-mate Jordan Nobbs wins the WSL Players' Player of the Year award which is held at the Grosvenor House hotel in London.

Mon 11 Sep: Senior FA executives are told they will face a parliamentary enquiry over the investigations into alleged "bullying and harassment" of former England striker Eniola Aluko by manager Mark Sampson. The enquiry will take place next month and will consider whether the investigations, which cleared Sampson, were properly conducted.

The BBC announces it will stream WSL 1 matches live on TV, radio and online when the season begins later this month. The BBC Red Button and BT Sport will also show matches with 14 games to be broadcast before 12 November.

Tue 12 Sep: In an interview with the BBC, England manager Mark Sampson says he still has the support of the players despite bullying allegations from former Lionesses striker Eniola Aluko.

WSL 1 side Sunderland announce they will no longer be training at the men's Academy of Light centre and will use facilities at Northumbria University in 2017/18. Home matches will also move from Eppleton Colliery FC's Hetton-le-Hole ground to South Shield FC's Mariners

Park. The news comes less than two weeks before the start of the season and follows confirmation in January 2017 that the club is reverting to part-time status.

Wed 13 Sep: Chelsea's Drew Spence tells the FA that she was the subject of a remark of a racist nature made by England manager Mark Sampson. She says she was left upset and offended by Sampson asking her, a mixed-race player, how many times she had been arrested. The incident, which is said to have happened in October 2015, formed part of Eniola Aluko's allegations of bullying against Sampson. Aluko did not name the player and this is the first time Spence has publicly backed Aluko's claim.

Sun 17 Sep: England pair Jessica Carter and Melissa Lawley withdraw from the squad for the upcoming World Cup qualifier with Russia because of injury.

Mon 18 Sep: Denmark's players say they have reached a partial agreement with the Danish Football Association in their dispute over employment rights. The team have been on strike, refusing to play last Friday's friendly against the Netherlands.

Tue 19 Sep: England beat Russia 6-0 in a World Cup qualifier at Prenton Park. Nikita Parris celebrates scoring the opening goal by rushing to embrace manager Mark Sampson. With the entire team joining in, it's viewed by many as a show of support for Sampson in the wake of bullying allegations from former England striker Eniola Aluko. Aluko says on twitter that the celebration is disrespectful. *NB: Aluko will later apologise for the tweet.*

Wed 20 Sep: Mark Sampson is sacked by England just a day after a 6-0 World Cup qualifying win over Russia. The FA insists the decision is not connected to the ongoing controversy and upcoming parliamentary enquiry into why he was cleared of a bullying allegation made by Eniola Aluko. Chief executive Martin Glenn says Sampson has been removed from his post because of "inappropriate and unacceptable" behaviour with female players during his previous role as manager of Bristol Academy. A 2015 FA assessment found that Sampson did not pose a risk, but the FA says it was only made aware of the full extent of the allegations last week.

Thu 28 Sep: WSL 1 side Manchester City confirm that Denmark international forward Nadia Nadim will join them in January 2018 when her deal with American side Portland Thorns expires. Nadim – who was born in Afghanistan – helped Denmark reach the final of Euro 2017.

Fri 29 Sep: Mo Marley steps up from her role as England Under-19s manager to take over the senior team on a temporary basis following the sacking of Mark Sampson. Prior to joining the England set-up Marley led Everton to their 2010 FA Cup triumph. As a player she won 42 caps for England, was captain at Euro 2001 and won the FA Cup in 1989.

Sat 7 Oct: In what's believed to be a first for international football, the Norwegian FA announces it will be paying male and female footballers exactly the same amount to represent their country. The money paid to the women's team will almost double from 31m krone

(£296,845) to 6m krone (£574,540). The amount includes 550,000 krone (£47,875) paid by male Norwegian players, money they receive for commercial activities.

Manchester City's Germany striker Pauline Bremer breaks her leg in a collision with Everton's Gabby George during their WSL 1 match at the Select Security Stadium. The serious injury mars City's 3-2 win.

Wed 18 Oct: FA chairman Greg Clarke and chief executive Martin Glenn appear at a parliamentary hearing where they are questioned about how an internal enquiry came to clear former England manager Mark Sampson after claims of bullying and harassment made against him. The allegations were made by former England striker Eniola Aluko who also appears at the hearing. The main revelation is that a third enquiry, led by barrister Katharine Newton, found that Sampson had indeed made discriminatory remarks to both Aluko and team-mate Drew Spence.

The Danish football association says Friday's upcoming World Cup qualifier with Sweden has been cancelled since their ongoing dispute with the players has left them unable to field a team.

Fri 20 Oct: England goalkeeper coach Lee Kendall will not attend tonight's friendly against France with the FA having announced an investigation into claims of inappropriate behaviour towards Eniola Aluko.

Mon 23 Oct: Chelsea manager Emma Hayes signs a new three-and-a-half year contract with the club.

Wed 25 Oct: Arsenal manager Pedro Martinez Losa leaves after three years in charge with his team having collected just four points from their opening three WSL 1 matches. After taking over in September 2014, the 41-year-old Spaniard led the Gunners to FA Cup success in 2016 and also won the 2015 WSL Continental Cup.

Thu 26 Oct: Arsenal and former England defender Alex Scott confirms she will retire from all football at the end of the 2017/18 season. Scott retired from England duty after Euro 2017 having won 140 caps.

Fri 3 Nov: Arsenal appoint Australian coach Joe Montemurro as their new manager. Montemurro leaves his position as assistant manager of current A-League men's side Melbourne City. Last season he led Melbourne City women's team to the title in their first year of existence.

Sat 4 Nov: England and Reading midfielder Jade Moore will be out of action for four months after sustaining a serious ankle injury in last weekend's WSL 1 win against Bristol City. She'll undergo surgery next week.

Tue 7 Nov: Former Arsenal women's manager Laura Harvey resigns as head coach of NWSL side Seattle Reign. Her announcement comes amid speculation that she is a candidate to become the new England manager, with the FA set to hold interviews on 4 December. Tier 2 side Watford say they will not be applying for a WSL licence under the FA's new criteria and will instead look to "re-energise a more community-focused approach to its ladies' football offering at all ages". *NB: Watford change their mind and apply before the second deadline in March, but are unsuccessful.*

Thu 9 Nov: WSL 1 side Sunderland confirm they will not apply for a WSL licence in the first wave of applications saying they will instead 'focus on a joint bid for a Tier 1 licence in March'.

Sweden and former Liverpool striker Emma Lundh reveals on Instagram that she has been diagnosed with multiple sclerosis.

Eniola Aluko gives her first interview since the DCMS parliamentary hearing. She tells the BBC she feels she has had no support from most of her England team-mates. She adds that returning to the England squad is not a priority at the moment and that she would be willing to work with the FA to help improve its culture and grievance process. Aluko also apologises for tweets which criticised the England players for their goal celebration with Mark Sampson in what turned out to be his last game in charge.

Fri 10 Nov: Yeovil Town, whose top-flight status appears under threat following the FA's new licence criteria, confirm they have applied for a WSL 1 licence on the final day of the deadline. London Bees also announce they have applied for a WSL 2 licence.

Tue 14 Nov: Current WSL 2 side Brighton confirm they have applied for a licence to join the top-flight when the FA restructures the Leagues next season.

Wed 15 Nov: Chelsea reach the quarter-finals of the Champions League for the first time. Ji So Yun's 54th-minute goal proves to be the winner as they beat Rosengard 1-0 in Sweden to complete a 4-0 aggregate win. In the night's Continental Cup group matches, Liverpool qualify for the quarter-finals with a 5-1 victory over Aston Villa, while Reading also make it through as they see off London Bees 4-0.

Meanwhile, midfield duo Kiera Walsh (Manchester City) and Leah Williamson (Arsenal) receive their first senior England call-ups. Interim boss Mo Marley names a 26-player squad for the upcoming World Cup qualifiers against Bosnia & Herzegovina and Kazakhstan. The pair both played under Marley for England Under-19s and were part of the Under-23s squad that won the Nordic Tournament in May 2017.

Thu 16 Nov: Manchester City qualify for the quarter-finals of the Champions League as they come from behind to beat Norwegian side LSK Kvinner 2-1 at the Academy Stadium. Izzy Christiansen and Nikita Parris score their goals as they prevail 7-1 on aggregate. In the evening's three Continental Cup group matches, Sheffield FC are knocked out of the competition after a 4-2 penalty shootout defeat at home to Sunderland. The match itself finished 1-1, with Sheffield's Melissa Johnson having a penalty saved by Rachel Laws in normal time. Jodie Taylor is on target twice in Arsenal's 6-0 win at Watford and Chloe Kelly racks up a hat-trick, including one from the spot, as Everton beat Oxford 4-0 at home.

England goalkeeping coach Lee Kendall – who was suspended last month after claims of inappropriate behaviour towards former international striker Eniola Aluko – resigns.

Mon 20 Nov: Chelsea sign Sweden international defender Jonna Andersson who will officially join when the transfer window opens on 29 December. The 24-year-old, who can play as left-back or wing-back, has spent the last nine years with Linkopings where she won six Swedish League titles and six Swedish Cups.

Thu 23 Nov: Midfielder Casey Stoney withdraws from the England squad for the upcoming World Cup qualifiers against Bosnia & Herzegovina and Kazakhstan due to a calf injury. Everton's Gabby George receives her first call-up in Stoney's place.

Fri 24 Nov: England make it two World Cup qualifying wins from two as they beat Bosnia & Herzegovina 4-0 at Bescot Stadium, home of Walsall FC. Captain Steph Houghton scores twice with Nikita Parris also on target and Fran Kirby adding the fourth late on from the penalty spot.

Mon 27 Nov: Speculation linking Laura Harvey with the vacant England manager's position ends after she is appointed as head coach of NWSL side Real Salt Lake City in the USA. Former Arsenal boss Harvey left Seattle Reign earlier this month. Chelsea forward Karen Carney withdraws from the England squad for tomorrow's World Cup qualifier against Kazakhstan with an ankle injury. Meanwhile, it's confirmed that Birmingham keeper Ann Katrin-Berger has been diagnosed with thyroid cancer. The 27-year-old will undergo surgery next month.

Sat 2 Dec: Two days after withdrawing his application for the vacant England position, Manchester City manager Nick Cushing signs a new three-and-a-half-year contract with the club.

Mon 4 Dec: Doncaster Rovers Belles – currently second in WSL 2 – confirm they have applied for a licence to play in Tier 2 in 2017/18, adding: 'Our current League position suggests that on footballing grounds we would deserve a place in Tier 1. However, the financial criteria set for entry into Tier 1 are simply beyond our means so we have applied for a Tier 2 Licence.'

Wed 6 Dec: WSL 2 side Oxford United confirm they have not applied for a WSL licence for 2017/18 adding: 'There will be a subsequent opportunity in March to reconsider our position.'

Sat 9 Dec: Keith Boanas announces tomorrow's match against Brighton will be his last as Watford manager. It's believed his decision to resign follows the club's announcement that they will not be applying for a WSL licence for 2018/19.

Sun 10 Dec: Snow and ice throughout the UK wipe out almost the entire day's fixtures. Everton beat Sunderland 5-1 in the only WSL 1 game to go ahead while Doncaster Rovers Belles are 3-2 winners over Sheffield FC in the sole WSL 2 match to survive the freeze. Just two matches involving WPL sides take place with Hull City beating WPL Northern Division One rivals Newcastle United 1-0 in the WPL Plate and table-toppers AFC Wimbledon beating 2nd-placed Leyton Orient 3-0 in WPL South East Division One.

Wed 13 Dec: The FA announces which WSL clubs have been successful in obtaining licences for WSL 1 and 2 for the 2018/19 season under its new criteria. Nine of the 10 existing WSL 1 sides (Arsenal, Birmingham City, Bristol City, Chelsea, Everton, Liverpool, Manchester City, Reading and Yeovil Town) will be joined by current WSL 2 side Brighton & Hove Albion. Sunderland did not apply for a licence. There are celebrations at Huish Park, where there had been real fears that Yeovil might lose their top-flight status. Seven of the existing WSL 2 teams will retain their place in the division – Aston Villa, Doncaster Rovers Belles, Durham, London Bees, Millwall Lionesses, Sheffield FC and Tottenham Hotspur (pictured with former Spurs player, Ledley King). Oxford United and Watford did not apply but can reconsider whether to do so in March. The process will now be moved on to consider applications from clubs currently outside of the WSL.

Fri 15 Dec: The FA confirms it will not appoint a new permanent manager before the end of the year, with Mo Marley to continue as interim boss. Meanwhile Everton striker Claudia Walker will miss the rest of the season after undergoing surgery on a hamstring injury sustained in a training match.

Mon 18 Dec: The draw for the WSL Continental Cup semi-finals is made. Current holders Manchester City will travel to fellow WSL 1 heavyweights Chelsea while Reading will host Arsenal. Ties to take place on the weekend of 13/14 January.

Tue 19 Dec: Chelsea confirm they will re-sign their former player Anita Asante, 32, when the transfer window opens on 29 December. The former England defensive midfielder will join from Swedish side Rosengard on a contract that will run until May 2020.

Sat 30 Dec: Liverpool announce Wales vice-captain Tash Harding will be leaving the club after turning down a new contract. The forward has been a regular since signing from Manchester City in 2016.

Mon 8 Jan: The draw for the FA Cup 4th round – the stage at which the WSL teams will enter – sees holders and WSL 1 leaders Manchester City handed an away tie at WSL 2 outfit Brighton. Arsenal, who have won the trophy a record 14 times, will travel to fellow WSL 1 side Yeovil.

Tue 9 Jan: Canada women's coach John Herdman, 42, leaves his position to take the job of Canada men's coach. In his six-year spell the Englishman took the team from 12th to 5th in the world, led them to the bronze medal at the 2012 and 2016 Olympics and reached the 2015 World Cup quarter-finals. He has been among the many names recently linked with the vacant England women's manager job.

Wed 10 Jan: Chelsea midfielder Drew Spence is included in England interim manager Mo Marley's 30-player squad for the upcoming La Manga training camp. It's her first call-up since she accused former manager Mark Sampson of making racially discriminating comments against her, an allegation that was later upheld by the FA. Gilly Flaherty, Ellen White and Rachel Daly also return to the squad. Casey Stoney will join the technical staff, working as a player-to-coach apprentice as part of her efforts to gain an A-Licence.

Fri 12 Jan: England left-back Demi Stokes, 26, signs a new three-year contract with her club Manchester City.

Sun 21 Jan: Another cold snap leads to a raft of postponements. No WSL fixtures were scheduled for today, but only one WPL match takes place as Chorley come from behind twice to beat Crewe Alexandra 4-2 in Northern Division One.

Tue 23 Jan: After days of speculation former Manchester United and England men's player Phil Neville is confirmed as England manager. The appointment is heavily criticised by numerous media commentators and fans who point out that Neville has not been a manager at any level, lacks experience of the women's game, and did not originally apply for the position. Others welcome his appointment saying it will raise the profile of the women's game.

Wed 24 Jan: Phil Neville apologises for historic social media posts after being accused of making sexist comments in tweets he posted back in 2012.

Thu 25 Jan: One of the biggest moves on transfer deadline day sees Watford's England Under-20 striker Rinsola Babajide, 19, sign for Liverpool. Elsewhere 20-year-old Arsenal striker Chloe Kelly – who has been on loan at Everton – makes the switch permanent. The Toffees also snap up 18-year-old Gunners full-back Taylor Hinds.

Mon 19 Feb: WPL South West One team Basingstoke are forced to withdraw from the League. They currently sit bottom of an 11-team division having picked up just two points from their 10 League games this season.

Wed 21 Feb: One day after being named as a new member of England manager Phil Neville's backroom staff, Casey Stoney plays the final game of her glittering career. She is afforded a guard of honour as she leads her Liverpool team out at home against Sunderland. The WSL 1 match finishes 3-1 to the Reds with Stoney receiving a standing ovation when she is substituted with a minute to play.

Fri 2 Mar: Phil Neville's first game as England manager finishes in a 4-1 win over France in the SheBelieves Cup in Columbus, Ohio. The goals come from Toni Duggan, Jill Scott, Jodie Taylor and Fran Kirby as the Lionesses beat France for only the second time in 44 years.

Mon 5 Mar: Ellen White scores a brace as England twice come from behind to draw 2-2 with Germany in New Jersey in their second SheBelieves Cup match. England now have four points, their highest tally in the competition's three-year history. They still have one match to play.

Tue 6 Mar: WPL North side Stoke City win their 10th consecutive Staffordshire FA County Cup as they beat WPL Midlands One side Sporting Khalsa 2-0 in the final at Evans Park, Stafford Town FC. Both goals come in the first half courtesy of Faye McCoy and Ashleigh Hayes.

Thu 8 Mar: England narrowly miss out on the draw they need to win the SheBelieves Cup as Karen Bardsley's 58th minute own goal sees them lose 1-0 to the USA in Orlando. The Lionesses finish as runners-up on four points behind the USA who win with seven points. France finish third behind England on goal difference, while Germany are fourth with a solitary point.

Sun 11 Mar: WPL South East One side Stevenage win their second consecutive Hertfordshire FA County Cup. As expected they prove too strong for Hoddesdon Town in the final at The County Ground, Letchworth Garden City. Amy Makewell hits a hat-trick, Chloe Gunn and Ashleigh Deacon both bag a brace and Leah Littlechild completes the scoring with a minute to go as Stevenage win 8-0.

Wed 14 Mar: Arsenal cause a mini-shock as they beat WSL 1 leaders and current holders Manchester City 1-0 in the WSL Continental Tyres Cup final at Adams Park. Vivianne Miedema scores the only goal of the game in the 33rd minute as the Gunners lift the trophy for a record-extending fifth time.

Sun 18 Mar: Another cold snap sees three of the four FA Cup quarter-finals postponed as Arsenal v Charlton, Durham v Everton and Sunderland v Manchester City are all called off. In the only tie that goes ahead Chelsea win 3-0 away to Liverpool with goals from Jonna Andersson, Katie Chapman and a Maren Mjelde penalty. The only WSL fixture scheduled for the day – Watford v Sheffield FC in WSL 2 – is also postponed, and the entire WPL programme is wiped out.

Wed 21 Mar: It's a great night for English clubs in the Champions League as both Manchester City and Chelsea win the first legs of their quarter-finals 2-0. Ji So-yun and Erin Cuthbert are on target as Chelsea win away to French side Montpellier, while City see off Swedish side Linkopings at home thanks to a Nikita Parris penalty and a Jane Ross header. Linkopings are reduced to 10 players when Liza Lantz receives her second yellow card for handball while conceding the 37th-minute penalty with which Parris gives City the lead.

Manchester United confirm they have applied for a licence to compete in WSL 2 (which will be rebranded as the FA Women's Championship) for 2018/19 despite the fact they have no women's team. As one of only two current men's Premier League clubs without a senior women's outfit (the other being Southampton), United have long been under pressure to form a team. Since scrapping their senior women's team in 2005 they have continued to run a women's section at junior age groups. WPL teams Charlton Athletic, Coventry United, Crystal Palace, Derby County, Leicester City Women, Lewes, Sheffield United and existing WSL 2 side Watford are among the other clubs known to have applied. A maximum of five will be successful with a decision from the FA due in May.

Thu 22 Mar: WPL Southern side Lewes win the Sussex FA County Cup with a 4-0 triumph over Crawley Wasps in the final at Culver Road. Georgia Bridges gets a brace while Rebecca Carter and Danielle Lane are also on target.

Fri 23 Mar: England climb to 2nd in the FIFA World Rankings, replacing Germany who drop to 3rd. USA remain in 1st place. It's the highest ever ranking achieved by an England men's or women's senior team. Men's rankings began in 1993, with England achieving their highest placing of 3rd in August 2012. Women's rankings started in 2003.

UEFA confirm former England manager Mark Sampson was banned for three matches for verbally abusing a female UEFA official during the Lionesses' 3-0 Euro 2017 semi-final defeat to the Netherlands. Sampson is alleged to have held a metal pole above his head while berating the venue director. It's revealed that UEFA charged Sampson in September 2017, the day after he was fired by the FA over a separate incident. The ban will be enforced should he ever return to a job in international football.

Men's Premier League club Southampton follow Manchester United by confirming they have applied to enter a team into the Championship (Tier 2) in 2018/19. The two clubs have – until now – been the only current men's Premier League clubs not to have a senior women's team.

Wed 28 Mar: Both England's Champions League representatives advance to the semi-finals. Chelsea, who are playing in the quarter-finals for the first time, beat French side Montpellier 3-1 at Kingsmeadow to complete a 5-1 aggregate win and book a last four spot against German outfit Wolfsburg who have knocked the Blues out in the last 16 in each of the previous two seasons. Meanwhile Manchester City are 5-3 winners away to Swedish side Linkopings and go through 7-3 on aggregate. They will take on Lyon – who have won the last two tournaments – just as they did in the semi-finals last season.

The FA confirms that WSL 1 attendances have fallen by 11% in 2017/18 with the move to a winter season and the bitterly cold weather thought to have played a part. There is good news though in that WSL 2 crowds have risen by 7% and peak viewing figures for live matches on BT Sport have increased from 46,000 to 103,000. The FA's head of women's football Baroness Sue Campbell also says she is "confident" that Great Britain will be allowed to field a women's team at the 2020 Tokyo Olympics.

Thu 29 Mar: As expected C&K Basildon, who are currently riding high in 2nd place in WPL Southern, prove too strong for Eastern Regional Football League side Brentwood Town in the Essex FA County Cup final which is played at Parkside, the new home of Aveley FC. Angela Addison nets four, Zoe Rushen gets a brace and Jay Blackie is also on target in a 7-0 victory. The score-line is harsh on Tier 5 Brentwood who are just 3-0 down with 13 minutes to play. It's a record-equalling fifth Essex FA County Cup win for C&K Basildon.

Fri 6 Apr: England are held to a goalless draw by Wales in their 2019 World Cup qualifier at St Mary's. Wales manager Jayne Ludlow describes it as the best result in the country's history. The Welsh feel they had a goal wrongly disallowed with Natasha Harding's ninth-minute shot appearing to cross the line before being hacked away by Lucy Bronze – goal-line technology is not in operation in the World Cup qualifiers. Wales remain at the top of Group 1, a point ahead of England but having played a game more.

Sat 7 Apr: The FA announce that WPL Plate finalists Fylde (of WPL Northern) have been expelled from the competition for fielding an ineligible player. Their defeated semi-final opponents Luton Town (of WPL South East One) will take their place in the final against WPL Southern side West Ham which will take place on Sunday 15 April at Hednesford Town.

Tue 10 Apr: England win 2-0 away to Bosnia & Herzegovina in their Group 1 World Cup qualifier. The Lionesses are reduced to 10 players when Alex Greenwood is sent off for a second yellow card two minutes into the second half. Toni Duggan gives them the lead nine minutes later before Bosnia & Herzegovina captain Amira Spahic also sees red. Jodie Taylor secures the points with a penalty three minutes into added time.

Wed 11 Apr: Manchester City confirm they will go on their first US tour this summer, visiting Portland and Miami where they will take part in the first Women's International Champions Cup. PSG and North Carolina Courage will also be involved in the tournament (in July it will be announced that Lyon will also compete).

Sun 15 Apr: History is made as the FA Cup semi-finals are televised live for the first time in the competition's 48-year history. In the lunch-time game – which is broadcast on the BBC red button – an injury-time header from Louise Quinn gives Arsenal a 2-1 win at Everton to see the Gunners reach their 16th final. The other semi-final is a showdown between current WSL 1 top two Chelsea and Manchester City at Kingsmeadow. A Fran Kirby double ensures Chelsea knock out the holders 2-0 in a match which is shown live on BBC Two.

Elsewhere WPL Southern side West Ham beat WPL South East One outfit Luton Town 5-0 in the WPL Plate final at Keys Park, the home of Hednesford Town. Earlier in the day, at the same venue, an Emily Curtis goal five minutes from time saw Stoke City reserves beat Portsmouth reserves 1-0 in the WPL Reserves Cup final. Meanwhile, Loughborough Foxes are confirmed as WPL Midlands One champions with four games to spare. The Foxes – who didn't even kick a ball today – secure the title courtesy of 3rd-placed The New Saints losing 4-1 at Radcliffe Olympic.

Tue 17 Apr: Millwall Lionesses – currently 2nd in WSL 2 and unbeaten in the League in 14 months – appeal to the public for funds, saying they may not survive until the end of the season.

WPL South West One side Poole Town win their fifth consecutive Dorset FA County Cup with a 7-0 victory over Tier 7 Dorset League outfit Dorchester Town at Hamworthy United FC.

Sun 22 Apr: In the Champions League semi-final first legs, Manchester City hold defending champions Lyon to a highly creditable goalless draw at the Academy Stadium. However, Chelsea go down to a 3-1 home defeat to Wolfsburg. The German side – who have knocked the Blues out of the last 2 Champions League tournaments – come from behind after Fran Kirby puts Chelsea ahead in the second minute. A Sara Bjork Gunnarsdottir header, an own goal from Maren Mjelde and a Lara Dickenmann volley give Wolfsburg a commanding lead ahead of the second leg.

At the 2017/18 PFA Player of the Year Awards, Chelsea's Fran Kirby scoops the main gong with Bristol City's Lauren Hemp winning the Young Player of the Year trophy. The men's prizes go to Liverpool's Mo Salah and Manchester City's Leroy Sane.

The nominees for the BBC Women's Footballer of the Year 2018 award are announced: Lucy Bronze (England & Lyon defender), Pernille Harder (Denmark & Wolfsburg forward), Sam Kerr (Australia & Chicago Red Stars/Perth Glory forward), Dzsenifer Marozsan (Germany & Lyon midfielder) and Lieke Martens (Netherlands & Barcelona midfielder/forward) make the shortlist.

WPL South East One side MK Dons win the Berks & Bucks FA County Cup with a 7-0 triumph over WPL South West One outfit Maidenhead United. The match takes place at Stadium:mk, home of MK Dons FC.

Tue 24 Apr: Chelsea forward Fran Kirby makes it a double as she wins the inaugural Football Writers' Player of the Year award to go with her PFA Player of the Year award.

Fri 27 Apr: WPL Northern One team Crewe Alexandra win their third successive Cheshire FA County Cup. Alex beat North West League leaders Tranmere Rovers 2-0 in the final at Cammell Laird FC. The Hampshire FA turn down an appeal from Southampton Women against a decision that they fielded an ineligible player in their County Cup semi-final. The complaint was raised by their defeated opponents Southampton FC Women. Southampton Women are expelled from the competition with Southampton FC Women taking their place in the final.

Sun 29 Apr: In the Champions League semi-finals there's disappointment for both English sides. Lyon's Lucy Bronze scores the only goal of the tie to knock out her former club Manchester City 1-0 on aggregate. Chelsea fail to overcome their 3-1 first-leg deficit away to Wolfsburg as they go down 2-0 in Germany to exit the competition 5-1 on aggregate. It all means a repeat of the 2016 final, with Lyon's hopes of a third straight title still alive. In domestic competition the WPL Cup final is contested between two WPL Northern sides at Chesterfield FC's Proact Stadium where Blackburn Rovers beat Leicester City Women 3-1. Elsewhere a Sasha Rowe penalty seven minutes from time secures Liverpool Marshall Feds their first ever trophy. Feds beat WPL Northern One rivals Mossley Hill Athletic 1-0 in the Liverpool FA County Cup final at Walton Hall Park.

Wed 2 May: Guiseley Vixens come from behind to beat WPL Northern rivals and holders Bradford City 3-1 in the West Riding FA County Cup final. It is only the second time City have been beaten in their seven appearances in the final to date.

Thu 3 May: With Chelsea not in action, Manchester City play their game in hand on the Blues and move back to the top of the table on goal difference thanks to a 6-1 win away to 9th-placed Bristol City. The score is only 1-0 at the break, but a second-half onslaught lifts City to the summit. Both teams have 32 points, with City's goal difference +28 to Chelsea's +26 with four games remaining.

In the Birmingham FA County Cup final, WPL Southern side Coventry prove far too strong for Birmingham & West Midlands of WPL Midlands One as they run out 15-0 winners at The Lamb ground. In the Durham FA County Cup final, North East Regional League side Norton & Stockton Ancients cause a shock against WPL Northern One outfit Chester-le-Street Town. Norton twice lead through Nyci Thorns – who nets her 100th goal for the club – and Shannon Reed. Chester-le-Street Town equalise on each occasion, but when it goes to penalties Norton prevail 5-4.

Elsewhere, WPL Midlands One side The New Saints win their 10th Shropshire FA County Cup by beating West Midlands Regional League Division One North outfit Shrewsbury Town 1-0. Louisa Anderson scores the winner in the fourth minute of injury-time. The Somerset FA County Cup is a WPL South West One derby and is won by Keynsham Town who see off Larkhall Athletic 3-0.

Fri 4 May: WPL North side Leicester City Women win the Leicestershire & Rutland FA County Cup with a 15-0 triumph over AFC Leicester.

Sat 5 May: A record FA Cup final crowd of 45,423 is at Wembley to see Chelsea beat Arsenal 3-1. Ramona Bachmann strikes twice in the 48th and 60th minutes before Vivianne Miedema gives the Gunners hope with 17 minutes to go. However, double Footballer of the Year

Fran Kirby quickly restores Chelsea's two-goal advantage. It's the Blues' second FA Cup triumph, repeating their 1-0 win over Notts County of 2015 which was the first final to be staged at Wembley. Chelsea manager Emma Hayes did not lead the teams out, or take part in the pre-match ceremonials, on medical advice because she is 33 weeks pregnant.

Sun 6 May: Buckland Athletic clinch promotion to Tier 4. A 7-1 win over AEK Boco sees them crowned champions of the South West Regional League Premier Division. The Lincolnshire FA County Cup is won by Nettleham who beat Grimsby Borough 7-0 at Sincil Bank.

Mon 7 May: Colchester United's Weston Homes Community Stadium hosts the Suffolk County FA Cup final and 456 are in attendance to see WPL South East high-flyers Ipswich Town beat AFC Sudbury of the Eastern Region Premier League. Sudbury take a shock early lead, but Ipswich hit back to win 5-1 and claim their fourth consecutive County Cup.

Men's National League outfit Salford City – co-owned by England manager Phil Neville, his brother Gary and former Manchester United team-mates Ryan Giggs, Paul Scholes and Nicky Butt – announce the club is to form a women's team called Salford City Lionesses.

Tue 8 May: Manchester City's title hopes suffer a huge blow as they lose 1-0 at Liverpool. City stay top of the table ahead of Chelsea on goal difference, but the Blues hope to take advantage tomorrow when they play their game in hand at home to Birmingham City.

WPL Northern side Nottingham Forest win the Nottingham FA County Cup as they run out 2-1 winners over WPL Midlands One outfit Radcliffe Borough.

Wed 9 May: Chelsea take full advantage of Manchester City's defeat yesterday as they win 2-1 at home to Birmingham to move to the brink of the WSL 1 title.

Thu 10 May: Chelsea captain Katie Chapman, 35, announces she will retire at the end of the season. Chapman – who joined from Arsenal in 2014 – won the FA Cup for what's believed to be a record 10th time on Saturday. She will take up an ambassadorial role with the Blues at the end of the season.

WPL Northern leaders Blackburn Rovers collect their second trophy of the season as they come from behind to beat WPL Northern One mid-table side Chorley 6-1 in the Lancashire FA County Cup final. Rovers have already lifted this season's WPL Cup.

WPL Southern side Portsmouth win their 10th Hampshire FA County Cup by seeing off Southampton FC 5-0 in the final at Alton Town FC.

Sat 12 May: Manchester City's title hopes are all but over as they suffer a second consecutive WSL 1 defeat, this time going down 2-1 away to Arsenal. The result means a draw for Chelsea at Bristol City this coming Tuesday will be enough for the Blues to claim the title.

A RECORD FA CUP FINAL CROWD OF 45,423 IS AT WEMBLEY TO SEE CHELSEA BEAT ARSENAL 3-1

Sun 13 May: Doncaster Rovers Belles are crowned WSL 2 champions before taking to the pitch away to 3rd-placed Millwall Lionesses. Their nearest rivals, Brighton, are surprisingly beaten 4-0 at Durham earlier in the day meaning the Belles have an unassailable lead. Belles beat Millwall 1-0.

Leicester City win 6-3 at Middlesbrough to leapfrog their opponents and move into 2nd place in WPL Northern. The result filters through to the Lee Westwood Sports Centre where divisional leaders Blackburn are currently 3-1 up away to Nottingham Forest with seven minutes to play and now know that a win will be enough to secure the title. They duly run out 4-1 winners meaning that neither Leicester nor Boro can catch them. It's the second year in a row that Rovers have claimed the title, and their success also means they have completed the Treble in 2017/18 having already claimed the WPL Cup and Lancashire FA County Cup. Rovers will meet Charlton in the Championship play-off final at Sheffield United FC's Bramall Lane on 27 May after the Addicks are confirmed as WPL Southern champions. The South London side win 4-0 at Crystal Palace, who were in 2nd place at kick-off. Kit Graham bags all four goals for Charlton meaning she has now scored 200 goals in 207 appearances for the club. Victory sees Charlton complete a Double for 2017/18 having already lifted the Capital Cup. C&K Basildon also kicked off their match at Chichester City with faint hopes of catching Charlton, but despite a 1-0 victory, they know that is no longer possible. Both C&K – who leapfrog Palace into 2nd place – and Palace have now completed all their fixtures, while Charlton are top with two games to play. C&K finish the season as runners-up, their highest ever position.

Hull City clinch the WPL Northern One title with a 4-0 home win over Mossley Hill Athletic. Hull's nearest challengers Brighouse Town beat Crewe 3-1 but can no longer catch the Tigresses.

In WPL Southern, Gillingham were not in action today but celebrate the fact that QPR's 6-1 defeat at Portsmouth has confirmed that they will not be relegated.
In WPL Northern One, a year after promotion Barnsley are relegated after losing 2-1 at home to Leeds – a result which sends them bottom for the first time this season with one game to play. The win ensures that Leeds themselves are safe.

Tue 15 May: Chelsea clinch the WSL 1 title thanks to a 2-0 win away to Bristol City. The Blues knew a draw tonight would be enough, after Manchester City slipped up at Arsenal on Saturday. Having beaten Arsenal in the FA Cup final 10 days ago, the result means Emma Hayes' side have completed the domestic Double for the second time, previously doing so in 2015.

WPL Northern side Huddersfield Town beat WPL Northern One outfit Barnsley 3-0 in the Sheffield & Hallamshire FA County Cup final at Doncaster's Keepmoat Stadium. A goal from Katie Nutter and two from Sarah Danby see Town retain the trophy they won last year. It's the first time this County Cup final has been held at a Football League stadium.

Wed 16 May: Arsenal midfielder Jordan Nobbs signs a new long-term contract with the club. The England vice-captain joined in 2010 and has helped the Gunners win two WSL titles, five Continental Cups and four FA Cups. Meanwhile, at Chelsea Eniola Aluko becomes the third player to announce she will be leaving the Double winners this summer with Claire Rafferty also set to depart and Katie Chapman having confirmed her retirement.

Thu 17 May: Chelsea Double-winning manager Emma Hayes gives birth to a baby boy. Hayes announced she was pregnant with twins last year, but a club statement reveals that sadly "one of them did not survive beyond the third trimester".

Sun 20 May: On the final day of WSL 1 action, Manchester City are 3-0 winners at home to Everton. The result confirms that they finish as runners-up and clinch qualification for the Champions League ahead of Arsenal who finish 3rd despite winning 6-1 at Bristol City. In WSL 2 Durham's 2-0 win at Watford means they equal their highest WSL finish of 4th and do so with a club record number of WSL points (35) and goals (44). London Bees finish the season with a WSL club record points haul of 23 thanks to a 1-1 draw at Tottenham which secures a 6th-place finish.

It's also the final day of WPL action. In WPL Northern, Leicester City Women secure runners-up spot. Rosie Axten converts a hat-trick of penalties as they win 4-1 at Bradford City. MK Dons clinch the WPL South East One title. A draw was all that was required away to bottom club Haringey Borough, but a 13-0 win sees them crowned champions in style. They finish ahead of AFC Wimbledon who led the table for much of the season.

Plymouth take the WPL South West One title with a 6-1 home win over Poole. It means they complete the season unbeaten and having won all but two of their League games. Southampton Women's – whose only defeat was at the hands of Plymouth – finish 2nd.

In WPL Midlands One Burton, who only came up to this level last summer, clinch runners-up spot courtesy of a 4-2 win at home to Sporting Khalsa. Sheffield United – who win 6-1 at Leicester City Ladies – finish a point back in 3rd place. Elsewhere in the division, Long Eaton United celebrate their highest ever finish of 6th thanks to a 4-2 win at Steel City Wanderers.

Tue 22 May: Lyon and England defender Lucy Bronze is named BBC Footballer of the Year. The award is voted for by fans around the world. The 26-year-old finishes ahead of 2nd-placed Netherlands forward Lieke Martens and 3rd-placed Australia striker Sam Kerr.

Wed 23 May: Chelsea announce they are changing their name from Chelsea Ladies to Chelsea Women's, a move Arsenal also took last year. The club will also stop referring to their men's team as the club's "first team".

Thu 24 May: Lyon win the Champions League for the third year in a row after a dramatic period of extra-time against Wolfsburg in Kiev. The match finishes goalless before Lyon run out 4-1 winners after the additional 30 minutes. Pernille Harder puts the German side 1-0 up just three minutes into extra-time, but three minutes later her team-mate Alexandra Popp is sent off. Lyon seize control with a flurry of three goals in five minutes from Amandine Henry, Eugenie Le Sommer and Ada Hergerberg. The French side complete the scoring four minutes from time through Camille Abily.

Sun 27 May: WPL Southern champions Charlton come from behind to beat their WPL Northern counterparts Blackburn in the national play-off final at Bramall Lane and win promotion to Tier 2. Lynda Shepherd gives Rovers the lead with a sixth-minute penalty, but two goals just before half-time from Kit Graham and Georgia Griffin win the day for Charlton who also see a last-minute Charlotte Gurr penalty saved by Rovers keeper Danielle Hill.

Mon 28 May: The FA confirms which clubs from outside the existing top two tiers have been successful in gaining a licence for 2018/19 under their new criteria. West Ham – who finished 2017/18 in 7th place in WPL Southern – are catapulted from Tier 3 to Tier 1 as they join WSL. The main headline is that Manchester United – with no existing women's team above youth level – will be joining the new 2nd Tier which will be called the FA Women's Championship. Manchester United Women will be based at The Cliff – United's historic training ground in Salford, once redevelopment is complete. They will be joined in the Championship by four other newcomers, three of whom are coming up from Tier 3: WPL play-off winners Charlton; fellow WPL Southern side Lewes; WPL Northern runners-up Leicester City Women; and one from Tier 4, Sheffield United who finished 3rd in WPL Midlands One. Existing WSL 2 sides Oxford and Watford, who did apply before the March deadline, have failed in their applications.

Tue 29 May: Willie Kirk stands down as manager of WSL 1 side Bristol City. Kirk was in charge for three years and most recently led City to an 8th place finish in 2017/18.

Wed 30 May: Manchester City confirm Scotland striker Jane Ross and Netherlands midfielder Tessel Middag have not had their contracts renewed. The pair helped City win three domestic trophies and reach two Champions League semi-finals.

Fri 1 Jun: FWA and Players' Player of the Year Fran Kirby signs a new contract with Chelsea, extending her stay with the Blues until at least 2021. Manchester City sign Scotland international Caroline Weir on a two-year contract. Weir has been with Liverpool since 2016. Birmingham City striker Ellen White is named Vauxhall England Player of the Year for her contribution to the national side, with Arsenal forward Beth Mead taking the Young Player of the Year award.

At the 20th annual FA Women's Football Awards, Chelsea's Emma Hayes is named FA WSL Head Coach of the Year.

Mon 4 Jun: England captain Steph Houghton, 30, will miss this week's World Cup qualifier against Russia. The Manchester City defender needs surgery on a knee injury. Former City team-mate Lucy Bronze, recently a Champions League winner with Lyon, will take the captain's armband in her place.

Wed 6 Jun: The FA confirms the names for its new divisions for 2018/19. Tier 1 is to be the FA Women's Super League, Tier 2 becomes The FA Women's Championship, Tier 3 will consist of the FA National League Southern Premier Division and Northern Premier Division, while Tier 4 is made up of FA Women's National League Division 1 North / Division 1 Midlands / Division 1 South East and Division 1 South West.

Eniola Aluko, who left Chelsea at the end of the season, signs for Italian champions Juventus. The 31-year-old striker won two WSL 1 titles and two FA Cups during her time with the Blues.

Thu 7 Jun: Matt Beard – who led Liverpool to the WSL title in 2013 and 2014 before leaving the club – is appointed the manager of top-flight newcomers West Ham who were granted a full-time licence last week. Beard, who has also previously managed Chelsea, returns to these shores after two-and-a-half years coaching Boston Breakers in America.

Fri 8 Jun: Casey Stoney is named as the manager of Tier 2 newcomers Manchester United. The 36-year-old former international defender and captain earned 130 caps for England and won 12 major trophies during her playing career before retiring earlier this season. She will leave her role as an assistant to England manager Phil Neville to take up the position.

Scott Rogers leaves Liverpool after nearly three years as manager. Rogers arrived as an assistant to Matt Beard in January 2014 and helped the club retain their WSL title that year, stepping up to the role of manager when Beard left for Boston Breakers in 2015.

Chelsea sign 24-year-old goalkeeper Lizzie Durack from Everton. The 2017/18 season was her second spell with the Toffees and she has previously played in Australia and the US. Durack will challenge Hedvig Lindahl and Carly Telford for the No.1 spot.

Mon 11 Jun: Liverpool trio Alex Greenwood, Martha Harris and Amy Turner leave the club after not having their contracts renewed. Greenwood joined from Notts County in 2016 and made 44 appearances for the Reds, scoring six goals. Defender Harris, who signed from Lincoln in 2013, was part of the WSL 1 title-winning side in 2014. Turner made seven appearances for the club following her departure from Notts County in May 2017.

Tue 12 Jun: Neil Redfearn – who led Doncaster Rovers Belles to the 2017/18 WSL 2 title – is named as the new manager of Liverpool. As former Leeds United men's boss, Redfearn became the first person to manage a men's Football League side and a WSL team when he took the job at Doncaster in December 2017.

England are knocked off top spot in their World Cup qualifying group by Wales who win 3-0 at home to Russia. Wales know that if they win their final game at home to England in August then they will take the only automatic qualifying spot. England have two games left to play. They can claim top spot either by winning in Wales, or drawing with them so long as they then avoid defeat in their final group match away to minnows Kazakhstan.

Wed 13 Jun: The BBC reports that Millwall Lionesses boss Lee Burch is set to leave the Tier 2 club and take over at top-flight Yeovil Town. Burch – who has been with Millwall since 2016 – was named League Managers' Association WSL 2 Manager of the Year for 2017/18 having led his side to 3rd place.

Chelsea winger Gemma Davison, 31, leaves the club after a four-year spell with the Blues in which she scored 14 goals in 78 appearances after signing from Liverpool. Goalkeeper Rebecca Spencer, who left Chelsea in May, signs for Tier 1 newcomers West Ham. The former Arsenal and Birmingham City keeper, 27, becomes the first new arrival at the Hammers since they were accepted into the top-flight. Spencer made four appearances for Chelsea in 2017/18.

Thu 14 Jun: As reported by the BBC yesterday, top-flight Yeovil confirm that Lee Burch has been appointed as their new manager.

Wales international captain Sophie Ingle, who can play in defence or midfield, re-joins Chelsea from Liverpool. The 26-year-old previously played for the Blues in 2012 and 2013.

Fri 15 Jun: It's another day of busy transfer activity as former England defender Claire Rafferty, 29, leaves Chelsea for Tier 1 newcomers West Ham and the Liverpool exodus continues as captain Gemma Bonner, 26, becomes the eighth player to leave this summer. The central defender signs a two-year deal with Manchester City having made 115 appearances for the Reds in her eight years with the club.

Sat 16 Jun: Top-flight newcomers Brighton sign 30-year-old utility player Kayleigh Green who is out of contract at WSL rivals Yeovil Town. Green – who has been capped by Wales – can play in defence or attack and becomes the Seagulls' first signing of the summer.

Tue 19 Jun: Chelsea continue their busy summer in the transfer market with their third signing as they snap up Birmingham City and England defender Jess Carter for an undisclosed fee. The 20-year-old – who is a former PFA Young Player of the Year – agrees a three-year deal with the Blues.

WSL newcomers West Ham sign free agent Vyan Sampson who left Arsenal in February after her contract expired. The 21-year-old defender has been with the Gunners since 2011 but several serious knee injuries restricted her to just four senior appearances.

Thu 21 Jun: Belgium striker Tessa Wullaert joins Manchester City. The 25-year-old, who played in the 2018 Champions League final for runners-up Wolfsburg, is her country's record goal scorer having hit 39 goals in 71 internationals.

Sun 24 Jun: Sheffield FC announce they have had to withdraw from the newly-launched Championship, saying it has become clear that the "financial commitments necessary to compete at this level are proving now too onerous". They add that the move towards a "full-time operation" in elite women's football is "no longer consistent" with their position as a club. It's unclear what level they will compete at in 2018/19.

Mon 25 Jun: West Ham continue their rebuilding ahead of their debut top-flight season by signing defender Gilly Flaherty from Chelsea. The England centre-back has been with the Blues for four years winning two WSL titles and two FA Cups.

Reading midfielder Jo Potter is announced as the new head coach of Tier 3 side Coventry United. Potter will continue to play for WSL side Reading while coaching United. At Coventry she'll be working under Jay Bradford who remains United manager.

Tue 26 Jun: With a host of players having left the club this summer, Liverpool make their first signing with 24-year-old defender Leighanne Robe arriving from Millwall Lionesses.

Chelsea announce that New Zealand international Ali Riley will join from Rosengard next month. The 30-year-old will arrive at Kingsmeadow when the Swedish season reaches its mid-season break. Riley can play in defence or midfield.

Thu 28 Jun: Willie Kirk – who stood down as manager of WSL side Bristol City – is confirmed as assistant manager at Tier 2 newcomers Manchester United. Manager Casey Stoney says of the 40-year-old: "Willie is a fantastic appointment and has a proven track record of developing young players."

Fri 29 Jun: England midfielder Jade Moore signs a new contract with Reading. The 27-year-old joined the Royals in 2017 but endured an injury-hit 2017/18 campaign. Remi Allen and Jo Potter also agree new deals.

Former Arsenal and England star Rachel Yankey joins manager Lee Swindlehurst's coaching staff at Tier 2 London Bees.

Chelsea announce they have reached agreement with Gothenburg FC to sign Finland international forward Adelina Engman next month.

Mon 2 Jul: Wales choose the venue for August's crucial World Cup qualifier against England. The match will be played at Rodney Parade, home of Newport County FC.

Arsenal sign Switzerland international midfielder Lia Walti from German club Turbine Potsdam.

Following the club's demotion to Tier 3, Sunderland goalkeeper Rachael Laws joins WSL outfit Reading as a replacement for Mary Earps who has left for Wolfsburg.

Tue 3 Jul: Liverpool sign Bristol City defender Jasmine Matthews. The 25-year-old, who was named Vixens' Players' Player of the Year for 2017/18, can also play in midfield.

Everton snap up former Sunderland midfielder Dominique Bruinenberg. The 25-year-old former Netherlands youth international scored five goals in 25 appearances for the Black Cats.

WSL side Birmingham City Ladies rename themselves Birmingham City Women. [Right] Aoife Mannion in action for Birmingham City during the 2017/18 campaign

Wed 4 Jul: WSL outfit Bristol City appoint former Nottingham Forest boss Tanya Oxtoby as their new manager. The 36-year-old from Australia replaces Willie Kirk who stood down at the end of the season and who has since become assistant manager at Manchester United.

For the second time in as many days Bristol City lose a player to WSL rivals Liverpool as 26-year-old Belgian international forward Yana Daniels signs for the Reds.

Arsenal sign 26-year-old Germany international Tabea Kemme. The 2016 Olympic gold medallist, who has won 44 caps for her country, can play in defence, midfield or attack.

Sun 8 Jul: Reading sign winger Gemma Davison and defender Sophie Howard. Davison, 31, was part of Chelsea's Double-winning squad last season while Howard has made the switch from German side 1899 Hoffenheim.

Mon 9 Jul: Scotland forward Jane Ross – who left Manchester City at the end of the season – signs for WSL newcomers West Ham.

Tue 10 Jul: Two more players leave Sunderland following their drop to Tier 3. Captain Lucy Staniforth signs for Birmingham City while German goalkeeper Anke Preuss joins Liverpool.

Wed 11 Jul: Thirty-three-year-old centre-back Leandra Little, who captained Doncaster Rovers Belles to the 2017/18 WSL 2 title, signs for Liverpool where she again teams up with former Belles boss Neil Redfearn.

Thu 12 Jul: The controversy over the FA's restructuring of the top two divisions continues as Doncaster Rovers Belles follow Sheffield FC in withdrawing from the Championship. Belles won the 2017/18 WSL 2 title by 10 points but were denied promotion having accepted that a Tier 1 licence was beyond them because they did not have the financial means to go full-time. A statement from Belles said they needed to leave the Championship to "ensure their continued viability". The FA confirms that both Doncaster and Sheffield FC will be placed into Tier 3 and that Crystal Palace will now take one of the available Tier 2 places. Palace had been left hugely disappointed when their original application to join the Championship was turned down. It's reported that Sunderland, Blackburn and one other unnamed club are also having appeals heard regarding inclusion in the Championship.

There are huge concerns for Doncaster with most their players having now left the club. Wales international defender Rhiannon Roberts, who was part of last season's WSL 2 title-winning squad, follows Leandra Little to Liverpool where she teams up with her former Belles boss Neil Redfearn.

Arsenal sign French goalkeeper Pauline Peyraud-Magnin from Champions League holders Lyon. The 26-year-old won three Champions League titles and three League titles in two spells with Lyon.

With a new board having taken control of Millwall Lionesses, and with manager Lee Burch having left for Yeovil, former Arsenal Women's boss Pedro Martinez Losa is named as director of football and Chris Phillips as manager.

Fri 13 Jul: The newly-formed Manchester United confirm their 21-player squad for their first season in the Championship. England left-back Alex Greenwood and goalkeeper Siobhan Chamberlain – both previously with Liverpool – are among the leading names. Also joining from Liverpool are Amy Turner, Martha Harris and Emily Harris. United, who have not had a senior women's team since 2005, also welcome back seven former youth players who previously had to leave when they turned 16, among them Katie Zelem who won Serie A with Juventus in 2017/18. Other players in a squad with an average age of 21 are Jessica Sigsworth – who was top scorer in WSL 2 with Doncaster Rovers Belles last season – and Scotland internationals Kirsty Smith and Lizzie Arnot.

Top-flight newcomers Brighton sign England Under-20 forward Ellie Brazil from Serie A side Fiorentina.

Sat 14 Jul: West Ham sign Dutch international midfielder Tessel Middag who left Manchester City at the end of last season.

Bristol City sign goalkeeper Sophie Baggaley, 21, from top-flight rivals Birmingham City. Meanwhile, Danique Kerkdijk, Loren Dykes, Frankie Brown, Flo Allen, Poppy Wilson and Carla Humphreys all sign new deals with the Vixens.

Liverpool sign four more players. Scotland international forward Christie Murray, 28, arrives from Glasgow City. Republic of Ireland international and defensive midfielder Niamh Fahey joins from French side Bordeaux. Doncaster Rovers Belles defender Sophie Bradley-Auckland links up with former boss Neil Redfearn and former England Under-23 striker Courtney Sweetman-Kirk arrives from Merseyside rivals Everton.

England international Lianne Sanderson, 30, joins Serie A side Juventus where she will link up with her former Three Lionesses team-mate Eniola Aluko who signed for the Italians earlier this summer.

Mon 16 Jul: Southampton FC announce former England international Marieanne Spacey-Cale as the new head of their Girls and Women's Football Technical Department. The men's Premier League club had their application for a Women's Championship licence for 2018/19 turned down by the FA. At the time of their application they were one of only two existing men's Premier League clubs – along with Manchester United – not to provide female football at senior level. United though were successful in their application, and Southampton say they are now committed to "providing a pathway for talented female players to fulfil their potential at Southampton FC."

Tue 17 Jul: England and Manchester United goalkeeper Siobhan Chamberlain is said to be recovering well after suffering a suspected neck injury in her new club's behind-closed doors friendly against Liverpool on Sunday. The match was abandoned while the 34-year-old was taken to hospital. A Manchester United statement reads: "Fortunately investigations confirmed no serious injury."

Wed 18 Jul: Reading attacking midfielder Brooke Chaplen, 29, extends her contract with the club.

Thu 19 Jul: West Ham sign Republic of Ireland forward Leanne Kiernan and American defender Brooke Hendrix.

Everton FC become the first men's Premier League club to use solely their women's team to launch their new kit.

Scotland international striker Erin Cuthbert signs a new three-year deal with champions Chelsea.

It's revealed that Germany captain and Lyon midfielder Dzsenifer Marozsan has a pulmonary embolism (meaning a blood vessel in her lungs is blocked). She says on facebook that she "will be out of training for a few weeks."

Fri 20 Jul: West Ham join the growing number of clubs to change their name from Ladies to Women. The Hammers also sign Germany international midfielder Julia Simic from SC Freiburg.

Bristol City sign Wales left-back Gemma Evans, 21, from Yeovil. Belgium international midfielder Julie Biesmans agrees a new deal with the club.

Tier 2 newcomers Crystal Palace strengthen midfield with the signing of Watford captain Anneka Nuttall.

Sat 21 Jul: The BBC breaks the news that England and Manchester City midfielder Izzy Christiansen is expected to sign for reigning European champions Lyon. It will be the second time in as many summers that a City player has made that switch with defender Lucy Bronze having done so last year.

Sun 22 Jul: Top-flight Reading sign Chelsea striker Millie Farrow. The 22-year-old, who has represented England at Under-19 and Under-23 level, joins from Bristol City.

Mon 23 Jul: As expected, Manchester City and England midfielder Izzy Christiansen completes her move to European champions Lyon. The 26-year-old signs a two-year deal with the French side and will link up with her former City team-mate Lucy Bronze who made the same switch last summer.

Mayumi Pacheco, who helped Doncaster Rovers Belles win WSL 2 last season, signs for Reading. The 19-year-old left-back, who has represented England at Under-17 and Under-19 level, started out at Liverpool before joining the Belles initially on loan.

Tue 24 Jul: The FA publishes what it says is "the final list of teams to compete in the FA Women's Super League and the FA Women's Championship for 2018/19". The list remains unchanged from the FA's most recent announcement, which effectively means any appeals have been unsuccessful. The BBC reports that Blackburn Rovers and Sunderland were among the clubs to have appeals rejected while other media outlets suggest that Southampton FC also appealed. The final divisions are as follows:

WSL: 11 teams – Arsenal, Birmingham City, Brighton & Hove Albion, Bristol City, Chelsea, Everton, Liverpool, Manchester City, Reading, Yeovil Town, West Ham United.

Championship: 11 teams: Aston Villa, Charlton Athletic, Crystal Palace, Durham, Leicester City Women, Lewes, London Bees, Millwall Lionesses, Manchester United, Sheffield United, Tottenham Hotspur.

It's confirmed that the revamped Leagues will kick-off on the weekend of 8-9 September and the Continental Tyres Women's League Cup will get under way on 18-19 August.

The constitution for the FA Women's National League can also now be finalised. With Sheffield FC and Doncaster Rovers Belles having both withdrawn from the Championship and been placed into WNL Northern Premier (Tier 3), that division had swelled to 14 teams. To alleviate some of the fixture congestion Loughborough Foxes are moved across to WNL Southern Premier (which had been reduced from 12 to 11 teams since Crystal Palace's promotion to the Championship earlier in the summer). So WNL Northern Premier now has 13 teams, and WNL Southern Premier 12. The final constitution for the divisions is as follows:

WNL Northern Premier: 13 teams – Blackburn Rovers, Bradford City, Derby County, Doncaster Rovers Belles, Fylde, Guiseley Vixens, Huddersfield Town, Hull City, Middlesbrough, Nottingham Forest, Sheffield FC, Stoke City, Sunderland.

WNL Southern Premier: 12 teams – C&K Basildon, Cardiff City Ladies, Chichester City, Coventry United, Gillingham, Loughborough Foxes, MK Dons, Oxford United, Plymouth Argyle, Portsmouth, Queens Park Rangers, Watford

Elsewhere in the news today, Bristol City sign left-back Ali Johnson, 19, who left Liverpool this week. The Vixens also snap up New Zealand international striker Katie Rood who won Serie A with Juventus last season.

Chelsea boss Emma Hayes – who led her club to the WSL and FA Cup Double last season – is included on the 10-strong shortlist for FIFA's Best Women's Coach 2018. The other nominees are Stephan Lerch (Vfl Wolfsburg), Mark Parsons (Portland Thorns), Reynald Pedros (Lyon), Alen Stajcic (Australia national team), Asako Takakura (Japan national team), Vadao (Brazil national team), Jorge Vilda (Spain national team), Martina Voss-Tecklenburg (Switzerland national team), Sarina Wiegman (Netherlands national team).

Lucy Bronze is the only English player on the shortlist for FIFA's Best Women's Player 2018. She's joined by five of her Lyon team-mates (Ada Hegerberg, Amandine Henry, Saki Kumagai, Dzsenifer Marozsan and Wendie Renard), as well as Pernille Harder (Vfl Wolfsburg), Sam Kerr (Sky Blue FC/Perth Glory/Chicago Red Stars), Marta (Orlando Pride), and Megan Rapinoe (Seattle Reign). Both the Best Coach and Best Player votes cover performances from 7 August 2017-24 May 2018 inclusive.

Wed 25 Jul: WSL outfit Everton sign Hannah Cain from Sheffield FC who recently had to withdraw from the Championship. The 19-year-old England Under-20 international came through Sheffield United's Centre of Excellence.

Scotland midfielder Chloe Arthur, 23, signs a two-year deal with Birmingham City following her departure from Bristol City.

Thu 26 Jul: Denmark international forward Nadia Nadim, 30, submits a surprise transfer request to her club Manchester City. Nadim, who is currently on City's tour of the US, joined them in January.

Brighton sign England Under-23 midfielder Jodie Brett from Everton.

Sat 28 Jul: Bristol City sign Scottish duo Lucy Graham and Eartha Cummings. Midfielder Graham, 21, joins from Hibernian with 19-year-old goalkeeper Cumings signing from Spartans FC.

Mon 30 Jul: Liverpool Ladies rebrand as Liverpool FC Women.

Tue 31 Jul: Brighton sign 28-year-old defender Victoria Williams who left Sunderland following their demotion to Tier 3. Williams agrees a one-year deal.

Wed 1 Aug: The FA releases the fixtures for the 2018/19 WSL and Championship seasons. Headline fixtures include WSL champions Chelsea at home to last season's runners-up Manchester City on the opening weekend and Tier 2 newcomers Manchester United away to Aston Villa. The season will begin on the weekend of September 8/9. The Continental

Cup fixtures are also released. The group stage will begin on August 18/19 with two groups of five teams and two groups of six teams.

Thu 2 Aug: The BBC learns that the FA would be open to either the Premier League or English Football League taking over the running of women's football. Both those bodies decline to comment on whether they have any interest.

Thu 9 Aug: The summer transfer window closes with Manchester City's signing of Canada international striker Janine Beckie (pictured) the highest profile deadline day signing. The 23-year-old agrees a one-year deal with City following her departure from American NWSL side Sky Blue FC.

FA WOMEN'S SUPER LEAGUE
TIER ONE

The structure of the women's club game in England has changed many times over the last two decades, but the most recent overhaul has proved to be the most controversial. It was in September 2017, just weeks after the start of the season, that the FA announced new licensing criteria for clubs to be allowed to compete in the top two tiers in 2018/19.

Tier 1 was to become the first fully professional division in women's football in England, with clubs needing to prove they had the financial means to support full-time players and staff. Coaches would be required to deliver a minimum of 16 hours' daytime contact per week (plus matches), increasing to 20 hours by the 2021/22 season.

In Tier 2 clubs would need to appoint full-time general managers and provide a minimum of 8 hours' daytime contact per week (plus matches) for semi-professional players.

The news shocked and split the women's game, with many in favour of the FA's plans and others fearful they were trying to grow the game too quickly for many clubs to keep up. The WSL 1 places of Yeovil Town and Sunderland immediately appeared under threat with WSL 2 outfits Oxford and Watford also looking particularly vulnerable. Yeovil eventually proved successful in crowdfunding the £350,000 they needed to maintain their top-flight status, but Sunderland missed out on a place in either of the top two divisions. They appealed but were unsuccessful and effectively relegated to Tier 3. Oxford and Watford were also unable to obtain Tier 2 licences and dropped to Tier 3.

Sunderland were the only existing top-flight club not to have their licence renewed. The other nine sides (Arsenal, Birmingham City, Bristol City, Chelsea, Everton, Liverpool, Manchester City, Reading and Yeovil) were joined by two newcomers for 2018/19: Brighton & Hove Albion, who finished 2017/18 as Tier 2 runners-up; and West Ham United who jumped two divisions having placed 7th in WPL Southern. With the name of Tier 2 having been changed from WSL 2 to The Championship, the top-flight would now be known simply as WSL instead of WSL 1. The club finishing bottom in 2018/19 will be relegated to the Championship. The top two clubs in the Championship will be eligible for promotion providing that all licence criteria can be met. From the end of 2019/20 there will be one up, one down between the WSL and the Championship.

This first club section of the book concentrates on the 11 teams who compete in the top division in 2018/19. The clubs appear in alphabetical order. The stadium listed is the main home ground the club played at in 2017/18. Some clubs will have changed stadiums for 2018/19 and where they have been able to notify us before our publishing deadlines these new venues have been listed. Some clubs may also have changed their managers since our deadlines.

Results of each team's WSL 1, FA Cup and Continental Cup matches for 2017/18 are listed. Where known the following information has been included for each game: scorers, goal times, penalties, missed penalties, own goals, attendances. The figure in the column on the far right is the club's League position after all the matches played that day have been completed. This has been included from their third fixture onwards. It's important to note that this isn't necessarily the position they started their next match in as other teams may have played matches in the interim. In the player appearance tables, an appearance counts as any match in which that player started or came on to play as a substitute.

PFA WOMEN'S PLAYER OF THE YEAR, FRAN KIRBY, HOLDING THE FA WSL TROPHY

ARSENAL

2018/19: WSL (Tier 1)

Nickname: The Gunners
Ground: Meadow Park, Boreham Wood FC
Manager: Joe Montemurro (since Nov 2017)

Season 2017/18:
WSL (Tier 1): 3rd
FA Cup: Runners-up
Continental Cup: Winners

Founded: 1987
National Honours: FA Cup Winners: (14)
1993, 95, 98, 99, 2001, 04, 06, 07, 08, 09, 11,
13, 14, 16 **FA Cup Runners-up: (2)** 2010, 18
WSL Champions: (2) 2011, 2012
WSL Continental Cup Winners: (5) 2011, 12,
13, 15, 18
WSL Continental Cup Runners-up: (1) 2014
UEFA Cup Winners: (1) 2007
WPL Champions (former top division): (12)
1993, 95, 97, 2001, 02, 04, 05, 06, 07, 08, 09,
10
WPL Cup Winners: (10)
1992, 93, 94, 98, 99, 2000, 01, 05, 07, 09
WPL Cup Runners-up: (3) 2003, 06, 08

Previous WSL Positions
2018 WSL 1 (Tier 1): 3rd
2017 WSL 1 (Tier 1): 3rd (Spring Series)
2016 WSL 1 (Tier 1): 3rd
2015 WSL 1 (Tier 1): 3rd
2014 WSL (Tier 1): 4th
2013 WSL (Tier 1): 3rd
2012 WSL (Tier 1): Champions
2011 WSL (Tier 1): Champions

As the only English team to have reigned as European champions and with 44 major trophies to their name, Arsenal remain the most decorated team in the country. The Champions League was won in 2007 when it was known as the UEFA Cup and the 44th of Arsenal's major trophies arrived in March 2018 when Vivianne Miedema struck the only goal of the game in the Continental Cup final against Manchester City at Adams Park. Hopes of a 45th were blown away by Chelsea in May's FA Cup final as the Blues swept to a 3-1 victory.

After their formation by Arsenal men's kitman Vic Akers in 1987 the club became the dominant force in English football. Akers collected a stunning 32 major trophies during his 22-year career as manager and now serves the club as honorary president.

The Gunners currently play the role of the major challengers to the new powers of the game: Chelsea and Manchester City. All in all, 2017/18 represented a successful first season under manager Joe Montemurro. The Australian replaced Spain's Pedro Martinez Losa in November 2017, leading the Gunners to Continental Cup glory, the FA Cup final and to 3rd in WSL 1, only missing out on qualification for the Champions League to Manchester City on the final day.

ARSENAL FACTS

- Arsenal are the only British side to win the Champions League, doing so when it was known as the UEFA Cup in 2007. Their 1-0 aggregate win over Swedish side Umea was part of a quadruple of major honours that season: League, FA Cup, League Cup and UEFA Cup.

- The only goal of that UEFA Cup final was scored by Alex Scott who was just 22 years old when she drilled home a stunning 25-yard effort in injury-time of the first leg in the Gammliavallen Stadium. Scott retired at the end of 2017/18 having won the Champions League, nine League titles, seven FA Cups, five League Cups and 140 caps for England.

- Arsenal have won the FA Cup a record 14 times. The Gunners have also won a record five Continental Cups, most recently beating Manchester City in the 2018 final at Adams Park.

Robin Parker / The FA

JORDAN NOBBS DOB: 08.12.92 MIDFIELDER

Since signing from Sunderland in 2010, Jordan Nobbs has helped Arsenal win two WSL titles, four Women's FA Cups and five Continental Tyres League Cups

Jordan Nobbs says she wants to become an Arsenal legend by the time she retires, and – after eight years with the Gunners – the quick-footed England star is surely well on her way to achieving that. The skilful playmaker from County Durham became Arsenal's longest-serving current player in 2018 following the retirement of long-serving right-back Alex Scott. "In our changing room, the lockers go in order of how long you've been at the club," Nobbs says. "I think it shows the respect that the club have for the people who have been here and their legacy. Since Alex left, I'm the one at the front of that line. That's a great feeling.

"I've been here for eight years and I signed a new two-year deal in May – I think that shows the love, the loyalty and the passion I have for putting on an Arsenal shirt. I want to become one of the best players they've had. It's hard work but that's my goal and my aim while I'm at this club. I want to keep on learning and I hope I can keep on improving but I feel like I'm on the right track to hopefully be an Arsenal legend. That's what I want to be."

And there is a long list of legends already among the Arsenal alumni, including England great Kelly Smith, who Nobbs admired, not just for her ability but for her club passion too.

"She was always Arsenal, through-and-through. She played for the badge on her shirt," Nobbs says. "I was very lucky to play with her while she was here. Her ability on the ball and her passion to want to win – both were indescribable.

"Another leader, great player and person at this club was Alex Scott. She was another one who I saw lead as a true captain at Arsenal. Alex set the standard for wanting to play for Arsenal, and reminding players how lucky you are to even play just once for this club."

A newer figure at Arsenal whose love for the club is equally clear is manager Joe Montemurro. The Australian – a lifelong Arsenal fan – took charge of the women's side in November 2017 and oversaw an immediate upturn in form, steering the team towards lifting the Continental Tyres League Cup in March with an impressive win over Manchester City.

"In the past few years we've been a little bit disjointed and a little bit inconsistent. Yes, we won the FA Cup [in 2016], but actually we weren't really playing as well as we wanted to," Nobbs admits. "Then, last year when Joe came in, we could immediately feel that we were playing better. We were coming off the pitch having enjoyed games.

"Coming over all the way from the other side of the world, I think that shows the love and the drive that Joe has for this club, and his desire to work for this club. He wants us to play the Arsenal way and to win trophies with good football. That's exciting for me. Whenever you chat to him, it's clear that he's a passionate guy who wants to win. I know managers don't have to be the nicest people, but he's genuinely one of the nicest guys in the game too.

"Yes, we were thrilled to win that final against Man City, but we were more excited by the way we played and performed, because that was how we want to be, as Arsenal. We're going in the right direction and I can't put in to words the love I have for being in London and for wearing red. I can't imagine ever leaving this club. The club has invested in me and changed my life. I can't thank them enough for that."

2017/18 WSL 1

Date	Opponent		Score	Scorers	Att	Pos
24.09	Birmingham C (h)	W	3-2	Jodie Taylor 35, (pen) 89, Lisa Evans 84, _Louise Quinn sent off 80_	837	
30.09	Manchester C (a)	L	2-5	Emma Mitchell 45+1, Heather O'Reilly 48	1,646	
08.10	Bristol City (h)	D	1-1	Danielle van de Donk 50	840	6
29.10	Everton (a)	W	2-0	Vivianne Miedema 23, Beth Mead 78	435	4
12.11	Sunderland (h)	W	3-0	Louise Quinn 58, Vivianne Miedema 68, Jordan Nobbs 76	400	5
10.12	Liverpool (h)		P-P			
07.01	Chelsea (a)	L	2-3	Vivianne Miedema 56, Dominique Janssen 63	2,570	4
28.01	Reading (a)	D	0-0		690	4

07.02	Liverpool (a)	W	3-0	*Vivianne Miedema missed pen (saved Rebecca Flaherty) 29*, Vivianne Miedema 29 (scored pen rebound), Dominique Janssen 45, Lisa Evans 62	461	4
11.02	Yeovil Town (h)	W	4-0	Danielle Carter 37, 71, Beth Mead 48, 85	740	3
23.02	Everton (h)	W	1-0	Beth Mead 38	813	3
01.04	Chelsea (h)	D	1-1	Beth Mead 45+1	1,807	4
18.04	Reading (h)	W	3-1	Kim Little 8, Dominique Janssen 27, Danielle van de Donk 64	610	3
21.04	Yeovil Town (a)	D	0-0		317	3
24.04	Liverpool (h)	W	3-0	Katie McCabe 65, Jordan Nobbs 74, 85	587	3
29.04	Birmingham C (a)	L	0-3		921	4
12.05	Manchester C (h)	W	2-1	Danielle van de Donk 52, Beth Mead 62	1,514	4
16.05	Sunderland (a)	W	2-0	Kim Little 9, Beth Mead 30	321	3
20.05	Bristol City (a)	W	6-1	Danielle van de Donk 21, 71, Kim Little (pen) 28, Leah Williamson 30, Beth Mead 38, Katie McCabe 44	724	3

2017/18 WSL Continental Cup: Group One South

12.10	London Bees (h)	W	7-0	Lisa Evans 24, Emma Mitchell 34, 37, Jodie Taylor 52, Beth Mead (pen) 58, (pen) 78, Louise Quinn 83	931
01.11	Millwall L (a)	W	5-2	Beth Mead 10, Jordan Nobbs 45, 75, Danielle Carter 78, Lauren James (pen) 89	451
05.11	Reading (h)	L	1-2	Beth Mead 59	380
16.11	Watford (a)	W	6-0	Jodie Taylor 15, 78, Danielle Carter 47, Emma Mitchell 60, Dominique Janssen 74, Danielle van de Donk 75	823
17.12 QF	Sunderland (h)	W	3-1	Jordan Nobbs 16, Vivianne Miedema 38, Beth Mead 77	400
14.01 SF	Reading (a)	W	3-2	Beth Mead 5, Vivianne Miedema 8, Jordan Nobbs 83	749
14.03	Manchester C (n)	W	1-0	Vivianne Miedema 33	2,136

(n) Played at Adams Park, Wycombe Wanderers FC

2017/18 FA Cup

04.02 R4	Yeovil Town (a)	W	3-0	Jordan Nobbs 12, *Beth Mead missed pen 22, Danielle Carter missed pen 44 (saved by Megan Walsh)*, Beth Mead 45, Hannah Miles (og) 59	323
18.02 R5	Millwall L (h)	W	1-0	Beth Mead 32	617
18.03 QF	Charlton A (h)		P-P		
25.03	Charlton A (h)	W	5-0	Kim Little (pen) 4, Heather O'Reilly 56, Vivianne Miedema 60 Danielle Carter 85, Jordan Nobbs 89	810
15.04 SF	Everton (a)	W	2-1	Danielle Carter 25, Louise Quinn 90+1	1,457
05.05 F	Chelsea (n)	L	1-3	Vivianne Miedema 73	45,423

ARSENAL PLAYER APPEARANCES & GOALS 2017/18

				WSL1		FAC		CC		Total	
				A	G	A	G	A	G	A	G
Carter, Danielle	F	ENG	18.05.93	17	2	5	2	6	2	28	6
Cooke, Shannon	D	ENG	02.02.00	2	-	-	-	-	-	2	-
Evans, Lisa	F	SCO	21.05.92	18	2	5	-	6	1	29	3
Filbey, Anne-Marie	M	ENG	11.10.99	1	-	-	-	1	-	2	-
Gibbon, Emma	G	WAL	06.02.99	-	-	-	-	-	-	-	-
Henning, Josephine	D	GER	08.09.89	3	-	-	-	-	-	3	-
Hinds, Taylor	M	ENG	25.04.99	-	-	-	-	2	-	2	-
James, Lauren	M	ENG	29.09.01	5	-	1	-	3	1	9	1
Janssen, Dominique	M	NED	17.01.95	17	3	4	-	7	1	28	4
Kuyken, Ava	M	ENG	15.06.01	3	-	1	-	1	-	5	-
Little, Kim	M	SCO	29.06.90	9	3	4	1	1	-	14	4
Lumsden, Bethany	F	ENG	n/a	2	-	-	-	2	-	4	-
McCabe, Katie	F	IRL	01.09.95	10	2	5	-	2	-	17	2
Mead, Beth	F	ENG	09.05.95	17	8	5	2	7	6	29	16
Miedema, Vivianne	F	NED	15.07.96	11	4	4	2	5	3	20	9
Mitchell, Emma	D	SCO	19.09.92	18	1	4	-	6	3	28	4
Moorhouse, Anna	G	ENG	30.03.95	4	-	3	-	4	-	11	-
Ngunga, Jessica	F	ENG	24.09.00	2	-	-	-	-	-	2	-
Nobbs, Jordan	M	ENG	08.12.92	17	3	5	2	7	4	29	9
O'Reilly, Heather	M	USA	02.01.85	16	1	5	1	7	-	28	2
Quinn, Louise	D	IRL	17.06.90	16	1	5	1	6	1	27	3
Rose, Jemma	D	ENG	19.01.92	4	-	-	-	6	-	10	-
Samuelson, Jessica	D	SWE	30.01.92	2	-	-	-	-	-	2	-
Scott, Alex	D	ENG	14.10.84	3	-	2	-	3	-	8	-
Taylor, Jodie	F	ENG	17.05.86	3	2	-	-	3	3	6	5
Thomas, Lucy	G	ENG	n/a	-	-	-	-	-	-	-	-
Van de Donk, Danielle	M	NED	05.08.91	18	5	4	-	5	1	27	6
Van Veenendaal, Sari	G	NED	03.04.90	14	-	2	-	3	-	19	-
Williamson, Leah	D	ENG	29.03.97	17	1	4	-	7	-	28	1

GOALSCORERS 2017/18

WSL 1: Mead (8), van de Donk (5), Miedema (4), Janssen (3), Little (3), Nobbs (3), Carter (2), Evans (2), McCabe (2), Taylor (2), Mitchell (1), O'Reilly (1), Quinn (1), Williamson (1)

FAC: Carter (2), Mead (2), Miedema (2), Nobbs (2), Little (1), O'Reilly (1), Quinn (1), own goals (1)

CC: Mead (6), Nobbs (4), Miedema (3), Mitchell (3), Taylor (3), Carter (2), Evans (1), James (1), Janssen (1), Quinn (1), van de Donk (1)

Total: Mead (16), Miedema (9), Nobbs (9), Carter (6), van de Donk (6), Taylor (5), Janssen (4), Little (4), Mitchell (4), Evans (3), Quinn (3), McCabe (2), O'Reilly (2), James (1), Williamson (1), own goals (1)

BIRMINGHAM CITY

2018/19: WSL (Tier 1)

Nickname: Blues
Ground: Damson Park, (Solihull Moors FC)
Manager: Marc Skinner (since Dec 2016)

Season 2017/18:
WSL (Tier 1): 5th
FA Cup: 5th Round
Continental Cup: Group Stage

Founded: 1968	**Previous WSL Positions**
National Honours: FA Cup Winners: (1)	**2018 WSL 1 (Tier 1):** 5th
2012, **Runners-up: (1)** 2017	**2017 WSL 1 (Tier 1):** 7th (Spring Series)
WSL Runners-up: (2) 2011, 12	**2016 WSL 1 (Tier 1):** 4th
WSL Continental Cup Runners-up: (3) 2011,	**2015 WSL 1 (Tier 1):** 6th
12, 16	**2014 WSL 1 (Tier 1):** 3rd
	2013 WSL (Tier 1): 4th
	2012 WSL (Tier 1): Runners-up
	2011 WSL (Tier 1): Runners-up

One FA Cup win, two League runners-up finishes and four more major Cup final appearances since the dawn of the WSL era is proof that Birmingham City are capable of holding their own among the elite of English football. If their achievements weren't impressive enough, it's worth bearing in mind that it's little more than a decade since a donation of £10,000 from a player's parent saved them from possible extinction. Blues overcame their financial difficulties of 2006 and went on to become founder members of the WSL for the 2011 summer season. They were long-time leaders of the League in that first WSL campaign only to be overhauled by eventual champions Arsenal in the title run-in. Champions League semi-finalists in 2014, the club has come a long way since being formed by a group of female Birmingham City fans in 1968. They had to get by on friendly matches alone for two years before joining the Heart of England League in 1970.

BIRMINGHAM FACTS

- Birmingham finished the 2017/18 season in 5th place and with a club record points return in the WSL era. Their tally of 30 points was greater even than the seasons when they finished runners-up in 2011 (29 points) and 2012 (26 points), although admittedly there were four fewer matches played in each of those earlier campaigns.

- Striker Ellen White finished 2017/18 as WSL 1 top scorer (15 goals) and was named the Vauxhall England Player of the Year for her performances for the national team in 2017/18. Goalkeeper Ann-Katrin Berger was joint winner of the WSL 1 Players' Player of the Year award alongside Manchester City's Jill Scott. Berger astounded her fellow pros with a string of sensational performances after returning to action within just two months of having undergone treatment for thyroid cancer.

- Along with Arsenal (six finals, five wins) and Manchester City (three finals, two wins), Birmingham are the only team to have played in at least three Continental Cup finals. Unfortunately for them, they have lost all three.

- In 2013/14, Birmingham became only the second British team (after Arsenal) to reach the Champions League semi-finals. They held Tyreso to a goalless draw in the first leg but went down 3-0 in the return leg in Sweden. Their only other Champions League campaign came in 2012/13 when they were knocked out in the Round of 32 by Italian side Bardolino Verona.

Birmingham City Ladies FC

AOIFE MANNION DOB: 24.09.95 DEFENDER

Aoife Mannion joined Birmingham City in 2013 and played Champions League football for the club before her 18th birthday.

"Up until I was about 12 years old, I genuinely believed that I was the only girl in the whole world that played football, which is absolutely crazy."

Birmingham City's Aoife Mannion's lack of a female footballing idol while she was growing up fittingly illustrates the true importance of the inspirational role that she plays for the Women's Super League club today.

"The contrast now is incredible. I remember the first time when one of the Blues fans, a little girl, had my name on the back of her shirt and I just thought 'wow', what a shift in women's football there has been in the last few years. I know when I was growing up, I would never have had a women's footballers' name on the back of my shirt, simply because I didn't really know that women and girls played football."

In 2018, clubs like Birmingham are helping to greatly reduce the chance of young girls growing up with the same initial misgivings about the game that Mannion had. And another top-half finish in 2017/18 saw the Blues continue to make an impression on the field as well as off it, finding superb form particularly in the latter part of the campaign.

"We're really happy with lots of our performances, especially in the second half of the season," Mannion says, hailing the coaching skills of manager Marc Skinner, who took charge in December 2016. "Marc has had a massive impact on the squad," former Aston Villa trainee Mannion continues, "He's had a positive impact on every single player and their development, technically and tactically on the pitch, plus he's starting to create a really positive culture and Birmingham is a really attractive club to be at at the moment, highlighted by the players that he's been able to bring in and also the players he's been able to retain."

Birmingham-born, Mannion describes herself as "Brummie, through and through" and her background shares a resemblance with that of a Blues legend – England winger Karen Carney, with both having attended St. Peter's secondary school in Solihull, albeit nine years apart, and Chelsea's Carney – like Mannion – is a life-long Birmingham fan.

Versatile England Under-23 international defender Mannion's education continued at the University of Birmingham, where she graduated with a degree in economics in December 2017 – a degree that she completed while playing regular, top-flight football.

"I was really lucky to be able to marry up my studies with my football in the same area," she says. "I feel quite fortunate to be from this area. It's a great place to live and I'm really passionate about it. I've got lots and lots of friends here.

"What's really nice is that it provides a platform for girls to come and watch us in Solihull.

"Even if football isn't what they want to do, that's fine, as long as we're encouraging girls and women to be active and play sport, and to show that it is an option for them and a really good thing to do as a form of exercise.

"I think that's a really powerful message. I would have loved to have role models when I was growing up so to think that we can do that for girls now is incredible."

WSL 1 2017/18

Date	Opponent	Result	Score	Scorers	Att	Pos
24.09	Arsenal (a)	L	2-3	Ellen White 12, 60	837	
01.10	Everton (h)	W	2-1	Ellen White 14, Charlie Wellings 31	821	
08.10	Reading (a)	D	2-2	Aoife Mannion (pen) 45+1, (og) 90+3	655	5
29.10	Manchester City (a)	L	1-3	Lucy Quinn 6, *Kerys Harrop sent off 79*	1,465	7
11.11	Liverpool (a)	L	0-1		843	7
10.12	Bristol City (h)	P-P				
06.01	Sunderland (a)	L	0-3		352	9
14.01	Bristol City (h)	W	2-0	Aoife Mannion (pen) 54, Charlie Wellings 61	517	7
28.01	Yeovil Town (h)+	W	3-0	Aoife Mannion (pen) 13, Meaghan Sargeant 45+1, Ellen White 47	405	5
10.02	Chelsea (h)	L	0-2		669	6

21.02	Manchester City (h)	W	2-0	Ellen White 23, 70	803	5
25.03	Liverpool (h)	W	4-0	Rachel Williams 12, Kate Longhurst (og) 19, Jessica Carter 33, Ellen White 82	869	5
28.03	Bristol City (a)	W	2-0	Ellen White 7, 67	500	4
01.04	Sunderland (h)	W	2-0	Ellen White 19, Rachel Williams 23	540	3
18.04	Yeovil Town (a)++	D	0-0		203	4
29.04	Arsenal (h)	W	3-0	Ellen White 10, 40, 86, *Aoife Mannion missed pen 77 (saved Sari van Veenendaal),*	921	5
09.05	Chelsea (a)	L	1-2	Hayley Ladd 62	934	6
13.05	Everton (a)*	W	3-0	Charlie Wellings 20, 58, Ellen White 86	337	5
20.05	Reading (h)**	D	1-1	Ellen White 29	1,120	5

+Fixture switched from Huish Park to avoid clash with Yeovil Town men's v Man U FA Cup R4 tie (played Fri 26.01)

++Played at Viridor Stadium, Taunton Town FC   *Played at Rossett Park, Marine FC **Played at St Andrews, Birmingham City FC

2017/18 WSL CONTINENTAL CUP: GROUP TWO NORTH

11.10	Oxford United (h)	W	4-0	Freda Ayisi 38, Lucy Quinn 55, Hayley Ladd 69, Charlie Wellings 89	445
02.11	Everton (a)	L	0-1		181
05.11	Doncaster R B (h)	W	3-2	Freda Ayisi 45+1, Charlie Wellings 58, Rachel Williams 75	682
03.12	Manchester C (a)	L	0-2		1,077

*Played at St Andrew's

2017/18 FA CUP

| 04.02 R4 | Reading (a) | W | 1-0 | Marisa Ewers 34 | 488 |
| 18.02 R5 | Manchester C. (h) | L | 1-3 (aet) | Ellen White 37 | 641 |

BIRMINGHAM CITY PLAYER APPEARANCES & GOALS 2017/18

				WSL1		FAC		CC		Total	
---	---	---	---	A	G	A	G	A	G	A	G
Ayisi, Freda	F	ENG	21.10.94	8	-	-	-	2	2	10	2
Berger, Ann-Katrin	G	GER	09.10.90	14	-	2	-	2	-	18	-
Carter, Jessica	D	ENG	27.10.97	18	1	2	-	3	-	23	1
Cusack, Maddy	M	ENG	28.10.95	-	-	-	-	2	-	2	-
Ewers, Marisa	D	GER	24.02.89	12	-	2	1	1	-	15	1
Follis, Emma	M	ENG	06.01.92	15	-	2	-	3	-	20	-
Hampton, Hannah	G	ENG	16.11.00	4	-	-	-	2	-	6	-
Harrop, Kerys	D	ENG	03.12.90	16	-	2	-	1	-	19	-
Hayles, Shania	M	ENG	22.12.99	-	-	-	-	1	-	1	-
Hegerberg, Andrine	M	NOR	06.06.93	4	-	-	-	3	-	7	-
Ladd, Hayley	D	WAL	06.10.93	17	1	2	-	4	1	23	2
Linden, Anna Isabelle	F	GER	15.01.91	1	-	-	-	2	-	3	-

				WSL 1		FAC		CC		Total	
				A	G	A	G	A	G	A	G
Mannion, Aoife	D	ENG	24.09.95	18	3	2	-	4	-	24	3
Mayling, Sarah	M	ENG	20.03.97	11	-	1	-	2	-	14	-
Quinn, Lucy	F	ENG	29.09.93	17	1	2	-	3	1	22	2
Sargeant, Meaghan	D	ENG	16.03.94	13	1	2	-	4	-	19	1
Scofield, Constance	M	ENG	26.05.99	-	-	-	-	2	-	2	-
Stenson, Frances	G	ENG	27.04.01	1	-	-	-	-	-	1	-
Stringer, Abbey-Leigh	M	ENG	17.05.95	11	-	1	-	2	-	14	-
Wellings, Charlie	F	ENG	18.05.98	18	4	2	-	4	2	24	6
Westwood, Emily	D	ENG	05.04.84	5	-	-	-	2	-	7	-
White, Ellen	F	ENG	09.05.89	14	15	2	1	-	-	16	16
Williams, Paige	D	ENG	10.03.95	11	-	-	-	3	-	14	-
Williams, Rachel	F	ENG	10.01.88	15	2	2	-	4	1	21	3

GOALSCORERS 2017/18

WSL 1: White (15), Wellings (4), Mannion (3), R.Williams (2), Carter (1), Ladd (1), Quinn (1), Sargeant (1), own goals (2)

FAC: Ewers (1), White (1)

CC: Ayisi (2), Wellings (2), Ladd (1), Quinn (1), R.Williams (1)

Total: White (16), Wellings (6), Mannion (3), R.Williams (3), Ayisi (2), Ladd (2), Quinn (2), own goals (2), Carter (1), Ewers (1), Sargeant (1)

BRIGHTON & HOVE ALBION

2018/19: WSL (Tier 1)

Nickname: The Seagulls
Ground: Culver Road, Lancing FC
Manager: Hope Powell (since July 2017)

Season 2017/18:
WSL 2 (Tier 2): Runners-up
FA Cup: 4th Round
Continental Cup: Group Stage

Founded: 1991
Honours: WPL 2 Runners-up: (1) 2018
WPL Southern Champions: (1) 2016
WPL National Play-off Winners: (1) 2016

Last 5 League Finishes:
2018 WSL 2 (Tier 2): Runners-up
2017 WSL 2 (Tier 2): 6th (Spring Series)
2016 WPL Southern (Tier 3): Champions
2015 WPL Southern (Tier 3): Runners-up
2014 WPL Southern (Tier 3): 7th

Brighton have made rapid progress in recent years and can now count themselves among the elite clubs of English football after confirmation in December 2017 that they were to be awarded with a licence for the newly-launched full-time top-flight for 2018/19. Their rise to prominence began in 2016 when they were crowned WPL Southern champions and then beat Sporting Albion (now West Bromwich Albion) 4-2 in the national play-off final at Adams Park to secure promotion to WSL 2.

They had to wait until the 2017 Spring Series to make their WSL 2 bow. Alessia Russo had the honour of scoring their first ever WSL goal when she put them ahead in the 14th minute of their match away to London Bees which ended up as a 1-1 draw. Brighton finished the Spring Series in a highly creditable 6th place, and then signalled their intentions to continue their progress by appointing former England manager Hope Powell. The vast experience of the long-time Lionesses boss played a key role in their successful 2017/18 campaign as they finished their first full WSL 2 season as runners-up behind Doncaster Rovers Belles.Their elevation to the top-flight was determined by off-field criteria but they will feel their lofty League position would have justified promotion anyway. Supporters will be confident the team has enough talent on the pitch, not to mention know-how in the dug-out, to mix it with the best.

BRIGHTON FACTS

- Summer 2017 signing Danielle Buet was named the club's Player of the Year for 2017/18. The former Chelsea and Arsenal midfielder previously played for England under Seagulls manager Hope Powell. She registered five goals in WSL 2 in 2017/18.

- The forerunners to Brighton & Hove Albion Women were Brighton GPO who reached the FA Cup semi-finals in 1975/76. The current club does not count that as part of its history, considering itself to have been formed in 1991 when they linked up with

Brighton & Hove Albion men's. They were founding members of the FA Women's Premier League starting life in Division One South in 1991/92.

- Brighton appointed former England boss Hope Powell as manager in the summer of 2017 ahead of their first full WSL season. She was Lionesses boss from 1998 to 2013, leading England to the final at Euro 2009 – where they lost to Germany – and also took charge of the Great Britain team at the London 2012 Olympics.

- After signing in the summer of 2017, Nigeria international Ini-Abasi Umotong scored eight WSL goals, and 11 in all competitions, in her debut season for Brighton. Umotong initially rose to prominence when she struck 25 goals in 29 games for Portsmouth in 2014/15. She then joined WSL 2 side Oxford in 2016 before moving on to Brighton.

The FA via Getty Images

KIRSTY BARTON DOB: 29.05.92 MIDFIELDER
Having joined the Seagulls in 2011, Barton is the
longest-serving current player at Brighton.

"When I was growing up, when people used to ask 'what do you want to be when you're older?' it wasn't an option for us as women to be professional footballers. But as the game has grown, I'm now very fortunate to be able to say that is my job. Dreams do come true!"

Brighton's transition from amateur football to becoming a professional top-flight women's team is arguably appreciated most by the club's longest-serving player, midfielder Kirsty Barton. That's partly because, during her primary school years, with no local girls' teams playing near her East Sussex home at the time, her football options were restricted to kick-abouts with her brother's team.

Then – aged 11 – Barton joined Crawley Wasps, before impressing Chelsea's scouts. "So then my poor Dad had to commute me up to Chelsea three times a week," she says. "I wouldn't be here in the position I am today if it wasn't for my Dad driving me around and always supporting me. I owe him so much."

However, after nearly seven years developing at Chelsea, Barton's promising career almost ended before it had a chance to get going, when she suffered a devastating anterior cruciate ligament knee injury in 2010, which saw her miss almost a year's worth of football.

Following extensive rehab, which came amid Chelsea's 2011 switch to join the then-newly-formed Women's Super League, a transfer to lower-League Brighton coincided with Barton's return to full fitness.

Success, and promotion through the divisions, has followed, including 2016's dramatic Tier 3 play-off final win over Sporting Club Albion which earned the Sussex club a Tier 2 spot, before last season's successful bid for a top-flight licence and an impressive second-placed finish.

During that time, Barton has studied at the University of Brighton's Eastbourne campus, spending three years training to be a teacher and working in a secondary school, alongside training with the Seagulls. So, after progressing through the pyramid, while only playing on a part-time basis, how does it feel to now be in the top tier and training every day?

"The mood in the camp is so, so positive because we know we're all so blessed to be in the position we are right now," Barton says. "There's not a single day when we wake up and think 'oh I've got to work'. We've got all the energy and motivation we could need, having given up full-time jobs or studies for this opportunity."

Overseeing the club's conversion to become a Tier 1 outfit has been one of the women's game's legends, former England head coach Hope Powell. "From the moment she stepped in the door, everyone completely respected her because of her background in the game and what she's done," Barton recalls. "Everyone wanted to impress her immediately.

"She has a very different approach to training – she doesn't need to shout at us to make us train hard. Everyone already does that without her needing to do that. She has a really calm approach, which I think works well for everyone here. It's because of that level of respect. Everyone trusts everything that she's saying."

Barton hopes of maintaining an even lengthier association with the Seagulls once her playing career ends, dreaming of earning a teaching role at the club's academy. However, for now, the versatile midfielder is simply enjoying the chance to play with and against some of the country's finest players, adding: "I feel so lucky to have this opportunity in life because I know there are so many female players who would love to be doing the same.

"To say that I've done it [played professionally], and to know that I'll always be able to say that, amazes me."

2017/18 WSL 2

					Att	Pos
24.09	Aston Villa (a)	W	1-0	Ini Umotong 46, *Sophie Perry missed pen (saved Sian Rogers) 46*	312	
01.10	Durham (h)	W	3-2	Felicity Gibbons 8, Ini Umotong 25, Danielle Buet (pen) 82, *Lucy Gillett sent off 55*	176	
08.10	Millwall L (a)	L	3-4	Aileen Whelan 21, Lucy Somes 67, Danielle Buet (pen) 88	304	6
29.10	Oxford U (a)	D	2-2	Ini Umotong 55, Sophie Perry 85	204	6
12.11	Sheffield FC (h)	W	1-0	Kirsty Barton 72		4
10.12	Watford (h)		P-P			
07.01	Tottenham H (a)	W	1-0	Sophie Perry 11	253	4
28.01	Doncaster R B (a)	L	1-4	Fern Whelan 45+2	602	4
11.02	London Bees (h)	W	3-1	Danielle Buet 5, Ini Umotong 22, Aileen Whelan 41	240	3
22.02	Oxford U (h)	W	5-1	Kate Natkiel 4, Aileen Whelan 28, 71, 84, Ini Umotong 81		3
25.03	Sheffield FC (a)	W	4-1	Ini Umotong 31, Kate Natkiel 57, Aileen Whelan 76, Danielle Buet (pen) 87	284	3
01.04	Tottenham H (h)	W	2-0	Chloe Peplow 44, Amanda Nilden 90+2		3
18.04	London Bees (a)	L	1-2	Aileen Whelan 64	321	3
22.04	Doncaster R B (h)*	W	1-0	Laura Rafferty 9	606	3
29.04	Aston Villa (h)	W	2-1	Kirsty Barton 16, Ini Umotong 42		3
06.05	Watford (h)	W	4-1	Danielle Buet (pen) 18, Ini Umotong 25, Bronwen Thomas 45+1, Kirsty Barton 74	202	2
09.05	Watford (a)	W	1-0	Aileen Whelan 40, *Brighton GK Lucy Gillett saved Helen Ward pen 80*	160	2
13.05	Durham (a)	L	0-4		386	2
20.05	Millwall L (h)	L	0-3		344	2

*Played at Checkatrade Stadium, Crawley Town FC

2017/18 WSL Continental Cup: Group Two South

					Att
11.10	Yeovil Town (h)	W	4-2	Felicity Gibbons 28, Ini Umotong 42, Kate Natkiel 44, 70	167
01.11	Chelsea (h)	L	0-3		364
05.11	Tottenham H (a)	W	4-1	Lucy Somes 18, Fern Whelan 31, Ini Umotong 85, 90+1	253
02.12	Bristol City (a)	L	0-3		224

2017/18 FA Cup

04.02 R4	Manchester City (h)	L	0-2		1,372

59

BRIGHTON & HOVE ALBION PLAYER APPEARANCES & GOALS 2017/18

				WSL 2		FAC		CC		Total	
				A	G	A	G	A	G	A	G
Ashton-Jones, Vicky	D	ENG	07.01.87	10	-	-	-	1	-	11	-
Barton, Kirsty	M	ENG	29.05.92	18	3	1	-	4	-	23	3
Buet, Danielle	M	ENG	31.10.88	16	5	1	-	4	-	21	5
Gibbons, Felicity	F	ENG	09.07.94	15	1	1	-	4	1	20	2
Gillett, Lucy	G	USA	23.10.93	11	-	1	-	3	-	15	-
Hartley, Laura	G	ENG	31.01.01	2	-	-	-	1	-	3	-
Hourihan, Marie	G	IRE	10.03.87	4	-	-	-	-	-	4	-
Legg, Jenna	M	ENG	23.06.97	14	-	1	-	3	-	18	-
Natkiel, Kate	M	ENG	24.09.92	17	2	1	-	2	2	20	4
Nesbeth, Leilanni	F	BER	17.07.01	1	-	-	-	-	-	1	-
Nilden, Amanda	D	SWE	07.08.98	6	1	1	-	-	-	7	1
Peplow, Chloe	M	ENG	03.12.98	11	1	1	-	-	-	12	1
Perry, Sophie	D	IRE	11.11.86	13	2	1	-	4	-	18	2
Pharoah, Sophia	M	ENG	11.09.00	4	-	-	-	1	-	5	-
Rafferty, Laura	D	ENG	29.04.96	17	1	1	-	3	-	21	1
Ritchie, Amelia	D	WAL	09.05.99	5	-	-	-	3	-	8	-
Roe, Bethan	D	ENG	03.11.99	9	-	1	-	4	-	14	-
Sansom, Chloe	G	ENG	17.10.96	2	-	-	-	1	-	3	-
Somes, Lucy	F	ENG	18.04.94	7	1	-	-	2	1	9	2
Taylor, Natalie	M	ENG	10.10.99	1	-	-	-	3	-	4	-
Thomas, Bronwen	F	WAL	10.02.00	10	1	-	-	2	-	12	1
Umotong, Ini-Abasi	F	NGA	15.05.94	15	8	1	-	4	3	20	11
Whelan, Aileen	F	ENG	18.08.91	17	8	1	-	3	-	21	8
Whelan, Fern	D	ENG	05.12.88	13	1	1	-	3	1	17	2

GOALSCORERS 2017/18

WSL 2: Umotong (8), A.Whelan (8), Buet (5), Barton (3), Natkiel (2), Perry (2), Gibbons (1), Nilden (1), Peplow (1), Rafferty (1), Somes (1), Thomas (1), F.Whelan (1)

FAC: None

CC: Umotong (3), Natkiel (2), Gibbons (1), Somes (1), F.Whelan (1)

Total: Umotong (11), A.Whelan (8), Buet (5), Natkiel (4), Barton (3), Gibbons (2), Perry (2), Somes (2), F.Whelan (2), Nilden (1), Peplow (1), Rafferty (1), Thomas (1)

BRISTOL CITY

2018/19: WSL (Tier 1)

Nickname: The Vixens
Ground: Stoke Gifford Stadium
Manager: Tanya Oxtoby (since July 2018)

Season 2017/18:
WSL 1 (Tier 1): 8th
FA Cup: 4th Round
Continental Cup: Quarter-finals

Founded: 1998 (as Bristol Rovers Women)
National Honours: FA Cup Runners-up: (2)
2011, 2013
WSL Runners-up: (1) 2013
WSL 2 Runners-up: (1) 2016

Previous WSL Positions
2018 WSL 1 (Tier 1): 8th
2017 WSL 1 (Tier 1): 8th Spring Series
2016 WSL 2 (Tier 2): Runners-up (Promoted)
2015 WSL 1 (Tier 1): 8th (Relegated)
2014 WSL 1 (Tier 1): 7th
2013 WSL (Tier 1): Runners-up
2012 WSL (Tier 1): 4th
2011 WSL (Tier 1): 5th

Season 2018/19 sees the dawn of a new era for Bristol City following manager Willie Kirk's decision, taken at the end of May, to stand down after three years at the helm. Kirk's first season in charge ended in relegation from the top-flight in 2015, but he immediately led them back up as WSL 2 runners-up in 2016. Then came two 8th-placed finishes in the 2017 Spring Series and the 2017/18 season as well as an FA Cup quarter-final appearance in 2017. At the beginning of July 2018 the Vixens appointed Tanya Oxtoby, 38, as their new manager. The Australian has previously been manager of Nottingham Forest and among the coaching staff at Perth Glory.

City will also have to adapt to life without the talents of young forward Lauren Hemp. She finished 2017/18 as the club's top scorer with seven goals in WSL 1 and nine in all competitions. Her efforts saw her crowned PFA Young Player of the Year, and within weeks of the season ending the England Under-19 international was snapped up by Manchester City.

The club are now affiliated with men's Championship outfit Bristol City. However, when they were founded in 1998, following a merger with Welsh side Cable-Tel, they were called Bristol Rovers Women. In 2005/06 the name was changed to Bristol Academy, with the current title of Bristol City Women being adopted ahead of the 2016 season.

BRISTOL CITY FACTS

- City's highest League finish came in 2013 when they were still known as Bristol Academy. They were WSL runners-up behind champions Liverpool and qualified for the Champions League. The Vixens beat Barcelona in the last 16 of the 2014/15 competition but were knocked out by eventual winners Frankfurt in the quarter-finals.

- Aside from that 2013 League campaign, the closest they have come to winning a national trophy is in the FA Cup where they have twice reached the final only to finish as runners-up to Arsenal. The Vixens were beaten 2-0 by the Gunners at Coventry's Ricoh Arena in 2011 and 3-0 at Doncaster Rovers' Keepmoat Stadium in 2013.

- Prior to the WSL era the club's greatest achievements were winning the South West Combination 1 title in 2000/01 and the Southern Premier 1 title in 2002/03 as well as 10 Gloucestershire FA County Cups between 1998/99 and 2010/11.

Rogan Thomson/JMP

CARLA HUMPHREY DOB 15.12.96 MIDFIELDER

Humphrey started out as a youth player at Arsenal, spending a decade at the club, making 23 appearances for the first team and scoring three goals.

When Bristol City signed Carla Humphrey from Arsenal in June 2017, they gained more than just a highly-rated young player, because a couple of particularly dedicated fans promptly joined the Vixens family too.

"My Dad and my Grandad won't miss a single game," Humphrey explains. "They both go to every one of our games, home and away, even if it's Sunderland away, or a three-hour drive each way. They always drive up themselves to support us. My mum gets too nervous to come though. She can't watch any of my games, even if it is a game that is being shown live on TV. She prefers to wait for my Dad to tell her how it went and then she'll watch it back afterwards with no stress."

Humphrey appreciates the role that family can play in football – and so, it seems, does the wider WSL community, with post-match opportunities for players to mingle with fans, friends and family remaining as popular as ever across the League, as players catch-up with loved ones and pose for selfies with fans for sometimes up to an hour after full-time. "It is lovely," Humphrey continued. "That's something that's really special about women's football, seeing friends, family and supporters after games and thanking them. It's really nice to show that you appreciate their support, and I believe and hope that it will continue, with such a nice, relaxed atmosphere."

The England youth international spent 2017/18 as a forward but is likely to be used in midfield in 2018/19. She is enjoying the atmosphere at Bristol City under new manager Tanya Oxtoby, following the former Birmingham City assistant coach's appointment in July 2018. "We all got behind Tanya's principles immediately," Humphrey said of Australian former Doncaster Rovers Belles player Oxtoby.

"We were extra motivated by a new manager coming in and we all just want to show everyone what we can do. Tanya came in with great ideas that we can buy in to. I feel as though the whole team know we have a clear direction and we know what's expected from us. There's a clarity there."

Born in Cambridgeshire, Humphrey's football career was significantly boosted by the support from her PE teachers at Hinchingbrooke School, as well as her time playing for Rushden & Diamonds between the ages of seven and nine. Then came a decade on Arsenal's books, moving up through the Gunners' age groups in an era when the London club largely dominated the top tier of the women's game in England.

Successes for Humphrey in the FA Youth Cup soon followed, before former Arsenal boss Shelley Kerr gave Humphrey her big break by including the youngster in Arsenal's senior squad for a Champions League trip to Kazakhstan in October 2013, learning from a Gunners team that featured England stars including Steph Houghton, Rachel Yankey and Katie Chapman.

"Those great experiences bring you to where you are today," Humphrey reflects. "Just being involved in the wider squad was amazing in itself. I had a really successful youth career at Arsenal and broke in to the first team, making my debut against Bristol of all teams."

And it's the West Country club that Humphrey now calls home, having become incredibly fond of the region, adding: "I absolutely love the city of Bristol. It's another bonus about being here. In the city, we all do things as a team, whether going out in town, trying the little porridge shop or getting some frozen yoghurt – we like to explore, because it's a lovely place."

Humphrey also voluntarily undertakes additional training of her own in a bid to get ahead of the game, going for extra runs on the Clifton Downs near the world-famous Clifton Suspension Bridge, from where – on most nights – you can see the sunset. "I do some extra training by myself because – this year – I really want to push on now. Now is the time for me to be trying to just get better and better."

2017/18 WSL 1

						Att	Pos
24.09	Chelsea (a)	L	0-6			1,540	
30.09	Yeovil Town (h)	W	1-0	Loren Dykes 29		621	
08.10	Arsenal (a)	D	1-1	Lauren Hemp 30		840	7
28.10	Reading (h)	L	0-5			573	7
12.11	Manchester C (a)	L	0-4			1,256	8
10.12	Birmingham C (a)	P-P					
06.01	Everton (h)	W	2-1	Lauren Hemp 10, (pen) 65		856	7
14.01	Birmingham C (a)	L	0-2			517	8
27.01	Liverpool (a)	L	0-2			461	8
10.02	Sunderland (h)	L	1-2	Lauren Hemp 14		448	9
21.02	Reading (a)	L	0-4			172	9
28.03	Birmingham C (h)	L	0-2			500	9
18.04	Liverpool (h)	L	0-2			518	9
21.04	Sunderland (a)	W	2-1	Millie Farrow 13, *Lauren Hemp missed pen 31 (saved Rachel Laws),* Lauren Hemp 31 (pen rebound)		172	9
03.05	Manchester C (h)	L	1-6	Millie Turner 65		568	9
06.05	Everton (a)*	W	2-1	Lauren Hemp 18, Julie Biesmans 90+2		143	7
12.05	Yeovil Town (a)	W	2-0	Lauren Hemp 60, Yana Daniels 73		505	7
15.05	Chelsea (h)	L	0-2			820	7
20.05	Arsenal (h)	L	1-6	Chloe Arthur 67		724	8

*Played at Rossett Park, Marine FC

2017/18 WSL CONTINENTAL CUP: GROUP TWO SOUTH

12.10	Tottenham H (a)	L	0-2			131
04.11	Chelsea (h)	L	1-2	Millie Turner 85		400
15.11	Yeovil Town (a)*	W	2-0	Lauren Hemp 36, Yana Daniels 63		264
02.12	Brighton & H A (h)	W	3-0	Danique Kerkdijk 24, Lauren Hemp (pen) 54, Yana Daniels 90		224
17.12 QF	Manchester C (h)+	L	0-2			352

*Played at Taunton Town FC   +Played at Oaklands Park Stadium

2017/18 FA CUP

04.02 R4	Everton (a)	L	1-3	Chloe Arthur 7		712

BRISTOL CITY PLAYER APPEARANCES & GOALS 2017/18

				WSL 1		FAC		CC		Total	
				A	G	A	G	A	G	A	G
Allen, Florence	D	ENG	21.01.99	13	-	-	-	5	-	18	-
Arthur, Chloe	M	SCO	21.01.95	14	1	1	1	4	-	19	2
Baggaley, Sophie	G	ENG	29.11.96	16	-	-	-	1	-	17	-
Biesmans, Julie	M	BEL	04.05.94	15	1	1	-	5	-	21	1
Brown, Frankie	D	SCO	08.10.87	11	-	1	-	2	-	14	-
Daniels, Yana	F	BEL	08.05.92	16	1	-	-	4	2	20	3
Dykes, Loren	D	WAL	05.02.88	14	1	1	-	3	-	18	1
Estcourt, Charlie	M	WAL	27.05.98	13	-	1	-	2	-	16	-
Farrow, Millie	F	ENG	08.03.96	8	1	-	-	-	-	8	1
Fergusson, Olivia	F	ENG	27.03.95	11	-	1	-	4	-	16	-
Hemp, Lauren	F	ENG	07.08.00	17	7	1	-	5	2	23	9
Humphrey, Carla	F	ENG	15.12.96	14	-	-	-	5	-	19	-
Kerkdijk, Danique	D	NED	01.05.96	17	-	1	-	5	1	23	1
Leach, Caitlin	G	ENG	16.11.96	1	-	-	-	3	-	4	-
Matthews, Jasmine	D	ENG	24.03.93	12	-	1	-	3	-	16	-
Palmer, Aimee	M	ENG	25.07.00	10	-	-	-	4	-	14	-
Turner, Millie	M	ENG	07.07.96	17	1	1	-	5	1	23	2
Van de Putte, Lorca	D	BEL	03.04.88	1	-	-	-	1	-	2	-
Watson, Aimee	G	WAL	04.08.00	-	-	1	-	1	-	2	-
Wilson, Eloise	D	ENG	11.05.97	1	-	-	-	1	-	2	-
Wilson, Poppy	M	ENG	06.08.99	5	-	-	-	1	-	6	-
Woodham, Lily	D	WAL	03.09.00	2	-	-	-	1	-	3	-
Woolley, Jesse	F	ENG	27.03.01	4	-	-	-	2	-	6	-

GOALSCORERS 2017/18

WSL 1: Hemp (7), Arthur (1), Biesmans (1), Daniels (1), Dykes (1), Farrow (1), Turner (1)

FAC: Arthur (1)

CC: Daniels (2), Hemp (2), Kerkdijk (1), Turner (1)

Total: Hemp (9), Daniels (3), Arthur (2), Turner (2), Biesmans (1), Dykes (1), Farrow (1), Kerkdijk (1)

CHELSEA

2018/19: WSL (Tier 1)

Nickname: The Blues
Ground: Kingsmeadow
Manager: Emma Hayes (since Jun 2012)

Season 2017/18:
WSL 1 (Tier 1): Champions
FA Cup: Winners
Continental Cup: Semi-finals
Champions League: Semi-finals

Founded: 1992
Honours: FA Cup Winners: (2) 2015, 2018
Runners-up: (2) 2012, 16
WSL 1 Champions: (2) 2015, 2018
WSL 1 Spring Series Champions: (1) 2017
WSL 1 Runners-up: (2) 2014, 16

Previous WSL Positions
2018 WSL 1 (Tier 1): Champions
2017 WSL 1 (Tier 1): Champions (Spring Series)
2016 WSL 1 (Tier 1): Runners-up
2015 WSL 1 (Tier 1): Champions
2014 WSL 1 (Tier 1): Runners-up
2013 WSL (Tier 1): 7th
2012 WSL (Tier 1): 6th
2011 WSL (Tier 1): 6th

In August 2015 – more than two decades after their formation – Chelsea won their first major trophy. South Korea striker Ji So-Yun scored the historic goal as Emma Hayes' side beat Notts County 1-0 in the first FA Cup final to be staged at Wembley. Two months later they followed it up by completing the Double as a 4-0 victory over Sunderland secured the WSL 1 title. Since then, they've hardly looked back. The club added the 2017 WSL 1 Spring Series title to their roll of honour and then another League and FA Cup Double in 2017/18.

Hayes described this second Double as the club's greatest achievement given the strength of title rivals Manchester City, and the fact that Chelsea matched the feat of Arsenal (2012) and Manchester City (2016) by going the entire League campaign unbeaten. On medical advice Hayes did not lead the team out at Wembley for the Cup final or take part in the pre-match ceremonials because she was heavily pregnant, but she was in the dugout. She then missed the match in which Chelsea clinched the WSL 1 title with a 2-0 win at Bristol City after being advised not to travel. Two days later she gave birth to a baby boy. In December 2017 it had been reported that she was expecting twins but a club statement said sadly one of the twins "did not survive beyond the third trimester".

The women's side is fully integrated into Chelsea FC who bought AFC Wimbledon's Kingsmeadow Stadium for the team to move into ahead of 2017/18. Last season also saw Chelsea's best Champions League campaign as they reached the semi-finals where they lost to Wolfsburg who have now knocked them out three years in a row.

CHELSEA FACTS

- Having already been crowned WSL 1 champions, Chelsea's hopes of finishing the 2017/18 season unbeaten in the League appeared slim when they trailed Liverpool 2-0 with just 20 minutes of their final match remaining. Substitute Eniola Aluko – playing her last match for the club – then reduced the arrears with Chelsea's 100th League goal of the campaign before a quick-fire double from Ji So-Yun saw the Blues win 3-2.

- Fran Kirby – who scored 26 goals in all competitions in 2017/18 – was named PFA Women's Player of the Year and also won the inaugural Football Writers' Association Women's Player of the Year award.

- Former Chelsea and England men's captain John Terry, who made nearly 500 Premier League appearances for the Blues, is president of Chelsea Women and is credited with helping to save them from going out of business in 2009 through financial donations.

Chelsea FC

FRAN KIRBY DOB: 29.06.93 FORWARD

Fran Kirby was the only member of England's bronze medal winning 2015 World Cup squad to be selected from a club who were then outside the top division – Reading.

There were 15 minutes left in the 2018 FA Cup final. Chelsea were 2-1 up but Arsenal, the competition's record 14-time winners, had just got themselves back in to the game. Then Fran Kirby gathered the ball on the edge of the Arsenal penalty area. The Blues could not have hoped for the ball to find a better player at that moment.

"Arsenal had just scored and suddenly everyone was a bit nervous, wondering 'are we going to throw this away?'" the England striker recalls. "I picked the ball up and luckily enough I got it on my left foot and managed to put it in the corner of the net. I'd been practising those shots hundreds of times in training. It was a bit of a blur, but that was a really special one for me, especially as I knew I'd been practising that one. All the practice paid off. Every kid who loves football wants to play at Wembley and to score there is even more special, so it was a dream come true."

With that goal, Chelsea's dreams of claiming their second FA Cup crown became reality as Kirby's confident finish secured a 3-1 win in front of a competition record crowd of 45,423, seeing them avenge their 1-0 loss from 2016's final against the Gunners.

"It's funny, as a footballer, sometimes you have those days when you wake up and you think 'everything is going to go right today' and I think all of us had one of those days that day," Kirby reflects. "We knew how it had felt to lose last time, so everyone was so focused. For me, it was really special to win the cup because I hadn't won that one before so I had really set my heart on it."

Team success is what Kirby says she is most proud of, in a year when Chelsea went an entire League campaign of 18 matches without a defeat, with a squad that she describes as having several real characters, from "the sly one" Drew Spence to England defender – and budding DJ – Millie Bright.

RnB, hip hop and rap can all be heard in the 'invincible' Blues' dressing room on the day of a game, Kirby reveals, plus with three Sweden national team members in the side, the squad often like to play ABBA songs too.

And the winner who seemingly took it all in the 2017-18 season was the clinical Kirby herself who – as well as helping champions Chelsea win the Double – saw her classy, vibrant displays rewarded with multiple individual awards.

The former Reading star was one of five players from Emma Hayes' side who were named in the Professional Footballers' Association's Women's Team of the Year for the English top flight and was voted as the PFA Women's Player of the Year for 2017-18, before being named as the first Football Writers' Association Women's Footballer of the Year.

Yet her "biggest critic" remains her Dad, who has been supporting her career even since it began with spells at Caversham Trents and Caversham Swans, before the future Lioness joined Reading at the age of seven.

"I will come off the pitch in the FA Cup and he is there telling me how I should have done this, how I should have done that, and saying I 'probably should have been booked in the second half' or stuff like that," Kirby jokes. "So he still gets on my back a bit, but he's very proud of me. Most of my trophies are at my Dad's place and a lot of my medals are there as well. He enjoys showing them off to his friends when they visit. But he still likes to be my biggest critic."

2017/18 WSL 1

Date	Opponent		Result	Scorers	Att	Pos
24.09	Bristol City (h)	W	6-0	Drew Spence 13, Fran Kirby 40, Maren Mjelde 52, 87, Magdalena Eriksson 87, Gilly Flaherty 90	1,540	
30.09	Sunderland (a)	W	6-0	Fran Kirby 22, Gemma Davison 57, 61, Ji So-Yun 73, Erin Cuthbert 82, Eniola Aluko 83	789	
07.10	Liverpool (h)	W	1-0	Maren Mjelde 14	2,114	1
29.10	Yeovil Town (h)	W	6-0	Crystal Dunn 7, 23, Eniola Aluko 19, 69, Karen Carney 22, 63	1,821	1
12.11	Reading (a)	D	2-2	Karen Carney 55, Eniola Aluko 75	1,012	2
10.12	Manchester C (h)		P-P			
07.01	Arsenal (h)	W	3-2	Maren Mjelde 23, Ji So-Yun 60, Sari van Veenendaal (og) 83	2,570	2
28.01	Everton (h)	W	1-0	Jonna Andersson 84	1,731	2
01.02	Manchester C (h)	D	0-0		2,648	2
10.02	Birmingham C (a)	W	2-0	Fran Kirby 17, Ji So-Yun 70	669	1
21.02	Yeovil Town (a)	W	2-0	Fran Kirby 62, Jonna Andersson 66	454	1
24.02	Manchester C (a)	D	2-2	Millie Bright 6, Ji So-Yun 24	1,417	1
25.03	Reading (h)	D	2-2	Joanna Andersson 51, Fran Kirby 77	1,652	1
01.04	Arsenal (a)	D	1-1	Fran Kirby 31	1,807	1
18.04	Everton (a)*	W	1-0	Magdalena Eriksson 12	580	1
09.05	Birmingham C (h)	W	2-1	Fran Kirby 20, Erin Cuthbert 90+1	934	1
12.05	Sunderland (h)	W	2-1	Fran Kirby 41, Eniola Aluko 55	1,940	1
15.05	Bristol City (a)	W	2-0	Drew Spence 9, Jonna Andersson 88	820	1C
20.05	Liverpool (a)+	W	3-2	Eniola Aluko 70, Ji So-Yun 80, 83	442	1C

*Played at Rossett Park, Marine FC   +Played at Prenton Park, Tranmere Rovers FC

2017/18 CHAMPIONS LEAGUE

Date	Opponent		Result	Scorers	Att
04.10 R32 1L	B Munich (GER) (h)	W	1-0	Drew Spence 10	2,136
11.10 R32 2L	B Munich (GER) (a)	L	1-2 Agg: 2-2, Chelsea win on away goals	Fran Kirby 60	1,285
08.11 R16 1L	Rosengard (SWE) (h)	W	3-0	Fran Kirby 33, Ramona Bachmann 66, Gilly Flaherty 73	1,861
15.11 R16 2L	Rosengard (SWE) (a)	W	1-0 Agg: 4-0	Ji So Yun 53	1,358
21.03 QF 1L	Montpellier (FRA) (a)	W	2-0	Ji So Yun 49, Erin Cuthbert 76	5,291

28.03 QF 2L	Montpellier (FRA) (h)	W	3-1 Agg: 5-1	Fran Kirby 4, (pen) 77, Ramona Bachmann 49	3,050
22.04 SF 1L	Wolfsburg (GER) (h)	L	1-3	Fran Kirby 2	3,329
29.04 SF 2L	Wolfsburg (GER) (a)	L	0-2 Agg: 1-5		3,813

2017/18 WSL CONTINENTAL CUP: GROUP TWO SOUTH

01.11	Brighton & H A (a)	W	3-0	Fran Kirby 13, Crystal Dunn 76, Ji So Yun 90+1	364
04.11	Bristol City (a)	W	2-1	Eniola Aluko 47, Karen Carney (pen) 90	400
02.12	Yeovil Town (h)	W	8-0	Crystal Dunn 5, Nicola Cousins (og) 19, Erin Cuthbert 45+4, 57, *Gemma Davison missed pen*, Drew Spence 45+13, 90+4, Fran Kirby (pen) 72, Gemma Davison 90+2	1,289
06.12	Tottenham H (h)	W	4-1	Hannah Blundell 24, Fran Kirby 44, 56 Drew Spence 77	1,541
17.12 QF	Liverpool (h)	W	5-1	Fran Kirby 4, 24, 62, Ramona Bachmann 23, Erin Cuthbert 77	1,161
14.01 SF	Manchester C (h)	L	0-1		2,595

2017/18 FA CUP

04.02 R4	London Bees (a)	W	10-0	Erin Cuthbert 19, 83, (pen) 89, Ji So Yun 22, Danielle Lea (og) 31, Fran Kirby 47, 68, Katie Chapman 73, 90, Millie Bright 77	486
18.02 R5	Doncaster R B (h)	W	6-0	Ji So Yun 12, Fran Kirby 49, Drew Spence 53, Erin Cuthbert 66, 88, Ramona Bachmann (pen) 79	1,564
18.03 QF	Liverpool (a)*	W	3-0	Jonna Andersson 21, Katie Chapman 45, Maren Mjelde (pen) 58	358
15.04 SF	Manchester C (h)	W	2-0	Fran Kirby 5, 74	3,048
05.05 F	Arsenal (n)	W	3-1	Ramona Bachmann 48, 60, Fran Kirby 76	45,423

*Played at Valerie Park, Preston Cables FC   (n) Played at Wembley Stadium

CHELSEA PLAYER APPEARANCES & GOALS 2017/18

				WSL 1		FAC		CC		CL		Total	
				A	G	A	G	A	G	A	G	A	G
Aluko, Eniola	F	ENG	21.02.87	13	6	4	-	4	1	4	-	25	7
Andersson, Jonna	D	SWE	02.01.93	10	4	4	1	1	-	-	-	15	5
Asante, Anita	D	ENG	27.04.85	4	-	1	-	-	-	-	-	5	-
Bachmann, Ramona	F	SUI	25.12.90	12	-	4	3	4	1	7	2	27	6
Blundell, Hannah	D	ENG	25.05.94	13	-	3	-	5	1	8	-	29	1
Bright, Millie	D	ENG	21.08.93	15	1	4	1	5	-	8	-	32	2
Carney, Karen	M	ENG	01.08.87	8	3	1	-	3	1	3	-	15	4
Chapman, Katie	M	ENG	15.06.82	16	-	5	3	4	-	8	-	33	3

				WSL 1		FAC		CC		CL		Total	
				A	G	A	G	A	G	A	G	A	G
Cooper, Deanna	D	ENG	20.06.93	1	-	-	-	-	-	-	-	1	-
Cuthbert, Erin	F	SCO	19.07.98	17	2	5	5	5	3	5	1	32	11
Davison, Gemma	M	ENG	17.04.87	13	2	3	-	4	1	4	-	24	3
Dunn, Crystal	F	USA	03.07.92	7	2	1	-	5	2	4	-	17	4
Eriksson, Magdalena	D	SWE	06.09.93	15	2	5	-	3	-	8	-	31	2
Flaherty, Gilly	D	ENG	24.08.91	10	1	1	-	5	-	7	1	23	2
Ji, So-Yun	M	KOR	21.02.91	14	6	3	2	5	1	6	2	28	11
Kirby, Fran	F	ENG	29.06.93	17	8	5	6	6	7	8	5	36	26
Lindahl, Hedvig	G	SWE	29.04.83	11	-	2	-	2	-	8	-	23	-
Mjelde, Maren	M	NOR	06.11.89	17	4	4	1	5	-	8	-	34	5
Rafferty, Claire	D	ENG	11.01.89	5	-	2	-	4	-	2	-	13	-
Spence, Drew	M	ENG	23.10.92	14	2	4	1	5	3	7	1	30	7
Spencer, Rebecca	G	ENG	22.02.91	2	-	-	-	2	-	-	-	4	-
Telford, Carly	G	ENG	07.07.87	5	-	2	-	2	-	-	-	9	-
Thorisdottir, Maria	D	NOR	05.06.93	10	-	5	-	4	-	7	-	26	-

GOALSCORERS 2017/18

WSL1: Kirby (8), Aluko (6), Ji (6), Andersson (4), Mjelde (4), Carney (3), Cuthbert (2), Davison (2), Dunn (2), Eriksson (2), Spence (2), Bright (1), Flaherty (1), own goals (1)

CL: Kirby (5), Bachmann (2), Ji (2), Cuthbert (1), Flaherty (1), Spence (1)

FAC: Kirby (6), Cuthbert (5), Bachmann (3), Chapman (3), Ji (2), Andersson (1), Bright (1), Mjelde (1), Spence (1), own goals (1)

CC: Kirby (7), Cuthbert (3), Spence (3), Dunn (2), Aluko (1), Bachmann (1), Blundell (1), Carney (1), Davison (1), Ji (1), own goals (1)

Total: Kirby (26), Cuthbert (11), Ji (11), Aluko (7), Spence (7), Bachmann (6), Andersson (5), Mjelde (5), Carney (4), Dunn (4), Chapman (3), Davison (3), own goals (3), Bright (2), Eriksson (2), Flaherty (2), Blundell (1)

EVERTON

2018/19: WSL (Tier 1)

Nickname: The Toffees

Ground: Select Security Stadium in 2017/18, moving to Merseyrail Community Stadium, (Southport FC) for first half of 2018/19

Manager: Andy Spence (since Nov 2012)

Season 2017/18:

WSL 1 (Tier 1): 9th

FA Cup: Semi-finals

Continental Cup: Quarter-finals

Founded: 1983 (as Hoylake WFC)	**Previous WSL Positions**
National Honours: FA Cup Winners: (2)	**2018 WSL 1 (Tier 1):** 9th
1989 (as Leasowe Pacific), 2010	**2017 WSL 2 (Tier 2):** 1st (Spring Series) Promoted
FA Cup Runners-up: (3) 1988 (as Leasowe	**2016 WSL 2 (Tier 2):** 3rd
Pacific), 2005, 14	**2015 WSL 2 (Tier 2):** 3rd
National Premier League Champions: (1)	**2014 WSL 1 (Tier 1):** 8th Relegated
1998	**2013 WSL (Tier 1):** 5th
National Premier League Runners-up: (5)	**2012 WSL (Tier 1):** 3rd
2006, 07, 08, 09, 10	**2011 WSL (Tier 1):** 3rd
WSL 2 Spring Series Champions: (1) 2017	
WPL Cup Winners: (1) 2008	
WPL Cup Runners-up: (3) 1997, 99, 2010	

Everton were founding members of the WSL and, as expected, they fared well in the inaugural 2011 season, finishing 3rd behind champions Arsenal and runners-up Birmingham. The Toffees had been the nearest challengers to the all-conquering Arsenal in the final seasons of the National Premier League, before that competition was replaced by the WSL. They were runners-up to the Gunners for five consecutive seasons from 2005/06 to 2009/10.

It was also in 2010 that they won their second FA Cup, and their first under the Everton name. Everton beat Arsenal 3-2 in a thrilling final at the City Ground in Nottingham with Natasha Dowie – who had earlier opened the scoring – hitting the winner with one minute of extra-time remaining. The club had previously lifted the famous trophy in their days as Leasowe Pacific when they beat Friends of Fulham – also by a 3-2 scoreline – in the final at Old Trafford in 1989.

Many of Everton's greatest achievements came under the management of former Everton and England captain Mo Marley who was in charge from 2002 to 2012. She led the club to those five consecutive Premier League runners-up positions and to that 2010 FA Cup triumph having also won the competition as a player in the Leasowe Pacific team of 1989. Marley's successor was her assistant Andy Spence who led Everton to the 2014 FA Cup final where they lost to Arsenal. They were also relegated that year but returned to the top-flight as WSL 2 Spring Series champions ahead of 2017/18.

EVERTON FACTS

- The club began life as Hoylake WFC in 1983 but became Leasowe Pacific following a merger with Dolphins FC. They took on the Everton name in 1995 and were crowned champions of England for the only time in 1998.

- The Toffees finished bottom of WSL 1 in 2014 and were relegated to WSL 2, but returned to the top-flight ahead of the 2017/18 season. They were 2017 WSL 2 Spring Series winners and, although no promotions had been scheduled between the divisions, they were chosen to fill the vacant WSL 1 spot left by Notts County who folded in April 2017.

- Everton have competed in the Champions League three times. They exited at the second group stage in 2007/08, went out in the Round of 32 to Norwegian outfit Roa in 2009/10 and reached the quarter-finals in 2010/11 only to lose to German side Duisburg.

Paul Greenwood / FA

FAYE BRYSON DOB 04.07.97 DEFENDER

Bryson captained Everton in the 2014 FA Youth Cup final. The closely-contested Merseyside derby took place at Stadium:mk and ended in a 1-0 defeat to Liverpool.

The 2018-19 season will be Faye Bryson's 10th year at Everton and that rare landmark is made even more remarkable by the fact that she only turned 21 in July. The young right-back's progression through the Toffees' Centre of Excellence since her arrival in 2009 has developed a deep-rooted bond between club and player. And throughout her time with the team, one coach hugely passionate about the club has always been there for guidance: Everton's first-team boss, Andy Spence.

"He's been part of everything in those past nine years for me," Bryson says. "It's a pleasure to be working with him still. Andy has always helped me or pushed me on with my game, so I'm so grateful for that. He's certainly aided my progress as a player and he's still doing that now, all the time. Everton is really close to my heart and it always will be, having been here for such a long time."

Bryson can still recall her senior debut from 2015 vividly. "Andy gave me the chance and he just said 'get on and do your thing'. We were 2-0 down when I came on, so I knew I had to do my best. We managed to get a point. It ended 2-2. That felt amazing to be part of, as well as the fact that I was developing as a player." Since that draw against London Bees, Bryson has gone on to become a familiar face for Everton fans and she made 20 appearances in all competitions last season.

Her targets for 2018/19 include cementing her place in the starting line-up and – to help her do that – she likes to observe and learn from the very best in the world. "The top right-back in the women's game at the minute is Lucy Bronze, someone who I've always looked up to. She's proven herself to be the best. You've got to mark yourself against the best players and she's someone who likes to get forward, which is something I like to do as well, so I try to pick things up from what she does.

"She's strong, she's got that physique, and she's got all the attributes. That's who you've got to base yourself on. If she's doing everything right – given all the things she's won – then I obviously aspire to be doing what she's doing."

And learning seems to be something that former Liverpool Feds youngster Bryson enjoys, having qualified as a Level Two football coach as well as obtaining coaches badges within handball, futsal and trampolining. All that – plus an honours degree from Liverpool John Moores University – makes Bryson a prime example of the modern professional Women's Super League player.

2017/18 WSL 1

Date	Opponent	Result	Score	Scorers	Att	Pos
22.09	Liverpool (h)	L	0-2		1,439	
01.10	Birmingham C (a)	L	1-2	Chloe Kelly 46	821	
07.10	Manchester C (h)	L	2-3	Claudia Walker 5, Simone Magill 66	735	9
29.10	Arsenal (h)	L	0-2		435	9
11.11	Yeovil Town (a)	W	2-0	Courtney Sweetman-Kirk 17, Chloe Kelly (pen) 60	683	9
10.12	Sunderland (h)	W	5-1	Chaney Boye-Hlorkah 36, Courtney Sweetman-Kirk 39, 51, Danielle Turner 55, 89	122	6
06.01	Bristol City (a)	L	1-2	Courtney Sweetman-Kirk 74	856	8
28.01	Chelsea (a)	L	0-1	*Courtney Sweetman-Kirk missed pen 23*	1,731	9
11.02	Reading (h)	W	2-1	Courtney Sweetman-Kirk 4, Chloe Kelly 21	274	8
23.02	Arsenal (a)	L	0-1		813	8

28.03	Sunderland (a)	D	1-1	Danielle Turner 48	224	8
18.04	Chelsea (h)*	L	0-1		580	8
22.04	Reading (a)	L	0-3		263	8
29.04	Liverpool (a)+	D	1-1	Jodie Brett 66	1,416	8
06.05	Bristol City (h)+	L	1-2	Danielle Turner 7	143	9
09.05	Yeovil Town (h)*	W	3-1	Danielle Turner 35, *Courtney Sweetman-Kirk missed pen (saved Megan Walsh 35),* Mollie Green 61, (pen) 73	130	7
13.05	Birmingham C (h)*	L	0-3		337	8
20.05	Manchester C (a)	L	0-3		1,605	9

*Played at Rossett Park, Marine FC   +Played at Prenton Park, Tranmere Rovers FC

2017/18 WSL CONTINENTAL CUP: GROUP TWO NORTH

12.10	Doncaster R B (a)	W	3-0	Chloe Kelly 6, Leandra Little (og) 24, Marthe Munsterman 86	482
02.11	Birmingham C (h)	W	1-0	Courtney Sweetman-Kirk 12	181
05.11	Manchester C (a)	L	1-2	Simone Magill 76	875
16.11	Oxford United (h)	W	4-0	Chloe Kelly 10, 81, (pen) 83, Claudia Walker 69	188
16.12 QF	Reading (h)	D	1-1 (aet) (L 3-4p)	Chloe Kelly 111	155

2017/18 FA CUP

04.02 R4	Bristol City (h)	W	3-1	Olivia Chance 52, 83, Georgia Brougham 56	712
18.02 R5	Lewes (a)	W	6-0	Chaney Boye-Hlorkah 8, 19, 40, Chloe Kelly 12, Danielle Turner 69, Megan Finnigan 89	975
18.03 QF	Durham (a)		P-P		
25.03 QF	Durham (a)	W	6-1	Courtney Sweetman-Kirk 15, 55, 63, Olivia Chance 42, Danielle Turner 58, Jodie Brett 90	502
15.04 SF	Arsenal (h)	L	1-2	Chloe Kelly (pen) 67	1,457

EVERTON PLAYER APPEARANCES & GOALS 2017/18

				WSL 1		FAC		CC		Total	
				A	G	A	G	A	G	A	G
Boye-Hlorkah, Chantelle	F	ENG	08.09.95	12	1	3	3	4	-	19	4
Brett, Jodie	M	ENG	09.03.96	15	1	3	1	4	-	22	2
Brougham, Georgia	D	ENG	18.03.96	12	-	4	1	5	-	21	1
Bryson, Faye	D	ENG	04.07.97	13	-	4	-	5	-	22	-
Chance, Olivia	M	NZL	05.10.93	13	-	4	3	5	-	22	3

				WSL 1		FAC		CC		Total	
				A	G	A	G	A	G	A	G
Doyle, Emma	M	ENG	30.11.99	2	-	-	-	1	-	3	-
Durack, Elizabeth	G	AUS	20.05.94	13	-	-	-	3	-	16	-
Finnigan, Megan	M	ENG	02.04.98	15	-	4	1	4	-	23	1
George, Gabrielle	D	ENG	02.02.97	17	-	2	-	5	-	24	-
Green, Mollie	F	ENG	04.08.97	13	2	3	-	1	-	17	2
Hinds, Taylor	D	ENG	25.09.99	7	-	3	-	-	-	10	-
Hughes, Elise	F	WAL	15.04.01	7	-	-	-	1	-	8	-
James, Angharad	M	WAL	01.06.94	15	-	3	-	4	-	22	-
Kelly, Chloe	F	ENG	15.01.98	15	3	5	2	5	5	25	10
Levell, Kirstie	G	ENG	07.01.97	10	-	4	-	5	-	19	-
Magill, Simone	F	NIR	01.11.94	7	1	-	-	5	1	12	2
Munsterman, Marthe	M	NED	19.02.93	12	-	2	-	4	1	18	1
Sweetman-Kirk, Courtney	F	ENG	16.11.90	17	5	3	3	5	1	25	9
Turner, Danielle	D	ENG	10.09.91	16	5	4	2	5	-	25	7
Walker, Claudia	F	ENG	10.06.96	5	1	-	-	4	1	9	2
Wilson, Olivia	D	ENG	28.04.99	1	-	-	-	-	-	1	-
Worm, Siri	D	NED	20.04.92	14	-	3	-	5	-	22	-

GOALSCORERS 2017/18

WSL 1: Sweetman-Kirk (5), Turner (5), Kelly (3), Green (2), Boye-Hlorkah (1), Brett (1), Magill (1), Walker (1)

FAC: Boye-Hlorkah (3), Chance (3), Sweetman-Kirk (3), Kelly (2), Turner (2), Brett (1), Brougham (1), Finnigan (1)

CC: Kelly (5), Magill (1), Munsterman (1), Sweetman-Kirk (1), Walker (1), own goals (1)

Total: Kelly (10), Sweetman-Kirk (9), Turner (7), Boye-Hlorkah (4), Chance (3), Brett (2), Green (2), Magill (2), Walker (2), Brougham (1), Finnigan (1), Munsterman (1), own goals (1)

LIVERPOOL

2018/19: WSL (Tier 1)

Women

Nickname: The Reds

Ground: Select Security Stadium (in 2017/18), possible ground move for 2018/19

Manager: Vacant

Season 2017/18:

WSL 1 (Tier 1): 6th

FA Cup: Quarter-finals

Continental Cup: Quarter-finals

Founded: 1989 (as Newton Ladies)	**Previous WSL Positions**
National Honours:	**2018 WSL 1 (Tier 1):** 6th
WSL 1 Champions: (2) 2013, 2014	**2017 WSL 1 (Tier 1):** 4th (Spring Series)
FA Cup Runners-up: (3) 1994 (as Knowsley),	**2016 WSL 1 (Tier 1):** 5th
95, 96	**2015 WSL 1 (Tier 1):** 7th
League Cup Runners-up: (1) 1993 (as Knowsley)	**2014 WSL 1 (Tier 1):** Champions
	2013 WSL (Tier 1): Champions
	2012 WSL (Tier 1): 8th
	2011 WSL (Tier 1): 8th

Liverpool's preparations for 2018/19 were far from ideal. With manager Scott Rogers departing at the end of 2017/18, there followed an exodus of players. Captain Gemma Bonner and Caroline Weir headed to Manchester City with Sophie Ingle joining Chelsea and Alex Greenwood, Martha Harris and Amy Turner all making the short trip to the newly-formed Manchester United.

Fresh from having led Doncaster Rovers Belles to the 2017/18 WSL 2 title, Liverpool appointed Neil Redfearn as Rogers' replacement. Redfearn – who played in the Premier League for Barnsley and managed Leeds and Rotherham in the Football League – lasted just weeks in the hot seat. Before departing he rebuilt the squad with his former Doncaster charges Rhiannon Roberts and Leandra Little among notable arrivals including Bristol City pair Jasmine Matthews and Yana Daniels and Sunderland goalkeeper Anke Preuss.

Liverpool began the 2018/19 season with a 1-0 defeat to Manchester United in the Continental Cup before slumping 5-0 away to Arsenal on the opening day of their WSL campaign. Five days later Redfearn quit with his goalkeeper coach Chris Kirkland taking over as caretaker manager.

It remains to be seen how quickly Liverpool can regroup as the club sets about trying to reclaim the glories of the early WSL era. Their title success of 2014 remains the most dramatic in the competition's history. The Reds kicked off the final game of the season in 3rd place but, with both Chelsea and Birmingham City above them failing to win, they finished the day as champions. A 3-0 victory over Bristol City in Widnes saw Liverpool pip Chelsea (beaten 2-1 by Manchester City) to the title on goal difference with Birmingham (who drew 2-2 with Notts County) just a point behind.

The unexpected set of results meant Liverpool had defended the WSL title they had won in 2013. That campaign also went to the wire with leaders Liverpool beating 2nd-placed Bristol City 2-0 on the final day. Back-to-back titles were an extraordinary achievement for manager Matt Beard who had taken over in 2012 after the club finished the first two seasons of the WSL bottom of the table. Beard left in October 2015. With Chelsea and Manchester City having transformed the WSL landscape, Liverpool's highest finish since has been 4th in the 2017 Spring Series.

LIVERPOOL FACTS

- Liverpool's first WSL title triumph of 2013 ended Arsenal's nine-year winning run as national champions. The following year Liverpool became only the third team (after Croydon and Arsenal) to successfully defend the national League title. The feat is yet to be matched over two full seasons although Chelsea were crowned WSL 1 Spring Series champions in 2017 (when teams played each other just once) and were top again in 2017/18.

- The Reds have twice competed in the Champions League. Both times they exited in the Round of 32, losing to Swedish side Linkoping in 2014/15 and to Italians Brescia in 2015/16.

- The club started life as Newton Ladies in 1989 and were known as Knowsley from 1991 before taking on the Liverpool name in 1995. They became fully integrated into Liverpool FC in 2013. The Reds have a history of heartache in knockout football having lost all four of their national finals. They were beaten League Cup finalists in 1993 and FA Cup runners-up on three consecutive occasions in 1994, 1995 and 1996.

"Until hearing about the interest from Liverpool I had spent my entire career at Bristol City," says Jas Matthews who joined the Reds in summer 2018. "I can't thank those at City enough for what they did in helping develop me into the player that I am today, but when Liverpool came in for me it just made sense for my career. It is a huge club with real ambitions to challenge for trophies, so I'm really excited."

The former England Under-21 defender has worked incredibly hard to rebuild her career after a terrible injury back in April 2015. With virtually the last kick of a game which ended in a goalless draw away to Birmingham City Matthews ruptured her Achilles'.

"I went to clear the ball and I just went down," she says. "I actually heard it happen, and I thought that someone must have smacked me from behind. In reality though, no-one had touched me. I was taken to A&E and in the morning the extent of the problem became clear."

Two operations followed. "It was horrible, horrendous. At one point I wanted to give the game up," she says. "If it hadn't been for the help of my team-mates, I think that would have been the end of my playing days. They supported me and kept me going. In truth though it was also difficult to be around them because they would be buzzing ahead of match-day and I would just be sat stewing in my room knowing there was no chance I could be involved."

It took more than two years of hard work for Matthews to be fully rehabilitated. She returned to City with a flourish and was named the Vixens' Players' Player of the Year for 2017/18. It was her solid and consistent form throughout the campaign which saw her signed by Neil Redfearn during his short-lived spell as Liverpool boss this summer. Matthews acknowledges a key factor in her revival was the faith shown in her by former manager Willie Kirk who also left Bristol City

JASMINE MATTHEWS DOB: 24.03.93 DEFENDER

In 2014/15 Matthews was part of a Bristol City side that beat Barcelona in the Champions League before being knocked out by Frankfurt in the quarter-finals.

this summer before becoming assistant coach at the newly-formed Manchester United. The pair came face to face when Liverpool met Manchester United in the Red Devils' historic first match on the opening day of 2018/19. United won that Continental Cup clash 1-0 at Prenton Park, but, having sustained her horror injury during Kirk's first game as City boss, Matthews will always be grateful to him. "He really didn't get to see me play much football before I was laid off, but he stood by me and gave me my chance when I was back to full fitness."

While getting her career back on track at City, Matthews also continued to work part-time in an Aldi super-market, but now she finds herself at a full-time club in England's first wholly professional division. "Those were tough times. I was doing seven to eight hours a day, starting at 7pm and finishing at 3 or 4pm. I would then go home, have a nap if I could, then eat before rushing to training. I wouldn't get home until 10 o'clock sometimes, and then it would be the same again the following day. At the end of the week of course you then have to go out and perform for the fans. You can't expect them to understand what you have been going through all week. They expect to see you and the team play well despite the fact that in the semi-professional set-up you don't have anywhere near the same preparation time as you do in the pro game."

Despite Liverpool's early season managerial unrest, the future is now looking brighter for Matthews. Having survived injury adversity and the challenges of a part-time career, who knows what she can go on to achieve in a professional setting.

WSL 1 2017/18

						Att	Pos
22.09	Everton (a)	W	2-0	Natasha Harding 69, Niamh Charles 90		1,439	
29.09	Reading (h)	L	0-3			481	
07.10	Chelsea (a)	L	0-1			2,114	6
28.10	Sunderland (a)	W	4-1	Natasha Harding 11, 60, 87, Alex Greenwood 57		429	4
11.11	Birmingham C (h)	W	1-0	Niamh Charles 30		843	3
10.12	Arsenal (a)	P-P					
06.01	Yeovil Town (h)	W	8-0	Annie Heatherson (og) 16, Bethany England 30, 39, 55, 60, Caroline Weir 51, Jessica Clarke 59, Laura Coombs 75		453	3
27.01	Bristol City (h)	W	2-0	Bethany England 46, 65		461	3
07.02	Arsenal (h)	L	0-3			461	3
11.02	Manchester City (a)	L	0-4			2,356	4
21.02	Sunderland (h)	W	3-1	Jessica Clarke 18, 50, Bethany England 55		497	3
25.03	Birmingham C (a)	L	0-4			869	4
01.04	Yeovil Town (a)*	W	4-0	Laura Coombs 1, Gemma Bonner 17, Ashley Hodson 19, Bethany England 64		312	5
18.04	Bristol City (a)	W	2-0	Bethany England 47, Alex Greenwood (pen) 85		518	4
24.04	Arsenal (a)	L	0-3			587	5
29.04	Everton (h)+	D	1-1	Laura Coombs 46		1,416	6
08.05	Manchester City (h)**	W	1-0	Bethany England 10		653	5
12.05	Reading (a)++	L	0-3			1,379	5
20.05	Chelsea (h)+	L	2-3	Jessica Clarke 1, Niamh Charles 8		442	6

*Played at Wordsworth Road, Taunton Town FC   +Played at Prenton Park, Tranmere Rovers FC

**Played at Deva Stadium, Chester FC   ++Played at Madejski Stadium, Reading FC

2017/18 WSL CONTINENTAL CUP: GROUP ONE NORTH

11.10	Sheffield FC (h)	W	6-0	Caroline Weir 10, 29, Ellie Gilliatt (og) 52, Sophie Ingle 65, Alicia Johnson 83, Bethany England 90	352	
05.11	Durham (a)	D	0-0 (W 5-4p)		351	
15.11	Aston Villa (h)	W	5-1	Ashley Hodson 17, Jessica Clarke 38, Alex Greenwood (pen) 48, Caroline Weir 85, Alicia Johnson 87	282	
02.12	Sunderland (a)	P-P				
05.12	Sunderland (a)	L	0-1		128	
17.12 QF	Chelsea (a)	L	1-5	Casey Stoney 51	1,161	

2017/18 FA CUP

04.02 R4	Watford (h)^	W	5-0	Alicia Johnson 7, Caroline Weir 19, Bethany England 22, 63, Martha Harris 29	252	
18.02 R5	Chichester C (a)	W	3-0	Rinsola Babajide 34, Ashley Hodson 39, Bethany England 47	1,300	

| 18.03 QF | Chelsea (h)* | L | 0-3 | | | | | | | 358 |

^Played at Walton Hall, Liverpool County FA   *Played at Valerie Park, Preston Cables FC

LIVERPOOL PLAYER APPEARANCES & GOALS 2017/18

					WSL1		FAC		CC		Total	
					A	G	A	G	A	G	A	G
Babajide, Rinsola	F	ENG	17.06.98		4	-	1	1	-	-	5	1
Blanchard, Annabel	F	ENG	07.05.01		1	-	-	-	-	-	1	-
Bonner, Gemma	D	ENG	13.07.91		14	1	-	-	5	-	19	1
Chamberlain, Siobhan	G	ENG	15.08.83		15	-	1	-	4	-	20	-
Charles, Niamh	F	ENG	21.06.99		11	3	-	-	3	-	14	3
Clarke, Jessica	F	ENG	05.05.89		13	4	3	-	5	1	21	5
Coombs, Laura	M	ENG	29.01.91		17	3	1	-	5	-	23	3
England, Bethany	F	ENG	03.06.94		16	10	2	3	3	1	21	14
Flaherty, Rebecca	G	SCO	06.03.98		3	-	1	-	1	-	5	-
Fletcher, Ellie	M	ENG	16.06.99		-	-	-	-	3	-	3	-
Greenwood, Alex	D	ENG	07.09.93		18	2	2	-	5	1	25	3
Harding, Natasha	F	WAL	02.03.89		5	4	-	-	3	-	8	4
Harris, Martha	D	ENG	19.08.94		16	-	2	1	3	-	21	1
Hartley, Naomi	D	ENG	12.01.01		-	-	1	-	-	-	1	-
Hodson, Ashley	F	ENG	05.05.95		13	1	3	1	5	1	21	3
Ingle, Sophie	M	WAL	02.09.91		18	-	3	-	5	1	26	1
Johnson, Alicia	M	ENG	24.12.98		12	-	3	1	3	2	18	3
Longhurst, Kate	M	ENG	02.05.89		14	-	3	-	3	-	20	-
Murray, Satara	D	ENG	01.07.93		14	-	2	-	2	-	18	-
Pike, Cassia	F	WAL	27.12.00		1	-	2	-	1	-	4	-
Ramsey, Emily	G	ENG	16.11.00		1	-	1	-	-	-	2	-
Roberts, Lucy	D	ENG	11.05.01		1	-	1	-	-	-	2	-
Rodgers, Amy	D	ENG	04.05.00		5	-	2	-	-	-	7	-
Stoney, Casey	D	ENG	13.05.82		9	-	-	-	3	1	12	1
Turner, Amy	D	ENG	04.07.91		6	-	1	-	-	-	7	-
Weir, Caroline	M	SCO	20.06.95		17	1	3	1	5	3	25	5

GOALSCORERS 2017/18

WSL1: England (10), Clarke (4), Harding (4), Charles (3), Coombs (3), Greenwood (2), Bonner (1), Hodson (1), Weir (1), own goals (1)

FAC: England (3), Babajide (1), Harris (1), Hodson (1), Johnson (1), Weir (1)

CC: Weir (3), Johnson (2), Clarke (1), England (1), Greenwood (1), Hodson (1), Ingle (1), Stoney (1), own goals (1)

Total: England (14), Clarke (5), Weir (5), Harding (4), Hodson (3), Charles (3), Coombs (3), Greenwood (3), Johnson (3), own goals (2), Babajide (1), Bonner (1), Harris (1), Ingle (1), Stoney (1)

MANCHESTER CITY

2018/19: WSL (Tier 1)

Nickname: City, The Blues
Ground: The Academy Stadium
Manager: Nick Cushing (since Nov 2013)

Season 2017/18:
WSL 1 (Tier 1): Runners-up
FA Cup: Semi-finals
Continental Cup: Runners-up
Champions League: Semi-finals

Founded: 1988
National Honours:
FA Cup Winners: (1) 2017
WSL 1 Champions: (1) 2016
WSL 1 Runners-up: (2) 2015, 18
WSL 1 Spring Series Runners-up: (1) 2017
WSL Continental Cup Winners: (2) 2014, 16
WSL Continental Cup Runners-up: (1) 2018

Previous WSL Positions
2018 WSL1 (Tier 1): Runners-up
2017 WSL1 (Tier 1): Runners-up (Spring Series)
2016 WSL1 (Tier 1): Champions
2015 WSL1 (Tier 1): Runners-up
2014 WSL1 (Tier 1): 5th

Manchester City Women became fully integrated into Manchester City FC in 2012 and, like their male counterparts, are now one of the dominant forces in the English game. They achieved entry into WSL 1 ahead of the 2014 season and, after a 5th-placed finish in that inaugural campaign, they have been in the top two every year since.

Manager Nick Cushing has been in charge throughout the WSL era. In 2017 City held all three domestic trophies at the same time. Having won the 2016 League title and Continental Cup (competitions which were played throughout the summer and autumn of that calendar year) they followed up by lifting the 2016/17 FA Cup with a 4-1 victory over Birmingham City at Wembley.

City's 2016 League triumph was all the more impressive given that they finished the season unbeaten, a feat only achieved in the WSL era by Arsenal in 2012 and matched by Chelsea in 2018. Given their high standards many viewed it as something of a disappointment to finish 2017/18 without silverware. They led WSL 1 throughout the middle of the season but faded in the final weeks as Chelsea overhauled them to claim the title. They were beaten 1-0 by Arsenal in the Continental Cup final in March, while Chelsea got the better of them in the FA Cup semi-finals the following month. In the Champions League they pushed defending champions and eventual winners Lyon all the way but lost 1-0 on aggregate, falling to a 2nd leg winner from former City player Lucy Bronze.

MANCHESTER CITY FACTS

- Manchester City have reached the semi-finals of the Champions League in both their European campaigns to date (2016/17 and 2017/18). On each occasion they were beaten by French side Lyon who went on to win the competition.

- Still reeling from the disappointment of missing out on the 2017/18 WSL 1 title to Chelsea, City composed themselves to secure qualification for the Champions League for a 3rd consecutive season by beating Everton 3-0 on the final day.

- Manager Nick Cushing was seen as a prime candidate for the England manager's job following the departure of Mark Sampson in September 2017. Cushing though withdrew his application for the post in late November and later in the week he signed a new three-and-a-half-year contract with City, stating: "My future is here. We can carry on being successful and continue the great work that we have shown over the last four years."

NIKITA PARRIS DOB: 10.03.94 FORWARD

**Nikita Parris made her senior debut for Everton in August 2010
in a Champions League qualifier in Lithuania**

The 2018-19 season is the year when England and Manchester City forward Nikita Parris says she wants to move from being referred to as a "rising star" to reaching her true potential. Having turned 24 in March 2018, Parris knows she is approaching the prime years of her career. She was one of the stars of last season's English top flight, finishing as the second-highest goalscorer in the division.

Netting 11 times in 18 League appearances as well as providing six assists, agile winger Parris helped City qualify for the Champions League with a second-placed finish. "We want to go one step further, regain trophies and be at the top of the pack, we don't want to be following anyone," she says.

"We'll be going out there to win all three domestic trophies and hopefully go one step further in the Champions League. We've got the quality to do that. If we could do the quadruple like Arsenal did in 2007, that would be fantastic.

"My aim this season is for us to be winning trophies. Every day I think about working hard and getting better, becoming no longer just a 'rising star' but moving past that potential and becoming a real stronghold within this team."

Parris, who joined Man City in 2015 – initially on loan from fellow WSL club Everton – has become a popular member of the side that won all three major domestic honours in 2016-17. "I've got a lot of friends on the team and I'm really close to Keira Walsh and Abbie McManus. But to be honest with you, I'm quite the joker on the team actually, so I'm in and out with every teammate, cracking jokes, and we just enjoy each other's company. I believe it's about the whole team gelling together, not just one or two players. That's how we, as a driving force, will grow together."

Parris is surrounded by fellow internationals at City, but that has been the case throughout her entire career, after progressing through Everton's centre of excellence and in to a Toffees squad which included Jill Scott, Toni Duggan as well as England internationals at the time Lindsay Johnson, Rachel Brown-Finnis, and Fara Williams. "I couldn't have had a more perfect way of coming in to football, with all those incredible role models," Parris recalls.

"Fara Williams became my best friend at Everton. She was kind of like my football mother, my big sister. She kept me in line. She joked with me at times but she also made sure that I easily settled in to the team because she allowed me to be myself while keeping me in line."

Parris began playing football with her local Under-8s Sunday-league side, Kingsley United, close to where she grew up in Toxteth in Merseyside. "My next-door neighbour was actually my first coach and then my other neighbour around the corner became my second coach, so it was a community-based team," she recalled.

So in those early years did she ever think she would one day play in the Champions League and for England at major international tournaments: "Definitely not. As a young kid, women's professional football wasn't talked about. It wasn't a thing. I was just concentrating on my studies and thinking 'at least I can be a PE teacher or I could work in a store' if I need a job."

Thankfully for the Lionesses, Everton spotted her talent as a teenager and now there are Under-8s asking for Parris' autograph at City's Academy Stadium after WSL games. "When they do come up to you asking for autographs you think 'are you talking to me?' It's a really surreal moment," she admits.

"It's also an obligation for us to continue the hard work that the pioneers of women's football did, like Fara Williams, who have paved the way for us to be professional footballers, because now also we've got to pave the way for the next generation."

2017/18 WSL 1

Date	Opponent		Result	Scorers	Att	Pos
24.09	Yeovil Town (a)	W	4-0	Isobel Christiansen (pen) 8, Jane Ross 44, Jill Scott 59, Georgia Stanway 83	1,302	
30.09	Arsenal (h)	W	5-2	Jane Ross 40, Stephanie Houghton 45+3, Georgia Stanway 70, Isobel Christiansen 74, Jill Scott 79	1,646	
07.10	Everton (a)	W	3-2	Stephanie Houghton 12, Nikita Parris 13, Pauline Bremer 18	735	2
29.10	Birmingham City (h)	W	3-1	Isobel Christiansen (pen) 75, (pen) 90+7, Jennifer Beattie 90+1	1,465	2
12.11	Bristol City (h)	W	4-0	Isobel Christiansen (pen) 7, Claire Emslie 37, Abbie McManus 58, Jennifer Beattie 86	1,256	1
10.12	Chelsea (a)		P-P			
07.01	Reading (a)	W	5-2	Nadia Nadim 6, Claire Emslie 32, Isobel Christiansen 43, Jill Scott 56, 58	951	1
28.01	Sunderland (a)	W	3-0	Nikita Parris 36, 72, Isobel Christiansen 56	978	1
01.02	Chelsea (a)	D	0-0		2,648	1
11.02	Liverpool (h)	W	4-0	Nikita Parris 2, 60, Isobel Christiansen (pen) 56, Abbie McManus 73	2,356	1
21.02	Birmingham City (a)	L	0-2		803	2
24.02	Chelsea (h)	D	2-2	Nikita Parris 49, Georgia Stanway 86	1,417	2
01.04	Reading (h)	L	0-2		1,274	2
18.04	Sunderland (h)	W	3-0	Georgia Stanway 13, 87, Nadia Nadim 90+4	943	2
03.05	Bristol City (a)	W	6-1	Jill Scott 41, Claire Emslie 47, Jane Ross 59, Nikita Parris 61, Nadia Nadim 81, Melissa Lawley 90+1	568	1
08.05	Liverpool (a)*	L	0-1		653	1
12.05	Arsenal (a)	L	1-2	Nadia Nadim 11	1,514	2
16.05	Yeovil Town (h)	W	5-0	Claire Emslie 44, Nikita Parris 47, 74, 76, Isobel Christiansen (pen) 81	715	2
20.05	Everton (h)	W	3-0	Jill Scott 22, 60, Nikita Parris 57	1,605	2

*Played at Deva Stadium, Chester FC

2017/18 CHAMPIONS LEAGUE

Date	Opponent		Result	Scorers	Att
04.10 R32 1L	St Polten (AUT) (a)	W	3-0	Demi Stokes 22, Stephanie Houghton 30, Nikita Parris 35	2,236
12.10 R32 2L	St Polten (AUT) (h)	W	3-0 Man City won 6-0 on aggregate	Jane Ross missed pen 6 (saved by Jasmin Boisits), Nikita Parris 34, Jill Scott 43, Melissa Lawley 85	1,041
09.11 R16 1L	LSK Kvinner (NOR) (a)	W	5-0	Demi Stokes 25, Isobel Christiansen (pen) 39, Claire Emslie 69, Jane Ross 73, 77	1,225

16.11 R16 2L	LSK Kvinner (NOR) (h)	W	2-1 Man City won 7-1 on aggregate	Isobel Christiansen 46, Nikita Parris 72	716
21.03 QF 1L	Linkopings FC (SWE) (h)	W	2-0	Nikita Parris (pen) 38, Jane Ross 55	1,259
28.03 QF 2L	Linkopings FC (SWE) (a)	W	5-3 Man City won 7-3 on aggregate	Jane Ross 14, Georgia Stanway 23, 33, Jennifer Beattie 42, Isobel Christiansen 63	1,903
22.04 SF 1L	Lyon (FRA) (h)	D	0-0		2,876
29.04 SF 2L	Lyon (FRA) (a)	L	0-1 Lyon won 1-0 on aggregate		20,837

2017/18 WSL CONTINENTAL CUP: GROUP TWO NORTH

02.11	Oxford United (a)	W	6-0	Isobel Christiansen (pen) 44, Georgia Stanway 45, 53, Claire Emslie 57, Jennifer Beattie 79, 86	777
05.11	Everton (h)	W	2-1	Isobel Christiansen 25, Nikita Parris 80	352
03.12	Birmingham C (h)	W	2-0	Nikita Parris 18, Claire Emslie 36	1,077
06.12	Doncaster R B (a)	W	3-2	Claire Emslie 4, Jane Ross 55, Georgia Stanway 55	924
17.12 QF	Bristol City (a)+	W	2-0	Nikita Parris 60, Jennifer Beattie 87	875
14.01 SF	Chelsea (a)	W	1-0	Nadia Nadim 18	2,595
14.03 F	Arsenal (n)	L	0-1		2,136

(n) Played at Adams Park, Wycombe Wanderers FC   +Played at Oaklands Park Stadium

2017/18 FA CUP

04.02 R4	Brighton & H A (a)	W	2-0	Isobel Christiansen 45, Claire Emslie 66	1,372
18.02 R5	Birmingham C (a)	W	3-1 (aet)	Nadia Nadim 13, Georgia Stanway 97, Claire Emslie 119	641
18.03 QF	Sunderland (a)		P-P		
25.03 QF	Sunderland (a)	W	4-2 (aet)	Demi Stokes 74, Jane Ross 90, 96, Ella Toone 114	552
15.04 SF	Chelsea (a)	L	0-2		3,048

MANCHESTER CITY PLAYER APPEARANCES & GOALS 2017/18

				WSL 1		FAC		CC		CL		Total	
				A	G	A	G	A	G	A	G	A	G
Bardsley, Karen	G	ENG	14.10.84	7	-	-	-	4	-	3	-	14	-
Beattie, Jennifer	D	SCO	13.05.91	18	2	4	-	6	3	8	1	36	6
Bremer, Pauline	F	GER	10.04.96	2	1	-	-	-	-	1	-	3	1
Campbell, Megan	D	IRL	28.06.93	4	-	-	-	2	-	4	-	10	-
Christiansen, Isobel	M	ENG	20.09.91	17	9	4	1	6	2	7	3	34	15
Emslie, Claire	F	SCO	08.03.94	17	4	4	2	6	3	8	1	35	10
Houghton, Stephanie	D	ENG	23.04.88	15	2	1	-	6	-	8	1	30	3
Hourihan, Marie	G	ENG	10.03.87	1	-	-	-	2	-	-	-	3	-
Jans, Mie	D	DEN	06.02.94	4	-	3	-	1	-	2	-	10	-
Lawley, Melissa	M	ENG	28.04.94	13	1	3	-	4	-	7	1	27	2
McManus, Abbie	D	ENG	14.01.93	16	2	4	-	6	-	8	-	34	2
Middag, Tessel	M	NED	23.12.92	1	-	1	-	-	-	1	-	3	-
Morgan, Esme	D	ENG	18.10.00	7	-	-	-	3	-	-	-	10	-
Nadim, Nadia	F	DEN	02.01.88	12	4	4	1	1	1	2	-	19	6
Park, Jessica	M	ENG	21.10.01	-	-	-	-	1	-	-	-	1	-
Parris, Nikita	F	ENG	10.03.94	18	11	4	-	5	3	8	4	35	18
Roebuck, Ellie	G	ENG	23.09.99	11	-	4	-	-	-	5	-	20	-
Ross, Jane	F	SCO	18.09.89	13	3	2	2	4	1	5	4	24	10
Scott, Jill	M	ENG	02.02.87	16	7	3	-	5	-	8	1	32	8
Spetsmark, Julia	F	SWE	30.06.89	3	-	-	-	1	-	-	-	4	-
Stanway, Georgia	F	ENG	03.01.99	14	5	4	1	4	3	6	2	28	11
Stokes, Demi	D	ENG	12.12.91	15	-	4	1	3	-	8	2	30	3
Toone, Ella	F	ENG	02.09.99	3	-	1	1	3	-	-	-	7	1
Walsh, Keira	M	ENG	08.04.97	18	-	3	-	6	-	8	-	35	-

GOALSCORERS 2017/18

WSL 1: Parris (11), Christiansen (9), Scott (7), Stanway (5), Emslie (4), Nadim (4), Ross (3), Beattie (2), Houghton (2), McManus (2), Bremer (1), Lawley (1)

CL: Parris (4), Ross (4), Christiansen (3), Stanway (2), Stokes (2), Beattie (1), Emslie (1), Houghton (1), Lawley (1), Scott (1)

FAC: Emslie (2), Ross (2), Christiansen (1), Nadim (1), Stanway (1), Stokes (1), Toone (1)

CC: Beattie (3), Emslie (3), Parris (3), Stanway (3), Christiansen (2), Ross (1), Nadim (1)

Total: Parris (18), Christiansen (15), Stanway (11), Emslie (10), Ross (10), Scott (8), Beattie (6), Nadim (6), Houghton (3), Stokes (3), Lawley (2), McManus (2), Bremer (1), Toone (1)

READING

2018/19: WSL (Tier 1)

Nickname: The Royals
Ground: Adams Park, (Wycombe Wanderers FC)
Manager: Kelly Chambers (since Aug 2012)

Season 2017/18:
WSL 1 (Tier 1): 4th
FA Cup: 4th Round
Continental Cup: Semi-finals

Founded: 2006
National Honours: WSL 2 Champions: (1) 2015

Previous WSL Positions
2018 WSL 1 (Tier 1): 4th
2017 WSL 1 (Tier 1): 6th (Spring Series)
2016 WSL 1 (Tier 1): 8th
2015 WSL 2 (Tier 2): Champions (Promoted)
2014 WSL 2 (Tier 2): 3rd

From 1988 Reading men's FC had an association with a club called Reading Royals Ladies FC but severed that link in 2006 to set up their own club which is the current Reading FC Women. In 2014 Reading FC Women were among the founding members of WSL 2. In terms of League finishes they have improved every season since then, placing 3rd in their first WSL 2 season, then gaining promotion to the top-flight as champions in 2015.

Since their elevation to WSL 1 they have finished 8th, 6th (in the Spring Series) and 4th. Indeed, Reading so nearly ended the 2017/18 campaign as the best-of-the-rest, behind super-powers Chelsea and Manchester City, but were edged out of 3rd place by Arsenal on the final day.

Fara Williams – who joined from Arsenal in 2017 – played a key role in Reading's 2017/18 success. The England midfielder bolstered a team already boasting the talents of Brooke Chaplen and Remi Allen with the trio racking up 24 WSL goals between them. Allen – whose haul of nine included a spectacular overhead kick in a 2-0 win against Manchester City at the start of April – ended the season by being named Reading's Player of the Year by her team-mates and also by the club's supporters.

England international Fran Kirby came through Reading's youth ranks. She joined the club at the age of seven. In 2015 she was the only player from a Tier 2 club to be included in the England squad that finished 3rd at the World Cup. After the tournament Kirby joined Chelsea where she has won a host of honours and was named the PFA and Football Writers' Player of the Year for 2017/18.

READING FACTS

- The 2017/18 season saw Reading come close to reaching their first national Cup final as they made it all the way to the semi-finals of the Continental Cup only to fall to a 3-2 defeat at home to eventual winners Arsenal.

- Reading were the only club to have two players short-listed for the 2017/18 WSL 1 Goal of the Year award. Remi Allen's bicycle kick in the 2-0 home win over Manchester City in April and Fara Williams' 25-yard dipping volley away to Liverpool in September were both among the nominees although the award was won by Manchester City's Georgia Stanway.

- Reading's WSL 2 title triumph in 2015 was achieved in dramatic fashion. They pipped Doncaster Rovers Belles to top spot on goal difference on the final day of the season thanks to a 3-2 win away to Aston Villa.

Kieran McManus / FA

JADE MOORE DOB: 22.10.90 MIDFIELDER

Jade Moore won the FA Cup with Birmingham City in 2012, with City beating Chelsea 3-2 on penalties after a 2-2 draw in the final at Ashton Gate.

In her own words, England midfielder Jade Moore had a bit of a "torrid season" because of an ankle injury in 2017/18, but thanks to her club Reading ensuring that she was treated by the "best ankle surgeon in the country", she knows she can be back at her best again this term.

"Previously I've had to lean on England with various medical issues whereas, here at Reading, everything was done in-house. I've had only the best medical people in contact with me, and Reading have organised it all," Moore says in praise of the club that signed her in 2017. "Off the field, the professionalism here is second to none. It's the best club that I've been at for that side of things." The Nottinghamshire-born star is also enjoying playing under respected Royals boss Kelly Chambers, who helped the side finish fourth in the top-flight last season.

"One of the biggest pulls from my side, when I first met Kelly, was that she's really normal," Moore recalls. "I know that doesn't always sound like a compliment but – when you're a player coming in to a team – you don't want anything too farfetched or under-played. Kelly understands exactly where the club wants to be.

"She's very level-headed, calm and collected and she likes to have a laugh as well. "She's definitely got a personality, which I think helps. She's really good to be around. Yet there's a fine balance between being too motivated and not motivated enough and – from the results last year – the team probably got the dressing room just right."

Moore, who grew up watching England's David Beckham and Michael Owen as a youngster, has been part of three major tournaments with the Lionesses, including helping her country finish third at the 2015 World Cup, drawing widespread acclaim for her reliable, disciplined and creative performances.

Having previously played for Lincoln City, Leeds United, Birmingham City and Notts County, Moore says she'll never truly leave her Northern roots, but she is glad to be settling in with the Royals. "I'm still a northerner – I don't think that will ever change – and I go back to see my family when I can," she continues. "But I really like where I live in Marlow, which is just around the corner from where we train at Bisham Abbey. It's really picturesque, right by the river Thames."

The Royals managed to get the wins flowing last season too, coming out on top in half of their WSL fixtures and losing just four League matches. "We probably achieved a little bit above our station as to what we potentially should have, which is always a promising thing," Moore adds. "Fifth place would have been something to aspire to, so beating that and finishing fourth was a credit to everyone involved."

Moore, who has previously stressed that football "saved her life" after the discovery of two holes in her heart in 2007 and subsequent surgery, remains grateful to have a professional career and fully appreciates the growth in the number of full-time contracts in the WSL. "Everyone at Reading is happy with where the quality of the football in the WSL has gone to and really is appreciating it and not taking it for granted," she adds.

"For the players that are now reaping the rewards with a full-time contract, they're really down to earth still, because they're the ones that are really thankful for the opportunity that they're getting. We're normal people. We aren't so high profile that you can't come within 10 feet of us. That's a crucial part of the women's game that's different to the men's. We are really appreciative of where the game has got to now, and the life it's allowing a lot of players to live."

2017/18 WSL 1

Date	Opponent	Result	Score	Scorers	Att	Pos
24.09	Sunderland (h)	L	0-1		502	
29.09	Liverpool (a)	W	3-0	Fara Williams 17, Remi Allen 33, Brooke Chaplen 73	481	
08.10	Birmingham C (h)	D	2-2	Brooke Chaplen (pen) 21, Jade Moore 29	655	4
28.10	Bristol City (a)	W	5-0	Fara Williams 3, Sophie Baggaley (og) 16, Remi Allen 17, *Brooke Chaplen missed pen 30,* Jade Moore 66, Rachel Rowe 75	573	3
12.11	Chelsea (h)	D	2-2	Remi Allen 34, Magda Ericsson (og) 90+2	1,012	5
10.12	Yeovil Town (a)		P-P			
07.01	Manchester C (h)	L	2-5	Remi Allen 34, Brooke Chaplen 41	951	6
28.01	Arsenal (h)	D	0-0		690	6
11.02	Everton (a)	L	1-2	Rachel Furness 38	274	7
21.02	Bristol City (h)	W	4-0	Kirsty Pearce 29, Fara Williams 51, 70, Brooke Chaplen 54	172	6
14.03	Yeovil Town (a)		P-P			6
25.03	Chelsea (a)	D	2-2	Brooke Chaplen (pen) 25, Fara Williams 47	1,652	6
28.03	Yeovil Town (h)	W	3-0	*Brooke Chaplen missed pen (saved by Megan Walsh) 34,* Remi Allen 41, Lauren Bruton 52, Kirsty Linnett 77	197	6
01.04	Manchester C (a)	W	2-0	Remi Allen 34, Kirsty Pearce 61, *Jo Potter sent off 81*	1,274	5
13.04	Yeovil Town (a)+	W	4-0	Remi Allen 10, 13, Rachel Furness 58, Rachel Rowe 84	223	4
18.04	Arsenal (a)	L	1-3	Fara Williams 50	610	5
22.04	Everton (h)	W	3-0	Remi Allen 47, Lauren Bruton 73, Kirsty Pearce 85	263	3
29.04	Sunderland (a)	W	2-0	Fara Williams 39, Rachel Furness 41, *Mary Earps sent off 75*		3
12.05	Liverpool (h)*	W	3-0	Brooke Chaplen 4, 73, Lauren Bruton 81	1,379	3
20.05	Birmingham C (a)++	D	1-1	Brooke Chaplen 4	1,120	4

+Played at Wordsworth Drive, Taunton Town FC   *Played at Madejski Stadium, Reading FC   ++Played at St Andrews, Birmingham City FC

2017/18 WSL CONTINENTAL CUP: GROUP ONE SOUTH

Date	Opponent	Result	Score	Scorers	Att
01.11	Watford (h)	W	4-0	Fara Williams 5, Molly Bartrip 45, Kirsty Linnett 69, Merrick Will (og) 90	211
05.11	Arsenal (a)	W	2-1	Fara Williams 52, 56	380
15.11	London Bees (h)*	W	4-0	Kirsty Pearce 52, Brooke Chaplen 55, Rachel Rowe 75, Rachel Furness 89	2,248
03.12	Millwall L (a)	W	5-0	Brooke Chaplen 38, 86, Rachel Furness 53, 66, Lauren Bruton 60	192
16.12 QF	Everton (a)	D	1-1 (aet) (W 4-3p)	Kirsty Linnett 94	155
14.01 SF	Arsenal (h)	L	2-3	Brooke Chaplen 7, Lauren Bruton 70	749

*Played at Madejski Stadium, Reading FC

2017/18 FA CUP

04.02 R4   Birmingham C (h)   L   0-1   488

READING PLAYER APPEARANCES & GOALS 2017/18

				WSL1		FAC		CC		Total	
				A	G	A	G	A	G	A	G
Allen, Remi	M	ENG	15.10.90	18	9	1	-	6	-	25	9
Bartrip, Molly	D	ENG	01.06.96	6	-	-	-	4	1	10	1
Bruton, Lauren	M	ENG	22.11.92	18	3	1	-	6	2	25	5
Chaplen, Brooke	M	ENG	16.04.89	18	8	1	-	6	4	25	12
De Bunsen, Tamsin	M	ENG	30.07.99	-	-	-	-	1	-	1	-
Earps, Mary	G	ENG	07.03.93	15	-	1	-	-	-	16	-
Fletcher, Melissa	F	ENG	28.01.92	2	-	-	-	1	-	3	-
Furness, Rachel	M	NIR	19.06.88	17	3	1	-	6	3	24	6
Gane, Evie	D	WAL	10.12.99	1	-	-	-	-	-	1	-
Green, Anna	D	NZL	20.08.90	5	-	1	-	5	-	11	-
Harding, Natasha	F	WAL	02.03.89	13	-	1	-	-	-	14	-
Jane, Rebecca	D	ENG	31.03.92	6	-	-	-	5	-	11	-
Kite, Rose	G	ENG	n/a	-	-	-	-	-	-	-	-
Linnett, Kirsty	F	ENG	24.09.93	13	1	1	-	6	2	20	3
Moloney, Grace	G	IRE	01.03.93	4	-	-	-	6	-	10	-
Moore, Jade	M	ENG	22.10.90	14	2	-	-	-	-	14	2
O'Rourke, Sophie	M	ENG	06.03.99	-	-	-	-	-	-	-	-
Pearce, Kirsty	D	ENG	19.04.87	18	3	1	-	5	1	24	4
Potter, Josanne	M	ENG	13.11.84	17	-	1	-	6	-	24	-
Rowe, Rachel	M	WAL	13.09.92	18	2	1	-	6	1	25	3
Sansom, Chloe	G	ENG	17.10.96	-	-	-	-	-	-	-	-
Scott, Harriet	D	IRE	10.02.93	9	-	1	-	3	-	13	-
Van den Berg, Mandy	D	NED	26.08.90	2	-	-	-	4	-	6	-
Williams, Fara	M	ENG	25.01.84	18	7	1	-	6	3	25	10

GOALSCORERS 2017/18

WSL1: Allen (9), Chaplen (8), Williams (7), Bruton (3), Furness (3), Pearce (3), Moore (2), Rowe (2), own goals (2), Linnett (1)

FAC: None

CC: Chaplen (4), Furness (3), Williams (3), Bruton (2), Linnett (2), Bartrip (1), Pearce (1), Rowe (1), own goals (1)

Total: Chaplen (12), Williams (10), Allen (9), Furness (6), Bruton (5), Pearce (4), Linnett (3), Rowe (3), Moore (2), Bartrip (1)

WEST HAM UNITED

2018/19: WSL (Tier 1)

Nickname: The Hammers
Ground: Rush Green, (WHUFC Training Ground)
Manager: Matt Beard (since June 2018)

Season 2017/18:
WSL Southern (Tier 3): 7th
FA Cup: 2nd Round
WPL Cup: Determining Round
WPL Plate: Winners
Capital Cup: 1st Round

Founded: 1991
National Honours: WPL Plate Winners (1):
2018

Last 5 League Finishes
2018 WPL Southern (Tier 3): 7th
2017 WPL Southern (Tier 3): 9th
2016 WPL Southern (Tier 3): 10th
2015 WPL Southern (Tier 3): 6th
2014 WPL Southern (Tier 3): 10th

In May 2018, the FA confirmed that West Ham were one of 11 clubs to be awarded with a licence for the newly-launched WSL, the first full-time professional division for female players in England. They were the only team from outside the existing top two divisions to be elected into the top-flight, having competed in the 3rd tier in 2017/18 where they finished 7th in WPL Southern. At the beginning of June 2018 West Ham named Matt Beard as their new manager. Beard led Liverpool to the WSL title in 2013 and 2014 before leaving for Boston Breakers in the US. Preparations for a new era began immediately with Chelsea pair Claire Rafferty and Gilly Flaherty among the first high-profile signings.

Managing director Jack Sullivan is the son of David Sullivan who co-owns West Ham United FC with long-time business partner David Gold. Sullivan Jr's response to the award of a WSL licence was: "This is a great day for the club and a proud one for all involved. The hard work from everyone has paid off and we are really excited for what lies ahead. We are very happy to be at the top of the women's footballing pyramid, but we all know that the hard work has only just started."

The Hammers won five of their final six WPL Southern fixtures and would surely have finished higher than 7th but for a sluggish start to 2017/18 when they won just one of their opening seven League games. They were also knocked out of the WPL Cup by Chichester City in the determining round, meaning they dropped into the WPL Plate. However, they responded in fine fashion by going on to win that competition, beating Luton 5-0 in the final. They also lifted the Isthmian Cup for teams in the South East with a 2-1 triumph over eventual WPL Southern champions Charlton in the final, Andria Georgiou and Molly Clark scoring the goals.

WEST HAM FACTS

- The WPL Plate triumph of 2017/18 was West Ham's first success in a national Cup competition, however they have twice won the Essex FA County Cup (in 2008/09 and 2010/11) and also added the Isthmian Cup for teams from the South East in 2017/18.

- The Hammers' elevation to the WSL marks a stunning turnaround for a club where – under a previous ownership structure – several players walked out in protest over a perceived lack of funding at the start of the 2015/16 season.

- Ellie Zoepfl celebrated being voted club Player of the Year with a 10-minute hat-trick on the final day of the season in the 7-1 home win over QPR which was watched by the club's biggest home attendance of the season – 1,356 – at Rush Green.

- West Ham men's legendary left-back Julian Dicks was manager of West Ham Ladies for the 2014/15 season in which the club finished 6th in WPL South.

GILLY FLAHERTY DOB 24.08.91 DEFENDER

Flaherty has spent her entire career in London. She started out as a youth player at Millwall Lionesses before moving to Arsenal, Chelsea and now West Ham.

Everybody "felt like the new girl" at the start of pre-season training at West Ham United, England centre-back Gilly Flaherty recalls, after her switch from West London to East London in the summer of 2018. Flaherty, who helped Chelsea win the Double last term, was one of the new arrivals at West Ham following their promotion from Tier 3 to the Women's Super League thanks to a successful licence application, which saw the Hammers turn professional.

The majority of the squad – recruited by new manager Matt Beard – were new summer signings like Flaherty. But what was it that attracted her to newcomers United? "I was offered a new contract at Chelsea and I could have stayed there and probably not really played a lot or sat on the bench. But I just want to play football. That's all," Flaherty explains. "It's about me playing, week-in, week-out. That's when I'm the happiest, when I'm playing. Chelsea and I both decided that it was best for both parties if we parted ways. Then my agent had a conversation with Beardy, who was very keen – along with Karen [Ray, West Ham's general manager until leaving in August 2018] to bring me down to West Ham. That meant a lot.

"For me, it was a bit of a weird feeling, because I've never known of interest from another club before. Then it all seemed a little bit more real when I went to see the great facilities, had a chat with Karen and Matt and then I knew straight away in my gut that it was the right decision for me to make, to get a new challenge and really try and push on again." Flaherty feels the fledgling scenario at West Ham reminds her of when she left Arsenal to join Chelsea – then still a relatively up-and-coming side, bidding for their first major trophy – in 2014.

Her time with the Blues saw them lift five major pieces of silverware, while she also scored 12 times in 96 appearances in all competitions while becoming a favourite for many Chelsea fans. Now she believes this carefully selected West Ham squad can compete at the very top too. "It took a few days for us all to remember everyone's names," she jokes, recalling the early parts of 2018-19's pre-season training." But credit goes to Beardy and Karen – they've put a team together where there are no egos, no big-time players. Everybody's just there to graft and there for the same goal – to push West Ham on.

"I don't really think you could have put a nicer bunch of girls together. They're all grafters, they all want to fight for each other. We're in it together and I couldn't be happier. You're going to see a team that will be tough to break down, resolute and together. I think we'll surprise a few people this year."

2017/18 WPL SOUTHERN

Date	Opponent		Result	Scorers		
20.08	Gillingham (a)+	L	0-1		250	
27.08	Cardiff City L (h)	W	4-3	Paige Anderson-James 15, 84, Amber Stobbs 24, Molly Peters 73	150	
10.09	C&K Basildon (a)	L	0-3		87	
17.09	Chichester City (a)	L	0-4		80	9
20.09	Charlton Athletic (h)	L	0-6		149	9
24.09	Portsmouth (a)	L	1-2	Chenise Austin (pen) 88	126	10
01.10	Lewes (a)	L	0-3		105	10
08.10	Swindon Town (h)	W	5-0	Hannah Wheeler 19, Molly Peters 34, Paige Anderson-James 66, 75, Kelly Wealthall 77	256	10
11.10	Charlton Athletic (a)*	W	3-1	Paige Anderson-James 32, Molly Peters 39, 60	452	9

15.10	Coventry United (h)	L	1-2	Andreya Ezekiel-Meade 36	264	9
12.11	Coventry United (a)	L	1-2	Ellie Zoepfl 18	75	8
26.11	C&K Basildon (h)	L	3-7	Molly Peters 40, Ellie Zoepfl 61, Rosie Kmita 82	253	9
17.12	Crystal Palace (h)	L	0-2		70	10
07.01	Gillingham (h)	D	0-0		133	10
28.01	Cardiff City L (a)	W	6-2	Rosie Kmita 12, 46, Elie Zoepfl 33, 72, Kelly Wealthall 68, Chloe Burr 80	85	8
04.02	Crystal Palace (a)	D	0-0		130	8
11.03	Chichester City (h)	W	2-0	Amber Stobbs 27, 88	198	8
18.03	Portsmouth (h)	P-P				8
25.03	Swindon Town (a)	W	6-0	Leanne Mabey 30, Kelly Wealthall 46, 71, Ellie Zoepfl 65, 87, Molly Clark 85,	102	8
08.04	QPR (a)	W	10-0	Amber Stobbs 10, 89, Chantelle Mackie 13, Kelly Wealthall 19, 69, 81, Ellie Zoepfl 34, 56, Rosie Kmita 70, Andria Georgiou 90	160	6
22.04	Portsmouth (h)	W	7-1	Hannah Wheeler 13, Kelly Wealthall 25, 60, 89, Rosie Kmita 37, Jasmine Auguste 55, Own Goal 85, *West Ham GK Cara Connatser saved Rachel Panting pen 82*	187	7
29.04	Lewes (h)	L	1-2	Kelly Wealthall 14, *Andria Georgiou sent off 69*	86	7
20.05	QPR (h)	W	7-1	Rosie Kmita 30, Kelly Wealthall 44, Jasmine Auguste 61, Ellie Zoepfl 63, 66, 73, Rebecca Dunning (pen) 90+1	1,356	7

*Played at The Valley, (Charlton Athletic FC)   +Played at Priestfield, (Gillingham FC)

2017/18 FA CUP

| 03.12 R2 | Coventry United (a) | L | 1-6 | Chenise Austin (pen) 52 | | |

2017/18 WPL CUP

| 03.09 DR | Chichester City (a) | L | 1-4 | Chloe Burr 77, *Charlotte Long sent off 65* | 70 | |

2017/18 WPL PLATE

29.10 R1	QPR (h)**	W	3-1	Chloe Burr 17, Amber Stobbs 44, Chenise Austin (pen) 56	1,052	
10.12 R2	Brislington (a)	P-P				
14.01 R2	Brislington (a)	W	6-0	Rosie Kmita 10, 26, 89, Molly Peters 60, Amber Stobbs 70, Kelly Wealthall 76	63	
11.02 QF	Keynsham Town (h)**	W	7-0	Kelly Wealthall 5, Leanne Mabey 18, 31, Amber Stobbs 34, 38, 79, Molly Peters 84	189	
04.03 SF	Hull City (a)	W	3-0	Kelly Wealthall 60, 63, Andria Georgiou 73	80	
15.04 F	Luton Town (n)	W	5-0	Amber Stobbs 25, Kelly Wealthall 29, Ellie Zoepfl 48, 73, Rosie Kmita 62	262	

**Played at Ship Lane, Thurrock FC   (n) Keys Park, Hednesford Town

2017/18 MIDDLESEX FA CAPITAL CUP

| 22.10 R1 | Crystal Palace (a) | | L | 1-3 | Julie Melfald 74 | 174 | |

WEST HAM UNITED PLAYER APPEARANCES & GOALS 2017/18

		WPL		FAC		WPLP		CapC		Total	
		A	G	A	G	A	G	A	G	A	G
Anderson-James, Paige	F	6	5	-	-	1	-	1	-	8	5
Auguste, Jasmine	D	20	2	1	-	5	-	1	-	27	2
Austin, Chenise	D	22	1	1	1	6	1	1	-	30	3
Bent, Stephaney	F	1	-	-	-	-	-	-	-	1	-
Brown, Demi	D	1	-	-	-	-	-	-	-	1	-
Burr, Chloe	F	15	1	1	-	6	2	1	-	23	3
Chitate-Samuriwo, Shona	M	3	-	-	-	-	-	-	-	3	-
Chong, Dayna	M	13	-	1	-	3	-	1	-	18	-
Clark, Molly	M	6	1	-	-	-	-	-	-	6	1
Connatser, Cara	G	5	-	-	-	1	-	-	-	6	-
Cooper, Amy	M	14	-	1	-	4	-	1	-	20	-
Dunning, Rebecca	D	1	1	-	-	-	-	-	-	1	1
Edwards, Shirvae	M	1	-	-	-	-	-	-	-	1	-
Ezekiel-Meade, Andreya	F	8	1	-	-	1	-	1	-	10	1
Georgiou, Andria	M	11	1	1	-	5	1	-	-	17	2
Ivison, Lottie	G	1	-	-	-	1	-	-	-	2	-
Kanto, Sindi	G	2	-	1	-	-	-	-	-	3	-
Kmita, Rosie	F	13	6	1	-	5	4	-	-	19	10
Kmita, Mollie	D	11	-	1	-	4	-	1	-	17	-
Locke, Whitney	F	-	-	-	-	1	-	-	-	1	-
Long, Charlotte	M	1	-	-	-	1	-	-	-	2	-
Mabey, Leanne	D	7	1	-	-	4	2	-	-	11	3
Mackie, Chantelle	D	20	1	-	-	6	-	1	-	27	1
Melfald, Julie	F	1	-	-	-	-	-	1	1	2	1
Miller, Georgia	M	2	-	-	-	1	-	-	-	3	-
Peters, Molly	F	16	5	1	-	5	2	-	-	22	7
Rowlands, Cherie	G	8	-	-	-	1	-	1	-	10	-
Salcedo, Carla	M	1	-	-	-	-	-	-	-	1	-
Sampson, Vyan	D	3	-	-	-	-	-	-	-	3	-
Staunton, Grace	G	5	-	-	-	3	-	-	-	8	-
Stobbs, Amber	F	16	5	1	-	5	6	1	-	23	11
Swift, Zoe	F	4	-	1	-	-	-	-	-	5	-
Waithe, Shakira	F	-	-	-	-	1	-	-	-	1	-
Walker, Portia	F	1	-	-	-	-	-	-	-	1	-
Wealthall, Kelly	F	17	12	-	-	4	5	1	-	22	17
Wheeler, Hannah	D	22	2	1	-	6	-	1	-	30	2
Yardley, Chanell	G	1	-	-	-	-	-	-	-	1	-
Zoepfl, Ellie	M	11	11	1	-	3	2	-	-	15	13

WPLP = WPL Cup & WPL Plate apps/goals combined   Total = WPL/FA Cup/WPL Cup/WPL Plate/Capital Cup. Does not include Isthmian Cup

GOALSCORERS 2017/18

WPL: Wealthall (12), Zoepfl (11), R.Kmita (6), Anderson-James (5), Peters (5), Stobbs (5), Auguste (2), Wheeler (2), Austin (1), Burr (1), Clark (1), Dunning (1), Ezekiel-Meade (1), Georgiou (1), Mabey (1), Mackie (1), own goals (1)

FAC: Austin (1)

WPLC/WPLP: Stobbs (6), Wealthall (5), R.Kmita (4), Burr (2), Mabey (2), Peters (2), Zoepfl (2), Austin (1), Georgiou (1)

CC: Melfald (1)

Total: Wealthall (17), Zoepfl (13), Stobbs (11), R.Kmita (10), Peters (7), Anderson-James (5), Austin (3), Burr (3), Mabey (3), Auguste (2), Georgiou (2), Wheeler (2), Clark (1), Dunning (1), Ezekiel-Meade (1), Mackie (1), Melfald (1), own goals (1)

YEOVIL TOWN

YEOVIL TOWN F.C.
ACHIEVE BY UNITY

2018/19: WSL (Tier 1)

Nickname: The Lady Glovers

Ground: Huish Park, Yeovil Town FC for 2017/18) moving to The Avenue (Dorchester Town FC for 2018/19)

Manager: Lee Burch (since June 2018)

Season 2017/18:

WSL 1 (Tier 1): 10th
FA Cup: 4th Round
Continental Cup: Group Stage

Founded: 1990 (as Yetminster)	**Previous WSL Positions**
National Honours: WSL 2 Champions: (1)	**2018 WSL 1 (Tier 1):** 10th
2016	**2017 WSL 1 (Tier 1):** 9th (Spring Series)
	2016 WSL 2 (Tier 2): Champions (Promoted)
	2015 WSL 2 (Tier 2): 4th
	2014 WSL 2 (Tier 2): 5th

The 2017/18 campaign was Yeovil's first full season in the top-flight, and while it proved a real struggle on the pitch, off it they achieved the most important victory in the club's history. There had been real fears that the FA's new licence criteria could see them frozen out of the WSL for 2018/19 with the semi-pro club needing to turn full-time and provide at least 16 hours of training a week. The Lady Glovers were even forced to turn to public donations as they launched a crowd-funding page to raise £350,000. When the FA confirmed in December 2017 that Yeovil would retain their status, the news was greeted with an understandable sense of pride as well as relief.

At the end of 2017/18 Jamie Sherwood ended his four-year spell as manager to become director of football, with Lee Burch replacing him in the dug-out. Burch led Millwall Lionesses to 3rd in WSL 2 in 2017/18 and won the WSL 2 Manager of the Year award. Under Sherwood Yeovil had clinched the WSL 2 title in 2016 and been promoted to the top-flight for the 2017 Spring Series in which teams played each other just once to fill the gap in the calendar before the switch to a winter season. Yeovil finished the Spring Series in 9th place

It took until matchday 13 of the 2017/18 WSL 1 season for Yeovil to pick up their first clean-sheet and first point of the campaign courtesy of a goalless draw at home to Birmingham in mid-April. Three days later came the greatest result to date in Yeovil's League history as they held two-time WSL champions Arsenal to a goalless draw at Huish Park. It took another game to register their first League goal of the season as Libby Piggott scored in a 3-1 defeat at Everton and Annie Heatherson grabbed their only other League goal of the season in the final day defeat at Sunderland.

YEOVIL FACTS

- Founded as Yetminster Ladies in 1990, the club then took on the name Sherbourne Ladies in 1993. It wasn't until 1999 that they became known as Yeovil Town Ladies.

- The Lady Glovers were among the founding members of WSL 2 in 2014 and have generally been on an upward trajectory ever since. They finished their first WSL 2 season in 5th place, then came 4th, and then went up to WSL 1 as champions. Life in the top-flight has been tough, finishing second to bottom of WSL 1 in the 2017 Spring Series and bottom in 2017/18.

- The opening match of the 2017 WSL 1 Spring Series at home to Liverpool was watched by a club record home crowd of 1,897 fans at Huish Park, beating the 1,483 who witnessed them defeat Sheffield FC 3-0 on the final day of the 2016 season as they secured promotion to the top-flight and clinched the WSL 2 title.

M Pearce / YTLFC

MEGAN WALSH DOB: 12.11.94 GOALKEEPER

Arsenal and Birmingham City had a combined 21 shots on target in their 0-0 draws against Yeovil in 2017/18, all of which were thwarted by an in-form Megan Walsh.

Megan Walsh didn't expect to be a goalkeeper. That was, at least not until she went in goal during one Saturday morning youth coaching session in the West Midlands and the coach quickly said: "Well, you need to go to trials." She was subsequently snapped up by Aston Villa's Centre of Excellence and a future Women's Super League star goalkeeper emerged, training at the club which she had always supported.

After spells at Villa, Everton and Notts County, the England Under-23 international joined Yeovil in May 2017 and was then one of the club's star performers in their 2017-18 top-flight campaign. The Lady Glovers, who were then training on a part-time basis, endured a testing season and finished bottom of the table, but their desire was never in doubt. "We never gave up, even if we were 5-0 down against Chelsea, we still keep going," Walsh says.

The Somerset side's never-say-die attitude was eventually rewarded with two clean sheets and 0-0 draws against Arsenal and Birmingham City, with Walsh producing player-of-the-match performances in both games. "It was such a good feeling at the final whistle," she recalls. "Arsenal chucked everything at us, even bringing their goalkeeper up for some corners at the end, but for us to hold out, it was amazing. It was a long, tough season but we all stuck together and then I was really pleased that I could do my bit for the team with saves in those games. But it wasn't just me – we all worked really hard and just never gave up."

For 2018/19, Yeovil have renewed hope, after making the transition to become a full-time, professional team during the summer, having earned a WSL licence, and Walsh believes the squad are fitter as a result. "We're a bit like a family already and that's only going to get stronger with us training more frequently and seeing each other more, because we'll get that personal connection. But also, we're fitter than last year, which is a positive, so we're hoping to get more points on the board than we did last year."

The summer break also saw changes in coaching personnel at Yeovil, with former first-team boss Jamie Sherwood moving to become director of football and ex-Millwall Lionesses boss Lee Burch arriving to take charge of the first team full-time. The club also have a new home ground, moving the majority of their fixtures to Dorchester Town's Avenue Stadium in Dorset, with the Lady Glovers hoping to "target Dorchester as a potential area to grow their fan base and commercial links", according to proud chairman Steve Allinson.

2017/18 WSL 1

Date	Opponent	Result	Score	Scorer	Att	Pos
24.09	Manchester C (h)	L	0-4		1,302	
30.09	Bristol City (a)	L	0-1		621	
08.10	Sunderland (h)	L	0-1		348	10
29.10	Chelsea (a)	L	0-6		1,821	10
11.11	Everton (h)	L	0-2		681	10
10.12	Reading (h)		P-P			
06.01	Liverpool (a)	L	0-8		453	10
28.01	Birmingham C (a)	L	0-3		405	10
11.02	Arsenal (a)	L	0-4		740	10
21.02	Chelsea (h)	L	0-2		454	10
14.03	Reading (h)		P-P			10
28.03	Reading (a)	L	0-3		197	10
01.04	Liverpool (h)+	L	0-4		312	10
13.04	Reading (h)+	L	0-4		223	10
18.04	Birmingham C (h)+	D	0-0		203	10
21.04	Arsenal (h)^	D	0-0		317	10
09.05	Everton (a)*	L	1-3	Libby Piggott 48	130	10

12.05	Bristol City (h)++	L	0-2		505	10
16.05	Manchester C (a)	L	0-5		715	10
20.05	Sunderland (a)	L	1-2	Annie Heatherson 16	226	10

+Played at Viridor Stadium, Taunton Town FC   *Played at Rossett Park, Marine FC
^Played at Woodspring Stadium, Weston-super-Mare FC

2017/18 WSL CONTINENTAL CUP: GROUP TWO SOUTH

11.10	Brighton & H A (a)	L	2-4	Paige Sawyer 90+1, Kayleigh Green 90+5	167
01.11	Tottenham H (h)	L	1-2	Gemma Evans 35	283
15.11	Bristol City (h)*	L	0-2		
02.12	Chelsea (a)	L	0-8		1,289

*Played at Viridor Stadium, Taunton Town FC

2017/18 FA CUP

| 04.02 R4 | Arsenal (h)^ | L | 0-3 | | 323 |

^Played at Woodspring Stadium, Weston-super-Mare FC

YEOVIL TOWN PLAYER APPEARANCES & GOALS 2017/18

				WSL 1		FAC		CC		Total	
				A	G	A	G	A	G	A	G
Aldridge, Kelly	M	ENG	22.09.80	15	-	1	-	2	-	18	-
Beales, Taylor-Jane	D	ENG	n/a	-	-	-	-	-	-	-	-
Bleazard, Helen	M	WAL	14.08.90	1	-	-	-	-	-	1	-
Burridge, Leah	D	ENG	03.01.97	14	-	1	-	3	-	18	-
Buxton, Charlotte	M	ENG	n/a	9	-	-	-	-	-	9	-
Cochrane, Chelsea	M	NIR	06.09.99	2	-	-	-	-	-	2	-
Cousins, Nicola	D	WAL	22.10.88	18	-	1	-	4	-	23	-
Curson, Ellen	M	WAL	18.02.94	4	-	-	-	3	-	7	-
Evans, Gemma	D	WAL	01.08.96	18	-	1	-	3	1	22	1
Evans, Georgia	M	WAL	16.10.95	16	-	1	-	4	-	21	-
Gauvain, Thierry-Jo	D	WAL	09.05.01	10	-	-	-	-	-	10	-
Green, Kayleigh	F	WAL	22.03.88	13	-	1	-	3	1	17	1
Heatherson, Ann-Marie	F	ENG	27.03.84	16	1	1	-	1	-	18	1
Hignett, Rachel	M	WAL	14.09.95	4	-	1	-	3	-	8	-
Howard, Bethany-May	G	ENG	06.05.95	-	-	1	-	2	-	3	-
Jackson, Bow	D	ENG	27.05.94	15	-	1	-	3	-	19	-
Jones, Jessie	M	ENG	12.05.99	11	-	1	-	2	-	14	-

				WSL 1		FAC		CC		Total	
				A	G	A	G	A	G	A	G
Jones, Katie	D	ENG	n/a	-	-	-	-	1	-	1	-
Lambe, Harriet	D	IRE	01.06.01	2	-	-	-	-	-	2	-
Lawrence, Nadia	F	WAL	29.11.89	7	-	-	-	3	-	10	-
Lloyd, Chloe	M	WAL	04.10.96	4	-	-	-	4	-	8	-
Melton, Chloe	F	ENG	n/a	5	-	-	-	1	-	6	-
Miles, Hannah	M	WAL	13.04.98	12	-	1	-	2	-	15	-
O'Sullivan, Laura	G	WAL	23.08.91	-	-	-	-	1	-	1	-
Piggott, Libby	F	WAL	n/a	4	1	-	-	-	-	4	1
Pusey, Ella	F	ENG	10.03.00	18	-	1	-	4	-	23	-
Robinson, Megan	F	ENG	n/a	3	-	-	-	-	-	3	-
Sawyer, Paige	F	ENG	15.04.99	3	-	-	-	4	1	7	1
Walsh, Megan	G	ENG	12.11.94	18	-	1	-	1	-	20	-

GOALSCORERS 2017/18

WSL 1: Heatherson (1), Piggott (1)

FAC: None

CC: Gemma Evans (1), Green (1), Sawyer (1)

Total: Gemma Evans (1), Green (1), Heatherson (1), Piggott (1), Sawyer (1)

FA WOMEN'S CHAMPIONSHIP
TIER TWO

Tier 2 – which had been known as WSL 2 – was renamed The Championship ahead of 2018/19. The FA's new licensing criteria saw major changes to the make-up of the division and initially an increase in numbers from 10 clubs to 12. The governing body demanded clubs must appoint full-time general managers and provide a minimum of eight hours' daytime contact per week (plus matches) for semi-professional players. That proved beyond existing Tier 2 sides Watford and Oxford who were placed into Tier 3 for 2018/19 after their applications were turned down.

The headline news was that Manchester United had been successful in their application despite the fact they were one of only two current men's Premier League clubs not to have a senior women's team. The award of a licence to Manchester United proved hugely controversial, especially as Tier 3 clubs such as Derby County and Crystal Palace (initially) missed out.

Alongside United – the only full-time team in a supposedly part-time division – there would be four more newcomers to Tier 2. Charlton Athletic were to be promoted as Tier 3 champions, having won WPL Southern and then beaten WPL Northern counterparts Blackburn in the national play-off final. The FA had maintained from the outset that the promotion place would remain open provided the triumphant club satisfied their licence criteria. Also coming up from Tier 3 would be Leicester City Women (who had finished 2017/18 as runners-up in WPL Northern), Lewes (5th in WPL Southern), and Sheffield United who would be jumping two divisions having finished 4th in WPL Midlands One.

Existing Tier 2 sides Aston Villa, Doncaster Rovers Belles, Durham, Millwall Lionesses, London Bees, Sheffield FC and Tottenham all initially retained their licences, although in late June Sheffield FC resigned their place stating the move towards a "full-time operation" was "no longer consistent" with their position as a club. In mid-July, reigning champions Doncaster Rovers Belles followed suite. Belles won the 2017/18 Tier 2 title by 10 points but stated they needed to give up their place in the newly-formed Championship to "ensure their continued viability". On the same day as Belles' resignation Crystal Palace were told they would now be awarded one of the vacant spots in Tier 2.

At the end of 2018/19, the top two clubs in the Championship will be promoted to the WSL provided they satisfy all licence criteria. The club finishing last in the WSL will be relegated to the Championship. There will be no relegation from the Championship. For one season only the winners of both WNL Northern Premier and WNL Southern Premier will be eligible for promotion to the Championship, subject to meeting licence criteria. A play-off between the two will still take place to determine the overall WNL champion. If either the WNL Northern Premier champion or WNL Southern Premier champion fails to meet the licence criteria, the runner-up in their division will be offered the promotion place. From the end of 2019/20 there will be one up, one down between the WSL and the Championship and between the Championship and the WNL.

**THE 2017/18 TOTTENHAM HOTSPUR LADIES SQUAD.
SPURS ARE ONE OF 11 SIDES COMPETING IN TIER 2 IN 2018/19**

This second club section of the book concentrates on the 11 teams who compete in Tier 2 in 2018/19. The clubs appear in alphabetical order. The stadium listed is the main home ground the club played at in 2017/18. Some clubs will have changed stadiums for 2018/19 and where they have been able to notify us before our publishing deadlines these new venues have been listed. Some clubs may also have changed their managers since our deadlines.

For clubs who were in Tier 2 in 2017/18 we have included their WSL 2, FA Cup and Continental Cup results from last season. For clubs who have come up from Tiers 3 and 4 we have included their League, FA Cup, WPL Cup/Plate and County Cup results from last season.

Where known the following information has been included for each game: scorers, goal times, penalties, missed penalties, own goals, attendances. The figure in the column on the far right is the club's League position after all the matches played that day have been completed. This has been included from their third or fourth fixture onwards. It's important to note that this isn't necessarily the position they started their next match in as other fixtures may have been played in the interim.

ASTON VILLA

2018/19: CHAMPIONSHIP (Tier 2)

Nickname: The Villans

Ground: The Lamb Ground, (Tamworth FC) in 2017/18, moving to Church Road (Boldmere St Michael's FC) for 2018/19

Manager: Gemma Davies (since Jun 2018)

Season 2017/18:

WSL 2 (Tier 2): 9th
FA Cup: 5th Round
Continental Cup: Group Stage

Founded: 1973 (as Solihull)

National Honours: WPL Cup Winners: (1) 2013

WPL Cup Runners-up: (1) 1995 (as Villa Aztecs)

Previous WSL Positions:

2018 WSL 2 (Tier 2): 9th

2017 WSL 2 (Tier 2): 4th (Spring Series)

2016 WSL 2 (Tier 2): 6th

2015 WSL 2 (Tier 2): 5th

2014 WSL 2 (Tier 2): 4th

#BackToBrum was the social media hashtag that hailed Aston Villa's return to Church Road for 2018/19 following a four-year absence. Having been successful in their application for a Tier 2 licence in the FA's newly-launched Championship, the Villans are confident that the recently upgraded 3G surface at the home of Boldmere St Michael's FC, and the plans to expand the stadium capacity, make it the perfect home for them to build towards a brighter future.

The 2017/18 campaign, (during which home games were played at the Lamb Ground, Tamworth FC), was a difficult one on the pitch. Director of football Dave Stevens and head coach Iain Sankey left at the end of a season which culminated with the club one place off the bottom of WSL 2. In June 2018 Gemma Davies was appointed the new head coach. The 25-year-old former assistant at WSL side Birmingham City will combine the job with her existing role as Head of Women's Football at the University of Birmingham.

There was also an emotional farewell for long-serving captain Chloe Jones, afforded a guard of honour as the teams entered the pitch for the final match of 2017/18 against Sheffield FC. Jones – who had announced her retirement a week previously, received a standing ovation when she was substituted with two minutes to play. In her first spell with the club she helped Villa win the 2013 WPL Cup, and returned in 2016 after a year playing in Finland. Fan favourite Beth Merrick also left after nearly 13 years' service and more than 100 appearances for Villa.

"I'm completely ecstatic and can't wait to get going. This is my hometown team, my family is full of Aston Villa fans and I'm over the moon to be the new head coach. It's a huge responsibility but it's one that I'm ready to take on. It's going to test me, it's going to be challenging, but it's a job I'm ready for and one that I'm going to relish."

Aston Villa's new manager Gemma Davies (pictured) talking to ladies.avfc.co.uk

ASTON VILLA FACTS

- Villa took part in an extraordinary penalty shootout in 2017/18. Their Continental Cup group stage match with Sheffield FC finished 2-2. With group stage games going straight to penalties, and the winners gaining a bonus point, Villa then prevailed 11-10. Chloe Beattie made what proved to be the crucial save before Jodie Hutton converted the winner.

- The club was founded as Solihull Ladies FC in 1973. In 1989, Aston Villa men's asked for help forming a ladies team. Solihull responded and changed their name to Villa Aztecs.

- Villa Aztecs reached the 1995 WPL Cup final where they were beaten 2-0 by Wimbledon.

- In 1996 they changed their name to Aston Villa Ladies and were officially recognised as the Premier League club's ladies team, but it wasn't until 2007 that they were fully integrated into the Aston Villa FC family.

- Promotion to the WPL Northern Division arrived in 1998. After 13 seasons at that level they won the 2011 WPL Northern Division and were promoted to the WPL National Division.

2017/18 WSL 2

Date	Opponent		Result	Scorers	Att	Pos
24.09	Brighton & H A (h)	L	0-1		312	
01.10	Tottenham H (a)	L	0-2		421	
08.10	Sheffield FC (a)	L	1-2	Kerri Welsh 88	303	8
29.10	Doncaster R B (a)	L	0-6		552	10
12.11	Watford (h)	W	4-0	Bethan Merrick 2, 77, Ebony Salmon 23, Chloe Jones 47	274	8
10.12	Durham (a)		P-P			
07.01	London Bees (h)	D	3-3	Ebony Salmon 31, 58, Elisha N'Dow 30	240	9
28.01	Oxford United (a)	L	1-3	Ebony Salmon 6	301	9
11.02	Millwall L (h)	L	0-2		167	9
21.02	Doncaster R B (h)	L	0-4			9
11.03	Durham (h)	L	1-3	Alice Hassall (pen) 76	109	9
25.03	Watford (a)	W	3-0	Alice Hassall 12, Jodie Hutton 47, Bethan Merrick 76	186	9
12.04	London Bees (a)	L	1-2	Ebony Salmon 89	218	9
18.04	Millwall L (a)	L	1-2	Ebony Salmon 81	341	9
22.04	Oxford United (h)	W	1-0	Ebony Salmon 76	127	9
29.04	Brighton & H A (a)	L	1-2	Natasha Baptiste 59		9
08.05	Durham (a)	L	0-3		434	9
13.05	Tottenham H (h)	D	1-1	Elisha N'Dow 58	208	9
20.05	Sheffield FC (h)	L	3-4	Jade Richards 7, Jodie Hutton 48, Bethan Merrick 71	259	9

2017/18 WSL CONTINENTAL CUP: GROUP ONE NORTH

Date	Opponent		Result	Scorers	Att
01.11	Sunderland (a)	L	1-3	Ashlee Brown 90+4	228
05.11	Sheffield FC (h)	D	2-2 (W 11-10p)	Kerri Welsh 39, Ebony Salmon 82	140
15.11	Liverpool (a)	L	1-5	Chloe Jones 67	282
03.12	Durham (h)	W	3-2	Natasha Baptiste 29, Ebony Salmon 62, Elizabeta Ejupi 87	82

2017/18 FA CUP

04.02 R4	Middlesbrough (h)	W	4-0	Ebony Salmon 4, 37, Elizabeta Ejupi 27, 48
18.02 R5	Sunderland (a)	L	2-3	Ebony Salmon 24, 57

ASTON VILLA PLAYER APPEARANCES & GOALS 2017/18

		WSL 2		FAC		CC		Total	
		A	G	A	G	A	G	A	G
Aguirre, Aja	G	8	-	-	-	-	-	8	-
Ale, Asmita	D	3	-	-	-	-	-	3	-
Baptiste, Natasha	F	10	1	1	-	2	1	13	2
Beattie, Chloe	G	-	-	-	-	2	-	2	-
Brown, Ashlee	D	9	-	-	-	2	1	11	1
Crackle, Hayley	D	13	-	2	-	4	-	19	-
Ejupi, Elizabeta	F	15	-	2	2	3	1	20	3
Elsmore, Ria	D	1	-	-	-	-	-	1	-
George, Hannah	D	2	-	-	-	-	-	2	-
Goddard, Amy	D	1	-	1	-	-	-	2	-
Harper, Chloe	M	-	-	-	-	-	-	-	-
Hassall, Alice	D	15	2	1	-	3	-	19	2
Hinchcliffe, Alys	F	1	-	-	-	-	-	1	-
Hurley, Aoife	D	18	-	2	-	4	-	24	-
Hutton, Jodie	M	18	2	2	-	4	-	24	2
Jewitt, Bethan	D	1	-	-	-	-	-	1	-
Jones, Chloe	M	18	1	2	-	4	1	24	2
Johnson, Sian	D	2	-	1	-	1	-	4	-
Martin, Ellen	M	2	-	1	-	-	-	3	-
Merrick, Bethan	F	18	4	1	-	4	-	23	4
Morphet, Anna	D	-	-	-	-	-	-	-	-
N'Dow, Elisha	D	18	2	2	-	4	-	24	2
Richards, Jade	D	18	1	2	-	4	-	24	1
Rogers, Sian	G	11	-	2	-	3	-	16	-
Salmon, Ebony	F	12	7	2	4	4	2	18	13
Smith, Tanisha	M	-	-	-	-	-	-	-	-
Walker, Lowri	M	1	-	-	-	-	-	1	-
Warner, Phoebe	M	7	-	-	-	-	-	7	-
Welsh, Kerri	F	4	1	-	-	2	1	6	2
West, Amy	M	13	-	2	-	3	-	18	-
Wilkinson, Katie	F	5	-	-	-	-	-	5	-

GOALSCORERS 2017/18

WSL 2: Salmon (7), Merrick (4), Hassall (2), Hutton (2), N'Dow (2), Baptiste (1), Jones (1), Richards (1), Welsh (1)

FAC: Salmon (4), Ejupi (1)

CC: Salmon (2), Baptiste (1), Brown (1), Ejupi (1), Jones (1), Welsh (1)

Total: Salmon (13), Merrick (4), Ejupi (3), Baptiste (2), Hassall (2), Hutton (2), Jones (2), N'Dow (2), Welsh (2), Brown (1), Richards (1)

CHARLTON ATHLETIC

2018/19: CHAMPIONSHIP (Tier 2)

Nickname: The Addicks

Ground: Bayliss Avenue, (Sporting Club Thamesmead FC) in 2017/18, moving to Oakwood, (VCD Athletic FC) in 2018/19

Manager: Riteesh Mishra (since 2016)

Season 2017/18:

WSL Southern (Tier 3): Champions
WPL National Play-off: Winners
FA Cup: Quarter-finals
WPL Cup: Quarter-finals
Capital Cup: Winners

Founded: 2000 (out of Croydon FC)

National Honours: FA Cup Winners: (1) 2005

FA Cup Runners-up: (3) 2003, 04, 07

WPL National Play-off Winners: (1) 2018

WPL National Division Runners-Up: (2) 2003/04, 2004/05

WPL Cup Winners: (3) 2004, 06, 15

WPL Cup Runners-up: (2) 2005, 2017

Last 5 League Positions:

2018 WPL South (Tier 3): Champions

2017 WPL South (Tier 3): 4th

2016 WPL South (Tier 3): Runners-up

2015 WPL South (Tier 3): 3rd

2014 WPL South (Tier 3): 5th

Having won their place in the inaugural Championship by means of their on-pitch achievements, Charlton are unique among the Tier 2 newcomers for 2018/19. On the announcement of their intentions to restructure the football pyramid in autumn 2017, the FA promised that promotion via the WPL play-offs would remain open so long as the victorious club also satisfied their licensing criteria.

Charlton led WPL Southern for almost the entire season, except for a spell in April when they dropped to 2nd then 3rd as Crystal Palace and C&K Basildon overhauled them. The Addicks recovered though thanks in no small part to the extraordinary goal-scoring exploits of Kit Graham and Charlotte Gurr.

Graham won the WPL Golden Boot with 32 goals in 22 League appearances (33 in 23 if you include the play-off final), while Gurr clocked up 24 in 21. In the national play-off final against WPL Northern champions Blackburn at Bramall Lane Lynda Shepherd's early penalty put Rovers ahead. Charlton held their nerve and two goals in quick succession just before half-time from Graham and then Georgia Griffin turned things round to send the Addicks up.

As well as promotion to celebrate, Charlton also claimed the Capital Cup, beating Crystal Palace in the final. At the end of a hugely entertaining and trophy-laden campaign Riteesh Mishra was named WPL Manager of the Year.

"Taking our place in the Championship for 2018/19 is the best thing that's happened in the last 10 years. This season, we've won the League, won the play-off final and been awarded a licence to compete in Tier 2. That's a brilliant achievement for the whole team and everybody connected with the club. We used to be one of the top two teams in the country along with Arsenal. We're not quite back up to that level yet but I think we've finally regained the ground we've lost. Let's hope 2018/19 is a season of consolidation and ultimately, of course, we want to move back to the top tier."

Stephen King – Charlton Athletic Women Chairman

CHARLTON FACTS

- Charlton were formed in 2000 when Croydon – who had just won the Double – were controversially brought under the umbrella of the Addicks. However, they do not consider Croydon's honours (English League champions in 1995/96, 1998/99 and 1999/2000 and FA Cup winners in 1996 and 2000) to be part of their own history.

- The Addicks were one of the most successful women's teams of the noughties. They won the FA Cup in 2005 and were runners-up on 3 other occasions. They also finished as runners-up to Arsenal in the top-flight in both 2003/04 and 2004/05.

- When Charlton Athletic men's team were relegated from the Premier League in 2007, the women's team was disbanded for financial reasons. A sponsorship announced in August of that year ensured the team was able to continue, but in the interim many of the players had joined other clubs.

2017/18 WPL SOUTHERN

20.08	Lewes (h)	W	6-1	Charlotte Lee 21, Lauren Dolbear (og) 38, Ellie Dorey 42, Kit Graham 73, 83, Charlotte Gurr 90	124	
27.08	Gillingham (a)+	W	2-1	Charlotte Lee 30, Charley Clifford 67	187	
10.09	Portsmouth (a)	W	1-0	Kit Graham 90+3, *Grace Coombs sent off 9*	147	
17.09	QPR (h)	W	7-0	Kim Dixson 20, Charlotte Gurr 49, Ellie Dorey 53, Katie Flack 74, Kit Graham 79, 85, Hope Nash 83	81	1
20.09	West Ham United (a)	W	6-0	Nicole Pepper 6, Charley Clifford 10, 60, Kit Graham 37, Georgia Griffin 77, Emma Sherwood 89	149	1
24.09	C&K Basildon (h)	W	4-1	Kit Graham 21, Charlotte Gurr 40, *Charlton GK Katie Startup saved Zoe Rushen pen 50*, Katie Flack 60, Emma Sherwood 72, *Ruby Southgate missed pen (saved by Nikita Runnacles) 88*	147	1
01.10	Cardiff City L (a)	W	3-1	Charlotte Gurr 14, 21, 33	85	1
08.10	Crystal Palace (h)	W	1-0	Charlotte Gurr 73	252	1
11.10	West Ham United (h)*	L	1-3	Kit Graham 53	452	1
29.10	C&K Basildon (a)	L	1-2	Charlotte Gurr 46	87	1
05.11	Coventry United (h)	W	2-0	Charlotte Gurr 20, Kit Graham 45+1	85	1
12.11	Lewes (a)	W	2-1	Charlotte Lee 70, Charley Clifford 75	407	1
26.11	Swindon Town (h)	W	11-0	Kit Graham 10, 16, 86, Charlotte Lee 17, 56, Charlotte Gurr 20, 35, 43, 47, Hannah Churchill 22, Grace Coombs 41	79	1
28.01	Swindon Town (a)	W	9-0	Charlotte Gurr 2, 18, (pen) 61, 90, Charley Clifford 9, Own Goal 43, Olivia Lukasewich 79, Georgia Griffin 83, Kit Graham 90+2	51	1
11.03	Cardiff City L (h)	W	5-1	Kit Graham 16, 41, Charlotte Gurr 20, 32, 57	94	1
15.04	Portsmouth (h)	W	1-0	Kit Graham 85	114	3
22.04	Coventry United (a)	W	3-0	Kit Graham 24, 54, Hope Nash 81		3
29.04	QPR (a)	W	11-0	Kit Graham 10, 20, 33, 36, 57, Georgia Griffin 12, 72, *Charlotte Gurr missed pen 15*, Hannah Churchill 30, Olivia Lukasewich 50, Kim Dixson 54, Charlotte Lee 86	120	2
02.05	Chichester City (a)	W	6-0	Nicole Pepper 7, Charley Clifford 16, 26, Georgia Griffin 28, Charlotte Gurr 61, Kit Graham 63	112	1
13.05	Crystal Palace (a)	W	4-0	Kit Graham 8, 47, 51, 59	258	1C
16.05	Gillingham (h)	W	8-1	Kim Dixson 30, Georgia Griffin 43, 45, 54, Kit Graham 70, (pen) 72, Charlotte Gurr 77, Charley Clifford 81	155	1C
20.05	Chichester City (h)	W	4-1	Charlotte Gurr 12, 81, Kit Graham 61, 90+5	203	1C

*Played at The Valley, (Charlton Athletic FC)   +Played at K Sports

2017/18 WPL PLAY-OFF FINAL

27.05	Blackburn Rovers (n)	W	2-1	Kit Graham 42, Georgia Griffin 45, *Charlotte Gurr missed pen (saved by Danielle Hill) 90*	917

(n)Played at Bramall Lane, Sheffield United FC

2017/18 FA CUP

03.12 R2	QPR (h)	W	5-0	Own goal 41, Charlotte Gurr 45, (pen) 52, 67, Kim Dixson 71	66
07.01 R3	Ipswich Town (a)	W	5-2 (aet)	Charlotte Gurr 69, Kit Graham 73, 98, Sam Pittuck 99, Charlotte Lee 116	110
04.02 R4	Blackburn R (a)	W	3-2 (aet)	Alex Taylor (og) 47, Charlotte Gurr 73, Georgia Griffin 100	157
18.02 R5	Cardiff City L (a)	W	3-1	Kit Graham 23, 29, Charlotte Gurr 32	295
18.03 QF	Arsenal (a)		P-P		
25.03 QF	Arsenal (a)	L	0-5		810

2017/18 WPL CUP

03.09 DR	Swindon Town (a)	W	11-0	Ellie Dorey 10, 17, 25, 85, Charlotte Lee 11, Charlotte Gurr 30, 49, 75, Charley Clifford 55, 63, Hope Nash 60	41
15.10 R1	AFC Wimbledon (h)	W	3-2	Charlotte Lee 31, 85, *Charlotte Gurr pen saved by Shanell Salgado 66*, Charlotte Gurr 90+8	88
10.12 R2	C&K Basildon (a)		P-P		
17.12 R2	C&K Basildon (a)		P-P		
14.01 R2	C&K Basildon (a)	W	2-1 (aet)	Charlotte Gurr 53, Kit Graham 111	147
11.02 QF	Lewes (h)	L	1-2 (aet)	Kit Graham 38	242

2017/18 MIDDLESEX FA CAPITAL CUP

22.10	Parkwood Rangers (a)	W	7-2	Charlotte Gurr 14, Kim Dixson 16, 83, Kit Graham 34, 56, 58, Daisy Monaghan 46	50 est
19.11 QF	Enfield Town (a)	W	6-0	Charlotte Lee 15, 30, Kit Graham 47, 52, Own goal 88, Florence Jackson 90+1	45 est
25.02 SF	Leyton Orient (h)	W	3-2	Georgia Griffin 14, Kit Graham 62, 72	114
06.05 F	Crystal Palace (n)	W	2-1	*Charlotte Lee missed pen (saved Megen Lynch) 10*, Kit Graham 59, Olivia Lukasewich 87	

(n) Played at Bedfont Sports Club

CHARLTON ATHLETIC PLAYER APPEARANCES & GOALS 2017/18

		WPL		FAC		WPLC		CapC		Total	
		A	G	A	G	A	G	A	G	A	G
Ashcroft, Emily	F	-	-	-	-	-	-	-	-	-	-
Baker, Alexandra	G	1	-	1	-	-	-	1	-	3	-
Bennett, Harley	M	6	-	-	-	-	-	-	-	6	-
Bottom, Katie	M	1	-	-	-	1	-	-	-	2	-
Brunton-Wilde, Chloe	D	19	-	5	-	2	-	4	-	30	-
Carpanini, Jessica	D	1	-	-	-	-	-	-	-	1	-
Churchill, Hannah	M	12	2	5	-	2	-	4	-	23	2
Clifford, Charley	M	22	8	5	-	4	2	4	-	35	10
Coombs, Grace	D	20	1	4	-	4	-	4	-	32	1
Dixson, Kimberley	M	21	3	5	1	4	-	4	2	34	6
Dorey, Ellie	F	7	2	-	-	1	4	-	-	8	6
Flack, Katie	D	12	2	-	-	2	-	1	-	15	2
Gardner, Hannah	G	-	-	-	-	-	-	-	-	1	-
Graham, Kit	F	23	33	5	4	3	2	4	8	35	47
Griffin, Georgia	F	15	9	5	1	3	-	3	1	26	11
Gurr, Charlotte	F	22	24	5	6	4	5	4	1	35	36
Jackson, Florence	M	3	-	3	-	2	-	2	1	10	1
Lee, Charlotte	F	17	6	5	1	4	3	4	2	30	12
Lukasewich, Olivia	M	10	2	3	-	1	-	2	1	16	3
Monaghan, Daisy	M	6	-	1	-	2	-	2	1	11	1
Nash, Amy	M	-	-	-	-	-	-	-	-	-	-
Nash, Hope	D	22	2	2	-	2	1	2	-	28	3
Nelson, Elle	M	1	-	-	-	-	-	-	-	1	-
Parreno-Espinosa, Melanie	M	2	-	-	-	-	-	-	-	2	-
Pepper, Nicole	M	20	2	5	-	3	-	4	-	32	2
Pittuck, Samantha	D	9	-	4	1	2	-	2	-	17	1
Sherwood, Emma	F	3	2	-	-	-	-	-	-	3	2
Smith, Latoya	G	-	-	-	-	-	-	-	-	-	-
Southgate, Ruby	D	6	-	2	-	2	-	1	-	11	-
Startup, Katie	G	22	-	4	-	4	-	3	-	33	-
Sullivan, Rosey	D	9	-	-	-	2	-	-	-	11	-
Walklett, Kerry	F	-	-	-	-	1	-	1	-	2	-
Weller, Bethany	M	-	-	-	-	-	-	-	-	-	-

WPL apps/goals includes national play-off final

Total apps/goals includes WPL/play-off final/FA Cup/WPL Cup/Capital Cup. Does not include Isthmian Cup

GOALSCORERS 2017/18:

WPL*: Graham (33), Gurr (24), Griffin (9), Clifford (8), Lee (6), Dixson (3), Churchill (2), Dorey (2), Flack (2), Lukasewich (2), H.Nash (2), Pepper (2), Sherwood (2), own goals (2), Coombs (1)

FAC: Gurr (6), Graham (4), own goals (2), Dixson (1), Griffin (1), Lee (1), Pittuck (1)

WPLC: Gurr (5), Dorey (4), Lee (3), Clifford (2), Graham (2), H.Nash (1)

CapC: Graham (8), Dixson (2), Lee (2), Griffin (1), Gurr (1), Jackson (1), Lukasewich (1), Monaghan (1), own goal (1)

Total: Graham (47), Gurr (36), Lee (12), Griffin (11), Clifford (10), Dixson (6), Dorey (6), own goals (5), H.Nash (3), Jackson (1), Lukasewich (3), Churchill (2), Flack (2), Pepper (2), Sherwood (2), Weller (2), Ashcroft (1), Coombs (1), Monaghan (1), Pittuck (1)

*includes national play-off final

CRYSTAL PALACE

2018/19: CHAMPIONSHIP (Tier 2)

Nickname: The Eagles
Ground: Hayes Lane, (Bromley FC)
Manager: Dean Davenport (since Jun 2013)

Season 2017/18:
WSL Southern (Tier 3): 3rd
FA Cup: 3rd Round
WPL Cup: 1st Round
Capital Cup: Runners-up

Founded: 1992	**Last 5 League Finishes:**
Regional Honours:	**2018 WPL Southern (Tier 3):** 3rd
WPL SE One (Tier 4) Champions: (1) 2016	**2017 WPL Southern (Tier 3):** 5th
L&SE Regional (Tier 5) Champions: (1) 2014	**2016 WPL SE One (Tier 4):** Champions (P)
Surrey FA County Cup Winners: (2) 2011,	**2015 WPL SE One (Tier 4):** 3rd
2016	**2014 L&SE Regional (Tier 5):** Champions (P)

Crystal Palace were the beneficiaries of Doncaster Rovers Belles' decision to withdraw from the Championship in mid-July. With Sheffield FC having also decided that they did not have the financial means to survive at that level, Palace were notified they could now take one of the two vacant spots in the newly launched 2nd Tier. The Eagles had been left hugely disappointed when their application was initially turned down in May.

Palace spent the 2017/18 season on the fringes of the title race in what is now the WNL Southern Premier (Tier 3) before having to settle for 3rd place behind champions Charlton and runners-up C&K Basildon. They were also Capital Cup runners-up, losing 2-1 to Charlton in the final. In 2018/19 they will have to adapt to life without their top-scorer Gemma Bryan who hit 31 League goals and 12 more in Cup competitions last term before leaving for Charlton in the summer.

The club was founded in 1992 and has enjoyed rapid progression in recent times with two promotions in the space of three seasons carrying them from Tier 5 to Tier 3 ahead of the 2016/17 season. Their award of a Tier 2 licence sees them start 2018/19 at the highest level in their history.

"The 2017/18 campaign was a fantastic season. Having set the foundations during our first WPL season in 2016/17, this was the year when the club wanted to build, progress and more importantly challenge for the top spots. In 2018/19 we hope to embrace the Championship. This is a special club because we literally are one big family. The association with the men's club has gone from strength to strength. Whatever team you are playing for when you are wearing the club badge you are expected to give 100% and the club and its fans will give the same back. South London & Proud."

Dean Davenport – Crystal Palace Manager

CRYSTAL PALACE FACTS

- The Eagles undeniably had a strong season on the pitch, finishing 3rd in WPL Southern behind champions Charlton and runners-up C&K Basildon. They topped the table at the end of March, but at that point their title rivals did have a number of games in hand. They also finished as runners-up to Charlton in the 2017/18 Capital Cup.

- Hot-shot striker Gemma Bryan scored 31 League goals and 43 in all competitions in 2017/18. She hit five goals in a single match on three occasions doing so against QPR (h), Swindon (a), and Poole Town (h) in the WPL Cup. She also notched up a further four hat-tricks against Chichester City (h), Swindon (h), Portsmouth (a), and Brislington (h) in the WPL Cup. She left the club in June 2018 before joining Charlton.

- In the 2015/16 season Palace clinched the WPL South East One (Tier 4) title without losing a single game. Manager Dean Davenport's side won 20 of their 22 League matches and drew the other two before being presented with the trophy in front of a capacity crowd at Selhurst Park before a Crystal Palace men's match.

2017/18 WPL SOUTHERN

20.08	QPR (h)	W	9-0	Nikita Whinnett 8, 54, 75, Gemma Bryan 30, 51, 57, 86, 89, Stefanie Simmons 74	105	
27.08	Chichester City (a)	W	4-2	Ciara Sherwood 12, Nikita Whinnett 18, Ellie Bailes 47, Gemma Bryan 79	81	
10.09	Swindon Town (a)	W	7-0	Gemma Bryan 5, 15, 24, 28, 58, Stefanie Simmons 29, 51	65	
17.09	Coventry United (h)	D	0-0		106	2
20.09	Lewes (a)	L	0-1		195	2
01.10	Portsmouth (h)	W	2-0	Gemma Bryan 26, (pen) 82	204	2
08.10	Charlton Athletic (a)	L	0-1		252	3
11.10	Lewes (h)	W	3-0	Gemma Bryan 11, 55, Ellie Bailes 73	107	4
05.11	Gillingham (a)*	W	1-0	Gemma Bryan 14	117	4
12.11	Chichester City (h)	W	4-1	Gemma Bryan 19, (pen) 71, (pen) 82, Nikita Whinnett 32	121	4
26.11	Cardiff City L (h)	W	2-0	Leesa Haydock 5, Gemma Bryan 79	70	4
10.12	QPR (a)		P-P			
17.12	West Ham United (a)	W	2-0	Ciara Sherwood 26, Ellie Stenning 87	70	2
14.01	Gillingham (h)	W	2-0	Ellie Stenning 53, Gemma Bryan 62	252	2
21.01	QPR (a)		P-P			2
28.01	C&K Basildon (a)	L	0-1	*Pamela McRoberts sent off 80*	172	2
04.02	West Ham United (h)	D	0-0		130	3
25.02	QPR (a)	W	2-1	Ciara Sherwood 36, Ellie Bailes 73	46	3
04.03	Swindon Town (h)	W	8-1	Gemma Bryan 6, 40, 90, Sarah Jones 27, Ellie Bailes 54, 85, Megan Chandler 80, Samantha Rowland 81	407	2
11.03	C&K Basildon (h)		P-P			2
25.03	Portsmouth (a)**	W	4-0	Gemma Bryan 1, (pen) 28, 69, Ellie Bailes 27	45	1
01.04	Coventry United (a)		P-P			1
08.04	Cardiff City L (a)	W	5-2	Amy Green 9, Sarah Jones 56, Gemma Bryan 76, Ellie Stenning 78, 85	85	1
15.04	C&K Basildon (h)	W	2-0	Ellie Bailes 42, Gemma Bryan (pen) 85	336	1
08.05	Coventry United (a)+	W	2-1	Gemma Bryan 7, 45	30	2
13.05	Charlton Athletic (h)	L	0-4		258	3

*Played at Priestfield, Gillingham FC   **Played at Littlehampton Town FC   +Played at Communications Park, Daventry Town FC

2017/18 FA CUP

03.12 R2	New London Lionesses (a)	W	3-0	Megan Chandler, Stefanie Simmons, Gemma Bryan
07.01 R3	Coventry United (h)+	D	1-1aet (L 2-3p)	Nikita Whinnett 58

+Played at Glebe FC

118

2017/18 WPL CUP

03.09 DR	Brislington (h)	W	10-1	Nikita Whinnett 2, 21, Rosie Paye 5, 79, Gemma Bryan 11, 37, 52, Ciara Sherwood 42, 71, Ellie Bailes 47	203
24.09 PR	Poole Town (a)	W	8-0	Gemma Bryan 18, 25, 30, 38, 45, Nikita Whinnett 65, Ellie Stenning 80, Sandra Martin 89	58
15.10 R1	Lewes (h)	L	1-2	Gemma Bryan 58	152

2017/18 MIDDLESEX FA CAPITAL CUP

22.10 R1	West Ham United (h)	W	3-1	Nikita Whinnett (pen) 13, Ellie Stenning 28, Ellie Bailes 81	174
19.11 R2	Carshalton Athletic (a)	W	6-0	Ellie Bailes 42, Gemma Bryan 57, Amy Green 69, 90, Ciara Sherwood 77, Ellie Stenning 78	
18.02 SF	QPR (a)	W	2-0	Ciara Sherwood 9, Lilli Maple 70	
06.05 F	Charlton Athletic (n)*	L	1-2	*Palace GK Megen Lynch saved Charlotte Lee pen 10,* Gemma Bryan 54	

*Played at Bedfont Sports Club

CRYSTAL PALACE PLAYER APPEARANCES & GOALS 2017/18

			WPL		FAC		WPLC		CapC		Total	
			A	G	A	G	A	G	A	G	A	G
Bailes, Ellie	M	ENG	20	7	2	-	2	1	4	2	28	10
Bryan, Gemma	F	ENG	22	31	2	1	3	9	2	2	29	43
Chandler, Megan	M	ENG	14	1	2	1	2	-	4	-	22	2
Collins, Ria	D	ENG	11	-	1	-	2	-	4	-	18	-
Davenport, Jade	M	ENG	15	-	1	-	3	-	4	-	23	-
Foreman, Tia	D	ENG	15	-	-	-	2	-	4	-	21	-
Goss, Megan	M	ENG	1	-	-	-	1	-	1	-	3	-
Green, Amy	M	ENG	9	1	2	-	-	-	1	2	12	3
Haydock, Leesa	M	ENG	11	1	1	-	2	-	1	-	15	1
Holdaway, Freya	D	WAL	16	-	2	-	3	-	3	-	24	-
Huntley, Lydia	D	ENG	5	-	-	-	-	-	-	-	5	-
Jones, Sarah	D	ENG	10	2	-	-	-	-	2	-	12	2
Lynch, Megen	G	ENG	21	-	2	-	3	-	4	-	30	-
Maple, Lilli	M	ENG	10	-	1	-	-	-	2	1	13	1
Martin, Sandra	M	ENG	-	-	-	-	1	1	-	-	1	1
McRoberts, Pamela	M	NIR	20	-	2	-	3	-	4	-	29	-
Paye, Rosie	D	ENG	20	-	2	-	2	2	2	-	26	2
Robinson, Mary	M	ENG	8	-	-	-	-	-	1	-	9	-
Rowland, Samantha	F	ENG	3	1	-	-	-	-	1	-	4	1

			WPL		FAC		WPLC		CapC		Total	
			A	G	A	G	A	G	A	G	A	G
Samuels, Hannah	M	ENG	6	-	-	-	2	-	-	-	8	-
Shakes, Roschelle	F	ENG	3	-	-	-	1	-	-	-	4	-
Sherwood, Ciara	M	NIR	18	3	2	-	3	2	4	2	27	7
Simmons, Stefanie	M	ENG	11	3	1	1	1	-	2	-	15	4
Stenning, Ellie	F	ENG	15	4	-	-	2	1	4	2	21	7
Whinnett, Nikita	F	ENG	13	5	1	1	3	3	1	1	18	10

GOALSCORERS 2017/18

WPL: Bryan (31), Bailes (7), Whinnett (5), Stenning (4), Sherwood (3), Simmons (3), Jones (2), Chandler (1), Green (1), Haydock (1), Rowland (1)

FAC: Bryan (1), Chandler (1), Simmons (1), Whinnett (1)

WPLC: Bryan (9), Whinnett (3), Paye (2), Sherwood (2), Bailes (1), Martin (1), Stenning (1)

CapC: Bailes (2), Bryan (2), Green (2), Sherwood (2), Stenning (2), Maple (1), Whinnett (1)

Total: Bryan (43), Bailes (10), Whinnett (10), Simmons (4), Green (3), Chandler (2), Paye (2), Maple (1), Martin (1)

DURHAM

2018/19: CHAMPIONSHIP (Tier 2)

Nickname: The Wildcats
Ground: New Ferens Park
Manager: Lee Sanders (since March 2014)

Season 2017/18:
WSL 2 (Tier 2): 4th
FA Cup: Quarter-finals
Continental Cup: Group Stage

Founded: 2013
National Honours: None

Previous WSL Positions
2018 WSL 2 (Tier 2): 4th
2017 WSL 2 (Tier 2): 5th (Spring Series)
2016 WSL 2 (Tier 2): 4th
2015 WSL 2 (Tier 2): 7th
2014 WSL 2 (Tier 2): 6th

With Scotland international forward Zoe Ness to the fore, Durham enjoyed their best ever WSL season in 2017/18, equalling their highest ever finish of 4th in Tier 2. They did so with a record points haul of 35, which was two more than they achieved in that 2016 season. Ness, who turned 22 in March, hit 8 League goals and 10 in all competitions, but it was her all-round game, and not just her form in front of goal, which saw her voted as the WSL 2 Players' Player of the Year 2017/18.

As well as a string of fine results on the pitch, there was plenty more to celebrate off it with confirmation that their application for a Tier 2 licence had been successful. For a club that has only existed in its current guise for five years, Durham have made rapid strides. They were founder members of WSL 2 (now the Championship) and have finished 4th in the last two full seasons.

In the summer the club was boosted by the decision of key players Beth Hepple and Nicki Gears to sign new deals. Midfielder Hepple is the Wildcats' longest-serving player having come through the youth ranks and played in every WSL 2 season. The 2017/18 season saw her become the first player to make 100 appearances for Durham and she also won her first call-up to the England Under-23 squad. Forward Gears enjoyed a productive 2017/18 too, clocking up her 50th Wildcats appearance and netting 5 goals.

"I love playing here and have the upmost respect for everyone who works behind the scenes. Personally, I enjoyed a good season in 2017/18, but I know I have plenty more in the tank and I can't wait to get going again. My personal aims are to stay injury free and support my team to the best of my ability. As a defender it's the clean sheets that count so that's my priority, however it is always good to get on the scoresheet too. We can go all the way in 2018/19. We have the quality in the squad and the support off the pitch too. I have a feeling it's going to be another good year for us."

Sarah Wilson, Durham Captain

DURHAM STATS

- As well as their club record WSL points tally of 35 in 2017/18, Durham also achieved a club record tally of WSL goals (44).

- The club was formed in 2013 as a collaboration between South Durham & Cestria Girls and Durham University and was immediately awarded a licence to compete in the first WSL 2 season of 2014.

- Their first competitive match as Durham was an FA Cup 3rd Round tie which ended in a 4-0 win over Chichester City on 14 February 2014.

- South Durham & Cestria Girls had themselves been founded in 2006 by Lee Sanders and quickly became one of the best teams in the region. They competed in international events in Portugal, Ghana and the USA and won a prestigious youth tournament, the World Peace Cup, in Oslo in 2010. In 2011 they were runners-up at the Gothia World Youth Cup.

2017/18 WSL 2

Date	Opponent	Result	Score	Scorers	Att	Pos
24.09	Tottenham H (h)	W	2-1	Beth Hepple 44, Nicki Gears 45+3	617	
01.10	Brighton & HA (a)	L	2-3	Beth Hepple 44, 57	176	
08.10	Watford (h)	W	4-0	Zoe Ness 39, Abigail Cottam 55, Beth Hepple 66, Kathryn Hill 78	487	2
29.10	Sheffield FC (a)	W	4-0	Nicola Worthington 46, Abigail Cottam 50, Rachel Lee 67, Jordan Atkinson 79	339	2
12.11	London Bees (h)	D	0-0		401	2
10.12	Aston Villa (h)	P-P				
07.01	Oxford United (a)	W	4-2	Beth Hepple 21, Zoe Ness 61, 83, Sarah Robson 68	158	2
28.01	Millwall L (a)	L	2-3	Beth Hepple 51, Jordan Atkinson 85	175	3
11.02	Doncaster R B (h)	L	1-2	Sarah Wilson 13	407	5
22.02	Sheffield FC (h)	W	3-2	Beth Hepple 32, Nicki Gears 69, Emily Roberts 70	347	3
11.03	Aston Villa (a)	W	3-1	Beth Hepple 45+1, Zoe Ness 89, Emily Roberts 90+1	109	3
01.04	Oxford United (h)	D	1-1	Jordan Atkinson 31	257	4
15.04	London Bees (a)	W	3-1	Sarah Robson 27, Beth Hepple 45, Emily Roberts 48	142	4
19.04	Doncaster R B (a)	L	1-3	Zoe Ness 50	310	4
22.04	Millwall L (h)	W	2-1	Zoe Ness 6, Emily Roberts 43	304	4
29.04	Tottenham H (a)	L	3-6	Beth Hepple 45, Nicki Gears 49, 54	453	4
08.05	Aston Villa (h)	W	3-0	Beth Hepple (pen) 18, Zoe Ness 71, Jordan Atkinson 86	434	4
13.05	Brighton & H A (h)	W	4-0	Zoe Ness 6, Nicki Gears 28, Emily Roberts 48, 74	386	4
20.05	Watford (a)	W	2-0	Rebecca Salicki 8, Jordan Atkinson 80	391	4

2017/18 WSL CONTINENTAL CUP: GROUP ONE NORTH

Date	Opponent	Result	Score	Scorers	Att
12.10	Sunderland (h)	D	0-0 (L 2-3p)		641
01.11	Sheffield FC (a)	L	1-5	Jordan Atkinson 26	122
05.11	Liverpool (h)	D	0-0 (L 4-5p)		351
03.12	Aston Villa (a)	L	2-3	Jordan Atkinson 21, Zoe Ness 90	82

2017/18 FA CUP

Date	Opponent	Result	Score	Scorers	Att
04.02 R4	Sheffield FC (h)	W	2-1	Beth Hepple 60, Sarah Robson 73, *Beth Hepple missed pen 78 (saved by Danielle Gibbons)*	244
18.02 R5	Leicester City W (h)	W	5-2	Zoe Ness 13, Ellie Christon 25, Abigail Cottam 43, 63, Emily Roberts 83	227
18.03 QF	Everton (h)	P-P			
25.03 QF	Everton (h)	L	1-6	Sarah Robson 67	502

DURHAM PLAYER APPEARANCES & GOALS 2017/18

		WSL 2		FAC		CC		Total	
		A	G	A	G	A	G	A	G
Alderson, Helen	G	17	-	3	-	3	-	23	-
Atkinson, Jordan	F	13	5	2	-	4	2	19	7
Blitzer, Jenny	D	3	-	-	-	-	-	3	-
Borthwick, Megan	G	2	-	-	-	1	-	3	-
Briggs, Lauren	M	17	-	2	-	3	-	22	-
Christon, Ellie	D	7	-	1	1	2	-	10	1
Cottam, Abigail	F	13	2	3	2	3	-	19	4
Dalgleish, Ellis	D	2	-	2	-	1	-	5	-
Dixon, Caroline	D	3	-	-	-	-	-	3	-
Drake, Daisy	F	-	-	-	-	1	-	1	-
Gears, Nicki	F	18	5	1	-	4	-	23	5
Gibson, Nicola	M	-	-	-	-	1	-	1	-
Hepple, Beth	M	17	11	3	1	4	-	24	12
Hill, Kathryn	D	16	1	3	-	3	-	22	1
Holder, Molly	F	-	-	-	-	1	-	1	-
Jennings, Jennifer	D	-	-	-	-	1	-	1	-
Johnson, Annabel	D	17	-	3	-	4	-	24	-
Jordinson, Lauren	D	1	-	-	-	1	-	2	-
Lee, Rachel	M	14	1	1	-	4	-	19	1
McCatty, Grace	D	6	-	3	-	-	-	9	-
Ness, Zoe	F	18	8	3	1	4	1	25	10
Podziute, Dominyka	G	-	-	-	-	-	-	-	-
Roberts, Emily	F	18	6	3	1	4	-	25	7
Robson, Sarah	M	13	2	3	2	1	-	17	4
Salicki, Rebecca	D	11	1	2	-	-	-	13	1
Todd, Rosanna	G	-	-	-	-	-	-	-	-
Wilson, Sarah	D	17	1	2	-	4	-	23	1
Worthington, Nicola	M	8	1	2	-	2	-	12	1

GOALSCORERS 2017/18

WSL 2: Hepple (11), Ness (8), Roberts (6), Atkinson (5), Gears (5), Cottam (2), Robson (2), Hill (1), Lee (1), Salicki (1), Wilson (1), Worthington (1)

FAC: Cottam (2), Robson (2), Christon (1), Hepple (1), Ness (1), Roberts (1)

CC: Atkinson (2), Ness (1)

Total: Hepple (12), Ness (10), Atkinson (7), Roberts (7), Gears (5), Cottam (4), Robson (4), Christon (1), Hill (1), Lee (1), Salicki (1), Wilson (1), Worthington (1)

LEICESTER CITY WOMEN

2018/19: CHAMPIONSHIP (Tier 2)

Nickname: The Foxes
Ground: Farley Way, (Quorn FC)
Manager: Jonathan Morgan

Season 2017/18:
WPL Northern (Tier 3): Runners-up
FA Cup: 5th Round
WPL Cup: Runners-up
County Cup: Winners

Founded: 2004
National Honours: WPL Cup Runners-up
(1): 2018

Last 5 League Positions
2018 WPL Northern (Tier 3): 2nd
2017 WPL Northern (Tier 3): 3rd
2016 WPL Midlands One (Tier 4): Champions
2015 WPL Midlands One (Tier 4): 2nd
2014 Midlands Combination (Tier 4): 2nd

A memorable 2017/18 season on the pitch was matched by great news off it in May when the FA confirmed that Leicester City Women had been successful in their application for a Tier 2 licence. The Foxes had finished as runners-up to Blackburn in both WPL Northern One and the WPL Cup and also celebrated silverware in the shape of the Leicestershire & Rutland FA County Cup.

The consistently high performance levels of forward Leigh Dugmore saw her voted as the WPL Players' Player of the Year for 2017/18, while another City star to excel throughout the campaign was Rosie Axten who finished as WPL Northern's top scorer, hitting 22 goals in 22 League appearances and 30 in 34 in all competitions.

The Foxes initially tried to join the elite of English football in 2011 but their bid for a WSL place was turned down. Their determination remained undiminished though. Manager Jonathan Morgan's response to gaining their place in the newly-formed Championship was: "I feel it's thoroughly deserved. We have quietly and patiently been setting up an infrastructure to rival many and we are delighted the FA has seen our vision."

"The 2017/18 season was one of growth and development. We achieved many things, most notably reaching the League Cup Final for the first time and finishing a strong 2nd in the League. We also claimed back the County Cup crown after four years without it. Leicester is a fantastic club, I've been here for a long time and I couldn't imagine playing anywhere else. The future is going to be busy, but we're prepared for everything we have to face and I know this group will meet everything head on and give it everything we've got."

Holly Morgan, Leicester City Women Captain

LEICESTER CITY WOMEN FACTS

- Leicester secured runners-up spot on the final day of the 2017/18 season with a 4-1 win at Bradford City where Rosie Axten scored a hat-trick of penalties.

- Manager Jonathan Morgan and assistant manager Michael Makoni celebrated their 100th game in charge of the team during the 3-2 home defeat to Guiseley on 8 April 2018.

- Captain Holly Morgan marked her 150th appearance for the Foxes in the 2-1 away win at Blackburn Rovers on 15 April 2018.

- Rosie Axten's goal in the 3-2 home defeat to Blackburn on 6 May 2018 was her 50th goal for Leicester City Women in all competitions.

- Leicester City Women are officially affiliated to Leicester City FC – the men's Premier League champions of 2015/2016 – and are not to be confused with grassroots club Leicester City Ladies.

2017/18 WPL NORTHERN

20.08	Bradford City (h)*	W	2-0	Rosie Axten 42, Charlotte Greengrass 50	124	
27.08	Stoke City (a)	W	3-1	Rosie Axten 78, 80, Sophie Domingo 88	60	
10.09	Middlesbrough (h)	L	1-2	Leigh Dugmore 21	72	
17.09	Nottingham Forest (h)	D	2-2	Natalie Johnson 25, Leigh Dugmore (pen) 68	158	5
20.09	Derby County (a)	D	1-1	Sophie Domingo 90	75	4
01.10	Fylde (h)	D	0-0		119	5
08.10	Huddersfield T (h)	W	3-2	Natalie Johnson 21, 51, Leigh Dugmore 64	89	4
11.10	Derby County (h)	W	4-0	Sophie Domingo 16, 56, Leigh Dugmore 63, Kim Farrow 82	103	2

22.10	Stoke City (h)	L	3-4	Leigh Dugmore 10, Sophie Domingo 46, Rosie Axten 56, *Charlotte Greengrass sent off 90+4*	123	3
05.11	Wolverhampton W (a)	W	4-3	Leigh Dugmore 7, Rachel Brown 35, Olivia Mitcham 64, Rosie Axten 89	80	2
12.11	Fylde (a)	W	7-2	Olivia Mitcham 20, 68, Hayley James 46, 59, 82, Rosie Axten (pen) 71, 88	47	2
26.11	West Brom (a)	W	4-1	Olivia Mitcham 16, Rosie Axten 18, (pen) 45, Shauna Cossens 79	82	2
14.01	Huddersfield T (a)	D	1-1	Paige Crossman 17	92	2
18.03	Wolverhampton W (h)		P-P			5
25.03	Nottingham Forest (a)	W	4-0	Rosie Axten 10, Leigh Dugmore 11, Nicole Nymoen 18, Paige Stewart 23	85	4
01.04	Wolverhampton W (h)	W	6-0	Leigh Dugmore 1, 55, Rosie Axten (pen) 32, (pen) 39, Nicole Nymoen 39, Ellie May 79	97	2
08.04	Guiseley Vixens (h)	L	2-3	Charlotte Greengrass 33, *Leicester missed penalty 82 (saved Bethan Davies),* Paige Crossman 90	72	3
15.04	Blackburn Rovers (a)	W	2-1	Sophie Domingo 57, 89	123	2
22.04	Guiseley Vixens (a)**	W	4-0	Leigh Dugmore 23, 70, Rosie Axten 50, 85	32	2
25.04	West Brom (h)	W	3-2	*Rosie Axten missed pen 11 (saved by Vanessa Kinnerley),* Sophie Domingo 71, Moriah Kennedy 80, Rosie Axten 90	89	2
06.05	Blackburn Rovers (h)	L	2-3	Rosie Axten 2, Leigh Dugmore 39	135	3
13.05	Middlesbrough (a)	W	6-3	Sophie Domingo 33, Own Goal 38, Charlotte Greengrass 42, Rosie Axten 49, 65, Nicole Myoen 61	167	2
20.05	Bradford City (a)+	W	4-1	Rosie Axten (pen) 18, (pen) 33, (pen) 86, Leigh Dugmore 41	47	2

*Played at Riverside   **Played at Woodhouse Grove   +Played at University of Bradford

2017/18 FA CUP

03.12 R2	Chorley (a)	W	3-0	Natalie Johnson 12, Leah Cudone 35, 53, *Leigh Dugmore missed pen 45*	78	
07.01 R3	Bradford City (h)	W	2-1	Rosie Axten (pen) 80, Leigh Dugmore 90	102	
04.02 R4	Plymouth Argyle (a)		P-P			
11.02 R4	Plymouth Argyle (a)	W	3-2	Charlotte Greengrass 12, Rosie Axten (pen) 59, Leigh Dugmore 90	208	
18.02 R5	Durham (a)	L	2-5	Leigh Dugmore 42, Sophie Domingo 45+2	227	

2017/18 WPL CUP

| 03.09 DR | Chorley (a) | W | 5-1 | Sophie Domingo 18, 26, Olivia Mitcham 32, Rosie Axten 81, Kimberley Farrow 83 | 66 | |
| 24.09 PR | The New Saints (a) | W | 5-2 | Leigh Dugmore 16, Nat Johnson 35, 72, Olivia Mitcham 53, Sophie Domingo 90 | 55 | |

29.10 R1	Bolton Wanderers (h)	W	3-0	Rosie Axten 9, 89, Olivia Mitcham 75	78
10.12 R2	Loughborough F (h)		P-P		
17.12 R2	Loughborough F (h)	W	3-1	Sophie Domingo 16, Paige Stewart 59, Rosie Axten 79	95
25.02 QF	Nottingham Forest (a)	D	1-1 aet (W 5-4p)	Ellie May 34	145
04.03 SF	Lewes (h)		P-P		
11.03 SF	Lewes (h)	W	4-2	Leigh Dugmore 12, Holly Morgan 16, Sophie Domingo 46, 52	148
29.04 F	Blackburn R (n)	L	1-3	Sophie Domingo 14	466

(n) Played at Proact Stadium, Chesterfield FC

2017/18 LEICESTERSHIRE FA COUNTY CUP

19.11 QF	Desford (h)	W	w/o		
28.01 SF	Loughborough F (h)	W	3-0	Leah Cudone 16, Ria Acton 74, Olivia Mitcham 87	76
04.05 F	AFC Leicester (n)	W	15-0	Leigh Dugmore 6, 52, Rosie Axten 17, 48, Sophie Domingo 20, 36, 80, Hayley James 27, Olivia Mitcham 30, 42, Charlotte Greengrass 67, 78, 88, Paige Crossman 74, Nicole Nymoen 90	200

(n) Played at Holmes Park, Leicestershire & Rutland County FA

LEICESTER CITY WOMEN PLAYER APPEARANCES & GOALS 2017/18

		WPL		FAC		WPLC		CouC		Total	
		A	G	A	G	A	G	A	G	A	G
Acton, Ria	D	18	-	3	-	6	-	2	1	29	1
Axten, Rosie	F	22	22	4	2	7	4	2	2	35	30
Benford, Jade	F	1	-	-	-	-	-	-	-	1	-
Brown, Rachel	D	7	1	3	-	5	-	1	-	16	1
Clarke, Charlotte	G	21	-	3	-	3	-	2	-	29	-
Clarke, Serena	G	-	-	1	-	1	-	-	-	2	-
Cossens, Shauna	M	11	1	2	-	2	-	-	-	15	1
Crossman, Paige	D	6	1	4	-	5	-	2	1	17	2
Cudone, Leah	F	2	-	4	2	2	-	1	1	7	3
Domingo, Sophie	F	22	9	4	1	7	7	2	3	35	20
Dugmore, Leigh	F	20	13	4	3	7	2	2	2	33	20
Farrow, Kimberley	F	2	1	-	-	1	1	-	-	3	2
Field, Scarlett	G	-	-	-	-	1	-	-	-	1	-

		WPL		FAC		WPLC		CouC		Total	
		A	G	A	G	A	G	A	G	A	G
Greengrass, Charlotte	D	17	3	1	1	3	-	1	3	22	7
Hannah, Erin	G	-	-	-	-	2	-	-	-	2	-
Hunt, Imogen	M	6	-	-	-	1	-	-	-	7	-
James, Hayley	D	17	3	3	-	5	-	2	1	27	4
Johnson, Natalie	M	21	3	3	1	6	2	1	-	31	6
May, Ellie	F	16	1	1	-	4	1	1	-	22	2
McGrother, Rebecca	F	4	-	-	-	2	-	-	-	6	-
McIntosh, Moriah	F	2	1	-	-	1	-	-	-	3	1
Mitcham, Olivia	F	18	4	2	-	4	3	2	3	26	10
Moncaster, Mai	M	6	-	1	-	3	-	-	-	10	-
Morgan, Holly	D	18	-	2	-	4	1	2	-	26	1
Nymoen, Nicole	M	18	3	3	-	4	-	2	1	27	4
O'Neill, Alex	D	1	-	-	-	-	-	-	-	1	-
Steggles, Charlotte	D	-	-	-	-	1	-	-	-	1	-
Stewart, Paige	M	22	1	3	-	6	1	1	-	32	2
Taylor, Annie	M	-	-	-	-	1	-	-	-	1	-
Williams, Gracie-mai	M	2	-	1	-	1	-	-	-	4	-

Total = WPL/FA Cup/WPL Cup/County Cup   Total apps/goals includes WPL/FA Cup/WPL Cup/County Cup

GOALSCORERS 2017/18

WPL: Axten (22), Dugmore (13), Domingo (9), Mitcham (4), Greengrass (3), James (3), Johnson (3), Nymoen (3), Cudone (2), Brown (1), Cossens (1), Crossman (1), Farrow (1), May (1). McIntosh (1), Stewart (1)

FAC: Dugmore (3), Axten (2), Domingo (1), Greengrass (1), Johnson (1)

WPLC: Domingo (7). Axten (4), Mitcham (3), Dugmore (2), Johnson (2), Farrow (1), May (1), Stewart (1)

County C: Greengrass (3), Mitcham (3), Axten (2), Domingo (2), Dugmore (2), Acton (1), Crossman (1), Cudone (1), James (1), Morgan (1), Nymoen (1)

Total: Axten (30), Domingo (20), Dugmore (20), Mitcham (10), Greengrass (7), Johnson (6), James (4), Nymoen (4), Cudone (3), Crossman (2), Farrow (2), May (2), Stewart (2), Acton (1), Brown (1), Cossens (1), McIntosh (1), Morgan (1)

LEWES

2018/19: CHAMPIONSHIP (Tier 2)

Nickname: The Rookettes
Ground: The Dripping Pan, (Lewes FC)
Manager: John Donoghue (since Jun 2014)

Season 2017/18:
WPL Southern (Tier 3): 5th
FA Cup: 5th Round
WPL Cup: Semi-finals
County Cup: Winners

Founded: 2002
National Honours: WPL Plate winners: (1)
2017

Last 5 League Positions
2018 WPL South (Tier 3): 5th
2017 WPL South (Tier 3): 7th
2016 WPL South (Tier 3): 7th
2015 WPL South (Tier 3): 7th
2014 WPL South (Tier 3): 6th

Lewes have made great strides both on and off the pitch in recent seasons and seen their hard work rewarded with a Tier 2 licence to join the newly-launched Championship. The 2017/18 season saw them equal their highest ever League finish of 5th in Tier 3, and also receive wide acclaim for their Equality FC initiative through which they claim to have become the first pro or semi-pro club in the world to pay its women's team the same as its men's team.

Many of the players who performed so well in 2017/18 have kept their place in the squad and will now get the chance to prove themselves at a higher level. While a 5th place finish was perfectly respectable, Lewes had actually been as high as 2nd in WPL Southern (now WNL Southern Premier) between September and mid-November and were only edged out of 4th place on goal difference by Coventry United who beat them on the final day.

As well as a successful League campaign in 2017/18, Lewes also had a fine season in the Cups. They made it to the 5th Round of the FA Cup where the draw handed them a glamour home tie against WSL side Everton. A crowd of almost 1000 was present to cheer Lewes on although two-time winners Everton eventually proved too strong with a 6-0 win. In the WPL Cup Lewes reached the semi-finals only to lose 4-2 to a very strong Leicester City Women team, but there was Cup glory in the Sussex FA County Cup where they beat Crawley Wasps 4-0 in the final at Culver Road.

"The 2017/18 season was our most successful yet; finishing 5th in the league with 41pts, winning the Sussex County Cup, and reaching the semi-finals of the League Cup and the last 16 of the FA Cup. I've played here for eight years now and I have watched the club grow year by year. That's down to the people who built the women's team, the management, volunteers, fans and dedicated players (past and present). The support we've been shown is what makes this club great. We hope we can maintain our WSL Championship status and really put Lewes FC Women on the map where I believe the club belongs. If we can pick up some trophies on the way… even better!"

Katie McIntyre – Lewes Captain

LEWES FACTS

- Lewes only failed to score in 3 of their 34 games in all competitions in 2017/18.

- Lewes twice went on runs in 2017/18 in which they won three successive League matches without conceding a goal, doing so against Coventry United, Portsmouth and Crystal Palace in September and QPR, Gillingham and QPR again in March and April.

- The club's only national Cup final appearance to date came in 2017 when they beat Huddersfield 4-0 in the WPL Plate final.

-

2017/18 WPL SOUTHERN

20.08	Charlton Athletic (a)	L	1-6	Katie McIntyre 7	124	
27.08	C&K Basildon (h)	D	1-1	Amy Taylor 60	112	
10.09	Coventry United (h)	W	1-0	Rebecca Carter 2	80	
17.09	Portsmouth (h)	W	1-0	Rebecca Carter 88	116	5
20.09	Crystal Palace (h)	W	1-0	Danielle Lane 80	195	3
24.09	Chichester City (a)	W	2-1	Katie McIntyre 35, Rebecca Carter 54	85	2
01.10	West Ham United (h)	W	3-0	Leeta Rutherford 43, Katie McIntyre 55, Rebecca Carter 85	105	2
08.10	Chichester City (h)	D	2-2	Leeta Rutherford 40, Danielle Lane 44	145	2
11.10	Crystal Palace (a)	L	0-3		107	2
29.10	Swindon Town (h)	W	7-0	Rebecca Carter 23, Charlotte Owen 38, Avilla Bergin 41, Rachel Palmer 58, Darcey James 68, Sarah Kempson 85, Danielle Lane 90+2	102	2

05.11	Cardiff City L (a)	W	3-2	Kelly Newton 8, 53, Georgia Bridges 80	70	2
12.11	Charlton Athletic (h)	L	1-2	Kelly Newton 29	407	3
19.11	Swindon Town (a)	W	3-1	Sarah Kempson 3, Georgia Bridges 60, Lisa Fulgence 78	45	2
26.11	Portsmouth (a)	L	2-3	Avilla Bergin (pen) 36, Leeta Rutherford 90	112	3
28.01	QPR (h)		P-P			4
25.02	Gillingham (h)		P-P			4
18.03	QPR (a)		P-P			4
25.03	QPR (h)	W	3-0	Rebecca Carter 43, Danielle Lane 55, Sarah Kempson 64	202	4
08.04	Gillingham (h)	W	2-0	Danielle Lane 31, 87	221	4
15.04	QPR (a)	W	3-0	Rebecca Carter 32, Danielle Lane 45, 59	50	4
22.04	C&K Basildon (a)	L	0-1		81	4
29.04	West Ham United (a)	W	2-1	Katie McIntyre 64, Amy Taylor 85	86	4
06.05	Gillingham (a)	W	2-0	Avilla Bergin 48, Katie McIntyre 69	57	4
13.05	Cardiff City (h)	W	4-0	Danielle Lane 39, 62, Rebecca Carter 56, Georgia Bridges 90+4	446	4
20.05	Coventry United (a)*	L	1-2	Avilla Bergin 9		5

*Played at Boldmere St Michaels FC

2017/18 FA CUP

03.12 R2	Enfield Town (h)	W	7-0	Danielle Lane 4, 39, 60, Rebecca Carter 13, Charlotte Owen 45+1, Kate McIntyre 51, Vicky Carleton 53	201
07.01 R3	Huddersfield T (a)	W	2-1	*Avilla Bergin had pen saved 10*, Rebecca Carter 10 (scored from penalty rebound), Kate McIntyre 80	96
04.02 R4	Keynsham Town (a)	W	3-0	Amy Taylor 30, Georgia Bridges 58, Sarah Kempson 62	75
18.02 R5	Everton (h)	L	0-6		975

2017/18 WPL CUP

03.09 DR	Southampton Saints (h)	W	3-1 (aet)	Amy Taylor 63, Leeta Rutherford 107, Danielle Lane 110	60
15.10 R1	Crystal Palace (a)	W	2-1	Amy Taylor 14, Avilla Bergin 33	
10.12 R2	Portsmouth (h)		P-P		
14.01 R2	Portsmouth (h)	W	5-1	Eilidh Currie (og) 19, Katie McIntyre 30, Sarah Kempson 31, Victoria Carleton 59, Georgia Bridges 83	196
11.02 QF	Charlton Athletic (a)	W	2-1 (aet)	Sarah Kempson 21, 110	242
04.03 SF	Leicester City W (a)		P-P		

| 11.03
SF | Leicester City W (a) | L | 2-4 | Amy Taylor 10, Sarah Kempson 90+4 | 148 |

2017/18 SUSSEX FA COUNTY CUP

17.12 QF	Bexhill United (a)	W	15-0	Vickey Carleton 6, Avilla Bergin 14, (pen) 61, Georgia Bridges 14, 28, 53, 57, 63, Rachel Palmer 22, Darcey James 27, Rebecca Carter 36, 65, 75, Natasha Wells 43, Kelly Newton 90	25
24.01 SF	Brighton & H.A. Development (a)*	W	4-1	Charlotte Owen 17, Own Goal 65, Georgia Bridges 72, Sarah Kempson (pen) 90	148
22.03 F	Crawley Wasps (n)**	W	4-0	Georgia Bridges 26, 67, Rebecca Carter 46, Danielle Lane 74	168

*Played at The Rookery 3G, Lewes   **Played at Culver Road, Sussex FA

LEWES PLAYER APPEARANCES & GOALS 2017/18

		WPL		FAC		WPLC		CouC		Total	
		A	G	A	G	A	G	A	G	A	G
Baker, Faye	G	13	-	4	-	3	-	2	-	22	-
Bergin, Avilla	M	20	4	2	-	4	1	3	2	29	7
Bridge, Hayley	M	-	-	-	-	-	-	-	-	-	-
Bridges, Georgia	F	12	3	3	1	2	1	3	8	20	13
Carleton, Victoria	M	14	1	4	1	5	1	2	1	23	4
Carter, Charlie	D	1	-	-	-	-	-	-	-	1	-
Carter, Rebecca	F	17	8	3	2	5	-	3	4	28	14
Dolbear, Lauren	G	1	-	-	-	-	-	-	-	1	-
Franchi, Kaysha	F	-	-	-	-	-	-	-	-	-	-
Fulgence, Lisa	F	3	1	-	-	-	-	-	-	3	1
Goldsmid, Jacqueline-Anne	G	3	-	-	-	1		1		5	-
Heather, Sian	M	2	-	-	-	1	-	-	-	3	-
James, Darcey	D	12	1	2	-	3	-	1	1	18	2
Johnson, Claire	D	13	-	4	-	4	-	2	-	23	-
Kempson, Sarah	M	12	3	4	1	4	4	2	1	22	9
Lane, Danielle	M	22	9	3	3	5	1	4	1	34	14
Larkin, Kellie	M	1	-	-	-	-	-	1	-	2	-
Love, Felicity	D	5	-	-	-	-	-	-	-	5	-
McCarthy, Kylie	D	5	-	3	-	3	-	1	-	12	-
McIntyre, Katie	M	21	5	4	2	5	1	3	-	33	8
Newton, Kelly	M	14	3	2	-	3	-	1	1	20	4
Owen, Charlotte	M	18	1	3	1	2	-	2	1	25	3
Palmer, Rachel	D	11	1	1	-	2	-	1	1	15	2
Rowbotham, Ava	M	3	-	-	-	-	-	-	-	3	-
Rutherford, Leeta	M	16	3	4	-	4	1	2	-	26	4
Samain, Leah	G	5	-	-	-	1	-	-	-	6	-

		WPL		FAC		WPLC		CouC		Total	
		A	G	A	G	A	G	A	G	A	G
Taylor, Amy	D	17	2	2	1	4	3	1	-	24	6
Thompson, Rebecca	D	21	-	4	-	4	-	3	-	32	-
Waine, Tammy	D	11	-	-	-	1	-	1	-	13	-
Wells, Natasha	D	12	-	3	-	3	-	3	1	21	1
Wingsutton, Meghann	M	1	-	-	-	-	-	-	-	1	-

Total = WPL/FA Cup/WPL Cup/County Cup

LEWES GOALSCORERS 2017/18

WPL: Lane (9), R.Carter (8), McIntyre (5), Bergin (4), Bridges (3), Kempson (3), Newton (3), Rutherford (3), Taylor (2), Carleton (1), Fulgence (1), James (1), Owen (1), Palmer (1)

FA Cup: Lane (3), R.Carter (2), McIntyre (2), Bridges (1), Carleton (1), Kempson (1), Owen (1), Taylor (1)

WPL Cup: Kempson (4), Taylor (3), Bergin (1), Bridges (1), Carleton (1), Lane (1), McIntyre (1), Rutherford (1), own goals (1)

County Cup: Bridges (8), R.Carter (4), Bergin (2), Carleton (1), James (1), Kempson (1), Lane (1), Newton (1), Owen (1), Palmer (1), Wells (1), own goals (1)

Total: R.Carter (14), Lane (14), Bridges (13), Kempson (9), McIntyre (8), Bergin (7), Taylor (6), Carleton (4), Newton (4), Rutherford (4), Owen (3), James (2), Palmer (2), own goals (2), Fulgence (1), Wells (1)

LONDON BEES

2018/19: CHAMPIONSHIP (Tier 2)

Nickname: The Bees
Ground: The Hive, Barnet FC
Manager: Luke Swindlehurst (since Jul 2017)

Season 2017/18:
WSL 2 (Tier 2): 6th
FA Cup: 4th Round
Continental Cup: Group Stages

Founded: 1975 (as District Line Ladies)
National Honours: FA Cup Runners-up: (1)
1997 (as Wembley)
WPL Cup Winners: (2) 1996 (as Wembley),
2011 (as Barnet)

Previous WSL Positions:
2018 WSL 2 (Tier 2): 6th
2017 WSL 2 (Tier 2): 7th (Spring Series)
2016 WSL 2 (Tier 2): 7th
2015 WSL 2 (Tier 2): 8th
2014 WSL 2 (Tier 2): 10th

London Bees had reason to celebrate at the end of 2017/18 after chalking up their highest ever points tally in WSL 2. The Bees collected 23 points to help them to a respectable 6th-placed finish, which was also their best ever WSL position. Amid the FA restructuring of the Leagues, the north London club were successful in their application to retain their Tier 2 licence.

Further good news followed over the summer as Harrow Borough Council approved plans to expand The Hive – the training base and stadium site London Bees share with men's outfit Barnet FC. Capacity is set to increase to over 8,000 with a newly-built South Stand and an extended East Stand. There will also be a new multi-purpose indoor sports hall, indoor football pitch and state of the art 5, 7 and 11-a-side pitches. Manager Luke Swindlehurst has also made a valuable addition to the coaching staff with the arrival of former England and Arsenal star Rachel Yankey.

They remain independent of Barnet FC but have a close relationship with them. In 2014 – the same year that they took on the name of London Bees – their application to join the first season of WSL 2 was successful. Perhaps their most notable result of the WSL era came in the 1st Round of the 2016 WSL Continental Cup when they beat Chelsea on penalties after a 3-3 draw. They then knocked out Sheffield FC in the quarter-finals before losing to Birmingham in the last four.

"We progressed again during 2017/18. Our highest points tally and League position were reasons to be proud but we also continued to move forward with the infrastructure and the playing squad. The team offered a new brand of football with an attacking, possession-based style. The main hope for 2018/19 is that we can jump forward again and climb up to an even higher League position. We'll be looking to develop all areas of the club to make us stronger for the future."

Luke Swindlehurst – London Bees Manager

MANAGER LUKE SWINDLEHURST GREETS NEW COACH RACHEL YANKEY IN JUNE 2018

LONDON BEES FACTS

- Set up by a group of Transport for London employees in 1975, the original name was District Line Ladies because that was the London Underground line many of the players worked on. They started out playing in the Hounslow & District League but enjoyed a rapid rise to reach the FA National League Southern Division by the early 90s.

- As they continued to go from strength to strength they merged with Wembley. It was as Wembley Ladies FC that they reached the 1997 FA Cup final where they took on one of the strongest teams in the country at the time, Millwall Lionesses. A side containing England's 1995 World Cup goalkeeper Lesley Higgs was narrowly beaten 1-0 at Upton Park.

- They first formed an informal affiliation with men's club Barnet FC in 1998 at which point they changed their name to Barnet Ladies. In 2010 they were unsuccessful in their application to be one of the founding members of the WSL, but succeeded in joining WSL 2 in 2014.

2017/18 WSL 2

						Att	Pos
24.09	Doncaster R B (h)	L	1-4	Tricia Gould 90		279	
30.09	Sheffield FC (a)	L	1-3	Paula Howells 24		314	
08.10	Tottenham H (h)	L	1-2	Jo Wilson 42		450	9
28.10	Millwall L (h)	L	2-3	Jo Wilson 6, Emma Beckett 7, *Ocean Ro-landsen sent off 50*		451	9
12.11	Durham (a)	D	0-0			401	9
09.12	Oxford United (h)	W	2-1	Paula Howells 4, Destiney Toussaint 90		178	8
07.01	Aston Villa (a)	D	3-3	Paula Howells 15, Danielle Lea 27, Katie Wilkinson 90+1		240	8
27.01	Watford (h)	W	3-1	Katie Wilkinson 39, Paula Howells 61, Destiney Toussaint 80		120	6
11.02	Brighton & H A (a)	L	1-3	Paula Howells 3		240	7
21.02	Millwall L (a)	D	1-1	Taylor O'Leary 10		217	8
29.03	Oxford United (a)	W	3-2	*Katie Wilkinson missed pen 11,* Paula Howells 23, Destiney Toussaint 59, Rosanna Lane 84		216	6
12.04	Aston Villa (h)	W	2-1	Katie Wilkinson 27, Destiney Toussaint 45		218	5
15.04	Durham (h)	L	1-3	Katie Wilkinson (pen) 75		142	5
18.04	Brighton & H A (h)	W	2-1	Katie Wilkinson 21, Tricia Gould 90		321	5
22.04	Watford (a)	W	4-0	Katie Wilkinson 14, (pen) 90, Destiney Toussaint 40, Tricia Gould 55		210	5
28.04	Doncaster R B (a)	L	1-3	Katie Wilkinson (pen) 4			5
12.05	Sheffield FC (h)	D	0-0			246	6
20.05	Tottenham H (a)	D	1-1	Taylor O'Leary 59		436	6

2017/18 WSL CONTINENTAL CUP: GROUP ONE SOUTH

					Att
12.10	Arsenal (a)	L	0-7		931
05.11	Millwall L (h)	L	3-4	Destiney Toussaint 2, 85, Jo Wilson 14, *(Paula Howells hit bar from pen 85 – Toussaint scored rebound)*	243
15.11	Reading (a)*	L	0-4		2,248
03.12	Watford (h)	D	1-1 (W 5-4p)	Emma Beckett (pen) 83	321

*Played at Madejski Stadium, Reading FC

2017/18 FA CUP

					Att
04.02 R4	Chelsea (h)	L	0-10		486

LONDON BEES PLAYER APPEARANCES & GOALS 2017/18

		WSL 2		FAC		CC		Total	
		A	G	A	G	A	G	A	G
Anderson, Rebecca	M	10	-	1	-	3	-	14	-
Beckett, Emma	M	18	1	1	-	4	1	23	2
Brayer, Alisha	M	-	-	-	-	-	-	-	-
Clarke, Evie	F	15	-	1	-	2	-	18	-
Fisher, Bolu	F	6	-	-	-	2	-	8	-
Fogarty, Sophie	D	9	-	1	-	4	-	14	-
Gibson, Kelsey	M	1	-	-	-	-	-	1	-
Goddard, Ashleigh	M	6	-	-	-	1	-	7	-
Gould, Tricia	F	6	3	-	-	-	-	6	3
Harris, Sophie	G	-	-	-	-	1	-	1	-
Hobbs, Nicola	G	17	-	1	-	3	-	21	-
Howells, Paula	M	17	6	1	-	4	-	22	6
Huggins, Katherine	M	1	-	-	-	2	-	3	-
Jumratie, Chelsea	D	1	-	-	-	-	-	1	-
Kinnane, Anya	D	1	-	-	-	-	-	1	-
Kmita, Rosie	F	2	-	-	-	-	-	2	-
Lalani, Hana	M	3	-	-	-	2	-	5	-
Lane, Rosanna	D	18	1	1	-	4	-	23	1
Lea, Danielle	D	13	1	1	-	2	-	16	1
Loomes, Lucy	F	3	-	-	-	4	-	7	-
Milliken, Lisa	M	1	-	-	-	-	-	1	-
O'Leary, Taylor	M	18	2	1	-	4	-	23	2
Rolandsen, Ocean	D	17	-	1	-	3	-	21	-
Stojko-Down, Alysha	M	-	-	-	-	-	-	-	-
Taylor, Grace	G	1	-	-	-	-	-	1	-
Toussaint, Destiney	F	17	5	1	-	4	2	22	7
Weston, Chelsea	D	13	-	1	-	3	-	17	-
Will, Merrick	M	10	-	1	-	-	-	11	-
Wilkinson, Katie	F	12	8	1	-	-	-	13	8
Wilson, Jo	F	4	2	-	-	2	1	6	3

GOALSCORERS 2017/18

WSL 2: Wilkinson (8), Howells (6), Toussaint (5), Gould (3), O'Leary (2), Wilson (2), Beckett (1), Lane (1), Lea (1)

FAC: None

CC: Toussaint (2), Beckett (1), Wilson (1)

Total: Wilkinson (8), Toussaint (7), Howells (6), Gould (3), Wilson (3), Beckett (2), O'Leary (2), Lane (1), Lea (1)

MANCHESTER UNITED

2018/19: CHAMPIONSHIP (Tier 2)

Nickname: The Red Devils
Ground: Leigh Sports Village
Manager: Casey Stoney (since Jun 2018)

Season 2017/18:
N/A

The inclusion of Manchester United in the Championship for 2018/19 was one of the most controversial events in the modern history of women's football in England. At the time that their licence application was approved in May 2018, United were one of just two existing men's Premier League clubs (along with Southampton) not to have a senior women's team.

United faced widespread criticism after disbanding their women's side in 2005, although they did continue with girls' football at age group level. More recently, as one of the biggest clubs in world football, they had come under increasing pressure to reform the team. While many welcomed their election to the Championship as an opportunity to raise the profile of women's football in England and across the globe, many queried why they had been given a perceived short cut to the top. Supporters of 2017/18 WSL 2 champions Doncaster Rovers Belles – who had seen their team not only miss out on promotion but eventually effectively relegated to Tier 3 because they were unable to satisfy the FA's new licensing criteria – may have felt particularly aggrieved. Others also argued that with United operating as the only full-time team in what was supposed to be a part-time division it was unfair on their Championship opponents and that they should instead be catapulted straight into the WSL.

The Cliff in Salford, the former training ground of Manchester United men's, was confirmed as their base, on the proviso that redevelopment work would need to be completed before they could move in. Home matches in 2018/19 will take place at Leigh Sports Village. A high-profile club demands a high-profile manager: Casey Stoney, capped 130 times by England and with 12 major honours to her name as a player, was appointed as the first manager of the new Manchester United Women.

Stoney, 36 at the time of taking on the role, played for Arsenal, Charlton, Chelsea, and Lincoln before ending her career at Liverpool where she hung up her boots in February 2018. A brief stint as an assistant to England head coach Phil Neville followed before she landed the United job.

"I think we have the potential to change the face of the game because of the fan base, the profile, the way we're going to do things on and off the pitch, which will excite people in the game to come and watch. Our short-term ambition is to recruit 21 players as well as staff, get them on the training ground, get them working, embed a philosophy, get playing in the Championship and make sure we're successful there. Long term, we want to be a successful team within women's football and that means Champions League football."

Casey Stoney – Manchester United manager (talking to BBC Sport, July 2018)

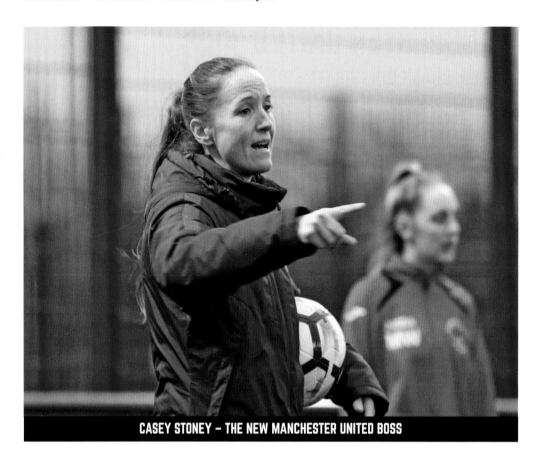

CASEY STONEY – THE NEW MANCHESTER UNITED BOSS

MANCHESTER UNITED FACTS

- The first match played by the new Manchester United Women team took place on 15 July 2018 when they faced Liverpool in a behind-closed-doors friendly. The match had to be abandoned (while it was still goalless) when United goalkeeper Siobhan Chamberlain was taken to hospital with what appeared to be a serious neck injury. Fortunately investigations confirmed no serious injury. Friendlies against Blackburn Rovers and West Ham United followed, but again the matches were behind closed doors and results were not made public.

- In the 1970s female fans of Manchester United formed their own team, Manchester United Ladies. Many recognized them as Manchester United FC's unofficial women's team and they were founding members of the North West Regional Women's Football League in 1999. In 2001 they became officially affiliated with Manchester United, but in 2005 they were disbanded when United decided to direct resources at girls football instead of a senior team.

- When United named their 21-player squad on 17 July 2018, it contained seven of their former youth players, among them midfielder Katie Zelem who won Serie A with Juventus

MILLWALL LIONESSES
2018/19: CHAMPIONSHIP (Tier 2)

Nickname: The Lionesses

Ground: St Paul's (Fisher FC) in 2017/18, moving to Princes Park (Dartford FC) for 2018/19

Manager: Chris Phillips (since July 2018)

Season 2017/18:

WSL 2 (Tier 2): 3rd

FA Cup: 5th Round

Continental Cup: Group Stages

Founded: 1971	**Previous WSL Positions**
National Honours:	**2018 WSL 2 (Tier 2):** 3rd
FA Cup Winners: (2) 1991, 97	**2017 WSL 2 (Tier 2):** 3rd (Spring Series)
WPL Cup Winners: (1) 1997	**2016 WSL 2 (Tier 2):** 8th
WPL Cup Runners-up: (1) 1992	**2015 WSL 2 (Tier 2):** 9th
	2014 WSL 2 (Tier 2): 8th

As two-time FA Cup winners and founding members of the FA's first national League (the Women's Premier League) in 1991, Millwall Lionesses are rightly proud of their long-held place among the elite clubs of English football. That status came under threat in 2017/18 when financial difficulties forced the club to crowdfund to raise enough money to survive until the end of the season. Their players – all part-timers – also agreed to forego their match fees to keep Millwall Lionesses alive.

The team refused to allow the off-field problems to become a distraction as they put in a string of stunning performances on the pitch, remaining unbeaten in League football for more than a year before being toppled by Durham in mid-April 2018. They kept the title race with eventual champions Doncaster Rovers Belles and Brighton going until the final weeks, only to finish 3rd. Millwall would have been runners-up ahead of Brighton on goal difference, but for being docked 3 points in November for fielding an ineligible player in the opening game against Watford. Finishing 3rd though was reason to be proud, even though celebrations were dampened when Lee Burch – voted WSL 2 Manager of the Year 2017/18 – left for top-flight Yeovil during the summer. A new board then took control of the club and appointed former Arsenal Women's boss Pedro Martinez Losa as director of football and Chris Phillips as manager. Hopes are high for a more stable future.

Founded in 1971, they became the first English team to be officially affiliated with a professional men's club in the 1980's when Millwall FC saw it as a good way to strengthen their ties with the local community. They were also the first club to open a Girls' Centre of Excellence. Famous names to have come through at Millwall include former England manager Hope Powell, Pauline Cope, Mary Phillip and Katie Chapman.

"To lead this amazing group to our highest place finish ever for Millwall Lionesses FC is a great honour. Millwall is a club with great history in women's football and it's good to see it back where it belongs and heading in the right direction."

Ashlee Hincks – Millwall Lionesses Captain before her departure in summer 2018

MILLWALL LIONESSES FACTS

- Millwall went 19 games unbeaten in WSL 2, a run which spanned more than a calendar year, before losing 2-1 to Durham on 22 April, 2018.

- The Lionesses collected their first piece of major silverware in 1991 when they beat Doncaster Belles in the FA Cup final with Yvonne Baldeo securing her place in club folklore by netting the winning goal. In 1997 they lifted the famous trophy again with a 1-0 win over Wembley in the final at Upton Park and they also completed a Cup Double that season thanks to a 2-1 triumph over Everton in the WPL Cup final which was held at Underhill.

- At the turn of the century Millwall dropped out of the top-flight but returned in 2009 a couple of years before the formation of the WSL. They were not among the WSL founding members in 2011, but when a 2nd tier was formed their application to join ahead of the inaugural 2014 season did prove successful.

2017/18 WSL 2

Date	Opponent		Score	Scorers	Att	Pos
24.09	Watford (h)	W	3-1	Billie Brooks 20, Leanne Cowan 45, Ella Rutherford 59, *Rianna Dean missed pen (saved by Jo Fletcher) 67*	393	
01.10	Doncaster R B (a)	D	2-2	Charlotte Devlin 45, Ashlee Hincks 88	807	
08.10	Brighton & H A (h)	W	4-3	Leanne Cowan 50, Bonnie Horwood 43, Ella Rutherford 71, Ashlee Hincks 80	304	1
28.10	London Bees (a)	W	3-2	Charlotte Devlin 38, 47, Ashlee Hincks (pen) 51	451	1
12.11	Oxford United (h)	W	1-0	Ella Rutherford 8	217	3
10.12	Tottenham H (h)		P-P			
07.01	Sheffield FC (h)	W	2-1	Ella Rutherford 35, 38	123	3
14.01	Tottenham H (h)	W	4-1	Amber Gaylor 4, Charlotte Devlin 71, 84, Megan Wynne 90+4	157	2
28.01	Durham (h)	W	3-2	Leigh Nicol 20, Billie Brooks 48, Ashlee Hincks 68	175	2
11.02	Aston Villa (a)	W	2-0	Charlotte Devlin 70, 90	167	2
21.02	London Bees (h)	D	1-1	Rianna Dean 17	217	2
25.03	Oxford United (a)	W	4-2	Rianna Dean 10, 35, *Millwall GK Sarah Quantrill saved Oxford pen 40,* Charlotte Devlin 73, 84	206	2
28.03	Tottenham H (a)		P-P			2
01.04	Sheffield FC (a)		P-P			2
18.04	Aston Villa (h)	W	2-1	Rianna Dean 83, Leighanne Robe 90	341	2
22.04	Durham (a)	L	1-2	Ellie Mason 19	304	2
29.04	Watford (a)	W	4-0	Ashlee Hincks 5, 8, Rianna Dean 59, Amber Gaylor 64, *Ashlee Hincks missed pen 68*	289	2
02.05	Tottenham H (a)	D	1-1	Billie Brooks 76	144	2
06.05	Sheffield FC (a)	L	0-3			2
13.05	Doncaster R B (h)	L	0-1		323	3
20.05	Brighton & H A (a)	W	3-0	Rianna Dean 25, Ashlee Hincks 81, Ella Rutherford 83		

2017/18 WSL CONTINENTAL CUP: GROUP ONE SOUTH

Date	Opponent		Score	Scorers	Att
12.10	Watford (a)	L	0-1		312
01.11	Arsenal (h)	L	2-5	Ellie Mason 19, Ella Rutherford 69	451
05.11	London Bees (a)	W	4-3	Rianna Dean 31, Ashlee Hincks 50, (pen) 73, Ellie Mason 60	243
03.12	Reading (h)	L	0-5		192

2017/18 FA CUP

Date	Opponent		Score	Scorers	Att
04.02 R4	Coventry United (h)	W	4-1	Megan Wynne 19, Rianna Dean 36, 48, 79	130
18.02 R5	Arsenal (a)	L	0-1		617

143

MILLWALL LIONESSES PLAYER APPEARANCES & GOALS 2017/18

		WSL 2		FAC		CC		Total	
		A	G	**A**	**G**	**A**	**G**	**A**	**G**
Alexander, Megan	D	18	-	1	-	4	-	23	-
Bailes, Freya	M	-	-	-	-	-	-	-	-
Booker, Samantha	M	1	-	-	-	1	-	2	-
Brooks, Billie	D	11	3	1	-	1	-	13	3
Butler, Jordan	D	11	-	-	-	2	-	13	-
Cowan, Leanne	D	14	2	2	-	3	-	19	2
Dean, Rianna	F	17	6	2	3	4	1	23	10
Devlin, Charlotte	M	18	9	2	-	3	-	23	9
Eligon, Simone	G	-	-	-	-	-	-	-	-
Fowle, Brionne	M	3	-	-	-	3	-	6	-
Gaylor, Amber	M	13	2	2	-	2	-	17	2
Giddings, Georgina	M	10	-	1	-	2	-	13	-
Hincks, Ashlee	F	17	7	1	-	4	2	22	9
Horwood, Bonnie	M	16	1	2	-	4	-	22	1
Mason, Ellie	M	18	1	2	-	3	2	23	3
Nicol, Leigh	M	14	1	2	-	4	-	20	1
Payne, Poppy	D	-	-	-	-	-	-	-	-
Powell, Beth	D	-	-	-	-	1	-	1	-
Quantrill, Sarah	G	18	-	2	-	3	-	23	-
Robe, Leighanne	D	17	1	2	-	3	-	22	1
Rutherford, Ella	F	11	6	1	-	2	1	14	7
Taylor, Grace	G	-	-	-	-	1	-	1	-
Wotton, Victoria	D	5	-	1	-	2	-	8	-
Wynne, Megan	M	18	1	2	1	4	-	24	2

GOALSCORERS 2017/18

WSL2: Devlin (9), Hinks (7), Dean (6), Rutherford (6), Brooks (3), Cowan (2), Gaylor (2), Horwood (1), Mason (1), Nicol (1), Robe (1), Wynne (1)

FAC: Dean (3), Wynne (1)

CC: Hincks (2), Mason (2), Dean (1), Rutherford (1)

Total: Dean (10), Devlin (9), Hincks (9), Rutherford (7), Brooks (3), Mason (3), Cowan (2), Gaylor (2), Wynne (2), Horwood (1), Nicol (1), Robe (1)

SHEFFIELD UNITED
2018/19: CHAMPIONSHIP (Tier 2)

Nickname: The Blades

Ground: Steelphalt Academy for 2017/18 moving to Sheffield Olympic Legacy Park for 2018/19

Manager: Carla Ward (since Jan 2018)

Season 2017/18:

WPL Midlands One (Tier 4): 3rd

FA Cup: 1st Round

WPL Cup: 1st Round

County Cup: 3rd Round

Founded: 1998 (as Sheffield United Community Ladies)

National Honours: None

Last 5 League Finishes:

2018 WPL Midlands 1 (Tier 4): 3rd

2017 East Mids Prem (Tier 5): Champions (P)

2016 NE Premier (Tier 5): 5th

2015 WPL North One (Tier 4): 12th (R)

2014 Northern Combination (Tier 3): 10th (R)

Sheffield United have jumped two divisions by virtue of impressing the FA with their application for a licence to join the newly-launched Championship for 2018/19. The Blades spent last season in Tier 4, finishing 3rd in WPL Midlands One (now WNL Division 1 Midlands) but have rocketed up to Tier 2 thanks to their successful bid.

Having faced a major overhaul in the summer of 2018 to prepare them for their place among the elite of the English game, manager Carla Ward will be confident her team will be able to compete. Ward herself played at Tier 2 level, making 221 appearances for local rivals Sheffield FC where she scored more than 100 goals.

She arrived at United as assistant manager to Dan O'Hearne in November 2017 before taking over as manager, initially on an interim basis, in January 2018.

While the FA's Tier 2 decisions were based almost entirely on off-field criteria, Sheffield United have made impressive progress on the pitch recently. They were promoted to Tier 4 by winning the 2016/17 East Midlands Regional Premier Division and also boast a development team and a regional talent centre which they hope will soon start feeding players to the senior team.

"For several years the profile and standard of the club has been growing both on and off the field. The infrastructure is in place and with the backing and support of all of Sheffield United FC we feel we are in a great position to move forward.

We believe our inclusion in the Championship will be a catalyst for further growth, development and success with homegrown players coming through our RTC and playing for the first-team at the top end of the women's game."

Lee Walshaw - General Manager 2017/18

SHEFFIELD UNITED FACTS

- Sheffield United striker Natalie Shaw hit 24 goals in 26 appearances in 2017/18 making her the 3rd-highest scorer for a WPL Midlands One club when it came to goals in all competitions. Charlotte Fisher (33 in 29 for Birmingham & West Midlands) and Jordan Atkin (29 in 24 for Burton Albion) were the only players to score more.

- Legendary Sheffield United men's player Tony Currie founded the club's girls team which first entered the South Yorkshire League in 1998. The opportunity to play women's football arose in 2002 when local side Sheffield Inter looked set to fold and were taken over by Sheffield United who claimed their place in the East Midlands Premier League.

- The club was known as Sheffield United Community Ladies until being granted permission to change its name to Sheffield United Ladies in 2016. Talent to have emerged through the Centre of Excellence includes England internationals Hannah Cain and Millie Bright.

2017/18 WPL MIDLANDS ONE

Date	Opponent		Score	Scorers		
20.08	Solihull Moors (h)	L	2-4	Jenifer Pearson 24, Taria Marsden 26	50	
27.08	Loughborough F (h)	D	1-1	Millie Kenyon 75	53	
10.09	Radcliffe Olympic (a)	D	0-0		42	
17.09	Rotherham United (a)	W	11-0	Taria Marsden 3, 37, Jodie Hartley 21, Sophie Bell 23, Kimberley Brown 27, 46, 88, Natalie Shaw 40, Evie Robinson 47, Alexandra Hickerman 90+1, Jenifer Pearson 90+2	63	6
21.09	Steel City W (h)	W	5-1	Taria Marsden 13, Natalie Shaw 50, 62, 77, Millie Kenyon 87	110	5
24.09	Sporting Khalsa (a)	W	3-1	Taria Marsden 6, 18, Natalie Shaw 19	35	5
01.10	Leicester City L (h)	W	4-0	Millie Kenyon 21, Natalie Shaw 68, 70, Jenifer Pearson 85	47	4
10.10	Steel City W (a)	D	2-2	Jenifer Pearson 9, Sophie Bell 74	76	3
22.10	The New Saints (h)	W	4-0	Natalie Shaw 19, 40, Kimberley Brown 75, Taria Marsden 77	61	3
05.11	Sporting Khalsa (h)	D	2-2	Jodie Hartley 30, Taria Marsden 62	60	3
03.12	Burton Albion (h)	W	5-1	Jenifer Pearson 18, Taria Marsden 27, 32, 63, Evie Robinson 76	41	4
10.12	Long Eaton United (h)		P-P			
14.01	Solihull Moors (a)	W	5-2	Taria Marsden 5, Sophie Bell 26, 55, 57, Millie Kenyon 69	45	3
28.01	B'ham & W M (h)	W	5-0	Hollie Barker 14, Taria Marsden 37, 70, Sophie Bell 60, Kimberley Brown 72	67	3
04.02	Rotherham United (h)	W	10-0	Natalie Shaw 13, 19, 68, Millie Kenyon 17, 52, 74, Sophie Bell 25, Jodie Hartley 53, Taria Marsden 88, Amy Beanland 89	102	3
11.02	Radcliffe Olympic (h)	W	2-1	Natalie Shaw 39, Sophie Bell (pen) 90+6	97	2

NAT SHAW (KNEELING) BEING CONGRATULATED BY KIM BROWN
AFTER SCORING AT BRAMALL LANE v LEEDS UTD IN THE FA CUP

18.02	Long Eaton United (h)	W	4-1	Natalie Shaw 42, 63, Natalie Froggatt 45, Georgia Stevens 85	106	2
04.03	The New Saints (a)		P-P			2
18.03	The New Saints (a)		P-P			2
25.03	Long Eaton United (a)	D	0-0			2
08.04	Burton Albion (a)	D	1-1	Hollie Barker 29	63	2
22.04	Loughborough F (a)	L	0-3		75	2
29.04	B'ham & W M (a)	W	5-1	Natalie Shaw 16, 41, 90, Hollie Barker 24, Jordan Spurr	20	2
13.05	The New Saints (a)	D	2-2	Natalia Frogatt 30, Taria Marsden 69	59	3
20.05	Leicester City L (a)	W	6-1	Jordan Spurr 43, Taria Marsden 44, 82, Sophie Bell 67, Natalie Shaw 78, Hollie Barker 84	80	3

2017/18 FA CUP

| 08.10 RQ3 | Leeds United (h)* | D | 3-3aet (W 3-2p) | Millie Kenyon 51, Natalie Shaw 76, Taria Marsden 93 | 546 |
| 12.11 R1 | Newcastle United (a) | L | 0-3 | | 110 |

*Played at Bramall Lane, (Sheffield United FC)

2017/18 WPL CUP

| 03.09 DR | B'ham & WM (h) | W | 6-0 | Millie Kenyon 9, Kimberley Brown 40, Natalie Shaw 64, 76, 90, Jenifer Pearson 81 | 43 |
| 15.10 R1 | Liverpool M F (h) | L | 1-2 | Own Goal 3 | 53 |

2017/18 SHEFFIELD & HALLAMSHIRE FA COUNTY CUP

| 17.12 R3 | Oughtibridge (a) | | P-P | |
| 07.01 R3 | Oughtibridge (a) | L | 1-2 | Natalie Shaw 59, *Jordan Spurr sent off 64* |

SHEFFIELD UNITED PLAYER APPEARANCES & GOALS 2017/18

		WPL		FAC		WPLC		CouC		Total	
		A	G	A	G	A	G	A	G	A	G
Ashton, Sheldon	D	6	-	-	-	-	-	-	-	6	-
Barker, Hollie	D	12	4	1	-	-	-	1	-	14	4
Beanland, Amy	D	13	1	-	-	1	-	1	-	15	1
Bell, Sophie	F	21	9	2	-	2	-	1	-	26	9
Brown, Kimberley	D	21	5	1	-	2	1	1	-	25	6
Cawthorn, Molly	D	6	-	1	-	2	-	-	-	9	-
Froggatt, Natalie	D	16	2	2	-	2	-	-	-	20	2
Hartley, Jodie	M	20	3	2	-	2	-	1	-	25	3

		WPL		FAC		WPLC		CouC		Total	
		A	G	A	G	A	G	A	G	A	G
Hickerman, Alexandra	M	13	1	1	-	-	-	-	-	14	1
Houldsworth, Jessica	G	22	-	2	-	2	-	1	-	27	-
Kenyon, Millie	F	22	7	2	1	2	1	1	-	27	9
Marsden, Taria	F	21	18	2	1	1	-	1	-	25	19
Marshall, Eve	D	17	-	2	-	2	-	1	-	22	-
Neary, Rosa	D	16	-	2	-	2	-	1	-	21	-
Pearson, Jenifer	M	19	5	2	-	2	1	1	-	24	6
Robinson, Evie	D	15	2	2	-	2	-	1	-	20	2
Ruddach, Rachael	M	1	-	-	-	-	-	-	-	1	-
Shaw, Natalie	F	21	19	2	1	2	3	1	1	26	24
Shugafi, Sydney	M	1	-	-	-	-	-	-	-	1	-
Spurr, Jordan	M	15	2	2	-	1	-	1	-	19	2
Stevens, Georgia	F	6	1	-	-	-	-	-	-	6	1

GOALSCORERS 2017/18

WPL: Shaw (19), Marsden (18), Bell (9), Kenyon (7), Brown (5), Pearson (5), Barker (4), Hartley (3), Froggatt (2), Robinson (2), Spurr (2), Beanland (1), Hickerman (1), Stevens (1)

FAC: Kenyon (1), Marsden (1), Shaw (1)

WPLC: Shaw (3), Brown (1), Kenyon (1), Pearson (1), own goals (1)

County Cup: Shaw (1)

Total: Shaw (24), Marsden (19), Bell (9), Kenyon (9), Brown (6), Pearson (6), Barker (4), Hartley (3), Froggatt (2), Robinson (2), Spurr (2), Beanland (1), Hickerman (1), Stevens (1)

TOTTENHAM HOTSPUR
2018/19: CHAMPIONSHIP (Tier 2)

Nickname: Spurs
Ground: Theobalds Lane (Cheshunt FC)
Manager: Karen Hills (since Aug 2009)

Season 2017/18:
WSL 2 (Tier 2): 7th
FA Cup: 4th Round
Continental Cup: 3rd Round

Founded: 1985 (as Broxbourne Ladies)	**Last 5 League Finishes:**
Significant Honours:	**2018 WSL 2 (Tier 2):** 7th
WPL Southern Champions: (1) 2016/17	**2017 WPL Southern (Tier 3):** Champions (P)
WPL Play-off Winners: (1) 2017	**2016 WPL Southern (Tier 3):** 6th
WPL Cup Winners: (2) 2016 & 2017	**2015 WPL Southern (Tier 3):** 5th
	2014 WPL Southern (Tier 3): 8th

The 2017/18 season marked Tottenham's debut in Tier 2 and it was a tough test, but one they ultimately passed with flying colours. Having been crowned 2016/17 WPL Southern Champions they beat Blackburn in the national play-off final at The Valley to take their place in WSL 2. Under the stewardship of long-serving manager Karen Hills and head coach Juan Amoros they set about proving their place among English football's established elite and impressed with a 7th-placed finish.

It was a history-making season: Bianca Baptiste scored Spurs' very first WSL 2 goal in a 2-1 defeat at Durham on the opening day; a first ever WSL 2 win followed a week later when Baptiste again and Coral-Jade Haines were on target in a 2-0 defeat of Aston Villa. They also achieved their very first wins against WSL 1 clubs with victories against Bristol City and Yeovil Town in the Continental Cup group stage.

For all those who played a part in it, and for all the fans who followed it, the 2017/18 season will remain one never to forget. There was even more to celebrate along the way with the news before Christmas that Spurs had been successful in their application to retain their Tier 2 licence for 2018/19 in the newly-launched Championship.

"I think the 2017/18 season was a positive one moving forward. We are a family and this club is so special because the team comes before anything. We had plenty of ups and downs but I believe we proved we can compete at the top level during our first season since promotion. Now we're striving to be the best."

Renee Hector -Tottenham Hotspur

TOTTENHAM HOTSPUR FACTS

- Long-time servant, goalkeeper Toni-Anne Wayne played her final game for the club in the last WSL fixture of the season which ended in a 1-1 draw at home to London Bees. One of the high points of Wayne's career was helping the club be promoted to WSL 2 at the end of the 2016/17 season. Her goal-kick in the play-off final against Blackburn set up Spurs' third in a 3-0 win.

- Forward Bianca Baptiste was Tottenham's leading scorer in 2017/18. She bagged 8 goals in WSL 2 and 2 more in the Continental Cup. Defender Ashleigh Neville won the club's Players' Player of the Year and Supporters' Club Player of the Season awards.

- On 19 April 2017 Tottenham Ladies played their first competitive match at White Hart Lane, just a month before demolition started on Spurs' famous home stadium. It proved to be a particularly special night as they beat West Ham 4-0 to clinch the 2016/17 WPL Southern title with 3 matches still to play. A crowd of 2,140 was present.

- Broxbourne Ladies was the club's original name when it was formed in 1985. In 1991/92 permission was granted to use the Tottenham Hotspur name. The team trains at the same world class venue as the men, Hotspur Way in Enfield.

2017/18 WSL 2

					Att	
24.09	Durham (a)	L	1-2	Bianca Baptiste 45	617	
01.10	Aston Villa (h)	W	2-0	Bianca Baptiste 19, Coral-Jade Haines 71	421	
08.10	London Bees (a)	W	2-1	Wendy Martin 17, 24	450	5
29.10	Watford (a)	D	1-1	Lucia Leon 61	579	5
12.11	Doncaster R B (h)	L	1-4	Wendy Martin 90	439	6
10.12	Millwall L (a)	P-P				
07.01	Brighton & H A (h)	L	0-1		253	6
14.01	Millwall L (a)	L	1-4	Sarah Wiltshire 54	57	6

28.01	Sheffield FC (a)	L	3-4	*Sarah Wiltshire missed pen (saved by Danielle Gibbons 15)* Coral-Jade Haines 15 (pen rebound), *Sophie Mclean sent off 42,* Bianca Baptiste 46, Sarah Wiltshire 68	443	8
11.02	Oxford United (h)	W	2-1	*Renee Hector missed pen (saved Demi Lambourne) 68,* Coral-Jade Haines 68 (pen rebound), Ryah Vyse 78	130	8
22.02	Watford (h)	W	6-0	Sarah Wiltshire 19, 45, 53, Lucia Leon 26, Bianca Baptiste 86, 89	242	5
25.03	Doncaster R B (a)	L	0-3		572	5
28.03	Millwall L (h)		P-P			5
01.04	Brighton & H A (a)	L	0-2			5
19.04	Oxford United (a)	W	2-1	Katie O'Leary 30, Coral-Jade Haines (pen) 89	335	6
22.04	Sheffield FC (h)	L	2-4	Ashleigh Neville 51, Sarah Wiltshire 80	368	6
29.04	Durham (h)	W	6-3	Wendy Martin 2, Bianca Baptiste 5, 7, Sarah Wiltshire 63, Ronnell Humes 84, Lucia Leon 90+3	453	6
02.05	Millwall L (h)	D	1-1	Wendy Martin 72	144	6
13.05	Aston Villa (a)	D	1-1	Jenna Schillaci 40	208	7
20.05	London Bees (h)	D	1-1	Bianca Baptiste 50	436	7

2017/18 WSL CONTINENTAL CUP: GROUP TWO SOUTH

12.10	Bristol City (h)	W	2-0	Lauren Pickett 41, Bianca Baptiste 66	131
01.11	Yeovil Town (a)	W	2-1	Sarah Wiltshire 63, Ronnell Humes 90+2	283
05.11	Brighton & H A (h)	L	1-4	Bianca Baptiste 15	253
06.12	Chelsea (a)	L	1-4	Lauren Pickett 64	1,541

2017/18 FA CUP

| 04.02 R4 | Doncaster R B (h) | L | 0-3 | *Toni-Anne Wayne sent off 84* | 105 |

TOTTENHAM HOTSPUR PLAYER APPEARANCES & GOALS 2017/18

		WSL 2		FAC		CC		Total	
		A	G	A	G	A	G	A	G
Baptiste, Bianca	F	17	8	1	-	4	2	22	10
Crook, Chloe	G	-	-	-	-	-	-	-	-
Ezekiel-Meade, Andreya	F	1	-	-	-	-	-	1	-
Green, Josie	M	14	-	1	-	3	-	18	-
Haines, Coral-Jade	M	17	4	-	-	4	-	21	4
Harvey, Shawna	F	1	-	-	-	-	-	1	-
Hector, Renee	D	17	-	1	-	4	-	22	-
Humes, Ronnell	F	4	1	1	-	3	1	8	2
Laudat, Rea	F	4	-	1	-	-	-	5	-
Leon, Lucia	D	13	3	1	-	3	-	17	3
Mackenzie, Hannah	D	15	-	1	-	4	-	20	-
Martin, Wendy	F	18	5	1	-	2	-	21	5
Mclean, Sophie	M	15	-	-	-	4	-	19	-
Morgan, Chloe	G	8	-	-	-	2	-	10	-
Neville, Ashleigh	D	17	1	-	-	4	-	21	1
O'Leary, Katie	F	13	1	1	-	1	-	15	1
Pickett, Lauren	F	13	-	1	-	2	2	16	2
Rawle, Leah	D	-	-	-	-	-	-	-	-
Schillaci, Jenna	D	16	1	-	-	4	-	20	1
Tudor, Sophie	D	-	-	-	-	-	-	-	-
Vio, Maya	M	10	-	1	-	4	-	15	-
Vyse, Ryah	D	12	1	1	-	2	-	15	1
Wayne, Toni-Anne	G	11	-	1	-	2	-	14	-
Wiltshire, Sarah	F	17	7	1	-	4	1	22	8

GOALSCORERS 2017/18

WSL 2: Baptiste (8), Wiltshire (7), Martin (5), Haines (4), Leon (3), Humes (1), Neville (1), O'Leary (1), Schillaci (1), Vyse (1)

FAC: None

CC: Baptiste (2), Pickett (2), Humes (1), Wiltshire (1)

Total: Baptiste (10), Wiltshire (8), Martin (5), Haines (4), Leon (3), Humes (2), Pickett (2), Neville (1), O'Leary (1), Schillaci (1), Vyse (1)

2018/19 WSL SQUAD NUMBERS &
SUMMER 2018 TRANSFER
WINDOW SIGNINGS

These are the squads that were lodged with the FA at the start of September 2018. However, there are circumstances under which transfers are possible after the transfer deadline, and clubs/players may also change squad numbers. Some youth players may also be introduced to the squad throughout the season.

ARSENAL 2018/19 SQUAD NUMBERS

1	Sari VAN VEENENDAAL	G	03.04.90	NED
3	Emma MITCHELL	D	19.09.92	SCO
6	Leah WILLIAMSON	D	29.03.97	ENG
7	Danielle VAN de DONK	M	05.08.91	NED
8	Jordan NOBBS	M	08.12.92	ENG
9	Danielle CARTER	F	18.05.93	ENG
10	Kim LITTLE	M	29.06.90	SCO
11	Vivianne MIEDEMA	F	15.06.96	NED
12	Jessica SAMUELLSON	D	03.01.92	SWE
15	Katie McCABE	F	01.09.95	IRE
16	Louise QUINN	D	17.06.90	IRE
17	Lisa EVANS	F	21.05.92	SCO
18	Pauline PEYRAUD-MAGNIN	G	17.03.92	FRA
19	Lia WALTI	M	19.04.93	SUI
20	Dominique BLOODWORTH *	M	17.01.95	NED
21	Tabea KEMME	D	14.12.91	GER
22	Viktoria SCHNADERBECK	M	04.01.91	AUT
23	Beth MEAD	F	09.05.95	ENG
24	Ava KUYKEN	M	15.06.01	ENG

*nee JANSSEN

ARSENAL SUMMER 2018 TRANSFER WINDOW

In: Viktoria Schnaderbeck (FC Bayern), Lia Walti (Turbine Potsdam), Tabea Kemme (Turbine Potsdam), Pauline Peyraud-Magnin (Lyon)

Out: Shannon Cooke (Louisiana State University), Josephine Henning (retired), Alex Scott (retired), Heather O'Reilly (NC Courage), Anna Moorhouse (West Ham), Lauren James (Manchester United), Emma Gibbon (Tottenham Hotspur), Jess N'Gunga (Tottenham Hotspur), Anna Filbey (Tottenham Hotspur), Vyan Sampson (West Ham United)

BIRMINGHAM CITY 2018/19 SQUAD NUMBERS

2	Paige WILLIAMS	D	10.03.95	ENG
3	Meaghan SARGEANT	D	16.03.94	ENG
4	Hayley LADD	D	06.10.93	WAL
6	Kerys HARROP	D	03.12.90	ENG
7	Chloe ARTHUR	M	21.01.95	SCO
8	Sarah MAYLING	M	20.03.97	ENG
9	Ellen WHITE	F	09.05.89	ENG
11	Lucy QUINN	F	29.09.93	ENG
13	Marisa EWERS	D	24.02.89	GER
14	Emma FOLLIS	M	06.01.92	ENG
15	Charlie WELLINGS	F	18.05.98	ENG
17	Rachel WILLIAMS	F	10.01.88	ENG
18	Connie SCOFIELD	M	20.05.99	ENG
19	Emily WESTWOOD	D	05.04.84	ENG
21	Shania HAYLES	M	22.12.99	ENG
23	Harriet SCOTT	D	10.02.93	IRE
24	Paris McKENZIE	M	17.01.01	ENG
25	Aoife MANNION	D	24.09.95	ENG
27	Hannah KENNY	M		ENG
28	Heidi LOGAN	M		ENG
29	Hannah HAMPTON	G	16.11.00	ENG
30	Ann-Katrin BERGER	G	09.10.90	GER
37	Lucy STANIFORTH	M	02.10.92	ENG

BIRMINGHAM CITY SUMMER 2018 TRANSFER WINDOW

In: Lucy Staniforth (Sunderland), Chloe Arthur (Bristol City), Harriet Scott (Reading)

Out: Emily Westwood (retired), Coral-Jade Haines (Tottenham Hotspur), Sophie Baggaley (Bristol City), Jess Carter (Chelsea), Fran Stenson (Manchester City), Madeline Cusack (released), Freda Ayisi (Leicester City Women), Abbey-Leigh Stringer (Everton)

BRIGHTON & HOVE ALBION 2018/19 SQUAD NUMBERS

1	Marie HOURIHAN	G	10.03.87	IRE
2	Beth ROE	D	03.11.99	ENG
3	Felicity GIBBONS	F	09.07.94	ENG
4	Danielle BUET	M	31.10.88	ENG
5	Fern WHELAN	D	05.12.88	ENG
6	Laura RAFFERTY	D	29.04.96	NIR
7	Aileen WHELAN	F	18.08.91	ENG
8	Kirsty BARTON	M	29.05.92	ENG
9	Ini UMOTONG	F	15.05.94	NGA
10	Kate NATKIEL	M	24.09.92	ENG
11	Amanda NILDEN	F	07.08.98	SWE
12	Chloe PEPLOW	M	03.12.98	ENG
13	Lucy GILLETT	G	28.10.93	USA
14	Jenna LEGG	M	23.06.97	ENG
15	Kayleigh GREEN	D	22.03.88	WAL
16	Ellie BRAZIL	F	10.01.99	ENG
17	Sophie PERRY	D	11.11.86	IRE
18	Jodie BRETT	M	09.03.96	ENG
19	Sophie HARRIS	G	25.08.94	ENG
20	Victoria WILLIAMS	D	05.04.90	ENG
21	Emily SIMPKINS	M	25.05.90	ENG

BRIGHTON & HOVE ALBION SUMMER 2018 TRANSFER WINDOW

In: Kayleigh Green (Yeovil Town), Ellie Brazil (Fiorentina), Jodie Brett (Everton), Sophie Harris (London Bees), Victoria Williams (Sunderland), Emily Simpkins (Doncaster Rovers Belles), Marie Hourihan (Manchester City)

Out: Lucy Somes (Lewes), Amelia Ritchie (Charlton Athletic), Chloe Sansom (released), Nina Wilson (Lewes)

BRISTOL CITY 2018/19 SQUAD NUMBERS

1	Sophie BAGGALEY	G	29.11.96	ENG
2	Loren DYKES	D	05.02.88	WAL
3	Gemma EVANS	D	01.08.96	WAL
4	Alicia JOHNSON	M	24.12.98	ENG
5	Frankie BROWN	D	08.10.87	SCO
6	Danique KERKDIJK	D	01.05.96	NED
7	Poppy PATTINSON	D	30.04.00	ENG
8	Carla HUMPHREY	F	15.12.96	ENG
9	Juliette KEMPPI	F	14.05.94	FIN
10	Ella RUTHERFORD	F	28.04.00	ENG
11	Katie ROOD	F	02.09.92	NZL
12	Flo ALLEN	D	21.01.99	ENG
13	Eartha CUMINGS	G	11.06.99	SCO
14	Lucy GRAHAM	M	10.10.96	SCO
16	Heather PAYNE	F	20.01.00	IRE
17	Rosella AYANE	F	16.03.96	ENG
18	Poppy WILSON	M	06.08.99	ENG
20	Julie BIESMANS	M	04.05.94	BEL
21	Ellie STRIPPEL	F		ENG
22	Aimee WATSON	G	04.08.00	WAL
27	Jess WOOLLEY	M	27.03.01	ENG

BRISTOL CITY SUMMER 2018 TRANSFER WINDOW

In: Sophie Baggaley (Birmingham City), Gemma Evans (Yeovil Town), Katie Rood (Juventus), Ali Johnson (Liverpool), Lucy Graham (Hibernian), Eartha Cumings (Spartans FC), Poppy Pattinson (Manchester City), Ella Rutherford (Millwall Lionesses)

Out: Lauren Hemp (Manchester City), Millie Farrow (Reading), Jasmine Matthews (Liverpool), Yana Daniels (Liverpool), Aimee Palmer (Manchester United), Charlie Estcourt (return to Reading after loan), Millie Turner (Manchester United), Chloe Arthur (Birmingham City), Corinne Yorston. Ellie Wilson (London Bees)

CHELSEA 2018/19 SQUAD NUMBERS

1	Hedvig LINDAHL	G	29.04.83	SWE
2	Maria THORISDOTTIR	D	05.06.93	NOR
3	Hannah BLUNDELL	D	25.05.94	ENG
4	Millie BRIGHT	D	21.08.93	ENG
5	Sophie INGLE	M	02.11.91	WAL
6	Anita ASANTE	D	27.04.85	ENG
7	Jess CARTER	D	27.10.97	ENG
8	Karen CARNEY	M	01.08.87	ENG
10	JI So-Yun	M	21.02.91	KOR
11	Ali RILEY	D	30.10.87	USA
12	Lizzie DURACK	G	20.05.94	AUS
14	Fran KIRBY	F	29.06.93	ENG
15	Beth ENGLAND	F	03.06.94	ENG
16	Magdalena ERIKSSON	D	06.09.93	SWE
17	Adelina ENGMAN	F	11.10.94	FIN
18	Maren MJELDE	M	06.11.93	NOR
20	Jonna ANDERSSON	D	02.01.93	SWE
21	Deanna COOPER	D	20.06.93	ENG
22	Erin CUTHBERT	F	19.07.98	SCO
23	Ramona BACHMANN	F	25.12.90	SUI
24	Drew SPENCE	M	23.10.92	ENG
25	Jade BAILEY	D	11.11.95	ENG
28	Carly TELFORD	G	07.07.87	ENG

CHELSEA SUMMER 2018 TRANSFER WINDOW

In: Beth England (returned from Liverpool after loan), Elizabeth Durack (Everton), Sophie Ingle (Liverpool), Jess Carter (Birmingham City), Ali Riley (FC Rosengard), Adelina Engman (Goteborg FC)

Out: Katie Chapman (retired), Claire Rafferty (West Ham United), Eniola Aluko (Juventus), Rebecca Spencer (West Ham United), Gemma Davison (Reading), Gilly Flaherty (West Ham United), Fran Kitching (Sheffield United, then straight to Liverpool)

EVERTON 2018/19 SQUAD NUMBERS

1	Kirstie LEVELL	G	07.01.97	ENG
2	Faye BRYSON	D	04.07.97	ENG
3	Danielle TURNER	D	10.09.91	ENG
4	Georgia BROUGHAM	D	18.03.96	ENG
5	Siri WORM	D	20.04.92	NED
6	Gabrielle GEORGE	D	02.02.97	ENG
7	Chantelle BOYE-HLORKAH	F	08.09.95	ENG
8	Inessa KAAGMAN	M	17.04.96	NED
9	Claudia WALKER	F	10.06.96	ENG
10	Simone MAGILL	F	01.11.94	NIR
11	Chloe KELLY	F	15.01.98	ENG
12	Angharad JAMES	M	01.06.94	WAL
13	Abbey-Leigh STRINGER	M	17.05.95	ENG
14	Taylor HINDS	D	25.09.99	ENG
16	Hannah CAIN	F	11.02.99	ENG
17	Olivia CHANCE	M	05.10.93	NZL
20	Megan FINNIGAN	M	02.04.98	ENG
22	Dominique BRUINENBERG	M	23.01.93	NED
25	Rebecca FLAHERTY	G	06.03.98	SCO
28	Elise HUGHES	F	15.04.01	WAL

EVERTON SUMMER 2018 TRANSFER WINDOW

In: Inessa Kaagman (Ajax), Dominique Bruinenberg (Sunderland), Hannah Cain (Sheffield FC), Abbey-Leigh Stringer (Birmingham City)

Out: Marthe Munsterman (Ajax), Mollie Green (Manchester United), Elizabeth Durack (Chelsea), Courtney Sweetman-Kirk (Liverpool), Jodie Brett (Brighton & Hove Albion), Amy Turner (Manchester United)

LIVERPOOL 2018/19 SQUAD NUMBERS

1	Anke PREUSS	G	22.09.92	GER
2	Jasmine MATTHEWS	D	24.03.93	ENG
3	Leighanne ROBE	D	26.12.93	ENG
4	Rhiannon ROBERTS	D	30.08.90	WAL
5	Niamh FAHEY	M	13.10.87	IRE
6	Sophie BRADLEY-AUCKLAND	D	20.10.89	ENG
7	Jessica CLARKE	F	05.05.89	ENG
8	Laura COOMBS	M	29.01.91	ENG
9	Courtney SWEETMAN-KIRK	F	16.11.90	ENG
10	Christie MURRAY	F	03.05.90	SCO
11	Yana DANIELS	F	08.05.92	BEL
12	Leandra LITTLE	D	08.11.84	ENG
15	Cassia PIKE	F	27.12.00	WAL
17	Niamh CHARLES	F	21.06.99	ENG
18	Fran KITCHING	G	17.02.98	ENG
19	Amy RODGERS	M	04.05.90	ENG
20	Rinsola BABAJIDE	F	17.06.98	ENG
21	Missy Bo KEARNS	F	14.04.01	ENG
22	Simran JHAMAT	F	22.01.01	ENG
23	Becky FLAHERTY	G	06.03.98	SCO
27	Annabel BLANCHARD	M	07.05.01	ENG
36	Ashley HODSON	F	05.05.95	ENG
44	Satara MURRAY	D	01.07.93	USA

LIVERPOOL SUMMER 2018 TRANSFER WINDOW

In: Leighanne Robe (Millwall Lionesses), Jasmine Matthews (Bristol City), Yana Daniels (Bristol City), Anke Preuss (Sunderland), Leandra Little (Doncaster Rovers Belles), Rhiannon Roberts (Doncaster Rovers Belles), Niamh Fahey (Bordeaux), Christie Murray (Glasgow City), Sophie Bradley-Auckland (Doncaster Rovers Belles), Courtney Sweetman-Kirk (Everton), Fran Kitching (Sheffield United), Kirsty Linnett (Reading)

Out: Beth England (returned to Chelsea after loan), Siobhan Chamberlain (Manchester United), Caroline Weir (Manchester City), Alex Greenwood (Manchester United), Amy Turner (Manchester United), Martha Harris (Manchester United), Emily Ramsey (Manchester United), Sophie Ingle (Chelsea), Gemma Bonner (Manchester City), Lucy Roberts (Manchester United), Ali Johnson (Bristol City), Kate Longhurst (West Ham United), Ellie Fletcher (Sheffield United on loan)

MANCHESTER CITY 2018/19 SQUAD NUMBERS

1	Karen BARDSLEY	G	14.10.84	ENG
2	Mie LETH JANS	D	06.02.94	DEN
3	Demi STOKES	D	12.12.91	ENG
4	Gemma BONNER	D	13.07.91	ENG
5	Jennifer BEATTIE	D	13.05.91	SCO
6	Stephanie HOUGHTON	D	23.04.88	ENG
7	Melissa LAWLEY	M	28.04.94	ENG
8	Jill SCOTT	M	02.02.87	ENG
9	Pauline BREMER	F	10.04.96	GER
10	Nadia NADIM	F	02.01.88	DEN
11	Janine BECKIE	F	20.08.94	CAN
12	Georgia STANWAY	F	03.01.99	ENG
13	Fran STENSON	G	27.04.01	ENG
14	Esme MORGAN	D	18.10.00	ENG
15	Lauren HEMP	F	07.08.00	ENG
16	Jessica PARK	F	21.10.01	ENG
17	Nikita PARRIS	F	10.03.94	ENG
19	Caroline WEIR	F	20.06.95	SCO

20	Megan CAMPBELL	D	28.06.93	IRE
22	Claire EMSLIE	M	08.03.94	SCO
23	Abbie McMANUS	D	14.01.93	ENG
24	Keira WALSH	M	08.04.97	ENG
25	Tessa WULLAERT	F	19.03.93	BEL
26	Ellie ROEBUCK	G	23.09.99	ENG
27	Katie BRADLEY	F		ENG

MANCHESTER CITY SUMMER 2018 TRANSFER WINDOW

In: Lauren Hemp (Bristol City), Caroline Weir (Liverpool), Gemma Bonner (Liverpool), Tessa Wullaert (Wolfsburg), Fran Stenson (Birmingham City), Janine Beckie (Sky Blue FC)

Out: Julia Spetsmark (KIF Orebro), Jane Ross (West Ham United), Tessel Middag (West Ham United), Ella Toone (Manchester United), Fran Bentley (Manchester United), Alethea Paul (Sheffield United), Isobel Christiansen (Lyon), Poppy Pattinson (Bristol City), Marie Hourihan (Brighton & Hove Albion), Serena Fletcher (Leicester City Women)

READING 2018/19 SQUAD NUMBERS

1	Grace MOLONEY	G	01.03.93	IRE
2	Rebecca JANE	D	31.03.92	ENG
3	Mayumi PACHECO	D	25.08.98	ENG
4	Fara WILLIAMS	M	25.01.84	ENG
5	Molly BARTRIP	D	01.06.96	ENG
6	Kirsty PEARCE	D	19.04.87	ENG
7	Rachel FURNESS	M	19.06.88	NIR
8	Remi ALLEN	M	15.10.90	ENG
9	Gemma DAVISON	M	17.04.87	ENG
10	Lauren BRUTON	M	22.11.92	ENG
11	Natasha HARDING	F	02.03.89	WAL
14	Millie FARROW	F	03.06.96	ENG
17	Charlie ESTCOURT	M	27.05.98	WAL
18	Jade MOORE	M	22.10.90	ENG
19	Brooke CHAPLEN	M	16.04.89	ENG
22	Josanne POTTER	M	13.11.84	ENG
23	Rachel ROWE	M	13.09.92	WAL
26	Sophie HOWARD	D	17.09.93	SCO
27	Rachael LAWS	G	05.11.90	ENG
28	Lily WOODHAM	D	03.09.00	WAL
29	Kiera SKEELS	D		ENG

READING SUMMER 2018 TRANSFER WINDOW

In: Charlie Estcourt (returned from Bristol City after loan), Rachael Laws (Sunderland), Sophie Howard (Hoffenheim), Gemma Davison (Chelsea), Millie Farrow (Bristol City), Mayumi Pacheco (Doncaster Rovers Belles)

Out: Harriet Scott (Birmingham City), Melissa Fletcher (retired), Kirty Linnett (Liverpool), Mary Earps (Wolfsburg), Sophie O'Rourke (released), Evie Gane (Aston Villa)

WEST HAM UNITED 2018/19 SQUAD NUMBERS

1	Rebecca SPENCER	G	22.02.91	ENG
2	Ria PERCIVAL	D	07.12.89	NZL
4	Brooke HENDRIX	D	06.05.93	USA
5	Gilly FLAHERTY	D	24.08.91	ENG
6	Tessel MIDDAG	M	23.12.92	NED
7	Alisha LEHMANN	F	21.01.99	SUI
8	Leanne KIERNAN	F	27.04.99	IRE
9	Jane ROSS	F	18.09.89	SCO
10	Julia SIMIC	M	14.05.89	GER
11	Claire RAFFERTY	D	11.01.89	ENG
12	Kate LONGHURST	M	02.05.89	ENG
13	Anna MOORHOUSE	G	30.03.95	ENG
14	Vyan SAMPSON	D	02.07.96	ENG
15	Brianna VISALLI	M	17.04.95	ENG
16	Rosie KMITA	F	27.07.94	ENG
17	Esmee DE GRAAF	F	02.08.97	NED
18	Lucienne REICHARDT	M	01.05.91	NED

WEST HAM UNITED SUMMER 2018 TRANSFER WINDOW

In: Rebecca Spencer (Chelsea), Claire Rafferty (Chelsea), Brianna Visalli (Chicago Red Stars), Gilly Flaherty (Chelsea), Esmee De Graaf (PEC Zwolle), Lucienne Reichardt (Ajax), Anna Moorhouse (Arsenal), Jane Ross (Manchester City), Tessel Middag (Manchester City), Leanne Kiernan (Shelbourne), Brooke Hendrix (Brescia), Julia Simic (Freiburg), Ria Percival (Basel), Alisha Lehmann (Young Boys), Kate Longhurst (Liverpool), Vyan Sampson (Arsenal)

Out: Amber Stobbs (Charlton Athletic), Georgia Miller (QPR), Whitney Locke (QPR), Mollie Kmita (Gillingham), Jasmine Auguste (released), Sindi Kanto (released), Cara Connatser (released), Amy Cooper (released), Chenise Austin (released), Stephaney Bent (released), Chloe Burr (Crystal Palace), Dayna Chong (Crystal Palace), Molly Clark (released), Kelly Wealthall (released), Ellie Zoepfl (released), Leanne Mabey (released), Chantelle Mackie (Millwall Lionesses), Molly Peters (released), Paige Anderson-James (released), Andria Georgiou (Crystal Palace), Hannah Wheeler (released)

YEOVIL TOWN 2018/19 SQUAD NUMBERS

1	Megan WALSH	G	12.11.94	ENG
3	Megan ALEXANDER	D	11.11.93	ENG
4	Emily SYME	M	23.07.00	ENG
5	Nicola COUSINS	D	22.10.88	WAL
6	Hannah SHORT	D	16.04.93	ENG
7	Olivia FERGUSSON	F	27.03.95	ENG
8	Bonnie HORWOOD	M	16.04.87	ENG
9	Annie HEATHERSON	F	27.03.84	ENG
10	Amber GAYLOR	M	22.02.95	ENG
12	Ellie MASON	M	16.02.96	ENG

23	Beth HOWARD	G	06.05.95	ENG
24	Charlotte BUXTON	M		ENG
25	Amy GODDARD	D	16.12.98	ENG
26	Emily DONOVAN	M	16.02.97	ENG
27	Leah BURRIDGE	D	03.01.97	ENG
28	Georgia EVANS	M	16.10.95	WAL
29	Megan ROBINSON	F		ENG

YEOVIL TOWN SUMMER 2018 TRANSFER WINDOW

In: Megan Alexander (Millwall Lionesses), Amber Gaylor (Millwall Lionesses), Olivia Fergusson (Bristol City), Emily Syme (Bishops Lydeard), Hannah Short (Oxford United), Bonnie Horwood (Millwall Lionesses), Amy Goddard (Aston Villa)

Out: Kayleigh Green (Brighton & Hove Albion), Gemma Evans (Bristol City), Bow Jackson (released)

2018/19 CHAMPIONSHIP SQUAD NUMBERS & SUMMER 2018 TRANSFER WINDOW SIGNINGS

ASTON VILLA 2018/19 SQUAD NUMBERS

1	Sian ROGERS	G
2	Hayley CRACKLE	D
3	Asmita ALE	D
4	Ria ELSMORE	D
5	Elisha N'DOW	D
6	Jade RICHARDS	D
7	Alice HASSALL	D
8	Aoife HURLEY	D
9	Alison HALL	F
10	Kerri WELSH	F
11	Amy WEST	M
12	Jodie HUTTON	M
14	Hollie GIBSON	D
16	Tanisha SMITH	M
17	Sophie HAYWOOD	M
18	Aja AGUIRRE	G
20	Phoebe WARNER	M
23	Nadine HANSSEN	M
24	Ashlee BROWN	D
	Evie GANE	D

ASTON VILLA SUMMER 2018 TRANSFER WINDOW

In: Hollie Gibson (Stoke City), Alison Hall (Coventry United), Nadine Hanssen (KRC Genk), Sophie Haywood (Texas A&M University), Evie Gane (Reading)

Out: Elizabeta Ejupi (Charlton Athletic), Beth Merrick (Sheffield United), Ebony Salmon (Manchester United)

CHARLTON ATHLETIC 2018/19 SQUAD NUMBERS

1	Katie STARTUP	G
2	Charlotte KERR	D
3	Chloe BRUNTON-WILDE	D
5	Amelia RITCHIE	D
6	Grace COOMBS	D
8	Charley CLIFFORD	M
9	Gemma BRYAN	F
10	Charlotte GURR	M
11	Amber STOBBS	M
13	Ellie BAILES	M
14	Nicole PEPPER	D
15	Hannah WHEELER	D
16	Kit GRAHAM	F
17	Harley BENNETT	M
19	Georgia GRIFFIN	F
22	Lily AGG	F
23	Hannah CHURCHILL	M
24	Lilli MAPLE	M
37	Elizabeta EJUPI	M

CHARLTON ATHLETIC SUMMER 2018 TRANSFER WINDOW

IN: Lily Agg (FFC Frankfurt), Ellie Bailes (Crystal Palace), Gemma Bryan (Crystal Palace), Elizabeta Ejupi (Aston Villa), Charlotte Kerr (Watford), Lilli Maple (Crystal Palace), Amelia Ritchie (Brighton & Hove Albion), Amber Stobbs (West Ham United)

OUT: Hope Nash (Crystal Palace)

CRYSTAL PALACE 2018/19 SQUAD NUMBERS

1	Megan LYNCH	G
2	Pamela McROBERTS	M
3	Anneka NUTTALL	D
4	Leesa HAYDOCK	M
5	Jordan BUTLER	D
6	Freya HOLDAWAY	D
7	Jade DAVENPORT	M
8	Ciara WATLING	M
9	Nikita WHINNETT	F
10	Ashlee HINCKS	F
11	Kallie BALFOUR	F
12	Chloe BURR	F

13	Shanell SALGADO	G
14	Francesca ALI	M
15	Andria GEORGIOU	M
16	Jade KEOGH	F
17	Amy GREEN	M
18	Megan CHANDLER	M
19	Dayna CHONG	M
20	Ria COLLINS	D
21	Hope NASH	D
22	Mary ROBINSON	M
26	Hannah MacKENZIE	F

CRYSTAL PALACE SUMMER 2018 TRANSFER WINDOW

IN: Kallie Balfour (Gillingham), Chloe Burr (West Ham United), Jordan Butler (Millwall Lionesses), Ashlee Hincks (Millwall Lionesses), Jade Keogh (Gillingham), Hannah Mackenzie (Tottenham Hotspur), Hope Nash (Charlton Athletic), Anneka Nuttall (Watford)

OUT: Ellie Bailes (Charlton Athletic), Gemma Bryan (Charlton Athletic), Lilli Maple (Charlton Athletic), Rosie Paye (Lewes), Ellie Stenning (Millwall Lionesses)

DURHAM 2018/19 SQUAD NUMBERS

1	Hannah REID	G
2	Kathryn HILL	D
5	Sarah WILSON	D
6	Sarah ROBSON	M
7	Beth HEPPLE	M
8	Zoe NESS	F
9	Nicki GEARS	F
10	Natalie GUTTERIDGE	M
12	Chloe KNOTT	M
13	Megan BORTHWICK	G
14	Rebecca SALICKI	D
16	Ellie CHRISTON	D
17	Emily ROBERTS	F
20	Lauren BRIGGS	M
22	Abigail COTTAM	F
24	Abby HOLMES	D
30	Rosanna TODD	G
96	Rachel LEE	M

DURHAM SUMMER 2018 TRANSFER WINDOW

In: Abby Holmes (PEC Zwolle), Chloe Knott (Georgetown University), Hannah Reid (Hibernian)

Out: Jenny Bitzer (AS Roma), Nicola Gibson (London Bees), Annabel Johnson (London Bees)

LEICESTER CITY 2018/19 SQUAD NUMBERS

1	Demi LAMBOURNE	G
2	Ella FRANKLIN-FRAITURE	D
3	Sarah JACKSON	D
4	Nicole NYMOEN	M
5	Holly MORGAN	D
6	Charlotte GREENGRASS	D
7	Sophie DOMINGO	F
8	Taome OLIVER	M
9	Melissa JOHNSON	F
10	Rosie AXTEN	F
11	Freda AYISI	F
12	Hayley JAMES	D
13	Charlotte CLARKE	G
14	Leigh DUGMORE	F
15	Fiona WORTS	F
16	Sherry McCUE	M
17	Freya THOMAS	M
19	Natalie JOHNSON	M
21	Natasha HUDSON	M
22	Serena FLETCHER	D
23	Lucy JOHNSON	D
24	Mai MONCASTER	M
28	Maddy CUSACK	M

LEICESTER CITY SUMMER 2018 TRANSFER WINDOW

In: Freda Ayisi (Birmingham City), Serena Fletcher (Manchester City), Ella Franklin-Fraiture (Oxford United), Sarah Jackson (Sheffield FC), Melissa Johnson (Sheffield FC), Taome Oliver (Oxford United)

Out: None

LEWES 2018/19 SQUAD NUMBERS

1	Faye BAKER	G
2	Rebecca THOMPSON-AGBRO	D
3	Natasha WELLS	D
4	Katie McINTYRE	M
5	Amy TAYLOR	D
6	Shannon MOLONEY	M
7	Victoria CARLETON	M
8	Leeta RUTHERFORD	M
9	Rebecca CARTER	F
10	Charlotte OWEN	M
11	Avilla BERGIN	M
12	Charley BOSWELL	D
13	Nina WILSON	G
14	Sarah KEMPSON	M

15	Georgia ROBERT	M
16	Samantha QUAYLE	M
17	Jacqueline-Anne GOLDSMID	G
18	Rosie PAYE	D
19	Danielle LANE	M

LEWES SUMMER 2018 TRANSFER WINDOW

In: Charley Boswell (Portsmouth), Shannon Moloney (Tottenham Hotspur), Rosie Paye (Crystal Palace), Samantha Quayle (Portsmouth), Georgia Robert (Des Moines Menace), Lucy Somes (Brighton & Hove Albion), Nina Wilson (Brighton & Hove Albion)

Out: None

LONDON BEES 2018/19 SQUAD NUMBERS

1	Sarah QUANTRILL	G
2	Annabel JOHNSON	D
3	Ellie WILSON	D
4	Destiney TOUSSAINT	F
5	Danielle LEA	D
6	Rosie LANE	D
7	Lucy LOOMES	F
8	Anne-Laure DAVY	F
9	Katie WILKINSON	F
10	Ruesha LITTLEJOHN	F
11	Paula HOWELLS	M
12	Lauren PICKETT	M
13	Taylor O'LEARY	M
14	Tricia GOULD	F
15	Ocean ROLANDSEN	D
16	Nicola GIBSON	M
17	Emma BECKETT	M
18	Brooke NUNN	M
19	Kelsey GIBSON	M
20	Connie FORMAN	F
22	Mollie DENCH	D
23	Merrick WILL	M

LONDON BEES SUMMER 2018 TRANSFER WINDOW

In: Anne-Laure Davy (Lille OSC), Nicola Gibson (Durham), Annabel Johnson (Durham), Ruesha Littlejohn (Celtic), Brooke Nunn (unattached), Lauren Pickett (Tottenham Hotspur), Sarah Quantrill (Millwall Lionesses), Ellie Wilson (Bristol City)

Out: Sophie Harris (Brighton & Hove Albion), Nicola Hobbs (Sheffield United), Anne Meiwald (Tottenham Hotspur)

MANCHESTER UNITED 2018/19 SQUAD NUMBERS

1	Siobhan CHAMBERLAIN	G
2	Martha HARRIS	D
3	Alex GREENWOOD	D
4	Amy TURNER	D
6	Aimee PALMER	M
7	Ella TOONE	F
8	Mollie GREEN	M
9	Jessica SIGSWORTH	F
10	Katie ZELEM	M
11	Leah GALTON	F
12	Naomi HARTLEY	D
13	Emily RAMSEY	G
14	Charlie DEVLIN	M
15	Lucy ROBERTS	D
16	Lauren JAMES	M
17	Lizzie ARNOT	F
18	Kirsty HANSON	F
19	Ebony SALMON	F
20	Kirsty SMITH	D
21	Millie TURNER	D
22	Fran BENTLEY	G

MANCHESTER UNITED SUMMER 2018 TRANSFER WINDOW

In: Leah Galton (Bayern Munich), Charlie Devlin (Millwall Lionesses), Mollie Green (Everton), Alex Greenwood (Liverpool), Kirsty Hanson (Doncaster Rovers Belles), Martha Harris (Liverpool), Ebony Salmon (Aston Villa), Jess Sigsworth (Doncaster Rovers Belles), Kirsty Smith (Hibernian), Ella Toone (Manchester City), Amy Turner (Everton), Millie Turner (Bristol City), Katie Zelem (Juventus)

MILLWALL LIONESSES 2018/19 SQUAD NUMBERS

1	Grace TAYLOR	G
2	Chantelle MACKIE	D
3	Leanne COWAN	D
4	Freya BAILES	M
5	Riva CASLEY	D
6	Ylenia PRIEST	D
8	Beth LUMSDEN	M
9	Gabby RAVENSCROFT	F
10	Lia CATALDO	M
11	Evie CLARKE	F
12	Beth POWELL	D
13	Chloe SAMSON	G

14	Georgie GIDDINGS	D
15	Jasmine AUGUSTE	D
16	Ellie STENNING	M
17	Lucy FITZGERALD	F
18	Michelle YOUNG	M
19	Beth HARFORD	F
20	Annie ROSSITER	F
21	Kalani PEART	D
22	Chloe WILKINSON	F
23	Caitlin HARTSHORNE	G
24	Asanteni CHARLES	D
25	Sara GUZOWSKA	F

MILLWALL LIONESSES SUMMER 2018 TRANSFER WINDOW

In: Riva Casley (Oxford United), Chantelle Mackie (West Ham United), Ellie Stenning (Crystal Palace)

Out: Megan Alexander (Yeovil Town), Jordan Butler (Crystal Palace), Rianna Dean (Tottenham Hotspur), Charlie Devlin (Manchester United), Ashlee Hincks (Crystal Palace), Sarah Quantrill (London Bees), Leighanne Robe (Liverpool), Ella Rutherford (Bristol City), Megan Wynne (Tottenham Hotspur)

SHEFFIELD UNITED 2018/19 SQUAD NUMBERS

1	Nicola HOBBS	G
2	Sophie BARKER	D
3	Samantha TIERNEY	M
4	Jade PENNOCK	M
5	Danielle COX	D
6	Nicole KEMP	D
7	Ellie GILLIATT	D
9	Rebecca RAYNER	F
10	Alethea PAUL	M
11	Chloe DIXON	F
12	Hollie BARKER	M
14	Jodie HARTLEY	M
15	Izzy FORD	F
16	Tania MARSDEN	F
17	Georgia STEVENS	F
18	Bethan MERRICK	F
19	Jodie MICHALSKA	F
20	Lisa RYAN	D
23	Lauren CRESSWELL	M
25	Nikki DAVIES	G
26	Ellie FLETCHER	D

SHEFFIELD UNITED SUMMER 2018 TRANSFER WINDOW

IN: Sophie Barker (Doncaster Rovers Belles), Danielle Cox (Sheffield FC), Lauren Cresswell (Derby County), Chloe Dixon (Sheffield FC), Ellie Fletcher (Liverpool – loan), Ellie Gilliatt (Sheffield FC), Nicola Hobbs (London Bees), Nicole Kemp (Sheffield FC), Beth Merrick (Aston Villa), Jodie Michalska (Sheffield FC), Alethea Paul (Manchester City), Jade Pennock (Doncaster Rovers Belles), Rebecca Rayner (Doncaster Rovers Belles), Sam Tierney (Doncaster Rovers Belles)

Out: Fran Kitching (Liverpool, soon after signing from Chelsea)

TOTTENHAM HOTSPUR 2018/19 SQUAD NUMBERS

1	Chloe MORGAN	G
2	Lucia LEON	D
3	Anne MEIWALD	D
4	Josie GREEN	M
5	Sophie MCLEAN	M
6	Renee HECTOR	D
7	Sarah WILTSHIRE	F
8	Bianca BAPTISTE	F
9	Rianna DEAN	F
10	Wendy MARTIN	F
11	Jenna SCHILLACI	D
12	Megan WYNNE	M
13	Emma GIBBON	G
14	Angela ADDISON	M
15	Anna FILBEY	M
16	Maya VIO	M
17	Jessica NAZ	F
18	Ryah VYSE	D
19	Ashleigh NEVILLE	D
20	Coral-Jade HAINES	M
	Jess NGUNGA	F

TOTTENHAM HOTSPUR SUMMER 2018 TRANSFER WINDOW

In: Angela Addison (C&K Basildon), Rianna Dean (Millwall Lionesses), Anna Filbey (Arsenal), Coral Haines (Birmingham City), Anne Meiwald (London Bees), Jess Ngunga (Arsenal), Megan Wynne (Millwall Lionesses)

Out: Hannah Mackenzie (Crystal Palace), Shannon Moloney (Lewes), Lauren Pickett (London Bees)

FA WOMEN'S NATIONAL LEAGUE
TIERS THREE & FOUR

The FA Women's Premier League was renamed the FA Women's National League ahead of the 2018/19 season, but the format remained the same. The WNL represents Tiers 3 and 4 of the club game in England, with teams organised into regional divisions. Tier 3 consists of WNL Northern Premier (formerly WPL Northern) and WNL Southern Premier (formerly WPL Southern). At the end of the season it has been traditional for the champions of each division to meet at a neutral venue in a one-game play-off with the winner promoted to Tier 2 (now the Championship) so long as they satisfy the FA's licence criteria. At the end of 2018/19 this play-off will still take place to determine an overall WNL champion but, for one season only, both the Southern and Northern champions will be eligible for promotion subject to meeting all licence criteria. If either champion is not eligible, the runner-up in their division will be offered the promotion place. There will be no relegation from the Championship to the WNL at the end of 2018/19. From the end of 2019/20 there will be one up, one down between the WNL and the Championship.

Tier 4 consists of four regional divisions: WNL Division 1 North (formerly WPL North 1); WNL Division 1 Midlands (formerly WPL Midlands 1); WNL Division 1 South East (formerly WPL South East 1); and WNL Division 1 South West (formerly WPL South West 1). The Southern Premier relegates into, and grants promotion out of, Division 1 South East and Division 1 South West while the Northern Premier does likewise with Division 1 North and Division 1 Midlands.

The four divisions at Tier 4 level grant promotion from, and relegate into, the eight Regional Premier Leagues at Tier 5. The champions at regional level may sometimes opt against promotion, usually because of the additional expense and logistics of travelling for away games over a wider area. However, in 2018/19 all eight Regional Premier League champions accepted promotion.

Throughout this section of the book all 72 of the clubs competing in Tiers 3 and 4 in 2018/19 are listed alphabetically. Also included are the four teams who were relegated from Tier 4 at the end of 2017/18, as well as Basingstoke (who withdrew from WPL South West 1 during 2017/18) and Radcliffe Olympic (who had been due to start 2018/19 in WPL Division 1 Midlands before folding in July).

ACTONIANS

2018/19: WNL DIVISION 1 SOUTH EAST (Tier 4)

Founded: 1998 (as Chiswick United)

Nickname: None

Ground: Berkeley Fields,

(North Greenford United FC)

Season 2017/18:

WPL South East One (Tier 4): 7th

FA Cup: 3rd Qualifying Round

WPL Cup: Preliminary Round

County Cup: 1st Round

HULL CITY CELEBRATE A GOAL ON THEIR WAY TO BECOMING 2017/18 WPL NORTHERN ONE

Underneath the club name is the division they compete in during 2018/19. The ground listed is the main home ground games were played at in 2017/18. Many clubs frequently change grounds between seasons. Where a club has been able to notify us (before publishing deadlines) of a new main home ground for 2018/19 this has also been listed. To the right is the club's form in each of the four main competitions in 2017/18 (League, FA Cup, WPL Cup/Plate, County Cup). Some teams also compete in other Cup competitions, but for reasons of space and uniformity of information presented, these have been excluded. For the teams who were promoted from Tier 5 (none of whom were eligible for the WPL Cup/Plate) we have included their regional League Cup results.

The following information – where known – is included for each game: scorers; goal times; penalties; missed penalties; sendings-off; attendances. Where goal times are unknown, if a player scored more than once it is listed such: (x2) or (x3) etc. Where an official attendance wasn't recorded, some clubs have provided us with an estimate which is denoted thus: 50 est The figure in the column to the far right is the club's position in the League at the end of all the matches played that day. This has been provided from the fourth League game of the season onwards. It's important to note that the team in question did not necessarily start its next match in that position as other games in their division may have been played in the interim.

Where matches are played at grounds other than the club's main home ground, or their opponent's main home ground, this information is listed at the bottom of the results table.

We asked every club for a summary of 2017/18 from their captain, manager or another leading figure. We are hugely grateful to those who had time to help us. In some cases the people who provided us with their thoughts may have left the club since speaking to us.

Cup matches key: DR = WPL Cup determining round (losers go into WPL Plate)
PR = Preliminary Round   RQ3 = 3rd Qualifying Round   R3 = 3rd Round

FA WOMEN'S NATIONAL LEAGUE 2018/19 CONSTITUTION

TIER 3:	NORTHERN PREMIER	SOUTHERN PREMIER
	Blackburn Rovers	C&K Basildon
	Bradford City	Cardiff City
	Derby County	Chichester City
	Doncaster R. Belles	Coventry United
	Fylde	Gillingham
	Guiseley Vixens	**Loughborough Foxes**
	Huddersfield Town	**MK Dons**
	Hull City	Oxford United
	Middlesbrough	**Plymouth Argyle**
	Nottingham Forest	Portsmouth
	Sheffield FC	QPR
	Stoke City	**Watford**
	Sunderland	

TIER 4:			
DIVISION 1 NORTH	**DIVISION 1 MIDLANDS**	**DIVISION 1 SOUTH EAST**	**DIVISION 1 SOUTH WEST**
Barnsley	**Bedworth United**	Actonians	Brislington
Bolton Wanderers	Birmingham & W M	AFC Wimbledon	**Buckland Athletic**
Brighouse Town	Burton Albion	**Billericay Town**	Cheltenham Town
Burnley	Long Eaton United	Cambridge United	**Chesham United**
Chester-le-Street T	**Nettleham**	**Crawley Wasps**	Keynsham Town
Chorley	Solihull Moors	Denham United	Larkhall Athletic
Crewe Alexandra	Sporting Khalsa	Enfield Town	Maidenhead United
Leeds United	Steel City Wanderers	Ipswich Town	Poole Town
Liverpool M Feds	The New Saints	Leyton Orient	St Nicholas*
Morecambe	**West Brom. Albion**	Luton Town	Southampton Saints
Newcastle United	**Wolverhampton W**	Norwich City	Southampton Women
Norton & Stockton		Stevenage	**Swindon Town**

Newcomers to each Tier in **bold**   *resigned from League on 21 Aug, 2018

NORTHERN PREMIER (TIER 3)

Doncaster Rovers Belles – Down from Tier 2 after withdrawing from Championship
Sheffield FC – Down from Tier 2 after withdrawing from Championship
Sunderland – Down from Tier 1 after application for WSL or Championship licence failed
Hull City – Promoted from Tier 4 as champions of WPL Northern 1

SOUTHERN PREMIER (TIER 3):

Loughborough Foxes – Promoted from Tier 4 as champions of WPL Midlands 1
MK Dons – Promoted from Tier 4 as champions of WPL South East 1
Oxford United – Down from Tier 2 after application for Championship licence failed
Plymouth Argyle – Promoted from Tier 4 as champions of WPL South West 1
Watford – Down from Tier 2 after opting not to apply for Championship licence

DIVISION 1 NORTH (TIER 4)

Burnley – Promoted from Tier 5 as champions of North West Regional Premier League
Norton & Stockton A. – Promoted from Tier 5 as champions of North East Regional Premier League

DIVISION 1 MIDLANDS (TIER 4)

Bedworth United – Promoted from Tier 5 as champions of West Midlands Regional Premier League
Nettleham – Promoted from Tier 5 as champions of East Midlands Regional Premier League
West Bromwich Albion – Relegated from Tier 3 after finishing bottom of WPL Northern
Wolverhampton Wanderers – Relegated from Tier 3 after finishing 11th in WPL Northern

DIVISION 1 SOUTH EAST (TIER 4)

Billericay Town – Promoted from Tier 5 as champions of Eastern Regional Premier League
Crawley Wasps – Promoted from Tier 5 as champions of London & SE Regional Premier League

DIVISION 1 SOUTH WEST (TIER 4)

Buckland Athletic – Promoted from Tier 5 as champions of South West Regional Premier League
Chesham United – Promoted from Tier 5 as champions of Southern Regional Premier League
Swindon Town – Relegated from Tier 3 after finishing bottom of WPL Southern

ACTONIANS

2018/19: WNL DIVISION 1 SOUTH EAST (Tier 4)

Founded: 1998 (as Chiswick United)

Nickname: None

Ground: Berkeley Fields, (North Greenford United FC), moving to Rectory Park, (Middlesex FA) for 2018/19

Season 2017/18:

WPL South East One (Tier 4): 7th

FA Cup: 3rd Qualifying Round

2017/18 WPL SOUTHERN

20.08	Haringey Borough (h)	W	13-0	Alessandra Barreca (x5), Caterina Kensbock, Catherine Murphy, Katrina Duncan-Marshalleck (x2), Lafe Uche, Mariko Engels, Sinthuja Sooriyakumar (x2)	35	
27.08	Leyton Orient (h)	W	5-1	Alessandra Barrecca (x2), Jessica Byrne, Katrina Duncan-Marshalleck, Sinthujah Soori-yakumar	30	
10.09	MK Dons (a)	L	0-4		85	
17.09	Norwich City (h)	W	7-2	Mariko Engels 10, 34, Carla Williams 20, 33, Alessandra Barrecca 74, 90+2, Katrina Duncan-Marshalleck 78	20	1
21.09	AFC Wimbledon (a)	L	0-3		50	4
01.10	Ipswich Town (a)	L	0-1		17	6
11.10	AFC Wimbledon (h)	L	1-2	Alessandra Barreca 68	50	7
15.10	Leyton Orient (a)*	W	4-3	Alessandra Barreca (x2), Jessica Byrne, Claire Hollingsworth	117	5
29.10	Stevenage (a)	L	1-2	Alessandra Barreca (pen)	25	7
05.11	Ipswich Town (h)	L	1-2	Sinead Friel 25	25	8
12.11	Denham United (a)	D	0-0		46	8
19.11	Luton Town (h)	L	2-3	Carla Williams 20, Alessandra Barreca 64	32	8
26.11	Cambridge United (h)	D	0-0		25	7
10.12	Stevenage (h)		P-P			
07.01	Enfield Town (a)	D	1-1	Catherine Murphy	26	8
21.01	MK Dons (h)		P-P			8
28.01	MK Dons (h)		P-P			8
04.02	Norwich City (a)		P-P			8
11.02	Denham United (h)		P-P			8
18.02	Enfield Town (h)	W	4-2	Carla Williams 20, 44, Alessandra Barrecca 35, 63		8
25.02	Stevenage (h)	L	1-2	Alessandra Barrecca 41	20	9

@sniperpose

04.03	Norwich City (a)		P-P			9
18.03	Haringey Borough (a)		P-P			9
25.03	Denham United (h)	W	3-0	Alessandra Barecca 45, 82, (pen) 90+3	40	8
08.04	Cambridge United (a)	W	2-0	Katrina Duncan 31, Carla Williams 57	74	8
15.04	MK Dons (h)		P-P			8
22.04	Norwich City (a)	W	1-0	Sara Lopez Ezzahiri	50	7
29.04	Haringey Borough (a)	W	10-0	Alessandra Barecca (x4), Sara Lopez Ezzahiri (x2), Carla Williams (x4)		5
08.05	MK Dons (h)	L	0-2		25	5
10.05	Luton Town (a)**	L	0-2		201	6

*Played at Matchroom Stadium, Leyton Orient FC   **Played at Kenilworth Road, Luton Town FC

2017/18 FA CUP

08.10 RQ3	MK Dons (a)	L	0-2		76

2017/18 WPL CUP

03.09 DR	Cheltenham Town (a)	W	2-1	Catherine Murphy, Jessica Byrne	35
24.09 PR	Southampton W (a)	L	0-2 (aet)		50

2017/18 MIDDLESEX FA CAPITAL CUP

22.10 R1   Leyton Orient (h)   L   0-2   30

"Although slightly disappointed with a 7th place finish, the 2017/18 season was a good one overall. We say farewell to long-serving first-team manager Daniel Chitty who we are sad to see go. He moves on to coach the men's teams at Actonians. Having done such a fantastic job for many years he leaves us in good shape and in good hands as Craig Brown takes over the team and we feel optimistic for the future. We are building a great coaching team with Jamie Daniel-Moon and Carley Lloyd also joining to take over the development team as we look to start integrating our Under-16's in 2018/19. Addison Tweed also moves to the reserves to assist John. Hopes are high for the future."

Linda Fox – Actonians Chairperson

- In 2017/18 Alessandra Barreca finished as the highest scorer in WPL South East 1 for League goals only, with 24. That tally included a hat-trick against Denham United, and four-goal and five-goal hauls in the matches against Haringey Borough.

- Everoy Johnson founded the club as Chiswick United in 1998 and they entered the Greater London League in Division Three West in their first season.

- They became known as Acton Sports Club when they moved to Acton in the summer of 2003. They were then taken under the wing of existing club Actonians FC when they found themselves without a home in 2008.

- Actonians won the London & South East Regional League and League Cup Double in 2014/15. It was their title success that season that saw them promoted to WPL South East Division One.

AFC WIMBLEDON

2018/19: WNL DIVISION 1 SOUTH EAST (Tier 4)

Founded: 1973 (as Friends of Fulham)
Nickname: The Dons
Ground: Gander Green Lane, (Sutton Utd FC) in 2017/18, moving to War Memorial Sports Ground, (Carshalton Athletic FC) for 2018/19

Season 2017/18:
WPL South East One (Tier 4): Runners-up
FA Cup: 2nd Round
WPL Cup: 1st Round
County Cup: n/a

2017/18 WPL SOUTH EAST ONE

Date	Opponent	Result	Score	Scorers		
20.08	Ipswich Town (h)	L	1-3	Kelly-Jade Whelan 5	50	
27.08	MK Dons (h)	W	4-2	Caroline Bisson 6, Rebecca Sargeant 17, Kelly-Jade Whelan 42, 80	70	
10.09	Denham United (a)	W	3-1	Rebecca Sargeant 2, 80, Caroline Bisson 18	20	
17.09	Luton Town (h)	W	4-1	Caroline Bisson 14, 63, Katie Stanley 60, Kelly-Jade Whelan 86	50	
21.09	Actonians (h)	W	3-0	Rebecca Sargeant 8, Kelly-Jade Whelan 34, Katie Stanley 79	50	1
01.10	Stevenage (a)	W	3-1	Laura Quinn-Low 4, 44, Rebecca Sargeant 82	40	1
11.10	Actonians (a)	W	2-1	Kelly Jade-Whelan 8, Rebecca Sargeant 65	50	1
22.10	Cambridge United (a)	W	1-0	Rebecca Sargeant 38	60	1
29.10	Enfield Town (a)	W	1-0	Katie Stanley 86	30	1
05.11	Stevenage (h)	L	2-3	Isi Asplund 84, Sian Wylie 87	30	1
19.11	Haringey Borough (h)	P-P				1
26.11	Denham United (h)	W	1-0	Katie Stanley 56	50	1
10.12	Leyton Orient (h)	W	3-0	Katie Stanley 14, Jordanne Hoesli-Atkins (pen) 51, Kelly Jade-Whelan 69	70	1
17.12	Leyton Orient (a)	P-P				1
07.01	Cambridge United (h)	W	2-0	Katie Stanley 2, Jenny Banfield 85	70	1
21.01	Norwich City (a)	P-P				1
28.01	Enfield Town (h)	W	2-1	Laura Quinn-Low 46, 56	70	1
04.02	MK Dons (a)	P-P				1
11.02	Haringey Borough (h)	W	12-2	Georgia Heasman 2, 65, 85, Kelly-Jade Whelan 25, Jess Trimnell 51, Laura Quinn-Low 53, 88, Hannah Searle 58, 60, Rebecca Sargeant 73, Hannah Billingham 78, 81	100	1
18.02	Norwich City (h)	W	8-2	Own Goal 2, Laura Quinn-Low 4, Rebecca Sargeant 15, Georgia Heasman 27, 88, Katie Stanley 53, 70, Caroline Bisson 65	100	1

Date	Opponent		Result		Scorers		
25.02	Haringey Borough (a)	W	9-1		Sarah Wentworth 10, *Jess Trimnell missed pen (saved)*, Katie Stanley 20, 60, Jess Trimnell 22, Georgia Heasman 28, Jordanne Hoesli-Atkins 81, Caroline Bisson 86, Rebecca Sargeant 90, Laura Quinn-Low 90+2	30	1
11.03	Norwich City (a)	W	2-1		Georgia Heasman 33, Caroline Bisson 42	56	1
18.03	Leyton Orient (a)		P-P				1
25.03	MK Dons (a)	L	0-1			85	1
15.04	Leyton Orient (a)	L	1-2		*Jordanne Hoesli-Atkins missed pen (saved)*, Caroline Bisson (pen) 35	74	1
06.05	Luton Town (a)	W	3-2		Katie Stanley 13, Caroline Bisson 29, 60	69	1
20.05	Ipswich Town (a)*	D	1-1		Caroline Bisson (pen) 47	60	2

*Played at Playford Road

2017/18 FA CUP

Date	Opponent		Result		Scorers	
08.10 RQ3	Woodley United (h)	W	14-1		Isi Asplund 3, 33, 47, Caroline Bisson 5, 16, 17, Georgia Heasman 11, Laura Quinn-Low 40, 80, Own Goal 51, Rebecca Sargeant 67, Hannah Billingham 74, Katie Stanley 85, 89	50
12.11 R1	Godalming Town (h)	W	5-0		Abbie Measures 5, Rebecca Sargeant 28, Kelly-Jade Whelan 41, Georgia Heasman 50, 85	90
03.12 R2	Portsmouth (h)	L	1-2		Isi Asplund 7	90

2017/18 WPL CUP

Date	Opponent		Result		Scorers	
03.09 DR	MK Dons (a)	W	1-0		Katie Stanley 47	85
15.10 R1	Charlton Athletic (a)	L	2-3		Rebecca Sargeant 4, Katie Stanley 90+7	88

- Female fans of professional side Fulham formed a women's team in 1973 and called it Friends of Fulham. They started out in the Hounslow & District League before progressing to the Greater London League and later into the Women's National Premier League.

- Friends of Fulham enjoyed their most successful year in 1984 when they won the Treble of FA Cup (beating Doncaster Belles in the final at Craven Cottage), the Home Counties League and the League Cup. They were also FA Cup runners-up in 1989 (losing to Leasowe Pacific, who later became Everton) and 1990 (when they were beaten by Doncaster Belles).

- In 1986 Friends of Fulham teamed up with professional men's outfit Wimbledon FC and became Wimbledon Ladies. In 1993 a 3-2 win at Plough Lane saw them become the first team to beat Doncaster Belles in a League game for 15 years.

- When the original men's Wimbledon football club relocated to Milton Keynes in 2003, the ladies instead teamed up with fans' phoenix club AFC Wimbledon.

"Over the last decade I have seen the club grow from one ladies team to three ladies and 13 girls squads. In this time we have also achieved success with promotion of the first-team to the WPL and numerous Surrey County Women's & Girls' League titles and County Cup triumphs. In 2017/18 our Under-15 side won their fourth straight County Cup title through the various age groups. Everyone at the club is a volunteer, we are a close-knit group and aim to continue to develop girls and women's football to ensure our success continues."

John Ivers – AFC Wimbledon Secretary

BARNSLEY

2018/19: WNL DIVISION 1 NORTH (Tier 4)

Founded: 1976
Nickname: None
Ground: Barnsley FC Academy

Season 2017/18:
WPL Northern One (Tier 4): 11th
FA Cup: 3rd Qualifying Round
WPL Cup: Determining Round

WPL Plate: First Round
County Cup: Runners-up

2017/18 WPL NORTHERN ONE

Date	Opponent		Result	Scorers		
20.08	Hull City (a)	L	1-6	Nikki Hogg 75	66	
27.08	Liverpool M F (h)	L	2-3	Demi Pringle (pen) 27, Amy Woodruff 43	90	
10.09	Chorley (h)	D	0-0		111	
17.09	Leeds United (a)	W	4-3	Danielle Lowe 47, Drew Greene 74, 86, Darcie Kendall Greene 81	219	7
20.09	Brighouse Town (h)	L	0-3		92	7
24.09	Bolton Wanderers (h)	L	1-3	Danielle Lowe	82	10
01.10	Chester-le-Street T (a)	W	5-2	Danielle Lowe (pen) 2, Amy Woodruff 6, Drew Greene 18, Demi Pringle 72, 89	30	6
11.10	Brighouse Town (a)	L	1-3	Demi Pringle 26	83	7
15.10	Morecambe (h)	L	1-4	Demi Pringle 88	60	9
29.10	Chorley (a)	L	1-5	Demi Pringle 65	53	10
12.11	Morecambe (a)	W	3-1	Demi Pringle 2, Abby Parkin 60, Drew Greene 89	20	8
19.11	Chester-le-Street T (h)	W	3-1	Anna Cairns 21, Drew Greene 34, Demi Pringle 75	30	5
26.11	Crewe Alexandra (a)	L	1-3	Anna Cairns 4	42	6
10.12	Mossley Hill A (a)		P-P			6
07.01	Hull City (h)	L	0-5		57	7
14.01	Newcastle United (a)	L	2-3	Rebecca Fevers 21, Darcie Kendall Greene 24	70	7
28.01	Liverpool M F (a)+	L	0-8		30	9
18.02	Mossley Hill A (h)	D	2-2	Lynn Goodman (pen) 7, Darcie Kendall Greene 89		8
11.03	Mossley Hill A (a)	L	0-3		25	9
08.04	Crewe Alexandra (h)	D	1-1	Kristie Ward (pen) 43	76	9
29.04	Bolton Wanderers (a)	D	2-2	Alayna Millard 77, 83		10
13.05	Leeds United (h)	L	1-2	Amy Woodruff 55	105	12
20.05	Newcastle United (h)	D	1-1	Amy Woodruff 33	60	11

+Played at Edge Hill University

2017/18 FA CUP

08.10 RQ3	Chester-le-Street T (a)	L	1-2	Abby Parkin 69	30

2017/18 WPL CUP

03.09 DR	Blackburn Rovers (a)	L	0-3		86

2017/18 WPL PLATE

22.10 R1	Chorley (h)	L	1-3	Amy Woodruff 53	65

2017/18 SHEFFIELD & HALLAMSHIRE FA COUNTY CUP

17.12 R3	AFC Dronfield (h)	W	w/o		
21.01 QF	Rovers Foundation (h)	W	w/o		
18.03 SF	Huddersfield Town Development (a)	P-P			
25.03 SF	Huddersfield Town Development (a)	W	1-0	Kristie Ward 58	120
15.05 F	Huddersfield Town (n)	L	0-3		250

(n) Played at Keepmoat Stadium, Doncaster Rovers FC

"I'm really excited about the opportunity to take over as manager of Barnsley. It's a really good set-up with good people involved at the club. The players are great in training and have proved themselves both physically and mentally in a tough pre-season. The team seems to be buying into what I am trying to achieve and we are confident that with effort and commitment we can have a successful season."

Chris Hamilton – appointed Barnsley manager in June 2018

- Following promotion at the end of 2016/17, Barnsley enjoyed a difficult season at a higher level and finished just one place off the bottom of WPL North One in 2017/18. They were spared relegation and are now hoping for happier times in 2018/19 having appointed Chris Hamilton as manager, fresh from him having led Nettleham to promotion to Tier 4.

- Barnsley acquitted themselves well in the 2017/18 Sheffield & Hallamshire FA County Cup final against a team from a higher division – Tier 3 outfit Huddersfield Town. However, Huddersfield eventually proved too strong winning 3-0. It was the first time this County Cup final had been held at a Football League ground with Doncaster Rovers FC's Keepmoat Stadium playing host to a proud evening for all involved.

- The 2016/17 season had been the most successful in Barnsley's history. As well as claiming the North East Regional Premier League title, they also won the North East League Cup final beating Wallsend 3-2.

- In 2016 Barnsley won the Sheffield & Hallamshire FA County Cup for the first time in their history thanks to a 4-2 win over Huddersfield. Netherwood schoolgirl Brittany Sanderson, aged 16, scored a hat-trick in the final.

BASINGSTOKE TOWN

2018/19: SOUTHERN REGIONAL PREMIER LEAGUE (Tier 5)

Founded: 1992

Nickname: Town

Ground: Winklebury Football Complex in

2017/18, moving to Queen Mary's College in 2018/19

Season 2017/18: Resigned

WPL South West One (Tier 4): 11th

FA Cup: 1st Round

WPL Cup: Determining Round

WPL Plate: Preliminary Round

County Cup: 2nd Round

2017/18 WPL SOUTH WEST ONE

20.08	Brislington (a)	L	0-3		53	
27.08	Larkhall Athletic (a)	P-P				
10.09	So'ton Women (a)	L	0-5		32	
17.09	Brislington (h)	D	2-2	Helen Ogle 50, Elizabeth Laws 62	25	9
20.09	Maidenhead U (a)	D	2-2	Charlotte Hull 68, Helen Ogle 72		9
01.10	Plymouth Argyle (h)	L	1-5	Katie Randell 5	30	10
11.10	Maidenhead U (h)	L	2-5	Helen Ogle 40, 52	25	10
15.10	Poole Town (h)	L	4-5	Sarah Wentworth 27, 31, Jade Bradley 56, Helen Ogle 90	28	10
29.10	Keynsham Town (h)	L	0-10		20	10
10.12	Larkhall Athletic (h)	P-P				10
17.12	St Nicholas (h)	L	3-6	Shannon King 5, Lianne Hill 15, Charlotte Hull 30	20	11
07.01	St Nicholas (a)	L	1-2		22	11
28.01	Cheltenham Town (a)	P-P				11
04.02	So'ton Saints (a)	P-P				11

All results expunged from the records following Basingstoke Town's resignation from the League.

2017/18 FA CUP

08.10 RQ3	FC Chippenham (a)	W	6-1	Charlotte Hull 24, Lianne Hill 29, 85, Helen Ogle 35, Vanessa Watson 42, Lindsey Beverley 82	
19.11 R1	Plymouth Argyle (a)	L	w/o	Basingstoke unable to fulfil fixture	

2017/18 WPL CUP

03.09 DR	C&K Basildon (a)	L	0-8		62

2017/18 WPL PLATE

| 24.09 PR | St Nicholas (a) | D | 2-2aet (L 2-4p) | Helen Ogle 61, 70 | 50 |

2017/18 HAMPSHIRE COUNTY FA CUP

| 26.11 R2 | Moneyfields | L | 0-4 |

- Basingstoke Town took the difficult decision to resign from the League in February 2018, meaning all their results were expunged from the records. Their difficulties attracted the sympathies of their WPL South West 1 rivals, with Southampton Saints tweeting: "So sorry to hear the news that our friends and @FAWPL family member @Basing_LadiesFC have had to withdraw from the league. We hope you return to better times."

- Basingstoke Town Ladies won promotion to WPL South West Division 1 (now WNL Division 1 South West) ahead of the 2016/17 season. They finished 9th in 2016/17 but were bottom of the table when they took the decision to withdraw in 2017/18.

- The team was formed in 1992 but almost went out of business in 1999. The efforts of then chairman Ian Walkom and secretary Clare Hodder ensured the club survived.

BEDWORTH UNITED

2018/19: WNL DIVISION 1 MIDLANDS (Tier 4)

Founded: 2014

Nickname: United

Ground: The Oval (Bedworth United FC)

Season 2017/18:

West Mids Reg Prem (Tier 5): Champions

FA Cup: 1st Round

League Cup: Runners-up

County Cup: 2nd Round

2017/18 WEST MIDLANDS REGIONAL PREMIER

20.08	Coundon Court (h)	W	3-1	Jodie McGuckin, Alexandra Shilton, Shanice Walsh
10.09	Kingshurst Sporting Club (h)	W	3-1	Kirsty Farnsworth, Shanice Walsh, Sophie Wilson
24.09	Leafield Athletic (h)	L	1-4	Jodie McGuckin
01.10	Leamington Lions (a)	W	11-0	Lydia Hackney, Leona McCook (x3), Milly Miller, Alexandra Shilton (x2), Chevette Steel (x2), Shanice Walsh (x2)
15.10	Knowle (a)	W	4-0	Jodi Hunter, Shanice Walsh (x3)
22.10	Stockingford AA Pavilion (a)	W	2-0	Jodi Hunter, Sophie Wilson
29.10	Wolverhampton Sporting (a)	W	5-0	Lydia Hackney, Jodie McGuckin, Chevette Steel (x2), Amanda Whalley
05.11	Worcester United (a)	W	5-0	Jodie McGuckin, Milly Miller, Chevette Steel, Shanice Walsh, Sophie Wilson
26.11	Coundon Court (a)	W	4-0	Jodi Hunter, Milly Miller, Sarah Elizabeth Rowles, Shanice Walsh
03.12	Crusaders (h)	W	4-1	Sarah Elizabeth-Rowles (x2), Sophie Wilson (x2)
17.12	Lye Town (h)	W	w/o	
14.01	Worcester United (h)	W	8-0	Jodie McGuckin, Milly Miller (x2), Sarah Elizabeth-Rowles (x3), Shanice Walsh, Amanda Whalley
28.01	Leamington Lions (h)	W	21-0	Evelina Buividaviciute (x3), Lydia Hackney, Jodi Hunter (x3), Jodie McGuckin, Nancy Mary Miles, Milly Miller (x4), Sarah Elizabeth Rowles (x6), Amanda Whalley (x2)
11.02	Wolverhampton Sporting (h)	W	6-1	Leona McCook, Jodie McGuckin, Milly Miller, Shanice Walsh (x2), Amanda Whalley
25.02	Kingshurst Sporting Club (a)	W	w/o	
25.03	Lye Town (a)	W	8-1	Kirsty Farnsworth (x2), Milly Miller, Sarah Elizabeth Rowles, Shanice Walsh (x3), Sophie Wilson
06.05	Knowle (h)	W	9-0	Kirsty Farnsworth, Misty McKinde, Milly Miller (x3), Sarah Elizabeth Rowles, Shanice Walsh (x2), Amanda Whalley

13.05	Leafield Athletic (a)	D	3-3	Kirsty Farnsworth, Sarah Elizabeth Rowles (x2)
15.05	Crusaders (a)	W	2-1	Kirsty Farnsworth, Shanice Walsh
22.05	Stockingford AA Pavilion (h)	W	6-1	Kirsty Farnsworth, Sarah Elizabeth Rowles (x2), Chevette Steel, Shanice Walsh, Amanda Whalley

2017/18 FA CUP

03.09 RQ1	Sutton Coldfield Town (a)	W	4-0	Jodi Hunter (x2), Jodie McGuckin, Milly Miller
17.09 RQ2	Gornal (h)	W	2-0 (aet)	Shanice Walsh, Sophie Wilson
08.10 RQ3	Birmingham & W M (h)	W	2-1	Chevette Steel, Jodie McGuckin
12.11 R1	The New Saints (h)	L	0-2	

2017/18 LEAGUE CUP

08.04 QF	Crusaders (h)	W	5-0	Kirsty Farnsworth (x2), Lydia Hackney, Jodi Hunter, Shanice Walsh
22.04 SF	Coundon Court (a)	W	5-3 (aet)	Kirsty Farnsworth, Jodie McGuckin (x2), Milly Miller, Sarah Elizabeth Rowles
29.04 F	Leafield Athletic (n)	L	0-1	

(n) Played at Yarnfield Lane, (Stone Dominoes FC)

2017/18 BIRMINGHAM FA COUNTY CUP

| 19.11 R2 | Stockingford AA Pavilion (h) | L | 2-4 | Amanda Whalley, Milly Miller |

"After a disappointing end to 2016/17 in the East Midlands Regional League, we were moved into the West Midlands Regional League where we knew we would have a real battle on our hands in 2017/18. We had a few new players come into the squad to strengthen the side. From the first minute of pre-season we had one goal in mind – promotion. It was a long season with a lot of games called off over the Christmas period. We kept on pushing and with a lot of grit and determination we achieved our aim. Nobody thinks 2018/19 will be easy. For many of the players it will be the highest level they have played at. As one of the older players I hope to bring my experience to the youngsters coming up from the development squad. We are excited about the challenge ahead."

Jodie McGuckin – Bedworth United Captain

- Bedworth pipped Leafield Athletic to the title in dramatic style, clinching the 2017/18 West Midlands Regional Premier League championship by a solitary point to secure their promotion to Tier 4 (the newly-named WNL Division 1 Midlands).

- Runners-up Leafield Athletic were indeed the only team to take points off Bedworth all season, with United going down 4-1 away in September and drawing 3-3 at home in May. Bedworth won all 18 of their other League fixtures.

- In Bedworth's 21-0 win over Leamington Lions in the League on 28 January, no fewer than 5 hat-tricks were scored with Sarah Elizabeth Rowles getting a double hat-trick, Milly Miller netting 4 goals and Evelina Buividaviciute and Jodi Hunter both grabbing 3 goals.

- Bedworth's run to the 1st Round Proper of the FA Cup in 2017/18 included a 2-1 home win over Tier 4 side Birmingham & West Midlands in the 3rd Qualifying Round.

BILLERICAY TOWN

2018/19: WNL DIVISION 1 SOUTH EAST (Tier 4)

Founded: 1986 (as Basildon Ladies)

Nickname: None

Ground: AGP Arena, (Billericay Town FC)

Season 2017/18:

Eastern Reg Prem (Tier 5): Champions

FA Cup: 3rd Qualifying Round

League Cup: Semi-finals

County Cup: Quarter-finals

2017/18 EASTERN REGIONAL PREMIER

20.08	Colney Heath (h)	W	12-1	Paris Smith (x5), Hayley Piggott, Lindsey Morgan (x4), Lauren Knight, Nicole Farmer
10.09	Acle United (a)	W	3-1	Paris Smith (x3)
24.09	AFC Sudbury (a)	W	3-1	Dempsey Favell, Lauren Knight, Lindsey Morgan
01.10	Bedford (h)	W	3-2	Sally Appleton, Lauren Knight, Lindsey Morgan
15.10	Brentwood Town (a)	W	4-1	Courtney Lumley, Lindsey Morgan, Paris Smith (x2)
22.10	Cambridge City (a)	L	1-2	Paris Smith
05.11	Royston Town (h)	D	3-3	Sally Appleton, Hayley Piggott, Sarah Dimambro
12.11	AFC Sudbury (h)	D	3-3	Georgia Box (x2), Courtney Lumley
19.11	Bedford (a)	D	1-1	Georgia Box
03.12	Acle United (h)	W	4-2	Georgia Box, Lindsey Morgan, Paris Smith (x2)
28.01	Cambridge City (h)	W	2-1	Paris Smith (x2)
04.02	AFC Dunstable (a)	W	1-0	Lauren Bourne
11.03	Brentwood Town (h)	W	4-1	Lindsey Morgan (x3), Paris Smith
01.04	Colney Heath (a)	D	2-2	Lindsey Morgan, Hayley Piggott
15.04	AFC Dunstable (h)	W	4-1	Courtney Clarke, Hayley Piggott, Paris Smith, Hope Strauss
29.04	Royston Town (a)	L	0-1	

2017/18 FA CUP

03.09 RQ1	Chelmsford City (h)	W	8-0	Nicole Farmer (x2), Lauren Knight (x2), Lindsey Morgan, Hayley Piggott, Paris Smith (x2)
17.09 RQ2	Brentwood Town (a)	W	3-2	Kirsty Knight, Lindsey Morgan (x2)
08.10 RQ3	Leyton Orient (a)	L	0-7	

2017/18 ESSEX FA COUNTY CUP

21.01 QF	Brentwood Town (h)	L	0-2	

180

2017/18 LEAGUE CUP

Date	Opponent	Result	Score	Scorers
07.01 R3	Ipswich Town Development (a)	W	9-0	Georgia Box (x2), Lindsey Morgan (x2), Paris Smith (x5)
25.02 QF	Wymondham Town (h)	W	1-0	Hope Strauss
08.04 SF	Acle United (a)	L	2-3	Lindsey Morgan, Hayley Piggott

"Season 2017/18 saw us achieve promotion to the FA WNL thanks to fantastic teamwork. After a number of seasons falling short, we got things right. We are a football family that strives to achieve team goals – a friendly bunch that enjoy banter in the changing rooms with great tunes blaring, it isn't just about the first-team but from all the teams from age 10 through to our senior side. The club ethic is that you play with a smile on your face, you win together and lose together."

Kim Coster – Billericay Town Manager

- Billericay were confirmed as Eastern Regional Premier Division champions for 2017/18 when nearest rivals Acle United lost 2-1 to Cambridge City. The Blues thus clinched the title by a solitary point and were promoted to the newly-formed WNL Division 1 South East for 2018/19.

- Paris Smith finished as the club's top scorer for 2017/18. She hit 17 goals in 9 League appearances, which also made her the division's top scorer for League goals. In all competitions she managed 24 in 13 in appearances.

- The club was founded as Basildon Ladies in 1986 and started life competing in the Greater London League 3rd Division. They changed their name to Billericay ahead of the 1996/97 season.

BIRMINGHAM & WEST MIDLANDS

2018/19: WPL
MIDLANDS ONE (Tier 4)

Founded: 2001 (as Bimingham University)

Nickname: None

Ground: The Vale Stadium, (Castle Vale FC)

Season 2017/18:

WPL Midlands One (Tier 4): 9th

FA Cup: 3rd Qualifying Round

WPL Cup: Determining Round

WPL Plate: Quarter-finals

County Cup: Runners-up

2017/18 WPL MIDLANDS ONE

20.08	Loughborough F (a)	L	0-3		42	
27.08	Leicester City L (h)		P-P			
10.09	Burton Albion (a)	L	1-4	Annie Collins 65	52	
17.09	Long Eaton United (a)	W	1-0	Valene Izon	30	7
20.09	Solihull Moors (h)	L	0-5		35	7
24.09	Loughborough F (h)	L	0-5	*Annie Collins missed pen (saved by Amy Burle) 48*	45	8
01.10	Radcliffe Olympic (a)	L	0-2		18	9
11.10	Solihull Moors (a)	D	2-2	Kwahjay-Tabia Mapp, Annie Collins	40	8
15.10	Steel City W (h)	W	7-0	Annie Collins 18, 81, Charlotte Fisher 29, 58, Amy Eastwood 45, Louise Price 45+1, Shannie Jennings 78	58	8
29.10	Leicester City L (a)	W	3-1	Charlotte Fisher 50, 69, 88	45	8
05.11	Radcliffe Olympic (h)	L	0-2		20	8
12.11	Burton Albion (h)	L	1-3	Katy Kirby 56	15	8
26.11	Sporting Khalsa (h)	L	0-3		20	9
03.12	Steel City W (a)	L	2-3	Natalie Dean, Charlotte Fisher	45	9
28.01	Sheffield United (a)	L	0-5		67	9
25.02	The New Saints (a)	D	2-2	Jodie Bragan, Charlotte Fisher	29	10
04.03	Rotherham United (a)		P-P			10
11.03	Leicester City L (h)	W	6-0	Shannie Jennings 16, Katy Kirby 18, Charlotte Fisher 25, 36, 88, Emily Painter 85	20	10
25.03	The New Saints (h)	W	1-1	Charlotte Fisher	20	10
15.04	Sporting Khalsa (a)	W	3-1	Charlotte Fisher (x2), Emily Painter	30	10
22.04	Long Eaton United (h)	L	1-2	Charlotte Fisher 47	25	10
29.04	Sheffield United (h)	L	1-5	Charlotte Fisher 80	20	10
06.05	Rotherham United (a)	W	5-2	Charlotte Fisher (x2), Emily Painter, Louise Price, Shannie Jennings	20	10
20.05	Rotherham United (h)	W	12-1	Charlotte Fisher (x5), Louise Price (x3), Katy Kirby (x2), Shannie Jennings, Lucy Gimson	30	9

2017/18 FA CUP

08.10 RQ3	Bedworth United (a)	L	1-2	Laura Parsons	53

2017/18 WPL CUP

03.09 DR	Sheffield United (a)	L	0-6		43

2017/18 WPL PLATE

22.10 R1	Sporting Khalsa (h)	W	3-1	Charlotte Fisher 21, 72, 88	30
10.12 R2	Crewe Alexandra (h)		P-P		
17.12 R2	Crewe Alexandra (h)	W	3-1	Harriet Shaw Roberts 21, Charlotte Fisher 48, Amy Eastwood 59	25
11.02 QF	Fylde (h)	L	1-5	Shannie Jennings	87

2017/18 BIRMINGHAM FA COUNTY CUP

19.11 R2	Leafield Athletic (h)	W	9-0	Charlotte Fisher 6, Amy Eastwood 25, Annie Collins 34, 41, Katy Kirby 43, 68, Harriet Shaw Roberts 52, 59, Natalie Dean 87	25
14.01 R3	Coventry Sphinx (a)	W	6-0	Charlotte Fisher (x5), Louise Price	15
18.02 QF	Wolverhampton United (h)	W	w/o		
18.03 SF	Redditch United (h)		P-P		
20.03 SF	Redditch United (h)	W	2-0	Charlotte Fisher, Louise Price	127
03.05 F	Coventry United (n)	L	0-15		

(n) Played at The Lamb, Tamworth FC

"The 2017/18 season was a rollercoaster, we struggled to get back on track after a really poor pre-season. Things then gradually started to turn after changes were made following our FA Cup defeat. Results soon followed with fantastic Cup runs in both the WPL Plate – where we reached the quarter-final – and the County cup, where we made it to the final for the first time in the club's history. The season wasn't up to the high standards we set ourselves, however we're proud we managed to salvage enough points, with a small squad, after a difficult start. The club formed as a university team in 2001, and in 2018 we are heading back to our roots as we partner again with the University of Birmingham in what is a huge development for us. These are exciting times for BWMLFC."

Helen Carver – Birmingham & W M General Manager

- Charlotte Fisher was the division's top scorer for goals in all competitions in 2017/18 with 33, and her 22 League goals were only bettered by Burton's Jordan Atkin (29). Fisher struck 15 goals in her final seven League matches of the season.

- Having announced her retirement, captain Lucy Gimson scored her first goal of the season in her very last match for the club – a final day 12-1 win over Rotherham.

- The club has had a number of former names. They were founded in 2001 as Birmingham University then became Birmingham Athletic and subsequently West Midlands Police before settling on Birmingham & West Midlands in 2014.

BLACKBURN ROVERS

2018/19: WNL
NORTHERN PREMIER (Tier 3)

Founded: 1991

Nickname: Rovers

Ground: Sir Tom Finney Stadium
(Bamber Bridge Football Club)

Season 2017/18:

WNL Northern Premier (Tier 3): Champions
Lost to Charlton in national play-off final

FA Cup: 4th Round

WPL Cup: Winners

County Cup: Winners

2017/18 WPL NORTHERN

20.08	Wolverhampton W (h)	W	3-0	Faye McCoy 27, 83, Kelsey Pearson 37	136	
27.08	West Brom (a)	W	2-0	Alexandra Taylor 8, Saffron Jordan 58	71	
10.09	Huddersfield Town (a)	W	2-1	Jess Holbrook 59, Kaylea Cunliffe 66	121	
01.10	Guiseley Vixens (h)*	W	3-1	Alex Taylor 8, Chelsey Jukes 43, Saffron Jordan 87	83	4
22.10	West Brom (h)+	W	2-0	Natasha Fenton 25, Saffron Jordan 82	96	2
29.10	Stoke City (a)	D	1-1	Kaylea Cunliffe 20	104	2
05.11	Nottingham Forest (h)	P-P				3
19.11	Huddersfield Town (h)	L	0-2	*Lynda Shepherd missed pen 56 (saved by Laura Carter)*	121	5
21.01	Nottingham Forest (h)	P-P				5
28.01	Nottingham Forest (h)	W	7-0	Saffron Jordan 14, Kelly Darby (og) 22, Natasha Flint 30, Kayleigh McDonald 56, Lagan Makin 62, Lynda Shepherd (pen) 74, Kelsey Pearson 75		5
30.01	Fylde (a)	P-P				5
25.02	Bradford City (a)	W	3-0	Natasha Flint 20, 65, Lynda Shepherd 45	84	5
15.03	Fylde (h)	W	3-0	Natasha Flint 33, Jess Holbrook 81, Lynda Shepherd 85	156	4
18.03	Nottingham Forest (a)	P-P				4
01.04	Derby County (a)	P-P				5
08.04	Derby County (h)	W	6-2	Natasha Flint 8, Lagan Makin 13, 73, Lynda Shepherd 15, (pen) 51, Jess Holbrook 32	103	5
10.04	Middlesbrough (h)	W	4-0	Natasha Flint 15, Lynda Shepherd 49, Saffron Jordan 56, Lagan Makin 84	86	3
15.04	Leicester City W (h)	L	1-2	Lynda Shepherd (pen) 45+1	123	5
17.04	Bradford City (h)	W	7-0	Lynda Shepherd 15, Lagan Makin 25, 67, Natasha Fenton 49, Jess Holbrook 58, Saffron Jordan 84, Hannah Walsh 87	103	2
22.04	Wolverhampton W (a)	D	1-1	Lynda Shepherd 55	80	3

26.04	Fylde (a)	W	6-1	Saffron Jordan 7, Ellie Cook 14, Natasha Flint 35, 81, 84, Kaylea Cunliffe 90+3	82	3
01.05	Derby County (a)	W	1-0	Natasha Fenton 40	53	2
06.05	Leicester City W (a)	W	3-2	Natasha Flint 27, 70, Saffron Jordan 67	135	1
13.05	Nottingham F (a)**	W	4-1	Lagan Makin 50, Jess Holbrook 71, Natasha Flint 81, Saffron Jordan 85	76	1C
15.05	Stoke City (h)++	W	3-0	Natasha Flint 23, Saffron Jordan 46, Jess Holbrook 69		1C
17.05	Guiseley Vixens (a)^	W	3-1	Natasha Fenton 29, Saffron Jordan 38, 54	48	1C
20.05	Middlesbrough (a)	W	3-2	Natasha Fenton 67, Natasha Flint 75, Saffron Jordan 79	103	1C

*Played Accrington & Rossendale College   +Played at Blackburn Rovers Senior Training Centre

**Played at Lee Westwood Sports Centre   ++Played at Ewood Park, Blackburn Rovers FC ^Played at John Craig Sports Centre

2017/18 WPL Play-off Final

27.05	Charlton A (n)	L	1-2	Lynda Shepherd (pen) 6		917

(n) Played at Bramall Lane, Sheffield United FC

2017/18 FA Cup

03.12 R2	Loughborough F (h)	W	4-1	Saffron Jordan 43, 53, 86, Kayleigh McDonald 78	77
07.01 R3	Portsmouth (h)	W	7-0	Kaylea Cunliffe 33, Natasha Flint 36, 57, 72, 75, Lagan Makin 45, 51	50est
04.02 R4	Charlton A (h)	L	2-3 (aet)	Natasha Flint 55, 81	157

2017/18 WPL CUP

03.09 DR	Barnsley (h)	W	3-0	Saffron Jordan 45, 63, Faye McCoy 60	86
15.10 R1	Stoke City (a)	D	2-2aet W 4-3p)	Lynda Shepherd (pen) 58, Alexandra Taylor 78	130
14.01 R2	Liverpool M F (a)	W	2-1	Kaylea Cunliffe 5, Alexandra Taylor 73	110
11.02 R3	Brighouse Town (a)		P-P		
18.02 R3	Brighouse Town (a)	W	2-1	Natasha Fenton 27, *Blackburn GK Danielle Hill saved Emily Starkie pen 83 – Brighouse scored rebound*, Ria Maire Montgomery 88	107
11.03 SF	Coventry United (h)		P-P		
25.03 SF	Coventry United (h)	D	2-2aet (W 4-2p)	Saffron Jordan 69, 90+1	197
29.04 F	Leicester City W (n)	W	3-1	Lynda Shepherd (pen) 33, Ellie Cook 74, Saffron Jordan 90	466

(n) Played at Proact Stadium, Chesterfield FC

2017/18 LANCASHIRE FA COUNTY CUP

24.09 R1	Blackburn Community Sports Club (a)	W	5-0	Jess Holbrook 1, 25, 52, Megan Taylor 43, Saffron Jordan 73	
08.10 QF	Fylde (h)	W	2-1	Megan Taylor 32, Saffron Jordan 41	176
26.11 SF	Bolton Wanderers (a)		P-P		
10.12 SF	Bolton Wanderers (a)		P-P		
17.12 SF	Bolton Wanderers (a)	W	5-1	Natasha Fenton (pen) 3, 52, Saffron Jordan 28, 39, 54	
10.05 F	Chorley (n)	W	6-1	Kayleigh McDonald 36, Saffron Jordan 49, 85, Hannah Walsh 54, Natasha Fenton 88, Chelsey Jukes 90+4	

(n) Played at Lancashire FA County Ground, Leyland

- Blackburn won the WPL Northern title in 2016/17 and 2017/18, but lost the national play-off final to their WPL Southern counterparts on both occasions, losing 3-0 to Tottenham at The Valley in 2017 and 2-1 to Charlton at Bramall Lane in 2018.

- Blackburn clinched the 2017/18 WPL Northern title with a 4-1 win at Nottingham Forest on 13 May. They were awarded the trophy after their next match which was a 3-0 home win over Stoke played at Ewood Park. Natasha Flint made it 1-0 with a 25-yard screamer which happened to be the club's 100th goal of the season.

- Past honours include the 2003/04 Northern Combination title when they went the entire League campaign without dropping a single point – they won every match to take the title and also lifted the Lancashire FA County Cup that season.

- They almost repeated the feat in the 2005/06 Women's Premier League Northern Division campaign. They claimed the title without losing a single game, winning 20 and drawing two of their 22 matches. On the back of that 2005/06 title success, manager Andy McNally became the first manager from outside the top-flight to win the FA Manager of the Year award.

BOLTON WANDERERS

2018/19: WNL
DIVISON ONE (Tier 4)

Founded: 1989

Nickname: None

Ground: Kensite Stadium
(Atherton Collieries FC)

Season 2017/18:

WPL Northern One (Tier 4): 4th

FA Cup: 1st Round

WPL Cup: 1st Round

County Cup: Semi-finals

2017/18 WPL NORTHERN ONE

20.08	Leeds United (h)	W	3-1	Michelle Kirkman-Ryan 8, Safron New-house 15, Emma Pilling 21	81	
27.08	Brighouse Town (a)	L	3-4	Michelle Saunders 12, Safron Newhouse 60, Michelle Kirkman-Ryan 74	53	
10.09	Morecambe (h)	L	1-4	Michelle Saunders 90	60	
20.09	Crewe Alexandra (a)	A-A		Abandoned in 24th min at 0-0 due to head injury to Bolton player		
24.09	Barnsley (a)	W	3-1	Ruby Howard 33, Saffron Newhouse 39, Emily Hockenhull 77	82	5
01.10	Chorley (h)	W	5-2	Safron Newhouse 3, 17, Emma Pilling 19, 37, Ruby Howard 64, *Ruby Howard missed pen 17*	126	5
17.10	Crewe Alexandra (h)	W	1-0	Emma Pilling 65	73	5
05.11	**Chester-Le-Street T (a)**	L	0-1	*Bolton GK saved penalty 60 but Chester-le-Street Town scored from rebound*	30	5
19.11	Liverpool M F (h)	P-P				5
03.12	Leeds United (a)	W	1-0	Safron Newhouse 72	35	5
07.01	Morecambe (a)	L	2-6	Emma Pilling 15, Ruby Howard 22	32	5
14.01	Hull City (h)	P-P				6
04.02	Mossley Hill A (a)	P-P				6
11.02	Newcastle United (h)	P-P				6
18.02	Hull City (a)	L	0-2		50	6
04.03	Newcastle United (h)	P-P				6
07.03	Crewe Alexandra (a)	W	1-0	Katie Nuttall (og) 67	76	6
11.03	Chester-le-Street T (h)*	W	2-1	Ruby Howard 28, *Chester-le-Street missed pen 90+3 (saved)*, Bethany Worth 90+3 (scored penalty rebound)	40	6
18.03	Newcastle United (a)	P-P				6
25.03	Mossley Hill A (h)	W	3-1	Safron Newhouse 4, 75, 80	104	5
08.04	Hull City (h)**	L	0-1			5

12.04	Newcastle United (h)	L	1-2		65	5
15.04	Brighouse Town (h)	L	2-3	Safron Newhouse 7, 56		5
18.04	Mossley Hill A (a)	L	1-2		30	5
22.04	Liverpool M F (a)	W	2-1	Emily Hockenhull 35, 75	45	5
29.04	Barnsley (h)	D	2-2	Olivia Hooper 10, Ruby Howard 60		5
06.05	Liverpool M F (h)	W	1-0	Emily Hockenhull 85	50	4
13.05	Newcastle United (a)	W	3-2	Ruby Howard 5, Emma Pilling 48, Safron Newhouse 76	41	4
20.05	Chorley (a)+	L	1-2		140	4

*Played at Lostock Academy   **Played at Eddie Davies Academy   +Played at Croston Sports Club

2017/18 FA CUP

15.10 RQ3	CMB Sports Club (a)	W	5-2	Michelle Kirkman-Ryan 3, 33, Emma Pilling (pen) 25, Safron Newhouse 53 *(rebound from her own saved pen)*, Gabby Yates 60	
12.11 R1	Liverpool M F (a)*	L	0-1 (aet)		60

*Match played at JMO Sports Park, Skelmerslade

2017/18 WPL CUP

03.09 DR	Leicester City L (a)	W	5-0	Michelle Kirkman-Ryan 22, 35, Safron New-house 51, 63, Rebecca Milner (og) 90	60
29.10 R1	Leicester City W (a)	L	0-3		75

2017/18 LANCASHIRE FA COUNTY CUP

17.09 R1	Morecambe (h)	W	4-2	Ruby Howard 55, 64, Michelle Kirkman-Ryan 78, Emma Pilling 90	90
22.10 QF	Burnley (a)	W	4-0	Ruby Howard 8, 33, Safron Newhouse 25, Emma Pilling 47	
26.11 SF	Blackburn R (h)		P-P		
10.12 SF	Blackburn R (h)		P-P		
17.12 SF	Blackburn R (h)	L	1-5	Emma Pilling 79	

- Bolton Wanderers won their first League title in 2016/17. They went up to Tier 4 as North West Regional Premier champions, securing the title with a game to spare thanks to a 3-0 win away to Blackpool when they needed only a point. Having been promoted, they then finished a highly creditable 4th in WPL Northern One in 2017/18.

- Safron Newhouse was Blackburn's top scorer in 2017/18. She hit 16 goals in 19 appearances in all competitions and 12 in 15 in the League.

- The Eddie Davies Academy – home of professional men's team Bolton Wanderers' academy side – was the site at which Bolton Wanderers Ladies played most of their home games in 2016/17. In June 2017 they announced they would spend 2017/18 at the 2,500 capacity Kensite Stadium, home of men's non-League side Atherton Collieries FC.

- The club was founded in 1989 and officially joined the Bolton Wanderers Football Club family in 2010.

BRADFORD CITY

2018/19: WNL
NORTHERN PREMIER (Tier 3)

Founded: 1988

Nickname: The Bantams

Ground: Plumpton Park, (Eccleshill Utd FC)

Season 2017/18:

WPL Northern (Tier 43): 8th

FA Cup: 3rd Round

WPL Cup: 1st Round

County Cup: Runners-up

2017/18 WPL NORTHERN

20.08	Leicester City W (a)	L	0-2		124	
27.08	Nottingham F (h)	D	0-0		71	
10.09	Wolverhampton W (h)	W	4-1	Ellie White 78, Charlotte Stuart 82, Abigail Lee 85, 90+3	63	
20.09	Huddersfield T (a)	D	2-2	Charlotte Stuart 36, Ellie White 58	137	8
01.10	Derby County (h)	L	1-2	Abigail Lee	67	10
08.10	Guiseley Vixens (a)	D	2-2	Charlotte Stuart 5, Laura Elford 70	40	10
17.10	Huddersfield T (h)	D	1-1	Ellie Olds 57	121	9
05.11	Fylde (h)	L	1-2	Charlotte Stuart 13	59	9
12.11	Middlesbrough (a)	L	2-3	Zoe Roberts 45, Hannah Smith 88	138	9
26.11	Wolverhampton W (a)	W	3-0	Hannah Campbell 38, Hannah Smith 52, Arianne Parnham 71	40	9
10.12	Derby County (a)	P-P				9
14.01	Stoke City (h)	L	2-6	Abigail Lee 14, Hannah Smith 33	65	10
21.01	Fylde (a)	P-P				10
28.01	Fylde (a)	P-P				10
04.02	Derby County (a)	W	1-0	Laura Elford 20	40	9
11.02	Middlesbrough (h)	P-P				9
18.02	Middlesbrough (h)	W	9-2	Laura Elford 10, 19, 31, (pen) 45, 73, 75, Arianne Parnham 59, Hannah Campbell 70, Ellie White 85	73	7
25.02	Blackburn Rovers (h)	L	0-3		84	8
04.03	West Brom (h)	P-P				8
11.03	Guiseley Vixens (h)	P-P				8
25.03	West Brom (a)	L	1-2	Abigail Lee 83	54	8
01.04	Fylde (a)	L	1-2	Ellie White 75	55	8
17.04	Blackburn Rovers (a)	L	0-7		103	8
19.04	Stoke City (a)	W	2-1	*Laura Elford missed pen 15 (saved by Natalie Hall),* Laura Elford 15 (scored pen rebound), Hannah Smith 45	103	8

22.04	West Brom (h)	W	4-2	Hannah Campbell 23, 24, 46, Laura Elford 74	47	7
29.04	Nottingham F (a)	L	0-1		374	8
10.05	Guiseley Vixens (h)	W	3-0	Hannah Campbell 36, 64, Laura Elford 57	74	8
20.05	Leicester City W (h)+	L	1-4	Arianne Parnham 23	47	8

+Played at University of Bradford

2017/18 FA CUP

| 03.12 R2 | Long Eaton United (h) | W | 5-0 | Laura Elford (pen) 48, Hannah Campbell 50, Ellie White 57, 64, Abigail Housecroft 72 | 26 |
| 07.01 R3 | Leicester City W (a) | L | 1-2 | Ellie White (pen) 9 | |

2017/18 WPL CUP

| 03.09 DR | Fylde (h) | D | 3-3aet (W 3-2p) | Laura Elford 81, 114, Ellie Olds 86, *Laura Elford sent off 115* | 81 |
| 22.10 R1 | Derby County (a) | L | 2-5aet | Ellie Olds 26, Ellie White 73, *Bradford miss pen (saved by Sophie Morgan) 107* | 106 |

2017/18 WEST RIDING FA CUP

15.10 R1	Brighouse Town (a)	D	2-2aet (W 4-2p)	Ellie Olds 13, Bryony Hanson 21	137
19.11 R2	Tyersal (a)	W	5-0	Laura Elford (x4), Amy Wood	
17.12 QF	Thackley (h)	W	15-0	Hannah Campbell 5, 15, 71, Laura Elford 10, 38, 40, 59, 70, 73, 90, Charlotte Stuart 26, 36, Bryony Hanson 28, 81, Abigail Lee (pen) 48	107
14.03 SF	Farsley Celtic (a)	W	2-0		
02.05 F	Guiseley Vixens (n)	L	1-3	Ellie White 17	

(n) Played at Fleet Lane, West Riding FA HQ

"We're in our 30th year and we have always aimed to bring good football and fun to Bradford, for as many girls and women as possible. Our most pleasing achievement in 2017/18 was seeing the development of our junior section of the club, in five years, coming from a handful of girls to seven competitive teams. The 2018/19 campaign will be an exciting one as we have a new senior management team who will be looking to further develop the players with the ambitious prospect of gaining membership at the next level – the FA Women's Championship."

Sally Thackray – Bradford City Women's Chair

- In 2017/18 striker Laura Elford was among the WPL Northern top scorers. Only Leicester's Rosie Axten (30), and Middlesbrough's Emily Scarr (28) scored more than Elford's 25 in all competitions. Elford hit a double hat-trick on two occasions, grabbing seven in the 15-0 County Cup win over Thackley and six in the 9-2 win against Middlesbrough in the League.

- In 1989 – a year after their formation – Bradford City were founder members of the Yorkshire and Humberside League. In 1997 they won promotion to the WPL for the first time after winning the Northern Division.

- Their best run in the WPL League Cup came in 1997/98 when they made it to the semi-finals before being knocked out on penalties by eventual winners Arsenal after a 2-2 draw.

BRIGHOUSE TOWN

2018/19: WNL
DIVISON 1 NORTH (Tier 4)

Founded: 2013

Nickname: Town

Ground: Yorkshire Payments Stadium
(Brighouse Town AFC)

Season 2017/18:

WPL Northern One (Tier 4): Runners-up

FA Cup: 4th Round

WPL Cup: Quarter-finals

County Cup: 1st Round

2017/18 WPL Northern One

Date	Opponent		Result	Scorers		
20.08	Newcastle United (a)	W	5-3	Charlotte Proud 14, Bridie Hannon 18, Jodie Redgrave 80, Aimi Beresford 83, 88	68	
27.08	Bolton Wanderers (h)	W	4-3	Jodie Redgrave 14, 41, Charlotte Proud 30, Rebecca Kendell 35	53	
10.09	Chester-le-Street T (a)	W	6-2	Jodie Redgrave 1, 23, 45, Cara Mahoney 34, Emily Starkie 44, Rebecca Kendell 61	40	
17.09	Hull City (h)	L	0-1		73	2
20.09	Barnsley (a)	W	3-0	Aimi Beresford 12, Emma Dobson 15, 40	92	3
01.10	Mossley Hill A (h)	W	5-1	Aimi Beresford 8, Jodie Redgrave 24, 44, Charlotte Proud 55, Emily Starkie 80	42	2
11.10	Barnsley (h)	W	3-1	Rebecca Kendell 5, Hannah Poulter 55, Jodie Redgrave 85	83	2
05.11	Leeds United (h)	W	3-1	Jodie Redgrave 16, 27, 37	112	1
19.11	Chorley (h)	W	2-1	Zoe Doherty 65, Jodie Redgrave 90+1	58	1
26.11	Morecambe (h)		P-P			1
25.02	Liverpool M F (a)	D	0-0		70	3
04.03	Crewe Alexandra (a)		P-P			3
07.03	Morecambe (a)	D	2-2	Anabelle Cass 9, Aimi Beresford 69	35	3
11.03	Newcastle United (h)		P-P			3
18.03	Chorley (a)		P-P			3
21.03	Leeds United (a)	W	5-2	Charlotte Proud 48, 72, Aimi Beresford 59, 82, Lauren Doyle 64	50	3
25.03	Chester-le-Street T (h)	W	4-2	Aimi Beresford (pen) 41, 85, Charlotte Proud 57, 73	92	3
08.04	Liverpool M F (h)		P-P			3
11.04	Liverpool M F (h)*	L	1-3	Jodie Redgrave 38	70	3
15.04	Bolton Wanders (a)	W	3-2	Charlotte Proud 3, Aimi Beresford 49, 72, Aimi Beresford missed pen 86		3
18.04	Newcastle United (h)	W	4-0	Charlotte Proud 11, 49, 53, Lauren Doyle 80	134	3
22.04	Morecambe (h)	L	1-2	Stephanie Jones sent off 48, Aimi Beresford 65	76	3

29.04	Hull City (a)	L	0-2		100	3
06.05	Crewe Alexandra (a)	W	1-0	Jodie Redgrave 71, Charlotte Proud missed pen 78	43	3
13.05	Crewe Alexandra (h)	W	3-1	Charlotte Proud 20, 82, Jodie Redgrave 76	102	2
16.05	Chorley (a)	W	3-0	Anabelle Cass 10, Emma Dobson 50, Jodie Redgrave 78	65	2
20.05	Mossley Hill A (a)	W	2-1	Jodie Redgrave 12, 38, Brighouse GK Stephanie Jones saved Mossley Hill Athletic pen 87	30	2

*Played at Woodhouse Grove School

2017/18 FA CUP

08.10 RQ3	Wakefield (h)	W	6-1	Charlotte Proud 10, (pen) 22, 51, 54, Lauren Doyle (pen) 15, Emily Starkie 90	104
12.11 R1	Chester-le-Street T (h)	W	6-1	Jodie Redgrave 10, 66, Aimi Beresford 18, 45+1, 80, Danielle Brown 70	43
03.12	Wolverhampton W (h)		P-P		
10.12	Wolverhampton W (h)		P-P		
17.12 R2	Wolverhampton W (h)	W	6-3	Jodie Redgrave 4, Dannielle Brown 16, 61, Lauren Doyle 58, *Jodie Redgrave missed pen 63,* Aimi Beresford (pen) 82, 88	123
07.01 R3	Derby County (a)		P-P		
14.01 R3	Derby County (a)	W	3-1	Jodie Redgrave 7, 55, Annabelle Cass 90	120
04.02 R4	Sunderland (a)	L	0-13		270 est

2017/18 WPL CUP

03.09 DR	Mossley Hill A (a)	W	1-0	Aimi Beresford 9	30
22.10 R1	Chester-le-Street T (h)		P-P		
29.10 R1	Chester-le-Street T (h)	W	5-1	Jodie Redgrave 11, 50, 70, Aimi Beresford 36, Charlotte Proud 80	65
21.01 R2	Derby County (h)		P-P		
28.01 R2	Derby County (h)	W	3-2	Jodie Redgrave 47, 90, Aimi Beresford (pen) 87	92
11.02 QF	Blackburn Rovers (h)		P-P		
18.02 QF	Blackburn Rovers (h)	L	1-2	*Emily Starkie missed pen (saved Danielle Hill) 83,* Lauren Doyle 83 (scored penalty rebound)	107

2017/18 WEST RIDING FA COUNTY CUP

15.10 R1	Bradford City (h)	D	2-2 (L 2-4p)	Jodie Redgrave 8, Zoe Doherty (pen) 82	137

Brighouse Town FC

 "Although, ultimately, we came up short in our quest for the title, we had a fantastic 2017/18. We managed to achieve 50 points (which was 13 more than in 2016/17), finished 2nd behind a very good Hull side and went further in both the League and FA Cups than the season before. It was undeniably a season of progression, offering plenty to build on."

Jodie Redgrave, Brighouse Town Captain

- Brighouse captain Jodie Redgrave finished 2017/18 as the joint top goalscorer in WPL Northern 1. She hit 19 League goals, the same number as Morecambe's Yasmine Swarbrick. She also notched a further 11 in the Cups, making her the division's outright top scorer in all competitions with 30 goals.

- In only their second season in the division, Town confirmed their runners-up League place for 2017/18 when they won their penultimate match 3-0 at Chorley on 16 May.

- The club has enjoyed a rapid rise since they were formed in 2013, going from the 6th tier to the 4th tier in three years. They were crowned North East Regional League South champions in 2013/14 and then North East Regional League Premier Division champions in 2015/16, an achievement which saw them promoted to Tier 4 – the level at which they are now.

- The team was established in 2013 when non-League men's side Brighouse was given the go-ahead to formalise their women's team. They merged with Kirklees Ladies to create Brighouse Town Ladies.

BRISLINGTON

2018/19: WNL
DIVISON 1 SOUTH WEST (Tier 4)

Founded: 2011

Nickname: None

Ground: Ironmould Lane
(Brislington FC)

Season 2017/18:

WPL South West One (Tier 4): 6th
FA Cup: 3rd Round
WPL Cup: Determining Round
WPL Plate: 2nd Round
County Cup: Quarter-finals

2017/18 WPL SOUTH WEST ONE

20.08	*Basingstoke Town (h)* **exp**	W	*3-0*	Jodie Arkell 35, Kim Maggs 48, Chelsea Heal 53	53	
27.08	Plymouth Argyle (h)	L	0-4		43	
17.09	*Basingstoke Town (a)* **exp**	D	*2-2*	*Unknown, Polly Wardle 89*	25	5
21.09	Keynsham Town (h)	L	1-2	Jodie Arkell 68	84	6
01.10	Poole Town (a)	W	3-2	Jodie Arkell 42, 65, 82	22	5
12.10	Keynsham Town (a)	L	0-4		105	5
29.10	So'ton Women (h)	L	1-5	Amy Jefferies 4	56	8
05.11	Cheltenham Town (a)	W	4-1	Jodie Arkell 31, 52, Chelsea Heal 35, 86	47	6
19.11	Larkhall Athletic (h)		P-P			
26.11	Maidenhead (h)		P-P			
28.01	St Nicholas (h)+	L	2-3	Kim Maggs 43, Zoe Gunter 55	62	7
11.02	So'ton Saints (h)		P-P			7
25.02	So'ton Saints (h)	L	0-3		42	8
04.03	Larkhall Athletic (a)		P-P			8
11.03	So'ton Saints (a)	L	1-3	Brodie Vogt 78	28	10
18.03	Larkhall Athletic (h)		P-P			10
22.03	Cheltenham Town (h)	D	0-0		62	9
25.03	So'ton Women (a)	L	0-6	*Chelsea Heal sent off 80*		9
08.04	St Nicholas (a)	L	1-3	Amy Jefferies 35, *Mollie Jones sent off 10*	61	10
15.04	Maidenhead U (h)	W	3-1	Kim Maggs 16, 21, Sophie Whelan 61	33	8
22.04	Plymouth Argyle (a)	L	1-9	Zoe Gunter 12		8
06.05	Poole Town (h)	W	4-3	Zoe Gunter 6, Polly Wardle 22, 60, Sophie Whelan 65	43	7
08.05	Larkhall Athletic (a)	W	3-1	Polly Wardle 50, Georgia Vandries 65, Amy Jefferies 85, *Polly Wardle sent off 85*	30	6
13.05	Larkhall Athletic (h)	D	1-1	Polly Wardle 65	63	6
20.05	Maidenhead U (a)	D	0-0		10	6

exp = Results expunged from records after Basingstoke withdrew from League   +Played at Keynsham Town FC

2017/18 FA CUP

08.10 RQ3	Torquay United (h)	D	0-0aet W(4-2p)		63
12.11 R1	Buckland Athletic (a)	W	4-1	Jodie Arkell 10, 78, Georgia Vandries 19, Kim Maggs 75	
03.12 R2	Swindon Town (h)	W	3-2 (aet)	Polly Wardle 49, Jodie Arkell 60, 117, *Georgia Vandries sent off 62*	67
07.01 R3	Keynsham Town (a)	L	1-8	Own goal 85	

2017/18 WPL CUP

03.09 DR	Crystal Palace (a)	L	1-10	Jodie Arkell 60	203

2017/18 WPL PLATE

22.10 R1	Cheltenham Town (a)	W	4-2	Jodie Arkell 8, 65, Chelsea Heal 29, Kim Maggs 34	63
10.12 R2	West Ham United (h)		P-P		
14.01 R2	West Ham United (h)	L	0-6		63

2017/18 SOMERSET FA COUNTY CUP

15.10 QF	Larkhall Athletic (h)	L	2-4	Sophie Whelan 18, Jodie Arkell 53

"The 2017/18 season was a mixed one. We started aiming high and changed a few things from previous years to see if we could reach the initial target set. We did learn a lot as individual players and as a team both on the field and off. We were playing good football in parts but something wasn't clicking. Towards the end of the season we reverted back to being the team we were before and enjoying the football we were playing which made a massive impact to the mood of the team resulting in a better atmosphere and results. Brislington is a club which is different to the rest as we are more of a family unit and all like to enjoy and have fun playing football whilst at a good standard."

Sophie Whelan, Brislington Captain

- Jodie Arkell was Brislington's top scorer in 2017/18, hitting six goals in the League and 14 in all competitions.

- Brislington won the South West Regional Premier Division in 2015/16 to gain promotion to WPL South West Division One (now WNL Division 1 South West) for 2016/17. During their first season at that level they enjoyed a comfortable 6th-place finish, a position they repeated in 2017/18.

- In 2011/12 – their first season after formation – Brislington competed in the Somerset County League Division Two. Despite most of their players being teenagers they won the title without dropping a point and with a goal difference of +186.

- The team groundshares Brislington Stadium at Ironmould Lane with the non-League men's club Brislington FC.

BUCKLAND ATHLETIC

2018/19: WNL
DIVISON 1 SOUTH WEST (Tier 4)

Founded: 2015

Nickname: The Bucks

Ground: Homers Heath,
(Buckland Athletic FC)

Season 2017/18:

WPL South West Reg Prem (Tier 5):
Champions
FA Cup: 1st Round
County Cup: 1st Round

2017/18 SOUTH WEST REGIONAL PREMIER

24.09	Middlezoy (h)	W	9-1	Courtney Butt, Hayley Chamberlain (x2), Amber Coates (x3), Laura Gough, Sarah Louise Stacey (x2)
29.10	Downend Flyers (a)	W	6-0	Kirsty Caunter, Laura Gough (x2), Kate Kine (x2), Gabrielle Trays
16.11	Exeter City (a)	W	5-0	Kirsty Caunter, Hayley Chamberlain (x3), Laura Gough
19.11	Ilminster Town (a)	W	2-0	Leah Brooks, Kirsty Caunter
26.11	Charleston (h)	W	10-1	Kirsty Caunter (x2), Hayley Chamberlain (x2), Amber Coates, Laura Gough (x2), Carla Staddon (x2), Corrine Potts
17.12	Keynsham Town Development (a)	W	5-4	Hayley Chamberlain (x2), Amber Coates (x2), Carla Staddon
21.01	Exeter City (h)	W	3-0	Hayley Chamberlain, Amber Coates, Carla Staddon
04.02	Downend Flyers (h)	W	8-0	Kirsty Caunter (x2), Hayley Chamberlain, Amber Coates, Laura Gough (x3), Kate Hine
18.02	Forest Green Rovers (a)	W	9-2	Kirsty Caunter (x5), Laura Gough (x2), Abigail Meyer, Leah Brooks
11.03	Marine Academy Plymouth (a)	W	6-1	Kirsty Caunter (x3), Hayley Chamberlain, Amber Coates, Laura Gough
18.03	Forest Green Rovers (h)	W	w/o	
25.03	Charleston (a)	W	w/o	
08.04	Keynsham Town Development (h)	W	3-0	Kirsty Caunter (x2), Amber Coates
15.04	Torquay United (a)	W	2-0	Amber Coates (x2)
22.04	Bishops Lydeard (a)*	W	6-0	Kirsty Caunter (x4), Hayley Chamberlain, Own Goal
22.04	Bishops Lydeard (h)*	W	5-0	Laura Gough (x2), Abigail Meyer, Sarah Louise Stacey, Kirsty Caunter
25.04	Ilminster Town (h)	W	3-0	Kirsty Caunter, Hayley Chamberlain, Laura Gough

29.04	AEK Boco (h)	W	w/o	
03.05	Marine Academy Plymouth (h)	W	3-0	Hayley Chamberlain, Laura Gough, Sarah Louise Stacey
06.05	AEK Boco (a)	W	7-1	Amber Coates (x3), Laura Gough (x2), Abigail Meyer (x2)
13.05	Middlezoy (a)	W	w/o	
20.05	Torquay United (h)	W	2-0	Amber Coates, Carla Staddon

*Double header (2 games of 60 minutes) played at Bishops Lydeard

2017/18 FA CUP

10.09 RQ1	Exeter City (h)	W	9-2	Kirsty Caunter (x3), Hayley Chamberlain, Laura Gough (x3), Emily Hannaford, Abigail Meyer
17.09 RQ2	Marine Academy Plymouth (a)	W	w/o	
08.10 RQ3	New Milton Town (a)	W	4-1	Kirsty Caunter, Laura Gough (x3)
12.11 R1	Brislington (h)	L	1-4	Emily Hannaford, *Gabrielle Trays sent off*

2017/18 DEVON FA COUNTY CUP

15.10 R1	Plymouth Argyle	L	3-4 (aet)	Hayley Chamberlain, Laura Gough (x2)

- Buckland Athletic Ladies have enjoyed a rapid rise since being founded as part of men's non-League club Buckland Athletic FC ahead of the 2015/16 season. In that debut campaign, under manager Grant Fisher, they won the Devon Women's League Division One without dropping a single point and lifted the League Cup.

- That 2015/16 title took them into the South West Regional League in which they became 2017/18 Premier champions without dropping a single point, winning all 18 of the matches they played and being handed four walkovers when opponents failed to fulfil fixtures.

- Kirsty Caunter finished 2017/18 as Buckland's top goalscorer. She hit 23 goals in 14 appearances in the League and 27 in 18 in all competitions.

BURNLEY

2018/19: WNL
DIVISION 1 NORTH (Tier 4)

Founded: 1995

Nickname: The Clarets

Ground: Barden Sports & Athletic Club in 2017/18, moving to Arbories Memorial Sports-Ground, (Padiham FC) for 2018/19

Season 2017/18:

North West Reg Prem (Tier 5): Champions

FA Cup: 3rd Round

League Cup: Semi-finals

County Cup: Quarter-finals

2017/18 NORTH WEST REGIONAL PREMIER

06.09	Accrington Sports (a)	W	11-0	Sarah Greenhalgh (x7), Vikki Eastwood, Lynette Craig, Lizzy Hamer, Joanna Rohman
10.09	Blackpool (h)^	W	6-1	Sarah Greenhalgh (x4), Vikki Eastwood, Lizzy Hamer
01.10	Tranmere R (a)	L	0-1	
05.11	Accrington Sports (h)*	W	4-0	Sarah Greenhalgh, Justine Wallace, Lynette Craig, Georgia Payton
19.11	Wigan Athletic (h) +	L	1-2	Georgia Payton
26.11	Stockport C (h)^	L	0-2	
17.12	Blackpool (a)	W	5-0	Sarah Greenhalgh (x2), Lynette Craig (x2), Evie Priestley
14.01	Wigan Athletic (a)	W	2-0	Evie Priestley, Own Goal
11.02	Fleetwood T W (h)^	W	4-0	Sarah Greenhalgh, Leah Embley, Evie Priestley (x2)
18.02	MSB Woolton (h)	W	7-1	Sarah Greenhalgh (x2), Lynette Craig (x2), Evie Priestley (x2), Sammy Fleck
11.03	Blackburn Comm. (h) ^^	W	2-1	Sarah Greenhalgh, Justine Wallace
11.03	Blackburn Comm. (a) ^^	W	1-0	Lynette Craig
25.03	MSB Woolton (a)	D	1-1	Leah Embley
01.04	Sir Tom Finney (h)*	W	5-0	Georgia Payton (x5)
04.04	Tranmere R (h)	W	5-0	Georgia Payton, Leah Embley (x4)
08.04	Sir Tom Finney (a)	W	5-1	Justine Wallace, Lynette Craig, Georgia Payton, Rebecca Hayton, Chloe Fell
11.04	Manchester Stingers (a)	W	4-0	Lynette Craig, Leah Embley, Rebecca Hayton, Holly Hunter
17.04	Manchester Stingers (h)	W	5-0	Lynette Craig, Georgia Payton (x2), Evie Priestley (x2)
19.04	Merseyrail Bootle (a)	W	2-0	Georgia Payton, Leah Embley
22.04	Fleetwood T W (a)	W	3-0	Lynette Craig, Leah Embley (x2)
25.04	Merseyrail Bootle (h)**	W	2-1	Lizzy Hamer, Georgia Payton
02.05	Stockport C (a)	W	2-0	Sarah Greenhalgh, Lynette Craig
13.05	CMB (h)++	W	4-0	Sarah Greenhalgh (x2, 1pen), Justine Wallace (pen), Vikki Eastwood
13.05	CMB (a)++	W	w/o	

*Played Hyndburn Leisure Centre 3G   +Played Cardinal Langley School 3G   ^Played Nelson & Colne College 3G
^^Double header, (2 games of 60 minutes played on same day at same venue)   **Played at Prairie Sports Village 3G
++Designated double header, but 2nd fixture did not take place due to CMB injuries

2017/18 FA CUP

03.09	RQ1	Fleetwood T W (a)	W	6-0	Sarah Greenhalgh (x4), Lizzy Hamer, Leah Embley
17.09	RQ2	Merseyrail Bootle (h)	W	4-3	Justine Wallace, Lizzy Hamer, Leah Embley, Evie Priestley
15.10	RQ3	Wigan A (h)	W	4-1	Sarah Greenhalgh (x2), Justine Wallace, Leah Embley
12.11	R1	Alnwick T J (a)	W	4-0	Sarah Greenhalgh, Lynette Craig (x2), Leah Embley
03.12	R2	Stoke City (a)	D	0-0aet (W 4-1p)	
07.01	R3	Cardiff City L (a)	L	2-3	Sarah Greenhalgh, Evie Priestley

2017/18 LEAGUE CUP

29.10	R1	Warrington Wolverines (a)	W	1-0	Sarah Greenhalgh
04.02	R2	Wigan A (a)	W	5-0	Justine Wallace (x2), Leah Embley (x2), Evie Priestley
25.02	QF	Fleetwood T W (a)	W	3-1 (aet)	Sarah Greenhalgh (x2), Evie Priestley
15.04	SF	Stockport C (h)	L	1-2	Justine Wallace

2017/18 LANCASHIRE FA COUNTY CUP

24.09	R1	Accrington Stanley C T (a)	W	11-0	Sarah Greenhalgh (x3), Vikki Eastwood, Georgia Payton (x3), Leah Embley (x2), Evie Priestley (x2)
22.10	QF	Bolton W (h)	L	0-4	

"The 2017/18 season was the most successful ever for the first-team as they topped the table and were promoted into the FA Women's National League Division 1 North. The team faced tough opposition from the beginning, however they worked tirelessly throughout the season to ultimately reign victorious. Alongside the League title, the squad made history by reaching the 3rd Round of the FA Cup, the furthest stage the club has ever got to. It rounded off quite the season for the Clarets, with exciting times ahead."

Matt Bee – Burnley Manager

- The 2017/18 season was the most successful in the club's history, as they won promotion to Tier 4 and reached the 1st Round proper of the FA Cup for the very first time, before going on to make it all the way to the 3rd Round.

- The North West Regional Premier title was clinched on the final day. Burnley were due to play CMB in a double header (when two games of 60 minutes' duration are played at the same venue on the same day because of fixture congestion) and needed one point from the six available. They won the opening fixture 4-0 to take the title, and the next match did not take place because CMB had sustained too many injuries.

- The Clarets' historic 2017/18 FA Cup run eventually ended at the 3rd Round Stage. They beat a team from two divisions higher along the way, knocking out Tier 3 Stoke City on penalties after a goalless draw in the 2nd Round. They were eventually beaten 3-2 by Cardiff City Ladies – also of Tier 3.

- The club was founded in 1995 by John Lister and was known as Burnley FC Girls and Ladies until being rebranded as Burnley FC Women at the end of 2017/18. They are formally affiliated with men's Premier League club Burnley FC.

BURTON ALBION

2018/19: WNL
DIVISON 1 MIDLANDS (Tier 4)

Founded: 2000

Nickname: The Brewers

Ground: Marston Road Ground,
 (Stafford Rangers FC) in 2017/18, moving to
The Lamb, (Tamworth FC) for 2018/19

Season 2017/18:

WPL Midlands One (Tier 4):
Runners-up

FA Cup: 3rd Qualifying Round
WPL Cup: Determining Round
WPL Plate: 1st Round
County Cup: 3rd Round

2017/18 WPL MIDLANDS ONE

Date	Opponent		Result	Scorers		
20.08	Leicester City L (a)	W	1-0	Jordan Atkin 41	85	
27.08	Sporting Khalsa (a)	W	2-1	Jordan Atkin 38, Charlotte Worth 90	60	
10.09	B'ham & W M (h)	W	4-1	Jordan Atkin 17, 71, 90, Jemma Grimadell 52	52	
20.09	Long Eaton United (h)	W	2-1	Jordan Atkin 49, 84	42	4
01.10	The New Saints (a)	L	1-7	Natasha Rothery 88	58	5
11.10	Long Eaton United (a)	W	1-0	Jemma Grimadell 48	52	5
05.11	Solihull Moors (a)	W	2-0	Yasmin Harris 56, 58	20	5
12.11	B'ham & WM (a)	W	3-1	Jordan Atkin 8, 80, Yasmin Harris 61	15	3
26.11	Radcliffe Olympic (a)	W	2-1	Hayleigh Sutton 35, Jordan Atkin 87	20	3
03.12	Sheffield United (a)	L	1-5	Charlotte Creswell 1	41	3
10.12	Sporting Khalsa (h)		P-P			3
17.12	The New Saints (h)		P-P			3
07.01	Loughborough F (a)	L	0-2		42	3
21.01	The New Saints (h)		P-P			4
28.01	Radcliffe Olympic (h)	L	1-2	Jordan Atkin 62	55	5
11.02	Loughborough F (h)	L	0-3		65	5
18.02	Rotherham United (h)	W	6-0	Jemma Grimadell 15, 73, Jordan Atkin 27, 76, 86, Lily Cocking 71	55	5
25.02	Leicester City L (h)	W	4-0	Hayleigh Sutton 9, 74, Jordan Atkin 24, Charlotte Cresswell 89	45	5
04.03	Steel City W (a)		P-P			5
11.03	Steel City W (a)	W	3-0	Sophia Bonser, Jordan Atkin 59, 88	60	4
18.03	Sporting Khalsa (h)		P-P			4
08.04	Sheffield United (h)	D	1-1	Jordan Atkin 31	63	4
15.04	Steel City W (h)	D	2-2	Jordan Atkin 14, 18	56	5
22.04	The New Saints (h)*	W	3-2	Jemma Grimadell 3, Jordan Atkin 14, 49	55	4

29.04	Rotherham United (a)	W	7-0	Sophia Bonser 26, Hannah Baines 50, Paris O'Connor 53, Amelia Robb 62, Jordan Atkin 71, 73, Lily Cocking 89	30	3
06.05	Solihull Moors (h)		P-P			3
13.05	Solihull Moors (h)	W	4-1	Hayleigh Sutton 18, Jordan Atkin missed pen 25 (saved by Kelly Woolley), Jordan Atkin 60, 84, Charlotte Cresswell 89	65	2
20.05	Sporting Khalsa (h)	W	4-2	Hayleigh Sutton 9, Jordan Atkin 36, 75, Hannah Baines 73	97	2

*Played at Etwall Leisure Centre

2017/18 FA CUP

| 08.10 RQ3 | Nettleham (h) | | L | 0-4 | | 30 |

2017/18 WPL CUP

| 03.09 DR | Middlesbrough (a) | | L | 0-5 | | 84 |

2017/18 WPL PLATE

| 22.10 R1 | Fylde (a) | | | P-P | | |
| 29.10 R1 | Fylde (a)+ | | L | 2-3 | Olivia Fuller (og) 9, Sophie Cordon 50 | 53 |

+Played at Leigh Sports Village

2017/18 COUNTY CUP

| 19.11 R2 | Kinghurst Sporting Club (h) | W | w/o |
| 14.01 R3 | Coventry United (a)* | L | 0-12 |

*Played at Warwick University

"Our players and staff are very proud to represent the town of Burton-upon-Trent on the national stage. Everyone understands that they are in a privileged position and are excellent role models for the young female footballers within our local community. The club's rise through the leagues over recent years has been remarkable. We were all delighted to finish as runners-up in 2017/18 and are determined to build on this success."

Jack White – Burton Albion Manager

- The 2017/18 season was a highly impressive first campaign in Tier 4 for Burton having been promoted as 2016/17 West Midlands Regional Premier League champions. Albion immediately adapted to life at a new level and finished as runners-up in WPL Midlands One (now WNL Division 1 Midlands). It was their 4-2 win at home to Sporting Khalsa on the final day that secured 2nd place.

- Burton striker Jordan Atkin finished 2017/18 as the highest scorer in the division (League goals only). She hit a stunning 29 in 22 appearances in WPL Midlands One, bagging three hat-tricks against Birmingham & West Midlands, Rotherham and Solihull Moors.

- Prior to their debut season in Tier 4 in 2017/18 the club enjoyed a rapid rise to prominence, winning four League titles in a row, including League and Cup Doubles in 2014/15, 2015/16 and 2016/17.

C&K BASILDON

2018/19: WNL
SOUTHERN PREMIER (Tier 3)

Founded: 2004 (as Basildon Town Ladies)

Nickname: None

Ground: The Frost Financial Stadium, (Canvey Island FC)

Season 2017/18:

WPL Southern (Tier 3): Runners-up

FA Cup: 2nd Round
WPL Cup: 2nd Round
County Cup: Winners

2017/18 WPL SOUTHERN

Date	Opponent		Result	Scorers	Att	
20.08	Chichester City (h)	W	2-0	April-Rose Bowers 28, Danica Revell 72	152	
27.08	Lewes (a)	D	1-1	Angela Addison 17	112	
10.09	West Ham United (h)	W	3-0	Angela Addison 23, Jay Blackie 48, Zoe Rusheen 71	87	
21.09	Gillingham (a)	W	3-1	Jay Blackie 7, Danica Revell 40, April-Rose Bowers (pen) 90+6	52	3
24.09	Charlton Athletic (a)	L	1-4	Angela Addison 78, *Zoe Rushen missed pen 50 (saved Katie Startup), C&K GK Nikita Runnacles saved Ruby Southgate pen 88*	147	4
01.10	QPR (h)	W	1-0	Zoe Rushen 15	71	4
08.10	Coventry United (a)	L	1-4	Therese Addison 61	102	5
11.10	Gillingham (h)	W	3-0	Angela Addison 33, April-Rose Bowers, Hayley West 87	63	4
29.10	Charlton Athletic (h)	W	2-1	Angela Addison 9, April-Rose Bowers	87	3
05.11	Swindon Town (a)	W	3-0	Angela Addison 50, Therese Addison 65, April-Rose Bowers 85	36	3
12.11	Cardiff City L (h)	W	5-0	Jay Blackie 11, 24, Angela Addison 41, 57 Danica Revell 68	52	2
26.11	West Ham United (a)	W	7-3	April-Rose Bowers 3, 11, 62, Danica Revell 7, Therese Addison 40, Jay Blackie 45, Angela Addison 89	253	2
28.01	Crystal Palace (h)	W	1-0	Angela Addison 37	172	3
04.02	Swindon Town (h)	W	3-1	Angela Addison 27, 35, Zoe Rushen 44	45	2
11.02	QPR (a)	W	3-1	Jay Blackie 15, Angela Addison 67, 73	52	1
04.03	Portsmouth (h)	P-P				1
11.03	Crystal Palace (a)	P-P				3
25.03	Cardiff City L (a)	W	4-2	Paige Wakefield 11, 81, Therese Addison 20, Angela Addison 48	80	2

08.04	Coventry United (h)	W	1-0	Zoe Rushen 48	47	2
15.04	Crystal Palace (a)	L	0-2	*Kerry-Anne Stimson sent off 87*	336	2
22.04	Lewes (h)	W	1-0	Hayley West 33	81	2
29.04	Portsmouth (h)	W	4-2	Angela Addison 8, Laken Duchar Clark 21, Jay Blackie 24, Therese Addison 71	61	1
06.05	Portsmouth (a)	L	1-2	Angela Addison 53, *Zoe Rushen missed penalty 54*	51	2
13.05	Chichester City (a)	W	1-0	Zoe Rushen 83	61	2

2017/18 FA CUP

03.12 R2	Chichester City (a)	L	2-4 (aet)	*Amy Nash sent off 16*, Zoe Rushen (pen) 25, Therese Addison 43	75

2017/18 WPL CUP

03.09 DR	Basinsgstoke Town (h)	W	8-0	Angela Addison (x5), Jay Blackie (x3)	62
22.10 R1	Ipswich Town (a)	W	w/o	Ipswich won 1-0 but were expelled from competition for fielding ineligible player	46
10.12 R2	Charlton Athletic (h)		P-P		
17.12 R2	Charlton Athletic (h)		P-P		
14.01 R2	Charlton Athletic (h)	L	1-2 (aet)	Angela Addison 38	147

2017/18 ESSEX COUNTY CUP

21.01 QF	Colchester Town (h)	W	w/o		
18.02 SF	Little Thurrock Dynamos (h)+	W	9-0	Zoe Rushen 10, 85, *Zoe Rushen missed pen 75*, Therese Addison 48, 87, Jay Blackie 59, 62, 70, 89, Therese Addison, April-Rose Bowers 83	72
29.03	Brentwood (n)	W	7-0	Angela Addison 13, 38, 48, 90+1, Jay Blackie 77, Zoe Rushen 81, 90+3	370

+Played at Basildon Sport & Leisure Club   (n) Played at Parkside, Aveley FC

"What we achieved in 2017/18 feels like a bit of a dream. To be runners-up in the WPL Southern, a team full of talented sides, was a magnificent achievement. I feel extremely lucky and proud to have been captain and leader of such an incredible group. The work-rate, team spirit and togetherness were key reasons why teams found it so hard to play against us. Bringing through so many talented players from our development squad was also something the club can be really proud of. We are a supportive, friendly and welcoming club that has stood together on and off the pitch."

Zoe Rushen, C&K Basildon Captain

- Despite having fewer resources than several of their divisional rivals, C&K have become one of the top teams in Tier 3 and enjoyed their best ever season in 2017/18 finishing as runners-up in WPL Southern (now WNL Southern Premier) and also winning the Essex FA County Cup. Their application to join Tier 2 (the newly-launched Championship) for 2018/19 was, however, unsuccessful.

- The manager who led C&K to that 2017/18 League runners-up position was Steve Tilson – formerly in charge of men's Football League side Southend United. He became C&K Basildon boss in 2015.

- The team started out as part of Basildon Town men's club before founder and former manager Peter King changed the name to C&K Basildon, naming it after his insurance company CKRE. In 2008 they were promoted out of the Essex County League with five League titles in seven seasons taking them into Tier 4 for the 2015/16 season.

- Their 2017/18 Essex FA County Cup triumph saw them lift the trophy for the fourth year in a row and the fifth time in six years (2012/13, 2014/15, 2015/16, 2016/17 and now 2017/18).

CAMBRIDGE UNITED

2018/19: WNL DIVISION ONE SOUTH EAST (Tier 4)

Founded: 2009 (as Cambridge Women)

Nickname: The U's

Ground: Recreation Way, (Mildenhall Town FC)

Season 2017/18:

WPL South East One (Tier 4): 8th

FA Cup: 1st Round
WPL Cup: 2nd Round
County Cup: Runners-up

2017/18 WPL South East One

Date	Opponent	Result	Score	Scorers	Att	Pos
20.08	Leyton Orient (h)	D	0-0		72	
27.08	Denham United (a)	W	3-1	Emma Whitter 17, Nuala Wayne 43, 60	105	
10.09	Ipswich Town (h)	D	2-2	Amy Howlett, Nuala Wayne	72	
17.09	Stevenage (a)	D	1-1	Emma Jenkins 90	70	7
20.09	MK Dons (a)	L	0-1		85	8
24.09	Denham United (h)	D	2-2	Lauren Gibson, Laura Bright 78	65	8
01.10	Haringey Borough (h)	W	12-2	Kelley Blanchflower 1, 45+3, 49, Amy Howlett 18, 23, 53 Laura Bright 38, Amber Cantwell 65, 71, 90+1, Emma Jenkins 76, Lauren Gibson 87	48	5
11.10	MK Dons (h)	L	0-2		85	6
22.10	AFC Wimbledon (h)	L	0-1		60	7
29.10	Norwich City (h)	W	2-1	Amy Howlett 9, Lauren Cartwright 40	45	6
05.11	Haringey Borough (a)	W	7-0	Emma Jenkins 8, 37, Nuala Wayne 39, *Lauren Cartwright missed pen 50 (saved)*, Laura Baker 59, Lauren Cartwright 67, Lauren Gibson 71, 80	25	5
26.11	Actonians (a)	D	0-0		25	6
07.01	AFC Wimbledon (a)	L	0-2		70	6
14.01	Stevenage (h)	W	2-1	Amber Cantwell, Amy Howlett	45	6
11.02	Enfield Town (a)	L	0-1		42	6
25.02	Ipswich Town (a)	L	1-3	*Amber Cantwell missed pen 44 (saved Sian Fagg)*, Amber Cantwell 59	55	6
11.03	Leyton Orient (a)	W	1-0	Faith Hewitt 21, *Lauren Cartwright sent off 56*	56	6
25.03	Luton Town (h)*	W	1-0	Amber Cantwell 85	50	5
08.04	Actonians (h)	L	0-2		74	7
29.04	Enfield Town (h)	W	1-0	Laura Baker (pen) 60	60	7
13.05	Norwich City (a)	L	2-3	Amy Howlett (pen) 45, Mollie Coupar 65	60	8
17.05	Luton Town (a)^	D	3-3	Kelley Blanchflower (x2), Victoria Neal	121	8

*Played at Clare College Sports Ground   ^Played at The Brache, Luton FC Training Ground

2017/18 FA Cup

08.10 RQ3	Norwich City (h)	W	4-0	Lauren Gibson (x2), Carolyn Sarafian, Nuala Wayne 89	48
12.11 R1	Long Eaton United (h)	L	0-1		

2017/18 WPL Cup

03.09 DR	St Nicholas (a)	W	5-0	Teonie Peyton 6, 43, Amy Howlett 53, Lauren Gibson 61, Emma Jenkins 75	40
15.10 R1	Enfield Town (a)	W	2-0	Laura Baker 29, Kelley Blanchflower 44	43
10.12 R2	Coventry United (h)		P-P		
17.12 R2	Coventry United (h)		P-P		
21.01 R2	Coventry United (h)		P-P		
28.01 R2	Coventry United (h)	L	0-5		70

2017/18 Cambridgeshire FA County Cup

18.02 R2	Wisbech St Mary (a)	W	12-0	Charlotte Crisp (x2), Laura Bright (x2) Faith Hewitt (x3), Laura Baker (x3), Teonie Peyton, Carolyn Sarafian
18.03 SF	Newmarket Town (h)	W	3-0	Lauren Gibson 41, Kelley Blanchflower 46, Faith Hewitt 50
10.05 F	Cambridge City (n)	L	1-3	

(n) Played at Bridge Road, Histon FC

- Lauren Gibson and Amy Howlett were joint top-scorers for the U's in 2017/18. They both hit eight goals in all competitions.

- Cambridge's teenage player Ruth Fox became a published author in 2018 and served as an inspiration to many when she went public with her battles against depression in her book: 'The Unseen Battle: One young footballer's struggle off the pitch.'

- Cambridge Women's FC merged with the Cambridge United men's professional outfit in May 2015 and changed their name to the same.

- Cambridge Women had themselves been formed when two clubs – Cambridge City and Cambridge United (who weren't affiliated to the men's club) joined forces in 2009. Today a new Cambridge City side also exists.

CARDIFF CITY LADIES

2018/19: WNL SOUTHERN PREMIER (Tier 3)

Founded: 1975 (as Llanedeyrn)

Nickname: The Bluebirds

Ground: CCB Centre for Sporting Excellence

Season 2017/18:

WPL Southern (Tier 3): 10th

FA Cup: 5th Round

WPL Cup: 2nd Round

2017/18 WPL SOUTHERN

20.08	Portsmouth (a)	L	1-4	Kelly Isaac 48, Laura Williams sent off 50	122	
27.08	West Ham United (a)	L	3-4	Cori Williams (x2), Chloe O'Connar	150	
10.09	Chichester City (h)	L	2-5	Cori Williams (pen) 7, Caitlin Morris 34	75	
21.09	Swindon Town (h)	W	4-1	Laura Williams 14, Cori Williams 25, 68, Ffion Price 64	80	9
01.10	Charlton Athletic (h)	L	1-3	Cori Williams 55	85	9
08.10	QPR (a)	W	4-3	Zoe Atkins 5, 14, Laura Williams 49, Ella Powell 52	27	9
05.11	Lewes (h)	L	2-3	Cori Williams 1, Chloe O'Connar 45	70	10
12.11	C&K Basildon (a)	L	0-5		52	10
14.11	Swindon Town (a)	W	6-0	Zoe Atkins, Cori Williams (x4), Jasmine Turner	36	9
19.11	Chichester City (a)	D	3-3	Daisy Evan-Watkins 8, Kelly Isaac 17, Cori Williams 74	80	8
26.11	Crystal Palace (a)	L	0-2		70	8
14.01	QPR (h)	D	1-1	Zoe Atkins 63	100	8
28.01	West Ham United (h)	L	2-6	Kelly Isaac 70, Estelle Randall 75	85	9
11.02	Gillingham (a)	D	1-1	Zoe Atkins 64	123	9
25.02	Portsmouth (h)	L	0-2		80	9
11.03	Charlton Athletic (a)	L	1-5	Cori Williams (pen) 31	94	10
25.03	C&K Basildon (h)	L	2-4	Cori Williams, Sophie Thomas	80	10
08.04	Crystal Palace (h)	L	2-5	Cori Williams (x2)	85	10
12.04	Coventry United (h)	D	2-2	Cori Williams 57, Ella Powell 90	75	10
15.04	Gillingham (h)	W	3-2	Kelly Isaac 7, Cori Williams 57, Ella Powell 68	95	9
06.05	Coventry United (a)	L	0-4	Nia Rees sent off 12	65	10
13.05	Lewes (a)	L	0-4		446	10

2017/18 FA CUP

03.12 R2	MK Dons (a)	W	1-0	Jasmine Turner 85	110
07.01 R3	Burnley (h)	W	3-2	Cori Williams 7, 86, Ella Powell 52	185
04.02 R4	Oxford United (h)	D	0-0aet (W 5-4p)		270
18.02 R5	Charlton Athletic (h)	L	1-3	Cori Williams 75	295

2017/18 WPL CUP

03.09 DR	Norwich City (a)	W	5-0	Kelly Isaac (x2), Cori Williams (x3)	72
29.10 R1	Leyton Orient (h)	W	3-1	Cori Williams 48, 61, Ella Powell 72	85
10.12 R2	Plymouth Argyle (h)		P-P		
17.12 R2	Plymouth Argyle (h)	L	1-2	Cori Williams	50

"Having played for the club for 10 years, 2017/18 was one of our most difficult seasons because we lost so many players at the start of the campaign to WSL clubs. Our great determination and spirit shone through in the end as we avoided relegation with a few games to spare. We also had a terrific run in the FA Cup, making it all the way to the 5th Round. We beat WSL 2 side Oxford on penalties and were eventually knocked out by a very good Charlton team who went on to win the WPL Southern title."

Cori Williams, Cardiff City Captain

- Cori Williams finished 2017/18 as Cardiff's top scorer. She hit 18 goals in the League and 28 in all competitions including a four-goal haul v Swindon and a hat-trick v Norwich in the WPL Cup.

- Cardiff City Ladies are not to be confused with Cardiff City Women who play in the Welsh Premier League. Formed as Llanedeyrn in 1975, Cardiff City Ladies are the oldest women's club in Wales. They were formerly affiliated to the men's professional Cardiff City between 2001 and 2003. It is now Cardiff City Women who are affiliated to Cardiff City men's club.

- Cardiff City Ladies were champions of the WPL Southern Division in 2005/06 and were promoted to the WPL National Division for the first time. The WPL National Division was scrapped when WSL 2 was introduced ahead of 2014/15.

CHELTENHAM TOWN

2018/19: WNL DIVISION 1 SOUTH WEST (Tier 4)

Founded: Circa 1997

Nickname: The Robins

Ground: Petersfield Park (Cheltenham Saracens FC)

Season 2017/18:

WPL South West One (Tier 4): 9th

FA Cup: 3rd Qualifying Round
WPL Cup: Determining Round
WPL Plate: 1st Round
County Cup: Runners-up

2017/18 WPL SOUTH WEST ONE

20.08	So'ton Saints (a)	L	0-2		50	
27.08	Keynsham Town (h)	L	0-4		62	
10.09	Maidenhead U (h)*	L	1-2	Ria Salleh 25	211	
17.09	So'ton Saints (h)	L	0-1		29	11
19.09	St Nicholas (h)	W	3-1	Sally Butterfield 55, Ella Hitchcox 60, Ria Salleh 68	42	7
24.09	Plymouth Argyle (h)	L	0-5		39	8
01.10	Larkhall Athletic (a)	L	4-5	Samantha Morris, Ella Hitchcox (x2), Jane Wiltshire	40	9
12.10	St Nicholas (a)+	W	3-0	Jennifer Brown Wealls (pen), Louise Fensome (x2)	40	7
05.11	Brislington (h)	L	1-4	Louise Fensome	47	9
12.11	Poole Town (a)	P-P				9
26.11	Larkhall Athletic (h)	W	1-0	Holly Rogers	36	8
03.12	Poole Town (a)	P-P				8
17.12	Maidenhead U (a)	L	2-3	Ella Hitchcox, Own Goal	15	9
28.01	Basingstoke T (h) (NB)	P-P				10
11.02	Poole Town (a)	L	1-6	Lydia Amarquay 10	17	10
25.02	Poole Town (h)	L	0-2		53	10
04.03	Plymouth Argyle (a)	P-P				10
11.03	So'ton Women (a)	L	0-2		35	8
22.03	Brislington (a)	D	0-0		62	8
22.04	Keynsham Town (a)	L	0-9		50	9
16.05	Plymouth Argyle (a)	L	0-9		32	9
20.05	So'ton Women (h)	L	1-3	Annabel Davies 49	78	9

*Played at Whaddon Road, Cheltenham Town FC   +Match abandoned after 87 mins after floodlight catches fire. Result stands

(NB) Match never rearranged because Basingstoke went on to resign from League

2017/18 FA Cup

08.10 RQ3	So'ton Saints (h)	L	1-4	Sally Butterfield	50

2017/18 WPL Cup

03.09 DR	Actonians (h)	L	1-2	Louise Fensome	35

2017/18 WPL Plate

22.10 R1	Brislington (h)	L	2-4	Jennifer Brown Wealls, Eleanor Marie Briscoe	63

2017/18 Gloucestershire FA County Cup

19.11	Forest Green R (a)*	W	1-0	Ella Hitchcox 16	148
18.02 QF	Downend Flyers (a)	W	2-0	Charlie Rowlands, Kayleigh Hateley	
25.03 SF	Cheltenham Civil Service (a)	W	w/o		
17.04 F	St Nicholas (n)	L	0-1		

*Played at Whaddon Road, Cheltenham Town FC   (n) Played at Almondsbury, Gloucester FA County Headquarters

"We are the leading senior ladies club in the region and have a youth set up from ages 10 and above. We are a self-funded club that takes pride in being part of our community. In 2017/18 we introduced a number of Under-18s into our first-team and while they are still settling in I am proud to say that they do not look out of place in our division."

Jen Brown-Wealls Current longest-serving Cheltenham player (more than 80 appearances)

- Cheltenham's final day crowd of 78 for their home game against Southampton Women was the 2nd-highest in the division that day and the 9th-highest in the whole of the WPL.

- The match away to St Nicholas on 12 October was abandoned with three minutes remaining after one of the floodlights caught fire. Cheltenham led 3-0 and the result stood.

- The 2018/19 season is Cheltenham Town's fifth consecutive s at Tier 4 level and 2019/20 will be their 30th anniversary season having been founded in 1989.

CHESHAM UNITED

2018/19: WNL DIVISION 1 SOUTH WEST (Tier 4)

Founded: 1995

Nickname: The Generals

Ground: The Meadow
(Chesham United FC)

Season 2017/18:

Southern Regional Prem (Tier 5): Champions

FA Cup: 1st Round

League Cup: Winners

County Cup: Semi-final

2017/18 SOUTHERN REGIONAL PREMIER

Date	Opponent		Result	Scorers
10.09	Ascot United (h)	W	6-0	Niamh Euman (x2), Stephanie Weston, Barbara Balint, Gemma Fraser (x2)
24.09	Winchester City Flyers (h)	W	4-1	Dawne Campbell, Gemma Fraser (x2), Joanne Horwood
22.10	Team Solent (a)	W	12-1	Emma Delves, Gemma Fraser (x5), Joanne Horwood, Tasha Smith, Sarah Hazell (x2), Natalie Adams, Sarah Harrison
29.10	New Milton T (h)	W	6-0	Gemma Fraser (x6)
05.11	Oxford City (a)	W	5-4	Niamh Euman, Gemma Fraser (x3), Sarah Hazell
26.11	Newbury (h)	W	4-0	Emma Delves, Stephanie Weston (x2), Lidia Niedertubbesing-Lopez
03.12	Milton Keynes City (a)	W	5-0	Lidia Niedertubbesing-Lopez, Tasha Smith, Sarah Hazell, Sarah Harrison (x2)
10.12	Team Solent (h)	W	w/o	
07.01	Ascot United (a)	W	7-1	Kate Bowers, Dawne Campbell, Emma Delves, Sarah Hazell, Gemma Fraser (x2), Lidia Niedertubbesing-Lopez
28.01	Milton Keynes City (h)	W	6-0	Kate Bowers (x3), Sarah Hazell, Gemma Fraser (x2)
04.02	Newbury (a)	W	5-1	Natalie Adams, Gemma Fraser (x2), Tasha Smith, Sarah Hazell
25.02	Winchester City Flyers (a)	W	7-0	Kate Bowers, Gemma Fraser (x5), Aoife Hanling
25.03	New Milton T (a)	W	w/o	
08.04	Shanklin (h)	W	w/o	
15.04	Shanklin (a)	W	10-0	Kate Bowers (x3), Emma Delves, Gemma Fraser (x3), Lidia Niedertubbesing-Lopez, Sara Harrison (x2)
26.04	Oxford City (h)	W	2-0	Gemma Fraser (x2)

2017/18 FA CUP

Date		Opponent		Result	Scorers
03.09	RQ1	Brentford (a)	W	7-1	Natalie Adams, Gemma Fraser (x4), Kirsty Gladwin, Barbara Blint
17.09	RQ2	Ascot United (a)	W	2-0	Tasha Smith, Kate Bowers
08.10	RQ3	Whyteleafe (h)	W	2-1	Paula Lambert, Natalie Adams
12.11	R1	New London Lionesses (h)	L	1-2 (aet)	Natalie Adams

2017/18 League Cup

01.10 PR	Oxford City (h)	W	2-1 (aet)	Dawne Campbell, Kate Bowers
15.10 R1	Winchester City Flyers (a)	W	4-0	Emma Delves, Kirsty Gladwin, Niamh Euman (x2)
14.01 QF	Ascot United (h)	W	11-0	Natalie Adams, Kate Bowers (x2), Paula Lambert, Tasha Smith (x2), Sarah Hazell, Gemma Fraser (x4)
11.03 SF	Woodley United (h)	W	4-0	Gemma Darvell, Sarah Harrison, Lidia Niedertub-besing-Lopez, Own Goal
20.05 F	Bournemouth CST (n)	W	3-1	Gemma Fraser (x3)

(n) Played at Alton Town FC

2017/18 Berks & Bucks FA County Cup

19.11 QF	Barton Rovers (a)	W	5-0	Kate Bowers (x2), Emma Delves, Niamh Euman, Own Goal
18.02 SF	MK Dons (h)	L	1-2	Gemma Darvell

"I've played for the club for more than 20 years and this was one of our best seasons. We came into 2017/18 buzzing after causing an upset against MK Dons in the 2017 Berks & Bucks FA County Cup final, and we just continued from where we had left off. An early victory against Oxford City in the League Cup made us believe we could win the League and we never looked back. Personally I was disappointed that I missed the last four or five games, as did a few others but our youngsters stepped up and we completed League and League Cup Double. We played well throughout the season and kept disciplined in the games that weren't very challenging. We are all looking forward to 2018/19 where we know we will be challenged in every single game."

Dawne Campbell – Chesham United Captain

- Chesham were crowned 2017/18 Southern Regional Premier League champions without dropping a single point and were promoted to WNL Division 1 South West. They completed the season with maximum points by beating runners-up Oxford City 2-0 on the final day of the season with a brace from Gemma Fraser. Three of their victories were walkovers as their opponents failed to fulfil the fixture.

- They went on to complete a League and Cup Double for 2017/18 as a hat-trick from Fraser saw them beat Bournemouth 3-0 in the Southern Regional Premier League Cup final.

- Fraser was the club's top goalscorer for 2017/18, hitting an astonishing 45 goals in 21 appearances in all competitions, a total which included 34 in 11 League appearances. These figures also made her the division's top scorer for League goals as well as for goals in all competitions.

CHESTER-LE-STREET TOWN

2018/19: WNL DIVISION 1 NORTH (Tier 4)

Founded: 2009

Nickname: Town / The Cestrians

Ground: Moor Park
(Chester-le-Street Town FC)

Season 2017/18:

WPL Northern One (Tier 4): 9th

FA Cup: 1st Round
WPL Cup: 1st Round
County Cup: Runners-up

2017/18 WPL NORTHERN ONE

Date	Opponent	Result	Score	Scorers		
20.08	Liverpool M F (a)	L	0-4		30	
27.08	Leeds United (a)*	L	0-1		840	
10.09	Brighouse Town (h)	L	2-6	Nichole Goundry-Havery 3, 35	40	
19.09	Newcastle United (h)	W	3-2	Nichole Goundry-Havery 21, Own Goal 44, Maddy Atkinson 66	90	11
24.09	Mossley Hill A (a)	W	2-0	Scorer unknown, Elisha Jones 86	20	7
01.10	Barnsley (h)	L	2-5	Chloe Johnson (pen) 40, Scorer Unknown 57	30	9
10.10	Newcastle United (a)+	D	3-3	Katie Ellison 18, Rachel Mellor 29, Brogan Prudhoe 36	72	8
05.11	Bolton Wanderers (h)	W	1-0	Katie Ellison 60 (Chester-le-Street missed pen, Ellison scored rebound)	30	7
19.11	Barnsley (a)	L	1-3	Maddy Atkinson 80	30	9
26.11	Hull City (a)	L	1-2	Nichole Goundry-Havery 10	40	9
03.12	Morecambe (h)	P-P				9
14.01	Crewe Alexandra (h)	L	1-2	Nichole Goundry-Havery 7	30	10
11.02	Mossley Hill A (h)	P-P				11
25.02	Crewe Alexandra (a)	L	2-6	Nichole Goundry-Havery (pen) 41, Brogan Prudhoe 80	50	11
04.03	Chorley (a)	P-P				11
11.03	Bolton Wanderers (a)++	L	1-2	Nichole Goundry-Havery 82	40	11
18.03	Morecambe (h)	P-P				11
25.03	Brighouse Town (a)	L	2-4	Nichole Goundry-Havery 47, Maddy Atkinson 58	92	11
01.04	Morecambe (a)	W	3-2	Nichole Goundry-Havery 36, 80, Brogan Prudhoe 73	25	11
03.04	Morecambe (h)	W	2-1	Nichole Goundry-Havery 3, Kacie Elson 29	30	8
08.04	Mossley Hill A (h)^	W	3-1	Nichole Goundry-Havery 51, 72, Kacie Elson 54	40	7
15.04	Hull City (h)	L	0-1		30	8

22.04	Chorley (h)	W	2-1	Nichole Goundry-Havery 26, Kacie Elson 59	40	7
29.04	Leeds United (h)	W	3-0	Laura Hockaday 32, Nichole Goundry-Havery 48, Kacie Elson 58	50	7
06.05	Chorley (a)	L	1-2	Nichole Goundry-Havery 65	55	9
20.05	Liverpool M F (h)	L	0-1		30	9

*Played at Elland Road, Leeds United FC   +Played at Whitley Park   ++Played at Lostock Academy   ^
Played at The Graham Sports Centre

2017/18 FA Cup

| 08.10 RQ3 | Barnsley (h) | W | 2-1 | Nichole Goundry-Havery 44, 53 | 30 |
| 12.11 R1 | Brighouse Town (a) | L | 1-6 | Elisha Jones 53 | 43 |

2017/18 WPL Cup

03.09 DR	Hull City (h)	W	3-2	Laura Hockaday 49, Elisha Jones 60, Nichole Goundry-Havery 75	30
22.10 R1	Brighouse Town (a)	P-P			
29.10 R1	Brighouse Town (a)	L	1-5	*Kimberley Wild sent off 39*, Nichole Goundry-Havery 76	65

2017/18 Durham FA County Cup

17.12 R1	South Shields (h)		P-P	
07.01 R1	South Shields (h)	W	3-1	
21.01 R2	Norton & Stockton A Reserves (a)		P-P	
28.01 R2	Norton & Stockton A Reserves (a)		P-P	
04.02 QF	Norton & Stockton A Reserves (a)	W	7-0	
18.02 SF	Consett (h)	W	7-0	
03.05 F	Norton & Stockton A (n)	D	2-2aet (L 4-5p)	

(n) Played at The Hetton Centre

- Chester-le-Street Town have been playing in Tier 4 since three successive promotions carried them up to that level ahead of the 2013/14 season. Their highest finish is 4th in 2016/17.

- In 2017/18, Town were a penalty shootout away from winning the Durham FA County Cup for the fourth year in a row. After a 2-2 draw they lost to Tier 5 Norton & Stockton Ancients on spot-kicks.

- The team is affiliated with Chester-le-Street Town FC men and plays its home games at the same Moor Park stadium.

CHICHESTER CITY

2018/19: WNL SOUTHERN PREMIER (Tier 3)

Founded: 1991

Nickname: Lilywhites / Green Army

Ground: Oaklands Park,
(Chichester City FC)

Season 2017/18:

WPL Southern Premier (Tier 3): 8th

FA Cup: 5th Round
WPL Cup: 1st Round

2017/18 WPL SOUTHERN

Date	Opponent		Result	Scorers	Att	Pos
20.08	C&K Basildon (a)	L	0-2		152	
27.08	Crystal Palace (h)	L	2-4	Charley Wilson-Blakely, Gemma Simmonds	81	
10.09	Cardiff City L (a)	W	5-2	Charley Wilson-Blakely (x2), Jess Lewry, Jenna Fowlie, Own Goal	75	
17.09	West Ham United (h)	W	4-0	Cherelle Khassal, Charley Wilson-Blakely (x2), Jade Widdows	80	6
20.09	Portsmouth (a)	D	2-2	Charley Wilson-Blakely 34, Cherelle Khassal 53, Kerrie Ryan sent off 73	271	6
24.09	Lewes (h)	L	1-2	Chloe Tucker 20	85	7
01.10	Swindon Town (a)	W	7-4	Charley Wilson-Blakely 19, 35, 48, Hollie Wride 27, Cherelle Khassal 37, 90, Alex Collighan 70	39	5
08.10	Lewes (a)	D	2-2	Charley Wilson-Blakely (x2)	145	6
12.10	Portsmouth (h)	W	3-2	Jess Lewry 28, Cherelle Khassal 30, Jenna Fowlie 54	290	5
05.11	QPR (a)	D	1-1	Kerrie Ryan missed pen 35, Gemma Simmonds 85	51	6
12.11	Crystal Palace (a)	L	1-4	Cherelle Khassal 81	121	7
19.11	Cardiff City L (h)	D	3-3	Jess Lewry 19, Hollie Wride 41, (pen) 58	80	6
26.11	Gillingham (a)	W	4-0	Hollie Wride 40, Hollie Wride missed pen 47, Jade Widdows 71, Laura Ingram 75, Jess Lewry 77	78	6
10.12	Gillingham (h)		P-P			6
21.01	Swindon Town (h)		P-P			6
28.01	Gillingham (h)		P-P			6
04.03	Gillingham (h)		P-P			7
11.03	West Ham United (a)	L	0-2		198	7
18.03	Swindon Town (h)		P-P			7
25.03	Gillingham (h)*	W	1-0	Jess Lewry 61	50	7
15.04	Coventry United (a)	L	1-3	Jade Widdows 46	60	8
22.04	Swindon Town (h)	W	2-1	Jade Widdows 62, Jess Lewry 90+4	50	8
29.04	Coventry United (h)	L	0-3		60	8
02.05	Charlton Athletic (h)	L	0-6		112	8
06.05	QPR (h)	W	3-0	Natasha Stephens missed pen 53 (saved by Lauren Dolbear), Laura Ingram 60, Jess Lewry 73, Alex Collighan 90	82	7

| 13.05 | C&K Basildon (h) | L | 0-1 | | 61 | 7 |
| 20.05 | Charlton Athletic (a) | L | 1-4 | Natasha Stephens 79 | 203 | 8 |

*Played at Nyewood Lane, Bognor Regis Town FC

2017/18 FA CUP

03.12 R2	C&K Basildon (h)	W	4-2 aet	Jess Lewry 7, Jade Widdows 53, *Jess Lewry sent off 56*, Emma Alexandre 104, Cherelle Khassal 105+3	
07.01 R3	Luton Town (h)	W	2-0	Alex Collinghan 85, Cherelle Khassal 89	
04.02 R4	The New Saints (a)	D	1-1 aet (W 5-4 p)	Cherelle Khassal 51	272
18.02 R5	Liverpool (h)	L	0-3		1,300

2017/18 WPL CUP

03.09 DR	West Ham United (h)	W	4-1	Jess Lewry 13, 60, Cherelle Khassal 87, Chloe Tucker 90	70
22.10 R1	Plymouth Argyle (a)		P-P		
29.10 R1	Plymouth Argyle (a)	L	1-3	Jade Widdows	63

"I think the fact we survived and beat teams nobody thought we could was a big achievement for us in 2017/18, being an underdog can be hard as it can go one of two ways. Our biggest achievement though as a club was playing Liverpool at home in the FA Cup 5th Round. So, we lost 3-0 but what a day! It wasn't like we sat on the back foot either we were just not clinical enough and in those games you need to be. In 2018/19, I have hopes that it will be the best season yet. Plenty of hard work and a good team ethos should make this a team hard to break down and see us produce the right results."

Lauren Cheshire – 2018/19 Chichester City Captain

- In 2017/18 Chichester City's reward for coming through FA Cup ties against C&K Basildon, Luton Town and The New Saints was arguably the biggest match in their history. They drew two-time WSL champions Liverpool at home in the 5th Round. A crowd of 1,300 was present at Oaklands Park as the part-timers took on one of the biggest clubs in English football and acquitted themselves well before going down 3-0.

- To set up the tie with Liverpool, Chichester had to come through a penalty shootout against Tier 5 side The New Saints in the 4th Round. They also had to do so without captain Emma Alexandre who had to go off with a head injury. "I was in the ambulance when they were taking their penalties. I've seen videos and I could hear the celebrations but then I was on the way to hospital so I couldn't be there," Alexandre told The Offside Rule podcast.

- Chichester City were promoted to Tier 3 for 2017/18 as WPL South West Division One champions. They won the title with a game to spare thanks to a 10-0 victory against St Nicholas in front of their own fans at Oaklands Park. The result meant they had racked up 23 goals in two games, having won 13-0 away at Exeter the previous Sunday.

- Chichester City's first-team did not compete in a County Cup competition in 2017/18. Their Development side was knocked out in the quarter-finals of the Sussex FA County Cup by eventual runners-up Crawley Wasps.

CHORLEY

2018/19: WNL DIVISION 1 NORTH (Tier 4)

Founded: 1983

Nickname: The Magpies

Ground: Jim Fowler Memorial Ground, (Euxton Villa FC) in 2017/18 moving to Victory Park (Chorley FC) for 2018/19

Season 2017/18:

WPL Northern One (Tier 4): 6th

FA Cup: 2nd Round
WPL Cup: Determining Round
WPL Plate: Quarter-finals
County Cup: Runners-up

2017/18 WPL NORTHERN ONE

Date	Opponent	Result	Score	Scorers		
20.08	Mossley Hill A (h)	W	6-1	Scarlett Smith 1, 76, Kerry Nickson 6, Lisa Topping 45+3, Rachel Wood 45+4, 64	78	
27.08	Hull City (h)	L	2-4	Jennifer King 25, Rachel Wood 36	59	
10.09	Barnsley (a)	D	0-0		111	
19.09	Morecambe (h)	L	0-1		80	6
01.10	Bolton Wanderers (a)	L	2-5	Laura Walker 22, Victoria Coope 85	126	11
11.10	Morecambe (a)	L	1-3	Victoria Coope 27	45	11
29.10	Barnsley (h)	W	5-1	Rachel Wood 1, Lisa Topping 5, Scarlett Smith 22, 78, Victoria Coope 83	53	8
05.11	Crewe Alexandra (h)	W	4-1	Karis Harrison 31, Madeline Cullin 56, Laura Walker 65, Scarlett Smith 82	68	6
19.11	Brighouse Town (a)	L	1-2	*Laura Walker missed pen 39,* Megan Fisher 54	58	8
07.01	Leeds United (h)	P-P				
21.01	Crewe Alexandra (a)	W	4-2	Lisa Topping 24, Rachel Wood 72, Victoria Coope 84, Madeline Cullin (pen) 88	42	7
28.01	Leeds United (h)	L	0-1		126	8
04.02	Newcastle United (h)	P-P				8
18.02	Liverpool M F (a)	L	0-1		50	9
04.03	Chester-le-Street T (h)	P-P				9
11.03	Liverpool M F (h)	D	1-1	Rachel Wood 14	70	7
18.03	Brighouse Town (h)	P-P				7
25.03	Hull City (a)	L	1-4	Demi Devereaux 67	60	8
08.04	Newcastle United (a)	P-P				10
15.04	Leeds United (a)	W	2-1	Rachel Wood 61, Katherine Bonner 74		9
22.04	Chester-le-Street T (a)	L	1-2	Scarlett Smith 84	40	9
25.04	Newcastle United (h)	W	3-1	Rachel Wood 12, Scarlett Smith 39, Melissa Ball 77	100	8
02.05	Mossley Hill A (a)*	W	2-1	Victoria Coope 78, Melissa Ball 82	35	8
06.05	Chester-le-Street T (h)	W	2-1	Scarlett Smith 2, Victoria Coope 49	55	6

16.05	Brighouse Town (h)	L	0-3		65	6
18.05	Newcastle United (a)	L	2-4	Madeline Cullin 15, 51	62	6
20.05	Bolton Wanderers (h)+	W	2-1	Rachel Wood 56, 68	140	6

*Played at Walton Hall Park   +Played at Croston FC

2017/18 FA CUP

08.10 RQ3	Altofts (a)		W	5-1	Rachel Wood 3, Lisa Topping 41, Scarlett Smith 54, Laura Walker 60, Kerry Nickson 73	200 est
12.11 R1	Norton & Stockton Ancients (a)	W	4-0		Rachel Wood 19, Victoria Coope 52, Madeline Cullin 66, Scarlett Smith 75	
03.12 R2	Leicester City W (h)		L	0-3		

2017/18 WPL CUP

| 03.09 DR | Leicester City W (h) | L | 1-5 | Laura Walker 12 | 66 |

2017/18 WPL PLATE

24.09 PR	Rotherham United (h)	W	2-1	Madeline Cullin 30, Laura Walker 76	72
22.10 R1	Barnsley (a)	W	3-1	Laura Walker 52, 69, Megan Searson 88	65
17.12 R2	Long Eaton United (a)	W	2-0	Rachel Wood 24, Scarlett Smith 62	44
11.02 QF	Hull City (a)	L	0-4		60

2017/18 LANCASHIRE FA COUNTY CUP

17.09 R1	Haslingden (h)	W	w/o		
15.10 QF	Blackpool FC (h)	W	3-0	Lisa Topping 2, Laura Walker 72, Kerry Nickson 77	77
26.11 SF	Fleetwood T W (a)		P-P		
10.12 SF	Fleetwood T W (a)		P-P		
14.01 SF	Fleetwood T W (a)	W	6-0	Scarlett Smith 13, 32, 44, 69, Rachel Wood 19, Janet Mitchell 86	65
10.05 F	Blackburn Rovers (n)	L	1-6	Rachel Wood 36	

(n) Played at Leyland, Lancashire FA County Ground

"After some major changes at the club during the summer of 2017 we were happy to have finished mid-table in WPL Northern 1 at the end of 2017/18. There are reasons to be positive and obviously we would hope to kick on in 2018/19 now that things have settled down, and we are reasonably confident we can do this."

Janet Mitchell, Chorley Captain

- For the 2018/19 season, Chorley are moving from Euxton Villa to Victory Park which is the home ground of Chorley FC men's.

- Chorley dedicated their 2017/18 final day victory over Bolton to the retiring Katherine Bonner. The team came from 1-0 down to win 2-1 and secure a 6th-place finish in WPL North 1 to cap a season in which they also finished as Lancashire FA County Cup runners-up.

- Chorley, founded in 1983, are the only women's club in the North West of England, apart from Manchester City, to have kept their original name since formation.

COVENTRY UNITED

2018/19: WNL SOUTHERN PREMIER (Tier 3)

Founded: 1991

Nickname: The Red and Greens / United / Cov

Ground: Butts Park Arena, (Coventry RUFC)

Season 2017/18:

WPL Southern (Tier 3): 4th

FA Cup: 4th Round
WPL Cup: Semi-Finals
County Cup: Winners

2017/18 WPL SOUTHERN

Date	Opponent	Result	Score	Scorers	Att	
20.08	Swindon Town (a)	W	8-0	Alison Hall 3, 30, 34, 54, Keeley Davies 4, Nikki Miles 61, Jade Brook 66, 82	73	
27.08	Portsmouth (h)	L	1-2	Stephanie Smith 31	50est	
10.09	Lewes (a)	L	0-1		80	
17.09	Crystal Palace (a)	D	0-0		106	8
01.10	Gillingham (a)	W	9-0	Alison Hall 11, Marie Gauntlett 26, (pen) 54, 77, 83, Amber Hughes 34, 50, Helen Dermody 65, Leah Seivwright 75	50	8
08.10	C&K Basildon (h)	W	4-1	Helen Dermody (x3), Alison Hall	102	7
15.10	West Ham United (a)	W	2-1	Alison Hall 20, 70	264	7
29.10	Portsmouth (a)*	W	2-0	Jade Brook 48, Amber Hughes 71	104	4
05.11	Charlton Athletic (a)	L	0-2		85	5
12.11	West Ham United (h)	W	2-1	Helen Dermody (pen) 44, Marie Gauntlett 70	75	5
26.11	QPR (a)	W	10-1	Stephanie Smith 5, Jade Brook 33, Alison Hall 37, Amber Hughes 48, Marie Gauntlett 50, 84, 87, Helen Dermody 62, (pen) 76, Laura Cooper 79	50	5
11.02	Swindon Town (h)	P-P				5
30.03	QPR (h)	P-P				6
01.04	Crystal Palace (h)	P-P				6
08.04	C&K Basildon (a)	L	0-1		47	7
12.04	Cardiff City L (a)	D	2-2	Alison Hall 32, Natalie Haigh (pen) 90+5	75	6
15.04	Chichester City (h)	W	3-1	Alison Hall 20, 22, 57		6
22.04	Charlton Athletic (h)	L	0-3			6
29.04	Chichester City (a)	W	3-0	Lois Jefferies 32, Amber Hughes 47, Marie Gauntlett 66	60	6
06.05	Cardiff City L (h)	W	4-0	Helen Dermody, Marie Gauntlett, Stephanie Smith, Jess Lundie		6
08.05	Crystal Palace (h)+	L	1-2	Marie Gauntlett, *Marie Gauntlett sent off*	30	6
13.05	Gillingham (h)+	W	5-0	Stephanie Smith, Jade Brook, Lois Jefferies, Keeley Davies, Marie Gauntlett		6

15.05	Swindon Town (h)+	W	7-0	Lois Jefferies (x3), Helen Dermody (x2, 1pen), Amber Hughes, Alison Hall	5
17.05	QPR (h)+	W	4-1	Marie Gauntlett (x2), Nikki Miles (x2)	5
20.05	Lewes (h)**	W	2-1	Jade Brook 60, Lois Jefferies 90	4

*Played at Privett Park   +Played at Communications Park, Daventry Town FC   **Played at Boldmere St Michaels FC

2017/18 FA CUP

03.12 R2	West Ham United (h)	W	6-1	Marie Gauntlett 16, Keeley Davies 54, Alison Hall 67, Anna Wilcox 70, Helen Dermody 76, Laura Cooper 84	
07.01 R3	Crystal Palace (a)+	D	1-1aet (W 3-2p)	Helen Dermody (pen) 7	
04.02 R4	Millwall L (a)++	L	1-4	Helen Dermody (pen) 85	

+Played at Glebe FC   ++Played at Beckenham Town FC

2017/18 WPL CUP

03.09 DR	Haringey Borough (h)	W	16-1	Stephanie Smith 6, 58, 62, 82, Keeley Davies 7, Alison Hall 11, 44, Leah Seivwright 21, 25, Helen Dermody 45, 61, 65, 76, Jade Brook 49, Marie Gauntlett 69, 87	93
22.10 R1	Stevenage (a)	W	2-0	Alison Hall 11, Helen Dermody (pen) 55	45
10.12 R2	Cambridge U (a)	P-P			
17.12 R2	Cambridge U (a)	P-P			
21.01 R2	Cambridge U (a)	P-P			
28.01 R2	Cambridge U (a)	W	5-0	Alison Hall 9, Jade Brook 50, 80 Natalie Haigh 59, Jessica Lundie 90	70
25.02 QF	Plymouth Argyle (a)	W	3-0	Nikki Miles 18, 70 Amber Hughes 58	55
11.03 SF	Blackburn Rovers (a)	P-P			
25.03 SF	Blackburn Rovers (a)	D	2-2aet (L 2-3p)	Keeley Davies 41, Helen Dermody 50	197

2017/18 BIRMINGHAM FA COUNTY CUP

19.11 R2	Coundon Court (a)	W	7-1	Laura Cooper (x2), Marie Gauntlett (x2), Alison Hall, Amber Hughes, Rosie McDonnell	
14.01 R3	Burton Albion (h)**	W	12-0	Helen Dermody (x3, 1pen), Jade Brook (x3), Marie Gauntlett, Laura Cooper, Amber Hughes, Jessica Lundie (x2), Alison Hall	
18.02 QF	Wolverhampton W (a)	W	3-1	Amber Hughes 7, Helen Dermody 22, Natalie Haigh 58	50
18.03 SF	West Brom (a)	P-P			
03.05 F	B'ham & W M (n)	W	15-0	Jade Brook (x3), Lois Jefferies (x3), Helen Dermody (x3, 1pen), Marie Gauntlett (x2), Amber Hughes, Stephanie Smith, Lauren Garner, Callan Barber (pen)	

**Played at Warwick University   (n) Played at The Lamb, Tamworth FC

"The 2017/18 season was one of mixed emotions. We were thrilled to regain the County Cup, however finishing 4th in the League was slightly disappointing. We set our standards high and winning the League was – and still is – a priority. Coventry United work really hard to be an inclusive club and it feels like a family. I love the support that is given to the women's section of the club. They support us wholeheartedly and I couldn't ask for anything more. We will set our standards high again in 2018/19 and look to retain the County Cup and try to win the League."

Jay Bradford – Coventry United Manager.

- In 2017/18 Coventry clinched 4th place in WPL Southern in the very last minute of the season. They came from behind to win 2-1 at home to Lewes courtesy of Lois Jefferies' 90th-minute winner. That goal saw them swap places with their opponents on goal difference alone. It was the first time Coventry had been as high as 4th in the table since October 2017.

- In summer 2018, Reading and England player Jo Potter joined the club as head coach, working with existing manager Jay Bradford. Potter will continue to play for Reading.

- A previous incarnation of the club was founded in 1921, but in 1991 they reformed and affiliated with Coventry City, who were then in the top-flight of the men's game. In July 2015 they broke away from Coventry City and affiliated with men's non-League team Coventry United, changing their name to the same.

- They recently achieved back-to-back promotions, winning the Midland Combination League in 2010 and the WPL Northern Division in 2011. That latter promotion took them into the FA National Premier League for the first time, before a restructuring of the women's game saw them placed into the WPL Southern Division. In 2013/14 they were WPL Southern Division champions.

CRAWLEY WASPS

2018/19: WNL DIVISION 1 SOUTH EAST (Tier 4)

Founded: 1991

Nickname: Wasps

Ground: Tinsley Lane, (Oakwood FC)

Season 2017/18:

London & SE Reg Prem (Tier 5): Champions

FA Cup: Did not enter

League Cup: Runners-up

County Cup: Runners-up

2017/18 London & South East Regional Premier

20.08	AFC Phoenix (h)	W	2-1	Naomi Cole 9, Suzy Davies 90
27.08	Parkwood Rangers (h)	W	6-1	Faye Rabson 4, 14, 18, Lauren Callaghan 45, Naomi Cole 62, Suzy Davies 71
03.09	Watford Development (a)		P-P	
10.09	London Kent Football United (h)		P-P	
17.09	Fulham FC Foundation (a)	W	7-2	Lauren Callaghan 8, 24, Rosanne Fine 26, Faye Rabson 42, Holly Walker 51, Suzy Davies 79, Naomi Cole 86
08.10	Fulham FC Foundation (h)	W	9-2	Faye Rabson 6, 26, 36, Kemina Webber 21, 39, 50, 53, Ariana Fleischman 29, Naomi Cole (pen) 88
15.10	London Kent Football United (a)	W	4-0	Toni Smith 7, Holly Walker 26, Naomi Cole 82, Lauren Callaghan 86
22.10	Aylesford (a)	W	6-1	Holly Walker 2, 28, Ariana Fleischman 4, Faye Rabson 13, Naomi Cole (pen) 59, 80
29.10	Carshalton Ath (h)	W	3-0	Naomi Cole 17, Faye Rabson 18, 27
05.11	AFC Phoenix (a)	D	1-1	Lauren Callaghan 39
19.11	Eastbourne Town (a)	W	7-0	Lauren Callaghan 6, Faye Rabson 27, 86, Suzy Davies 30, 82, Own Goal 42, Holly Walker 52
26.11	Aylesford (h)	W	8-0	Ariana Fleischman 12, 70, Danielle Boyd 27, Faye Rabson 36, 45, 80, Naomi Cole 78, Suzy Davies 82
07.01	Eastbourne Town (h)		P-P	
14.01	Carshalton Ath (a)	W	5-2	Kemina Webber 1, 32, Faye Rabson 46, Naomi Cole 66, Jade Elphick 88
21.01	Watford Development (h)		P-P	
28.01	Parkwood Rangers (a)	W	3-0	Naomi Cole, Faye Rabson, Kemina Webber
04.02	Watford Development (a)		P-P	

11.03	Watford Development (h)*	W	21-0	Kemina Webber 2, 60, 88, Naomi Cole 6, 40, 48, 81, Faye Rabson 12, 45, 87, Rachel Palmer 22, 54, 56, Ariana Fleischman 23, 33, 83, Catherine O'Hagan 35, Toni Smith 52, 66, 78, Jenny Drury 65
18.03	London Kent Football United (h)		P-P	
08.04	Watford Development (a)	W	w/o	
15.04	Eastbourne Town (h)*	W	3-2	Faye Rabson 4, Rachel Palmer 50, Naomi Cole (pen) 82
22.04	London Kent Football United (h)+	W	5-1	Faye Rabson 14, 16, 38, Rachel Palmer 31, Naomi Cole 56

*Played at Shooting Field, Steyning Town Community Football Club 3G   +Played at The Haven, Crawley Down Gatwick FC

2017/18 LEAGUE CUP

01.10 Group	Carshalton Ath (h)	W	9-0	Naomi Cole 9, Rosanne Fine 26, Danielle Boyd 23, Hayley Fowle 38, 40, 66, Suzy Davies 82, Nicholle Smith 84, Kemina Webber 87
12.11 Group	Fulham FC Foundation (a)	W	3-1	Danielle Boyd 31, 65, Jenny Drury (pen) 42
04.02 QF	Watford Development (a)	W	w/o	
04.03* SF	Parkwood Rangers (h)	W	3-0	Naomi Cole (pen) 45, Kemina Webber 70, Faye Rabson 74
20.05 F	AFC Phoenix (n)	L	2-3	Faye Rabson 14, Ariana Fleischman 17

*Played at Shooting Field, Steyning Town Community Football Club 3G   (n) Played at The Gallagher Stadium, Maidstone United FC

2017/18 SUSSEX FA COUNTY CUP

17.12 QF	Chichester City Development (h)	W	2-0	Naomi Cole 28, Faye Rabson 86
11.02 SF	Eastbourne (a)	W	2-0	Naomi Cole 25, Suzy Davis 67
22.03 F	Lewes (n)	L	0-4	

"After what we did in 2017/18, I've got the self-belief that this team can go very, very far. It's going to be another competitive step for us but the capabilities of this squad are very strong. Hopefully we can go in to 2018/19 as underdogs, there'll be no pressure, and we'll see what we can do."

Naomi Cole – Crawley Wasps Captain

- Crawley Wasps won promotion to the newly-named WNL Division 1 South East for 2018/19 by being crowned champions of the 2017/18 London & South East Regional Premier League. They finished the season unbeaten in the League and only dropped two points, winning every game except for their 1-1 draw away to eventual runners-up AFC Phoenix in November.

- Wasps were also runners-up in two Cup competitions in 2017/18, losing to AFC Phoenix in the London & South East Regional Premier League Cup final and to Tier 3 outfit Lewes in the Sussex FA County Cup final. An administrative error meant they did not compete in the 2017/18 FA Cup.

- Faye Rabson scored 24 goals in 15 appearances in the League in 2017/18 making her the division's highest scorer for League goals only.

- Crawley Wasps were founded in 1991 and celebrated their 25th year as an all-female club in 2016. In 2016-17, the then Wasps Under-15s created headlines by opting to enter a boys league - the Mid Sussex Youth League - having gone unbeaten in girls football for two years. That team's captain Eleanor Keegan went on to join Millwall's youth set up, and her successor Chanelle Gainsford was shortlisted for England Schools.

CREWE ALEXANDRA

2018/19: WNL DIVISION 1 NORTH (Tier 4)

Founded: 2000 (as Crewe Cardinals)

Nickname: The Alex

Ground: Cumberland Arena, (Crewe FC)

Season 2017/18:

WPL Northern One (Tier 4): 8th

FA Cup: 3rd Qualifying Round
WPL Cup: Determining Round
WPL Plate: 2nd Round
County Cup: Winners

2017/18 WPL NORTHERN ONE

27.08	Morecambe (h)	D	2-2	Beth Ragdale 10, Laura Callis (og) 38	33	
10.09	Hull City (a)	D	1-1	Laura Garner 41	60	
17.09	Mossley Hill A (a)	W	1-0	Laura Garner 86	44	4
20.09	Bolton Wanderers (h)	A-A		Abandoned in 24th min at 0-0 due to head injury to Bolton player		6
01.10	Newcastle United (a)*	L	0-2		53	10
15.10	Mossley Hill A (h)	W	2-0	Leanne Derry 64, Megan Booth 83	44	6
17.10	Bolton Wanderers (a)	L	0-1		73	6
05.11	Chorley (a)	L	1-4	Own Goal 10	68	9
19.11	Morecambe (a)	W	4-2	Amanda Fallon 3, Laura Garner 7, 45, Michelle Saunders 80	58	7
26.11	Barnsley (h)	W	3-1	Michelle Saunders 23, Laura Garner 77, Emma Lambourne 84	42	5
14.01	Chester-Le-Street T (a)	W	2-1	Amanda Fallon 24, Laura Garner 42	30	5
21.01	Chorley (h)	L	2-4	Megan Booth 18, Michelle Saunders 65	42	5
28.01	Hull City (h)	P-P				5
04.02	Leeds United (h)	D	0-0		36	5
11.02	Liverpool M F (h)	P-P				5
25.02	Chester-le-Street T (h)	W	6-2	Amanda Fallon 10, 61, Michelle Saunders 34, Laura Garner 47, 51, Abbie Chapman 67	50	5
04.03	Brighouse Town (h)	P-P				5
07.03	Bolton Wanderers (h)	L	0-1	Laura Garner missed pen 80	76	5
08.04	Barnsley (a)	D	1-1	Beth Ragdale 67	76	6
15.04	Liverpool M F (a)	L	1-2	Amanda Fallon 65	60	6
22.04	Hull City (h)	W	2-1	Michelle Saunders 65, Georgina Stebbings (pen) 87	37	6

29.04	Newcastle United (h)	L	0-2		45	6
02.05	Liverpool M F (h)	L	0-1		40	6
06.05	Brighouse Town (h)	L	0-1		43	8
13.05	Brighouse Town (a)	L	1-3	Georgina Stebbings 51	102	8
20.05	Leeds United (a)+	D	1-1	Amanda Fallon 63	100	8

*Played at University of Northumbria +Played at Leeds United FC Training Ground

2017/18 FA CUP

08.10 RQ3	Hull City (h)	L	1-4	Leanne Derry 32	32

2017/18 WPL CUP

03.09 DR	The New Saints (a)	D	3-3aet (L 4-5p)	Emma Lambourne 27, Laura Garner 36, Georgina Stebbings 110	54

2017/18 WPL PLATE

29.10 R1	Mossley Hill A (a)	W	3-2	Bethany Grice 8, Leanne Derry 19, Amanda Fallon 75	35
10.12 R2	Birmingham & W M (a)		P-P		
17.12 R2	Birmingham & W M (a)	L	1-3	Megan Booth 55	25

2017/18 CHESHIRE FA COUNTY CUP

18.02 QF	Altrincham (a)	W	2-1	Amanda Fallon 11, Georgina Stebbings 29	37
18.03 SF	Chester (h)		P-P		
25.03 SF	Chester (h)	W	7-0	Laura Garner 16, Megan Booth 26, 28, Bethany Grice 39, Michelle Saunders 56, Beth Ragdale 64, Amanda Fallon 76	108
27.04 F	Tranmere Rovers (n)	W	2-0	Amanda Fallon 40, Laura Garner 66	96

(n) Played at Kirklands, Cammell Laird 1907 FC

"The 2017/18 season was our most successful to date with fantastic signings who boosted the squad and who influenced some of our most notable results and performances throughout the campaign. Beating the promoted champions Hull at home, having also collected a point at their place, were two matches in particular that highlighted the potential of this team. We have a superb squad of players with a mixture of youth and experience that aims to be competing at the top of the table in 2018/19."

Katie Nuttall, Crewe Alexandra Captain

- The 2-0 win over Tranmere in the 2017/18 Cheshire FA County Cup final meant Alex lifted the trophy for the third season in a row. A club record home crowd of 108 had watched the semi-final win against Chester FC at the Cumberland Arena.

- During the 2017/18 campaign, six players made their first-team debuts having come through the club's youth system, progressing all the way from the Under-16s to senior football.

- The original Crewe Ladies club joined the North West Regional League in 1985 but folded before the end of 1992/93. A new club was formed, called Crewe Alexandra, which was elected into the North West Regional League in 1999/00. They also folded in August 2001.

- A rival club named Crewe Vagrants, which had been set up in 2000/01, won the West Midlands Regional League Premier Division in 2002/03. In 2005/06 they became the Crewe Alexandra which exists today and also won the Midlands Combination title that season.

DENHAM UNITED

2018/19: WNL DIVISION 1 SOUTH EAST (Tier 4)

Founded: 1987

Nickname: None

Ground: The Den

Season 2017/18:

WPL South East One (Tier 4): 9th

FA Cup: 3rd Qualifying Round
WPL Cup: Determining Round
WPL Plate: 1st Round
County Cup: Quarter-finals

2017/18 WPL SOUTH EAST ONE

20.08	MK Dons (a)	D	1-1	Alissa Down	80	
27.08	Cambridge United (h)	L	1-3	Jenny Banfield	105	
10.09	AFC Wimbledon (h)	L	1-3	Kara Howes	20	
17.09	Haringey Borough (a)	W	5-2	Chontele Lawrence 14, Jenny Banfield, Sophie Cheadle (x2), Annie Hewitt 90	31	8
20.09	Luton Town (a)	P-P				
24.09	Cambridge United (a)	D	2-2	Sophie Cheadle 48, Annie Hewitt 84	65	10
01.10	Enfield Town (a)	D	1-1	Annie Hewitt 44	29	10
04.10	Luton Town (a)*	L	4-5	Lauren Cox 7, 42, Jenny Banfield 44, Kayleigh Currivan 80	325	10
15.10	MK Dons (h)	D	1-1	Alissa Down 17	87	10
18.10	Luton Town (h)	L	1-5	Jenny Banfield 28	124	10
29.10	Haringey Borough (h)	W	5-0	Jenny Banfield (x2), Emma Bebbington, Annie Hewitt, Celine O'Halloran	66	9
05.11	Leyton Orient (h)	L	0-2		42	9
12.11	Actonians (h)	D	0-0		46	9
26.11	AFC Wimbledon (a)	L	0-1		50	10
03.12	Norwich City (a)	D	2-2	Alissa Down, Sophie Cheadle	45	9
10.12	Enfield Town (h)	P-P				
07.01	Leyton Orient (a)	L	1-2	Sophie Cheadle	61	10
14.01	Norwich City (h)	W	3-1	Annie Hewitt, Alissa Down (x2, 1pen)	35	9
21.01	Enfield Town (h)	P-P				9
04.02	Ipswich Town (a)	L	2-4	Kayleigh Currivan 15, 49	60	9
11.02	Actonians (a)	P-P				9
11.03	Enfield Town (h)	W	4-1	Sophie Cheadle, Alissa Down (x2), Kayleigh Currivan	58	10
18.03	Stevenage (a)	P-P				10
25.03	Actonians (a)	L	0-3		40	10
15.04	Ipswich Town (h)	L	1-6	Alissa Down 75	46	10

| 06.05 | Stevenage (a) | D | 1-1 | Hattie Kettle | 45 | 9 |
| 20.05 | Stevenage (h) | W | 2-1 | Kayleigh Currivan (x2) | | 9 |

*Played at Kenilworth Rd, Luton Town FC

2017/18 FA CUP

| 08.10 RQ3 | Harlow Town (a) | L | 0-1 | | 90 |

2017/18 WPL CUP

| 03.09 DR | Southampton W (a) | L | 2-4 | Sophie Cheadle, Alissa Down | 34 |

2017/18 WPL PLATE

| 22.10 R1 | MK Dons (a) | L | 0-2 | | 85 |

2017/18 MIDDLESEX FA CAPITAL CUP

| 19.11 QF | Leyton Orient (a) | L | 1-4 | Sophie Cheadle |

"We started the 2017/18 season off with a draw against Milton Keynes. After that result we were positive we would finish in the top three, but eventually that was not to be. We had far too many draws, and players leaving left us with a mountain to climb, we picked it up again in the last couple of games and finished the League with respectable form. Fingers crossed for a better 2018/2019 season."

Joanne Currivan – Denham Secretary

- Based in Uxbridge in North West London, Denham United are recognised as the largest all-female football club in the South East of England.

- In 2017/18, Alissa Down finished as the club's top goalscorer in all competitions for the fourth year in a row, hitting nine goals in 26 appearances. Prior to that she notched eight in 28 (2016/17), seven in 27 (2015/16) and nine in 20 (2014/15).

- One of Denham's most dramatic matches of 2017/18 was their away League fixture at Luton which was played at Kenilworth Road in front of 325 fans and ended in a 5-4 defeat.

DERBY COUNTY

2018/19: WNL NORTHERN PREMIER (Tier 3)

Founded: 1989

Nickname: Ewe Rams

Ground: Don Amott LG Arena, (Mickleover Sports FC)

Season 2017/18:

WPL Northern (Tier 3): 7th

FA Cup: 3rd Round
WPL Cup: 2nd Round
County Cup: n/a

2017/18 WPL NORTHERN

20.08	Stoke City (a)	W	4-1	Andrea Bell 34, Nicole Ledgister 37, 42, Kelly Kennaugh 51	131	
10.09	Nottingham Forest (a)	L	0-1		162	
17.09	Huddersfield T (h)	L	0-1		102	9
20.09	Leicester City W (h)	D	1-1	Andrea Bell 6	75	9
24.09	Fylde (a)	D	1-1	Camilla Newton 85	64	10
01.10	Bradford City (a)	W	2-1	Kelly Kennaugh 27, Georgia Hewitt 52	67	8
08.10	West Brom (h)	D	1-1	Karagh Tait 66	107	6
11.10	Leicester City W (a)	L	0-4		103	6
29.10	Wolverhampton W (a)	P-P				6
05.11	Middlesbrough (h)*	L	0-3		97	8
12.11	Nottingham F (h)	W	3-2	Amy Sims 63, Molly Johnson 71, Leanne De Silva 84, *Derby GK Sarah Morgan saved Summer Holmes penalty 89*	226	7
26.11	Huddersfield T (a)	W	3-0	Nikki Ledgister 14, Leanne De Silva 49, Andrea Bell 87	76	6
10.12	Bradford City (h)	P-P				6
04.02	Bradford City (h)	L	0-1		40	6
11.02	Guiseley Vixens (h)	D	2-2	Andrea Bell 29, 90+3	20	6
18.02	Fylde (h)	W	1-0	Lauren Cresswell 65	75	6
25.02	Middlesbrough (a)	L	1-3	Andrea Bell 32	122	6
11.03	Wolverhampton W (a)	P-P				6
25.03	Guiseley Vixens (a)	W	2-0	Shannon Weston 14, Lauren Cresswell 66	40	6
01.04	Blackburn Rovers (h)	P-P				6
08.04	Blackburn Rovers (a)	L	2-6	Shannon Weston 28, Kirsty Allen 87	103	6
26.04	Wolverhampton W (h)	D	1-1	Kirsty Allen 85	72	7
29.04	West Brom (a)	W	2-1	Andrea Bell 33, (pen) 90+5	54	7
01.05	Blackburn Rovers (a)	L	0-1		53	7

| 06.05 | Wolverhampton W (a) | L | 1-2 | *Andrea Bell missed pen 50,* Andrea Bell 55 | 100 | 7 |
| 20.05 | Stoke City (h)+ | L | 0-4 | | 75 | 7 |

*Played at Etwall Leisure Centre   +Played at Derby University

2017/18 FA CUP

03.12 R2	Hull City (h)	D	1-1aet (W 3-2p)	Nicole Ledgister 29	77
07.01 R3	Brighouse Town (h)		P-P		
14.01 R3	Brighouse Town (h)	L	1-3	Lisa Giampalma 42	120

2017/18 WPL CUP

03.09 DR	Rotherham United (h)*	W	7-0	Nicole Ledgister 13, Lisa Giampalma 15, Karagh Tait 44, Georgia Hewitt 53, Andrea Bell 55, 90, Leanne De Silva 63	63
22.10 R1	Bradford City (h)	W	5-2 (aet)	Sophia Bonserr 87, Andrea Bell (pen) 90+4, 103, (pen) 105, *Derby GK Sophie Morgan saved Bradford pen 107,* Karagh Tait 116	106
21.01 R2	Brighouse Town (a)		P-P		
28.01 R2	Brighouse Town (a)	L	2-3	Karagh Tait 25, Hannah Ward 30	92

*Played at Derby University

"We worked tremendously hard throughout 2017/18 to pick up results after a stop/start campaign where we struggled to get any momentum due to fixture changes. We had an excellent mix in the squad of senior pros and youngsters that will only see us improve and we are excited about our plans heading into 2018/19. We hope to bring in a few players that will enhance us further and get us challenging up at the top end of the table."

Hannah Ward, Derby County Captain

- Derby won the WPL Club of the Year award for 2017/18, having also done so at the end of 2015/16. CEO Duncan Gibbs said: "It's always nice to get recognised as a club moving forward. Though we missed out on a place in the new FA Women's Championship, we are already working very hard to put a team together on the pitch to get there as soon as possible and the foundations are in place for us to build over the next year both on and off the pitch."

- Andrea Bell was Derby's top scorer in 2017/18. She hit nine goals in the League and ended up with a total of 14 in all competitions, with three coming from the penalty spot.

- Derby County's breakthrough season came in 2008/09 when they won the Midland Combination League for the first time in their history. The Ewe Rams sealed the title that season, (and promotion to Tier 4), in the final game of the season when they beat Crewe 4-2 in a match that was played at Pride Park.

- In 2013/14 a home friendly against an Arsenal team containing England internationals Rachel Yankey, Kelly Smith and Casey Stoney was watched by a then club record crowd of 600. The Gunners won 5-0. That record has twice been beaten, first when 700 attended a prestige friendly against WSL champions Liverpool in 2015 and then when more than 800 came to watch the FA Cup tie against Nottingham Forest in February 2017.

DONCASTER ROVERS BELLES

2018/19: WNL NORTHERN PREMIER (Tier 3)

Founded: 1969 (as Belle Vue Belles)

Nickname: Belles

Ground: Keepmoat Stadium, (Doncaster Rovers FC) in 2017/18, moving to Oxford Street, (Rossington Main FC) for 2018/19

Season 2017/18:

WSL 2 (Tier 2): Champions

FA Cup: 5th Round
Continental Cup: Group Stage

2017/18 WSL 2

Date	Opponent		Result	Scorers	Att	Pos
24.09	London Bees (a)	W	4-1	Rebecca Rayner 10, 88, Kirsty Hanson 37, Christie Murray 82	279	
01.10	Millwall L (h)	D	2-2	Rebecca Rayner 12, Rhiannon Roberts 29	807	
08.10	Oxford United (a)	D	2-2	Christie Murray 22, 83	231	7
29.10	Aston Villa (h)	W	6-0	Kirsty Hanson 5, 59, Rebecca Rayner 14, Leandra Little 50, Jessica Sigsworth 90, 90+3	552	3
12.11	Tottenham H (a)	W	4-1	Ryah Vyse (og) 19, Jessica Sigsworth 34, Monique Watson 66, Christie Murray 78	439	1
10.12	Sheffield FC (h)	W	3-2	Kirsty Hanson 18, Jessica Sigsworth 21, Sophie Jones (og) 74		1
07.01	Watford (a)	W	2-0	Leandra Little 10, Jessica Sigsworth 44	241	1
28.01	Brighton & H A (h)	W	4-1	Jessica Sigsworth (pen) 33, Kirsty Hanson 45+5, 78, Rebecca Rayner 90	602	1
11.02	Durham (a)	W	2-1	Emily Simpkins 27, Jessica Sigsworth 61	407	1
21.02	Aston Villa (a)	W	4-0	Rhiannon Roberts 12, Rebecca Rayner 67, Jessica Sigsworth 76, Kirsty Hanson 79	410	1
25.03	Tottenham H (h)	W	3-0	Kirsty Hanson 34, Rebecca Rayner 54, Jessica Sigsworth 82	572	1
31.03	Watford (h)	W	3-1	Jessica Sigsworth 9, Sam Tierney 13, Maz Pacheco 32	321	1
19.04	Durham (h)	W	3-1	Kirsty Hanson 4, 45, Sophie Bradley-Auckland 16	310	1
22.04	Brighton & H A (a)*	L	0-1		606	1
28.04	London Bees (h)	W	3-1	Jessica Sigsworth (pen) 18, 49, Kirsty Hanson 80		1
09.05	Sheffield FC (a)	W	2-1	Rebecca Rayner 55, Emily Simpkins 64		1
13.05	Millwall L (a)	W	1-0	Jade Pennock 75	323	1C
20.05	Oxford United (h)	W	4-0	Jessica Sigsworth (pen) 16, (pen) 44, 75, Rhiannon Roberts 25	310	1C

*Played at Checkatrade Stadium, Crawley Town FC

2017/18 WSL CONTINENTAL CUP: GROUP TWO NORTH

12.10	Everton (h)	L	0-3		482
05.11	Birmingham C (a)*	L	2-3	Christie Murray 36, Kirsty Hanson 76	682
03.12	Oxford U (a)	W	5-1	Rebecca Rayner 2, 4, Christie Murray 69, 87, Jessica Sigsworth 73	172
06.12	Manchester C (h)	L	2-3	Jessica Sigsworth 54, Christie Murray 77	924

*Played at St Andrew's

2017/18 FA CUP

04.02 R4	Tottenham H (a)	W	3-0	Sophie Walton 2, Emily Simpkins 45, Rebecca Rayner 90+5	105
18.02 R5	Chelsea (a)	L	0-6		1,564

- Doncaster Rovers Belles were among the high-profile casualties of the FA's controversial new licensing criteria for 2018/19. Belles, one of the most successful clubs in the history of women's football in England, won the 2017/18 WSL 2 title by 10 points. They already knew they would be denied promotion having decided they did not have the financial means to apply for a Tier 1 licence. They were originally placed into the newly-formed Championship but on 12 July they resigned their place stating they needed to do so "to ensure their continued viability". The 2018/19 season is their 50th anniversary season.

- Jessica Sigsworth won the 2017/18 Golden Boot for WSL 2, hitting 15 goals. She also scored two more in the Continental Cup. In summer 2018 she signed for the newly-formed Manchester United.

- Doncaster Belles changed their name to Doncaster Rovers Belles when they formed a partnership with Doncaster Rovers FC, the men's professional club, in 2005. They worked alongside Doncaster Rovers FC, Doncaster Lakers Rugby Club, Doncaster Athletics Club and Doncaster Council to develop the 15,000-seat Keepmoat Stadium which opened in 2006 and is now their home.

- Prior to the rise of Arsenal in the 1990s, Doncaster Belles – as they were then known – were the dominant force in English football. They lifted the FA Cup six times between 1983 and 1994 and were the champions of the FA's inaugural national division – the Women's Premier League – in 1991/92, before winning it again in 1993/94. They were founding members of the WSL in 2011, but were controversially "relegated" to the newly-formed WSL 2 in 2014 to make way for Manchester City in the top-flight.

ENFIELD TOWN

2018/19: WNL DIVISION 1 SOUTH EAST (Tier 4)

Founded: 1985 (as Merryhill Midgets)

Nickname: Town

Ground: Queen Elizabeth II Stadium, (Enfield Town FC)

Season 2017/18:

WPL South East One (Tier 4): 10th

FA Cup: 2nd Round
WPL Cup: 1st Round
Capital Cup: Quarter-finals

2017/18 WPL South East One

20.08	Norwich City (a)	W	4-2	Lisa Kline 67, 70, Robyn Amy Brown 75, Amira Martin 77	52	
27.08	Luton Town (h)	L	1-2	Nuala McKevitt	41	
10.09	Leyton Orient (a)	L	0-9		65	
17.09	MK Dons (h)	L	1-3	Donjeta Krasnici	42	11
20.09	Stevenage (a)	L	0-3		50	11
24.09	Ipswich Town (h)	W	3-2	Alena Beganovic 9, Lisa Kline 31, Regan Coleman 33	25	9
01.10	Denham United (h)	D	1-1	Danielle Smith 56	29	9
11.10	Stevenage (h)	D	1-1	Danielle Smith 35	57	9
29.10	AFC Wimbledon (h)	L	0-1		30	10
05.11	Luton Town (a)	D	0-0		37	10
26.11	Haringey Borough (a)	W	3-1	Danielle Smith 35, Regan Coleman 48, 88	18	9
10.12	Denham United (a)	P-P				9
17.12	Haringey Borough (h)	W	6-0	Own Goal 22, Sheryce Slater 26, Daisy Jenkins 66, Andrea Vivas 71, 88, Danielle Smith 87	28	7
07.01	Actonians (h)	D	1-1	Own Goal 71	26	7
21.01	Denham United (a)	P-P				7
28.01	AFC Wimbledon (a)	L	1-2	Katherine Long 87	70	7
11.02	Cambridge United (h)	W	1-0	Stavroula Panayiotou 36	42	7
18.02	Actonians (a)	L	2-4	Nuala McKevitt 61, Lisa Kline 72		7
25.02	Norwich City (h)	L	2-3	Katherine Long 1, Sheryce Slater 36	43	8
11.03	Denham United (a)	L	1-4	Regan Coleman 56, *Nuala McKevitt sent off 58*	58	8
18.03	MK Dons (a)	P-P				8
01.04	Ipswich Town (a)	L	2-5	Katherine Long 24, 39	40	9
11.04	MK Dons (a)	L	1-5	Andrea Vivas 72		9
29.04	Cambridge United (a)	L	0-1		60	9
20.05	Leyton Orient (h)	D	0-0		105	10

2017/18 FA CUP

08.10 RQ3	AFC Sudbury (h)	W	1-0	Stavroula Panayiotou	
12.11 R1	Wymondham Town (h)	W	3-2	Nuala McKevitt 53, Lisa Kline 70, Stavroula Panayiotou 90	45
03.12 R2	Lewes (a)	L	0-7		201

2017/18 WPL CUP

03.09 DR	Keynsham Town (h)	W	3-2	Regan Coleman (x3)	23
15.10 R1	Cambridge United (h)	L	0-2	*Emma Thomas sent off 89*	43

2017/18 MIDDLESEX FA CAPITAL CUP

22.10 R1	Haringey Borough (a)	W	7-2	Lisa Kline (x5), Kerrie Malborough, Regan Coleman	
19.11 QF	Charlton Athletic (h)	L	0-6		47

"The 2017/18 campaign was a mixture of emotions. We hit many challenges and our main problem was availability of players. If it wasn't for the hard work of manager Claire Ford and the staff, there would have been many games we wouldn't have been able to play. Many reserve team players stepped up and some played senior football for the first time. Our greatest achievement was that after all of this we were able to stay in the division. That's what makes this club so special, everyone comes together to do what they can to help. For a community club where every-thing is done on a voluntary basis, we've achieved so much. I love this club. It does fantastic things for all age groups and I just want it to keep growing and get the recognition it deserves."

Photo: @MikeyTheTowner

Kerrie Marlborough – former Enfield Town captain

- When the club was founded in 1985 it was known as Merryhill Midgets. The team then formed an alliance with Enfield men's and became known as Enfield. In 2001, Enfield men's split. One club continued under the same name, while some fans formed a sup-porter-led club called Enfield Town. The ladies' team aligned with the latter and took on the same name.

- Enfield Town reached their very first national Cup final in 2015/16 when they made it to the WPL Plate final under manager Kyri Neocleous. They took on Coventry United at Keys Park in Hednesford but were beaten 5-1.

- In Town's 7-2 win over Haringey Borough in the 2017/18 Middlesex FA Capital Cup 1st round, Lisa Kline scored five goals.

FYLDE

2018/19: WNL NORTHERN PREMIER (Tier 3)

Founded: 1971 (as Duke of York)

Nickname: The Coasters

Ground: Kellamergh Park, (AFC Fylde)

Season 2017/18:

WPL Northern (Tier 3): 5th

FA Cup: 3rd Round
WPL Cup: Determining Round
WPL Plate: Semi-finals
County Cup: Quarter-finals

2017/18 WPL NORTHERN

Date	Opponent		Result	Scorers	Att	
20.08	Middlesbrough (a)	W	3-0	Hannah Forster 56, Veatriki Sarri 58, Lauren Davies 66	125	
10.09	Guiseley Vixens (h)+	W	2-0	Lauren Davies 15, Danielle Young 81	46	
24.09	Derby County (h)+	D	1-1	Lagan Makin 87	64	6
01.10	Leicester City W (a)	D	0-0		119	6
15.10	Wolverhampton W (a)	W	1-0	Natasha Flint 39	50	6
05.11	Bradford City (a)	W	2-1	Natasha Flint 45, Sophie Charlton 83	59	6
12.11	Leicester City W (h)	L	2-7	Charlotte Farrell 12, Lauren Davies 90	47	6
19.11	Middlesbrough (h)		P-P			7
26.11	Stoke City (h)		P-P			7
21.01	Bradford City (h)		P-P			8
28.01	Bradford City (h)		P-P			8
30.01	Blackburn R (h)		P-P			8
04.02	Huddersfield T (a)	L	0-1		73	8
18.02	Derby County (a)	L	0-1		75	9
25.02	West Brom (a)	W	5-0	Lauren Davies 33, Leah Foster 49, Hollie Kelsh 65, Sophie Charlton 85, 88	64	7
15.03	Blackburn R (a)	L	0-3		156	7
18.03	Guiseley Vixens (a)		P-P			7
25.03	Stoke City (h)	D	0-0		42	7
01.04	Bradford City (h)+	W	2-1	Alys Hinchcliffe 32, Jenna Carroll (pen) 70	55	7
08.04	Nottingham Forest (h)		P-P			7
15.04	Wolverhampton W (h)	D	0-0		33	6
19.04	Huddersfield T (h)+	D	2-2	Sophie Charlton 14, 16	29	6
22.04	Nottingham Forest (a)	W	4-3	Laura Merrin 7, Olivia Wilkes 31, Leah Foster 69, Sophie Charlton 85	54	6
26.04	Blackburn R (h)+	L	1-6	Hannah Forster 75	82	6

29.04	Middlesbrough (h)	W	4-3	Jenna Carroll 28, 61, (pen) 68, Leah Foster 32	62	6
06.05	Stoke City (a)	L	1-3	Danielle Young 28	143	6
13.05	Guiseley Vixens (a)	D	2-2	Sophie Charlton (pen) 19, Emily Hollinshead 55	33	6
15.05	Nottingham Forest (h)*	W	1-0	Danielle Young 70		6
20.05	West Brom (h)	W	2-1	Own Goal 65, Sophie Charlton 83	43	5

*Played at Moss Farm Leisure Complex   +Played at Mill Lane, AFC Fyld

2017/18 FA CUP

| 03.12 R2 | Guiseley Vixens (h) | W | 2-0 | Sophie Charlton 44, Lauren Davies 87 | 43 |
| 07.01 R3 | Plymouth Argyle (h)* | L | 1-3 | Laura Merrin 12 | |

*Played at UCLAN Sports Arena

2017/18 WPL CUP

| 03.09 DR | Bradford City (a) | D | 3-3 aet (L 2-3 pens) | Sophie Charlton 13, Veatriki Sarri 62, 90+5 | 81 |

2017/18 WPL PLATE

22.10 R1	Burton Albion (h)		P-P		
29.1 R1	Burton Albion (h)+	W	3-2	Sophie Charlton 7, Lauren Davies 30, Hollie Kelsh 75	53
10.12 R2	Leeds United (h)		P-P		
14.01 R2	Leeds United (h)	D	0-0 aet (W 4-3p)		58

11.02 QF	Birmingham & WM (a)	W	5-1	Sophie Charlton (x2), Olivia Fuller (x2), Laura Merrin	
04.03 SF	Luton Town (a)		P-P		
11.03 SF	Luton Town (a)*	W	2-1	Olivia Wild 78, Alys Hinchcliffe 82	61

*Fylde expelled from WPL Plate on 07.04 for fielding ineligible player in semi-final v Luton Town. Luton handed walkover.

+Played at Leigh Sports Village

2017/18 LANCASHIRE FA COUNTY CUP

| 17.09 R1 | Bury (h)+ | W | 10-0 | Olivia Wilkes 5, Leah Foster 7, Lagan Makin 13, 42, 60, 69, 76, Danielle Lea 55, Sophie Charlton 82, Charlotte Farrell 86 | 53 |
| 08.10 QF | Blackburn Rovers (a) | L | 1-2 | Lagan Makin 82 | 176 |

+Played at Mill Lane

- Fylde were called Duke of York when they were founded in 1971. They became Preston Rangers in 1977 and then Preston North End in 1997. In May 2016 they switched their association from Preston North End to AFC Fylde who offered them the chance to play at Mill Farm and made funds available. As Preston Rangers they reached the semi-finals of the FA Women's Cup in 1982/83 and 1989/90.

- In 2005/06 they were promoted to the FA Women's Premier League Northern Division (Tier 3) for the first time having won the Northern Combination Football League in their days as Preston North End.

- The club's first national Cup final success came when they won the 2014/15 WPL Plate, beating League rivals Huddersfield Town 3-0 in the final. They looked to have made it back to the final in 2017/18 but, having beaten Luton in the semi-final, were expelled from the competition for fielding an ineligible player.

- In January 2017 Fylde appointed Conrad Prendergast, then aged just 24, as manager. He joined from Manchester City women's coaching staff.

GILLINGHAM

2018/19: WNL SOUTHERN PREMIER (Tier 3)

Founded: 1995

Nickname: The Gills

Ground: The Sports Ground, (Chatham Town FC)

Season 2017/18:

WPL Southern (Tier 3): 9th

FA Cup: 2nd Round
WPL Cup: Determining Round
WPL Plate: 1st Round
County Cup: Semi-finals

2017/18 WPL SOUTHERN

Date	Opponent	Result	Score	Scorers	Att	Pos
20.08	West Ham United (h)*	W	1-0	Kallie Balfour 89	250	
27.08	Charlton Athletic (h)+	L	1-2	Kallie Balfour 49	187	
10.09	QPR (a)	W	4-0	Jenny Newman 28, 76, Danielle Farmer 39, Jade Keogh 60	35	
17.09	Swindon Town (h)*	W	5-0	Jenny Newman 12, Kallie Balfour 18, 29, 59, Jade Keogh 85	102	3
21.09	C&K Basildon (h)	L	1-3	Jenny Newman 35	52	5
01.10	Coventry United (h)	L	0-9	*Jade Keogh sent off 58*	50	7
08.10	Portsmouth (a)	L	1-3	Jenny Newman 65	110	8
11.10	C&K Basildon (a)	L	0-3		63	8
05.11	Crystal Palace (h)*	L	0-1		117	8
12.11	Portsmouth (h)	L	0-4		97	9
26.11	Chichester City (h)	L	0-4		78	10
10.12	Chichester City (a)	P-P				
17.12	QPR (h)	P-P				
07.01	West Ham United (a)	D	0-0		133	9
14.01	Crystal Palace (a)	L	0-2		252	10
28.01	Chichester City (a)	P-P				10
12.02	Cardiff City L (h)	D	1-1	Kallie Balfour 90+2	123	10
25.02	Lewes (a)	P-P				10
04.03	Chichester City (a)	P-P				10
11.03	Swindon Town (a)	W	4-0	Kallie Balfour 20, 31, 70, Jade Keogh 38	22	10
25.03	Chichester City (a)**	L	0-1		50	9
08.04	Lewes (a)	L	0-2		221	9
15.04	Cardiff City L (a)	L	2-3	Millie Waud 29, Maddison Farrand 52	95	10
22.04	QPR (h)*	W	3-0	Kallie Balfour (pen) 44, *Courtney Gibson sent off 55*, Jade Keogh 80, 88	82	9
06.05	Lewes (h)^	L	0-2		57	9

13.05	Coventry United (a)++	L	0-5			9
16.05	Charlton Athletic (a)	L	1-8	Jade Keogh 70	155	9

*Played at Priestfield, Gillingham FC   **Played at Nyewood Lane, Bognor Regis Town FC   +Played at K Sports

++Played at Communications Park, Daventry Town FC   ^Played at Meridian Sports and Social Club

2017/18 FA CUP

03.12 R2	Plymouth Argyle (h)*	L	1-3 (aet)	Jade Keogh 33	

*Played at Priestfield (Gillingham FC)

2017/18 WPL CUP

03.09 DR	Stevenage (h)	L	0-1		152

2017/18 WPL PLATE

22.10 R1	Luton Town (h)+	L	3-4 (aet)	Danielle Farmer (pen) 70, Kylie Manktelow 107, 109	73

+Played at K Sports

2017/18 KENT FA COUNTY CUP

19.11 QF	Herne Bay (a)	W	8-0	Jade Keogh 16, Jenny Newman 32, 37, 45, 66, Esther Anu 47, 60, Bethany Nugent 64	
21.01 SF	London Kent Football United (a)	L	1-2	Sharna Giordani 33	35

"We came up as 2016/17 WPL South East champions but then lost so many players, and then had to face the daunting prospect of competing in a higher division without them. But we stuck together throughout 2017/18, we had each other's backs and we achieved our aim of staying up. Our team spirit got us through a lot of games. We feel as though we are building something at the club and that we can push on in 2018/19. We want to establish ourselves in Tier 3 and we feel like we are capable of finishing higher up the table."

Jade Keogh, Gillingham Captain

- Gillingham were runaway Tier 4 champions (when the division was known as WPL South East One) in 2016/17. They would have completed the entire season unbeaten but for a final day defeat away to AFC Wimbledon. It took them a while to acclimatise to life in Tier 3 in 2017/18, but eventually they stayed up quite comfortably.

- Kallie Balfour top scored for Gillingham in 2017/18 with 10 goals, including a hat-trick against Swindon in mid-September. All 10 of them were scored in the League.

- Gillingham Ladies come under the umbrella of Gillingham FC, the men's professional outfit. It is the third link-up with the club in their history. The first came in 1995 when Gillingham FC chairman Paul Scally co-opted a local team called Borstal 88. After a period of independence they were brought back into the Gillingham FC fold in 2008 and then again, after another break, in 2014.

GUISELEY VIXENS

2018/19: WNL NORTHERN PREMIER (Tier 3)

Founded: 1993 (as Meanwood Vixens)

Nickname: The Vixens

Ground: Nethermoor Park, (Guiseley AFC)

Season 2017/18:

WPL Northern (Tier 3): 10th

FA Cup: 2nd Round

WPL Cup: 2nd Round

County Cup: Winners

2017/18 WPL NORTHERN

Date	Opponent	Result		Scorers		
20.08	Nottingham Forest (a)	L	0-1		82	
27.08	Huddersfield Town (a)	L	0-6	*Charlotte Higginson sent off 72*	96	
10.09	Fylde (a)	L	0-2		46	
17.09	Stoke City (h)	D	3-3	Chantelle O'Hara 34, 38, Alarna Fuller 90+5	41	10
20.09	Middlesbrough (a)	L	1-3	Chantelle O'Hara 75	130	11
24.09	Wolverhampton W (h)++	D	2-2	Nikki Berko 68, 76	30	11
01.10	Blackburn Rovers (a)*	L	1-3	Own Goal 60	83	12
08.10	Bradford City (h)	D	2-2	Emily Scott 20, Danica Roberts 45+7, *Manager Glenn Pearson sent to stands 72*	40	11
05.11	West Brom (a)	L	1-3	Nikki Berko (pen) 58	84	12
15.11	Middlesbrough (h)	L	1-5	Fiona Worts 18	98	12
26.11	Nottingham Forest (h)	A-A		Abandoned at 0-0 after 20 mins due to serious neck injury		*12*
28.01	Stoke City (a)	L	2-3	Nikki Berko 53, Natalie Brace 70	82	12
04.02	West Brom (h)	P-P				12
11.02	Derby County (a)	D	2-2	Fiona Worts 50, Debbie Hastings 77	20	12
04.03	Wolverhampton W (a)	P-P				12
11.03	Bradford City (a)	P-P				12
18.03	Fylde (h)	P-P				12
25.03	Derby County (h)	L	0-2		40	12
08.04	Leicester City W (a)	W	3-2	Jessica Heald 10, Emily Heckler 67, 87	72	11
15.04	West Brom (h)	W	3-2	Ellie Olds 33, Natalie Brace 55, Nikki Berko 75	24	11
22.04	Leicester City W (h)**	L	0-4		32	11
29.04	Wolverhampton W (a)	L	1-2	Emily Heckler 12	75	12
06.05	Nottingham F (h)++	W	6-0	Emily Heckler 10, Nikki Berko 32, 40, 45, 65, 80	31	12
10.05	Bradford City (a)	L	0-3		74	12
13.05	Fylde (h)	D	2-2	Charlotte Blythe 6, Emily Heckler 54	33	10
17.05	Blackburn Rovers (h)^	L	1-3	Ellie Olds 71	48	10
20.05	Huddersfield Town (h)	W	2-1	Nikki Berko 41, Beth Stanfield 79	67	10

*Played at Accrington & Rossendale College   **Played at Woodhouse Grove

^Played at John Craig Sports Centre ++Played at Fleet Lane, West Riding CFA Headquarters

2017/18 FA Cup

03.12 R2	Fylde (a)	L	0-2	43

2017/18 WPL CUP

03.09 DR	Solihull Moors (a)	W	2-1 (aet)	Danica Roberts 107, Chantelle O'Hara 117	40
22.10 R1	Huddersfield Town (h)		P-P		
29.10 R1	Huddersfield Town (h)+++	W	3-2	Ebony Njie 67, Nikki Berko 72, Emily Scott 90	75
10.12 R2	Nottingham F (a)		P-P		
14.01 R2	Nottingham F (a)	L	0-5		73

+++Played at Livesedge

2017/18 WEST RIDING FA COUNTY CUP

15.10 R1	Brighouse Athletic (a)	W	6-0	Harriet Jakeman 38, Megan Maxted 42, Demi Wisher 55, Elizabeth White 65, Ebony Njie 74, Hannah Brierley 80	
19.11 R2	Harrogate Town (a)	W	2-0	Nikki Berko 33, 47, *Lauren Griffiths sent off 70*	
17.12 QF	Altofts (a)		P-P		
07.01 QF	Altofts (a)	W	w/o		
21.03 SF	Leeds United Res (a)*	W	4-0	Nikki Berko 16, 55, 63, Debbie Hastings 83	
02.05 F	Bradford City (n)*	W	3-1	Beth Stanfield 44, Olivia Da Costa 65, Emily Heckler 70	150

*Played at Fleet Lane, West Riding FA Headquarters

"There's no denying that 2017/18 was a tough season, especially with losing so many players to injury in the first half of the campaign. It was great to see that despite that adversity we stuck together and continued to believe in ourselves. The management never stopped trying, and in the second half of the season we turned it around to produce some amazing results against big teams in the League which resulted in us meeting out target of staying up."

Alarna Fuller, Guiseley Vixens Club Captain

- The club that was founded as Meanwood Vixens in 1993 quickly grew and became known as Leeds City Vixens before affiliating with men's non-League team Guiseley AFC in 2005.

- The Vixens were promoted to the WPL Northern Division (Tier 3) ahead of 2017/18 as champions of WPL Northern Division One. They wrapped up the 2016/17 title when they won 3-2 at Blackpool Wren Rovers on April 23, becoming champions of that division for the second time in three seasons.

- Nikki Berko was the Vixens' top-scorer in 2017/18. She bagged 11 goals in the League, including five in the 6-0 win over Nottingham Forest on 6 May. She also scored once in the WPL Cup and five in the County Cup, making it a total of 17 in all competitions.

HARINGEY BOROUGH

2018/19: EASTERN REGIONAL PREMIER (Tier 5)

Founded: 1999

Nickname: Borough

Ground: Coles Park,
(Haringey Borough FC)

Season 2017/18:

WPL South East One (Tier 4): 12th (R)

FA Cup: 3rd Qualifying Round
WPL Cup: Determining Round
WPL Plate: 1st Round
Capital Cup: 1st Round

2017/18 WPL SOUTH EAST ONE

20.08	Actonians (a)	L	0-13	Stephanie Cooper sent off		35	
27.08	Norwich City (a)	L	0-7			60	
10.09	Luton Town (a)	L	1-5	Julia Carruthers		30	
17.09	Denham United (h)	L	2-5	Julia Carruthers, Aisa Jabbi-Jaiteh		31	12
01.10	Cambridge United (a)	L	2-12	Julie Carruthers, Shanice Nourrice		48	12
04.10	Leyton Orient (a)	L	0-8			35	12
29.10	Denham United (a)	L	0-5			66	12
05.11	Cambridge United (h)	L	0-7	Haringey GK saved Lauren Cartwright pen 50		25	12
07.11	Leyton Orient (h)	L	0-8			26	12
12.11	Norwich City (h)	P-P					12
19.11	AFC Wimbledon (a)	P-P					12
26.11	Enfield Town (h)	L	1-3	Jonea Peter		18	12
10.12	Ipswich Town (a)	P-P					12
17.12	Enfield Town (a)	L	0-6	Lynda Dunphy sent off		28	12
14.01	Ipswich Town (a)	L	0-9			40	12
28.01	Norwich City (h)	L	3-4	Julia Carruthers (x2), Jonea Peter		15	12
04.02	Stevenage (a)	P-P					12
11.02	AFC Wimbledon (a)	L	2-12	Julia Carruthers, Brooke Hills		100	12
18.02	Stevenage (a)	L	0-10			60	12
25.02	AFC Wimbledon (h)	L	1-9	Brooke Hills (pen)		30	12
04.03	Ipswich Town (h)	L	0-10	Julia Carruthers sent off 38		12	12
18.03	Actonians (h)	P-P					12
25.03	Stevenage (h)	L	2-10	Jonea Peter, Shanice Nourrice			12
08.04	Luton Town (h)	L	0-14				12
29.04	Actonians (h)	L	0-10				12
13.05	MK Dons (a)*	L	1-16	Julia Carruthers		80	12
20.05	MK Dons (h)	L	0-13				12

*Played at Wootton Blue Cross

2017/18 FA Cup

08.10 RQ3   Godalming Town (a)   L   0-5

2017/18 WPL Cup

03.09 DR   Coventry United (a)   L   1-16   Jonea Peter   93

2017/18 WPL Plate

15.10 R1   Norwich City (a)   L   0-5   *Naomi Graham sent off*   40

2017/18 Middlesex FA Capital Cup

22.10 R1   Enfield Town (h)   L   2-7   Madison Alexander 49, Julia Carruthers 89

"I've never been prouder of a group of players than those who stuck it out throughout the 2017/18 season. These have been difficult times for our club. On New Year's Day 2017 we suffered the devastating loss of our inspirational manager Steve Browne, 52, who had been battling cancer for five years. The team was top of the Eastern Regional Premier at the time and went on to claim the title and win the League Cup in Steve's honour. In summer 2017 more than 14 of our players left and we had to rebuild from scratch. Our new manager departed after a few months and I took on the job alongside my secretarial role. I even returned to play 18 games despite having retired three years ago. Results show that it was an incredibly tough challenge in Tier 4, but we always managed to get 11 players out and were commended by many of our opponents for never giving up. Ahead of 2018/19, and our return to Tier 5, we have a new management team, new players, and the pleasure of playing on our own 4G pitch. Haringey is in my blood having captained the side for more than 10 years. We are so grateful to our fans and after a tough couple of years we are now starting to turn the corner."

Karla Parker – Haringey Borough Manager 2017/18

- As 2016/17 Eastern Regional Premier champions, Haringey Borough were promoted to WPL South East One (now WNL Division 1 South East) for the 2017/18 season. It was their first ever season in Tier 4, and it was always going to be hugely difficult. They finished bottom of the table without collecting a point.

- Haringey Borough Women's club was set up ahead of the 1999/2000 season but played only occasional friendlies that year.

- In 2000 they merged with Mill Hill United who had been accepted into the Eastern Region League, Division Two. The new club continued with the Haringey Borough name and their groundshare of Coles Park with the men's team, something they still do today.

- Coles Park is a stone's throw from Tottenham Hotspur football club and is actually situated on White Hart Lane, which Spurs' now demolished stadium of the same name never was. White Hart Lane stadium was on Tottenham High Road, as is Tottenham's new ground.

HUDDERSFIELD TOWN

2018/19: WNL NORTHERN PREMIER (Tier 3)

Founded: 1988 (as Huddersfield Ladies)

Nickname: Town

Ground: The Stafflex Arena, (Shelley FC)

Season 2017/18:

WPL Northern (Tier 3): 6th

FA Cup: 3rd Round
WPL Cup: 1st Round
County Cup: Winners

2017/18 WPL NORTHERN

20.08	West Brom (h)	W	4-0	Charley Evans 44, Emily Heckler 45+3, Kate Mallin 48, 90+2	67	
27.08	Guiseley Vixens (h)	W	6-0	Kate Mallin 4, Emily Heckler 23, 24, Hannah Campbell 70, 79, Danielle Whitham 72	96	
10.09	Blackburn Rovers (h)	L	1-2	Kate Mallin 42	121	
17.09	Derby County (a)	W	1-0	Emily Heckler 55	102	1
20.09	Bradford City (h)	D	2-2	Sarah Danby 67, Brittany Sanderson 89	137	2
24.09	West Brom (a)	L	1-2	Sarah Danby 40	56	2
01.10	Middlesbrough (h)	L	0-1		146	3
08.10	Leicester City W (a)	L	2-3	Hannah Campbell 33, Brittany Sanderson 45+3	89	5
15.10	Middlesbrough (a)	W	3-0	Katie Nutter 27, 39, Own Goal 83	85	4
17.10	Bradford City (a)	D	1-1	Hannah Campbell 23	121	3
05.11	Stoke City (h)	W	2-0	Kate Mallin 62, 90	78	3
12.11	Wolverhampton W (a)	W	5-3	Emily Heckler 6, 13, Kate Mallin 31, Brittany Sanderson 52, Danielle Whitham 56	60	3
19.11	Blackburn Rovers (a)	W	2-0	Emily Heckler 45, 76, *Vicky Abbott sent off 56, Huddersfield GK Laura Carter saved Lynda Shepherd pen 56*	121	2
26.11	Derby County (h)	L	0-3		76	3
14.01	Leicester City W (h)	D	1-1	Brittany Sanderson 29	92	3
04.02	Fylde (h)	W	1-0	Lucy Sowerby 37	73	2
11.02	Nottingham F (h)	W	4-0	Kate Mallin 6, Emily Heckler 20, 26, Lucy Sowerby 33	56	2
18.02	Stoke City (a)	L	2-3	Lucy Sowerby 48, Kate Mallin 86	105	2
08.04	Wolverhampton W (h)	W	2-0	Danielle Whitham 27, Ella Harris 90+2	73	2
15.04	Nottingham F (a)	D	2-2	Katie Nutter 42, Brittany Sanderson 58	67	3
19.04	Fylde (a)	D	2-2	Lucy Sowerby 72, Charley Evans 79	29	2
20.05	Guiseley Vixens (a)	L	1-2	Brittany Sanderson 55	67	6

2017/18 FA CUP

03.12 R2	West Brom (h)	W	7-0	*Kate Mallin missed pen (saved) 26,* Emily Heckler 34, 86, Brittany Sanderson 45, Sarah Danby (pen) 46, 69, 78, Lucy Sowerby 67	79
07.01 R3	Lewes (h)	L	1-2	Brittany Sanderson 61	96

2017/18 WPL Cup

03.09 DR	Newcastle United (a)	W	3-0	Kate Mallin 5, 83, Hannah Campbell 86	69
22.10 R1	Guiseley Vixens (a)		P-P		
29.10 R1	Guiseley Vixens (a)*	L	2-3	Katie Nutter 40, Sarah Danby 56	75

*Played at Liversedge

2017/18 SHEFFIELD & HALLAMSHIRE FA COUNTY CUP

17.12 R3	AFC Doncaster (a)	W	w/o		
21.01 QF	Harworth Colliery (h)		P-P		
28.01 QF	Harworth Colliery (h)	W	8-0	Emily Heckler 2, 10, Britanny Sanderson 18, 40, Kate Mallin 51, Ella Harris 55, 74, Sarah Danby 62	65
18.03 SF	Oughtibridge War Memorial (a)		P-P		
25.03 SF	Oughtibridge War Memorial (a)	W	2-1	Lucy Sowerby 21, 47	55
15.05 F	Barnsley (n)	W	3-0	Katie Nutter 15, Sarah Danby 25, 83	250

(n) Played at Keepmoat Stadium, Doncaster Rovers FC

"Finishing with our highest points total since coming up to the WPL some four seasons ago, made 2017/18 a decent campaign. We came 6th and, had it not been for a late dip in form, we would have been higher up the table. We retained the Sheffield & Hallamshire FA County Cup, once again taking on our South Yorkshire rivals Barnsley in the final and coming out 3-0 winners. I have been involved with the club for nearly 20 years, since I was 10. I have no desire to play anywhere else and my loyalties are to my home town club, because it's a special place. I'm staying here to see what we can achieve, with our ultimate aim being to gain promotion to the new Championship."

Kate Mallin, Huddersfield Town Captain

- Huddersfield retained the Sheffield & Hallamshire FA County Cup in 2017/18 by beating Barnsley 3-0 in the final at Doncaster Rovers FC's Keepmoat Stadium. Katie Nutter gave them the lead, and Sarah Danby was then on target twice. It was the first time this County Cup final had been held at a Football League stadium.

- The club's longest-serving manager was Mickey Booth who was in charge for 14 years before standing down at the end of the 2012/13 season.

- Huddersfield Ladies became Huddersfield Town Ladies ahead of the 1993/94 season and went on to win the Treble of North East Regional Division One, League Cup and Yorkshire Cup in their first season.

- The following year they claimed the League title again, winning all 16 of their games and scoring 101 goals.

HULL CITY

2018/19: WNL NORTHERN PREMIER (Tier 3)

Founded: 2001

Nickname: City / The Tigresses

Ground: Hull University Sports Ground

Season 2017/18:

WPL Northern One (Tier 4): Champions

FA Cup: 2nd Round
WPL Cup: Determining Round
WPL Plate: Semi-finals
County Cup: Runners-up

2017/18 WPL NORTHERN ONE

Date	Opponent	Result	Score	Scorers	Att	
20.08	Barnsley (h)	W	6-1	Hope Knight 29, 36, 80, 90, Ellie Harding 24, Rebecca Beech 19	66	
27.08	Chorley (a)	W	4-2	Joanne Symington 50, Katie Thompson 58, 68, Rachael Ackroyd 74	59	
10.09	Crewe Alexandra (h)	D	1-1	Katie Thompson 70	60	
17.09	Brighouse Town (a)	W	1-0	Natasha Cooke 13	73	1
20.09	Leeds United (h)	W	5-1	Joanne Symington 59, Ellie Tanser 62, Katie Thompson, Rebecca Beech, Sophie Stamp 90	60	1
01.10	Liverpool M F (h)	W	3-0	Sophie Stamp 24, 66, Hope Knight 84	80	1
11.10	Leeds United (a)	W	1-0	Joanne Symington 42	80	1
05.11	Mossley Hill A (a)	P-P				2
26.11	Chester-le-Street T (h)	W	2-1	Ellie Tanser 12, Katie Thompson 60	40	2
17.12	Mossley H A (a)	P-P				2
07.01	Barnsley (a)	W	5-0	Eden Pedersen, Joanne Symington, Hope Knight, Rachel Ackroyd (x2)	57	1
14.01	Bolton Wanderers (a)	P-P				1
21.01	Morecambe (h)	P-P				1
28.01	Crewe Alexandra (a)	P-P				2
04.02	Liverpool M F (a)	D	2-2	Ellie Tanser 35, Rebecca Beech 51	80	2
18.02	Bolton Wanderers (h)	W	2-0	Eden Pedersen, Hope Knight	50	2
25.02	Newcastle United (h)	W	4-1	Rebecca Beech 11, 30, Sophie Stamp 80, Rachael Ackroyd 88	50	1
11.03	Morecambe (h)	W	7-0	Hope Knight 4, 15, 43, Katie Thompson 27, 60, (pen) 80, Rebecca Beech 88	60	1
18.03	Mossley Hill A (h)	P-P				1
25.03	Chorley (h)	W	4-1	Rachael Ackroyd (x3), Hope Knight	60	1

01.04	Mossley Hill A (a)	D	1-1	Rachael Ackroyd 75	20	1
08.04	Bolton Wanderers (a)*	W	1-0	Hope Knight 75		1
15.04	Chester-le-Street T (a)	W	1-0	Katie Thompson (pen) 90	30	1
22.04	Crewe Alexandra (a)	L	1-2	Joanne Symington 5, *Eden Pedersen sent off 87*	37	1
29.04	Brighouse Town (h)	W	2-0	Natalie Bell 10, Katie Thompson 55	100	1
06.05	Newcastle United (a)	L	0-1			1
13.05	Mossley Hill A (h)	W	4-0	Hope Knight 22, 52, Rachel Ackroyd 53, Liberty Bott 86	100	1C
20.05	Morecambe (a)	W	9-0	Hope Knight 7, 25, 44, Liberty Bott 15, 30, Rebecca Beech 32, 55, 80, 90	25	1C

*Played at Eddie Davies Academy

2017/18 FA CUP

08.10 RQ3	Crewe Alexandra (a)	W	4-1	Hope Knight 44, Rebecca Beech, Rachael Ackroyd 82, Katie Thompson 90+1	32
12.11 R1	Steel City W (h)	W	4-1	**Natalie Bell 62, Hope Knight 68, 80, 88**	80
03.12 R2	Derby County (a)	D	1-1aet (L 2-3p)	**Natalie Bell 78**	77

2017/18 WPL CUP

| 03.09 DR | Chester-le-Street T (a) | L | 2-3 | Ellie Tanser 52, Joanne Symington 65 | 30 |

2017/18 WPL PLATE

24.09 PR	Leicester City L (h)	W	w/o		
29.10 R1	Morecambe (a)	W	5-1	Katie Thompson (x2), Hope Knight, Rachael Ackroyd, Liberty Bott, *Amy Halloran sent off 82*	35
10.12 R2	Newcastle U (h)	W	1-0	Rachael Ackroyd 30	20
11.02 QF	Chorley (h)	W	4-0	Rebecca Beech, Ellie Tanser, Hope Knight, Joanne Symington	60
04.03 SF	West Ham United (h)	L	0-3		80

2017/18 EAST RIDING FA COUNTY CUP

19.11 QF	Mill Lane United (a)	W	w/o	
25.03 SF	East Yorkshire Carnegie (h)	W	w/o	
25.04 F	AFC Preston (n)	L	w/o	Hull concede match after being refused County FA permission to field development players

"The 2017/18 season was a fantastic one. We worked extremely hard to achieve our goal of promotion. We had many ups and a few downs, but what is special about our club is that we stick together. A quote that sums up our team is, 'Talent wins games, but teamwork and intelligence wins championships'. Hull City Ladies isn't just a football club, it's a football family."

Jo Symington – Hull City Captain

- The 2017/18 season was a year of progress for Hull. Having finished a highly creditable 3rd in 2016/17, they topped that by being crowned WPL Northern 1 champions, losing just two of their 22 League games and scoring 66 goals on their way to the title.

- There were two hat-trick scorers in the final day 9-0 win over Morecambe – Rebecca Beech and Hope Knight for whom it was a fourth hat-trick of the season.

- City went out of the FA Cup in dramatic circumstances as they lost on penalties to higher division opponents Derby in the 2nd Round. Hull trailed 1-0 to the Ewe Rams before Nat Bell's equaliser on her 18th birthday forced extra-time. With no goals in the additional period it went to penalties where Katie Thompson, Jo Symington and Hope Knight all failed to convert as Hull lost the shootout 3-2.

- Hull were technically East Riding FA County Cup runners-up for 2017/18, but did not play a game in the competition. After their quarter-final and semi-final opponents were unable to fulfil the fixtures, the Tigresses advanced to the final against AFC Preston on walkovers. With a number of injuries they sought to field development players in the final but were refused permission by the County FA, and so conceded the game.

- Hull City's recent progress, and promotion to the WPL Northern Division 1 in 2014/15 is in part thanks to their merger with Beverley Town Ladies in 2011/12.

IPSWICH TOWN

2018/19: WNL DIVISION 1 South East (Tier 4)

Founded: Unknown

Nickname: Town

Ground: Goldstar Ground, (Felixstowe & Walton United FC)

Season 2017/18:

WPL South East One (Tier 4): 3rd

FA Cup: 3rd Round
WPL Cup: 1st Round
County Cup: Winners

2017/18 WPL SOUTH EAST ONE

20.08	AFC Wimbledon (a)	W	3-1	Natasha Thomas (x2), Lindsey Cooper	50	
27.08	Stevenage (h)	W	1-0	Lindsey Cooper 55	50	
10.09	Cambridge United (a)	D	2-2	Amanda Crump, Cassandra Craddock	72	
17.09	Leyton Orient (h)	L	0-2		38	6
20.09	Norwich City (a)	W	5-0	Zoe Cossey 3, 82, Natasha Thomas 39, Cassandra Craddock 44, Miagh Downey 54	82	1
24.09	Enfield Town (a)	L	2-3	Natasha Thomas, Jacqueline Ball	25	3
01.10	Actonians (h)	W	1-0	Roxanne Small	17	3
11.10	Norwich City (h)	W	8-1	Roxanne Small 6, Zoe Cossey 16, 71, 73, Amanda Crump, Lindsey Cooper, Miagh Downey 29, Sophie Welton 55	105	3
05.11	Actonians (a)	W	2-1	Zoe Cossey 45, 64	25	4
26.11	MK Dons (a)	D	2-2	Sophie Welton, Jade Henry	55	5
10.12	Haringey Borough (h)	P-P				5
14.01	Haringey Borough (h)	W	9-0	Sophie Welton 9, 25, 40, 62, Miagh Downey 12, Amanda Crump 38, 72, Cassandra Craddock 67, Natasha Thomas 90	40	4
28.01	Leyton Orient (a)	L	1-2	Natasha Thomas 41	57	4
04.02	Denham United (h)	W	4-2	Own Goal 12, Miagh Downey 38, Amanda Crump (pen) 62, Zoe Cossey 76	60	4
11.02	Stevenage (a)	P-P				4
25.02	Cambridge United (h)	W	3-1	Natasha Thomas 14, 78, *Ipswich GK Sian Fagg saved Amber Cantwell pen 44,* Miagh Downey 49	12	3
04.03	Haringey Borough (a)	W	10-0	Natasha Thomas 14, 40, 51, 65, 89, Zoe Cossey 21, 27, Amanda Crump 59, Miagh Downey 67, Sophie Welton 68		2
11.03	MK Dons (h)	L	0-1		77	2
01.04	Enfield Town (h)	W	5-2	Sophie Welton 19, Amanda Crump (pen) 39, (pen) 71, Lindsey Cooper 49, Gemma Moore 89	40	2

08.04	Stevenage (a)		P-P			2
15.04	Denham United (a)	W	6-1	Zoe Cossey 1, 26, 87, Amanda Crump (pen) 53, Gemma Moore 68, Natasha Thomas 85	46	2
22.04	Luton Town (h)	W	2-1	Cassie Craddock 8, Natasha Thomas 26	101	2
29.04	Stevenage (a)*	W	7-2	Zoe Cossey 4, Natasha Thomas 7, 42, 61, 81, Miagh Downey 14, Roxy Small 85	20	2
13.05	Luton Town (a)	W	2-1	Natasha Thomas 30, Miagh Downey 77	40	3
20.05	AFC Wimbledon (h)+	D	1-1	Zoe Cossey 72	60	3

*Played at Crofters End, Sawbridgeworth Town FC   +Played at Playford Road

2017/18 FA CUP

08.10 RQ3	Cambridge City (a)	W	5-1	Jordan Arnoup 6, Natasha Thomas 23, 66, Lindsey Cooper 72, Roxanne Small 75	
12.11 R1	Leyton Orient (h)	W	4-2 (aet)	**Sophie Welton 45, Cassandra Craddock 73, Gemma Moore 99,** *Ipwich GK saved Orient pen 104,* **Zoe Cossey 117**	
03.12 R2	Stevenage (a)	D	1-1aet (W 3-0p)	Natasha Thomas 69	
07.01 R3	Charlton Athletic (h)	L	2-5 (aet)	Cassandra Craddock 47, 75	110

2017/18 WPL Cup

03.09 DR	Larkhall Athletic (a)	W	8-1	Victoria Campbell, Cassandra Craddock (x3), Jade Henry, Roxanne Small, Sophie Welton (x2)	20
22.10 R1	C&K Basildon (h)	L	w/o	*NB: Ipswich won 1-0 (Zoe Cossey) but were later expelled for fielding an ineligible player*	46

2017/18 SUFFOLK FA COUNTY CUP

15.10 R1	Walsham Le Willows (h)	W	11-0	Sophie Welton (x4), Natasha Thomas (x4), Cassandra Craddock, Jade Henry, Amanda Crump	45
19.11 R2	Hadleigh United (a)	W	w/o		
18.02 QF	Bungay Town (h)	W	7-1	Jordan Arnoup 1, Amanda Crump 3, 20, Sophie Welton 14, Zoe Cossey 31, 78, Miagh Downey 70	30
18.03 SF	Ipswich Wanderers (h)*		A-A	Abandoned after 25 mins due to serious injury to a Wanderers player. Town leading 1-0 (Jordan Arnoup (pen) 16)	
25.03 SF	Ipswich Wanderers (h)*	W	7-0	Sophie Welton 12, 63, Miagh Downey 50, Zoe Cossey 56, 84, Amanda Crump 62, Natasha Thomas 74	
07.05 F	AFC Sudbury (n)	W	5-1	Natasha Thomas 19, 65, Amanda Crump 35, Sophie Welton 55, Lindsey Cooper 61	456

*Played at Ransomes Sports Pavilion   (n) Played at Weston Homes Communities Stadium, Colchester United FC

"In 2017/18 we had a really successful season and narrowly missed out on promotion. Once again we lifted the Suffolk FA County Cup after beating AFC Sudbury 5-1 in the final. We had a great run in the FA Cup and made it to the 3rd Round and extra-time before bowing out to a really strong Charlton side who went on to win the League above us and are now in the Championship. We are the biggest women's side in East Anglia with a great support network, a very talented squad and a variety of characters which makes playing for Ipswich really enjoyable. Our hope for 2018/19 is to build on last season's success and gain promotion."

Amanda Crump – Ipswich Town captain

•

- Ipswich Town manager Ralph Pruden stood down after the final game of the 2017/18 season following four years in charge of the club. His final season culminated in an impressive 3rd place finish in WPL South East One (now WNL Division 1 South East) and a County Cup triumph.

- It was the fourth year in a row that Town have won the Suffolk FA County Cup, doing so in 2015 (W 2-0 v AFC Sudbury), 2016 (W 8-0 Kirkley & Pakefield), 2017 (W 5-0 Lowestoft Town) and 2018 (W 2-0 AFC Sudbury).

- Ipswich striker Natasha Thomas scored 30 goals in 2017/18 making her the division's highest scorer in all competitions. She was the division's second-highest scorer when it came to League goals only, with 20, behind Alessandra Barreca (24) of Actionians.

- Ipswich Town's formal association with the men's professional club of the same name was announced in February 2012.

KEYNSHAM TOWN

2018/19: WNL DIVISION 1 South West (Tier 4)

Founded: 1993 (as Super Strikers Girls)

Nickname: The K's

Ground: AJN Stadium, (Keynsham Town FC)

Season 2017/18:

WPL South West One (Tier 4): 3rd

FA Cup: 4th Round
WPL Cup: Determining Round
WPL Plate: Quarter-finals
County Cup: Winners

2017/18 WPL SOUTH WEST ONE

27.08	Cheltenham Town (a)	W	4-0	Kerry Bartlett 31, 77, Katie Cook 56, Justine Lorton 60	62	
10.09	St Nicholas (h)	W	11-0	Kerry Bartlett 1, 7, 16, 46, 87, Katie Cook 13, Jade Radburn 24, Justine Lorton 28, 59, Christina Vega Leandro 33, 85	45	
17.09	Poole Town (h)	W	5-1	Kerry Bartlett 12, Katie Cook 61, Michelle Munro 41, Nadine Grogan 87, Justine Lorton 43	40	3
21.09	Brislington (a)	W	2-1	Kerry Barlett 13, 58	84	2
24.09	Maidenhead U (a)	W	2-1	Emily Plummer 19, Kerry Bartlett 66		2
01.10	St Nicholas (a)	W	9-0	Kerry Bartlett 10, 20, 26, 45+1, 65, Andreea Alexandru 12, Michelle Munro 29, Clarice White 42, Jessie Osborne 69	35	2
12.10	Brislington (h)	W	4-0	Kerry Bartlett 38, 67, 85, Katie Cook 43	105	1
29.10	*Basingstoke Town (a)* **exp**	W	10-0	Justine Lorton 4, 42, Kerry Bartlett 6, 17 27, 30, 83, 85, Christine Vega Leandro 61, Katie Cook 64	20	1
05.11	Plymouth Argyle (a)	L	2-5	Katie Cook 34, Kerry Bartlett 63	111	1
26.11	So'ton Women (a)	L	0-1		35	1
21.01	Poole Town (a)		P-P			2
25.02	Larkhall Athletic (h)	W	2-0	Sandy Abi-Elias 76, Justine Lorton 78	50	2
04.03	Poole Town (a)		P-P			2
11.03	Poole Town (a)		P-P			4
18.03	So'ton Saints (a)		P-P			4
25.03	Maidenhead U (h)	W	11-0	Christine Vega Leandro 3, 77, Kerry Bartlett 17, 88, Clarice White 28, Ellie Curson 35, 38, 83, Justine Lorton 45, 45+2, Carly Bryant 48	45	3
08.04	Plymouth Argyle (h)	L	1-6	Kerry Bartlett 5	70	4
15.04	So'ton Women (h)	D	4-4	Kerry Barlett 12, Justine Lorton 80, 90+1, Jade Radburn 86	60	4
22.04	Cheltenham Town (h)	W	9-0	Jade Radburn 27, Kerry Bartlett 37, 53, 70, Justine Lorton 39, 41, Ellie Curson 45+2, Christine Vega Leandro 72, (pen) 88	50	4

29.04	Poole Town (a)*	W	6-1	Kerry Bartlett 27, 32, Justine Lorton 39, Michelle Munro 44, Christine Vega Leandro 75, (pen) 80	28	3
06.05	Larkhall Athletic (a)	W	4-1	Kerry Bartlett 10, 55, Justine Lorton 30, Ellie Curson 38	30	3
13.05	So'ton Saints (h)	W	4-1	Kerry Bartlett 16, 86, Christine Vega Leandro 75, 81	25	3
20.05	So'ton Saints (a)	L	2-3	Christine Vega Leandro 58, Jade Radburn 85	21	3

*Played at Tatnam Ground, Poole Town FC   exp = Result expunged from records when Basingstoke withdrew from League

2017/18 FA CUP

08.10 RQ3	St Nicholas (a)	W	1-0	Michelle Munro 69	55
12.11 R1	So'ton Saints (a)	W	3-1	Katie Cook 27, Kerry Bartlett 65, Justine Lorton 83	
03.12 R2	So'ton Women (h)	W	2-1	Kerry Bartlett 18, Justine Lorton 82	
07.01 R3	Brislington (h)	W	8-1	Kerry Bartlett 12, 21, 27, 72, Justine Lorton 42, Christine Vega Leandro 78, Katie Cook 76, Own Goal 85	
04.02 R4	Lewes (h)	L	0-3		75

2017/18 WPL CUP

03.09 DR	Enfield Town (a)	L	2-3	Christina Vega Leandro 41, Katie Cook 70	23

2017/18 WPL PLATE

22.10 R1	St Nicholas (h)	W	4-0	Katie Cook 6, 86, Carly Bryant 31, Asia Brown 81	45
10.12 R2	Swindon Town (a)		P-P		
17.12 R2	Swindon Town (a)		P-P		
14.01 R2	Swindon Town (a)	W	10-1	Kerry Bartlett 20, 22, 24, 41, 43, Justine Lorton 8, 45, Christine Vega Leandro 12, 82, Clarice White 62	44
11.02 QF	West Ham United (a)	L	0-7		189

2017/18 SOMERSET FA COUNTY CUP

15.10 QF	Frome Town (a)	W	w/o	
18.02 SF	Hamilton (a)	W	w/o	
03.05 F	Larkhall Athletic (n)	W	3-0	Clarice White 40, Justine Lorton 55, Kerry Bartlett (pen) 74

(n) Played at Bishop Sutton FC

- In 2017/18 Keynsham Town improved on their 4th place finish of the previous season by placing 3rd in WPL South West One (now WNL Division 1 South West). They topped the table in October and November but eventually finished behind champions Plymouth Argyle and runners-up Southampton Women.

- They also had silverware to celebrate in 2017/18 with a 3-0 win over Larkhall Athletic in the Somerset FA County Cup final, although admittedly it was the only game they played in the competition after walkovers in the quarter-finals and semi-finals.

- Kerry Bartlett was the division's second-highest scorer in 2017/18 hitting 33 goals in the League and 45 in all competitions. Only Natasha Knapman of Plymouth got more, with 40 League goals and 61 in all competitions. Bartlett's tally included five-goal hauls in both League games against St Nicholas and also against Swindon in the WPL Plate, a four-goal haul against Brislington in the FA Cup and hat-tricks in League games against Brislington and Cheltenham.

- The club was initially formed as an Under-11's six-a-side team in 1993 by pupils of Chandag Junior School in Bristol under the name Super Strikers Girls. The name was later changed to Protel Super Strikers following sponsorship by a local telecoms company. At that point the club also adopted Celtic's green and white colours.

- In 1998/99 the club became closely affiliated with Keynsham Town men's team and was granted use of their facilities. They changed their name to the same.

LARKHALL ATHLETIC

2018/19: WNL DIVISION 1
South West (Tier 4)

Founded: 2008

Nickname: The Larks

Ground: Plain Ham,
(Larkhall Athletic FC))

Season 2017/18:

WPL South West One (Tier 4): 7th

FA Cup: 1st Round
WPL Cup: Determining Round
WPL Plate: 1st Round
County Cup: Runners-up

2017/18 WPL SOUTH WEST ONE

Date	Opponent	Result	Score	Scorers		
20.08	So'ton Women (a)		P-P			
27.08	Basingstoke Town (h)		P-P			
10.09	Plymouth Argyle (a)	L	1-9	Lizzie Barrett 35, *Kate German sent off*	32	
17.09	St Nicholas (a)	D	2-2	Lizzie Barrett (x2)	55	8
01.10	Cheltenham Town (h)	W	5-4	Lizzie Barrett (x2), Kate German, Ann-Marie Hervey, Katie-May O'Hara Nash	40	7
29.10	Maidenhead U (h)	W	1-0	Charlotte Morrison	45	6
05.11	Poole Town (a)	W	3-1	Kate German (x2), Katy-May O'Hara Nash	21	5
19.11	Brislington (a)		P-P			5
26.11	Cheltenham Town (a)	L	0-1		36	6
03.12	So'ton Saints (a)		P-P			6
10.12	Basingstoke Town (a)		P-P			6
17.12	So'ton Women (h)*	L	0-6		25	8
07.01	Poole Town (h)		P-P			8
14.01	Plymouth Argyle (h)	L	0-3		20	8
21.01	Maidenhead U (a)		P-P			8
28.01	Poole Town (h)		P-P			8
04.02	So'ton Women (a)	L	1-6	Lizzie Barrett	20	8
25.02	Keynsham Town (a)	L	0-2		50	9
04.03	Brislington (h)		P-P			9
11.03	Maidenhead U (a)	L	0-1		15	7
18.03	Brislington (a)		P-P			7
21.03	St Nicholas (h)	W	5-0	Lizzie Barrett (x3), Kate German, Jodie Sheppard	30	7
08.04	So'ton Saints (h)	L	0-3		15	6
15.04	Poole Town (h)	L	0-1		20	6
22.04	So'ton Saints (a)	L	0-3		10	6
06.05	Keynsham Town (h)	L	1-4	Emily Harrington	30	6

08.05	Brislington (h)	L	1-3	Ann-Marie Hervey	30	7
13.05	Brislington (a)	D	1-1	Kate German	63	7

*Played at Bath University

2017/18 FA CUP

08.10 RQ3	Forest Green Rovers (a)	W	3-0	Lizzie Barrett, Kate German, Katie May-O'Hara Nash	
12.11 R1	So'ton Women (h)	L	2-3	Kate German 37, Ann-Marie Hervey 49	40

2017/18 WPL CUP

03.09 DR	Ipswich Town (h)	L	1-8	Kate German	20

2017/18 WPL PLATE

22.10 R1	So'ton Saints (a)	L	0-3		15

2017/18 SOMERSET FA COUNTY CUP

15.10 QF	Brislington (a)	W	4-2	Kate German (x2), Katy-May O'Hara Nash, Charlotte Morrison	
18.02 SF	Bishops Lydeard (h)	W	3-0	Lizzie Barrett, Kate German, Katy-May O'Hara Nash	30
03.05 F	Keynsham Town (n)	L	0-3		

(n) Played at Bishop Sutton FC

- Larkhall Athletic's Nicola O'Connell won the respect of her peers in 2017/18 as she was voted WPL Division One Players' Player of the Year.

- Lizzie Barrett was the club's top scorer as regards League goals in 2017/18, with nine. In all competitions she was joint top-scorer with Kate German – they both hit 11. Both scored during Larkhall's run to the Somerset FA County Cup final in which the team beat Brislington and Bishops Lydeard only to lose to Keynsham Town in the final.

- Larkhall Athletic Ladies were formed in 2008 following their move across from Bath City Ladies.

LEEDS UNITED

2018/19: WNL DIVISION 1 North (Tier 4)

Founded: 1989

Nickname: The Pheonix

Ground: Wheatley Park, (Garforth Town FC) in 2017/18 moving to Thorp Arch (Leeds United Academy) for 2018/19

Season 2017/18:

WPL North One (Tier 4): 10th

FA Cup: 3rd Qualifying Round
WPL Cup: Determining Round
WPL Plate: 2nd Round
County Cup: Quarter-finals

2017/18 WPL NORTHERN ONE

Date	Opponent		Result	Scorers	Att	Pos
20.08	Bolton W (a)	L	1-3	Carly Hoyle 41	81	
27.08	Chester-le-Street T (h)	W	1-0	Liuli Dyson 84	840*	
10.09	Liverpool M F (a)	L	1-2	Carey Huegett	45	
17.09	Barnsley (h)	L	3-4	Carey Huegett 43, Rebecca Hunt 63, Liuli Dyson 74	219	10
20.09	Hull City (a)	L	1-5	Martina Petrova 78	60	10
24.09	Newcastle United (a)	W	4-3	Martina Petrova 3, Arianne Parnham 8, 79, Charlotte Adams 54	75	6
01.10	Morecambe (h)**	L	1-3	Charlotte Adams	35	8
11.10	Hull City (h)	L	0-1		80	9
29.10	Liverpool M F (h)	L	0-2		108	11
05.11	Brighouse Town (a)	L	1-3	Carey Huegett 70	112	11
12.11	Mossley Hill A (a)	L	1-2	Rebecca Hunt 2	35	11
03.12	Bolton W (h)	L	0-1		35	11
10.12	Fylde (a)		P-P			11
07.01	Chorley (a)		P-P			11
21.01	Newcastle United (h)		P-P			11
28.01	Chorley (a)	W	1-0	Bridie Hannon 3, *Olivia Smart sent off*	126	11
04.02	Crewe Alex (a)	D	0-0		36	11
11.02	Morecambe (a)	W	2-1	Shelbey Morris 56, Rebecca Hunt 66	35	9
04.03	Mossley Hill A (h)		P-P			10
21.03	Brighouse Town (h)	L	2-5	Holly Findlay 9, 41	50	10
25.03	Newcastle United (h)	W	1-0	Carey Huegett 18	75	7
15.04	Chorley (h)	L	1-2	Shelbey Morris 22		10
29.04	Chester-le-Street T (a)	L	0-3	*Rebecca Hunt sent off*	50	11
06.05	Mossley Hill A (h)	W	2-1	Carey Huegett, Holly Findlay	150	10
13.05	Barnsley (a)	W	2-1	Shelbey Morris 18, 20	105	10
20.05	Crewe Alex (h)+	D	1-1	Jenny Clark 87	100	10

*Played at Elland Road, (Leeds United FC)   **Played at Batley Sports and Tennis Centre   +Played at Leeds United Training Ground

2017/18 FA CUP

| 08.10 RQ3 | Sheffield United (a)+ | D | 3-3aet (L 2-3p) | Carey Huegett (x2), Liuli Dyson | 546 |

+Played at Bramall Lane, (Sheffield United FC)

2017/18 WPL CUP

| 03.09 DR | Nottingham F (a) | L | 1-7 | Laura Porritt (pen) 75 | 94 |

2017/18 WPL PLATE

| 22.10 R1 | Solihull Moors (h) | W | 3-2 | Rachel Stuart (x2, 1pen), Shelbey Morris | 79 |
| 14.01 R2 | Fylde (a) | D | 0-0aet (L 3-4 p) | | 58 |

2017/18 WEST RIDING FA COUNTY CUP

15.10 R1	Ripon City (a)	W	13-0	Carey Huegett 5, 6, 44, 65, 73, Marty Petrova 7, Rebecca Hunt 20, 27, Arrianne Parnham 30, Shannon Beal 45+1, Shelbey Morris 85, Beth Davies 86, Rachel Stuart 89
19.11 R2	Lower Hopton (a)	W	5-0	
17.12 QF	Farsley Celtic (h)	D	1-1 L 5-6p)	Laura Porritt 23

"There's no doubting 2017/18 was a difficult season, but we managed to get the results we needed and keep our place in the division. This means a lot as Leeds United is a massive club with so much history, just like the men aiming for the Premier League. Our goal is to keep on pushing for a higher level. It's an honour and a privilege to wear the Leeds United badge."

Cath Hamill – Leeds United Captain

- In June 2017 Leeds Ladies re-established their association with Leeds United men's team. The agreement saw them again take on the name of Leeds United Ladies, handed the same kit as the men, and return to the same Thorp Arch training ground. In 2018/19 they will be playing their home matches at Thorp Arch.

- The club was initially formed as Leeds United Ladies in 1989 and previously had intermittent funding and support from the men throughout its lifetime. In 2013/14 that support was withdrawn, and the club was known as Leeds Ladies until the summer of 2017.

- Leeds' have twice reached the FA Women's Cup final (2006 & 2008) only to lose both times to overwhelming favourites Arsenal.

- Former England forward Sue Smith is the best known player ever to have represented the club. Smith won 93 caps for her country and played for Leeds from 2002 to 2010.

LEICESTER CITY LADIES

2018/19: EAST MIDLANDS REGIONAL PREMIER (Tier 5)

Founded: 1966

Nickname: The Foxes / Blues / City

Ground: Linwood Playing Fields

Season 2017/18:

WPL Midlands One (Tier 4): 12th (R)

FA Cup: 3rd Qualifying Round
WPL Cup: Determining Round
WPL Plate: Preliminary Round
County Cup: 1st Round

2017/18 WPL MIDLANDS ONE

Date	Opponent	Result	Score	Scorers		
20.08	Burton Albion (h)	L	0-1		85	
27.08	B'ham & W M (a)	P-P				
10.09	Steel City W (h)	L	0-6		30	
17.09	Solihull Moors (a)	L	1-4	Carmelina Colange Lo 50	40	11
20.09	Loughborough F (h)	L	0-4		65	12
01.10	Sheffield United (a)	L	0-4		47	11
12.10	Loughborough F (a)	L	0-7		65	11
29.10	B'ham & W M (h)	L	1-3	Erica Kilby	45	11
05.11	Long Eaton United (a)	L	0-4		32	11
12.11	Radcliffe Olympic (a)	L	1-5	Bayleigh Newby	25	12
26.11	Rotherham Utd (h)*	L	2-3	Carmelina Colange Lo (x2)	15	12
03.12	Solihull Moors (h)	L	1-4	Gemma Ball	20	12
10.12	The New Saints (a)	P-P				
07.01	Rotherham Utd (a)	D	1-1	Ellise Newby 35	35	12
14.01	The New Saints (a)	L	0-5		51	12
21.01	Steel City W (a)	P-P				12
28.01	Sporting Khalsa (h)	L	0-6		30	12
04.02	Radcliffe Olympic (h)	L	0-1		20	12
25.02	Burton Albion (a)	L	0-4		45	12
04.03	Sporting Khalsa (a)	P-P				12
11.03	B'ham & WM (a)	L	0-6		20	12
08.04	The New Saints (h)	L	0-12		15	12
22.04	Steel City W (a)	W	3-1	Katie Connor (x2) Bayleigh Newby	57	12
29.04	Long Eaton United (h)	L	0-3		40	12
06.05	Sporting Khalsa (a)	L	0-6		20	12
20.05	Sheffield United (h)	L	1-6	Gemma Ball	80	12

*Played at Saffron Lane, (Aylestone Park FC)

2017/18 FA CUP
08.10 RQ3   Long Eaton United (a)   L   1-3

2017/18 WPL CUP
03.09 DR   Bolton Wanderers (h)   L   0-5   60

2017/18 WPL PLATE
24.09 PR   Hull City (a)   L   w/o

2017/18 LEICESTERSHIRE & RUTLAND FA COUNTY CUP
15.10 R1   Leicester City W Development   L   1-3

"The beginning of 2017/18 was incredibly difficult for us when a strong group of players signed on proved to be unreliable and we could never keep any consistency. Great credit should be given to a small core of senior players who did all they could to maintain the team and support less experienced and younger players who stepped up to keep the first-team alive. The new management team brought in talented youngsters and a consistent pattern of play. Performances improved steadily but there was just too much to do to survive the season. We are optimistic of better results to come."

Amie Cattell – Leicester City Ladies Captain

- A tricky 2017/18 season saw Leicester City Ladies finish bottom of WPL Midlands One and suffer relegation to the East Midlands Regional Premier League. However, the club continued to do great work for the community and to forge links with women's football abroad, even travelling to Bulgaria for a successful three-game tour in May 2018.

- Formed in 1966, Leicester City Ladies is believed to be the oldest women's club in the country still existing in its original guise. It is a grassroots club and a separate entity to Leicester City Women which is affiliated to the men's Premier League side Leicester City.

- In 1992, well before the creation of Leicester City Women, Leicester City Ladies did have a close relationship with the men's Leicester City. In 1996 Leicester City Ladies played Crystal Palace Ladies at Wembley before their male counterparts faced each other in the Championship play-off final.

LEYTON ORIENT

2018/19: WNL DIVISION 1 SOUTH EAST (Tier 4)

Founded: 2004 (as KIKK United)

Nickname: The O's

Ground: Mile End Stadium

Season 2017/18:

WPL South East One (Tier 4): 4th

FA Cup: 1st Round

WPL Cup: 1st Round

Capital Cup: Semi-final

2017/18 WPL SOUTH EAST ONE

Date	Opponent		Result	Scorers		
20.08	Cambridge United (a)	D	0-0		72	
27.08	Actonians (a)	L	1-5	Egle Trezzi 68	30	
10.09	Enfield Town (h)	W	9-0	Chanel Richards 1, 50, Sophie Le Marchand 3, 76, Daniele Griffiths 8, Egle Trezzi 15, Hayley Barton 65, Ella Meadowcroft 72, 82	65	
17.09	Ipswich Town (a)	W	2-0	Lisa Holmback 24, Chanel Richards 31	38	4
24.09	Luton Town (a)	W	4-0	Sarka Stryhalova 17, 33 Sophie Le Marchand 39, Chanel Richards 66	34	2
01.10	Norwich City (a)	W	5-2	Sophie Le Marchand 16, Lisa Holmbeck 51, Sarka Stryhalova 56, 79, Danielle Griffiths (pen) 61	48	2
04.10	Haringey Borough (h)	W	8-0	Hayley Barton 11, 40, Chloe McNee 14, Sophie Le Marchand 22, Danielle Griffiths (pen) 35, Belen Ripoll Doulton 45, 66, Egle Trezzi 48	35	2
15.10	Actonians (h)*	L	3-4	Chloe McNee 23, Sophie Le Marchand 67, Sarka Stryhalova 70	117	3
05.11	Denham United (a)	W	2-0	Belen Ripoll Doulton 36, Sophie Le Marchand 43	42	3
07.11	Haringey Borough (a)	W	8-0	Danielle Griffiths (pen) 4, Egle Trezzi 22, Kayleigh Xidhas 29, Francesca Cagetti 41, Sarka Stryhalova 44, 56, Sophie Le Marchand 45, 54,	26	2
26.11	Stevenage (a)	W	2-0	Danielle Griffiths (pen) 63, Sarka Stryhalova 87, *Lisa Holmback sent off 90+2*	30	2
10.12	AFC Wimbledon (a)	L	0-3		70	2
17.12	AFC Wimbledon (h)	P-P				2
07.01	Denham United (h)	W	2-1	Sophie Le Marchand 12, Rebecca Hirst 21	61	2
14.01	MK Dons (a)	L	1-2	Vanessa Wilson 33	85	2
28.01	Ipswich Town (h)	W	2-1	Sophie Le Marchand 20, 60	57	2
04.02	Luton Town (h)	L	0-4	*Vanessa Wilson sent off 78*	61	2
11.02	Norwich City (h)	P-P				2
11.03	Cambridge United (h)	L	0-1		56	3
18.03	AFC Wimbledon (h)	P-P				3
25.03	Norwich City (h)	W	4-1	Sophie Le Marchand 1, 11, 41 Hayley Barton 60	63	2
15.04	AFC Wimbledon (h)	W	2-1	Lisa Fulgence 19, 25	74	3

29.04	MK Dons (h) *	L	2-6	Sophie Le Marchand 29, Lisa Holmback 32,	202	4
13.05	Stevenage (h)	D	2-2	Sarka Stryhalova 60, Hannah Porter 73, *Danielle Griffiths missed pen 85*	55	4
20.05	Enfield Town (a)	D	0-0		105	4

*Played at Matchroom Stadium, Leyton Orient FC

2017/18 FA Cup

| 08.10 RQ3 | Billericay Town (h)* | W | 7-0 | Sophie Le Marchand 8, 33, 55, 60, Chloe McNee 11, Vanessa Wilson 50, Egle Trezzi 70 | 207 |
| 12.11 R1 | Ipswich Town (a) | L | 2-4 (aet) | Kayleigh Xidhas 86, Own Goal 90, *Danielle Griffiths missed pen 104 (saved)* | |

*Played at Matchroom Stadium, Leyton Orient FC

2017/18 WPL Cup

| 03.09 DR | Luton Town (a) | W | 4-2 | Sophie Le Marchand 37, Belen Ripoll Douton 43, Ellie Davies 67, Ella Meadowcroft 87 | 59 |
| 29.10R1 | Cardiff City L (a) | L | 1-3 | Leyre Bastyr 85 | 85 |

2017/18 Middlesex FA Capital Cup

22.10 R1	Actonians (a)	W	2-0	Ellie Davies 18, Leyre Bastyr 38	30
19.11 QF	Denham United (h)	W	4-1	Hayley Barton 33, Belen Ripoll Douton 47, Sophie Le Marchand 49, 54	
25.02 SF	Charlton Athletic (a)	L	2-3	Belen Ripoll-Douton 22, Lisa Holmbeck 46	114

"Finishing 4th in our first season in the WPL was a fantastic achievement and really set the marker for a promotion push in 2018/19. We showed the rest of the teams in the League that we can perform and get a result against anyone: that comes from a team spirit and environment which is second to none. All of the girls work for each other, help each other and want to succeed as a club. It is a real pleasure to be a part of this team and I hope we can step on and show our true potential."

Danielle Griffiths – Leyton Orient Captain

- As 2016/17 London & South East Premier Division winners, Orient were promoted to WPL South East One (now WNL Division 1 South East) ahead of the 2017/18 season. They had a great first campaign in Tier 4, ultimately finishing in 4th place having been as high as 2nd at various points throughout the season. One of the reasons behind their success was the goalscoring prowess of Sophie Le Marchand. She hit 23 goals to finish as the division's 3rd-highest scorer in all competitions.

- The club began life as KIKK United in 2004, founded by a group of Swedish women who took its name from the Swedish expression Kick In Kulan I Krysset, which means 'scoring in the top corner'.

- KIKK United became officially affiliated with the men's professional outfit Leyton Orient in the summer of 2015. They took the club's name and played their first League match as Leyton Orient Women on August 23rd that year, beating Fulham 1-0. They regularly play

LIVERPOOL FEDS

2018/19: WNL DIVISION 1 NORTH (Tier 4)

Founded: 1991

Nickname: Feds

Ground: IM Marsh Campus in 2017/18, moving to South Liverpool Football Hub in 2018/19

Season 2017/18:

WPL Northern One (Tier 4): 3rd

FA Cup: 3rd Round
WPL Cup: 2nd Round
County Cup: Winners

2017/18 WPL NORTHERN ONE

Date	Opponent		Score	Scorers		
20.08	Chester-leStreet T (h)	W	4-0	Carla Lee 26, 29, 37, Carina Mendes 55	30	
27.08	Barnsley (a)	W	3-2	Nicole Johnston 52, Chantelle Thompson 60, Roisin Havelin 61, *Helen Griffiths sent off 90*	90	
10.09	Leeds United (h)	W	2-1	Roisin Havelin 64, Amy Seagraves 66	45	
20.09	Mossley Hill A (h)	W	4-0	Carla Lee (pen) 23, 31, Rosie Kinvig 51, Nicole Johnston 61	50	2
01.10	Hull City (a)	L	0-3		80	3
11.10	Mossley Hill A (a)*	W	3-0	Roisin Havelin 3, 90, Carla Lee 73	49	3
22.10	Newcastle United (a)	D	1-1	Charlotte Gill 2	63	4
29.10	Leeds United (a)	W	2-0	Sasha Rowe 46, Roisin Havelin 80	108	2
19.11	Bolton Wanderers (a)		P-P			2
26.11	Newcastle United (h)+	W	3-0	Nicole Johnston 43, Abby Pope 64, Sasha Rowe 65	40	3
28.01	Barnsley (h)+	W	8-0	Laura Bartup 9, 89, Rosie Kinvig 45, 75, 81, 88, Carla Lee (pen) 54, Nicole Johnston 82	30	1
04.02	Hull City (h)	D	2-2	Laura Bartup 18, Carla Lee 78	80	1
11.02	Crewe Alexandra (a)		P-P			1
18.02	Chorley (h)	W	1-0	Sasha Rowe (pen) 85	50	1
25.02	Brighouse Town (h)	D	0-0		70	2
04.03	Morecambe (h)	W	5-0	Helen Griffiths 16, Chantelle Thompson 23, Rosie Kinvig 50, 74, Laura Bartup 70	30	1
11.03	Chorley (a)	D	1-1	Sasha Rowe (pen) 84	70	2
25.03	Morecambe (a)	L	1-3	Sasha Rowe 39	32	2
08.04	Brighouse Town (a)		P-P			2
11.04	Brighouse Town (a)**	W	3-1	Chantelle Thompson 55, Laura Bartup 72, 78	70	2
15.04	Crewe Alexandra (h)	W	2-1	Carla Lee 71, Georgina Stebbings (og) 87	60	2
22.04	Bolton Wanderers (h)	L	1-2	Sasha Rowe 5	45	2
02.05	Crewe Alexandra (a)	W	1-0	Carla Lee 70	40	2
06.05	Bolton Wanderers (a)	L	0-1		50	2
20.05	Chester-le-Street T (a)	W	1-0	Laura Bartup 62, *Laura Bartup sent off 88*	30	3

*Played at Litherland Sports Club   +Played at Edge Hill University   **Played at Woodhouse Grove School

2017/18 FA CUP

08.10 RQ3	Mossley Hill A (h)	W	7-0	Sasha Rowe 10, 14, 18, Laura Bartup 42, 89, *Carla Lee missed pen 53*, Carla Lee 66, Nicole Johnston 80	100
12.11 R1	Bolton Wanderers (h)+	W	1-0 (aet)	Carina Mendes 112	60
03.12 R2	Nettleham (a)	W	3-1	Lynsey Longhurst 48, Roisin Havelin 68, Abby Pope 83	225
07.01 R3	Middlesbrough (a)	L	3-4 (aet)	Sasha Rowe (pen) 4, Laura Bartup 11, 83	113

+Played at Skelmersdale

2017/18 WPL CUP

03.09 DR	Wolverhampton W (a)	W	2-0	Carla Lee 44, Chantelle Thompson 62	45
24.09 PR	Steel City W (h)	W	3-1	Sasha Rowe 28, Chantelle Thompson 36, Roisin Havelin 85	40
15.10 R1	Sheffield United (a)	W	2-1	Laura Bartup 68, 87	53
14.01 R2	Blackburn Rovers (h)	L	1-2	Carla Lee 16	110

2017/18 LIVERPOOL FA COUNTY CUP

21.01 SF	Burscough Dynamo (h)	W	13-0	Laura Bartup 6, 15, 73, 78, Sasha Rowe 16, 26, 41, Carla Lee 47, Rosie Kinvig 64, 75, 81, 82, Roisin Havelin 68	35
29.04 F	Mossley Hill A (n)	W	1-0	Sasha Rowe (pen) 83	100

(n) Played at Walton Hall Park, Liverpool County FA

"The 2017/18 season was another fantastic campaign for us; 3rd in the League and great runs in the WPL and FA Cups where we tested ourselves against brilliant sides from the division above, pushing them both all the way. Eventual WPL Northern champions Blackburn beat us 2-1 in the WPL Cup and Middlesbrough – who finished 3rd in that division – edged us out 4-3 after extra-time in the FA Cup. Winning the County Cup – the club's first piece of silverware – was a special moment for everyone involved. We are so excited for 2018/19 with a special group of players hungry for more."

Chantelle Thompson, Liverpool Feds Captain

- With just seven minutes of the Liverpool FA County Cup final remaining, Sasha Rowe held her nerve to score an historic penalty. Her goal meant Feds beat Mossley Hill Athletic 1-0 to lift the first silverware in the club's history. They had previously made it to the final four times only to lose to Mossley twice and Everton twice.

- The team was formed at the Liverpool Institute of Higher Education (now known as Liverpool Hope University) in 1991. The 'Feds' part of the name originates from the fact that sports teams at the Institute of Higher Education competed as a Federation of the St Katherine's and Christ Notre Dame Colleges.

- Carla Lee was the club's top scorer in the League in 2017/18 with 10 goals, while Laura Bartup top scored in all competitions, hitting 17.

- Formerly known as Liverpool Marshall Feds, the club dropped the Marshall part of its name in summer 2018.

LONG EATON UNITED

2018/19: WNL DIVISION 1 MIDLANDS (Tier 4)

Founded: c1996

Nickname: The Blues

Ground: Grange Park (Long Eaton United FC)

Season 2017/18:

WPL Midlands One (Tier 4): 6th

FA Cup: 2nd Round
WPL Cup: Determining Round
WPL Plate: 2nd Round
County Cup: Semi-final

2017/18 WPL MIDLANDS ONE

20.08	Rotherham United (a)		P-P			
27.08	The New Saints (a)	L	0-5		65	
10.09	Loughborough F (h)	L	0-2		82	
17.09	B'ham & W M (h)	L	0-1	*Michelle Kilmartin sent off*	30	10
20.09	Burton Albion (a)	L	1-2	Cara Newton 22	42	10
24.09	Radcliffe Olympic (h)	L	0-3		65	10
01.10	Sporting Khalsa (h)	W	2-0	Viki Adams, Elle Rowson	54	8
11.10	Burton Albion (h)	L	0-1		52	10
15.10	Solihull Moors (h)	L	3-7	Amy Pashley (x3)	43	10
29.10	Rotherham United (h)	W	2-0	Jade Arber 22, Viki Adams 65	52	10
05.11	Leicester City L (h)	W	4-0	Cara Newton (x2), Amy Pashley, Viki Adams	32	9
26.11	The New Saints (h)	L	2-3	Elle Rowson 25, Laura Sears 35	32	10
10.12	Sheffield United (a)		P-P			
07.01	Radcliffe Olympic (a)	L	0-1		30	10
14.01	Loughborough F (a)	L	0-6		46	10
11.02	Solihull Moors (a)		P-P			10
18.02	Sheffield United (a)	L	1-4	Viki Adams 64	106	10
25.02	Steel City W (h)	W	3-0	Viki Adams (x2), Cara Newton	42	9
11.03	Sporting Khalsa (a)	W	2-0	Katherine Clarke, Viki Adams	10	9
18.03	Solihull Moors (a)		P-P			9
25.03	Sheffield United (h)	D	0-0			9
08.04	Rotherham United (a)	W	6-0	Jade Arber (x3), Viki Adams (x3)	25	9
22.04	B'ham & W M (a)	W	2-1	Viki Adams, Anya Cresswell	25	9
29.04	Leicester City L (a)	W	3-0	Jade Arber, Viki Adams, Rebecca Lindley	40	7
02.05	Solihull Moors (a)*	W	3-1	Viki Adams, Jade Arber, Katherine Clarke	70	6
20.05	Steel City W (a)	W	4-2	Jade Arber, Cara Newton (x3)	84	6

*Played at ATG Stadium, Solihull Moors FC

2017/18 FA CUP

08.10 RQ3	Leicester City L (h)	W	3-1	Amy Pashley, Viki Adams, Jade Arber	
12.11 R1	Cambridge United (a)	W	1-0	Jade Arber 35	
03.12 R2	Bradford City (a)	L	0-5		26

2017/18 WPL CUP

| 03.09 DR | West Brom (h) | L | 1-2 (aet) | Eve Williams 39 | 65 |

2017/18 WPL PLATE

| 22.10 R1 | Wolverhampton W (a) | W | 2-1 (aet) | Viki Adams 35, Jade Arber 95 | 50 |
| 17.12 R2 | Chorley (h) | L | 0-2 | | 44 |

2017/18 DERBYSHIRE FA COUNTY CUP

19.11 R2	Bye			
28.01 QF	Pride Park Juniors & Ladies (h)	W	4-2	
18.02 SF	Woodlands (h)	L	1-4	

"A lot has changed at the club over the last year. The 2017/18 season was our first running two senior teams with the inclusion of a new development side so it took some time to bed both teams in. On the pitch it was a season of ups and downs. First-team results were poor in the first half of the season and we lost our manager in October so everyone had to pull together. With the recruitment of Stuart Wilson as interim manager in January until the end of the season we went on a run of 7 wins, 1 draw and 1 loss in our last 9 games and ended up finishing in the top half of the table with our highest ever points tally and League position at this level. We recruited John Bennett as our new first-team manager. He has had two successful spells in charge at Derby County and we are confident we can build for the future under him."

Kat Clarke, Long Eaton United Captain

- Long Eaton United's 4-2 win away to Steel City Wanderers on the final day of the 2017/18 season secured 6th place, their highest ever finish in WPL Midlands One (now WNL Division 1 Midlands).

- In 2015/16 Long Eaton United reached the FA Cup 1st Round proper for the first time in their history. As a Tier 5 team they beat Tier 4 Wolverhampton Wanderers 3-2 and were knocked out in the 2nd round by Tier 3 Sporting Albion.

- Long Eaton United secured promotion to the WPL Midlands Division One (now WNL Division 1 Midlands) for the first time in their history when they were crowned East Midlands Regional League champions in 2015/16 with three games to spare.

LOUGHBOROUGH FOXES

2018/19: WNL SOUTHERN PREMIER (Tier 3)

Founded: 2006

Nickname: The Foxes

Ground: The Stadium Pitch, Loughborough University

Season 2017/18:

WPL Midlands One (Tier 4): Champions

FA Cup: 2nd Round
WPL Cup: 2nd Round
County Cup: Semi-final

2017/18 WPL MIDLANDS ONE

Date	Opponent	Result		Scorers		
20.08	B'ham & W M (h)	W	3-0	Charlotte Cooper 47, 55, Lindsey Tugby 65	42	
27.08	Sheffield United (a)	D	1-1	Eva Rogers 25	53	
10.09	Long Eaton United (a)	W	2-0	Chloe Young 70, Shauna Chambers 85	82	
17.09	Radcliffe Olympic (h)	W	4-1	Charlotte Cooper 14, 70, Becky Matlock 21, Lindsey Tugby 44	37	2
20.09	Leicester City L (a)	W	4-0	Chloe Young 29, Eva Rogers 35, 45, Harriet Simes 41	25	2
24.09	B'ham & W M (a)	W	5-0	Lindsey Tugby 6, *Loughborough GK Amy Burle saved Annie Collins pen 48,* Chloe Young (pen) 52, Siobhan Eastham 55, Charlotte Cooper 63, Simran Singh 88	45	1
01.10	Solihull Moors (a)	W	1-0	Charlotte Cooper (pen) 56	70	1
12.10	Leicester City L (h)	W	7-0	Chloe Young 25, 38, 60, Laura Dexter 35, Laura Steele 55, Becky Matlock 70, Frankie Wilson 75	65	1
29.10	Sporting Khalsa (a)	W	4-1	Charlotte Cooper 32, Jodie Bartle 79, Eva Rogers 82, 87	20	1
05.11	Rotherham United (h)	W	5-0	Chloe Young 22, 89, Own Goal 39, Laura Dexter 65, Charlotte Cooper 75	32	1
07.01	Burton Albion (h)	W	2-0	Chloe Young 62, Laura Dexter 77	42	1
14.01	Long Eaton United (h)	W	6-0	Charlotte Cooper 20, 36, Victoria Brackenbury 26, Lindsey Tugby 48, 55, Tiana Hicks 62	46	1
11.02	Burton Albion (a)	W	3-0	Charlotte Cooper 25, 66, 74	65	1
18.02	Steel City W (h)	W	9-0	Charlotte Cooper 9, 15, 51, Rebecca Knight 12, 79, Olivia Bramley 20, 42, Laura Dexter 28, Tiana Hicks 32	39	1
25.02	Rotherham United (a)	W	4-0	Rebeca Knight 24, Jodie Bartle 68, Charlotte Cooper 75, Laura Steele 83	40	1
04.03	Solhiull Moors (h)	P-P				1
11.03	The New Saints (h)	W	5-1	Eva Rogers 2, 90+2, Laura Steele 58, Rebecca McGrother 75, 90+5	43	1
25.03	Solihull Moors (h)	W	3-1	Chloe Young 20, Charlotte Cooper 63, Eva Rogers 90+2	20	1
08.04	Steel City W (a)	W	6-1	Laura Steele 6, Chloe Young 22, 75, Becky Matlock 31, Rebecca McGrother 60, Rebecca Knight 86	54	1
22.04	Sheffield United (h)	W	3-0	Chloe Young 58, 65, Charlotte Cooper 80	75	1C

29.04	The New Saints (a)	W	4-1	Charlotte Cooper 35, Olivia Bramley 49, 57, Laura Steele 70	39	1C
13.05	Sporting Khalsa (h)	W	6-0	Victoria Brackenbury 22, Eva Rogers 33, Tiana Hicks 45, Chloe Young 45+2, Charlotte Cooper 78, Laura Steele 90	75	1C
20.05	Radcliffe Olympic (a)	W	4-2	Laura Steele 9, Rebecca Knight 12, 56, Jodie Bartle 77		1C

2017/18 FA CUP

08.10 RQ3	Radcliffe Olympic (a)	W	w/o		
12.11 R1	Redditch United (a)	W	4-2	Chloe Young 33, 37, 77, Shauna Chambers 73	312
03.12 R2	Blackburn Rovers (a)	L	1-4	Charlotte Cooper 71	77

2017/18 WPL CUP

03.09 DR	Sporting Khalsa (h)	W	5-0	Chloe Young 30, 80, Laura Steele 55, 75, Victoria Brackenbury 60	40
22.10 R1	Middlesbrough (h)	W	2-0	Lindsey Tugby 20, Charlotte Cooper 43	60
10.12 R2	Leicester City W (a)		P-P		
17.12 R2	Leicester City W (a)	L	1-3	Rebecca Knight 57	95

2017/18 LEICESTERSHIRE FA COUNTY CUP

15.10 R1	Castle Donington (h)		W	17-0	Francesca Wilson (pen) 5, 12, 86, Eva Rogers 6, 16, 44, 55, Harriet Simes 15, Victoria Brackenbury (pen) 28, 35, 53 Charlotte Cooper 31, Chloe Young 41, 42, Jodie Bartle 49, Siobhan Eastham 57, Own Goal 89	35
19.11 QF	Leicester City W Development (a)		W	3-1	Victoria Brackenbury 19, Own Goal 21, Shauna Chambers 63	
28.01 SF	Leicester City W (a)		L	0-3		

"The 2017/18 season was fantastic. We overcame the disappointment of the previous year to go up as champions. To go the entire League season unbeaten, and to only drop two points, was amazing. Having the best defensive record in the League's history was also something to be really proud of. We played some great football and scored some great goals. Most importantly the team spirit and hard work of the staff has forged a strong unit to take us into 2018/19 in a very positive frame of mind."

Shauna Chambers – Loughborough Foxes Captain

- Loughborough Foxes completed the 2017/18 WPL Midlands One season as Invincibles, going up as unbeaten champions. Indeed they would have won every game but for a 1-1 draw at Sheffield United on the second weekend – those were the only points they dropped.

- Foxes were confirmed as WPL Midlands One champions with four games to spare. They didn't kick a ball the day the title was secured, with The New Saints' 4-1 defeat at Radcliffe Olympic meaning no one could catch them.

- The club started out playing in Shepshed but was reformed and renamed as Loughborough Foxes in 1999 in memory of player Rachael Fox who died that year. At that time the club only had a junior team but a ladies first team was added in 2006. They have been promoted six times in their 12-year history.

LUTON TOWN

2018/19: WNL DIVISION 1 SOUTH EAST (Tier 4)

Founded: 1997

Nickname: The Lady Hatters

Ground: Stockwood Park Athletics Stadium

Season 2017/18:

WPL South East One (Tier 4): 5th

FA Cup: 3rd Round

WPL Cup: Determining Round

WPL Plate: Runners-up

County Cup: Runners-up

2017/18 WPL SOUTH EAST ONE

20.08	Stevenage (h)*	W	5-2	Jess McKay, Nicola Henman (x2), Zara Carroll (x2)	140
27.08	Enfield Town (a)	W	2-1	Joanne Rutherford, Dionne Manning	41
10.09	Haringey Borough (h)	W	5-1	Joanne Rutherford (x2, 1pen), Jodie Bellinger (x2), Rebecca Wilson-Kane	30
17.09	AFC Wimbledon (a)	L	1-4	Zara Carroll	50
20.09	Denham United (h)	P-P			
24.09	Leyton Orient (h)	L	0-4		34	6
01.10	MK Dons (h)	L	1-2	Jess McKay 4	76	7
04.10	Denham United (h)**	W	5-4	Jess McKay 22, 64, 85, Joanne Rutherford 39, 52	324	7
18.10	Denham United (a)	W	5-1	Stephanie Gale 7, Dionne Manning 17, Nicola Henman 49, Zara Carroll (pen) 60, Funmi Babalola 90	124	6
29.10	MK Dons (a)	L	1-2	Joanne Rutherford (pen)	85	5
05.11	Enfield Town (h)	D	0-0		37	6
19.11	Actonians (a)	W	3-2	Dionne Manning 34, Own Goal 38, Zara Carroll 46	32	5
26.11	Norwich City (h)	W	8-2	Lisa Nixon, Nicola Henman (x2), Jess McKay, Amy Summerfield, Zara Carroll, Joanne Rutherford, Natasha Fensome	34	4
04.02	Leyton Orient (a)	W	4-0	Stephanie Gale, Natasha Fensome (x2), Lisa Nixon, *Joanne Rutherford missed pen*	61	5
11.03	Norwich City (a)	P-P				5
25.03	Cambridge U (a)+	L	0-1		50	6
04.04	Stevenage (a)++	L	0-1		75	6
08.04	Haringey Borough (a)	W	14-0	Natasha Fensome (x5), Jess McKay (x4), Nicola Henman (x2), Zara Carroll, Dionne Manning, Funmi Babalola		5
22.04	Ipswich Town (a)	L	1-2	*Zara Carroll missed pen 56*, Funmi Babalola 90+1	101	6
06.05	AFC Wimbledon (h)	L	2-3	Funmi Babalola, Nicola Henman	69	8
10.05	Actonians (h)**	W	2-0	Jess McKay, Nicola Henman	201	5
13.05	Ipswich Town (h)	L	1-2	Jess McKay	40	5

| 17.05 | Cambridge United (h)^ | D | 3-3 | Lucy Webster (x2), Jodie Whitford-Stark | 121 | 5 |
| 20.05 | Norwich City (a) | W | 3-2 | Nicola Henman, Jess McKay, Zara Carroll | 60 | 5 |

*Played at Caddington   **Played at Kenilworth Road, (Luton Town FC)   +Played at Clare College Sports Ground
++Played at Colney Heath FC   ^Played at The Brache, Luton FC Training Ground

2017/18 FA CUP

08.10	RQ3	Maidenhead United (a)	W	1-0	Jess McKay	
12.11	R1	AFC Dunstable (a)	W	4-0	Jess McKay (x2), Nicola Henman, Dionne Manning	
03.12	R2	Harlow Town (h)	W	3-2 (aet)	Jess McKay (x2), Kim Farrow	
07.01	R3	Chichester City (a)	L	0-2		

2017/18 WPL CUP

| 03.09 | DR | Leyton Orient (h) | L | 2-4 | Nicola Henman 10, Jess McKay 61 | 59 |

2017/18 WPL PLATE

22.10	R1	Gillingham (a)+	W	4-3 (aet)	Nicola Henman 12, 96, Jess McKay 101, 113	
10.12	R2	Southampton Saints (h)	P-P			
17.12	R2	Southampton Saints (h)	P-P			
14.01	R2	Southampton Saints (h)	W	3-1	Natasha Fensome, Jess McKay (x2)	27
11.02		MK Dons (h)	P-P			

25.02	MK Dons (h)	W	3-2	Zara Carroll, Natasha Fensome, Nicola Henman	71
04.03	Fylde (h)		P-P		
11.03	Fylde (h)**	W	w/o	(Luton originally lost 1-2 with a goal from Nicola Henman but Fylde were later expelled for fielding an ineligible player)	61
15.04 F	West Ham United (n)	L	0-5		262

+Played at K Sports   (n) Keys Park, Hednesford Town FC

2017/18 Bedfordshire FA County Cup

21.01 QF	Woburn & Wavendon (a)		P-P	
28.01 QF	Woburn & Wavendon (a)	W	17-0	Kim Farrow 4, 26, Stephanie Gale 12, Natasha Fensome 17, 43, 54, 70, 72, Nicola Henman 20, 25, 86, Jess McKay 28, Zara Carroll 40, Rachel Kosky 73, Dionne Manninng 74, 89, Lisa Nixon 83
18.02 SF	AFC Dunstable (h)	W	2-1	Own Goal, Zara Carroll (pen)
29.04 F	Bedford (n)	L	1-3	Joanne Rutherford, *Rachel Kosky sent off*

(n)Played at Biggleswade FC

"Our 2017/18 season had some ups and downs but over all we maintained 5th position in the League. We feel we are capable of being a top two club and have proved that time and again by taking points off of the top teams over the past two to three seasons. We also had a great couple of Cup rins and were proud of our achievements, especially in the WPL Plate final against West Ham. We hope that in 2018/19 we can be more consistent in our results and this could take us a couple of places up the League."

Nikki Baker – Luton Town Manager

- Competing against teams with bigger budgets, Luton have put in a series of good performances in Tier 4 over recent years, finishing 4th in 2014/15 and 2015/16, and then 5th in 2016/17 and 2017/18.

- Jess McKay was Luton's top scorer in 2017/18, she hit 13 goals in the League and 24 in all competitions.

- Luton Town Ladies became officially affiliated with Luton Town men's in 2000.

MAIDENHEAD UNITED

2018/19: WNL DIVISION 1 SOUTH WEST (Tier 4)

Founded: 2013

Nickname: The Magpies

Ground: York Road,
(Maidenhead United FC)

Season 2017/18:

WPL South West One (Tier 4): 8th

FA Cup: 3rd Qualifying Round
WPL Cup: Determining Round
WPL Plate: 1st Round
County Cup: Runners-up

2017/18 WPL SOUTH WEST ONE

Date	Opponent	Result		Scorers	Att	
20.08	Poole Town (h)	L	0-1		30	
27.08	So'ton Saints (a)	L	0-4		45	
10.09	Cheltenham Town (a)	W	2-1	Claire Rogers 65, Alex Dover 80	211	
17.09	Plymouth Argyle (h)	L	0-4		28	7
20.09	*Basingstoke Town (h)* **exp**	D	2-2	Alex Dover, Tina Brett		7
24.09	Keynsham Town (h)	L	1-2			7
11.10	*Basingstoke Town (a)* **exp**	W	5-2	Olivia Buzalo (x4), Hannah Summers	25	6
29.10	Larkhall Athletic (a)	L	0-1		45	7
05.11	So'ton Saints (h)	L	1-3	Tina Brett 70	25	8
12.11	St Nicholas (h)		P-P			8
19.11	Poole Town (a)	D	2-2	Olivia Buzalo 20, 50	26	8
26.11	Brislington (a)		P-P			8
03.12	St Nicholas (h)	W	5-2	Hannah Summers (pen), Zoe Clifford (x2), Own Goal, Clare Rogers	20	5
10.12	So'ton Women (a)		P-P			5
17.12	Cheltenham Town (h)	W	3-2	Alex Dover 10, Lucy Casey 74, 83	15	5
21.01	Larkhall Athletic (h)		P-P			5
28.01	Plymouth Argyle (a)		P-P			5
11.02	So'ton Women (h)		P-P			6
25.02	St Nicholas (a)	L	1-3	Natalie Barnes 5	30	6
04.03	So'ton Women (a)		P-P			6
11.03	Larkhall Athletic (h)	W	1-0	Tina Brett 55	15	6
25.03	Keynsham Town (a)	L	0-11		45	7
01.04	So'ton Women (a)	L	0-3		40	7
08.04	So'ton Women (h)	L	0-10		35	7
15.04	Brislington (a)	L	1-3	Natalie Barnes 19	33	7
29.04	Plymouth Argyle (a)		P-P			7
19.05	Plymouth Argyle (a)	L	w/o			8
20.05	Brislington (h)	D	0-0		10	8

exp = results expunged from records after Basingstoke Town withdrew from the League

2017/18 FA CUP

| 08.10 RQ3 | Luton Town (h) | L | 0-1 | | |

2017/18 WPL CUP

| 03.09 DR | Poole Town (h) | L | 0-1 (aet) | | 53 |

2017/18 WPL PLATE

| 22.10 R1 | Swindon Town (a) | L | 1-7 | Lucy Casey | 47 |

2017/18 BERKS & BUCKS FA COUNTY CUP

19.11 QF	Bye			
18.02 SF	Woodley United (h)	W	2-1	Lucy Casey 38, Tina Brett 90+2
22.04 F	MK Dons (n)	L	0-7	Maidenhead GK Eleanor Parker saved Heather McDonnell pen 30

(n) Played at Stadium:mk, MK Dons FC

- Maidenhead were runners-up in the 2017/18 Berks & Bucks FA County Cup final, losing to eventual WPL South East One champions MK Dons. The final officially took place on neutral territory, but the stadium that had been chosen to host it was in fact Stadium:mk, home of MK Dons men's team.

- Maidenhead United Ladies play at the home ground of Maidenhead United men's team – York Road. The stadium is recognised by FIFA and the FA as being the oldest ground continuously used by the same club, with Maidenhead having played there since 1871.

- Maidenhead Ladies' first ever match was a friendly against Reading Women. Around 100 fans attended the fixture at York Road in the summer of 2013.

MIDDLESBROUGH

2018/19: WNL NORTHERN PREMIER (Tier 3)

Founded: 1976 (as Cleveland Spartans)

Nickname: Boro

Ground: Teesdale Park (Thornaby FC) for 2017/18, moving to Bedford Terrace, (Billingham Town FC) for 2018/19

Season 2017/18:

WPL Northern (Tier 3): 3rd

FA Cup: 4th Round
WPL Cup: 1st Round
County Cup: Not eligible

2017/18 WPL NORTHERN

Date	Opponent		Score	Scorers	Att	
20.08	Fylde (h)	L	0-3		125	
27.08	Wolverhampton W (a)	W	4-3	Anna Birtwhistle 2, Emily Scarr 57, 65, Emma Foster 88	100	
10.09	Leicester City W (a)	W	2-1	Ellie Dobson 19, Emily Scarr 81	72	
17.09	West Brom (h)	W	4-0	Holly Manders 52, Ellie Dobson 57, Leonie Hutchinson 66, Emma Foster 79	82	3
20.09	Guiseley Vixens (h)	W	3-1	Holly Manders 19, Emily Scarr 41, Leonie Hutchinson 71	130	1
01.10	Huddersfield T (a)	W	1-0	Emma Kelly 57	146	2
08.10	Stoke City (h)	W	3-0	Millie Bell 27, Bianca Owens 39, Emily Scarr 55	75	1
15.10	Huddersfield T (h)	L	0-3		85	1
29.10	Nottingham F (a)	W	5-1	Emily Scarr 16, 51, 88, Emma Foster 22, Bianca Owens 45+2	106	1
05.11	Derby County (a)*	W	3-0	Emily Scarr 22, Emma Kelly 83, Eve Gatens 85	97	1
12.11	Bradford City (h)	W	3-2	Emily Scarr 20, 40, Jessica Havelock 35	138	1
15.11	Guiseley Vixens (a)	W	5-1	Ellie Dobson 3, Emily Scarr 67, Holly Manders 66, 74, Millie Bell 87	98	1
19.11	Fylde (a)		P-P			
10.12	Stoke City (a)		P-P			
28.01	Wolverhampton W (h)	W	7-1	Emily Scarr 10, 54, 87, Jessica Havelock 13, Emma Kelly 82, Bianca Owens 84, 86	234	1
11.02	Bradford City (a)		P-P			1
18.02	Bradford City (a)	L	2-9	Jessica Havelock 17, Holly Manders 55	73	1
25.02	Derby County (h)	W	3-1	Millie Bell 2, Emily Scarr 7, 90+3	122	1
04.03	Stoke City (a)		P-P			1
11.03	Nottingham Forest (h)+	W	4-1	Jess Havelock 44, 81, Eleanor Dale 49, Emily Scarr 56		1
18.03	Stoke City (a)		P-P			1
08.04	West Brom (a)	W	3-2	Bianca Owens 22, 61, (pen) 82	67	1
10.04	Blackburn Rovers (a)	L	0-4		86	1
15.04	Stoke City (a)	L	3-6	Emily Scarr 45+1, Bianca Owens (pen) 59, Eleanor Dale 79	142	1

29.04	Fylde (a)	L	3-4	Unknown 3, Unknown 35, Tyler Dodds 50	62	1
13.05	Leicester City W (h)	L	3-6	Bianca Owens 3, Emily Scarr 36, Ellie Dobson 90	167	3
20.05	Blackburn Rovers (h)	L	2-3	Emma Foster 8, Tyler Dodds 45+2	103	3

*Played at Etwall Leisure Centre   +Played at Middlesbrough College

2017/18 FA Cup

03.12 R2	Farsley Celtic (h) +	W	8-1	Millie Bell 43, Emily Scarr 47, 62, 64, Holly Manders 76, 87, Bianca Owens 79, 82	103
07.01 R3	Liverpool M F (h)	W	4-3 (aet)	Bianca Owens 43, Emily Scarr 72, 120+4, Jessica Havelock 90+4	113
04.02 R4	Aston Villa (a)	L	0-4		

+Played at Middlesbrough Foundation, Eston 3G

2017/18 WPL Cup

| 03.09 DR | Burton Albion (h) | W | 5-0 | Emily Scarr 55, 78, 85, Jessica Havelock 59, Emma Kelly 75 | 84 |
| 22.10 R1 | Loughborough F (a) | L | 0-2 | | 60 |

"Finishing 3rd in WPL Northern in 2017/18 was such an achievement for us in only our second season at this level after promotion. This year we have had numerous young players making their debuts from our regional talent club, who have exceeded expectations and established themselves as regular starters for the first-team. The talent filtering through from the RTC has created solid foundations for the club and we now have the quality and balance to better what we have achieved so far. This club gives young players the opportunity to play in the 3rd tier of women's football and everything they need to assist with achieving and reaching their full potential."

Laura Wareham – Middlesbrough Captain

- Boro have certainly made an impression on Tier 3 since their promotion ahead of the 2016/17 campaign. They finished that season as runners-up behind champions Blackburn and then followed that up with 3rd place in 2017/18 behind Blackburn and Leicester City Women.

- Emily Scarr scored 20 League goals and 28 in all competitions in 2017/18. Only Leicester City Women player Rosie Axten got more (22 and 30).

- Middlesbrough did not compete in the County Cup in 2017/18 because the North Riding FA rules prohibit teams at their level from taking part.

- In their early days as Cleveland Spartans the team was coached by Middlesbrough men's players Mark Proctor and David Hodgson. Middlesbrough's longest-serving manager to date has been former central midfielder Marrie Wieczorek who remained in charge for 20 years.

- In autumn 2015, Boro forward Bianca Owens twice achieved the feat of scoring eight goals in one game, doing so in an 11-0 win against Lowick United in the FA Cup 3rd Qualifying Round on 11 October and again in the 10-2 League victory against Stockport County on 15 November.

MILTON KEYNES DONS

2018/19: WNL SOUTHERN PREMIER (Tier 3)

Founded: 2009

Nickname: The Dons

Ground: Willen Road (Newport Pagnell FC) in 2017/18, moving to Stadium:mk (MK Dons FC) for 2018/19

Season 2017/18:

WPL South East One (Tier 4): Champions

FA Cup: 2nd Round
WPL Cup: Determining Round
WPL Plate: Quarter-finals
County Cup: Winners

2017/18 WPL SOUTH EAST ONE

20.08	Denham United (h)	D	1-1	Kerry Newman	80	
27.08	AFC Wimbledon (a)	L	2-4	Charly Wright, Charley Clarke	70	
10.09	Actonians (h)	W	4-0	Charly Wright 4, Dawn Mallett (pen) 36, 90, Anna Loftus 78	85	
17.09	Enfield Town (a)	W	3-1	Amelia Hazard (x2), Charly Wright	42	5
20.09	Cambridge United (h)	W	1-0	Alice Hughes 84	85	2
01.10	Luton Town (a)	W	2-1	Laura Mills, Charly Wright 90+6	76	4
11.10	Cambridge United (a)	W	2-0	Alice Hughes, Laura Mills	85	4
15.10	Denham United (a)	D	1-1	Alice Hughes	87	2
29.10	Luton Town (h)	W	2-1	Laura Mills 16, 31	85	2
05.11	Norwich City (a)	W	1-0	Amelia Hazard	41	2
26.11	Ipswich Town (h)	D	2-2	Charley Clarke, Amelia Hazard	55	3
14.01	Leyton Orient (h)	W	2-1	Charley Clarke, Louise Naylor	85	3
21.01	Actonians (a)		P-P			3
28.01	Actonians (a)		P-P			3
04.02	AFC Wimbledon (h)		P-P			3
04.03	Stevenage (a)		P-P			4
11.03	Ipswich Town (a)	W	1-0	Charley Clarke 87	77	4
18.03	Enfield Town (h)		P-P			4
25.03	AFC Wimbledon (h)	W	1-0	Kim Farrow	85	3
11.04	Enfield Town (h)	W	5-1	Charly Wright, Alice Hughes, Kimberley Farrow, Heather McDonnell (x2)		2
15.04	Actonians (a)		P-P			4
25.04	Stevenage (h)		P-P			4
29.04	Leyton Orient (a)*	W	6-2	Vicky Holland, Heather McDonnell (x2), Laura Mills, Louis Naylor, Anna Loftus	202	3
02.05	Stevenage (a)	W	2-0	Kim Farrow 56, Heather McDonnell 85	43	3
06.05	Norwich City (h)+	W	6-2	Heather McDonnell 1, 52, 70, Laura Mills 34, Charley Clarke 65, Kim Farrow 87	200	2

08.05	Actonians (a)	W	2-0	Leah Cudone 49, 75	25	2
13.05	Haringey Borough (h)**	W	16-1	Laura Mills 6, Leah Cudone 15, 24, Dawn Mallett 31, Kim Farrow (pen) 45, Heather McDonnell 51, 53, 74, Alice Hughes 58, Louise Naylor 59, 82, 90, Leanna Doyle missed pen 62 (saved by Talisha Hickson), Anna Loftus 68, Zoe Boote 70, Leanna Doyle 78, 85, Anna Loftus sent off 89	80	1
16.05	Stevenage (h)+	W	1-0	Leah Cudone 74	450	1
20.05	Haringey Borough (a)	W	13-0	Own Goal 15, Leah Cudone 25, 43, Leanna Doyle 28, Laura Mills 32, 51, 55, Kim Farrow 57, 61, 90, Amy Gooderham 80, Zoe Boote 87, 88		1C

*Played at Matchroom Stadium, Leyton Orient FC +Played at Stadium:mk, MK Dons FC **Played at Wootton Blue Cross

2017/18 FA CUP

08.10 RQ3	Actonians (h)	W	2-0	Charly Wright 4, Laura Mills 82	76
12.11 R1	Ashford Town (Middx) (a)	W	6-0	Dawn Mallett (x4), Amelia Hazard, Alice Hughes	55
03.12 R2	Cardiff City L (h)	L	0-1		110

2017/18 WPL CUP

03.09 DR	AFC Wimbledon (h)	L	0-1		85

2017/18 WPL PLATE

22.10 R1	Denham United (h)	W	2-0	Amelia Hazard, Kerry Newman	85
10.12 R2	Norwich City (a)	0	P-P		
17.12 R2	Norwich City (a)		P-P		
07.01 R2	Norwich City (a)	W	4-2	Heather McDonnell, Sasha Newsome, Charly Wright, Amelia Hazard	35
11.02 QF	Luton Town (a)		P-P		
25.02 QF	Luton Town (a)	L	2-3	Vicky Holland, Heather McDonnell	71

2017/18 Berks & Bucks FA County Cup

19.11 QF	Wargrave (h)	W	11-0	Heather McDonnell 2, 51, Alice Hughes 21, Leanna Doyle 27, Sasha Newsome 29, Charley Clarke 34, 40, Anna Loftus 36, Charly Wright 38, Louise Naylor 62, 78
18.02 SF	Chesham United (a)	W	2-1	Kerry Newman 48, Sasha Newsome 62
22.04 F	Maidenhead United (n)	W	7-0	Alice Hughes 22, *Heather McDonnell missed pen 30 (saved Eleanor Parker),* Anna Loftus 51, 60, Heather McDonnell 55, Charly Wright 70, Amy Gooderham 78, Laura Mills 90+3

(n) Played at Stadium MK, MK Dons FC

"We had a fantastic 2017/18 achieving the Double, by winning the League and County Cup. The passion, drive and commitment by the ladies was phenomenal and I am incredibly proud to have captained MK Dons FC Ladies throughout the campaign. The togetherness shown by an incredible group of women throughout the season is why this club is so special to be a part of. We had a fantastic amount of support from the club which helped us to achieve promotion. I am thoroughly looking forward to the challenges that lie ahead and can't wait to ply our trade in a higher division."

Leanna Doyle – MK Dons Captain

- MK Dons were crowned WPL South East One champions after overhauling AFC Wimbledon in the title run-in. With three games to go MK Dons trailed AFC Wimbledon by three points and a vastly inferior goal difference, but they wiped that out within one game by beating bottom club Haringey Borough 16-1 to go top (on GD) for the first time all season.

- They then went three points clear by beating Stevenage 1-0 in their penultimate game with Leah Cudone hitting a late winner. It all meant that MK Dons needed just a draw against Haringey when they met again on the final day. They romped to another heavy win, this time 13-0, to secure the title.

- After defeat in their second game of the season, MK Dons then went 20 League games unbeaten on their way to wrapping up the title.

- As well as their title win, there was also Cup success as MK Dons beat Maidenhead United 7-0 in the Berks & Bucks FA County Cup final. It was the fourth time they have won the trophy having previously done so in 2014, 2015 and 2016.

MORECAMBE

2018/19: WNL DIVISION 1 NORTH (Tier 4)

Founded: 2005

Nickname: The Seagals

Ground: Lancaster & Morecambe College

Season 2017/18:

WPL Northern One (Tier 4): 7th

FA Cup: 3rd Qualifying Round
WPL Cup: Determining Round
WPL Plate: 1st Round
County Cup: 1st Round

2017/18 WPL NORTHERN ONE

27.08	Crewe Alexandra (a)	D	2-2	Becky Whittingham 18, 87	33	
10.09	Bolton Wanderers (a)	W	4-1	Beth Fisher, Emma Kay, Yasmine Swarbrick (x2)	60	
19.09	Chorley (a)	W	1-0	Emma Kay 10	80	4
01.10	Leeds United (a)*	W	3-1	Yasmine Swarbrick (x3)	35	4
11.10	Chorley (h)	W	3-1	Emma Kay, Yasmine Swarbrick, Louise Gibbins	45	4
15.10	Barnsley (a)	W	4-1	Charlotte Higginson, Emily Hutton, Yasmine Swarbrick, Melissa Martin	60	3
12.11	Barnsley (h)	L	1-3	Emma Kay	20	4
19.11	Crewe Alexandra (h)	L	2-4	Hannah Paling 36, Yasmine Swarbrick 44	58	4
26.11	Brighouse Town (a)	P-P				4
03.12	Chester-le-Street T (a)	P-P				
17.12	Newcastle United (h)	L	2-4	Charlotte Higginson 56, Hannah Paling 59	24	4
07.01	Bolton Wanderers (h)	W	6-2	Beth Fisher, Charlotte Higginson (x2), Emily Hutton, Hannah Paling, Yasmine Swarbrick	32	4
14.01	Mossley Hill A (h)	W	8-2	Melissa Brown, Louise Gibbins, Charlotte Higginson, Hannah Paling, Yasmine Swarbrick (x3), Elizabeth Chapman	25	3
21.01	Hull City (a)	P-P				3
28.01	Newcastle United (a)	L	1-2	Yasmine Swarbrick 1	42	4
11.02	Leeds United (h)	L	1-2	Yasmine Swarbrick 16	35	4
25.02	Mossley Hill A (a)	L	1-5	Charlotte Higginson	20	4
04.03	Liverpool M F (a)	L	0-5		30	4
07.03	Brighouse Town (h)	D	2-2	Charlotte Higginson, Becky Whittingham	35	4
11.03	Hull City (a)	L	0-7		60	4
18.03	Chester-le-Street T (a)	P-P				4
25.03	Liverpool M F (h)	W	3-1	Megan Doherty 42, Charlotte Higginson 56, 79, *Emily Hutton sent off 75*	32	4
01.04	Chester-le-Street T (h)	L	2-3	Yasmine Swarbrick (x2)	25	4
03.04	Chester-le-Street T (a)	L	1-2	Yasmine Swarbrick	30	4

| 22.04 | Brighouse Town (a) | W | 2-1 | *Megan Doherty sent off 55,* Charlotte Higginson 81, Yasmine Swarbrick 88 | 76 | 4 |
| 20.05 | Hull City (h) | L | 0-9 | | 25 | 7 |

*Played at Batley Sports and Tennis Centre

2017/18 FA CUP

08.10 RQ3	Steel City W (a)	L	1-2	Yasmine Swarbrick	40

2017/18 WPL CUP

03.09 DR	Stoke City (h)	L	1-3	Emma Kay	48

2017/18 WPL PLATE

29.10R1	Hull City (h)	L	1-5	Melissa Brown	35

2017/18 LANCASHIRE COUNTY FA CUP

17.09 R1	Bolton Wanderers (a)	L	2-4	Emma Kay 37, 86	90

"Given the circumstances, we feel we performed as well as could have been expected in 2017/18. We lost two keepers through injury, and our striker moved on after only seven games, leaving us to find a replacement. Throughout the campaign we lacked consistency and were often playing without our strongest team. On our day we proved good enough to beat some good teams and we can take a lot of pride in the fact that we beat five of the six teams that finished above us."

Nick Barrett – Morecambe Manager

• Yasmine Swarbrick was WPL Northern One's joint top goalscorer for League goals in 2017/18. She hit 19 in 21 appearances, the same total as Brighouse Town's Jodie Redgrave who made 22 appearances.

• Morecambe were promoted from the North West Regional League Premier Division as champions in time for the first season of the WPL Northern Division One in 2014/15 and have been at that level ever since.

• Morecambe have had two cup successes over the years, winning the North West Regional League Cup in 2013/14 and the Lancashire County Cup in 2009/10.

(Left) Hannah Paling, Morecambe's inspirational captain, lost her mum this year but still managed to continue playing and has completed 300 games for the club.

MOSSLEY HILL ATHLETIC

2018/19: NORTH WEST REGIONAL PREMIER LAGUE (Tier 5)

Founded: 2005

Nickname: The Maroons

Ground: Mossley Hill Athletic Club

Season 2017/18:

WPL Northern One (Tier 4): 12th (R)

FA Cup: 3rd Qualifying Round
WPL Cup: Determining Round
WPL Plate: 1st Round
County Cup: Runners-up

2017/18 WPL NORTHERN ONE

Date	Opponent	Result	Score	Scorers	Att	Pos
20.08	Chorley (a)	L	1-6	Ceri Ogdon 30	78	
10.09	*Newcastle U (h)* **exp**	L	1-2	Erin Slade 33	35	
17.09	Crewe Alexandra (h)	L	0-1		44	11
20.09	Liverpool M F (a)	L	0-4		50	12
24.09	Chester-le-Street T (h)*	L	0-2		20	12
01.10	Brighouse Town (a)	L	1-5	Caroline Charlton (pen) 36	42	12
11.10	Liverpool M F (h)	L	0-3		49	12
15.10	Crewe Alexandra (a)	L	0-2		44	12
05.11	Hull City (h)		P-P			12
12.11	Leeds United (h)	W	2-1	Amy Hughes 61, 65	35	12
10.12	Barnsley (h)		P-P			12
17.12	Hull City (h)		P-P			12
14.01	Morecambe (a)	L	2-8	Amy Hughes 2, 60	25	12
04.02	Bolton Wanderers (h)		P-P			12
11.02	Chester-le-Street T (a)		P-P			12
18.02	Barnsley (a)	D	2-2	Kirstie Pickin 57, Amy Hughes 83		12
25.02	Morecambe (h)	W	5-1	Nicola James 6, 12 Amy Hughes 16, 88 Rachel Davison 55	20	12
04.03	Leeds United (a)		P-P			12
11.03	Barnsley (h)	W	3-0	Caroline Charlton (pen) 30, Amy Hughes 60, 83	25	12
18.03	Hull City (a)		P-P			12
25.03	Bolton Wanderers (a)	L	1-3	Amy Hughes 86	104	12
01.04	Hull City (h)	D	1-1	Olivia Ellinson 25	20	12
08.04	Chester-le-Street T (a)**	L	1-3	Amy Hughes 17	40	12
15.04	Newcastle United (a)	L	1-5	Stephanie Lockhart 43	42	12
18.04	Bolton Wanderers (h)	W	2-1	Jodie Mortimer 43, Amy Hughes 75, *Nikki James sent off 90+3*	30	11
22.04	Newcastle United (h)	W	3-2	Amy Hughes 48, Caroline Charlton (pen) 77, Nicola James 80	30	10
02.05	Chorley (h)++	L	1-2	Amy Hughes 18	35	10

06.05	Leeds United (a)	L	1-2	Olivia Ellinson 82		150	11
13.05	Hull City (a)	L	0-4			100	11
20.05	Brighouse Town (h)	L	1-2	Olivia Ellinson 85, *Mossley Hill Athletic missed pen (saved by Stephanie Jones) 87*		30	12

*Played at JMO Sports Club   +Played at Litherland Sports Club   **Played at The Graham Sports Centre

++Played at Walton Hall Park   exp = Expunged from records due to Newcastle making too many substitutions. Replayed 22.04

2017/18 FA CUP

| 08.10 RQ3 | Liverpool M F (a) | L | 0-7 | | 100 |

2017/18 WPL CUP

| 03.09 DR | Brighouse Town (h) | L | 0-1 | | 30 |

2017/18 WPL Plate

| 29.10 R1 | Crewe Alexandra (h) | L | 2-3 | Eve Davenport 55, Jodie Mortimer 73 | 35 |

2017/18 LIVERPOOL FA COUNTY CUP

19.11 QF	MSB Woolton (h)	W	5-1	Olivia Ellinson 19, Chelsea Wharton 53, Amy Hughes 60, Erin Slade 65, 68	20
21.01 SF	Merseyrail (h)		P-P		
28.01 SF	Merseyrail (h)	D	2-2 (W 6-5p)	Caroline Charlton 75, Kirstie Pickin 85	30
29.04 F	Liverpool M F (n)	L	0-1		100

(n) Played at Walton Hall Park, Liverpool County FA

"Our club is special because we aren't just a bunch of players, we are friends. You can see that on the pitch from the drive, passion and determination of each and every player. To be still fighting in the League right up until our last game was quite something. Having started with zero points from our first seven games, we couldn't have imagined that we would still have a chance of staying up on the final day, even though it didn't go our way in the end. If we approach 2018/19 with the same mentality then I am certain that we will be looking at a top three finish or even winning the League. I have 100% belief in the players and management we have."

Amy Fisher – Mossley Hill Athletic Captain

- In the League, Mossley Hill Athletic had a tough 2017/18 season, finishing bottom of WPL Northern One and being relegated to Tier 5.

- They also narrowly missed out on winning what would have been their sixth Liverpool FA County Cup. They reached the final but were beaten 1-0 by Liverpool Marshall Feds.

- Past honours include being crowned Lancashire FA County 1st Division Champions in 2005/06, North West League Division 1 North Champions in 2006/07 and North West Premier Division Champions in 2009/10.

- The most famous player to come through the youth ranks at Mossley Hill Athletic is England and Barcelona winger Toni Duggan.

NETTLEHAM

2018/19: WNL DIVISION 1 MIDLANDS (Tier 4)

Founded: Unknown

Nickname: The Netts

Ground: Mulsanne Park (Nettleham FC)

Season 2017/18:

East Mids reg Prem (Tier 5): Champions

FA Cup: 2nd Round
League Cup: 3rd Round
County Cup: Winners

2017/18 EAST MIDLANDS REGIONAL PREMIER

07.09	Ollerton Town (a)	W	3-2	Abbie Murrell 20, 62, Katie Davison 81
24.09	Mansfield Town (a)	L	1-2	Hollie Newman 66
01.10	Rise Park (h)	W	4-0	Annie Ward 1, Sophie Crosby 28, Rebecca Hornsey 77, Abbie Murrell 80
04.10	Mansfield Hosiery Mills (h)	W	5-0	Shelly Futter 14, Daisy Marsh 43, Courtney Limb 60, 64, 75
15.10	Kettering Town (h)	W	7-0	Katy Thornley 23, Nicola Symons 35, Abbie Murrell 56, 60, 75, Sophie Crosby 61, Rebecca Hornsey 66,
22.10	Loughborough Students (a)	W	3-2	Sophie Crosby 14, 42, Tia Johnson 83
05.11	Arnold Town (h)	W	5-1	Abbie Murrell 25, Tia Johnson 52, 67, Holly Newman 71, Jess Hogg 78
19.11	Mansfield Town (h)	W	4-2	Tia Johnson (x3), Holly Newman
26.11	Oughtibridge W M (h)	D	0-0	
14.01	Loughborough Students (h)	W	3-0	Sophie Crosby 33, Katy Thornley 47, 83
11.03	Peterborough N S (h)	D	1-1	Abbie Murrell 76
25.03	Arnold Town (a)	W	8-0	Rebecca Hornsey 6, 81, 85, Annie Ward 18, 89, Leighanne Powles (og) 40, Courtney Limb 55, 86
28.03	Leicester City W Development (a)	W	6-0	Annie Ward 19, Francesca Wilson 27, 81, Holly Newman 29, Stephanie Lee 49, Rebecca Hornsey 76
04.04	Ollerton Town (h)	D	0-0	
08.04	Kettering Town (a)	W	1-0	Own Goal 70
11.04	Mansfield Hosiery Mills (a)	W	3-1	Sophie Crosby 14, 20, Francesca Wilson 32
15.04	Leicester City W Development (h)	W	3-0	Francesca Wilson 14, Abbie Murrell 42, 56
18.04	Eastwood (h)	W	8-0	Abbie Murrell 26, 32, 72, 74, Annie Ward 40, Courtney Limb 47, Tia Johnson 65, Rebecca Hornsey 79
22.04	Eastwood (a)	W	5-1	Rebecca Hornsey 35, Annie Ward 41, Tia Johnson 63, Sophie Crosby 65, Own Goal 71
29.04	Oughtibridge W M (a)	W	2-0	Francesca Wilson 23, Tia Johnson 63
10.05	Rise Park (a)	W	9-0	Holly Newman 3, 21, 9, 58, 83, Katy Thornley 35, Francesca Wilson 48, 60, Annie Ward 87
13.05	Peterborough N S (a)	W	3-1	Abbie Murrell 41, 60, Annie Ward 53

2017/18 FA CUP

03.09 RQ1	Market Warsop (a)	W	5-0	Katy Thornley, Abbie Murrell (x2), Stacey Aisthorpe, Own Goal
17.09 RQ2	Leicester City W Development (a)	W	3-2 (aet)	
08.10 RQ3	Burton Albion (a)	W	4-0	Becky Hornsey, Elise Keyworth, Nicola Symons, Sophie Crosby
12.11 R1	Loughborough Students (h)	W	3-0	
03.12 R2	Liverpool Marshall Feds (h)	L	1-3	Katy Thornley

2017/18 LEAGUE CUP

10.09 R1	Rise Park (a)	W	5-1	Holly Newman 37, 71, 80, Tia Johnson 45, Rebecca Hornsey 65
29.10 R2	Peterborough U (h)	D	1-1 (W 5-4p)	Courtney Limb 31
20.12 R3	Leicester City W Development (a)	D	1-1 (L 4-5p)	Shelly Futter 50

2017/18 LINCOLNSHIRE FA COUNTY CUP

28.01 QF	Lincoln Moorlands-Railway (h)	W	4-0	
18.02 SF	Boston United (a)	W	6-0	Holly Newman (x3), Tia Johnson, Shelly Futter, Katy Thornley
06.05 F	Grimsby Borough (n)	W	7-0	Holly Newman, Abbie Murrell (x2), Imogen Burnley, Annie Ward (x2), Sophie Crosby

(n) Played at Sincil Bank, Lincoln City FC

"This is a special club; a small village team on the outskirts of Lincoln that has gone from strength to strength in recent years. We have a mixture of experience and youth as well as very good technical players. With the arrival in summer 2018 of new manager Richard Cooper we are buzzing for the season ahead in the Women's National League."

Katie Davison, Nettleham Vice-Captain

- Nettleham went into their final game of 2017/18 needing a point to clinch the East Midlands Regional Premier League title and were crowned champions in style thanks to a 3-1 win at Peterborough Northern Star in which Abbie Murrell scored twice and Annie Ward was also on target. The Netts had finished as runners-up in the League in the previous three seasons but can now finally take their place in the newly-formed WNL Division 1 Midlands.

- The Netts completed a League and Cup Double in 2017/18 as they added to their title by winning the Lincolnshire FA County Cup, beating Grimsby Borough 7-0 in the final.

- In the FA Cup they made it all the way to the 2nd Round, beating Tier 3 Burton Albion 4-0 away in the 2nd Qualifying Round. Their run was ended by Tier 3 Liverpool Marshall Feds.

NEWCASTLE UNITED

2018/19: WNL DIVISION 1 NORTH (Tier 4)

Founded: 1989

Nickname: The Lady Magpies

Ground: Newcastle University in 2017/18, moving to Druid Park, Woolsington for 2018/19

Season 2017/18:

WPL Northern One (Tier 4): 5th

FA Cup: 3rd Round
WPL Cup: Determining Round
WPL Plate: 2nd Round
County Cup: Winners

2017/18 WPL NORTHERN ONE

20.08	Brighouse Town (h)	L	3-5	Annece Legg, Stephanie Lyons, Megan McKenzie	68	
10.09	*Mossley Hill A (a)* ***exp***	W	2-1	Jade Anderson, Stephanie Ord	35	
19.09	Chester-le-Street T (a)	L	2-3	Siobhan Jones 75, Beth Gardener 88	90	9
24.09	Leeds United (h)	L	3-4	Stephanie Ord 2, 70, Emma Hewitt 33	75	11
01.10	Crewe Alexandra (h)+	W	2-0	Stephanie Ord 11, Beth Ragdale (og) 77	53	7
10.10	Chester-le-Street T (h)*	D	3-3	Jessica Foster 7, 88, Siobhan Jones 51	72	6
22.10	Liverpool M F (h)	D	1-1	Jessica Foster 10	63	7
26.11	Liverpool M F (a)**	L	0-3		40	10
17.12	Morecambe (a)	W	4-2	Christina Deverdics 2, Stephanie Ord 16, Siobhan Jones (pen) 75, Nicole Dack 86	24	8
14.01	Barnsley (h)	W	3-2	Stephanie Ord 28, Megan McKenzie 69, 75	70	8
21.01	Leeds United (a)		P-P			9
28.01	Morecambe (h)	W	2-1	Rebecca Olley 3, Megan McKenzie 16	42	7
04.02	Chorley (a)		P-P			7
11.02	Bolton Wanderers (a)		P-P			7
25.02	Hull City (a)	L	1-4	Stephanie Ord 27	50	7
04.03	Bolton Wanderers (a)		P-P			7
11.03	Brighouse Town (a)		P-P			8
18.03	Bolton Wanderers (h)		P-P			8
25.03	Leeds United (a)	L	0-1		75	9
08.04	Chorley (h)		P-P			11
12.04	Bolton Wanderers (a)	W	2-1	Shiobhan Jones, Jessie Ellison	65	8
15.04	Mossley Hill A (h)	W	5-1	Rebecca Olley 15, Stephanie Ord 30, Megan McKenzie 48, Rebecca Hanson 82, Jessie Ellison	42	7
18.04	Brighouse Town (a)	L	0-4		134	7
22.04	Mossley Hill A (a)	L	2-3	Jess Foster 21, Brooke Cochrane 45	30	8
25.04	Chorley (a)	L	1-3	Megan McKenzie 21	100	9
29.04	Crewe Alexandra (a)	W	2-0	Stephanie Ord (pen) 7, Rhiannon Gray 35	45	8

06.05	Hull City (h)	W	1-0	Rhiannon Gray 1		7
13.05	Bolton Wanderers (h)	L	2-3	Stephanie Ord, Megan McKenzie	41	7
18.05	Chorley (h)	W	4-2	Own Goal 13, Stephanie Ord 30, 80, Jessica Foster 60	62	6
20.05	Barnsley (a)	D	1-1	Rebecca Olley	60	5

+Played at University of Northumbria *Played at Whitley Park **Played at Edge Hill University

exp = Expunged from records due to Newcastle making too many substitutions. Replayed 22.04

2017/18 FA CUP

08.10 RQ3	Carlisle United (h)	W	9-1	Siobhan Jones 10, 68, Jessica Foster 32, 38, Stephanie Ord 36, 81, 87, Nicole Dack 75, Stephanie Lyons 83	84
12.11 R1	Sheffield United (h)	W	3-0	Own Goal 42, Megan McKenzie 49, Stephanie Lyons 82	110
03.12 R2	Nottingham Forest (a)	W	2-0	Megan McKenzie 49, 61	76
07.01 R3	The New Saints (h)	L	1-2	Stephanie Ord 59	115

2017/18 WPL CUP

| 03.09 DR | Huddersfield T (h) | L | 0-3 | | 69 |

2017/18 WPL PLATE

| 29.10 R1 | Radcliffe Olympic (h) | W | 2-0 | Stephanie Ord 55, 70 | 30 |
| 10.12 R2 | Hull City (a) | L | 0-1 | | 20 |

2017/18 NORTHUMBERLAND FA COUNTY CUP

15.10 R1	Newbiggin Hill (a)	W	w/o		
19.11 QF	Ashington Town (a)	W	w/o		
18.02 SF	Wallsend B C (h)	W	9-0	Brooke Cochrane, Jessica Foster (x4), Megan McKenzie (x3), Stephanie Ord	84
11.05 F	Newcastle United Reserves (n)	W	2-0	Jessica Foster (x2)	

(n) Played at Whitley Park, Benton

"The 2017/18 campaign was a great first season as a new team. It has opened a bright future ahead of us as a club. We had a few ups and downs throughout the year but we finished strongly, and to lift the County Cup – my first trophy as NUWFC captain – was amazing. To pull on a black and white shirt every Sunday is an unbelievable feeling and one I can't wait to have again in 2018/19."

Brooke Cochrane – Newcastle United Captain

- Newcastle climbed into their highest League position of the 2017/18 season on the final day when they drew 1-1 away to Barnsley and moved up to 5th place.

- Newcastle United Women became officially affiliated with the men's Newcastle United FC in 2016.

- In 1996 the club played a Manchester United women's team at Wembley before the men's Community Shield match (then known as the Charity Shield) between the same two clubs.

- The Lady Magpies reached the FA Cup quarter-finals for the first time in 2006/07 where they lost to Liverpool 9-8 on penalties after a 2-2 draw.

NORTON & STOCKTON ANCIENTS

2018/19: WNL DIVISION 1
NORTH (Tier 4)

Founded: 2006

Nickname: None

Ground: Station Road,
(Norton & Stockton Ancients FC)

Season 2017/18:

North East Regional Prem (Tier 5): Champions

FA Cup: 1st Round
League Cup: Runners-up
County Cup: Winners

2017/18 NORTH EAST REGIONAL PREMIER

24.09	Tynedale (a)	W	7-3	Courtney Corrie, Heather Johnson, Anna Mawston (x3), Sian Williams, Nyci Thorns
01.10	Wakefield (h)	W	12-0	Courtney Corrie, Anna Mawston (x3), Kate McSorley (x2), Nyci Thorns (x3), Victoria Burton (x2), Kira Whittle
29.10	Farsley Celtic (h)	W	2-0	Nyci Thorns, Sian Williams
26.11	York City (a)	W	3-0	Courtney Corrie, Sian Williams (x2)
04.02	Wakefield (a)	W	13-0	Anna Mawston (x5), Kate McSorley, Sian Williams (x4), Courtney Corrie, Shannon Reed (x2)
11.02	Tynedale (h)	W	5-1	Nyci Thorns (x3), Sian Williams, Shannon Reed
11.03	Castleford White Rose (a)	W	9-1	Anna Mawston (x2), Nyci Thorns (x4), Shannon Reed (x3)
25.03	Durham Cestria (a)	W	4-2	Victoria Burton, Kate McSorley, Nyci Thorns (x2)
28.03	Wallsend B C (h)	W	w/o	
18.04	Hartlepool United (h)	W	4-0	Shannon Reed, Nyci Thorns (x3, 1pen)
22.04	Castleford White Rose (h)	W	8-1	Courtney Corrie (x3), Kate McSorley (x2), Nyci Thorns (x3)
25.04	Wallsend B C (a)	W	15-0	Victoria Burton (x6), Kate McSorley, Shannon Reed, Aimee Stabler, Nyci Thorns (x5), Sian Williams
08.05	Durham Cestria (h)	D	2-2	Nyci Thorns, Sian Williams
16.05	York City (h)	W	w/o	
20.05	Hartlepool United (a)	L	1-4	Shannon Reed
23.05	Farsley Celtic (a)	W	6-0	Chelsea Beetch, Victoria Burton, Kate McSorley, Shannon Reed, Nyci Thorns (x2)

2017/18 FA CUP

03.09	RQ1	Tynedale (a)	W	w/o	
17.09	RQ2	Penrith (h)	W	3-2 (aet)	Victoria Burton, Jessica White, Sian Williams
08.10	RQ3	South Shields (a)	W	3-0	Courtney Corrie, Kate McSorley, Jessica White
12.11	R1	Chorley (h)	L	0-4	

2017/18 LEAGUE CUP

10.09 R1	Tynedale (a)	W	w/o	
25.02 R2	Wallsend B C (h)	W	9-0	Victoria Burton, Anna Mawston, Nyci Thorns (x6), Sian Williams
01.04 QF	South Shields (h)	W	3-2	Victoria Burton, Nyci Thorns (x2)
29.04 SF	Farsley Celtic (h)	W	2-1	Chelsea Beetch, Victoria Burton
13.05 F	Durham Cestria (n)	L	0-2	Rachel Chisnall sent off 70

(n) Played at Wilberfoss Sports & Social

2017/18 DURHAM FA COUNTY CUP

19.11R1	Washington (h)	W	7-0	Courtney Corrie, Victoria Burton, Anna Mawston (x2), Kira Whittle, Sian Williams, Jessica White
14.01 R2	Boldon CA Villa (a)	W	7-0	Shannon Reed (x2), Nyci Thorns (x3), Sian Williams, Connie Smith
28.01QF	Chester-le-Street Waldridge Park (a)	W	15-0	Chelsea Beetch, Victoria Burton (x3), Anna Mawston (x3), Kate McSorley, Lizzie Rodger, Aimee Stabler, Nyci Thorns (x3), Keeley Wilkinson, Sian Williams
18.02 SF	Tynedale (h)	W	3-1	Victoria Burton, Nyci Thorns, Sian Williams
F	Chester-le-Street T (n)	D	2-2 (W 5-4p)	Shannon Reed, Nyci Thorns

(n) Played at The Hetton Centre, Houghton-le-Spring

"The 2017/18 season was fantastic across the whole club. Our junior teams won two League titles and reached a Cup final, whilst our senior reserve team won the League Cup and were runners-up in the Durham FA Women's League, securing promotion into the North East Regional League North. This is a fantastic achievement for a team in which most of the players are experiencing women's football for the first time. The first-team had a phenomenal campaign, winning the Durham FA County Cup for the first time in four years, winning the League and dropping only five points all season, and coming runners-up in the League Cup. We are delighted that the club is back playing in Tier 4 for 2018/19; when we got relegated it was our target to get back within three seasons, and we've done exactly that. With a strong junior section behind us we are looking to cement ourselves as a strong team in the WNL Division 1 North and retain the Durham County Cup."

Chris Burton – Manager 2017/18

- Norton's top-scorer in 2017/18 was Nyci Thorns. She managed 50 goals, a tally which also saw her finish the campaign as the League's highest scorer. She hit a double hat-trick in the 9-0 League Cup win over Wallsend, a feat also achieved by team-mate Victoria Burton against the same opponents in a 15-0 win in the League.

- As well as being promoted to the new WNL Division 1 North as champions, Norton & Stockton Ancients also won the 2017/18 Durham FA County Cup, beating Chester-le-Street Town on penalties in the final. Their spot-kicks were scored by Victoria Burton, Shannon Reed, Courtney Corrie, Sian Williams and Nyci Thorns. Goalkeeper Rachel Chisnall saved Chester-le-Street Town's first effort.

- Captain Kate McGuire has only ever played for Norton & Stockton Ancients and has been captain at various age groups since joining when she was eight years old.

- The club has seven junior girls teams and a senior reserve team who are competing in the NERWFL Northern Division in 2018/19 following promotion in their debut season in women's football. Norton & Stockton Ancients' junior teams are coached by eight of the club's female players with the support of a number of other qualified coaches.

- The most famous player to have come through the club is Jordan Nobbs, currently of Arsenal and England, who played for Norton as a junior.

NORWICH CITY

2018/19: WNL DIVISION 1 SOUTH EAST (Tier 4)

Founded: 1998

Nickname: The Canaries

Ground: Plantation Park, (Norwich United FC)

Season 2017/18:

WPL South East One (Tier 4): 11th

FA Cup: 3rd Qualifying Round
WPL Cup: Determining Round
WPL Plate: 2nd Round
County Cup: 2nd Round

2017/18 WPL SOUTH EAST ONE

Date	Opponent		Result	Scorers		
20.08	Enfield Town (h)	L	2-4	Aimee Durrant 14, Chelsea Garrett 53	52	
27.08	Haringey Borough (h)	W	7-0	Chelsea Garrett 7, 25, 35, Aimee Durrant 23, 45+1, Charlotte Broad 49, Natasha Snelling 57	60	
10.09	Stevenage (a)	L	1-4	Aimee Durrant 45	45	
17.09	Actonians (a)	L	2-7	Chelsea Garrett 12, Aimee Durrant 90+8	20	10
20.09	Ipswich Town (h)	L	0-5		82	10
01.10	Leyton Orient (h)	L	2-5	Millie Daviss 21, Charlotte Broad (pen) 74	48	11
11.10	Ipswich Town (a)	L	1-8	Sasha Diston (pen) 48	105	11
29.10	Cambridge United (a)	L	1-2	Chelsea Garrett 7	45	11
05.11	MK Dons (h)	L	0-1		41	11
12.11	Haringey Borough (a)	P-P				11
26.11	Luton Town (a)	L	2-8	Natasha Snelling 9, Millie Daviss 78	34	11
03.12	Denham United (h)	D	2-2	Natasha Snelling 16, 70	45	11
14.01	Denham United (a)	L	1-3	Natasha Snelling 87	35	11
21.01	AFC Wimbledon (h)	P-P				11
28.01	Haringey Borough (a)	W	4-3	Vivian Moyo 35, 57, Sasha Diston 70, Chelsea Garrett 83	15	11
04.02	Actonians (h)	P-P				11
11.02	Leyton Orient (a)	P-P				11
18.02	AFC Wimbledon (a)	L	2-8	Aimee Durrant 25, Jodie Drake 60	100	11
25.02	Enfield Town (a)	W	3-2	Aimee Durrant 32, 40, Brydie Siryj 60	43	11
04.03	Actonians (h)	P-P				11
11.03	AFC Wimbledon (h)	L	1-2	Chelsea Garrett 50	56	11
18.03	Luton Town (h)	P-P				11
25.03	Leyton Orient (a)	L	1-4	Millie Daviss 53	63	11
15.04	Stevenage (h)	L	0-1		46	11
22.04	Actonians (h)	L	0-1		50	11
06.05	MK Dons (a)*	L	2-6	Chelsea Garrett 47, Natasha Snelling 90	200	11

| 13.05 | Cambridge United (h) | W | 3-2 | Chelsea Garrett 20, 88, Aimee Durant 33 | 60 | 11 |
| 20.05 | Luton Town (h) | L | 2-3 | Chelsea Garrett 14, 81 | 60 | 11 |

*Played at Stadium:mk, MK Dons FC

2017/18 FA CUP

| 08.10 RQ3 | Cambridge United (a) | L | 0-4 | | 48 |

2017/18 WPL CUP

| 03.09 DR | Cardiff City L (h) | L | 0-5 | | 72 |

2017/18 WPL PLATE

15.10 R1	Haringey Borough (h)	W	5-0	Natasha Snelling 13, Charlotte Broad 30, Aimee Durant 56, 85, Laura Thacker 90+4	40
10.12 R2	MK Dons (h)		P-P		
17.12 R2	MK Dons (h)		P-P		
07.01 R2	MK Dons (h)	L	2-4	Chelsea Garrett 42, Jodie Drake 49	35

2017/18 NORFOLK COUNTY CUP

| 19.11R2 | King's Lynn Town (a) | L | 1-2 | Vivian Moyo 84 |

- Season 2017/18 was a difficult one for Norwich as they finished in 11th place, just one spot off the bottom of WPL South East One. Chelsea Garrett was the club's top scorer. She hit 13 goals in the League and 14 in all competitions.

- The club is officially affiliated to the men's professional side Norwich City and proudly claims that 90% of its players have progressed through its youth ranks.

- Past honours include winning the South East Combination League Cup and Norfolk County Cup. The Canaries are also three-time winners of the Suffolk FA County Cup, beating Ipswich on penalties in the 2007 final, running out 5-0

NOTTINGHAM FOREST

2018/19: WNL NORTHERN PREMIER (Tier 3)

Founded: 1990

Nickname: The Reds

Ground: Mill Street, (Basford United FC) in 2017/18, moving to CTFC Stadium (Carlton Town FC) for 2018/19

Season 2017/18:

WPL Northern (Tier 3): 9th

FA Cup: 2nd Round
WPL Cup: Quarter-finals
County Cup: Winners

2017/18 WPL NORTHERN

Date	Opponent	Result	Score	Scorers	Att	Pos
20.08	Guiseley Vixens (h)	W	1-0	Hazzana Parnell 14	82	
27.08	Bradford City (a)	D	0-0		71	
10.09	Derby County (h)	W	1-0	Hazzana Parnell 57	162	
17.09	Leicester City W (a)	D	2-2	Samantha Conroy 20, Natasha Hudson 62	158	4
20.09	Stoke City (a)	L	1-3	Kelly Darby 47, *Summer Holmes sent off 72*	110	5
01.10	West Brom (h)	W	5-1	Trina Greaves 7, Hazzana Parnell 17, 79, Nicola Emery 53, Natasha Hudson 65	87	2
08.10	Wolverhampton W (a)	W	1-0	Trina Greaves 26, *Amy Dicken sent off 59*	100	2
24.10	Stoke City (h)	L	0-1		156	3
29.10	Middlesbrough (h)	L	1-5	Samantha Conroy 19	106	6
05.11	Blackburn Rovers (a)	P-P				6
12.11	Derby County (a)	L	2-3	Samantha Conroy 28, Natasha Hudson 47, *Summer Holmes missed penalty (saved by Sarah Morgan) 89*	226	7
26.11	Guiseley Vixens (a)	A-A		Abandoned at 20 mins due to serious neck injury		8
07.01	West Brom (a)	D	1-1	Amy Dicken 83	85	7
21.01	Blackburn Rovers (a)	P-P				7
28.01	Blackburn Rovers (a)	L	0-7			7
11.02	Huddersfield Town (a)	L	0-4		56	7
11.03	Middlesbrough (a)+	L	1-4	Kelly Highman 31		9
18.03	Blackburn Rovers (h)	P-P				9
25.03	Leicester City W (h)	L	0-4		85	9
08.04	Fylde (a)	P-P				9
15.04	Huddersfield Town (h)	D	2-2	Hazzana Parnell (pen) 52, Leanne Robinson 71	67	9
22.04	Fylde (h)	L	3-4	Leanne Robinson 18, Kelly Darby 74, Hazzana Parnell (pen) 75	54	9
29.04	Bradford City (h)**	W	1-0	Hazzana Parnell 36	354	9

Photo: Lee Samcro

06.05	Guiseley Vixens (a)*	L	0-6		31	9
13.05	Blackburn Rovers (h)**	L	1-4	Hazzana Parnell 29	76	9
15.05	Fylde (a)++	L	0-1			9
20.05	Wolverhampton W (h)**	L	0-5	Kelly Darby sent off	70	9

+Played at Middlesbrough College *Played at Fleet Lane, West Riding CFA Headquarters
**Played at Lee Westwood Sports Centre   ++Played at Moss Farm Leisure Complex

2017/18 FA CUP

03.12 R2	Newcastle U (h)	L	0-2		76

2017/18 WPL Cup

03.09 DR	Leeds United (h)	W	7-1	Kelly Darby 16, Amy Dicken 35, 48, Charlotte Griffin 46, Hazzana Parnell 50, Rebecca Kemp 70, Trina Greaves 79	94
15.10 R1	West Brom (h)	W	5-0	Nicola Emery 39, 89, Natasha Hudson 44, Trina Greaves 48, Samantha Conroy 70	124
10.12 R2	Guiseley Vixens (h)	P-P			
14.01 R2	Guiseley Vixens (h)	W	5-0	Nicola Emery 8, 48, Charlotte Griffin 52, 66, Summer Holmes 63	73
25.02 QF	Leicester City W (h)	D	1-1 aet (L 4-5p)	Natasha Hudson 55	145

2017/18 NOTTINGHAMSHIRE FA COUNTY CUP

Date	Round	Opponent	Result	Score	Scorers
22.10	R1	Ollerton Town (a)	W	3-2	Trina Greaves 24, Hazzana Parnell 39, Samantha Conroy 48
19.11	R2	Nottingham F Reserves (a)	W	11-0	Natasha Hudson 3, 26, 41 Trina Greaves 35, 47, 67, 90, Kelly Darby 38, Ellis Cullen 54, Nicola Emery 59, Amy Dicken 85
18.02	SF	Arnold Town (h)	W	w/o	
08.05	F	Radcliffe Olympic (n)	W	2-1	Natasha Hudson, Amy Dicken

(n) Played at Greenwich Avenue, Basford United FC

- Forest won the 2017/18 Nottinghamshire FA County Cup, beating Tier 4 side Radcliffe Olympic 2-1 in the final with goals from Natasha Hudson and Amy Dicken.

- Hazzana Parnell was Forest's leading scorer in 2017/18. She hit eight goals in the League and 10 in all competitions.

- The club reached the WPL Cup final in 2010/11 but had to settle for runners-up spot as they were beaten on penalties by Barnet.

- When the club was founded in 1990 they advertised for players in the official matchday programme for Nottingham Forest's men's Division One match against Everton.

- Forest were among the teams who applied to join the WSL for the 2014 season, but they were unsuccessful.

315

OXFORD UNITED
2018/19: WNL SOUTHERN PREMIER (Tier 3)

Founded: c1990

Nickname: The U's

Ground: Court Place Farm, (Oxford City FC)

Season 2017/18:

WSL 2 (Tier 2): 8th

FA Cup: 4th Round

Continental Cup: Group Stage

WSL 2 2017/18

						Att	Pos
24.09	Sheffield FC (h)	W	1-0	Ellie Gilliatt (og) 60		220	
01.10	Watford (a)	W	3-1	Hannah Short 7, Kayleigh Hines 33, Emily Allen 81		170	
08.10	Doncaster R B (h)	D	2-2	Chloe Chivers 59, Kayleigh Hines 90+3		231	2
29.10	Brighton & H A (h)	D	2-2	Chloe Chivers 63, Taome Oliver 71		204	4
12.11	Millwall L (a)	L	0-1			217	5
09.12	London Bees (a)	L	1-2	Kayleigh Hines 23		178	5
07.01	Durham (h)	L	2-4	Hannah Short 4, Ellis Hillman 78		158	5
28.01	Aston Villa (h)	W	3-1	Taome Oliver 35, Kayleigh Hines 49, Dan Carlton 51		301	5
11.02	Tottenham H (a)	L	1-2	Chloe Chivers 24		130	4
22.02	Brighton & H A (a)	L	1-5	Chloe Chivers 57			6
25.03	Millwall L (h)	L	2-4	Kayleigh Hines 38, *Oxford missed pen 40 (saved Sarah Quantrill)*, Chloe Chivers 90		206	6
29.03	London Bees (h)	L	2-3	Emily Allen 13, Taome Oliver 18		216	7
01.04	Durham (a)	D	1-1	Imogen Lancaster 45+1		257	7
19.04	Tottenham H (h)	L	1-2	Hannah Short 71		335	8
22.04	Aston Villa (a)	L	0-1			127	8
29.04	Sheffield FC (a)	L	1-4	Georgia Timms 86			8
13.05	Watford (h)	L	1-2	Fran Kitching (og) 15		525	8
20.05	Doncaster R B (a)	L	0-4			310	8

2017 WSL CONTINENTAL CUP: GROUP TWO NORTH

					Att
11.10	Birmingham C (a)	L	0-4	*Hannah Short sent off 62*	445
02.11	Manchester C (h)	L	0-6		777
16.11	Everton (a)	L	0-4		
03.12	Doncaster R B (h)	L	1-5	Hannah Short 12	172

2017 FA CUP

					Att
04.02 R4	Cardiff City (a)	D	0-0 (L 4-5 p)		270

- The U's were founder members of WSL 2 in 2014 and played at that level until the end of 2017/18. Their application for a Tier 2 licence under the FA's new criteria for 2018/19 was turned down. It was a decision which understandably left many at the club hugely disappointed and saw them forced to drop down to Tier 3.

- Founded in the early 1990s, Oxford United women's had a loose affiliation with Oxford United men's club until 2008 when that relationship became formalised. At that point the men's club founded a girls' Centre of Excellence and fully integrated the women's team into the Oxford United FC set-up.

- The U's are 3-time winners of the Oxfordshire FA Cup (2010/11, 2011/12, and 2012/13), were South Regional Premier League winners in 2011/12 and lifted the South Regional League Cup in 2010/11 and 2011/12. Other honours include the South West Counties League Cup in 2012/13 and runners-up position in the South Regional League Division One in 2008/09.

- Oxford's best FA Cup run to date came in 2012/13. Having beaten Keynsham Town in the 2nd Round they then caused a shock away to Charlton. For the 4th Round tie at home to Newcastle they were granted use of Oxford United men's Kassam Stadium. A crowd of 700 saw them dispatch Newcastle to reach the 5th Round for the first time in the club's history. The reward was a home tie against top-flight Everton. Although the WSL 1 outfit proved too strong, (winning 7-0), another impressive crowd of 945 came to the Kassam as Oxford's 'never-say-die' Cup spirit won them many new admirers.

PLYMOUTH ARGYLE

2018/19: WNL SOUTHERN PREMIER (Tier 3)

Founded: 1975 (as Plymouth Pilgrims)

Nickname: The Lady Pilgrims / Argyle

Ground: Haye Road,
(Elburton Villa FC)

Season 2017/18:

WPL South West One (Tier 4):
Champions

FA Cup: 4th Round
WPL Cup: Quarter-finals
County Cup: Winners

2017/18 WPL SOUTH WEST ONE

Date	Opponent	Res	Score	Scorers		
20.08	St Nicholas (a)	W	8-0	Natasha Knapman 30, 36, 45, 78, 90, Kayley Lane 56, Ezme Wells 64, 87	35	
27.08	Brislington (a)	W	4-0	Kayley Lane 45, Zoe Cunningham 48, Natasha Knapman 52, 67	43	
10.09	Larkhall Athletic (h)	W	9-1	Natasha Knapman 25, 30, 59, 84, Katie Middleton 44, Amber Pollock 65, Danielle Barr 75, Jessie Boston 83, Rebecca Dandridge 90	32	
17.09	Maidenhead U (a)	W	4-0	Katie Middleton 25, Natasha Knapman 30, 39, Zoe Cunningham 56	28	1
24.09	Cheltenham T (a)	W	5-0	Natasha Knapman 30, 32, 55, 85, Ezme Wells 68	39	1
01.10	Basingstoke T (a) exp	W	5-1	Natasha Knapman 22, 68, 77, 83, Zoe Cunningham 71	30	1
05.11	Keynsham Town (h)	W	5-2	Kaylee Lane 14, 85 Katie Middleton 60, Natasha Knapman 70, Phoebe Baker 68	111	2
14.01	Larkhall Athletic (a)	W	3-0	Zoe Cunningham 54, 58, 80	20	3
28.01	Maidenhead U (h)	P-P				3
18.02	Poole Town (a)	P-P				3
04.03	Cheltenham Town (h)	P-P				3
11.03	St Nicholas (h)*	W	13-0	Natasha Knapman 1, 10, 22, 30, 35, 67, 73, Danielle Barr 5, Kirsten Prior (og) 53, Zoe Cunningham 60, 84, Rebecca Atkins 65, 85	35	3
18.03	So'ton Women (a)	P-P				3
25.03	So'ton Saints (h)+	W	6-0	Amber Pollock 4, Natasha Knapman 9, 40, 48, Zoe Cunningham 19, Rebecca Dandridge 30	40	2
01.04	Poole Town (a)**	W	3-2	Zoe Cunningham 15, 30, Natasha Knapman 55	52	2
08.04	Keynsham Town (a)	W	6-1	Natasha Knapman, 20, 38, 45+1, 55, Amber Pollock 22, Katie Middleton (pen) 82	70	2
15.04	So'ton Saints (a)	D	1-1	Katie Middleton 77	15	2
22.04	Brislington (h)	W	9-1	Kayley Lane 14, 71, Rebecca Dandridge 16, 55, Natasha Knapman 19, Amber Pollock 63, Katie Middleton 67, Kayleigh Brown 75, Rebecca Atkins 82		2

29.04	Maidenhead U (h)		P-P			2
06.05	So'ton Women (h)	W	7-1	Amber Pollock 13, 18, Rebecca Dandridge 30, Katie Middleton (pen) 42, Natasha Knapman 50, 54, Zoe Cunningham 60,	88	2
13.05	So'ton Women (a)^	D	2-2	Rebecca Dandridge 27, Zoe Cunningham 76	70	2
16.05	Cheltenham Town (h)	W	9-0	Natasha Knapman 3, Zoe Cunningham 34, 78, Rebecca Dandridge 45, 63, Katie Middleton 56, Danielle Barr 59, Darcey Hepworth 64, Ebony Dover (pen) 90+1	32	1
19.05	Maidenhead U (h)	W	w/o			
20.05	Poole Town (h)++	W	6-1	Natasha Knapman 14, 65, 71, Kayley Lane 42, 56, Katie Middleton (pen) 87	450	1C

exp = Result expunged from records following Basingstoke's resignation from the League   *Played at University of St Mark & St John
+Played at Marjon Sports & Health Centre   **Played at Dorset FA County Ground 3G   ++Played at Home Park, Plymouth Argyle FC
^Played at Alton Ladies

2017/18 FA CUP

08.10 RQ3	Poole Town (a)	W	5-2	Natasha Knapman 22, 55, 80, Zoe Cunningham 47, 90	34
19.11 R1	Basingstoke Town (h)	W	w/o		
03.12 R2	Gillingham (a)*	W	3-1 (aet)	Zoe Cunningham 2, Natasha Knapman 102, Ezme Wells 110	

07.01 R3	Fylde (a)+	W	3-1	Natasha Knapman 4, 43, Amber Pollock 35, *Katie Middleton missed pen 65*	
04.02 R4	Leicester City W (h)		P-P		
11.02 R4	Leicester City W (h)	L	2-3	Natasha Knapman 49, Katie Middleton 90+5	208

*Played at Priestfield, Gillingham FC   +Played at UCLAN Sports Arena

2017/18 WPL CUP

03.09 DR	Bye				
22.10 R1	Chichester City (h)		P-P		
29.10 R1	Chichester City (h)	W	3-1	Natasha Knapman 38, 65, Tori Marks 60	63
10.12 R2	Cardiff City L (a)		P-P		
17.12 R2	Cardiff City L (a)	W	2-1	Rebecca Atkins 20, Natasha Knapman 68	50
25.02 QF	Coventry United (h)	L	0-3		55

2017/18 DEVON FA COUNTY CUP

15.10 R1	Buckland Athletic (a)	W	4-3 (aet)	Natasha Knapman 50, 101, 115, Amber Pollock 22	150est
26.11 QF	Alphington (a)	W	11-1	Darcey Hepworth, Natasha Knapman (x5), Katie Middleton, Kayleigh Brown, Zoe Cunningham, Jessie Boston, Rebecca Atkins	
21.01 SF	Marine Academy Plymouth (h)	W	w/o		
06.04 F	Torquay United (n)	W	8-0	Katie Middleton 12, 24, Kayley Lane 38, 70, 87, Natasha Knapman 48, 82, 90	377

(n) Played at Newton Abbot, Devon FA HQ

"There has been no person who can be singled out as playing a more important role in Argyle's success than anyone else. Everybody, from those behind the scenes, the committee, to the managers, coaches, physio and players on the pitch. We are an all-encompassing club and when we have needed to call on the promising youngsters we have not been afraid to do so because we have so much confidence in their ability. The door is always open to them, that is who we are as a club."

Travis Rowland, Plymouth Argyle Manager

- Season 2017/18 was one of huge success as Plymouth won the WPL South West One title – going the entire campaign unbeaten – and picked up the Devon County Cup. Natasha Knapman was crowned the division's top scorer with an astonishing 40 goals in the League and 61 in all competitions. The title brought them promotion to Tier 3 for 2018/19.

- Argyle scored exactly 100 goals in their title-winning 2017/18 League campaign. Katie Middleton – who has now played over 200 games for the Lady Pilgrims – notched up the century with a penalty on the final day in a 6-1 win over Poole. They also conceded just 12 goals thanks in no small part to the efforts of goalkeeper Michaela Phillips who has been at the club for 10 years.

- Following a five-a-side competition at the Mayflower Leisure Centre, two teams joined forces in 1975 to create an 11-a-side team called Plymouth Pilgrims. With the team at the time playing their home matches at Saltash United's Kimberly Stadium, they changed their name to Saltash Pilgrims in the late 1990s. In 2001/02 they were invited to compete as part of the men's professional club, Plymouth Argyle, and changed their name to the same.

POOLE TOWN
2018/19: WNL DIVISION 1 SOUTH WEST (Tier 4)

Founded: 1980s

Nickname: The Dolphins

Ground: Milborne St Andrew

Season 2017/18:

WPL South West One (Tier 4): 5th

FA Cup: 3rd Qualifying Round
WPL Cup: Preliminary Round
County Cup: Winners

2017/18 WPL SOUTH WEST ONE

Date	Opponent		Result	Scorers		
20.08	Maidenhead U (a)	W	1-0	Samantha Gubb 52	30	
27.08	St Nicholas (h)	W	6-0	Samantha Gubb 7, 21, Charlotte Eastman 65, Jessica Fowell 78, Rachel Anderson 82, 87	33	
10.09	So'ton Saints (h)	L	0-4		22	
17.09	Keynsham Town (a)	L	1-5	Samantha Gubb 44	40	4
20.09	So'ton Women (h)*	L	0-5		52	5
01.10	Brislington (h)	L	2-3	Samantha Gubb 10, Jessica Fowell 25	22	6
11.10	So'ton Women (a)	L	1-3	Own Goal 2	39	7
15.10	*Basingstoke Town (a)* **exp**	W	5-4	Jemma Tewkesbury 5, 21, Faye Rolfe-Hawkins 12, 28, Samantha Gubb 78	*28*	5
29.10	So'ton Saints (a)	D	0-0		22	5
05.11	Larkhall Athletic (h)	L	1-3	Jemma Tewkesbury 75	21	7
12.11	Cheltenham Town (h)		P-P			7
19.11	Maidenhead U (h)	D	2-2	Faye Rolfe-Hawkins 1, Jemma Tewkesbury 56, *Samantha Gubb sent off 59*	26	5
03.12	Cheltenham Town (h)		P-P			5
10.12	St Nicholas (a)		P-P			5
07.01	Larkhall Athletic (a)		P-P			5
21.01	Keynsham Town (h)		P-P			6
28.01	Larkhall Athletic (a)		P-P			6
04.02	St Nicholas (a)		P-P			6
11.02	Cheltenham Town (h)	W	6-1	Jemma Tewkesbury 16, 23, 82, 90, Sacha Paynter 44, Katelyn Wyatt 68	17	5
18.02	Plymouth A (h)		P-P			5
25.02	Cheltenham Town (a)	W	2-0	Charlotte Eastman 56, 68	53	5
04.03	Keynsham Town (h)		P-P			5
11.03	Keynsham Town (h)		P-P			5
01.04	Plymouth A (h)**	L	2-3	Jemma Tewkesbury 21, Faye Rolfe-Hawkins 45	52	5
15.04	Larkhall Athletic (a)	W	1-0	Maisy Smith 82	20	5
22.04	St Nicholas (a)	W	2-1	Rebecca Miles 44, Jessica Fowell 63	30	5
29.04	Keynsham Town (h)+	L	1-6	Jemma Tewkesbury 25	28	5

Photo: Nadia Lonnen

06.05	Brislington (a)	L	3-4	Katie Paul 3, Alexis Bussell 74, 82	43	5
20.05	Plymouth Argyle (a)++	L	1-6	Rebecca Miles 17	450	5

exp = Result expunged from records after Basingstoke Town resigned from the League.   *Played at Verwood Town FC
**Played at Dorset FA County Ground 3G   +Played at Tatnam Ground, Poole Town FC   ++Played at Home Park, Plymouth Argyle FC

2017/18 FA CUP

08.10 RQ3	Plymouth Argyle (h)	L	2-5	Jemma Tewkesbury 29, Faye Rolfe-Hawkins 46	34

2017/18 WPL CUP

03.09 DR	Maidenhead United (a)	W	1-0 (aet)	Rachel Anderson 101	53
24.09 PR	Crystal Palace (h)	L	0-8		58

2017/18 DORSET FA COUNTY CUP

14.01 QF	Wool & Winfrith (a)	W	19-0	Sacha Paynter 5, 20, 78, Shelley Towers 11, Charlotte Eastman 26, Rebecca Miles 38, Faye Rolfe-Hawkins 46, 49, 64, 67, Jemma Tewkesbury 55, 60, 70, 77, Emma Samways 56, 68, 85, Siena White 71, 80
18.03	Wareham Rangers (a)	P-P		
25.03 SF	Wareham Rangers (a)	W	12-1	Rebecca Miles 1, 15, Faye Rolfe-Hawkins 8, 17, 44, 81, Emma Samways 10, Sacha Paynter 34, Jemma Tewkesbury 39, 43, 80, Samantha Gubb 67
17.04 F	Dorchester Town (n)	W	7-0	Maisy Smith (x3), Rebecca Miles, Faye Rolfe-Hawkins, Sacha Paynter, Jemma Tewkesbury

(n) Played at Hamworthy United FC

"Our achievements in 2017/18 were more than we expected going into the season. To finish mid-table in our first WPL season proved how our team share the same passion, drive and goal to get better week in and week out and to take Poole Town Ladies to the next level."

Rebecca Witherington – Poole Town Captain

- Back-to-back promotions carried Poole Town from Tier 6 to the Tier 4 for the start of the 2017/18 season. They went up to WPL South West One (now WNL Division 1 South West) after finishing 3rd in the South West Regional League in 2016/17, taking the promotion spot because Champions Yeovil Town Intermediate were not eligible to do so and runners-up Marine Academy Plymouth decided to continue competing in Tier 5.

- In 2017/18 they finished a highly-creditable 5th in their first season in Tier 4. The goals of Jemma Tewkesbury played a key role in their success, she notched eight in the League and 17 in all competitions.

- The Dolphins have won the Dorset FA County Cup five years in a row. They beat Dorchester Town 7-0 in the final in 2017/18.

PORTSMOUTH
2018/19: WNL SOUTHERN PREMIER (Tier 3)

Founded: 1987

Nickname: Pompey

Ground: Westleigh Park, (Havant & Waterlooville FC) in 2017/18, moving to PMC Stadium (Baffins Milton Rovers) for 2018/19

Season 2017/18:

WPL Southern (Tier 3): 6th

FA Cup: 3rd Round
WPL Cup: 2nd Round
County Cup: Winners

2017/18 WPL SOUTHERN

Date	Opponent		Result	Scorers	Att	
20.08	Cardiff City L (h)	W	4-1	Shannon Albuery 3, Natasha Stephens 16, Samantha Quayle 43, Molly Clark 88, *Michelle Beazley sent off 64*	122	
27.08	Coventry United (a)	W	2-1	Samantha Quayle 11, Rachel Panting 13	80est	
10.09	Charlton Athletic (h)	L	0-1		147	
17.09	Lewes (a)	L	0-1		116	7
20.09	Chichester City (a)	D	2-2	Shannon Albuery 76, Molly Clark 81	271	7
24.09	West Ham United (h)	W	2-1	Shannon Seivwright 84, Rachel Panting (pen) 90+3	126	5
01.10	Crystal Palace (a)	L	0-2		204	6
08.10	Gillingham (h)*	W	3-1	Nadine Bazan 3, Samantha Quayle 50, 61	110	4
12.10	Chichester City (a)	L	2-3	Samantha Quayle 31, *Shannon Seivwright missed pen 85,* Shannon Albuery 90+1	290	6
29.10	Coventry United (h)	L	0-2		104	7
12.11	Gillingham (a)	W	4-0	Natasha Stephens 12, Molly Clark 25, Samantha Quayle 42, Shannon Albuery 45	97	6
26.11	Lewes (h)	W	3-2	Samantha Quayle 49, 66, Molly Clark 55	112	7
04.02	QPR (a)	W	1-0	Katie James 76	60	6
25.02	Cardiff City (a)	W	2-0	Daisy McLachlan 48, Eilidh Currie 84	80	5
04.03	C&K Basildon (a)		P-P			5
11.03	QPR (h)		P-P			5
18.03	West Ham United (a)		P-P			5
25.03	Crystal Palace (h)**	L	0-4		45	5
01.04	Swindon Town (h)+	W	5-0	*Rachel Panting missed pen 17,* Shannon Albuery 22, 28, 87, Samantha Quayle 39, Katie James 90+1	54	5
08.04	Swindon Town (a)	W	3-0	Daisy McLachlan 68, Katie James 80, Samantha Quayle 88	45	5
15.04	Charlton Athletic (a)	L	0-1		114	5
22.04	West Ham United (a)	L	1-7	Daisy McLachlan 80, *Rachel Panting missed pen 82 (saved Cara Connaster)*	187	5
29.04	C & K Basildon (a)	L	2-4	Daisy McLachlan 49, Shannon Albuery 76	61	5

| 06.05 | C & K Basildon (h)+ | W | 2-1 | Daisy McLachlan 15, 41 | 51 | 5 |
| 13.05 | QPR (h)++ | W | 6-1 | Charley Boswell 25, Samantha Quayle 38, 81, Daisy McLachlan 40, Rachel Panting (pen) 71, Emma-Jane May (pen) 89 | 397 | 5 |

*Played at Privett Park   **Played at Littlehampton Town FC   +Played at Bognor Regis Town
++Played at Fratton Park, Portsmouth FC

2017/18 FA CUP

| 03.12 R2 | AFC Wimbledon (a) | W | 2-1 | Samantha Quayle 52, Amelia Southgate 55 | 90 |
| 07.01 R3 | Blackburn Rovers (a) | L | 0-7 | | 50est |

2017/18 WPL CUP

03.09 DR	QPR (a)	W	3-0	Jade Widdowson 28, Molly Clark 35, Natasha Stephens 47	50
15.10 R1	Southampton W (a)	W	3-1	Gemma Hillier 13, Shannon Albuery 24, Natasha Stephens 63	108
10.12 R2	Lewes (a)		P-P		
14.01 R2	Lewes (a)	L	1-5	Rachel Panting 57	196

2017/18 HAMPSHIRE FA COUNTY CUP

| 19.11 R2 | Winchester City Flyers (a) | W | 7-0 | Rachel Panting 13, 57, 59, Samantha Quayle 45+1, 81, Natasha Stephens 55, Shannon Seivwright 83 | 40 est |
| 21.01 QF | Warsash Wasps (a) | | P-P | | |

28.01 QF	Warsash Wasps (a)	W	10-0	Samantha Quayle 10, 37, 90+5, Amelia Southgate 13, Katie James 16, 28, Rachel Panting 37, 62, Daisy McLachlan 45, Emma-Jane May 81	60 est
18.02 SF	Southampton Saints (a)	W	3-0	Shannon Albuery 64, Rachel Panting 75, Ellie Russell (og) 78	80 est
10.05 F	Southampton FC (n)	W	5-0	Shannon Albuery 26, 45, 47, Daisy McLachlan (pen) 32, Rachel Panting 54	200 est

(n) Played at Alton Town FC

"I couldn't be any prouder of this group of players; the ones that wear the iconic Pompey shirt each week. Not only have they all bought into our philosophy, but the progression they have made as a team has been fantastic to see. They've had to deal with some adversity along the way, but it has been their reaction to this that has defined their character and built a strong team culture. It is a fitting reward that the last game of 2017/18 was played at Fratton Park in front of such a large crowd."

Jay Sadler, *Portsmouth Manager*

- In June 2018 it was announced that Portsmouth Ladies will officially come under the umbrella of Portsmouth FC (the men's professional outfit) from 2018/19 onwards. A busy summer also saw the club switch stadiums, meaning they will be playing back in their home city in 2018/19 at the PMC Stadium, home of non-League Baffins Milton Rovers.

- Samantha Quayle was top scorer for Portsmouth in 2017/18, hitting 12 goals in the WPL and 18 in all competitions.

- Portsmouth won the WPL Southern Division title in 2011/12 (when it was Tier 4) and 2014/15 (Tier 3). Prior to that their first silverware arrived in 2002/03 when they won the South West Combination League and South West Combination League Cup.

- In 2014/15, Nigeria striker Ini Umotong became the first Portsmouth player to be capped at senior level when she made her debut in a 2-2 draw with Mali. She hit 29 goals in 25 games (all comps) in 2014/15 before leaving for Oxford and later joining Brighton.

QUEENS PARK RANGERS
2018/19: WNL SOUTHERN PREMIER (Tier 3)

Founded: 2001

Nickname: Rangers

Ground: Honeycroft, (Uxbridge FC)

Season 2017/18:

WPL Southern (Tier 3): 11th

FA Cup: 2nd Round
WPL Cup: Determining Round
WPL Plate: 1st Round
Capital Cup: Semi-finals

2017/18 WPL SOUTHERN

Date	Opponent	Result	Score	Scorers / Notes		
20.08	Crystal Palace (a)	L	0-9		105	
27.08	Swindon Town (h)	W	2-0	Elly Maggs 43, 66	45	
10.09	Gillingham (h)	L	0-4	Mara Deluca sent off 58	35	
17.09	Charlton Athletic (a)	L	0-7		81	10
01.10	C&K Basildon (a)	L	0-1		71	11
08.10	Cardiff City L (h)	L	3-4	Laura Hennessy 22, Kasha Petit 79, Rae Roberts 88	27	11
05.11	Chichester City (h)	D	1-1	Katie Knell 2	51	11
26.11	Coventry United (h)	L	1-10	Pauline Adeyemo 80	50	11
10.12	Crystal Palace (h)		P-P			11
17.12	Gillingham (a)		P-P			11
07.01	Swindon Town (a)	W	4-1	Helen Ogle 17, 27, 51, Kasha Petit 62	33	11
14.01	Cardiff City L (a)	D	1-1	Dominkia Netschova 38	100	11
21.01	Crystal Palace (h)		P-P			11
28.01	Lewes (a)		P-P			11
04.02	Portsmouth (h)	L	0-1		60	11
11.02	C&K Basildon (h)	L	1-3	Cherrelle Albert 4	52	11
25.02	Crystal Palace (h)	L	1-2	Mara Deluca 63	46	11
11.03	Portsmouth (a)		P-P			11
18.03	Lewes (h)		P-P			11
25.03	Lewes (a)	L	0-3		202	11
30.03	Coventry United (a)		P-P			11
08.04	West Ham United (h)	L	0-10		160	11
15.04	Lewes (h)	L	0-3		50	11
22.04	Gillingham (a)	L	0-3		82	11
29.04	Charlton Athletic (h)	L	0-11		120	11
06.05	Chichester City (a)	L	0-3	QPR GK Lauren Dolbear saved Natasha Stephens pen 53	82	11
13.05	Portsmouth (a)*	L	1-6	Chontelle Lawrence 90+1	397	11

| 17.05 | Coventry United (a)+ | L | 1-4 | Helen Ogle 34 | | 11 |
| 20.05 | West Ham United (a) | L | 1-7 | Helen Ogle 84 | 1,356 | 11 |

*Played at Fratton Park, Portsmouth FC   +Played at Communications Park, Daventry Town FC

2017/18 FA CUP

| 03.12 R2 | Charlton Athletic (a) | L | 0-5 | | 66 |

2017/18 WPL CUP

| 03.09 DR | Portsmouth (h) | L | 0-3 | | 50 |

2017/18 WPL PLATE

| 29.10 R1 | West Ham United (a)** | L | 1-3 | Katie Knell 48 | 1,052 |

**Played at Ship Lane, Thurrock FC

2017/18 MIDDLESEX FA CAPITAL CUP

22.10 R1	AFC Phoenix (h)+	W	1-0	Kasha Petit
19.11 QF	Fulham Foundation (h)*	W	1-0	Dominika Netschova 67
18.02 SF	Crystal Palace (h)	L	0-2	

+Played at Middlesex Stadium   *Drawn at home, but played at Motspur Park, Fulham FC training ground

"I'm excited to be playing at QPR because I have played for the club before in my youth years and my experience before was just amazing. I am quite sure this time around it is going to be equally good, and hopefully even better. The 2018/19 season excites me so much and I just can't wait to be on the pitch every weekend with my team-mates."

Courtnay Ward-Chambers, QPR (signed June 2018)

- The 2017/18 season was a tough one on the pitch as QPR finished second-from-bottom of WPL Southern. Their only League wins both came against bottom club Swindon.

- QPR Ladies were formed out of the merger of Wembley Mill Hill and QPR Women's in May 2001. They were relegated from the WPL at the end of 2001/02 but finally returned to that level when they were promoted at the end of 2008/09. In June 2018 they officially changed the suffix of their name from Ladies to Women, joining a growing number of clubs doing so.

- The team has twice collected silverware; the Middlesex County FA Women's Senior Cup in 2009/10 and the South West Combination League Cup in 2006/07. They were runners-up in the South East Combination League in 2002/03.

RADCLIFFE OLYMPIC
2018/19: Folded in July 2018

Founded: 1999 (as Dayncourt Ladies)

Nickname: Olympic

Ground: The Recreation Ground,
(Radcliffe Olympic FC)

Season 2017/18:

WPL Midlands One (Tier 4): 4th

FA Cup: 3rd Qualifying Round
WPL Cup: Determining Round
WPL Plate: 1st Round
County Cup: Runners-up

2017/18 WPL MIDLANDS ONE

Date	Opponent		Score	Scorers		
20.08	Sporting Khalsa (h)		P-P			
27.08	Solihull Moors (a)	L	3-4	Brogan Jones 12, 80, Alex Saulter 37	35	
10.09	Sheffield United (h)	D	0-0		42	
17.09	Loughborough F (a)	L	1-4	Rania Turner-Ramadan 25	37	8
21.09	Rotherham United (h)	W	5-1	Linnea Kremer 2, 51, Ellie Readman 9, 78, Alice Kempski 40	22	7
24.09	Long Eaton United (a)	W	3-0	Linnea Kremer 25, 52 Ellie Readman 75	65	6
01.10	B'ham & W M (h)	W	2-0	Alice Kempski 11, Rania Turner-Ramdan (pen) 80	18	6
12.10	Rotherham United (a)	W	3-1	Rania Turner-Ramadan 13, Sarah Saxon (og) 34, Beth Bailey 70	65	6
15.10	The New Saints (a)	L	2-4	Linnea Kremer 15, Georgia Gladwin 70	55	6
05.11	B'ham & W M (a)	W	2-0	Beth Bailey 32, Georgia Gladwin 50	20	6
12.11	Leicester City L (h)	W	5-1	Rania Turner-Ramadan 20, Beth Bailey 25, Alice Kempski 27, Ellie Readman 48, Georgia Gladwin 89	25	5
26.11	Burton Albion (h)	L	1-2	Alex Saulter 71	20	5
10.12	Steel City W (h)		P-P			5
07.01	Long Eaton United (h)	W	1-0	Catherine Jackson 67	30	5
28.01	Burton Albion (a)	W	2-1	Rania Turner-Ramadan 10, Alice Kempski 20, *Georgina Shaw sent off 20*	55	4
04.02	Leicester City L (a)	W	1-0	Beth Bailey 52	20	4
11.02	Sheffield United (a)	L	1-2	Beth Bailey 30	97	4
25.02	Sporting Khalsa (h)	W	2-1	Rania Turner-Ramadan 32, Alex Saulter 43	25	4
18.03	Steel City W (h)		P-P			5
25.03	Sporting Khalsa (a)	L	1-2	Ellie Readman 50	20	5
08.04	Solihull Moors (h)	D	3-3	Brogan Jones, Beth Bailey (x2)		5
15.04	The New Saints (h)	W	4-1	Own Goal, Rania Turner-Ramadan, Beth Bailey, Kayleigh Aylmer	35	4
29.04	Steel City W (a)	W	7-0	Beth Bailey (x3), Christina Brewer, Honor Cantrell, Rania Turner-Ramadan, Dannielle Saulter	43	5

331

| 13.05 | Steel City W (h) | W | w/o | | 4 |
| 20.05 | Loughborough F (h) | L | 2-4 | Rania Turner-Ramadan (pen), Beth Bailey | 5 |

2017/18 FA CUP

| 08.10 RQ3 | Loughborough F (h) | L | w/o | |

2017/18 WPL CUP

| 03.09 DR | Steel City W (a) | L | 2-5 (aet) | Ashleigh Evans 18, Ellie Readman 25 | 33 |

2017/18 WPL PLATE

| 29.10 R1 | Newcastle United (a) | L | 0-2 | | 30 |

2017/18 NOTTS FA COUNTY CUP

Date	Round	Opponent	Result	Score	Scorers
22.10	R1	Eastwood Community (h)	W	3-1	Linnea Kremer (x3)
19.11	QF	Teversal (a)	W	8-0	Beth Bailey, Emily Hallam, Linnea Kremer, Rania Turner-Ramadan (x3), Ellie Readman (x2)
18.02	SF	Market Warsop (a)	W	6-0	Rania Turner-Ramadan (x2), Beth Bailey (x2), Georgia Gladwin, Kimmie Harford
08.05	F	Nottingham Forest (n)	L	1-2	L Robinson

On 25 July 2018 came the sad news that Radcliffe Olympic – a club which had existed since 1999 – had been forced to fold. They had been due to start 2018/19 in WNL Division 1 Midlands, but a spokesperson revealed: "Unfortunately we have had to fold. We were struggling for players last year and the core group have got to an age where other things take priority. Furthermore our manager had to leave due to her personal circumstances and we were unable to find a replacement in time for the start of preseason."

- It was while having a kickabout on Bingham Road in Radcliffe that Kate Tinsley and friends came up with the idea of forming a women's football side, and thus the team that would go on to become Radcliffe Olympic was founded.

- Tinsley, and other volunteers, have played a key role in the development of the club which has gone from strength to strength since merging with Radcliffe Olympic. The women's team groundshare with Radcliffe Olympic men's at The Rec.

- Ex-Notts County player Mick Vinter was among those who founded the club, then known as Daynscourt Ladies, in August 1999. The club started life playing in the Third Division of the East Midlands Unison Women's Football League. They enjoyed many Cup finals and promotions on their route up to Tier 4.

ROTHERHAM UNITED

2018/19: NORTH EASTERN REGIONAL PREMIER LEAGUE (Tier 5)

Founded: 1969 (as Kilnhurst Shooting Stars)

Nickname: The Millers

Ground: Roundwood Sports Club, (Parkgate FC)

Season 2017/18:

WPL Midlands One (Tier 4): 11th (R)

FA Cup: 3rd Qualifying Round
WPL Cup: Determining Round
WPL Plate: Preliminary Round
County Cup: Quarter-final

2017/18 WPL MIDLANDS ONE

Date	Opponent		Score	Scorers		
20.08	Long Eaton United (h)		P-P			
27.08	Steel City W (a)		P-P			
10.09	The New Saints (h)	L	1-3	Kirsty Louise-Richardson	35	
17.09	Sheffield United (h)	L	0-11		63	12
21.09	Radcliffe Olympic (a)	L	1-5	Amy Booth	22	12
01.10	Steel City W (h)	L	1-7	Samantha Hale	60	12
12.10	Radcliffe Olympic (h)	L	1-3	Libby Hallam	65	12
15.10	Sporting Khalsa (a)	L	0-5		20	12
29.10	Long Eaton United (a)	L	0-2		52	12
05.11	Loughborough F (a)	L	0-5		32	12
12.11	Solihull Moors (h)	W	3-1	Phoebe Hallam, Kirsty Louise Richardson, Sarah Saxon	36	11
19.11	The New Saints (a)+	L	1-4	Bryher Taylor	45	11
26.11	Leicester City L (a)*	W	3-2	Phoebe Hallam, Samantha Hale, Catherine McDuff Viau	15	11
10.12	Solihull Moors (a)		P-P			11
07.01	Leicester City L (h)	D	1-1	Sarah Saxon	35	11
14.01	Sporting Khalsa (h)	L	0-2		35	11
04.02	Sheffield United (a)	L	0-10		102	11
18.02	Burton Albion (a)	L	0-6		55	11
25.02	Loughborough F (h)	L	0-4		40	11
04.03	B'ham & W M (h)		P-P			11
11.03	Solihull Moors (a)	L	0-9		20	11
25.03	Steel City W (a)	L	0-4		62	11
08.04	Long Eaton United (h)	L	0-6		25	11
29.04	Burton Albion (h)	L	0-7		30	11
06.05	B'ham & WM (h)	L	2-5	Libby Hallam (x2)	20	11
20.05	B'ham & WM (a)	L	1-12	Sarah Saxon	30	11

+Match played at Four Crosses   *Played at Saffron Lane, (Aylestone Park FC)

2017/18 FA CUP
08.10 RQ3	Alnwick T Juniors (a)	L	0-5		82

2017/18 WPL CUP
03.09 DR	Derby County (a)	L	0-7		63

2017/18 WPL PLATE
24.09 PR	Chorley (a)	L	1-2	Catherine McDuff Viau	72

2017/18 SHEFFIELD & HALLAMSHIRE FA COUNTY CUP
17.12 R3	Doncaster Belles (a)	W	2-1	Amy Booth 20, Phoebe Hallam 50	
21.01 QF	Huddersfield Town Development (h)	P-P			
28.01 QF	Huddersfield Town Development (h)	L	1-6	Catherine McDuff Viau	45

- After a couple of tough seasons in WPL Midlands One (Tier 4), Rotherham United are back in Tier 5. They finished 11th in 2016/17 but were spared relegation, however another 11th-place finish in 2017/18 saw them suffer the drop.

- In June 2018 the club appointed Scott Duncanson as their new general manager. Duncanson has previously coached at Sheffield United Academy and Doncaster Rovers Belles.

- The club originated out of Kilnhurst Shooting Stars youth club in 1969 where football was one of a number of sports played. In the early 70s the name was changed to Kilnhurst Ladies and then to Millmoor Ladies in 1989 when they formed their first links with men's professional club Rotherham United.

- A further change of name followed when the FA devised a new pyramid system in 1999. The team competed as Parkgate Ladies in the Midland Combination League. In 2003 they renewed their links with Rotherham United men's club and took the same name.

- Current chair Val Hoyle has been with the club since it was formed and has served as a player, worked on the management committee, and even stood in as caretaker manager in 2016/17.

SHEFFIELD FC

2018/19: WNL NORTHERN PREMIER (Tier 3)

Founded: 2003

Nickname: The Club

Ground: Dronfield, (Sheffield FC)

Season 2017/18:

WSL 2 (Tier 2): 5th

FA Cup: 4th Round

Continental Cup: Group Stage

2017/18 WSL 2

						Att	Pos
24.09	Oxford United (a)	L	0-1			220	
30.09	London Bees (h)	W	3-1	Katie Anderson 15, Jenna Dear 33, Melissa Johnson 58		314	
08.10	Aston Villa (h)	W	2-1	Chloe Dixon 1, 45		303	4
29.10	Durham (h)	L	0-4			339	7
12.11	Brighton & H A (a)	L	0-1				7
10.12	Doncaster R B (a)	L	2-3	Sophie Jones 48, *Sophie Jones missed pen 86 (saved by Bethan Davies)*, Emma Johnson 90			7
07.01	Millwall L (a)	L	1-2	Hannah Cain 7		123	7
28.01	Tottenham H (h)	W	4-3	Melissa Johnson 12, 18, 45+2, Katie Anderson 54, *Hannah Cain sent off 42, Jenna Dear sent off 60*		443	6
11.02	Watford (a)		P-P				6
22.02	Durham (a)	L	2-3	Katie Anderson 72, Melissa Johnson 81		347	7
04.03	Watford (a)		P-P				7
18.03	Watford (a)		P-P				7
25.03	Brighton & H A (h)	L	1-4	Emma Johnson (pen) 89		284	8
01.04	Millwall L (h)		P-P				8
15.04	Watford (h)	W	4-0	Beth Donoghue 17, Hannah Cain 42, Emma Johnson (pen) 45, Rhema Lord-Mears 75			7
22.04	Tottenham H (a)	W	4-2	Melissa Johnson 5, 43, Chloe Dixon 73, Sarah Wiltshire (og) 87		368	7
29.04	Oxford United (h)	W	4-1	Emma Johnson 48, 60, Hannah Cain 54, Jenna Dear 64			7
06.05	Millwall L (h)	W	3-0	Melissa Johnson 6, Niamh Cashin 15, Chloe Dixon 47			5
09.05	Doncaster R B (h)	L	1-2	Hannah Cain 28			5
12.05	London Bees (a)	D	0-0			246	5
16.05	Watford (a)	W	5-0	Hannah Cain 52, Melissa Johnson 68, Ellie Gilliatt 84, 88, 90+4		129	5
20.05	Aston Villa (a)	W	4-3	Melissa Johnson 9, 31, 45+1, Chloe Dixon 43		259	5

2017/18 WSL CONTINENTAL CUP: GROUP ONE NORTH

11.10	Liverpool (a)	L	0-6		352
01.11	Durham (h)	W	5-1	Danielle Cox 2, Melissa Johnson 24, 29, 66, Holly Housley 36	122
05.11	Aston Villa (a)	D	2-2 L (10-11p)	Holly Housley 16, Melissa Johnson 90+4	140
16.11	Sunderland (h)	D	1-1 L (2-4p)	Rhema Lord-Mears 44, *Melissa Johnson missed penalty 73 (saved by Rachel Laws)*	203

2017/18 FA CUP

04.02 R4	Durham (a)	L	1-2	Melissa Johnson 48	244

- Sheffield FC were one of the major casualties of the controversial new FA licensing criteria ahead of 2018/19. Having been in Tier 2 since 2016, they were initially successful in their application for a place in the newly-formed Championship. However, in July 2018 they took the difficult decision to withdraw stating the "move towards a full-time operation" in women's elite football was "no longer consistent" with their position as a club.

- Sheffield FC ended the 2017/18 season in fine form with six wins in their final eight WSL 2 matches, having won just three in the League up until that point.

- In the 2017/18 Continental Cup group stage they lost a marathon penalty shootout 11-10 to Aston Villa. Shootouts were used to determine which team would win a bonus point after drawn matches. They were also beaten by Sunderland on spot-kicks in another group match.

- Sheffield FC Ladies were formed in 2003 when Norton Ladies were taken under the umbrella of Sheffield FC men's. They began life in Division One East of the Yorkshire & Humberside League which was the bottom level of the women's football pyramid at the time.

- They rapidly rose to reach the elite ranks by 2016. They were the first club to be promoted to WSL 2 via a play-off, doing so thanks to Lisa Giampalma's stoppage-time winner against Portsmouth in 2015.

SOLIHULL MOORS
2018/19: WNL DIVISION 1 MIDANDS (Tier 4)

Founded: 1994 (as Shirley Town)

Nickname: Moors

Ground: West Midlands Sports & Social Club

Season 2017/18:

WPL Midlands One (Tier 4): 7th

FA Cup: 3rd Qualifying Round
WPL Cup: Determining Round
WPL Plate: 1st Preliminary Round
County Cup: 2nd Round

2017/18 WPL MIDLANDS ONE

20.08	Sheffield United (a)	W	4-2	Lois Jefferies 3, 26, 64, Abbie Taylor 75	50	
27.08	Radcliffe Olympic (h)	W	4-3	Phillippa Harmison 6, 35, Lois Jefferies 70, Jessica Howard 90	35	
10.09	Sporting Khalsa (a)	W	2-0	Lois Jefferies 13, Melissa Pugh 61	20	
17.09	Leicester City L (h)	W	4-1	Victoria Grieve 21, Lois Jefferies 39, Samantha White 43, Abbie Taylor 63	40	1
20.09	B'ham & W M (a)	W	5-0	Ashlea Hargreaves 7, Lois Jefferies 18, 87 Samantha White 23, Philippa Harmison 36	35	1
01.10	Loughbrough F (h)	L	0-1		70	3
11.10	B'ham & W M (h)	D	2-2	Chloe Bickley 30, Victoria Grieve 38	40	2
15.10	Long Eaton United (a)	W	7-3	Lois Jefferies 1, 16, 32, Carly Davies 40, Samantha White 62, Victoria Gutteridge 72, 84	43	2
29.10	The New Saints (h)	L	0-4		45	3
05.11	Burton Albion (h)	L	0-2		20	4
12.11	Rotherham United (a)	L	1-3	Claire Lester 34	36	6
26.11	Steel City W (a)	L	1-3	Amelia Kirk 75	57	6
03.12	Leicester City L (a)	W	4-1	Natalie Courtney 32, 64, Victoria Grieve 61, Abbie Taylor 75	20	5
10.12	Rotherham United (h)		P-P			5
14.01	Sheffield United (h)	L	2-5	Abbie Taylor 1, Georgia Jones 36	45	6
04.02	Steel City W (h)	L	2-3	Georgia Jones 20, 73 *Amy Pashley sent off 42*	60	6
11.02	Long Eaton United (h)		P-P			6
04.03	Loughborough F (a)		P-P			6
11.03	Rotherham United (h)	W	9-0	Natalie Courtney 11, 62, Samantha White 18, 68, Chloe Bickley 43, Tanya Dickinson 49, 75, Amelia Kirk 53, Victoria Grieve 82,	20	6
18.03	Long Eaton United (h)		P-P			6
25.03	Loughborough F (a)	L	1-3	Georgia Jones 22	20	6
08.04	Radcliffe Olympic (a)	D	3-3	Abbie Taylor 31, Phillippa Harmison 36, Carly Davies 65	15	6
22.04	Sporting Khalsa (h)	D	0-0		40	6

02.05	Long Eaton United (h)*	L	1-3	Amy Pashley 71	70	7
06.05	Burton Albion (a)		P-P			7
13.05	Burton Albion (a)	L	1-4	Samantha White 5, *Solihull GK Kelly Woolley saved Jordan Atkin pen 25*	65	7
20.05	The New Saints (a)	W	2-1	Ashlea Hargreaves 12, Phillippa Harmison 57	25	7

*Played at ATG Stadium, Solihull Moors FC

2017/18 FA CUP

| 08.10 RQ3 | Redditch United (a) | L | 2-5 | Victoria Grieve 60, Samantha White 67 | 70 |

2017/18 WPL CUP

| 03.09 DR | Guiseley Vixens (h) | L | 1-2 aet | Carly Davies 112 | 40 |

2017/18 WPL PLATE

| 22.10 R1 | Leeds United (a) | L | 2-3 | Tanya Dickinson 18, Abbie Taylor 80 | 79 |

2017/18 COUNTY CUP

| 19.11 R2 | Redditch United (a) | L | w/o | | |

"We are a growing club, with a focus on promoting youth and developing our junior section to be the biggest in the local area. Our players become friends here, and that is an important focus for us, as well as winning matches."

Sarah Westwood, Solihull Moors Manager

- Lois Jefferies was the club's top scorer in the 2017/18 season, she hit 11 goals – all of them coming in League matches. She notched hat-tricks in the 4-2 win over Sheffield United on the opening day and in the 7-3 win at Long Eaton United in October.

- The club was founded as Shirley Town in 1994. Ground relocations saw them change their name to Woodbourne United in 1996, Billesley United in 1998 and Solihull Glades in 2003 before becoming Solihull in 2005. In December 2016, they confirmed they would be joining up with men's National League side Solihull Moors from the start of the 2017/18 season.

- They have won two League titles, finishing top of the West Midlands Division One Central during their days as Solihull Glades in 2003/04 and top of the West Midlands Premier Division as Solihull in 2012/13.

SOUTHAMPTON SAINTS
2018/19: WNL DIVISION 1
SOUTH WEST (Tier 4)

Founded: 1979 (as Red Star Southampton)

Nickname: The Saints

Ground: Universal Stadium, (Sholing FC)

Season 2017/18:

WPL South West One (Tier 4): 4th

FA Cup: 1st Round
WPL Cup: Determining Round
WPL Plate: 2nd Round
County Cup: Semi-finals

2017/18 WPL South West One

Date	Opponent		Res		Scorers		
20.08	Cheltenham T (h)	W	2-0		Gemma Woodford 36, Krystal Whyte 65	50	
27.08	Maidenhead U (h)	W	4-0		Libby O'Dell 10, Krystal Whyte 11, Emma King 70, Gemma Woodford 79	45	
10.09	Poole Town (a)	W	4-0		Catherine Browning 2, 23, Libby O'Dell 33, Alisha Buckingham 47	22	
17.09	Cheltenham T (a)	W	1-0		Libby O'Dell 41	29	2
01.10	So'ton Women (h)	L	1-3		Libby O'Dell	65	3
29.10	Poole Town (h)	D	0-0			22	4
05.11	Maidenhead U (a)	W	3-1		Libby O'Dell 55, Emma King 69, Alisha Buckingham 80	25	4
26.11	St Nicholas (a)	W	2-0		Libby O'Dell 63, Chloe Melton 85	30	4
03.12	Larkhall Athletic (h)	P-P					4
07.01	So'ton Women (a)	L	0-1			62	4
04.02	Basingstoke Town (h)	P-P					4
11.02	Brislington (a)	P-P					4
25.02	Brislington (a)	W	3-0		Sabrina Morriss-Manosalva (x2), Alisha Buckingham	42	4
04.03	St Nicholas (h)	P-P					4
11.03	Brislington (h)	W	3-1		Catherine Browning 4, Krystal Whyte 8, Alisha Buckingham	28	2
18.03	Keynsham Town (h)	P-P					2
25.03	Plymouth Argyle (a)*	L	0-6			40	3
08.04	Larkhall Athletic (a)	W	3-0		Libby O'Dell 10, Sabrina Morriss-Manosalva 20, Alisha Buckingham 75	15	3
15.04	Plymouth Argyle (h)	D	1-1		Libby O'Dell 22	15	3
22.04	Larkhall Athletic (h)	W	3-0		Emma Eldridge 27, Roxy Stewart 53, Catherine Browning 89	10	3
29.04	St Nicholas (h)	P-P					4
06.05	St Nicholas (h)	W	4-1		Catherine Browning (x2), Alisha Buckingham, Libby O'Dell	6	4

| 13.05 | Keynsham Town (a) | L | 1-4 | Catherine Browning | 25 | 4 |
| 20.05 | Keynsham Town (h) | W | 3-2 | Catherine Browning 10, Krystal Whyte 23, Libby O'Dell 72 | 21 | 4 |

*Played at Marjon Sports and Health Centre

2017/18 FA CUP

| 08.10 RQ3 | Cheltenham Town (a) | W | 4-1 | Nicole Matthews 1, Alisha Buckingham 44, Libby O'Dell 48, Catherine Browning 85 | 50 |
| 12.11 R1 | Keynsham Town (h) | L | 1-3 | Alisha Buckingham 23 | |

2017/18 WPL CUP

| 03.09 DR | Lewes (a) | L | 1-3 (aet) | Sabrina Morriss-Manosalva 60 | 60 |

2017/18 WPL PLATE

22.10 R1	Larkhall Athletic (h)	W	3-0	Nicole Matthews 34, Alisha Buckingham 41, Libby O'Dell 78	15
10.12 R2	Luton Town (a)		P-P		
17.12 R2	Luton Town (a)		P-P		
14.01 R2	Luton Town (a)	L	1-3	Krystal Whyte 60	27

2017/18 HAMPSHIRE FA COUNTY CUP

19.11 R2	Fleet Town (a)	W	w/o		
28.01 QF	Moneyfields (a)	W	2-0	Chloe Melton 79, 86	
18.02 SF	Portsmouth (h)	L	0-3		80est

- Southampton Saints' top scorer in League competition in 2017/18 was Catherine Browning who hit eight goals. In all competitions Browning was joint top-scorer with Alisha Buckingham, they both scored nine.

- The first club in the region – Southampton Women – was founded in 1970 and went on to win the FA Cup eight times before folding in 1985/86. At that point many of their players joined Red Star Southampton, which had been founded in 1979 and would go on to become Southampton Saints. Southampton Women then also reformed in 2003.

- Southampton Saints and Southampton Women should not be confused with Southampton FC Women which is attached to men's Premier League club Southampton FC. However, in 1995 Southampton Saints did form an affiliation with Southampton FC, but that ended when the men's club withdrew its support after being relegated from the Premier League in 2005.

SOUTHAMPTON WOMEN
2018/19: WNL DIVISION 1
SOUTH WEST (Tier 4)

Founded: 2003

Nickname: None

Ground: Testwood Stadium, (AFC Totton) for 2017/18, moving to Gangwarily (Blackfied & Langley FC) for 2018/19

Season 2017/18:

WPL South West One (Tier 4): Runners-up

FA Cup: 2nd Round
WPL Cup: 1st Round
County Cup: Semi-finals

2017/18 WPL SOUTH WEST ONE

Date	Opponent		Result	Scorers		
20.08	Larkhall Athletic (h)		P-P			
10.09	*Basingstoke Town (a)* **exp**	W	5-0	Sheree Bell-Jack 15, Emma Pinner 20, 54, Jane Yeates 36, Laura Vokes 65	32	
20.09	Poole Town (a)*	W	5-0	Jane Yeates 8, 25, Emma Pinner 33, 39, Sheree Bell-Jack 60	52	4
01.10	So'ton Saints (a)	W	3-1	Kirsty Bell 35, 44, Emma Pinner 90+4	65	4
11.10	Poole Town (h)	W	3-1	Emma Pinner 7, 19, Jane Yeates 58	39	3
29.10	Brislington (a)	W	5-1	Laura Vokes 45+2, Emma Pinner 50, Natalie Bavister 66, Cassie Thorp 85, Sheree Bell-Jack 87	56	3
05.11	St Nicholas (a)	W	3-2	Chelsie Hay 25, Emma Pinner 89, Kellie Warren 90+6	55	3
26.11	Keynsham Town (h)	W	1-0	Jane Yeates 77	35	3
10.12	Maidenhead U (h)		P-P			
17.12	Larkhall Athletic (a)	W	6-0	Emma Pinner 19, 44, 62, Philippa Holden 60, 86, Sheree Bell-Jack 70	25	2
07.01	So'ton Saints (h)	W	1-0	Emma Pinner 29	62	1
14.01	St Nicholas (h)	W	4-0	Natasha Angel 36, Karleen Hellard 67, Emma Pinner 78, Sophie Solloway 90+1	55	1
04.02	Larkhall Athletic (h)	W	6-1	Cassie Thorp, Manuela Nprta, Jane Yeates (x3), *Jane Yeates missed pen at 4-1*, Emma Pinner	20	1
11.02	Maidenhead U (a)		P-P			1
04.03	Maidenhead U (h)		P-P			1
11.03	Cheltenham Town (h)	W	2-0	Manuela Nprta (pen) 42, Kellie Warren 67	35	1
18.03	Plymouth Argyle (h)		P-P			1
25.03	Brislington (h)	W	6-0	Jane Yeates, Sheree Bell-Jack (x2), Natasha Angel, Own Goal, Chelsie Hay (pen)		1
01.04	Maidenhead U (h)	W	3-0	Emma Pinner 14, Kirsty Whitton 55, Jane Yeates 77	40	1
08.04	Maidenhead U (a)	W	10-0	Chelsie Hay (x3), Lavinia Nkomo (x2), Emma Pinner (x4, 1pen), Philippa Holden	35	1

15.04	Keynsham Town (a)	D	4-4	Emma Pinner 28, Chelsie Hay 58, Cassie Thorp 60, Natasha Angel 65	60	1
06.05	Plymouth Argyle (a)	L	1-7	Laura Vokes 65	88	1
13.05	Plymouth Argyle (h)^	D	2-2	Laura Vokes 26, Philippa Holden 65	70	1
20.05	Cheltenham Town (a)	W	3-1	Laura Vokes 8, 45+3, Sophie Solloway 90	78	2

*Played at Verwood Town FC   ^Played at Alton Ladies

2017/18 FA CUP

08.10 RQ3	Winchester C Flyers (a)	W	7-0	Jane Yeates 20, Natasha Angel 41, Chelsie Hay 62, Kirsty Bell 71, Manuela Nprta 76, Own Goal 82, Sheree Bell-Jack 90	
12.11 R1	Larkhall Athletic (a)	W	3-2	Sheree Bell-Jack 12, 39, Jane Yeates 67	40
03.12 R2	Keynsham Town (a)	L	1-2	Sheree Bell-Jack 30	

2017/18 WPL CUP

03.09 DR	Denham United (h)	W	4-2	Laura Vokes 13, 17 Emma Pinner 23, Kellie Warren 31	34
24.09 PR	Actonians (h)	W	2-0 (aet)	Own Goal 95, Jane Yeates 101	50
15.10 R1	Portsmouth (h)	L	1-3	Laura Vokes 49	108

2017/18 HAMPSHIRE FA COUNTY CUP

19.11 QF	Bournemouth (a)			P-P	
21.01 QF	Bournemouth (a)			P-P	
28.01 QF	Bournemouth (a)		W	3-0	Emma Pinner 12, Philippa Holden 34, Sheree Bell-Jack
18.02 SF	Southampton FC (a)		L	w/o	NB: Southampton Women's initially won 4-0 (Emma Pinner 20, 75, Jane Yeates 55, Manuela Nprta 90+3) but were expelled after it was ruled they fielded an ineligible player.

"We are a club that celebrates success together and always aims to build and grow everyone in the club. From the domination of the Under-16s, the promotion and progress of the senior team, the resilience and development of the reserves to the passion of our army of volunteers."

Tash Angel – Southampton Women Captain

- Southampton Women were promoted to WPL South West One (now WNL Division 1 South West) ahead of the 2017/18 season as champions of the 2016/17 Southern Regional Premier League. They had a tremendous debut season in Tier 4, finishing as runners-up behind Plymouth who were the only team to beat them. Emma Pinner finished as the League's 3rd-highest scorer with 23 goals in 21 games.

- They won their opening 14 League games before dropping their first points in a 4-4 draw at Keynsham on 15th April. Their first defeat came in their next match against eventual champions Plymouth who overhauled Southampton right at the end of the season.

- Kirsty Bell made her 150th appearance (42 goals in that time) for Southampton Women in the 3-1 win at Cheltenham on the final day of the 2017/18 season.

- It's a matter of dispute as to whether the current Southampton Women is a separate entity to the Southampton Women that won eight FA Cups between 1971-1981 or a continuation of the club. The original Southampton Women folded in 1985/86 with the current outfit founded in 2003. Only Arsenal (14) have won more FA Cups than the original Southampton Women.

- Southampton Women are not to be confused with Southampton FC Women, who are affiliated to men's Premier League club Southampton FC. Southampton FC Women applied to join the FA Women's Championship ahead of 2018/19, despite at that point being (along with Manchester United) one of only two existing men's Premier League clubs not to have a women's team above Under-21 level. Manchester United's application was accepted, Southampton FC Women's was rejected. .

SPORTING KHALSA

2018/19: WNL DIVISION 1 MIDLANDS (Tier 4)

Founded: 2004 (as FC Reedswood)

Nickname: Sporting

Ground: University of Wolverhampton 3G in 2017/18, returning to Aspray Arena (Sporting Khalsa FC) for 2018/19

Season 2017/18:

WPL Midlands One (Tier 4): 8th

FA Cup: 2nd Round
WPL Cup: Determining Round
WPL Plate: 1st Round
County Cup: Runners-up

2017/18 WPL MIDLANDS ONE

20.08	Radcliffe Olympic (a)		P-P			
27.08	Burton Albion (h)	L	1-2	Sophie Richards 72	60	
10.09	Solihull Moors (h)	L	0-2		20	
17.09	Steel City W (a)	L	0-2		31	9
20.09	The New Saints (h)	L	0-2		50	9
24.09	Sheffield United (h)	L	1-3	Megan Wilton 75	35	9
01.10	Long Eaton United (a)	L	0-2		54	10
11.10	The New Saints (a)	W	5-2	Rebecca Gill-Parsons, Lyndsey Glover, Lauren Walker, Megan Wilton, Own Goal	69	9
15.10	Rotherham United (h)	W	5-0	Lyndsey Glover, Natalie Morris, Julie Stirrup, Lauren Walker, Rebecca Gill-Parsons	20	9
29.10	Loughborough F (h)	L	1-4	Rebecca Gill-Parsons 76	20	9
05.11	Sheffield United (a)	D	2-2	Lyndsey Glover, Jodie Lewis	60	10
26.11	B'ham & W M (a)	W	3-0	Lyndsey Glover (pen), Megan Wilton, Kyrie Ball 85	20	8
10.12	Burton Albion (a)		P-P			8
14.01	Rotherham United (a)	W	2-0	Stephanie Speck 65, Jodie Lewis 80	35	8
28.01	Leicester City L (a)	W	6-0	Kyrie Ball, Jodie Lewis, Natalie Morris (x3), Lauren Walker	30	7
11.02	Steel City W (h)	W	2-0	Jodie Lewis 35, 57	20	7
25.02	Radcliffe Olympic (a)	L	1-2	Stephanie Speck	25	7
04.03	Leicester City L (h)		P-P			7
11.03	Long Eaton United (h)	L	0-2		10	7
18.03	Burton Albion (a)		P-P			7
25.03	Radcliffe Olympic (h)	W	2-1	Lyndsey Glover, Gurjit Dulay	20	7
15.04	B'ham & W M (h)	L	1-3	Kiera Mae	30	8
22.04	Solihull Moors (a)	D	0-0		40	7
06.05	Leicester City L (h)	W	6-0	Rebecca Gill-Parsons (x3), Lyndsey Glover, Katie Nardone, Lauren Walker	20	8
13.05	Loughborough F (a)	L	0-6		75	8
20.05	Burton Albion (a)	L	2-4	Rebecca Gill-Parsons 8, 14	97	8

2017/18 FA CUP

Date	Round	Opponent	Result	Score	Scorers	
08.10 RQ3		Lye Town (h)	W	6-1	Kyrie Ball, Gurjit Dulay, Rebecca Gill-Parsons, Lauren Walker (x2), Katie Nardone	
12.11 R1		Eastwood Community (h)	W	5-1	Lauren Walker (x4)	
03.12 R2		The New Saints (h)	D	2-2 aet (L 1-4p)		45

2017/18 WPL CUP

03.09 DR	Loughborough F (a)	L	0-5		40

2017/18 WPL PLATE

22.10 R1	B'ham & W M (a)	L	1-3	Lyndsey Glover	30

2017/18 STAFFORDSHIRE COUNTY CUP

19.11 R1		Leek Town (a)	W	4-1		
17.12 QF		Wyrley (h)	W	18-0	Kyrie Ball (x3), Jodie Lewis, Stephanie Speck (x3), Julie Stirrup, Lauren Walker (x3), Megan Wilton (x5), Melody Lewis, Ellie Walker	
21.01 SF		Wolves Sporting (h)		P-P		
04.02 SF		Wolves Sporting (h)	W	5-0	Lauren Walker, Jodie Lewis (x3), Sophie Richards	25
06.03 F		Stoke City (n)	L	0-2		

(n) Played at Evans Park, Stafford Town FC

• After a difficult start to the 2017/18 season, Sporting Khalsa recovered in style. They lost their opening six League matches but then went on a run when they lost just one in eight, and eventually finished in a respectable 8th position in the table. They also made it to the final of the Staffordshire County Cup where they lost 2-0 to WPL Northern (Tier 3) outfit Stoke City.

• Sporting Khalsa men's club was formed as a grassroots team in 1991 and began life in the Walsall & District Sunday Leagues. They quickly grew and between 1995 and 1997 they were playing at semi-professional level.

• After a season playing at the University of Wolverhampton's Walsall Campus, Sporting Khalsa Women have returned to the Aspray Arena for 2018/19. They have resumed their groundshare with Sporting Khalsa men's team at a venue which has seen improvements including extra seating.

• FC Reedswood Ladies team was founded in 2004 and was integrated into Sporting Khalsa men's club in 2015, becoming Sporting Khalsa Women.

ST NICHOLAS
Resigned from League on Tue 21 Aug 2018

Founded: 2009

Nickname: St Nicks

Ground: Lodge Road, (Yate Town FC)

Season 2017/18:

WPL South West One (Tier 4): 10th

FA Cup: 3rd Qualifying Round
WPL Cup: Determining Round
WPL Plate: 1st Round
County Cup: Winners

2017/18 WPL SOUTH WEST ONE

Date	Opponent		Result	Scorers		
20.08	Plymouth Argyle (h)	L	0-8		35	
27.08	Poole Town (a)	L	0-6		33	
10.09	Keynsham Town (a)	L	0-11		45	
17.09	Larkhall Athletic (h)	D	2-2	Rhian Robbins 55, 78	55	10
19.09	Cheltenham Town (a)	L	1-3	Poppy Coles 80	42	11
01.10	Keynsham Town (h)	L	0-9		35	11
12.10	Cheltenham Town (h)	L	0-3*		40	11
05.11	So'ton Women (h)	L	2-3	Rhian Robbins 35, 65	55	11
12.11	Maidenhead U (a)		P-P			11
26.11	So'ton Saints (h)	L	0-2		30	11
03.12	Maidenhead U (a)	L	2-5	Hannah Summers (og) 5, Sophie Sweet 53	20	11
10.12	Poole Town (h)		P-P			
17.12	Basingstoke Town (a) **exp**	W	6-3	Adele Hooper 10, 75, Rhian Robbins 35, (other scorers unknown)	20	10
07.01	Basingstoke Town (h) **exp**	W	2-1	Rhian Robbins 21, Adele Hooper 90+2	22	10
14.01	So'ton Women (a)	L	0-4		55	10
28.01	Brislington (a)+	W	3-2	Rhian Robbins 30, Cheryl Baber 44, Adele Hooper 82	62	9
04.02	Poole Town (h)		P-P			9
25.02	Maidenhead U (h)	W	3-1	Rhian Robbins 15, 24, Kirsten Rendall 37	30	7
04.03	So'ton Saints (a)		P-P			7
11.03	Plymouth Argyle (a)	L	0-13		35	9
21.03	Larkhall Athletic (a)	L	0-5		30	9
08.04	Brislington (h)	W	3-1	Rhian Robbins 18, 77, Adele Hooper 61	61	9
22.04	Poole Town (h)	L	1-2	Cheryl Baber 11	30	10
29.04	So'ton Saints (a)		P-P			10
06.05	So'ton Saints (a)	L	1-4	Rhian Robbins 38	6	10

exp = Results expunged from the records following Basingstoke Town's resignation from League.

*Match abandoned after 87 mins after floodlight catches fire. Result stands   +Played at Keynsham Town FC

2017/18 FA CUP

08.10 RQ3	Keynsham Town (h)	L	0-1		55

2017/18 WPL CUP

03.09 DR	Cambridge United (h)	L	0-5		40

2017/18 WPL PLATE

24.09 PR	Basingstoke Town (h)	D	2-2 aet (W 4-2p)	Rhian Robbins 14, Kirsten Rendall 90+2	50
22.10 R1	Keynsham Town (a)	L	0-4		45

2017/18 GLOUCESTERSHIRE FA COUNTY CUP

15.10 R1	Bristol & West (h)	W	10-0	Cheryl Baber 6, 25, Rhian Robbins 10, 55, Sophie Morgan 33, Adele Hooper 35, Kirsten Rendell 49, Sophie Bull 66, 78, Danielle Shiner 84	30
19.11 R2	Oldland Abbotonians (a)	W	6-3	Adele Hooper 35, Rhian Robbins 44, 59, 61, Cheryl Baber 65, Sophie Bull 88	32
18.02 QF	Forest of Dean (h)	W	w/o		
18.03 SF	Almondsbury UWE (h)	P-P			
25.03 SF	Almondsbury UWE (h)	W	4-2	Rhian Robbins 17, Adele Hooper 27, 65, 79	26
17.04 F	Cheltenham Town (n)	W	1-0	Cheryl Baber 86	86

(n) Played at Almondsbury , GFA Headquarters

- Rhian Robbins scored the team's first and last goals of 2017/18. She was on target in a 2-2 draw with Larkhall Athletic on 17 September and also in a 4-1 defeat to Southampton Saints on the final day. She was also the club's top scorer with 16 goals in all competitions.

- St Nicholas FC was founded as a boys' club in 1974 to provide the chance to play for those aged 9-18yrs in the Yate and Chipping Sodbury region.

- St Nicholas announced two days after the start of the 2018/19 season, but before themselves playing a match, that they would not be able to field a first team in WNL Division 1 South West because of a lack of playing numbers. Their reserve team will continue to play in the Gloucester County League Division One.

STEEL CITY WANDERERS

2018/19: WNL DIVISION 1
MIDLANDS (Tier 4)

Founded: 1993 (as Loxley Girls)

Nickname: Steels

Ground: SGP Thorncliffe, High Green

Season 2017/18:

WPL Midlands One (Tier 4): 10th

FA Cup: 1st Round

WPL Cup: Preliminary Round
County Cup: 3rd Round

2017/18 WPL MIDLANDS ONE

Date	Opponent		Result	Scorers		
20.08	The New Saints (a)	L	1-8	Lucy Ridley 39	32	
27.08	Rotherham United (h)		P-P			
10.09	Leicester City L (a)	W	6-0	Hannah Wright 5, 31, Cheryl Mawhood 16, Zoe Beresford 44, Jodie Whitford-Stark 83, Lucy Ridley 84	30	
17.09	Sporting Khalsa (h)	W	2-0	Lucy Ridley 16, 52	31	5
21.09	Sheffield United (a)	L	1-5	Sarah Middleton 44	110	6
01.10	Rotherham United (a)	W	7-1	Lauren Brown 8, 69, Cheryl Mawhood 17, 72, Jodie Whitford-Stark 31, Lucy Smith, Claire Bratton 87	60	7
10.10	Sheffield United (h)	D	2-2	Cheryl Mawhood 33, Lucy Ridley 62	76	7
15.10	B'ham & W M (a)	L	0-7		58	7
05.11	The New Saints (h)	L	5-6	Cheryl Mawhood, Sarah Middleton, Abby Pike, Hannah Wright (x2)	40	7
26.11	Solihull Moors (h)	W	3-1	Cheryl Mawhood 18, Paris Wagstaff 54, 69	57	7
03.12	B'ham & W M (h)	W	3-2	Cheryl Mawhood 22, Lucy Ridley 65, 73	45	7
10.12	Radcliffe Olympic (a)		P-P			
21.01	Leicester City L (h)		P-P			7
04.02	Solihull Moors (a)	W	3-2	Claire Attrill 10, 47, Lucy Smith 12	60	7
11.02	Sporting Khalsa (a)	L	0-2		20	8
18.02	Loughborough F (a)	L	0-9		39	8
25.02	Long Eaton United (a)	L	0-3		42	8
04.03	Burton Albion (h)		P-P			8
11.03	Burton Albion (h)	L	0-3	*Claire Bratton sent off 61*	60	8
18.03	Radcliffe Olympic (a)		P-P			8
25.03	Rotherham United (h)	W	4-0	Lucy Ridley 19, Paige Unwin 53, Claire Attrill 77, Abby Pike (pen) 85	62	8
08.04	Loughborough F (h)	L	1-6	Sarah Middleton 54	54	8
15.04	Burton Albion (a)	D	2-2	Hannah Wright 71, Louise Webster 85	56	7
22.04	Leicester City L (h)	L	1-3	Maria Burns 16	57	8
29.04	Radcliffe Olympic (h)	L	0-7		43	9

13.05	Radcliffe Olympic (a)	L	w/o			9
20.05	Long Eaton United (h)	L	2-4	Cheryl Mawhood 40, Abby Pike 78	84	10

2017/18 FA CUP

08.10 RQ3	Morecambe (h)	W	2-1	Cheryl Mawhood 56, 83	40
12.11 R1	Hull City (a)	L	1-4	Hannah Wright 82, *Steel City W player sent off after final whistle*	80

2017/18 WPL CUP

03.09 DR	Radcliffe Olympic (h)	W	5-2 aet	Claire Bratton 38, Lucy Ridley 42, Sarah Middleton 93, Zoe Beresford 101, Cheryl Mawhood 112	33
24.09 PR	Liverpool M F (a)	L	1-3	Lucy Ridley 53, *Claire Keats sent off 81*	40

2017/18 SHEFFIELD & HALLAMSHIRE FA COUNTY CUP

17.12 R3	Harworth Colliery (a)		P-P	
07.01 R3	Harworth Colliery (a)	L	1-4	Zoe Beresford 34

- The Sheffield-based club took the name Steel City Wanderers in 1995, two years after forming as Loxley Girls.

- The club was founded by Steve and Sue Odams who wanted their triplet daughters Cheryl, Johanna and Selina to be able to play football.

- Cheryl Mawhood was the team's top scorer in 2017/18 with 11 goals in 21 appearances in all competitions.

STEVENAGE

2018/19: WNL DIVISION 1 SOUTH EAST (Tier 4)

Founded: 2001

Nickname: Boro

Ground: Hertingfordbury Park, (Hertford Town FC)

Season 2017/18:

WPL South East One (Tier 4): 6th

FA Cup: 2nd Round
WPL Cup: 1st Round
County Cup: Winners

2017/18 WPL SOUTH EAST ONE

20.08	Luton Town (a)*	L	2-5	Amy Josland, Donna McGuigan	140	
27.08	Ipswich Town (a)	L	0-1			
10.09	Norwich City (h)	W	4-1	Kristi Burling, Leah Littlechild (x2), Donna McGuigan	45	
17.09	Cambridge United (h)	D	1-1	Cara Breckenridge	70	9
20.09	Enfield Town (h)	W	3-0	Amy Makewell (x2), Donna McGuigan	50	7
01.10	AFC Wimbledon (h)	L	1-3	Donna McGuigan	40	8
11.10	Enfield Town (a)	D	1-1	*Donna McGuigan missed pen,* Chloe Gunn 90	57	8
29.10	Actonians (h)	W	2-1	Leah Littlechild, Kristi Burling	25	8
05.11	AFC Wimbledon (a)	W	3-2	Ellie Searle, Chloe Gunn, Nicole Emmings	30	7
26.11	Leyton Orient (h)	L	0-2		30	8
10.12	Actonians (a)		P-P			
14.01	Cambridge United (a)	L	1-2	Chloe Gunn (pen)	45	10
04.02	Haringey Borough (h)		P-P			10
11.02	Ipswich Town (h)		P-P			10
18.02	Haringey Borough (h)	W	10-0	Nicole Emmings (x3), Amy Makewell (x3), Ellie Searle, Paige Logie (x3)	60	9
25.02	Actonians (a)	W	2-1	Paige Logie, Donna McGuigan	20	7
04.03	MK Dons (h)		P-P			7
18.03	Denham United (h)		P-P			7
25.03	Haringey Borough (a)	W	10-2	Leah Littlechild (x4), Donna McGuigan (2) Chloe Gunn (pen), Own Goal, Amy Makewell, Amy Josland		7
04.04	Luton Town (h)**	W	1-0	Amy Makewell 55	75	5
08.04	Ipswich Town (h)		P-P			6
15.04	Norwich City (a)	W	1-0	Nicole Emmings	46	5
25.04	MK Dons (a)		P-P			5
29.04	Ipswich Town (h)+	L	2-7	Nicole Emmings 39, Kristi Burling 70	20	6
02.05	MK Dons (h)	L	0-2		40	6
06.05	Denham (h)	D	1-1	Donna McGuigan	45	6

13.05	Leyton Orient (a)	D	2-2	Rebecca Scola, Amy Makewell (pen) 80	55	6
16.05	MK Dons (a)++	L	0-1		450	6
20.05	Denham United (a)	L	1-2	Donna McGuigan		6

*Played at Caddington   **Played at Colney Heath FC

+Played at Crofters End, Sawbridgeworth Town FC   ++Played at Stadium:mk, MK Dons FC

2017/18 WPL CUP

| 03.09 DR | Gillingham (a) | W | 1-0 | Nicole Emmings 40 | 152 |
| 22.10 R1 | Coventry United (h) | L | 0-2 | | 45 |

2017/18 HERTFORDSHIRE FA COUNTY CUP

15.10 R1	Garston (a)	W	14-1	Cara Breckenridge, Chloe Gunn (x2), Rebecca Scola, Nicole Emmings (x3), Ellie Searle, Leah Littlechild (x3), Kristi Burling, Amy Josland, Dominique Godbeer
19.11 R2	Evergreen Eagles (a)	W	14-0	Amy Josland (x3), Donna McGuigan (x5, 1pen), Amy Makewell, Leah Littlechild, Rebecca Scola (x2), Katherine Long (x2)
17.12 QF	Hemel Hempstead Town (a)	P-P		
07.01 QF	Hemel Hempstead Town (a)	W	3-0	Ellie Searle, Donna McGuigan, Amy Makewell
21.01 SF	Royston Town (h)	P-P		
28.01 SF	Royston Town (h)	W	3-0	Ashleigh Deacon, Leah Littlechild, Chloe Gunn (pen)
11.03 F	Hoddesdon Town Owls (n)	W	8-0	Amy Makewell 16, 20, 68, Chloe Gunn 30, 41, Ashleigh Deacon 51, 52, Leah Littlechild 89

(n) Played at The County Ground, Letchworth Garden City

"I have been with Stevenage Ladies for 13 seasons and this has been the most successful one on and off the pitch. Both the first-team and reserves squad have great fun but know when to get to work. It's that ethos that brings teams together and enables us to get the best out of each and every player. The firsts finished in the highest position in our history and also made the County Cup final for the fourth year in a row. The reserves also had great success winning 11 games in a row, scoring 64 and clinching the League title with four games to go as well as reaching the League Plate final."

Dave Potter – Stevenage Secretary and Reserves Manager

- Manager Reece Buck led Stevenage to their highest ever League finish in 2017/18 as they secured 6th place in Tier 4. Under the stewardship of Dave Potter there was also success for the reserves as they clinched their League title with four games to spare.

- There was also Cup glory as Stevenage won the Hertfordshire County Cup for the third time in four seasons in 2017/18. They collected the trophy for the very first time in 2015 and won it again in 2017. They were also runners-up in 2016.

- Stevenage Ladies were officially formed as Stevenage Borough Ladies in 2001 and moved under the umbrella of the men's professional outfit in 2014. Like the men's team the club's nickname remains Boro, despite the fact the 'Borough' part of the club's name was dropped in 2010. Although they have support from the men's club, they continue to fund themselves fully with player subs and fundraising.

STOKE CITY
2018/19: WNL NORTHERN PREMIER (Tier 3)

Founded: 2001

Nickname: The Potters

Ground: Community Drive, (Norton Utd FC)

Season 2017/18:

WPL Northern (Tier 3): 4th

FA Cup: 2nd Round
WPL Cup: 1st Round
County Cup: Winners

2017/18 WPL NORTHERN

Date	Opponent		Result	Scorers	Att	
20.08	Derby County (h)	L	1-4	Hannah Keryakoplis 10	131	
27.08	Leicester City W (h)	L	1-3	Holly Morgan (og) 3	60	
10.09	West Brom (a)	W	5-0	Ashleigh Hayes 11, Louise Roberts 39, Hannah Keryakoplis 52, 64, Tash Tezgel 68	107	
17.09	Guiseley Vixens (a)	D	3-3	Ashleigh Hayes 16, 46, Hannah Keryakoplis 55, *Emily Owens sent off 90+9*	41	8
20.09	Nottingham F (h)	W	3-1	Cassie Hyde 27, Kate Asher 45+2, Louise Roberts 68	110	6
01.10	Wolverhampton W (h)	D	1-1	Cassie Hyde 48	131	7
08.10	Middlesbrough (a)	L	0-3		75	8
22.10	Leicester City W (a)	W	4-3	Hannah Keryakoplis 16, Rachael Ball 34, Ashleigh Hayes 89, Kelsey Richardson 90+2	123	7
24.10	Nottingham F (a)	W	1-0	Hannah Keryakoplis 59	156	6
29.10	Blackburn Rovers (h)	D	1-1	Emily Owen 22	104	4
05.11	Huddersfield T (a)	L	0-2		78	5
12.11	West Brom (h)	W	2-1	Ashleigh Hayes 21, Kate Asher 36	163	5
26.11	Fylde (a)		P-P			5
10.12	Middlesbrough (h)		P-P			5
14.01	Bradford City (a)	W	6-2	Hannah Keryakoplis 3, 12, 74, 85, Ashleigh Hayes 23, Emily Owen 61	65	4
28.01	Guiseley Vixens (h)	W	3-2	Hannah Keryakoplis 34, Ashleigh Hayes 38, Rachael Ball 68	82	4
18.02	Huddersfield T (h)	W	3-2	Faye McCoy 17, Kate Asher 36, Hannah Keryakoplis 55, *Kate Asher sent off 62*	105	3
25.02	Wolverhampton W (a)	W	4-1	Kate Asher 8, Cassie Hyde 18, Hannah Keryakoplis 45+2, Faye McCoy 68	50	3
04.03	Middlesbrough (h)		P-P			3
18.03	Middlesbrough (h)		P-P			3
25.03	Fylde (a)	D	0-0		42	2
15.04	Middlesbrough (h)	W	6-3	Ashleigh Hayes 16, 55, Faye McCoy 25, (pen) 29, Cassie Hyde 50, Hannah Keryakoplis 67	142	4

19.04	Bradford City (h)	L	1-2	*Stoke GK Natalie Hall saved Laura Elford's pen 15 (Bradford scored rebound),* Hannah Keryakoplis 43	103	5
06.05	Fylde (h)	W	3-1	Ashleigh Hayes 3, Hannah Keryakoplis 45+1, Beth Roberts 81	143	4
15.05	Blackburn Rovers (a)*	L	0-3			4
20.05	Derby County (a)+	W	4-0	Ashleigh Hayes 28, 36, Ella Pemberton 45, Hannah Keryakoplis 66	75	4

*Played at Ewood Park, Blackburn Rovers FC   +Played at Derby University

2017/18 FA CUP

03.12	R2	Burnley (h)	D	0-0 aet (L 1-4p)	108

2017/18 WPL CUP

03.09	DR	Morecambe (a)	W	3-1	Jamilla Palmer 52, Hannah Keryakoplis 69, 81	48
15.10	R1	Blackburn R (h)	D	2-2aet (L 3-4p)	Kate Asher 1, Emily Owen (pen) 67	130

2017/18 STAFFORDSHIRE FA COUNTY CUP

19.11 R2	Brereton Town (a)	W	w/o		
17.12 QF	Stoke City Reserves (h)	W	2-1	Own Goal 61, Rachael Ball 81	90
01.02 SF	Stoke City Development (a)	W	7-0	Meg Bowyer 15, Faye McCoy 17, Ashleigh Hayes 25, Millie Elson 65, 70, Tash Tezgel 72, Hollie Gibson 80	75
06.03 F	Sporting Khalsa (n)	W	2-0	Faye McCoy 17, Ashleigh Hayes 35	

(n) Played at Evans Park, Stafford Town FC

"The 2017/18 season was a strange one in many ways. A slow start meant our target of challenging for the title became virtually impossible but our final few months were really positive, including memorable wins against Bradford and Middlesbrough. We proved in our performances and results that on our day we can beat anyone and we're looking forward to continuing that in 2018/19. The success of our reserve team (winning the Double) shows there is great depth in the squad and a number of those players will be challenging for first-team spots in the very near future. The future is extremely bright at Stoke City."

Meg Bowyer, Stoke City Captain

- Stoke finished 2017/18 in 4th place in WPL Northern, the third season in a row that they have done so. Their points total of 40 was 10 superior to their tally of 2016/17.

- The first known women's team in Stoke was founded in 1921 by Len Bridgett, a director at Stoke City men's football club. They were known as Stoke United and played against the legendary Dick, Kerr's Ladies side from Preston twice in April 1921 before beating French side Les Sportives de Paris in two exhibition matches played in Barcelona.

- The modern Stoke City Ladies team was formed in 2001 and enjoyed a breakthrough season in 2012/13 when they won a treble of trophies and gained promotion to the WPL Northern Division.

- Stoke City Ladies are now formally affiliated with men's professional Premier League club Stoke City and played one match at the Bet365 Stadium during the 2016/17 season – a League fixture against Nottingham Forest which ended in a 1-1 draw.

357

SUNDERLAND
2018/19: WNL NORTHERN
PREMIER (Tier 3)

Founded: 1989 (as The Kestrels)

Nickname: The Lady Black Cats / The Lasses

Ground: Mariners Park, (South Shields FC) in 2017/18, moving to Hetton Centre for 2018/19

Season 2017/18:

WSL 1 (Tier 1): 7th

FA Cup: Quarter-finals

Continental Cup: Quarter-finals

2017/18 WSL 1

						Att	Pos
24.09	Reading (a)	W	1-0	Simona Koren 5		502	
30.09	Chelsea (h)	L	0-6			789	
08.10	Yeovil Town (a)	W	1-0	Kiera Ramshaw 36		348	3
28.10	Liverpool (h)	L	1-4	Lucy Staniforth 10			5
12.11	Arsenal (a)	L	0-3				6
10.12	Everton (a)	L	1-5	Bridget Galloway 90+1			7
06.01	Birmingham City (h)	W	3-0	Dominique Bruinenberg 55, Hayley Sharp 88, Abbey Joice 90+5			5
28.01	Manchester City (h)	L	0-3			978	7
09.02	Bristol City (a)	W	2-1	Bridget Galloway 11, Rachel Pitman 58		448	5
21.02	Liverpool (a)	L	1-3	Dominique Bruinenberg 32			7
28.03	Everton (h)	D	1-1	Lucy Staniforth 62			7
01.04	Birmingham C (a)	L	0-2			540	7
18.04	Manchester City (a)	L	0-3				7
21.04	Bristol City (h)	L	1-2	Lucy Staniforth 56			7
29.04	Reading (h)	L	0-2				7
12.05	Chelsea (a)	L	1-2	Kiera Ramshaw 86		1,940	9
16.05	Arsenal (h)	L	0-2			321	9
20.05	Yeovil Town (h)	W	2-1	Kiera Ramshaw 58, Bridget Galloway 63		226	7

2017/18 WSL CONTINENTAL CUP: GROUP ONE NORTH

					Att
12.10	Durham (a)	D	0-0 (W 3-2p)		641
01.11	Aston Villa (h)	W	3-1	Lucy Staniforth 28, 57, Dominique Bruinenberg 78	
16.11	Sheffield FC (a)	D	1-1 (W 4-2p)	Lucy Staniforth 33	
02.12	Liverpool (h)	P-P			
05.12	Liverpool (h)	W	1-0	Bridget Galloway 13	
17.12 QF	Arsenal (a)	L	1-3	Bridget Galloway 56	

2017/18 FA CUP

04.02 R4	Brighouse Town (h)	W	13-0	Dominique Bruinenberg 7, 27, Bridget Galloway 24, Hayley Sharp 35, 84, Lucy Staniforth 62, 68, 80, Mollie Lambert 69, 76, 85, Abbey Joice 72, Georgia Gibson 82	270 est
18.02 R5	Aston Villa (h)	W	3-2	Victoria Williams 5, Rachel Pitman 79, Kiera Ramshaw 84	
18.03 QF	Manchester City (h)		P-P		
25.03 QF	Manchester City (h)	L	2-4 aet	Victoria Williams 33, Lucy Staniforth 76	552

- The FA's controversial new licensing criteria ahead of the 2018/19 season worked against Sunderland whose application for a Tier 1 licence was rejected. It meant huge disappointment for all those involved with a club which had been in WSL 1 since 2015, but now finds itself in Tier 3. Sunderland won promotion to WSL 1 as the first champions of WSL 2 in 2014. Their best top-flight finish of the WSL era was the 4th place they achieved in 2015.

- The club began life as a five-a-side team called Kestrels in 1989. Over the next decade, competing in full-scale football in the Northern Premier League, they were variously known as Cowgate Kestrels, RTM Kestrels and Blyth Spartans Kestrels. In 1999 they merged with an existing Sunderland Ladies club to become Sunderland Women's.

- They had a fleeting relationship with Sunderland men's at the start of the century, which ceased in 2004. In 2013 they came back under the Sunderland men's umbrella and changed their name from Sunderland Women to Sunderland Ladies.

- Current England and Manchester City captain Steph Houghton was born in Durham and began her career with Sunderland before leaving for Leeds in 2007.

SWINDON TOWN

2018/19: WNL DIVISION 1 SOUTH WEST (Tier 4)

Founded: 1993

Nickname: The Robins

Ground: Cinder Lane, (Fairford Town FC)

Season 2017/18:

WPL Southern (Tier 3): 12th (R)

FA Cup: 2nd Round
WPL Cup: Determining Round
WPL Plate: 2nd Round
County Cup: Did not enter

2017/18 WPL SOUTHERN

20.08	Coventry United (h)	L	0-8		73	
27.08	QPR (a)	L	0-2		45	
10.09	Crystal Palace (h)	L	0-7		65	
17.09	Gillingham (a)*	L	0-5		102	12
21.09	Cardiff City L (a)	L	1-4	Annie Martin 84	80	12
01.10	Chichester City (h)	L	4-7	Abby Picton 45+1, Mia Mugford 54, Annie Martin 62, Sophie Barrett 64	39	12
08.10	West Ham United (a)	L	0-5		256	12
29.10	Lewes (a)	L	0-7		102	12
05.11	C&K Basildon (h)	L	0-3		36	12
14.11	Cardiff City L (h)	L	0-6		36	12
19.11	Lewes (h)	L	1-3	Milly Colford 10	45	12
26.11	Charlton Athletic (a)	L	0-11		79	12
07.01	QPR (h)	L	1-4	Mia Mugford 90+1	33	12
21.01	Chichester City (a)	P-P				12
28.01	Charlton Athletic (h)	L	0-9		51	12
04.02	C&K Basildon (a)	L	1-3	Mia Mugford 17	45	12
11.02	Coventry United (a)	P-P				12
04.03	Crystal Palace (a)	L	1-8	Victoria Taylor 19	407	12
11.03	Gillingham (h)	L	0-4		22	12
18.03	Chichester City (a)	P-P				12
25.03	West Ham United (h)	L	0-6		102	12
01.04	Portsmouth (a)	L	0-5		54	12
08.04	Portsmouth (h)	L	0-3		45	12
22.04	Chichester City (a)	L	1-2	Sophie Roberts 25	50	12
15.05	Coventry United (a)+	L	0-7		50	12

*Played at Priestfield, (Gillingham FC)   +Played at Communications Park, Daventry Town FC

2017/18 FA CUP

03.12 R2	Brislington (a)	L	2-3 (aet)		67

2017/18 WPL CUP

03.09 DR	Charlton Athletic (h)	L	0-11		41

2017/18 WPL PLATE

22.10 R1	Maidenhead United (h)	W	7-1	*Samantha Hallsworth missed pen at 0-0,* Annie Martin 36, 49, 90+2, Mia Mugford (pen) 44, 59, Emily Arrell 62, Natalie Jo Goodright 65	47
10.12 R2	Keynsham Town (h)		P-P		
17.12 R2	Keynsham Town (h)		P-P		
14.01 R2	Keynsham Town (h)	L	1-10	Emily Arrell 13	44

@SwindonTownLFC

"Swindon is a town deserving of a women's club playing at a high level and our aim is to get back to where we feel we belong. The 2018/19 season will see us looking to continue the development of our younger players, improve the quality of our senior players and look to establish ourselves in a new division."

Dan Jones – Swindon Town Manager

- Swindon endured a really tough 2017/18 season, losing all their League games to finish bottom of WPL Southern and suffer relegation to Tier 4. The high point of their campaign came in the WPL Plate 1st Round when they recovered from missing an early penalty to beat Maidenhead United 7-1 with Annie Martin scoring a hat-trick.

- In June 2018, Swindon appointed Dan Jones as their new manager. Jones spent 2017/18 working as part of the coaching staff at WPL Southern side Portsmouth and has previously had spells with Salisbury and Maidenhead.

- The first women's club to be established in the region were the Swindon Spitfires who were formed in 1967. Several players broke away from the Spitfires to help set up Swindon Town Women in 1993. The club started life in the South West Regional League.

- The team would have won the inaugural FA WPL South West Division One title in 2014/15 but for a three-point deduction for fielding an ineligible player.

THE NEW SAINTS

2018/19: WNL DIVISION 1 MIDLANDS (Tier 4)

Founded: 2002

Nickname: The Saints

Ground: Park Hall Stadium, (The New Saints FC)

Season 2017/18:

WPL Midlands One (Tier 4): 5th

FA Cup: 4th Round
WPL Cup: Determining Round
WPL Plate: 2nd Round
County Cup: Winners

2017/18 WPL MIDLANDS ONE

Date	Opponent	Result	Score	Scorers		
20.08	Steel City W (h)	W	8-1	Kimberley Bebbington 7, Emily Ridge 11, 33, 76, Emma Roden 16, 30, Sophie Davies 71, 84	32	
27.08	Long Eaton United (h)	W	5-0	Madison Jones 19, Emily Ridge 30, Sophie Davies 58, 75, Taylor Davis 86	65	
10.09	Rotherham United (a)	W	3-1	Emily Ridge 8, Chloe Wilkinson 44, Charlotte Canlett 57	35	
20.09	Sporting Khalsa (a)	W	2-0	Kimberley Bebbington 34, 47	50	3
01.10	Burton Albion (h)*	W	7-1	Emily Ridge 25, Charlotte Canlett 28, Laura Morris 38, Sophie Davies 44, 79, Kimberley Bebbington 55, 67	58	2
11.10	Sporting Khalsa (h)	L	2-5	Emily Ridge 6, 15	69	4
15.10	Radcliffe Olympic (h)	W	4-2	Charlotte Canlett 22, Emily Ridge 35, 45, 61	55	3
22.10	Sheffield United (a)	L	0-4		61	4
29.10	Solihull Moors (a)	W	4-0	Sophie Davies 36, 44, Kimberley Bebbington 56, 75	45	2
05.11	Steel City W (a)	W	6-5	Charlotte Canlett 25, 55, Kimberley Bebbington 37, Laura Morris 56, 64, 86,	40	2
19.11	Rotherham United (h)+	W	4-1	Emily Ridge (pen) 5, 32, Phoebe Davies 12, Kimberley Bebbington 53	45	2
26.11	Long Eaton United (a)	W	3-2	Laura Morris 43, Charlotte Canlett 46, 63	32	1
10.12	Leicester City L (h)	P-P				
17.12	Burton Albion (a)	P-P				
14.01	Leicester City L (h)	W	5-0	Emily Ridge 16, Kimberley Bebbington 19, Laura Morris 27, Charlotte Canlett 45+2, Louisa Anderson 76	51	2
21.01	Burton Albion (a)	P-P				2
25.02	B'ham & WM (h)	D	2-2	Kimberley Bebbington 11, Louisa Anderson 38	29	3
04.03	Sheffield United (h)	P-P				3
11.03	Loughborough F (a)	L	1-5	Emily Ridge 21	43	3
18.03	Sheffield United (h)	P-P				3
25.03	B'ham & W M (a)	D	1-1	Laura Morris 75	20	3

08.04	Leicester City L (a)	W	12-0	Sarah Jackson 1, 23, 49, Katherine Huntbach 7, Own Goal 43, Phoebe Davies 56, Stacey Garnham 58, Kimberley Bebbington 68, Laura Morris 77, Lia Lewis 81, Hannah Yates 84, Sara Bengtsson 85	15	3
15.04	Radcliff Olympic (a)	L	1-4	Kimberley Bebbington 82	35	3
22.04	Burton Albion (a)**	L	2-3	Kimberley Bebbington 26, Emily Ridge 40	55	3
29.04	Loughborough F (h)	L	1-4	Charlotte Canlett 2	39	4
13.05	Sheffield United (h)	D	2-2	Louisa Anderson 60, Laura Morris 68	59	5
20.05	Solihull Moors (h)	L	1-2	Laura Morris 63	25	4

*Played at Foxen Manor +Played at Four Crosses   **Played at Etwall Leisure Centre

2017/18 FA CUP

08.10 RQ3	Shrewsbury Town (h)	W	3-1	Kimberley Bebbington 40, 63, Emily Ridge 52	147
12.11 R1	Bedworth United (a)	W	2-0	Emily Ridge 5, 90+5	85
03.12 R2	Sporting Khalsa (a)	D	2-2 aet (W 4-1p)	Lia Lewis 20, Emily Ridge 83	45
07.01 R3	Newcastle United (a)	W	2-1	Kimberley Bebbington 10, Emily Ridge 76	115
04.02 R4	Chichester City (h)	D	1-1aet (L 4-5 p)	Kimberley Bebbington 32	272

2017/18 WPL CUP

| 03.09 DR | Crewe Alexandra (h) | D | 3-3aet (W 5-4p) | Stephanie Taylor 19, Charlotte Canlett 30, Emily Ridge 106 | 54 |
| 24.09 PR | Leicester City W (h) | L | 2-5 | Kimberley Bebbington 58, Charlotte Canlett (pen) 61 | 55 |

2017/18 Shropshire FA County Cup

28.01 R1	Shrewsbury Juniors (h)	W	w/o		
11.02 QF	Shifnal Town (a)	W	2-1	Chloe Wilkinson 10, Emily Ridge 70	38
14.03 SF	Ellesmere Rangers (a)	W	9-0	Charlotte Canlett (x3), Sarah Jackson (x2), Holly Turbill (x2), Laura Morris, Sophie Edwards	
04.05 F	Shrewsbury Town (n)	W	1-0	Louisa Anderson 90+4	169

(n) Played at The New Bucks Head, Telford United FC

"We can hold our heads high after a memorable 2017/18 season. The main highlight was beating Newcastle on the road to move into the 4th Round of the FA Cup. It has been a privilege to captain TNS Ladies and to have worked with a knowledgeable and future-thinking management team."

Charlotte Canlett – TNS Captain

- Season 2017/18 was the most successful in the history of the club. The New Saints topped the table at the end of August and the beginning of September, meaning they had risen to their highest ever League position of 1st in Tier 4. More importantly they achieved their best ever League finish, placing 5th come the end of the season.

- They also had their best ever FA Cup run in 2017/18, reaching the 4th Round for the first time. They came through four rounds and only lost to Tier 3 Chichester City on penalties. A club record home crowd of 272 watched that match against Chichester.

- Despite the success, manager Andy Williams left at the end of the season because the demands of his full-time job as a headteacher had increased. He told the club's website: "I am incredibly proud of what the team has achieved together – I am confident that I leave the team and the club in a better place than before I arrived."

- TNS hailed their Shropshire FA County Cup win (in which they beat Shrewsbury Town in the final) as La Decima, because it was their 10th triumph in the competition.

- They scored in 31 of their 32 matches across all competitions in 2017/18 with 20 different players on the scoresheet in those matches.

WATFORD
2018/19: WNL SOUTHERN PREMIER (Tier 3)

Founded: 1970
(as Watford Supporters' Ladies Club)
Nickname: The Lady Hornets / The Golden Girls
Ground: The CRY Community Stadium,
(Kings Langley FC)

Season 2017/18:

WSL 2 (Tier 2): 10th

FA Cup: 2nd Round

Continental Cup: Group Stage

2017/18 WSL 2

						Att	Pos
24.09	Millwall L (a)	L	1-3	Simona Petkova 5, *Laura May Walkley sent off 81*		393	
01.10	Oxford United (h)	L	1-3	Sarah Jones 36		170	
08.10	Durham (a)	L	0-4			487	10
29.10	Tottenham H (h)	D	1-1	*Rinsola Babajide missed pen 16*, Adekite Fatuga-Dada 53		579	8
12.11	Aston Villa (a)	L	0-4			274	10
10.12	Brighton & H A (a)		P-P				
07.01	Doncaster R B (h)	L	0-2			241	10
27.01	London Bees (a)	L	1-3	Anneka Nuttall 87		120	10
11.02	Sheffield FC (h)		P-P				10
22.02	Tottenham H (a)	L	0-6			242	10
04.03	Sheffield FC (h)		P-P				10
18.03	Sheffield FC (h)		P-P				10
25.03	Aston Villa (h)	L	0-3			186	10
31.03	Doncaster R B (a)	L	1-3	Anneka Nuttall 45		410	10
15.04	Sheffield FC (a)	L	0-4			321	10
22.04	London Bees (h)	L	0-4			210	10
29.04	Millwall L (h)	L	0-4			289	10
06.05	Brighton & H A (a)	L	1-4	Simona Petkova 16		202	10
09.05	Brighton & H A (h)	L	0-1	*Helen Ward missed pen (saved Lucy Gillett) 80*		160	10
13.05	Oxford United (a)	W	2-1	Helen Ward 17, Simona Petkova 64		525	10
16.05	Sheffield FC (h)	L	0-5			129	10
20.05	Durham (h)	L	0-2			391	10

2017/18 WSL CONTINENTAL CUP: GROUP ONE SOUTH

						Att	
12.10	Millwall L (h)	W	1-0	Adekite Fatuga-Dada 73		312	
01.11	Reading (a)	L	0-4			211	
16.11	Arsenal (h)	L	0-6			823	
03.12	London Bees (a)	D	1-1 (L 4-5p)	Rinsola Babajide 45		321	

AW Images

2017/18 FA CUP

04.02 R4   Liverpool (a)^   L   0-5   252

^Played at Walton Hall, Liverpool County FA

"The 2017/18 season was one of opportunity. A lot of young players stepped up to the plate and made the most of the fantastic chance to play top level football. Attendances increased and we saw a successful Sister Club campaign through which we help inspire local girls to aim for the top."

Anneka Nuttall, Watford Captain (before leaving in July 2018)

- There was disappointment in autumn 2017 when Watford announced that the new FA licence criteria meant they would not be applying to remain in the newly-launched Tier 2. They now find themselves in Tier 3. The 2017/18 season also proved to be a tough one on the pitch as they finished bottom of WSL 2. The Lady Hornets were founding members of WSL 2 but finished bottom in three of their five campaigns at that level. Their best finishes were 7th in 2014 and 8th in the 2017 Spring Series.

- Watford were Premier League runners-up (behind champions Sunderland) in 2012/13. That was the final season that the division represented the 2nd tier of English football, operating directly under WSL. At the end of that season a WSL 2 was introduced for 2014.

- Female fans of Watford FC formed their own team in 1970, calling it the Watford Supporters' Ladies Club. For a while the name was changed to the "Willy Walker Wonders" in homage to manager Doug Hewish and coaches John Williams and Mike Walker. In 1997 they merged with Watford Town Girls, and then came their first link-up with Watford FC via the men's Community, Sports and Education Trust. It wasn't until early 2016 that Watford Ladies were formally brought under the Watford FC umbrella.

WEST BROMWICH ALBION

2018/19: WNL DIVISION 1 MIDLANDS (Tier 4)

Founded: 1989

Nickname: Albion

Ground: Church Road,
(Boldmere St Michaels FC)

Season 2017/18:

WPL Northern (Tier 3): 12th (R)

FA Cup: 2nd Round
WPL Cup: 1st Round
County Cup: Semi-finals

2017/18 WPL NORTHERN

Date	Opponent	Result	Score	Scorers	Att	
20.08	Huddersfield T (a)	L	0-4		67	
27.08	Blackburn Rovers (h)	L	0-2		71	
10.09	Stoke City (h)	L	0-5		107	
17.09	Middlesbrough (a)	L	0-4		82	8
20.09	Wolverhampton W (a)	W	4-2	Nicole Dale 26, Gina Burton 37, Brodie Vincze 75, Leanne Mitchell 85, *Antonia Smith sent off 40*	300	10
24.09	Huddersfield T (h)	W	2-1	Leanne Mitchell 41, Antonia Smith 45, *Brode Vincze sent off 89*	56	8
01.10	Nottingham Forest (a)	L	1-5	Leanne Mitchell 2	87	9
08.10	Derby County (a)	D	1-1	Sophie Hull 57	107	9
17.10	Wolverhampton W (h)	L	1-2	Jennifer Kikomeko 74	236	10
22.10	Blackburn Rovers (a)	L	0-2		96	10
05.11	Guiseley Vixens (h)	W	3-1	Leanne Mitchell 44, 88, Harriet James 60	84	8
12.11	Stoke City (a)	L	1-2	Leanne Mitchell 65	163	8
26.11	Leicester City W (h)	L	1-4	Leah Seivwright (pen) 63	82	10
07.01	Nottingham F (h)	D	1-1	Cheryl Edwards 70	85	9
04.02	Guiseley Vixens (a)		P-P			10
25.02	Fylde (h)	L	0-5		64	10
04.03	Bradford City (a)		P-P			10
25.03	Bradford City (h)	W	2-1	Jennifer Kikomeko 14, 26	54	10
08.04	Middlesbrough (h)	L	2-3	Laura Davies 23, Gina Burton 67	67	10
15.04	Guiseley Vixens (a)	L	2-3	Jennifer Kikomeko (pen) 25, 58	24	10
22.04	Bradford City (a)	L	2-4	Laura Davies 37, Hannah George 48	47	10
25.04	Leicester City W (a)	L	2-3	Leanne Mitchell 18, Laura Davies 83	89	10
29.04	Derby County (h)	L	1-2	Natalie Murray 70	54	10
20.05	Fylde (a)	L	1-2	Lucy Finch 49	43	12R

2017/18 FA CUP

Date		Opponent	Result	Score	Notes	Att
03.12	R2	Huddersfield Town (a)	L	0-7	West Brom GK saved Kate Mallin pen 26	79

2017/18 WPL CUP

03.09 DR	Long Eaton United (a)	W	2-1 (aet)	Sophie Hull 65, Leanne Mitchell 118	65
15.10 R1	Nottingham Forest (a)	L	0-5		124

2017/18 BIRMINGHAM FA COUNTY CUP

19.11 R2	Crusaders (a)	W	3-1	Lucy Finch 3, Harriet James 61, 80	
14.01 R3	Solihull United (a)	W	2-1	Own goal 25, Natasha Merritt 81	30 est
18.02 QF	Stockington AA Pavilion (h)	W	9-1	Laura Davies 4, Hannah George 30, Natalie Murray 44, Nicole Dale 50, 58, Gina Burton 55, Justine Buckmire 64, Jennifer Kikomeko 73, 85	
18.03 SF	Coventry United (h)		P-P		
05.04 SF	Coventry United (h)	L	0-2		171

"The 2017/18 season was always going to be tough due to events that unravelled towards the end of the previous campaign. An entirely new backroom team and playing cohort had to be assembled, along with development on all other operational aspects that gets the team functioning in the WPL. The culture we developed was effective at times yet wasn't robust enough to see us collect enough points. We had an excellent period after Christmas where we allowed ourselves to believe that staying in the League

would be a formality, and complacency crept in. Lessons have been learnt which means we will benefit from the experience of relegation. The bigger the challenge, the greater the opportunity. Thank you to all the fans and parents for their support throughout a tough campaign and hopefully we can give them more to shout about in 2018/19."

Dave Lawrence – West Brom, Head of Women and Girls

- West Brom went into their final match of the 2017/18 season away to Fylde needing to win and hope for other results elsewhere to go their way to stay in Tier 3. They went ahead four minutes after half-time through Lucy Finch, but an own goal saw Fylde equalise before Albion eventually lost 2-1 and were relegated.

- West Bromwich Albion FC Women competed under the name Sporting Club Albion between 2009 and 2016.

- It was as Sporting Club Albion that they won the WPL Northern Division title in 2015/16 for the first time in their history. Having claimed the title they met WPL Southern Division Champions Brighton & Hove Albion in a one-off play off for promotion to WSL 2, but they were beaten 4-2 at Adams Park.

WOLVERHAMPTON WANDERERS

2018/19: WNL DIVISION 1
MIDLANDS (Tier 4)

Founded: 1975 (as Heathfield Rovers)

Nickname: The Wolfettes

Ground: Keys Park, (Hednesford Town FC) in 2017/18, moving to Queen Street, (Bilston Town FC) for 2018/19

Season 2017/18:

WPL Northern (Tier 3): 11th (R)

FA Cup: 2nd Round
WPL Cup: Determining Round
WPL Plate: 1st Round
County Cup: Quarter-finals

2017/18 WPL NORTHERN

20.08	Blackburn Rovers (a)	L	0-3		136	
27.08	Middlesbrough (h)	L	3-4	Jade Cross 1, Jennifer Anslow 44, 77	100	
10.09	Bradford City (a)	L	1-4	Jade Cross 29, *Jennifer Anslow sent off 90*	63	
20.09	West Brom (h)	L	2-4	Leanne Robinson 78, Jade Cross 88, *Kirsty Bavington sent off 44*	300	12
24.09	Guiseley Vixens (a)	D	2-2	Leanne Robinson 3, Laura McQuilkin 80	30	12
01.10	Stoke City (a)	D	1-1	Jade Cross 7	131	11
08.10	Nottingham F (h)	L	0-1		100	12
15.10	Fylde (h)	L	0-1		50	12
17.10	West Brom (a)	W	2-1	Anna Price 18, Billie Haynes 44	236	11
29.10	Derby County (h)	P-P				
05.11	Leicester City W (h)	L	3-4	Anna Price 13, Leanne Robinson 64, Jade Cross 80	80	11
12.11	Huddersfield T (h)	L	3-5	Jade Cross 21, Anna Price 38, Jennifer Anslow 47	60	11
26.11	Bradford City (h)	L	0-3		40	11
28.01	Middlesbrough (a)	L	1-7	Laura McQuilkin 29	234	11
25.02	Stoke City (h)	L	1-4	Jennifer Anslow 23	50	11
04.03	Guiseley Vixens (h)	P-P				11
11.03	Derby County (h)	P-P				11
18.03	Leicester City W (a)	P-P				11
01.04	Leicester City W (a)	L	0-6		97	11
08.04	Huddersfield T (a)	L	0-2		73	12
15.04	Fylde (a)	D	0-0		33	12
22.04	Blackburn Rovers (h)	D	1-1	Andrea Whetton 16	80	12
26.04	Derby County (a)	D	1-1	Jade Cross 82	72	12
29.04	Guiseley Vixens (h)	W	2-1	Jennifer Anslow 23, Charlotte Criddle 89	75	11
06.05	Derby County (h)*	W	2-1	Anna Price 21, Jennifer Anslow 88	100	11
20.05	Nottingham F (a)+	W	5-0	Anna Price 7, Billie Haynes 12, Jade Cross 16, Chloe Williams 75, Charlotte Criddle (pen) 79	70	11

*Played at Queen Street Stadium, Bilston Town FC   +Played at Lee Westwood Sports Centre

Simon Faulkner

2017/18 FA CUP

03.12 R2	Brighouse Town (a)		P-P		
10.12 R2	Brighouse Town (a)		P-P		
17.12 R2	Brighouse Town (a)	L	3-6	Charlotte Criddle 2, 12, 50	123

2017/18 WPL CUP

03.09 DR	Liverpool M F (h)	L	0-2		45

2017/18 WPL PLATE

22.10 R1	Long Eaton United (h)	L	1-2 (aet)	Billie Haynes 40	50

2017/18 BIRMINGHAM FA COUNTY CUP

19.11 R2	Lye Town (a)		P-P		
05.12 R2	Lye Town (a)	W	8-1	Jade Cross 22, 40, 59, 71, Charlotte Criddle 25, 31, Jennifer Anslow 51, Nikki Lal 86	45 est
14.01 R3	Sutton Coldfield T (h)	W	5-0	Jade Cross 10, 72, Anna Price 42, 81, Jade Hewitt 62	75
18.02 QF	Coventry United (h)	L	1-3	Jade Cross 72	50

"Our six-game unbeaten run to close the season was our biggest achievement this year. With a new management team arriving in February, they invested time in some of our extremely talented younger players, who are graduates of our Regional Talent Centre. This created an excellent balance of energetic youth, as well as experienced heads. This was highlighted in our final game where we beat Nottingham Forest 5-0 away from home. With the quality of the players coming through, the future of Wolves Women is extremely bright."

Anna Price, Wolverhampton Wanderers Captain

- Having come up as WPL Midlands One champions ahead of the 2017/18 season, Wolves endured a difficult campaign in Tier 4 and suffered immediate relegation. There were though a number of high points, among them the form of the club's top scorer Jade Cross who hit eight goals in the League and a total of 15 in all competitions.

- Summer 2018 also marked the end of an era as long-serving defender Claire Hakeman announced her retirement. The 38-year-old former Birmingham City player had been with the club for more than a decade.

- Wolves started out as Heathfield Rovers in 1975 and have also been known in the past as Wolverhampton & Wednesbury Tube and Wolverhampton Ladies. In 1993 they were granted permission from Wolverhampton Wanderers men's club to call themselves by the same name. Today they are officially affiliated to the men's club.

- At the end of 1993/94 they were promoted to the top-flight – the FA Women's Premier League National Division – where they spent two years before being relegated.

- Aston Villa's 1982 European Cup-winning captain Dennis Mortimer was appointed manager in 2000 and narrowly missed out on promotion to the top-flight during his three seasons in charge.

ENGLAND 2017/18

Having been knocked out of Euro 2017 by hosts Netherlands at the semi-final stage, England set out about qualifying for the 2019 World Cup in France. The build-up to the qualification campaign was beset by problems with the FA facing intense media scrutiny for how it had come to clear manager Mark Sampson of allegations of bullying by Eniola Aluko. The FA stuck by Sampson whose players also showed their support by celebrating with him en masse when Nikita Parris opened the scoring in the first qualifier against Russia which England went on to win 6-0. However, the following day Sampson was sacked on a separate matter, the FA stating he had been removed from post because of evidence of "inappropriate and unacceptable behaviour" with female players in a previous role.

Former England captain Mo Marley stepped up from her role as boss of the England Under-19s to become interim manager of the senior side. Marley oversaw a friendly defeat in France and healthy home World Cup qualifying wins over Bosnia & Herzegovina (4-0) and Kazakhstan (5-0). In January 2018 former Manchester United and England men's player Phil Neville was named as the new manager. His appointment had a mixed reaction with critics pointing to his lack of previous managerial experience and the fact that he had not initially applied for the role. His tenure began in March with a 4-1 win over France in the SheBelieves Cup in the US. England finished the round-robin tournament in 2nd place after a draw with Germany and a defeat to the USA.

The World Cup qualifiers resumed with a goalless home draw against Wales at St Mary's Stadium (a result which left the two teams battling it out for the only automatic qualifying spot in the group) and wins away to Bosnia & Herzegovina and Russia.

Key: WCQ = World Cup Qualifier   F = Friendly SBC = SheBelieves Cup

ENGLAND RESULTS & LINE-UPS – ALL MATCHES 2017/18

19.09   Russia (h)   W 6-0   WCQ   Prenton Park, Tranmere Rovers FC   7,047
Nikita Parris 11, Jodie Taylor 14, *Kirby missed pen 31,* Jordan Nobbs 36, Lucy Bronze 44, Toni Duggan 57, 84

England (4-2-3-1): Siobhan Chamberlain (Liverpool); Lucy Bronze (Lyon), Stephanie Houghton © (Man City), Millie Bright (Chelsea), Demi Stokes (Man City); Jordan Nobbs (Arsenal), Jade Moore (Reading); Nikita Parris (Man City) (sub Karen Carney 61 (Chelsea)), Fran Kirby (Chelsea) (sub Isobel Christiansen (Man City) 70), Toni Duggan (Barcelona); Jodie Taylor (Arsenal) (sub Ellen White 65 (Birmingham City)).

Unused: Laura Bassett (Unattached), Carly Telford (Chelsea), Alex Greenwood (Liverpool), Jill Scott (Man City).

Head coach: Mark Sampson

Russia: Shcherbak, Kovalenko, Tsybutovich (sent off 30), Kozhnikova, Ziyastinova, Morozova, Fedorova, Smirnova, Cholovyaga (Belomyttseva 33), Sochneva (Pantyukhina 79), Danilova.

Unused: Sheikina, Mashina, Podshibyakina, Galay, Belyaeva, Belomyttseva, Pantyukhina.

Head coach: Elena Fomina

Referee: Stephanie Frappart (France)

20.10   France (a)   **L 0-1**   F   Stade du Hainaut, Valenciennes   20,059

Asseyi 89

France: Sarah Bouhaddi, Marion Torrent, Hawa Cissoko, Wendie Renard, Amel Majri, Onema Grace Geyoro, Aminata Diallo, Kadidiatou Diani (Vivianne Asseyi 81), Ines Jaurena (Lea Le Garrec 69), Eugenie Le Sommer©, Valerie Gauvin (Ouleymata Sarr 69).

Unused: Elisa Launay, Charlotte Lorgere, Laura Georges, Estelle Cascarino, Amandine Henry, Camille Catala, Elise Bussaglia, Griedge Mbock Bathy.

Head coach: Corinne Diacre

England 4-3-3: Siobhan Chamberlain (Liverpool); Lucy Bronze (Lyon), Stephanie Houghton © (Man City), Millie Bright (Chelsea), Demi Stokes (Man City); Jill Scott (Man City), Fara Williams (Reading) (sub Jade Moore 61 (Reading)), Jordan Nobbs (Arsenal); Karen Carney (Chelsea) (sub Melissa Lawley 62 (Man City)), Jodie Taylor (Arsenal) (sub Nikita Parris 84 (Man City)), Toni Duggan (Barcelona).

Unused: Alex Greenwood (Liverpool), Carly Telford (Chelsea), Casey Stoney (Liverpool), Gemma Bonner (Liverpool),Jo Potter(Reading), Mary Earps(Reading), Danielle Carter (Arsenal).

Interim head coach: Mo Marley

Refeee: Jana Adamkova (Czech Republic)

24.11   Bosnia & H (h)   **W 4-0**   WCQ   Banks's Stadium, Walsall FC   10,026

Houghton 19, Parris 46, Houghton 54, Kirby (pen) 83

England (4-3-3): Siobhan Chamberlain (Liverpool); Lucy Bronze (Lyon), Stephanie Houghton © (Man City), Millie Bright (Chelsea), Alex Greenwood (Liverpool); Jordan Nobbs (Arsenal), Fran Kirby (Chelsea), Isobel Christiansen (Man City) (sub Jo Potter 73 (Reading)); Nikita Parris (Man City) (sub Melissa Lawley 81 (Man City)), Danielle Carter (Arsenal), Toni Duggan (Arsenal)

Unused: Demi Stokes (Man City), Karen Bardsley (Man City), Jodie Taylor (Arsenal), Karen Carney (Chelsea).

Interim head coach: Mo Marley

Bosnia & H: Almina Hodzic, Antonela Radeljic, Amira Spahic © (Nikola Milovic 90), Melisa Hasanbegovic, Lidija Kulis, Alisa Spahic (Aida Hadzic 77), Amela Krso, Marija Aleksic, Dajana Spasojevic, Milena Nikolic, Andela Seslija (Valentina Sakotic 45).

Unused: Arnela Sabanovic, Amna Lihovic, Marina Lukic, Alma Kameric.

Head coach: Samira Hurem

Referee: Ewa Augustyn (Poland)

28.11   Kazakhstan (h)   **W 5-0**   WCQ   Weston Homes Community Stadium, Colchester United FC   9,643

Lawley 15, Kirby (pen) 64, Parris 68, 75, Christiansen 76

England (4-3-3): Karen Bardsley (Man City); Lucy Bronze (Lyon) (sub Jess Carter 77 (Birmingham City)), Stephanie Houghton © (Man City), Gemma Bonner (Liverpool), Alex Greenwood (Liverpool); Keira Walsh (Man City), Fara Williams (Reading) (sub Isobel Christiansen 63 (Man City)), Jill Scott (Man City); Nikita Parris (Man City), Jodie Taylor (Arsenal) (sub Fran Kirby 63 (Chelsea)), Melissa Lawley (Man City).

Unused: Jo Potter (Reading), Carly Telford (Chelsea), Leah Williamson (Arsenal), Jordan Nobbs (Arsenal).

Interim head coach: Mo Marley

Kazakhstan: Oksana Zheleznyak (Irina Sandalova 45), Shokhista Khojasheva, Bibigul Nurusheva, Yekaterina Krasyukova, Yekaterina Babshuk, Svetlana Bortnikova, Karina Zhumabaikyzy, Adilya Vyldanova, Begaim Kirgizbaeva ©, Aida Gaistenova (Anastassiya Vlassova 70), Saule Karibayeva (Asselkhan Turlybekova 81).

Unused: Mariya Demidova, Zuleira Turlybekova, Arailym Orynbasarova, Aigerim Alimkulova, Zuleira Abisheva.

Head coach: Aitpay Jamantayev

Referee: Lois Otte (Belgium)

| 01.03 | France (n) | W 4-1 | SBC | Mapfre Stadium, Columbus; Ohio, USA | 7,566 |

Duggan 7, Scott 28, Taylor 39, Kirby 46; Thiney 77

England (4-3-3): Karen Bardsley (Man City) (sub Carly Telford 83 (Chelsea)); Lucy Bronze© (Lyon), Anita Asante (Chelsea) (sub Abbie McManus 14 (Man City)), Millie Bright (Chelsea), Demi Stokes (Man City) (sub Alex Greenwood 87 (Liverpool)); Jill Scott (Man City), Keira Walsh (Man City), Fran Kirby (Chelsea) (sub Isobel Christiansen 71 (Man City)); Nikita Parris (Man City) (sub Melissa Lawley (61 Man City), Jodie Taylor (Melbourne City), Toni Duggan (Barcelona) (sub Ellen White 71 (Birmingham City)).

Unused: Fara Williams (Reading), Hannah Blundell (Chelsea), Siobhan Chamberlain (Liverpool), Rachel Daly (Houston Dash), Georgia Stanway (Man City), Gabrielle George(Everton).

Head coach: Phil Neville

France: Karima Benameur, Eve Perisset, Griedge Mbock Bathy, Laura Georges, Sakina Karchaoui, Aminata Diallo, Kadidiatou Diani (Viviane Asseyi 61), Amandine Henry ©, Faustine Robert (Gaetane Thiney 61), Eugenie Le Sommer, Ouleymata Sarr (Valerie Gauvin 74).

Unused: Aissatou Tounkara, Estelle Cascarino, Amel Majri, Maeva Clemaron, Marie-Charlotte Leger, Sarah Bouhaddi, Marion Torrent, Solene Durand, Onema Grace Geyoro.

Head coach: Corinne Diacre

Referee: Christina Unkel (USA)

| 04.03 | Germany (n) | D 2-2 | SBC | Red Bull Arena, New Jersey, USA | 7,882 |

Kayikci 17, Bright (og) 51; White 18, 73

Germany: Almuth Schult, Tabea Kemme (Sara Doorsoun 90), Kathrin Hendrich, Lena Goessling (Johanna Elsig 87), Verena Faisst, Svenja Huth (Carina Schuller 75), Linda Dallmann (Lina Magull 45), Dzsenifer Marozsan ©, Sara Dabritz (Mandy Islacker 72), Hasret Kayikci (Anna Blasse 45), Alexandra Popp.

Unused: Leonie Maier, Jacqueline Klasen, Laura Benkarth, Carina Schluter, Sharon Beck.

Head coach: Steffi Jones

England (4-3-3): Siobhan Chamberlain (Liverpool); Lucy Bronze© (Lyon), Abbie McManus (Man City), Millie Bright (Chelsea), Demi Stokes (Man City); Jill Scott (Man City) (sub Isobel Christiansen 67 (Man City)), Fara Williams (Reading) (sub Keira Walsh 59 (Man City)), Fran Kirby (Chelsea) (sub Jodie Taylor 90 (Melbourne City)); Melissa Lawley (Man City) (sub Rachel Daly 85 (Houston Dash)), Ellen White (Birmingham City), Toni Duggan (Barcelona) (sub Nikita Parris 67 (Man City)).

Unused: Karen Bardsley (Man City), Hannah Blundell (Chelsea), Alex Greenwood (Liverpool), Georgia Stanway (Man City), Carly Telford (Chelsea), Gabrielle George (Everton).

Head coach: Phil Neville

ENGLAND'S TONI DUGGAN IN ACTION AT ST MARY'S STADIUM AGAINST WALES

Referee: Stephanie Frappart (France)

| 08.03 | USA (a) | L 0-1 | SBC | Orlando City Stadium, Florida; USA | 12,351 |

Bardsley (og) 58

USA: Alyssa Naeher, Emily Sonnett, Abby Dahlkemper, Tierna Davidson, Crystal Dunn, Carli Lloyd ©, Allie Long (Sofia Huerta 74), Lindsey Horan (Morgan Brian 74), Mallory Pugh (Lynn Williams 90+2), Alex Morgan, Megan Rapinoe (Savannah McCaskill 80). **Unused:** Casey Short, Andi Sullivan, Kelley O'Hara, Julie Ertz, Jane Campbell, Taylor Smith, Christen Press, Ashlyn Harris.

Head coach: Jill Ellis

England (4-2-3-1): Karen Bardsley (Man City); Lucy Bronze © (Lyon), Millie Bright (Chelsea), Abbie McManus (Man City), Demi Stokes (Man City) (sub Hannah Blundell 87 (Chelsea)); Keira Walsh (Man City) (sub Jill Scott 87 (Man City)), Isobel Christiansen(Man City); Melissa Lawley (Man City) (sub Toni Duggan 52 (Barcelona)), Fran Kirby (Chelsea) (sub Rachel Daly 75 (Houston Dash)), Ellen White (Birmingham City); Jodie Taylor (Melbourne City) (sub Nikita Parris 52 (Man City)). **Unused:** Siobhan Chamberlain (Liverpool), Fara Williams (Reading), Alex Greenwood (Liverpool), Georgia Stanway (Man City), Carly Telford (Chelsea), Gabrielle George (Everton).

Head coach: Phil Neville

Referee: Carol Anne Chenard (Canada)

| 06.04 | Wales (h) | D 0-0 | WCQ | St Mary's, Southampton | 25,603 |

England: Carly Telford (Chelsea); Lucy Bronze (Lyon), Steph Houghton ©; (Man City), Abbie McManus (Man City), 3 Demi Stokes (Man City); 8 Jordan Nobbs (Arsenal), 4 Keira Walsh (Man City), 10 Fran Kirby (Chelsea); 7 Nikita Parris (Man City) (sub Melissa Lawley 55 (Man City)), 9 Jodie Taylor (Seattle Reign) (sub Ellen White 55 (Birmingham City)), 11 Toni Duggan (Barcelona) (sub Beth Mead 80 (Arsenal)). **Unused:** Karen Bardsley (Man City), Rachel Daly (Houston Dash), Gabby George (Everton), Isobel Christiansen (Man City)

Head coach: Phil Neville

Wales: Laura O'Sullivan, Loren Dykes, Sophie Ingle (c) , Rhiannon Roberts, Natasha Harding, Angharad James, Kayleigh Green, Jess Fishlock, Rachel Rowe, Hayley Ladd, Charlotte Estcourt. **Unused:** Claire Skinner, Alice Griffiths, Nadia Lawrence, Elise Hughes, Melissa Fletcher, Hannah Miles, Helen Ward.

Head coach: Jayne Ludlow

Referee: Pernilla Larsson (Sweden)

| 10.04 | Bosnia & H (a) | W 2-0 | WCQ | Football Centre, Zenica |

Duggan 56, Taylor (pen) 90+2.   Sent-off: Greenwood 47; Amira Spahic 59

Bosnia & Herzegovina (5-4-1): Envera Hasanbegovic; Amira Spahic (sub Merjema Medic 90+2), Melisa Hasanbegovic, Marija Aleksic, Antonela Radeljic, Lidija Kulis; Valentina Sakotic (sub Marina Lukic 74), Aida Hadzic, Alisa Spahic, Amela Krso (sub Selma Kapetanovic 66); Milena Nikolic (capt). **Unused:** Jelena Gvozderac, Zerina Piskic, Dragica Denda, Amna Lihovic

Head coach: Samira Huren

England (4-3-3): Carly Telford (Chelsea); Lucy Bronze (Lyon), Steph Houghton ©; (Man City), Abbie McManus (Man City), Alex Greenwood (Liverpool); Jordan Nobbs (Arsenal), Jade Moore (Reading), Isobel Christiansen (Man City) (sub Rachel Daly 80 (Houston Dash)); Melissa Lawley (Man City) (sub Beth Mead 57 (Arsenal)), Ellen White (Birmingham City), Toni Duggan (Barcelona) (sub Jodie Taylor 87 (Seattle Reign). **Unused:** Karen Bardsley (Man City), Gabby George (Everton), Fara Williams (Reading), Nikita Parris (Man City).

Head coach: Phil Neville

Referee: Andromachi Tsiofliki (Greece)

| 08.06 | **Russia (a)** | **W 3-1** | **WCQ** | **Sapsan Arena, Moscow** |

Elena Danilova 31; Nikita Parris 22, Jill Scott 27, 36

Russia (4-1-4-1): Yulia Grichenko; Anastasiya Akimova, Irina Podshibyakina, Anna Belomyttseva, Elvira Ziyastinova; Anna Kozhnikova; Ekaterina Pantyukhina (sub 72 Nelli Korovkina), Nadezhda Smirnova, Lipa Yakupova (sub 45 Margarita Chernomyrdina), Elena Morozova; Elena Danilova (sub 81 Ekaterina Sochneva). **Unused:** Elvira Todua, Ekaterina Bratko, Alsu Abdullina, Nadezhda Koltakova,

Head coach: Elena Fomina

England (4-2-3-1): Carly Telford (Chelsea); Lucy Bronze © (Lyon), Abbie McManus (Man City), Millie Bright (Chelsea), Rachel Daly (Houston Dash); Jill Scott (Man City),Keira Walsh (Man City) (sub Leah Williamson 84 (Arsenal)); Nikita Parris (Man City),Fran Kirby (Chelsea), Toni Duggan (Barcelona) (sub Beth Mead 62 (Arsenal)); Ellen White (Birmingham City) (sub Jodie Taylor 67 (Seattle Reign)). **Unused:** Hannah Blundell (Chelsea), Karen Bardsley (Man City), Lauren Bruton (Reading), Mel Lawley (Man City).

Head coach: Phil Neville

Referee: Dr Riem Hussein (Germany)

SHEBELIEVES CUP 2018 - FULL RESULTS AND STANDINGS

The SheBelieves Cup is an invitational event held in the US. It has been staged every year since 2016, featuring the same four teams, the USA, England, France and Germany. The teams play each other once in a round-robin format. In common with regular friendly international matches, a maximum of six substitutions can be made in each match.

RESULTS

01.03	England	4-1	France
01.03	USA	1-0	Germany
04.03	USA	1-1	France
04.03	Germany	2-2	England
07.03	France	3-0	Germany
07.03	USA	1-0	England

FINAL STANDINGS

Pos	Team	P	W	D	L	F	A	GD	Pts
1.	USA	3	2	1	0	3	1	2	7
2.	England	3	1	1	1	6	4	2	4
3.	France	3	1	1	1	5	5	0	4
4.	Germany	3	0	1	2	2	6	-4	1

If two or more teams are level on points, their rankings are decided by the following criteria in this order: 1) goal difference from all games; 2) goals scored in all games; 3) points from matches solely between the teams who are level on points; 4) goal difference from matches solely between the teams who are level on points; 5) goals scored in matches solely between the teams who are level on points; 6) FIFA Ranking

2019 FIFA WOMEN'S WORLD CUP QUALIFIERS – GROUP 1 RESULTS & FIXTURES

17.09.17	Kazakhstan	0-1	Wales
19.09.17	England	6-0	Russia
21.10.17	Kazakhstan	0-2	Bosnia & Herzegovina
24.10.17	Russia	0-0	Wales
24.11.17	Wales	1-0	Kazakhstan
24.11.17	England	4-0	Bosnia & Herzegovina
28.11.17	Bosnia & Herzegovina	0-1	Wales
28.11.17	England	5-0	Kazakhstan
05.04.18	Bosnia & Herzegovina	1-6	Russia
06.04.18	England	0-0	Wales
09.04.18	Kazakhstan	0-3	Russia
10.04.18	Bosnia & Herzegovina	0-2	England
07.06.18	Wales	1-0	Bosnia & Herzegovina
08.06.18	Russia	1-3	England
12.06.18	Bosnia & Herzegovina	0-2	Kazakhstan
12.06.18	Wales	3-0	Russia
30.08.18	Russia	V	Kazakhstan
31.08.18	Wales	V	England
04.09.18	Kazakhstan	V	England
04.09.18	Russia	V	Bosnia & Herzegovina

GROUP 1 TABLE – LAST UPDATED 13.06.18

Pos	Team	P	W	D	L	F	A	GD	Pts
1.	Wales	7	5	2	0	7	0	7	17
2.	England	6	5	1	0	20	1	19	16
3.	Russia	6	2	1	3	10	13	-3	7
4.	Kazakhstan	6	1	0	5	2	12	-10	3
5.	Bosnia & Herz.	7	1	0	6	3	16	-13	3

If England and Wales finish level on points, head-to-head record will determine who finishes top. If still level, away goals in the matches between the teams will determine the outcome. If still level the ranking will be determined by the following criteria in the order given: a) group goal difference, b) group goals scored, c) group away goals scored, d) best disciplinary record, e) UEFA national team coefficient ranking.

In total there are seven European qualifying groups for the 2019 FIFA Women's World Cup. The winners of each group qualify automatically for France 2019. One further qualifier will be determined via the following play-off system.

The four group runners-up with the best records against the teams which finish 1st, 3rd and 4th in their groups will go into the play-offs. The play-offs consist of two semi-finals played over two legs in October 2018 with the winners going into a two-legged play-off final. The winner of the play-off final qualifies for the World Cup. In total there will be nine European teams competing at the World Cup including hosts France who have qualified by right.

The finals take place 7 June – 7 July 2019 and include 24 teams from across the world. There will be six groups of four teams. The top two in each group progress to the knockout phase along with the four best third-placed teams.

2017/18 LEAGUE TABLES

WSL 1 (TIER 1)

Pos	Team	P	W	D	L	F	A	GD	Pts	
1.	Chelsea	18	13	5	0	44	13	31	44	
2.	Manchester City	18	12	2	4	51	17	34	38	
3.	Arsenal	18	11	4	3	38	18	20	37	
4.	Reading	18	9	5	4	40	18	22	32	
5.	Birmingham City	18	9	3	6	30	18	12	30	
6.	Liverpool	18	9	1	8	30	27	3	28	
7.	Sunderland	18	5	1	12	15	40	-25	16	R
8.	Bristol City	18	5	1	12	13	47	-34	16	
9.	Everton	18	4	2	12	19	30	-11	14	
10.	Yeovil Town	18	0	2	16	2	54	-52	2	

Champions Chelsea and runners-up Manchester City qualify for 2018/19 Champions League. Sunderland did not apply for a Tier 1 licence for 2018/19 and their Tier 2 application was unsuccessful. They were placed into Tier 3 for 2018/19.

WSL 2 (TIER 2)

Pos	Team	P	W	D	L	F	A	GD	Pts	
1.	Doncaster Rovers Belles	18	15	2	1	52	15	37	47	R
2.	Brighton & Hove Albion	18	12	1	5	35	26	9	37	P
3	Millwall Lionesses	18	12	3	3	40	23	17	36*	
4.	Durham	18	11	2	5	44	26	18	35	
5.	Sheffield FC	18	9	1	8	40	31	9	28	R
6.	London Bees	18	6	5	7	29	32	-3	23	
7.	Tottenham Hotspur	18	6	4	8	32	34	-2	22	
8.	Oxford United	18	3	3	12	24	41	-17	12	R
9.	Aston Villa	18	3	2	13	21	40	-19	11	
10.	Watford	18	1	1	16	8	57	-49	4	R

*Docked 3pts for fielding ineligible player

Brighton's application to join Tier 1 for 2018/19 was approved. Watford's and Oxford's applications for a Tier 2 licence were unsuccessful. Doncaster Rovers Belles and Sheffield FC were initially successful in their applications but later withdrew. All four teams were placed into Tier 3 for 2018/19.

WPL NORTHERN (TIER 3)

Pos	Team	P	W	D	L	F	A	GD	Pts	
1.	Blackburn Rovers	22	18	2	2	68	17	51	56	
2.	Leicester City W	22	14	4	4	68	32	36	46	P
3.	Middlesbrough	22	14	0	8	63	52	11	42	
4.	Stoke City	22	12	4	6	52	38	14	40	
5.	Fylde	22	10	6	6	35	35	0	36	
6.	Huddersfield Town	22	10	5	7	45	27	18	35	
7.	Derby County	22	7	5	10	27	37	-10	26	
8.	Bradford City	22	7	4	11	40	45	-5	25	
9.	Nottingham Forest	22	5	4	13	23	57	-34	19	
10.	Guiseley Vixens	22	4	5	13	33	56	-23	17	
11.	Wolverhampton W	22	4	5	13	30	56	-26	17	R
12.	West Brom. Albion	22	4	2	16	27	59	-32	14	R

Blackburn Rovers missed out on the only Tier 2 place for 2018/19 to be awarded partly on merit when they lost the national play-off final to Charlton Athletic. Their Tier 2 application was also unsuccessful. Leicester City Women's application for a Tier 2 licence for 2018/19 was successful. Wolves and West Brom were relegated to Tier 4 for 2018/19 after finishing in the bottom two.

WPL SOUTHERN (TIER 3)

Pos	Team	P	W	D	L	F	A	GD	Pts	
1.	Charlton Athletic	22	20	0	2	98	13	85	60	P
2.	C&K Basildon	22	17	1	4	51	24	27	52	
3.	Crystal Palace	22	16	2	4	59	15	44	50	P
4.	Coventry United	22	14	2	6	69	20	49	44	
5.	Lewes	22	14	2	6	45	25	20	44	P
6.	Portsmouth	22	12	1	9	44	35	9	37	
7.	West Ham United	22	9	2	11	57	42	15	29	P
8.	Chichester City	22	8	4	10	43	48	-5	28	
9.	Gillingham	22	5	2	15	24	53	-29	17	
10.	Cardiff City	22	4	4	14	40	69	-29	16	
11.	QPR	22	2	2	18	17	94	-77	8	
12.	Swindon Town	22	0	0	22	10	119	-109	0	R

Charlton were promoted to Tier 2 for 2018/19 after beating Blackburn Rovers in the national play-off final and satisfying the FA licence criteria. West Ham were promoted to Tier 1 for 2018/19 after their application was successful. Lewes were promoted to Tier 2 for 2018/19 after their application was successful. Crystal Palace were originally unsuccessful in their application to join Tier 2 but were later awarded a place. Swindon were relegated to Tier 3 for 2018/19 after finishing bottom.

WPL NORTHERN DIVISION 1 (TIER 4)

Pos	Team	P	W	D	L	F	A	GD	Pts	
1.	Hull City	22	17	3	2	66	14	52	54	P
2.	Brighouse Town	22	16	2	4	60	30	30	50	
3.	Liverpool M Feds	22	14	4	4	48	18	30	46	
4.	Bolton Wanderers	22	11	1	10	38	38	0	34	
5.	Newcastle United	22	9	3	10	44	47	-3	30	
6.	Chorley	22	9	2	11	41	41	0	29	
7.	Morecambe	22	9	2	11	49	60	-11	29	
8.	Crewe Alexandra	22	7	5	10	30	33	-3	26	
9.	Chester-le-Street T	22	8	1	13	35	49	-14	25	
10.	Leeds United	22	7	2	13	26	43	-17	23	
11.	Barnsley	22	4	5	13	32	64	-32	17	
12.	Mossley Hill Ath	22	5	2	15	28	60	-32	17	R

Hull City were promoted to Tier 3 for 2018/19 after finishing top. Mossley Hill Athletic were relegated to Tier 5 for 2018/19 after finishing bottom.

WPL MIDLANDS DIVISION 1 (TIER 4)

Pos	Team	P	W	D	L	F	A	GD	Pts	
1.	Loughborough F	22	21	1	0	91	9	82	64	P
2.	Burton Albion	22	15	2	5	54	32	22	47	
3.	Sheffield United	22	13	7	2	79	24	55	46	P
4.	Radcliffe Olympic	22	13	2	7	51	31	20	41	
5.	The New Saints	22	12	3	7	76	45	31	39	
6.	Long Eaton United	22	10	1	11	38	39	-1	31	
7.	Solihull Moors	22	9	3	10	55	47	8	30	
8.	Sporting Khalsa	22	8	2	12	40	39	1	26	
9.	B'ham & WM	22	7	3	12	48	52	-4	24	
10.	Steel City W	22	7	2	13	43	73	-30	23	
11.	Rotherham United	22	2	1	19	15	114	-99	7	R
12.	Leicester City L	22	1	1	20	11	96	-85	4	R

Loughborough Foxes were promoted to Tier 3 for 2018/19 after finishing top. Sheffield United were promoted to Tier 2 for 2018/19 after their application for a licence was successful. Rotherham United and Leicester City Ladies were relegated to Tier 5 for 2018/19 after finishing in the bottom two.

WPL SOUTH EAST DIVISION 1 (TIER 4)

Pos	Team	P	W	D	L	F	A	GD	Pts	
1.	MK Dons	22	18	3	1	76	18	58	57	P
2.	AFC Wimbledon	22	17	1	4	68	25	43	52	
3.	Ipswich Town	22	15	3	4	76	26	50	48	
4.	Leyton Orient	22	12	3	7	59	33	26	39	
5.	Luton Town	22	11	2	9	66	39	27	35	
6.	Stevenage	22	9	4	9	48	37	11	31	
7.	Actonians	22	9	3	10	56	32	24	30	
8.	Cambridge United	22	8	6	8	40	28	12	30	
9.	Denham United	22	5	7	10	38	47	-9	22	
10.	Enfield Town	22	5	5	12	31	50	-19	20	
11.	Norwich City	22	4	1	17	39	81	-42	13	
12.	Haringey Borough	22	0	0	22	15	196	-181	0	R

MK Dons were promoted to Tier 3 after finishing top. Haringey Borough were relegated to Tier 5 for 2018/19 after finishing bottom.

WPL SOUTH WEST DIVISION 1 (TIER 4)

Pos	Team	P	W	D	L	F	A	GD	Pts	
1.	Plymouth Argyle	18	16	2	0	100	12	88	50	P
2.	Southampton W	18	15	2	1	68	20	48	47	
3.	Keynsham Town	18	13	1	4	82	25	57	40	
4.	Southampton Saints	18	12	2	4	38	20	18	38	
5.	Poole Town	18	6	2	10	32	46	-14	20	
6.	Brislington	18	5	3	10	25	51	-26	18	
7.	Larkhall Athletic	18	4	2	12	21	50	-29	14	
8.	Maidenhead United	18	4	2	12	17	52	-35	14	
9.	Cheltenham Town	18	3	1	14	17	58	-41	10	
10.	St Nicholas	18	3	1	14	18	84	-66	10	

Basingstoke Town resigned from WPL South West 1 in Feb 2018 and all their results were expunged from the records. Plymouth Argyle were promoted to Tier 3 for 2018/19 after finishing top.

EASTERN REGIONAL LEAGUE PREMIER DIVISION (TIER 5)

Pos	Team	P	W	D	L	F	A	GD	Pts	
1.	Billericay Town	16	10	4	2	50	23	27	34	P
2.	Cambridge City	16	10	3	3	37	19	18	33	

3.	Acle United	16	10	1	5	42	24	18	31
4.	Bedford	16	8	3	5	31	19	12	27
5.	Royston Town	16	7	4	5	29	28	1	25
6.	AFC Dunstable	16	5	2	9	16	25	-9	17
7.	Brentwood Town	16	5	2	9	25	49	-24	17
8.	AFC Sudbury	16	3	4	9	24	33	-9	13
9.	Colney Heath	16	0	5	11	9	43	-34	5

EAST MIDLANDS REGIONAL LEAGUE PREMIER DIVISION (TIER 5)

Pos	Team	P	W	D	L	F	A	GD	Pts
1.	Nettleham	22	18	3	1	84	13	71	57 **P**
2.	Oughtibridge War Memorial	22	17	3	2	75	14	61	54
3.	Peterborough Northern Star	22	16	3	3	67	24	43	51
4.	Leicester City Women Dev.	22	14	3	5	80	34	46	45
5.	Loughborough Students	22	9	5	8	52	45	7	32
6.	Ollerton Town	22	11	2	9	56	30	26	26*
7.	Mansfield Town 2015	22	8	1	13	38	66	-28	25
8.	Kettering Town	22	7	2	13	30	46	-16	23
9.	Eastwood CFC	22	6	5	11	42	75	-33	23
10.	Mansfield Hosiery Mills	22	4	3	15	22	70	-48	15
11.	Rise Park	22	3	3	16	17	73	-56	12
12.	Arnold Town	22	2	1	19	20	93	-73	7

*Ollerton Town docked 9pts for failing to fulfil 3 fixtures.

LONDON & SOUTH EAST REGIONAL LEAGUE PREMIER DIVISION (TIER 5)

Pos	Team	P	W	D	L	F	A	GD	Pts
1.	Crawley Wasps	16	15	1	0	90	13	77	46 **P**
2.	AFC Phoenix	16	13	2	1	61	17	44	41
3.	London Kent Football United	16	10	2	4	42	34	8	32
4.	Parkwood Rangers	16	8	3	5	39	31	8	27
5.	Carshalton Athletic	16	6	4	6	40	32	8	22
6.	Aylesford	16	5	1	10	34	52	-18	15*
7.	Fulham FC Foundation	16	4	1	11	37	56	-19	13
8.	Eastbourne Town	16	3	2	11	15	42	-27	11
9.	Camden Town	0	0	0	0	0	0	0	0
10.	Watford Ladies Development	16	0	0	16	4	85	-81	-2*

*Aylesford docked 1pt for failing to play Eastbourne Town 22/04
*Watford Development docked 1pt for failing to play Aylesford 28/08 and 1pt for failing to play London Kent Football United 29/10
Camden Town withdrew from League and all results were expunged

NORTH EAST REGIONAL LEAGUE PREMIER DIVISION (TIER 5)

Pos	Team	P	W	D	L	F	A	GD	Pts
1.	Norton & Stockton Ancients	16	14	1	1	91	14	77	43 P
2.	Durham Cestria	16	13	1	2	83	12	71	40
3.	Hartlepool United	16	11	1	4	73	27	46	34
4.	Farsley Celtic	16	10	1	5	50	36	14	31
5.	Ryton & Crawcrook Albion Tynedale	16	7	0	9	44	51	-7	18*
6.	York City	16	6	1	9	45	36	9	16*
7.	Wallsend Boys' Club	16	5	1	10	38	85	-47	13*
8.	Castleford White Rose	16	2	0	14	26	93	-67	6
9.	Wakefield	16	0	2	14	18	114	-96	2

*Ryton & Crawcrook docked 3pts for failing to play Durham Cestria 20/05/18
*York City docked 3pts for failing to play Norton & Stockton 16/05/18
*Wallsend Boys' Club docked 3pts for failing to play Norton & Stockton 28/3/18

NORTH WEST REGIONAL LEAGUE PREMIER DIVISION (TIER 5)

Pos	Team	P	W	D	L	F	A	GD	Pts
1.	Burnley	24	20	1	3	81	11	70	61 P
2.	Stockport County	24	17	4	3	88	23	65	55
3.	Wigan Athletic	24	16	4	4	85	33	52	52
4.	Tranmere Rovers	24	15	5	4	66	42	24	50
5.	Merseyrail Bootle	24	11	5	8	66	43	23	38
6.	Fleetwood Town Wrens	24	10	5	9	57	47	10	35
7.	Manchester Stingers	24	9	5	10	50	62	-12	32
8.	MSB Woolton	24	8	5	11	43	69	-26	29
9.	Sir Tom Finney	24	9	3	12	45	66	-21	28*
10.	Accrington Sports & FC	24	6	6	12	35	75	-40	24
11.	Blackburn Community	24	4	5	15	32	60	-28	17
12.	Blackpool FC	24	3	2	19	22	76	-54	11
13	CMB	24	2	2	20	14	77	-63	8

*Sir Tom Finney docked 2pts for failing to play Tranmere 03/12/17

SOUTHERN REGIONAL LEAGUE PREMIER DIVISION (TIER 5)

Pos	Team	P	W	D	L	F	A	GD	Pts
1.	Chesham United	16	16	0	0	79	8	71	48 P
2.	Oxford City	16	13	0	3	69	17	52	39
3.	Winchester City Flyers	16	10	1	5	40	36	4	31
4.	New Milton Town	16	9	2	5	42	28	14	27*

5.	Newbury	16	6	3	7	21	31	-10	21
6.	Ascot United	16	6	1	9	33	37	-4	19
7.	Milton Keynes City	16	5	1	10	22	40	-18	14*
8.	Shanklin	16	3	0	13	10	50	-40	7*
9.	Team Solent	16	0	0	16	5	74	-69	-4*

*New Milton docked 1pt for failing to play Chesham 25/03 and 1pt for failing to play Oxford City 06/05
*Milton Keynes City docked 1pt for failing to play Winchester City Flyers 06/05 and 1pt for failing to play Oxford City 13/05
*Shanklin docked 2pts for failing to fulfil fixtures
*Team Solent docked 1pt for failing to play Shanklin 17/09, 1pt for failing to play MK City 08/10, 1pt for failing to play Shanklin 29/10 and 1pt for failing to play Newbury 11/02

SOUTH WEST REGIONAL LEAGUE PREMIER DIVISION (TIER 5)

Pos	Team	P	W	D	L	F	A	GD	Pts
1.	Buckland Athletic	22	22	0	0	94	10	84	66 P
2.	Marine Academy Plymouth	22	18	1	3	60	24	36	55
3.	Torquay United	22	14	4	4	45	13	32	46
4.	Exeter City	22	11	6	5	62	39	23	39
5.	Middlezoy	22	9	2	11	43	48	-5	29
6.	Forest Green Rovers	22	8	2	12	45	46	-1	26
7.	Ilminster Town	22	8	2	12	33	47	-14	26
8.	Bishops Lydeard	22	6	6	10	43	46	-3	24
9.	Keynsham Town Development	22	9	3	10	40	49	-9	22*
10.	Charlestown	22	4	7	11	19	35	-16	19
11.	Downend Flyers	22	3	1	18	14	69	-55	10
12.	AEK Boco	22	2	2	18	23	95	-72	8

*Keynsham Town Development docked 8pts for fielding ineligible players

WEST MIDLANDS REGIONAL LEAGUE PREMIER DIVISION (TIER 5)

Pos	Team	P	W	D	L	F	A	GD	Pts
1.	Bedworth United	20	18	1	1	105	14	91	55 P
2.	Leafield Athletic	20	17	3	0	81	22	59	54
3.	Stockingford AA Pavilion	20	14	2	4	64	26	38	44
4.	Crusaders	20	13	1	6	56	37	19	40
5.	Lye Town	20	9	1	10	40	43	-3	28
6.	Wolverhampton Sporting	20	9	0	11	49	50	-1	27
7.	Coundon Court	20	8	0	12	41	53	-12	24
8.	Kingshurst Sporting Club	20	7	0	13	50	29	21	21
9.	Knowle	20	6	2	12	22	63	-41	20
10.	Worcester United	20	1	2	17	9	56	-47	5
11.	Leamington Lions	20	1	2	17	8	132	-124	5

2017/18 TOP GOALSCORERS – LEAGUE GOALS ONLY

WSL 1 (TIER 1)

	Player	Club	Goals (Assists)
1.	Ellen White	Birmingham City	15 (2)
2.	Nikita Parris	Manchester City	11 (6)
3.	Beth England	Liverpool	10 (1)
4.	Remi Allen	Reading	9 (6)
5.	Isobel Christiansen	Manchester City	9 (3)
6.	Francesca Kirby	Chelsea	8 (6)
7.	Brooke Chaplen	Reading	8 (2)
8.	Beth Mead	Arsenal	8 (1)
9.	Fara Williams	Reading	7 (5)
10.	Jill Scott	Manchester City	7 (4)
11.	Lauren Hemp	Bristol City	7 (0)

WSL 2 (TIER 2)

	Player	Club	Goals
1.	Jessica Sigsworth	Doncaster Rovers Belles	15
2.	Melissa Johnson	Sheffield FC	12
=3.	Kirsty Hanson	Doncaster Rovers Belles	11
=3.	Beth Hepple	Durham	11
5.	Charlotte Devlin	Millwall Lionesses	9
=6.	Bianca Baptiste	Tottenham Hotspur	8
=6.	Zoe Ness	Durham	8
=6.	Rebecca Rayner	Doncaster Rovers Belles	8
=6.	Ini Umotong	Brighton & Hove Albion	8
=6	Aileen Whelan	Brighton & Hove Albion	8
=6.	Katie Wilkinson	London Bees	8

WPL NORTHERN (TIER 3)

	Player	Club	Goals
1.	Rosie Axten	Leicester City Women	22
2.	Emily Scarr	Middlesbrough	20
3.	Hannah Keryakoplis	Stoke City	17
4.	Natasha Flint	Blackburn Rovers/Fylde	16
5.	Emily Heckler	Huddersfield Town/Guiseley Vixens	15
=6.	Leigh Dugmore	Leicester City Women	13
=6.	Saffron Jordan	Blackburn Rovers	13
8.	Ashleigh Hayes	Stoke City	12
=9.	Nikki Berko	Guiseley Vixens	11

=9.	Hannah Campbell	Huddersfield Town/Bradford City	11
=9.	Laura Elford	Bradford City	11

WPL SOUTHERN (TIER 3)

	Player	Club	Goals
1.	Kit Graham	Charlton Athletic	32*
2.	Gemma Bryan	Crystal Palace	31
3.	Charlotte Gurr	Charlton Athletic	24
4.	Cori Williams	Cardiff City Ladies	18
5.	Angela Addison	C&K Basildon	17
=6.	Marie Gauntlett	Coventry United	14
=6.	Alison Hall	Coventry United	14
=8.	Samantha Quayle	Portsmouth	12
=8.	Kelly Wealthall	West Ham United	12
=10.	Charley Wilson-Blakeley	Chichester City	11
=10.	Ellie Zoepfl	West Ham United	11

*Does not include 1 goal in WPL national play-off final

WPL NORTHERN 1 (TIER 4)

	Player	Club	Goals
=1.	Jodie Redgrave	Brighouse Town	19
=1.	Yasmine Swarbrick	Hull City/Morecambe	19
3.	Hope Knight	Hull City	17
4.	Nichole Goundry-Havery	Chester-le-Street Town	16
5.	Amy Hughes	Mossley Hill Athletic	14
6.	Charlotte Proud	Brighouse Town	13
=7.	Aimi Beresford	Brighouse Town	12
=7.	Safron Newhouse	Bolton Wanderers	12
=9.	Charlotte Higginson	Morecambe	11
=9.	Stephanie Ord	Newcastle United/Barnsley	11

WPL MIDLANDS 1 (TIER 4)

	Player	Club	Goals
1.	Jordan Atkin	Burton Albion	29
2.	Charlotte Fisher	Birmingham & West Midlands	22
3.	Charlotte Cooper	Loughborough Foxes	21
4.	Natalie Shaw	Sheffield United	19
5.	Taria Marsden	Sheffield United	18
6.	Emily Ridge	The New Saints	16
7.	Chloe Young	Loughborough Foxes	15

8.	Kimberley Bebbington	The New Saints	14
9.	Viki Adam	Long Eaton United	13
=10.	Beth Bailey	Radcliffe Olympic	11
=10.	Lois Jefferies	Solihull Moors	11

WPL SOUTH EAST 1 (TIER 4)

	Player	Club	Goals
1.	Alessandra Barreca	Actonians	24
2.	Natasha Thomas	Ipswich Town	20
3.	Sophie Le Marchand	Leyton Orient	16
4.	Zoe Cossey	Ipswich Town	15
=5.	Chelsea Garrett	Norwich City	13
=5.	Jess McKay	Luton Town	13
=7.	Caroline Bisson	AFC Wimbledon	11
=7.	Heather McDonnell	Milton Keynes Dons	11
=7.	Katie Stanley	AFC Wimbledon	11
=10.	Nicola Henman	Luton Town	10
=10.	Laura Mills	Cambridge United/MK Dons	10
=10.	Rebecca Sargeant	AFC Wimbledon	10
=10.	Carla Williams	Actonians	10

WPL SOUTH WEST 1 (TIER 4)

	Player	Club	Goals
1.	Natasha Knapman	Plymouth Argyle	40
2.	Kerry Bartlett	Keynsham Town	33
3.	Emma Pinner	Southampton Women	19
4.	Zoe Cunningham	Plymouth Argyle	14
5.	Justine Lorton	Keynsham Town	13
6.	Christine Vega Leandro	Keynsham Town	11
=7.	Libby O'Dell	Southampton Saints	10
=7.	Rhian Robbins	St Nicholas	10
=9.	Lizzie Barrett	Larkhall Athletic	9
=9.	Katie Middleton	Plymouth Argyle	9

CHAMPIONS LEAGUE 2017/18

Lyon were crowned European champions for the third year in a row following a remarkable period of extra-time in the final against German outfit Wolfsburg. Goalless at full-time, the match finished 4-1 after the additional 30 minutes. Pernille Harder's deflected shot put Wolfsburg ahead, but moments later they lost Alexandra Popp who was sent off for a second yellow card offence.

The defending champions immediately capitalised as they equalised through Amandine Henry. Shanice van de Sanden then set up two goals with crosses for Eugenie Le Sommer and Ada Hegerberg respectively before Camille Abily's low finish completed the scoring.

Lyon defender Lucy Bronze, who on leaving Manchester City last summer said she was doing so in order to win this trophy, became the first England player to do so since the competition became known as the Champions League ahead of the 2009/10 season.

Bronze had scored the only goal across two legs in the semi-finals as Lyon knocked out her former club Manchester City at the same stage for the second year in succession. Chelsea enjoyed their best season in Europe as they advanced beyond the Round of 32 for the first time before exiting to Wolfsburg in the semi-finals. It was the third year in a row that Wolfsburg had knocked them out.

PRELIMINARY STAGE

In the preliminary stage, 40 teams were split into 10 groups of 4. Each group has a host team. Most matches are played in the same stadium, where that isn't possible, they are played close by. The final group games kick-off at the same time and thus take place in different stadiums. Teams play the other teams in their group once. The 10 group winners and best runner-up advanced to the Round of 32 knock-out stage.

GROUP 1 - HOST TEAM: MARTVE (GEORGIA)

	P	W	D	L	F	A	Pts	
1.Gintra Universitetas (Lithuania)	3	3	0	0	13	1	9	Q
2.Konak Belediyespor (Turkey)	3	2	0	1	11	4	6	
3.Partizan Bardejov (Slovakia)	3	1	0	2	4	9	3	
4.Martve (Georgia)	3	0	0	3	0	14	0	

22 Aug	Konak Belediyespor	5-0	Martve	Tbilsi	350
22 Aug	Gintra Universitetas	4-0	Partizan Bardejov	Tbilsi	40
25 Aug	Gintra Universitetas	6-0	Martve	Tbilsi	72
25 Aug	Partizan Bardejov	1-5	Konak Belediyespor	Tbilsi	40
28 Aug	Konak Belediyespor	1-3	Gintra Universitetas	Tbilsi	44
28 Aug	Martve	0-3	Partizan Bardejov	Tbilsi	31

GROUP 2 – HOST TEAM: OLIMPIA CLUJ (ROMANIA)

	P	W	D	L	F	A	Pts	
1.Olimpia Cluj (Romania)	3	2	1	0	**5**	**1**	**7**	**Q**
2.Hibernian (Scotland)	3	1	2	0	7	2	5	
3.Zhytlobud-2 Kharkiv (Ukraine)	3	1	1	1	10	2	4	
4.Swansea City (Wales)	3	0	0	3	0	17	0	

22 Aug	Hibernian	5-0	Swansea City	Cluj	102
22 Aug	Olimpia Cluj	1-0	Zhytlobud-2	Cluj	350
25 Aug	Zhytlobud-2	1-1	Hibernian	Cluj	100
25 Aug	Olimpia Cluj	3-0	Swansea City	Cluj	350
28 Aug	Hibernian	1-1	Olimpia Cluj	Cluj	250
28 Aug	Swansea City	0-9	Zhytlobud-2	Cluj	60

GROUP 3 - HOST TEAM: PARNU (ESTONIA)

	P	W	D	L	F	A	Pts	
1.Ajax (Netherlands)	3	3	0	**0**	**11**	**1**	**9**	**Q**
2.Standard Liege (Belgium)	3	2	0	1	10	3	6	
3.Parnu (Estonia)	3	1	0	2	3	4	3	
4.Riga FS (Latvia)	3	0	0	3	0	16	0	

22 Aug	Ajax	6-0	Riga FS	Parnu	119
22 Aug	Standard Liege	2-0	Parnu	Parnu	630
25 Aug	Standard Liege	8-0	Riga FS	Parnu	120
25 Aug	Parnu	1-2	Ajax	Parnu	750
28 Aug	Ajax	3-0	Standard Liege	Vandra	250
28 Aug	Riga FS	0-2	Parnu	Parnu	353

GROUP 4 - HOST TEAM: LINFIELD (NORTHERN IRELAND)

	P	W	D	L	F	A	Pts	
1.Medyk Konin (Poland)	3	2	**1**	**0**	**6**	**2**	**7**	**Q**
2.Shelbourne (Rep. Ireland)	3	1	2	0	3	1	5	
3.PK-35 Vantaa (Finland)	3	1	1	1	2	2	4	
4.Linfield (N.Ireland)	3	0	0	3	2	8	0	

22 Aug	Medyk Konin	0-0	Shelbourne	Belfast	213
22 Aug	PK-35 Vantaa	1-0	Linfield	Belfast	252

25 Aug	Medyk Konin	4-1	Linfield	Belfast	102
25 Aug	Shelbourne	0-0	PK-35 Vantaa	Belfast	157
28 Aug	PK-35 Vantaa	1-2	Medyk Konin	Belfast	58
28 Aug	Linfield	1-3	Shelbourne	Belfast	281

GROUP 5 - HOST TEAM: APOLLON LIMASSOL (CYPRUS)

	P	W	D	L	F	A	Pts	
1.Apollon Limassol (Cyprus)	3	**3**	**0**	**0**	**14**	**1**	**9**	Q
2.Sturm Graz (Austria)	3	2	0	1	8	5	6	
3.NSA Sofia (Blugaria)	3	1	0	2	2	7	3	
4.Noroc Nimoreni (Moldova)	3	0	0	3	0	11	0	

22 Aug	Apollon Limassol	4-0	NSA Sofia	Nicosia	99
22 Aug	Sturm Graz	4-0	Noroc Nimoreni	Nicosia	20
25 Aug	NSA Sofia	1-3	Sturm Graz	Nicosia	25
25 Aug	Apollon Limassol	6-0	Noroc Nimoreni	Nicosia	110
28 Aug	Sturm Graz	1-4	Apollon Limassol	Nicosia	230
28 Aug	Noroc Nimoreni	0-1	NSA Sofia	Nicosia	5

GROUP 6 – OLIMPIJA LJUBLJANA: (SLOVENIA)

	P	W	D	L	F	A	Pts	
1.FC Minsk (Belarus)	**3**	**2**	**1**	**0**	**13**	**0**	**7**	Q
2.Zurich (Switzerland)	**3**	**2**	**1**	**0**	**7**	**1**	**6**	Q
3.Olimpija Ljubljana (Slovenia)	3	1	0	2	2	7	3	
4.Birkirkara (Malta)	3	0	0	3	0	14	0	

22 Aug	Zurich	2-1	O.Ljubljana	Ljubljana	250
22 Aug	FC Minsk	8-0	Birkirkara	Ljubljana	50
25 Aug	Zurich	5-0	Birkirkara	Ljubljana	100
25 Aug	O.Ljubljana	0-5	FC Minsk	Ljubljana	280
28 Aug	FC Minsk	0-0	Zurich	Ljubljana	50
28 Aug	Birkirkara	0-1	O.Ljubljana	Ljubljana	120

GROUP 7 - HOST TEAM: OSIJEK (CROATIA)

	P	W	D	L	F	A	Pts	
1.Stjarnan (Iceland)	**3**	**3**	**0**	**0**	**21**	**0**	**9**	Q
2.Osijek (Croatia)	3	2	0	1	11	1	6	
3.Ki Klaksvik (Faroe Islands)	3	1	0	2	6	14	3	

4.Istatov (Macedonia)		3	0	0	3	1	24	0	

22 Aug	Stjarnan	9-0	Ki Klaksvik	Osijek	43
22 Aug	Osijek	7-0	Istatov	Osijek	178
25 Aug	Stjarnan	11-0	Istatov	Osijek	39
25 Aug	Ki Klaksvik	0-4	Osijek	Osijek	350
28 Aug	Osijek	0-1	Stjarnan	Osijek	400
28 Aug	Istatov	1-6	Ki Klaksvik	Vinkovci	100

GROUP 8 - HOST TEAM: MTK HUNGARIA (HUNGARY)

	P	W	D	L	F	A	Pts	
1.BIIK Kazygurt (Kazakhstan)	3	3	0	0	6	1	9	**Q**
2.Sporting CP (Portugal)	3	2	0	1	7	3	6	
3.MTK Hungaria (Hungary)	3	1	0	2	2	5	3	
4.Hajvalia (Kosovo)	3	0	0	3	1	7	0	

22 Aug	BIIK Kazygurt	2-1	Sporting CP	Budapest	300
22 Aug	MTK Hungaria	2-0	Hajvalia	Budapest	250
25 Aug	BIIK Kazygurt	1-0	Hajvalia	Budapest	150
25 Aug	Sporting CP	2-0	MTK Hungaria	Budapest	500
28 Aug	MTK Hungaria	0-3	BIIK Kazygurt	Budapest	250
28 Aug	Hajvalia	1-4	Sporting CP	Budapest	150

GROUP 9 - HOST TEAM: BREZNICA PLJEVLJA (MONTENEGRO)

	P	W	D	L	F	A	Pts	
1.Avaldsnes (Norway)	3	3	0	0	10	3	9	Q
2.Sparak Subotica (Serbia)	3	2	0	1	13	3	6	
3.Breznica Pljevlja (Montenegro)	3	0	1	2	3	10	1	
4.Kiryat Gat (Israel)	3	0	1	2	5	15	1	

22 Aug	Spartak Subotica	7-1	Kiryat Gat	Niksic	70
22 Aug	Avaldsnes	2-1	Breznica Pljevlja	Podgorica	200
25 Aug	Kiryat Gat	2-6	Avaldsnes	Niksic	50
25 Aug	Spartak Subotica	6-0	Breznica Pljevlja	Podgorica	150
28 Aug	Avaldsnes	2-0	Spartak Subotica	Niksic	70
28 Aug	Breznica Pljevlja	2-2	Kiryat Gat	Podgorica	62

GROUP 10 - HOST TEAM: SFK 2000 (BOSNIA & HERZEGOVINA)

	P	W	D	L	F	A	Pts	
1.PAOK (Greece)	3	3	0	0	12	0	9	Q
2.Vllaznia (Albania)	3	2	0	1	3	1	6	

3.SFK 2000 (Bosnia & Herz.)	3	1	0	2	3	4	3
4.Bettembourg (Luxembourg)	3	0	0	3	0	13	0

22 Aug	PAOK	8-0	Bettembourg	Sarajevo	50
22 Aug	SFK 2000	0-1	Vllaznia	Sarajevo	350
25 Aug	SFK 2000	3-0	Bettembourg	Sarajevo	125
25 Aug	Vllaznia	0-1	PAOK	Sarajevo	32
28 Aug	PAOK	3-0	SFK 2000	Sarajevo	280
28 Aug	Bettembourg	0-2	Vllaznia	Sarajevo	50

ROUND OF 32

The 10 group winners from the preliminary stage and best runner-up were joined by 21 teams which qualified directly. They played over two legs with the winners advancing to the Round of 16.

5 Oct	Stjarnan (Iceland)	1-1	Rossiyanka (Russia)	Garoabaer	287
11 Oct	Rossiyanka (Russia)	0-4	Stjarnan (Iceland)	Khimki	162
Agg:	**Stjarnan won 5-1**				

4 Oct	Fiorentina (Italy)	2-1	Fortuna Hjorring (Denmark)	Florence	2,881
11 Oct	Fortuna Hjorring (Denmark)	0-0	Fiorentina (Italy)	Hjorring	1,024
Agg:	**Fiorentina won 2-1**				

4 Oct	Apollon Limassol (Cyprus)	0-1	Linkoping (Sweden)	Nicosia	100
11 Oct	Linkoping (Sweden)	3-0	Apollon Limassol (Cyprus)	Linkoping	1,402
Agg:	**Linkoping won 4-0**				

4 Oct	Montpellier (France)	0-1	Zvezda Perm (Russia)	Montpellier	1,600
11 Oct	Zvezda Perm (Russia)	0-2	Montpellier (France)	Moscow	300
Agg:	**Montpellier won 2-1**				

4 Oct	BIIK Kazygurt (Kazakhstan)	3-0	Glasgow City (Scotland)	Shymkent	1,500
12 Oct	Glasgow City (Scotland)	4-1	BIIK Kazygurt (Kazakhstan)	Glasgow	552
Agg:	**4-4: BIIK won on away goals**				

4 Oct	Gintra Universitetas (Lithuania)	1-1	Zurich (Switzerland)	Siauliai	1,500
11 Oct	Zurich (Switzerland)	1-2	Gintra Universitetas (Lithuania)	Zurich	2,520
Agg:	**Gintra won 3-2**				

4 Oct	Atletico Madrid (Spain)	0-3	Wolfsburg (Germany)	Majada-honda	823
11 Oct	Wolfsburg (Germany)	12-2	Atletico Madrid (Spain)	Wolfsburg	1,753

Agg: **Wolfsburg won 15-2**

4 Oct	Lillestrom (Norway)	0-0	Brondby (Denmark)	Lillestrom	820
11 Oct	Brondby (Denmark)	1-3	Lillestrom (Norway)	Brondby	1,336

Agg: **Lillestrom won 3-1**

4 Oct	Ajax (Netherlands)	1-0	Brescia (Italy)	Ouder-Amstel	1,700
11 Oct	Brescia (Italy)	2-0	Ajax (Netherlands)	Brescia	2,030

Agg: **Brescia won 2-1**

4 Oct	St Polten (Austria)	0-3	Manchester City (England)	St Polten	2,236
12 Oct	Manchester City (England)	3-0	St Polten (Austria)	Manchester	1,041

Agg: **Manchester City won 6-0**

4 Oct	Chelsea (England)	1-0	Bayern Munich (Germany)	Kingston	2,136
11 Oct	Bayern Munich (Germany)	2-1	Chelsea (England)	Munich	1,285

Agg: **2-2: Chelsea won on away goals**

4 Oct	FC Minsk (Belarus)	1-3	Slavia Prague (Czech Rep.)	Minsk	2000
11 Oct	Slavia Prague (Czech Rep.)	4-3	FC Minsk (Belarus)	Prague	1,535

Agg: **Slavia Prague won 7-4**

4 Oct	Medyk Konin (Poland)	0-5	Lyon (France)	Konin	1,200
11 Oct	Lyon (France)	9-0	Medyk Konin (Poland)	Decines-Charpieu	4,822

Agg: **Lyon win 14-0**

4 Oct	PAOK (Greece)	0-5	Sparta Prague (Czech Rep.)	Thessaloniki	810
11 Oct	Sparta Prague (Czech Rep.)	3-0	PAOK (Greece)	Prague	526

Agg: **PAOK won 8-0**

5 Oct	Olimpia Cluj (Romania)	0-1	Rosengard (Sweden)	Cluj	250
11 Oct	Rosengard (Sweden)	4-0	Olimpia Cluj (Romania)	Malmo	633

Agg: **Rosengard won 5-0**

4 Oct	Avaldsnes (Norway)	0-4	Barcelona (Spain)	Haugesund	4,528
11 Oct	Barcelona (Spain)	2-0	Avaldsnes (Norway)	Barcelona	957

Agg: **Barcelona won 6-0**

ROUND OF 16

8 Nov	Sparta Prague (Czech Rep.)	1-1	Linkoping (Sweden)	Prague	489
15 Nov	Linkoping (Sweden)	3-0	Sparta Prague (Czech Rep.)	Linkoping	701
Agg:	**Linkoping won 4-1**				

8 Nov	Gintra Universitetas (Lithuania)	0-6	Barcelona (Spain)	Siauliai	3,500
15 Nov	Barcelona (Spain)	3-0	Gintra Universitetas (Lithuania)	Barcelona	707
Agg:	**Barcelona won 9-0**				

8 Nov	Chelsea (England)	3-0	Rosengard (Sweden)	Kingston	1,861
15 Nov	Rosengard (Sweden)	0-1	Chelsea (England)	Malmo	1,358
Agg:	**Chelsea won 4-0**				

9 Nov	Lillestrom (Norway)	0-5	Man. City (England)	Lillestrom	1,225
16 Nov	Man. City (England)	2-1	Lillestrom (Norway)	Manchester	716
Agg:	**Man. City won 7-1**				

8 Nov	Brescia (Italy)	2-3	Montpellier (France)	Lumezzane	1,100
15 Nov	Montpellier (France)	6-0	Brescia (Italy)	Montpellier	1,263
Agg:	**Montpellier won 9-2**				

8 Nov	BIIK Kazygurt (Kazakhstan)	0-7	Lyon (France)	Shymkent	250
15 Nov	Lyon (France)	9-0	BIIK Kazygurt (Kazakhstan)	Decines-Charpieu	509
Agg:	**Lyon won 16-0**				

8 Nov	Fiorentina (Italy)	0-4	Wolfsburg (Germany)	Florence	2,369
15 Nov	Wolfsburg (Germany)	3-3	Fiorentina (Italy)	Wolfsburg	1,226
Agg:	**Wolfsburg won 7-3**				

9 Nov	Stjarnan (Iceland)	1-2	Slavia Prague (Czech Rep.)	Garoabaer	372
16 Nov	Slavia Prague (Czech Rep.)	0-0	Stjarnan (Iceland)	Prague	1,306
Agg:	**Slavia Prague won 2-1**				

QUARTER-FINALS

21 Mar	Montpellier (France)	0-2	Chelsea (England)	Montpellier	5,291
28 Mar	Chelsea (England)	3-1	Montpellier (France)	Kingston	3,050
Agg:	**Chelsea won 5-1**				

| 22 Mar | Wolfsburg (Germany) | 5-0 | Slavia Prague (Czech Rep.) | Wolfsburg | 1,326 |

| 28 Mar | Slavia Prague (Czech Rep.) | 1-1 | Wolfsburg (Germany) | Prague | 1,712 |
| Agg: | **Wolfsburg won 6-1** | | | | |

21 Mar	Manchester City (England)	2-0	Linkoping (Sweden)	Manchester	1,259
28 Mar	Linkoping (Sweden)	3-5	Manchester City (England)	Linkoping	1,903
Agg:	**Manchester City won 7-3**				

22 Mar	Lyon (France)	2-1	Barcelona (Spain)	Decines-Charpieu	15,104
28 Mar	Barcelona (Spain)	0-1	Lyon (France)	Barcelona	12,178
Agg:	**Lyon won 3-1**				

SEMI-FINALS

22 Apr	Chelsea (England)	1-3	Wolfsburg (Germany)	Kingston	3,329
29 Apr	Wolfsburg (Germany)	2-0	Chelsea (England)	Wolfsburg	3,813
Agg:	**Wolfsburg won 5-1**				

22 Apr	Manchester City (England)	0-0	Lyon (France)	Manchester	2,876
29 Apr	Lyon (France)	1-0	Manchester City (England)	Decines-Charpieu	20,837
Agg:	**Lyon won 1-0**				

FINAL

Valeriy Lobanovskiy Dynamo Stadium, Kiev;   **Thu 24 May**

Wolfsburg (Germany) 1-4 Lyon (France) (aet)   Attendance: 14,237

Pernille Harder 93   Amandine Henry 98, Eugenie Le Sommer 99

Ada Hegerberg 103, Camille Abily 116

Wolfsburg (4-4-2): Almuth Schult; Anna Blasse, Nilla Fischer, Lena Goessling, Noelle Maritz; Caroline Graham Hansen (sub Tessa Wullaert 46), Sara Bjork Gunnarsdottir (sub Joelle Wedemeyer 57), Alexandra Popp (sent off 96), Lara Dickenmann (sub Isabel Kerschowski 89); Ewa Pajor, Pernille Harder

Manager: Stephan Lerch

Lyon (4-4-2): Sarah Bouhaddi; Lucy Bronze, Griedge M'Bock Bathy, Wendie Renard, Selma Bacha (sub Delphine Cascarino 75); Dzsenifer Maroszan, Saki Kumagai (sub Shanice van de Sanden 95), Amandine Henry, Amel Majri; Ada Hegerberg, Eugenie Le Sommer (sub Camille Abily 114)

Manager: Reynald Pedros

Referee: Jana Adamkova (CZE)

THE SSE WOMEN'S FA CUP 2017/18

Chelsea lifted the FA Cup for the second time as they won a London derby against Arsenal 3-1 in front of a competition-record crowd of 45,423 at Wembley. The game burst into life early in the second half thanks to two fine goals by Chelsea's Ramona Bachmann.

Dutch international Vivianne Miedema gave Arsenal hope when she reduced the arrears with a low finish, but Fran Kirby's curling effort put the Blues back in control. It proved to be the first leg of a second domestic Double for Chelsea who would also go on to claim the WSL 1 title in May. The competition had got under way back in early September 2017 with a 1st Qualifying Round. In total, the FA accepted 276 entrants into the 2017/18 Women's FA Cup. The women's FA Cup has been sponsored by energy firm SSE since 2015.

In the tables below the tier the team plays its League football in is given in parentheses. Attendances are provided in the final column where known. (aet) denotes after extra-time. (4-2p) denotes 4-2 on penalties after extra-time. Hw/o denotes home walkover Aw/o denotes away walkover

FIRST QUALIFYING ROUND; 3RD SEP 2017

The 1st Qualifying Round consisted of 174 teams competing across 87 ties

Alnwick Town Juniors (7)	3-2	Washington (7)	53
Blyth Town Lions (6)	0-3	South Shields (6)	
RACA Tynedale (5)	Aw/o	Norton & Stockton Ancients (5)	
Penrith (6)	4-2	South Park Rangers (7)	
Workington Reds (6)	1-2	Redcar Town (7)	
Prudhoe Town (6) **A-A**	2-5 (aet)	Chester-le-Street SCFC (7)	
Bishop Auckland (7)	4-2	Gateshead Leam Rangers (7)	
Carlisle United (6)	3-1	Wallsend Boys Club (5)	48
Sheffield Wednesday (6)	2-1	Yorkshire Amateur (7)	
Altofts (6)	Hw/o	Bradford Park Avenue (8)	
Malet Lambert (6)	4-5 (aet)	Wakefield (5)	
Ossett Albion (6)	0-5	Farsley Celtic (5)	
Dronfield Town (7) **A-A2**	0-5	Harworth Colliery (7)	
Nelson (8)	0-14	Blackpool (5)	
Merseyrail Bootle (5)	4-2	Stockport County (5)	
Wigan Athletic (5)	7-0	Accrington (5)	
FC United of Manchester (6)	13-1	Altrincham (6)	
West Didsbury & Chorlton (6)	3-2	Warrington Wolverines (6)	
Manchester Stingers (5)	2-1	Blackburn Community Sports Club (5)	
Fleetwood Town Wrens (5)	0-6	Burnley (5)	

Lincoln Moorlands Railway (6)	4-3	Cosby United (6)	
Loughborough Students (5)	4-2	Mansfield Town (5)	20
AFC Leicester (6)	0-2	Leicester City Women Development (5)	
Rise Park (5)	7-3	Teversal (6)	
Market Warsop (6)	0-5	Nettleham (5)	
Eastwood Ladies (5)	3-0	Arnold Town (5)	
Leafield Athletic (5)	5-1	Knowle (5)	39
Leek Town (6)	2-1	Solihull United (6)	68
Wyrley (6)	0-3	Lye Town (5)	
Redditch United (6)	2-1	Stockingford AA Pavilion (5)	
Shrewsbury Town (6)	4-2	Wolverhampton Sporting Community (5)	68
Solihull Sporting (6)	0-8	Coventry Sphinx (6)	
Crusaders (5)	6-2	Abbey Hulton United (7)	30
Shrewsbury Juniors (6)	0-3	Brereton Town (6)	
Coundon Court (5)	2-6	Goldenhill Wanderers (6)	42
Rugby Town (6)	1-4	Worcester United (5)	
Sutton Coldfield Town (6)	0-4	Bedworth United (5)	
Gornal (6)	Hw/o	Stone Dominoes (6)	
Newmarket Town (7)	4-2	Histon (6)	85
Kettering Town (5)	10-0	Woodford United (8)	35
Sprowston (7)	0-4	Wymondham Town (6)	
Roade (7)	0-1	St Ives Town (7)	
Oadby & Wigston (6)	1-3	King's Lynn Town (6)	
Peterborough Northern Star (5)	Hw/o	Netherton United (7)	
Cambridge City (5)	8-2	Moulton (7)	
Riverside (6)	2-1	Corby Town (6)	
March Town United (7)	0-5	Peterborough United (6)	80
Acle United (5)	4-1	Thrapston Town (6)	85
Colchester Town (5)	2-4	Bungay Town (7)	
Harlow Town (6)	4-0	Little Thurrock Dynamos (6)	
Brentwood Town (5)	6-0	Corringham Cosmos (7)	
AFC Sudbury (5)	4-3	Writtle (5)	
Billericay Town (5)	8-0	Chelmsford City (7)	
Milton Keynes City (5)	2-4 (aet)	Bedford (5)	50
Sandy (7)	Aw/o	Hemel Hempstead Town (6)	
AFC Dunstable (5)	5-0	Houghton Athletic (7)	
Royston Town (5)	7-0	Watford Ladies Development (5)	80
Hertford Town (6)	0-1	Bishop's Stortford (6)	
Garston (7)	1-4	Colney Heath (5)	
Brentford (7)	1-7	Chesham United (5)	25
Headington (7)	0-17	Ashford Town (Middx) (7)	

Ascot United (5)	1-1 (4-3p)	Newbury (5)	73
Benson Lionesses (6)	4-2	Wargrave (6)	
Fleet Town (6)	1-8	Alton (6)	
Oxford City (5) ^	Aw/o	Woodley United (6)	
Chinnor (7)	0-12	New London Lionesses (7)	
Queens Park Rangers Girls (6)	0-1	Hampton & Richmond Borough (7)	
Meridian (6)	2-1	Fulham Foundation (5)	
Ashford (6)	2-3 (aet)	Aylesford (5)	25
Kent Football United (6)	0-4	London Kent Football United (5)	30
Worthing (6)	1-2	Godalming Town (7)	
Eastbourne Town (5)	7-0	Dartford (7)	
Worthing Town (8)	1-7	Parkwood Rangers (5)	
Victoire (6)	2-2 (2-4p)	Burgess Hill Town (7)	
Whyteleafe (6)	1-0	Bexhill United (6)	
Abbey Rangers (8)	1-2	Eastbourne (6)	
Carshalton Athletic (5)	Aw/o	Herne Bay (6)^^	35
Frampton Rangers (7)	2-3	New Milton Town (5)	
Buckland Athletic (5)*	9-2	Exeter City (5)	
AEK Boco (5)	0-9	Downend Flyers (5)	
FC Chippenham (6)	4-3 (aet)	Team Solent (5)	
Middlezoy Rovers (5)	1-7	Marine Academy Plymouth (5)	20
Royal Wootton Bassett Town (6)	2-5	AFC Bournemouth (6)	
Warsash Wasps (6)	4-0	Ilminster Town (5)	54
Winchester City Flyers (5)	5-0	Frome Town (6)	
Bournemouth Sports (7)	3-1	Keynsham Town Development (5)	
Eastleigh (6)	0-6	Torquay United (5)	

*Played 10th September 2017   A-A = Prudhoe Town 2-5 (aet) Chester-le-Street SCFC abandoned after 116 minutes, result stands A-A2 = Dronfield Town 0-5 Harworth Colliery abandoned after 68 minutes, result stands   ^Oxford City beat Woodley United 9-0, but were disqualified for fielding an unregistered player   ^^Carshalton Athletic beat Herne Bay 3-0 but were later disqualified

SECOND QUALIFYING ROUND; 17TH SEP 2017

The 87 winners from the 1st Qualifying Round were joined by 11 teams exempted to this stage, making a total of 98 teams competing across 49 ties.

Alnwick Town Juniors (7)	1-0	Redcar Town (7)	57
Cramlington United (6)	1-7	Carlisle United (6)	
Bishop Auckland (7)	1-6	South Shields (6)	48
Chester-le-Street SCFC (7)	0-9	Hartlepool United (5)	
Norton & Stockton Ancients (5)	3-2 (aet)	Penrith (6)	150
Worksop Town (8)	3-5	Farsley Celtic (5)	
Altofts (6)	4-3 (aet)	Sheffield Wednesday (6)	
Wakefield (5)	4-3	Harworth Colliery (7)	

Blackpool (5)	2-2 (2-3p)	West Didsbury & Chorlton (6)	52
CMB Ladies (5)	2-1	Tranmere Rovers (5)	40
Burnley (5)	4-3	Merseyrail Bootle (5)	40
Manchester Stingers (5)	0-6	MSB Woolton (5)	
Wigan Athletic (5)	1-0	FC United of Manchester (6)	
Eastwood Ladies (5)	4-0	Rise Park (5)	
Loughborough Students (5)	6-3	Lincoln Moorlands Railway (6)	25
Leicester City Women Development (5)	2-3 (aet)	Nettleham (5)	45
Shrewsbury Town (6)	5-2	Leek Town (6)	
Redditch United (6)	5-1	Goldenhill Wanderers (6)	
Leafield Athletic (5)	1-2	Lye Town (5)	
Bedworth United (5)	2-0 (aet)	Gornal (6)	62
Worcester United (5)	2-8	Coventry Sphinx (6)	
Brereton Town (6)	2-1	Crusaders (5)	
Newmarket Town (7)	4-3 (aet)	King's Lynn Town (6)	
Acle United (5)	Hw/o	Riverside (6)	
Cambridge City (5)	5-2	Kettering Town (5)	
Peterborough Northern Star (5)	4-2	Peterborough United (6)	
Wymondham Town (6)	7-1	St Ives Town (7)	
Frontiers (7)	1-8	AFC Sudbury (5)	49
Harlow Town (6)	3-2	Bungay Town (7)	45
Brentwood Town (5)	2-3	Billericay Town (5)	
Colney Heath (5)	0-4	Royston Town (5)	
Hemel Hempstead Town (6)	0-12	Bedford (5)	
AFC Dunstable (5)	7-1	Bishop's Stortford (6)	
Benson Lionesses (6)	1-12	Ashford Town (Middx) (7)	
New London Lionesses (7)	2-0	Hampton & Richmond Borough (7)	
Ascot United (5)	0-2	Chesham United (5)	
Woodley United (6)+	2-1	Alton (6)	35
Eastbourne Town (5)	5-2	Aylesford (5)	
Godalming Town (7)	3-2 (aet)	Eastbourne (6)	
Meridian (6)	2-3	London Kent Football United (5)	20
Hassocks (6)	5-1	Margate (7)	
Herne Bay (6)	1-3	Parkwood Rangers (5)	32
Whyteleafe (6)	6-0	Burgess Hill Town (7)	
Marine Academy Plymouth (5)	Aw/o	Buckland Athletic (5)	
FC Chippenham (6)	2-1	Bournemouth Sports (7)	
New Milton Town (5)	5-4	Downend Flyers (5)	50
Pen Mill (7)	1-4	Forest Green Rovers (5)	76
Torquay United (5)	1-0	AFC Bournemouth (6)	
Winchester City Flyers (5)	5-1	Warsash Wasps (6)	

+Played 24th September

THIRD QUALIFYING ROUND; 8TH OCT 2017

This round consisted of 48 ties. The 49 winners from the 2nd Qualifying Round were joined by 47 teams from the WPL Division One level (the 4th tier of English football).

Alnwick Town Juniors (7)	5-0	Rotherham United (4)	82
Farsley Celtic (5)	Hw/o	Hartlepool United (5)^	
Burnley (5)	4-1	Wigan Athletic (5)	35
West Didsbury & Chorlton (6)_	6-3	MSB Woolton (5)	
Brighouse Town (4)	6-1	Wakefield (5)	104
Altofts (6)	1-5	Chorley (4)	
Chester-le-Street Town (4)	2-1	Barnsley (4)	
Crewe Alexandra (4)	1-4	Hull City (4)	32
South Shields (6)	0-3	Norton & Stockton Ancients (5)	
CMB Ladies (5)	2-5	Bolton Wanderers (4)	42
Liverpool Marshall Feds (4)	7-0	Mossley Hill Athletic (4)	
Steel City Wanderers (4)	2-1	Morecambe (4)	40
Sheffield United (4)	3-3 (3-2p)	Leeds United (4)	
Newcastle United (4)	9-1	Carlisle United (6)	84
Redditch United (6)	5-2	Solihull Moors (4)	
Sporting Khalsa (4)	6-1	Lye Town (5)	40
The New Saints (4)	3-1	Shrewsbury Town (6)	147
Eastwood Ladies (5)	5-3	Coventry Sphinx (6)	
Long Eaton United (4)	3-1	Leicester City Ladies (4)	
Bedworth United (5)	2-1	Birmingham & West Midlands (4)	53
Radcliffe Olympic (4)	Aw/o	Loughborough Foxes (4)	
Loughborough Students (5)	3-0	Brereton Town (6)	83
Burton Albion (4)	0-4	Nettleham (5)	30
Milton Keynes Dons (4)	2-0	Actonians (4)	76
Cambridge City (5)	1-5	Ipswich Town (4)	
Maidenhead United (4)	0-1	Luton Town (4)	
Cambridge United (4)	4-0	Norwich City (4)	48
Peterborough Northern Star (5)	1-3	Acle United (5)	
Harlow Town (6)	1-0	Denham United (4)	90
Wymondham Town (6)	9-2 (aet)	Newmarket Town (7)	175
Enfield Town (4)	1-0	AFC Sudbury (5)	
Godalming Town (7)	5-0	Haringey Borough (4)	
Ashford Town (Middx) (7)	6-4	London Kent Football United (5)	
AFC Dunstable (5)	2-0	Eastbourne Town (5)	49
New London Lionesses (7)	3-1 (aet)	Parkwood Rangers (5)	
Leyton Orient (4)	7-0	Billericay Town (5)	207
Hassocks (6)	0-8	Stevenage (4)	
Bedford (5)	2-3	Royston Town (5)	

Chesham United (5)	2-1	Whyteleafe (6)	
AFC Wimbledon (4)	14-1	Woodley United (6)	50
Cheltenham Town (4)	1-4	Southampton Saints (4)	
FC Chippenham (6)	1-6	Basingstoke Town (4)	
Poole Town (4)	2-5	Plymouth Argyle (4)	34
St Nicholas (4)	0-1	Keynsham Town (4)	55
New Milton Town (5)	1-4	Buckland Athletic (5)	60
Winchester City Flyers (5)	0-7	Southampton Women (4)	
Forest Green Rovers (5)	0-3	Larkhall Athletic (4)	
Brislington (4)	0-0 (4-2p)	Torquay United (5)	63

^Hartlepool United beat Farsley Celtic 3-1 but were disqualified for fielding ineligible player

FIRST ROUND; 12TH NOVEMBER 2017

The 24 matches that took place in the 1st Round proper consisted of the 48 winners from the 3rd Qualifying Round.

Alnwick Town Juniors (7)	0-4	Burnley (5)	
Liverpool Marshall Feds (4)	1-0 (aet)	Bolton Wanderers (4)	
Hull City (4)	4-1	Steel City Wanderers (4)	
Norton & Stockton Ancients (5)	0-4	Chorley (4)	70
Farsley Celtic (5)	6-4 (aet)	West Didsbury & Chorlton (6)	
Newcastle United (4)	3-0	Sheffield United (4)	
Brighouse Town (4)	6-1	Chester-le-Street Town (4)	43
Bedworth United (5)	0-2	The New Saints (4)	85
Redditch United (6)	2-4	Loughborough Foxes (4)	312
Nettleham (5)	3-0	Loughborough Students (5)	
Sporting Khalsa (4)	5-1	Eastwood Ladies (5)	
Cambridge United (4)	0-1	Long Eaton United (4)	85
Enfield Town (4)	3-2	Wymondham Town (6)	
Harlow Town (6)	2-1	Royston Town (5)	133
Stevenage (4)	4-1	Acle United (5)	25
Ipswich Town (4)	4-2 (aet)	Leyton Orient (4)	65
Ashford Town (Middx) (7)	0-6	Milton Keynes Dons (4)	55
Chesham United (5)	1-2 (aet)	New London Lionesses (7)	
AFC Wimbledon (4)	5-0	Godalming Town (7)	90
AFC Dunstable (5)	0-4	Luton Town (4)	102
Larkhall Athletic (4)	2-3	Southampton Women (4)	40
Buckland Athletic (5)	1-4	Brislington (4)	
Plymouth Argyle (4)	Hw/o	Basingstoke Town (4)	
Southampton Saints (4)	1-3	Keynsham Town (4)	

SECOND ROUND; 3RD DEC 2017

The 24 teams from the WPL North and WPL South (Tier 3 of English football) entered at this stage to join the 24 match winners from the 1st Round proper.

Middlesbrough (3)	8-1	Farsley Celtic (5)	
Sporting Khalsa (4)	2-2 (1-4p)	The New Saints (4)	45
Derby County (3)	1-1 (3-2p)	Hull City (4)	81
Huddersfield Town (3)	7-0	West Bromwich Albion (3)	79
Nettleham (5)	1-3	Liverpool Marshall Feds (4)	
Nottingham Forest (3)	0-2	Newcastle United (4)	76
Bradford City (3)	5-0	Long Eaton United (4)	
Blackburn Rovers (3)	4-1	Loughborough Foxes (4)	77
Fylde (3)	2-0	Guiseley Vixens (3)	43
Stoke City (3)	0-0 (1-4p)	Burnley (5)	108
Brighouse Town (4)^	6-3	Wolverhampton Wanderers (3)	123
Chorley (4)	0-3	Leicester City Women (3)	102
Keynsham Town (4)	2-1	Southampton Women (4)	
Milton Keynes Dons (4)	0-1	Cardiff City Ladies (3)	110
Lewes (3)	7-0	Enfield Town (4)	
Charlton Athletic (3)	5-0	QPR (3)	66
Gillingham (3)	1-3 (aet)	Plymouth Argyle (4)	
Brislington (4)	3-2 (aet)	Swindon Town (3)	67
AFC Wimbledon (4)	1-2	Portsmouth (3)	70
New London Lionesses (7)	0-3	Crystal Palace (3)	
Luton Town (4)	3-2 (aet)	Harlow Town (6)	51
Coventry United (3)	6-1	West Ham United (3)	
Chichester City (3)	4-2 (aet)	C&K Basildon (3)	120
Stevenage (4)	1-1 (0-3p)	Ipswich Town (4)	80

^Played 17th December

THIRD ROUND; 5TH FEB 2018

The 12 matches that took place at this stage consisted of the 24 match winners from the 2nd Round proper.

Cardiff City Ladies (3)	3-2	Burnley (5)	185
Fylde (3)	1-3	Plymouth Argyle (4)	58
Keynsham Town (4)	8-1	Brislington (4)	70
Huddersfield Town (3)	1-2	Lewes (3)	96
Leicester City Women (3)	2-1	Bradford City (3)	78
Newcastle United (4)	1-2	The New Saints (4)	115
Blackburn Rovers (3)	7-0	Portsmouth (3)	50est
Brighouse Town (4)	3-1	Derby County (3)	

Ipswich Town (4)	2-5 (aet)	Charlton Athletic (3)	110
Crystal Palace (3)	1-1 (2-3p)	Coventry United (3)	
Middlesbrough (3)	4-3 (aet)	Liverpool Marshall Feds (4)	
Chichester City (3)	2-0	Luton Town (4)	100

FOURTH ROUND; 4TH FEB 2018

The 20 teams from WSL 1 and WSL 2 (Tiers 1 and 2 of English football) entered at this stage to compete with the 12 winners from the 3rd Round proper across 16 ties.

Durham (2)	2-1	Sheffield FC (2)	
Aston Villa (2)	4-0	Middlesbrough (3)	
Sunderland (1)	13-0	Brighouse Town (4)	270est
Keynsham Town (4)	0-3	Lewes (3)	75
Tottenham Hotspur (2)	0-3	Doncaster Rovers Belles (2)	105
Liverpool (1)	5-0	Watford (2)	252
Cardiff City Ladies (3)	0-0 (5-4p)	Oxford United (2)	270
The New Saints (4)	1-1 (4-5p)	Chichester City (3)	
Millwall Lionesses (2)	4-1	Coventry United (3)	130
Reading (1)	0-1	Birmingham City (1)	488
Plymouth Argyle (4)**	2-3	Leicester City Women (3)	208
Brighton & Hove Albion (2)	0-2	Manchester City (1)	1,400
Blackburn Rovers (3)	2-3 (aet)	Charlton Athletic (3)	
Yeovil Town (1)	0-3	Arsenal (1)	
London Bees (2)	0-10	Chelsea (1)	486
Everton (1)	3-1	Bristol City (1)	712

**Played 11th February

FIFTH ROUND; 18TH FEB 2018

| **Arsenal (1)** | **1-0** | **Millwall Lionesses (2)** | 617 |
| Beth Mead 32 | | | |

| **Cardiff City Ladies (3)** | **1-3** | **Charlton Athletic (3)** | 295 |
| Cori Williams 75 | | Kit Graham 23, 29, Charlotte Gurr 32 | |

| **Lewes (3)** | **0-6** | **Everton (1)** | 975 |
| Amy Taylor 30, Georgia Bridges 58, Sarah Kempson 62 | | | |

| **Sunderland (1)** | **3-2** | **Aston Villa (2)** | |
| Victoria Williams 5, Rachel Pitman 79, Kiera Ramshaw 84 | | Ebony Salmon 24, 57 | |

405

Chichester City (3)	0-3	**Liverpool (1)**	1,300
		Rinsola Babajide 34, Ashley Hodson 39, Bethany England 47	

Birmingham City (1)	1-3 (aet)	**Manchester City (1)**	641
Ellen White 37		Nadia Nadim 13, Georgia Stanway 97, Claire Emslie 119	

Chelsea (1)	6-0	**Doncaster Rovers Belles (2)**	1,564
Ji So-Yun 12, Fran Kirby 49, Drew Spence 53, Erin Cuthbert 66, 88, Ramona Bachmann (pen) 79			

Durham (2)	5-2	**Leicester City Women (3)**	227
Zoe Ness 13, Ellie Christon 25, Abigail Cottam 43, 63, Emily Roberts 83		Leigh Dugmore 42, Sophie Domingo 45+2	

QUARTER-FINALS; 18TH MAR 2018

Sunderland (1)*	2-4 (aet)	**Manchester City (1)**	552
Victoria Williams 33, Lucy Staniforth 76		Demi Stokes 74, Jane Ross 90, 96, Ella Toone 114	

Liverpool (1)	0-3	**Chelsea (1)**	358
		Jonna Andersson 21, Katie Chapman 45, Maren Mjelde (pen) 58	

Arsenal (1)*	5-0	**Charlton Athletic (3)**	810
Kim Little (pen) 4, Heather O'Reilly 56, Vivianne Miedema 60, Danielle Carter, 85, Jordan Nobbs 89			

Durham (2)*	1-6	**Everton (1)**	502
Sarah Robson 67		Courtney Sweetman-Kirk 15, 55, 63, Olivia Chance 42, Danielle Turner 58, Jodie Brett 90	

*Played on 25th March

SEMI-FINALS; 15TH APR 2018

Everton (1)   **1-2**   **Arsenal (1)**   1,457

Chloe Kelly (pen) 67   Danielle Carter 25 Louise Quinn 90+1

Chelsea (1)   **2-0**   **Manchester City (1)**   3,048

Fran Kirby 5, 74

FINAL; 13TH MAY 2017

Wembley Stadium

Arsenal (1)   **1-3**   **Chelsea (1)**

Att: 45,423

Vivianne Miedema 73   Ramona Bachmann 48, 60
Fran Kirby 76

Arsenal (4-1-4-1): Sari van Veenendaal; Lisa Evans (sub Danielle Carter 85), Leah Williamson, Louise Quinn, Emma Mitchell (sub Katie McCabe 85); Dominique Janssen (sub Heather O'Reilly 63); Jordan Nobbs, Danielle van de Donk, Kim Little, Beth Mead; Vivianne Miedema

Manager: Joe Montemurro

Chelsea (3-4-1-2): Hedvig Lindahl; Millie Bright, Maren Mjelde, Magdalena Eriksson; Hannah Blundell, Ji So-Yun, Katie Chapman, Jonna Andersson (sub Maria Thorisdottir 70); Drew Spence (sub Erin Cuthbert 75); Ramona Bachmann (sub Eniola Aluko 85), Fran Kirby

Manager: Emma Hayes

Referee: Lindsey Robinson

WSL CONTINENTAL TYRES CUP 2017/18

The first silverware of the season was carried off by Arsenal as they won the Continental Cup for a record-extending fifth time, denying favourites and holders Manchester City in a tight final at Adams Park on 14th March. Netherlands international Vivianne Miedema scored the only goal after fine build-up play from England's Jordan Nobbs. Miedema's compatriot Dominique Janssen had earlier rattled the crossbar as the Gunners impressed. City's best chances fell to Nikita Parris and substitute Jane Ross after half-time, but they couldn't find an equaliser.

This competition is effectively the League Cup for England's elite teams and has been played since the creation of the WSL in 2011. It has been sponsored by Continental Tyres for all eight editions and its official title is the FA WSL Continental Tyres Cup.

Prior to 2017/18, the previous edition of the competition was played in the autumn of 2016 and was run entirely as a straight knockout. For 2017/18 it reverted to an opening group stage, as had been the format in previous seasons. Where group matches finished in a draw both teams were awarded one point, but a penalty shootout then took place to determine which side would collect a bonus point. Victories inside 90 minutes were worth the traditional three points. In the knockout stages drawn matches progressed to 30 minutes' extra-time before penalties.

GROUP 1 NORTH

11.10	Liverpool (WSL 1)	6-0	Sheffield FC (WSL 2)
	Caroline Weir 10, 29, Ellie Gilliatt (og) 52, Sophie Ingle 65, Alicia Johnson 83, Bethany England 90	Att: 352	
12.10	Durham (WSL 2)	0-0 (2-3p) Att: 641	Sunderland (WSL 1)
01.11	Sunderland (WSL 1)	3-1	Aston Villa (WSL 2)
	Lucy Staniforth 28, 57, Dominique Bruinenberg 78	Att: 228	Ashlee Brown 90+4
01.11	Sheffield FC (WSL 2)	5-1	Durham (WSL 2)
	Danielle Cox 2, Melissa Johnson 24, 29, 66, Holly Housley 36	Att: 122	Jordan Atkinson 26
05.11	Durham (WSL 2)	0-0 (4-5p) Att: 351	Liverpool (WSL 1)
05.11	Aston Villa (WSL 2)	2-2 (11-10p)	Sheffield FC (WSL 2)
	Kerri Welsh 39, Ebony Salmon 82	Att: 140	Holly Housley 16, Melissa Johnson 90+4

15.11	Liverpool (WSL 1)	5-1	Aston Villa (WSL 2)
	Ashley Hodson 17, Jessica Clarke 38, Alex Greenwood (pen) 48, Caroline Weir 85, Alicia Johnson 87	Att: 282	Chloe Jones 67
16.11	Sheffield FC (WSL 2)	1-1 (2-4p)	Sunderland (WSL 1)
	Rhema Lord-Mears 44, *Melissa Johnson missed penalty 73 (saved by Rachel Laws)*	Att: 203	Lucy Staniforth 33
03.12	Aston Villa (WSL 2)	3-2	Durham (WSL 2)
	Natasha Baptiste 29, Ebony Salmon 62, Elizabeta Ejupi 87	Att: 82	Jordan Atkinson 21, Zoe Ness 90
05.12	Sunderland (WSL 1)	1-0	Liverpool (WSL 1)
	Bridget Galloway 13	Att: 128	

FINAL STANDINGS – GROUP 1 NORTH

Team	P	W	WPens	LPens	L	F	A	GD	Pts	
1.Sunderland	4	2	2	0	0	5	2	+3	10	Qualify
2.Liverpool	4	2	1	0	1	11	2	+9	8	Qualify
3.Sheffield FC	4	1	0	2	1	8	10	-2	5	
4.Aston Villa	4	1	1	0	2	7	12	-5	5	
5.Durham	4	0	0	2	2	3	8	-5	2	

GROUP 2 NORTH

11.10	Birmingham City (WSL 1)	4-0	Oxford United (WSL 2)
	Freda Ayisi 38, Lucy Quinn 55, Hayley Ladd 69, Charlie Wellings 89	Att: 445	Hannah Short sent off 60
12.10	Doncaster R B (WSL 2)	0-3	Everton (WSL 1)
		Att: 482	Chloe Kelly 6, Leandra Little (og) 24, Marthe Munsterman 86
02.11	Everton (WSL 1)	1-0	Birmingham City (WSL 1)
	Courtney Sweetman-Kirk 12	Att: 181	
02.11	Oxford United (WSL 2)	0-6	Manchester City (WSL 1)
		Att: 777	Isobel Christiansen (pen) 44, Georgia Stanway 45, 53, Claire Emslie 57, Jennifer Beattie 79, 86
05.11	Birmingham City (WSL 1)	3-2	Doncaster Rovers Belles (WSL 2)
	Freda Ayisi 45+1, Charlie Wellings 58, Rachel Williams 75	Att: 682	Christie Murray 36, Kirsty Hanson 76
05.11	Manchester City (WSL 1)	2-1	Everton (WSL 1)
	Isobel Christiansen 25, Nikita Parris 80	Att: 875	Simone Magill 76
16.11	Everton (WSL 1)	4-0	Oxford United (WSL 2)

	Chloe Kelly 10, 81, (pen) 83, Claudia Walker 69		Att: 188	
03.12	Manchester City (WSL 1)	2-0		Birmingham City (WSL 1)
	Nikita Parris 18, Claire Emslie 36		Att: 1,077	
03.12	Oxford United (WSL 2)	1-5		Doncaster R B (WSL 2)
	Hannah Short 12		Att: 172	Rebecca Rayner 2, 4, Christie Murray 69, 87, Jessica Sigsworth 73
06.12	Doncaster R B (WSL 2)	2-3		Manchester City (WSL 1)
	Jessica Sigsworth 54, Christie Murray 77		Att: 924	Claire Emslie 4, Jane Ross 55, Georgia Stanway 55

FINAL STANDINGS – GROUP 2 NORTH

Team	P	W	WPens	LPens	L	F	A	GD	Pts	
1.Manchester City	4	4	0	0	0	13	3	+10	12	Qualify
2.Everton	4	3	0	0	1	9	2	+7	9	Qualify
3.Birmingham City	4	2	0	0	2	7	5	+2	6	
4.Doncaster R B	4	1	0	0	3	9	10	-1	3	
5.Oxford Utd	4	0	0	0	4	1	19	-18	0	

GROUP 1 SOUTH

12.10	Arsenal (WSL 1)	7-0		London Bees (WSL 2)
	Lisa Evans 24, Emma Mitchell 34, 37, Jodie Taylor 52, Beth Mead (pen) 58, (pen) 78, Louise Quinn 83		Att: 931	
13.10	Watford (WSL 2)	1-0		Millwall Lionesses (WSL 2)
	Adekite Fatuga-Dada 73		Att: 312	
01.11	Reading (WSL 1)	4-0		Watford (WSL 2)
	Fara Williams 5, Molly Bartrip 45, Kirsty Linnett 69, Merrick Will (og) 90		Att: 211	
01.11	Millwall Lionesses (WSL 2)	2-5		Arsenal (WSL 1)
	Ellie Mason 19, Ella Rutherford 69		Att: 451	Beth Mead 10, Jordan Nobbs 45, 75, Danielle Carter 78, Lauren James (pen) 89
05.11	London Bees (WSL 2)	3-4		Millwall Lionesses (WSL 2)
	Destiney Toussaint 2, 85, Jo Wilson 14, *(Paula Howells hit bar from pen 85 – Toussaint scored rebound)*		Att: 243	Rianna Dean 31, Ashlee Hincks 50, (pen) 73, Ellie Mason 60
05.11	Arsenal (WSL 1)	1-2		Reading (WSL 1)

| | Beth Mead 59 | | Att: 380 | Fara Williams 52, 56 |

| 15.11 | Reading (WSL 1) | 4-0 | London Bees (WSL 2) |
| | Kirsty Pearce 52, Brooke Chaplen 55, Rachel Rowe 75, Rachel Furness 89 | Att: 2,248 | |

| 16.11 | Watford (WSL 2) | 0-6 | Arsenal (WSL 1) |
| | | Att: 823 | Jodie Taylor 15, 78, Danielle Carter 47, Emma Mitchell 60, Dominique Janssen 74, Danielle van de Donk 75 |

| 03.12 | Millwall Lionesses (WSL 2) | 0-5 | Reading (WSL 1) |
| | | Att: 192 | Brooke Chaplen 38, 86, Rachel Furness 53, 66, Lauren Bruton 60 |

| 03.12 | London Bees (WSL 2) | 1-1 (5-4p) | Watford (WSL 2) |
| | Emma Beckett (pen) 83 | Att: 321 | Rinsola Babajide 45 |

FINAL STANDINGS – GROUP 1 SOUTH

Team	P	W	WPens	LPens	L	F	A	GD	Pts	
1.Reading	4	4	0	0	0	15	1	+14	12	Qualify
2.Arsenal	4	3	0	0	1	19	4	+15	9	Qualify
3.Watford	4	1	0	1	2	2	11	-9	4	
4.Millwall Lionesses	4	1	0	0	3	6	14	-8	3	
5.London Bees	4	0	1	0	3	4	16	-12	2	

GROUP 2 SOUTH

| 11.10 | Brighton & H A (WSL 2) | 4-2 | Yeovil Town (WSL 1) |
| | Felicity Gibbons 28, Ini Umotong 42, Kate Natkiel 44, 70 | Att: 167 | Paige Sawyer 90+1, Kayleigh Green 90+5 |

| 12.10 | Tottenham Hotspur (WSL 2) | 2-0 | Bristol City (WSL 1) |
| | Lauren Pickett 41, Bianca Baptiste 66 | Att: 215 | |

| 01.11 | Yeovil Town (WSL 1) | 1-2 | Tottenham Hotspur (WSL 2) |
| | Gemma Evans 35 | Att: 283 | Sarah Wiltshire 63, Ronnell Humes 90+2 |

| 01.11 | Brighton & H A (WSL 2) | 0-3 | Chelsea (WSL 1) |

Fran Kirby 13, Crystal Dunn 76, Ji So Yun 90+1

Att: 364

04.11	Bristol City (WSL 1)	1-2	Chelsea (WSL 1)
	Millie Turner 85	Att: 400	Eniola Aluko 47, Karen Carney (pen) 90
05.11	Tottenham Hotspur (WSL 2)	1-4	Brighton & H A (WSL 2)
	Bianca Baptiste 15	Att: 215	Lucy Somes 18, Fern Whelan 31, Ini Umotong 85, 90+1

| 15.11 | Yeovil Town (WSL 1) | 0-2 | Bristol City (WSL 1) |
| | | Att: 264 | Lauren Hemp 36, Yana Daniels 63 |

| 02.12 | Bristol City (WSL 1) | 3-0 | Brighton & H A (WSL 2) |
| | Danique Kerkdijk 31, Lauren Hemp 53, Yana Daniels 90 | Att: 224 | |

| 02.12 | Chelsea (WSL 1) | 8-0 | Yeovil Town (WSL 1) |
| | Crystal Dunn 5, Nicola Cousins (og) 19, Erin Cuthbert 45+4, 57, *Gemma Davison missed pen,* Drew Spence 45+13, 90+4, Fran Kirby (pen) 72, Gemma Davison 90+2 | Att: 1,289 | |

| 06.12 | Chelsea (WSL 1) | 4-1 | Tottenham Hotspur (WSL 2) |
| | Hannah Blundell 24, Fran Kirby 44, 56 Drew Spence 77 | Att: 1,541 | Lauren Pickett 64 |

FINAL STANDINGS – GROUP 2 SOUTH

Team	P	W	WPens	LPens	L	F	A	GD	Pts	
1.Chelsea	4	4	0	0	0	17	2	+15	12	Qualify
2.Bristol City	4	2	0	0	2	6	4	+2	6	**Qualify**
3.Brighton & H A	4	2	0	0	2	8	9	-1	6	
4.Tottenham H	4	2	0	0	2	6	9	-3	6	
5.Yeovil Town	4	0	0	0	4	3	16	-13	0	

QUARTER-FINALS

		1-1	
16.12	Everton (WSL 1)		Reading (WSL 1)
		(3-4p)	
	Chloe Kelly 111	Att: 155	Kirsty Linnett 94

17.12	Chelsea (WSL 1)	5-1	Liverpool (WSL 1)
	Fran Kirby 4, 24, 62, Ramona Bachmann 23, Erin Cuthbert 77	Att: 1,161	Casey Stoney 51
17.12	Bristol City (WSL 1)	0-2	Manchester City (WSL 1)
		Att: 352	Nikita Parris 60, Jennifer Beattie 87
17.12	Arsenal (WSL 1)	3-1	Sunderland (WSL 1)
	Jordan Nobbs 16, Vivianne Miedema 38, Beth Mead 77	Att: 400	Bridget Galloway 56

SEMI-FINALS

14.01	Chelsea (WSL 1)	0-1	Manchester City (WSL 1)
		Att: 2,595	Nadia Nadim 18
14.01	Reading (WSL 1)	2-3	Arsenal (WSL 1)
	Brooke Chaplen 7, Lauren Bruton 70	Att: 749	Beth Mead 5, Vivianne Miedema 8, Jordan Nobbs 83

FINAL

14 MARCH 2018

			Adams Park, Wycombe Wanderers FC
Arsenal (WSL 1)	**1-0**	**Man City (WSL 1)**	Att: 2,136

Vivianne Miedema 33

Arsenal (4-2-3-1): Sari van Veenendaal, Lisa Evans, Leah Williamson, Louise Quinn, Emma Mitchell, Dominique Janssen, Danielle van de Donk, Beth Mead (sub Heather O'Reilly 81), Jordan Nobbs, Kim Little (sub Katie McCabe 89), Vivianne Miedema (Danielle Carter 73)
Manager: Joe Montemurro

Manchester City (4-3-3): Ellie Roebuck, Demi Stokes, Jennifer Beattie, Steph Houghton, Abbie McManus, Kiera Walsh, Jill Scott (sub Melissa Lawley 81), Isobel Christiansen (Claire Emslie 61), Nikita Parris, Georgia Stanway, Nadia Nadim (Jane Ross 46)
Manager: Nick Cushing

Referee: Amy Fearn

413

WOMEN'S PREMIER LEAGUE CUP
2017/18

THE FA WOMEN'S **PREMIER LEAGUE CUP**

The WPL Cup (renamed WNL Cup for 2018/19) is the primary League Cup competition for teams in Tiers 3 and 4 of English football. It is a straight knockout competition with all ties played as one-off matches. It begins with the Determining Round. The teams who win at this stage continue in the Cup, while the losers drop into the Plate. Drawn matches go to extra-time and then penalties.

The 2017/18 WPL Cup final was contested by WPL Northern (Tier 3) rivals Blackburn Rovers and Leicester City Women. City took an early lead through Sophie Domingo before Lynda Shepherd equalised from the spot just after the half-hour mark. Ellie Cook gave Rovers the lead with about a quarter of an hour to play and a last-minute goal from Saffron Jordan clinched a 3-1 win.

A few weeks later Rovers went on to win the WPL Northern title, but they missed out on promotion to the newly-formed Championship when they lost to Charlton in the national play-off final. Leicester finished as runners-up in the League but were awarded a Championship licence for 2018/19.

DETERMINING ROUND: 3RD SEPTEMBER

Blackburn Rovers (N) — **3-0** — **Barnsley (N1)**
Saffron Jordan 45, 63, Faye McCoy 60
Att: 86

Bradford City (N) — **3-3 (aet)** / **(3-2p)** — **Fylde (N)**
Laura Elford (x2), Ellie Olds,
Ellie Olds sent off
Att: 81
Sophie Charlton 13, Veatriki Sarri 62, 90+5

C & K Basildon (S) — **8-0** — **Basingstoke Town (SW1)**
Angela Addison (x5), Jay Blackie (x3)
Att: 62

Cheltenham Town (SW1) — **1-2** — **Actonians (SE1)**
Louise Fensome
Att: 35
Jessica Byrne, Catherine Murphy

Chester-le-Street Town (N1) — **3-2** — **Hull City (N1)**
Laura Hockaday 49, Elisha Jones 60, Nichole Goundry-Havery 75
Att: 30
Ellie Tanser, Joanne Symington

Chichester City (S) — **4-1** — **West Ham United (S)**
Jess Lewry 13, 60, Cherelle Khassal 87, Chloe Tucker 90
Att: 70
Chloe Burr 77, *Charlotte Long sent off 65*

Chorley (N1)	**1-5**	**Leicester City Women (N)**
Laura Walker 12	Att: 66	Sophie Domingo 18, 26, Olivia Mitcham 32, Rosie Axten 81, Kimberley Farrow 83
Coventry United (S)	**16-1**	**Haringey Borough (SE1)**
Stephanie Smith 6, 58, 62, 82, Keeley Davies 7, Alison Hall 11, 44, Leah Seivwright 21, 25, Helen Dermody 45, 61, 65, 76, Jade Brook 49, Marie Gauntlett 69, 87	Att: 93	Jonea Peter
Crystal Palace (S)	**10-1**	**Brislington (SW1)**
Nikita Louise Whinnett 2, 21, Rosie Paye 5, 79, Gemma Bryan 11, 37, 52, Ciara Sherwood 42, 71, Ellie Bailes 47	Att: 203	Jodie Arkell 60
Derby County (N)	**7-0**	**Rotherham United (M1)**
Nicole Ledgister 13, Lisa Giampalma 15, Karagh Tait 44, Georgia Hewitt 53, Andrea Bell 55, 90, Leanne de Silva 63	Att: 63	
Enfield Town (SE1)	**3-2**	**Keynsham Town (SW1)**
Regan Coleman (x3)	Att: 23	Christina Vega Leandro 41, Katie Cook 70
Gillingham (S)	0-1	Stevenage (SE1)
	Att: 152	Nicole Emmings
Larkhall Athletic (SW1)	**1-8**	**Ipswich Town (SE1)**
Kate German	Att: 20	Victoria Campbell, Cassandra Craddock (x3), Jade Henry, Roxanne Small, Sophie Welton
Leicester City Ladies (M1)	0-5	Bolton Wanderers (N1)
	Att: 60	Michelle Kirkman-Ryan 22, 35, Safron Newhouse 51, 63, Rebecca Milner (og) 90
Lewes (S)	**3-1 (aet)**	**Southampton Saints (SW1)**
Amy Taylor 63, Leeta Rutherford 92, Danielle Lane 110	Att: 60	Sabrina Morriss-Manosalva
Long Eaton United (M1)	**1-2 (aet)**	**West Bromwich Albion (N)**
Eve Williams 39	Att: 65	Sophie Hull 65, Leanne Mitchell 118

Loughborough Foxes (M1)	**5-0**	**Sporting Khalsa (M1)**
Chloe Young 30, 80, Laura Steele 55, 75, Victoria Brackenbury 60	Att: 40	

Luton Town (SE1)	**2-4**	**Leyton Orient**
Nicola Henman, Jess McKay	Att: 59	Sophie Le Marchand 37, Belen Ripoll Douton 43, Ellie Davies 67, Ella Meadowcroft 87

Maidenhead United (SW1)	**0-1 (aet)**	**Poole Town (SW1)**
	Att: 53	Rachel Anderson 110

Middlesbrough (N)	**5-0**	**Burton Albion (M1)**
Emily Scarr 55, 78, 85, Jessica Havelock 59, Emma Kelly 75	Att: 84	

Milton Keynes Dons (SE1)	**0-1**	**AFC Wimbledon (SE1)**
	Att: 85	Katie Stanley 47

Morecambe (N1)	**1-3**	**Stoke City (N)**
Emma Kay	Att: 48	Hannah Keryakoplis 69, 81, Jamilla Palmer 52

Mossley Hill Athletic (N1)	**0-1**	**Brighouse Town (N1)**
	Att: 30	Aimi Beresford 9

Newcastle United (N1)	**0-3**	**Huddersfield Town (N)**
	Att: 69	Kate Mallin 5, 83, Hannah Campbell 86

Norwich City (SE1)	**0-5**	**Cardiff City (S)**
	Att: 72	Kelly Issac (x2), Cori Williams (x3)

QPR (S)	**0-3**	**Portsmouth (S)**
	Att: 50	Molly Clark, Natasha Stephens, Jade Widdowson

Sheffield United (M1)	**6-0**	**Birmingham & West Mids (M1)**
Millie Kenyon 9, Kimberley Brown 40, Natalie Shaw 64, 76, 90, Jenifer Pearson 81	Att: 43	

Solihull Moors (M1)	1-2 (aet)	Guiseley Vixens (N)
Carly Davies 112	Att: 40	Danica Roberts 107, Chantelle O'Hara 117

Southampton Women (SW1)	4-2	Denham United (SE1)
Laura Vokes (x2), Emma Pinner, Kellie Warren	Att: 34	Sophie Cheadle, Alissa Down

St Nicholas (SW1)	0-5	Cambridge United (SE1)
	Att: 40	Lauren Gibson, Amy Howlett, Emma Jenkins, Teonie Peyton (x2)

Steel City Wanderers (M1)	5-2 (aet)	Radcliffe Olympic (M1)
Claire Bratton 38, Lucy Ridley 42, Sarah Middleton 93, Zoe Beresford 101, Cheryl Mawhood 112	Att: 33	Ashleigh Evans 18, Ellie Readman 25

Swindon Town (S)	0-11	Charlton Athletic (S)
	Att: 41	Ellie Dorey 10, 17, 25, 85, Charlotte Lee 11, Charlotte Gurr 30, 49, 75, Charley Clifford 55, 63, Hope Nash 60

The New Saints (M1)	3-3 (aet) (5-4p)	Crewe Alexandra (N1)
Stephanie Taylor 19, Charlotte Canlett 30, Emily Ridge 106	Att: 54	Emma Lambourne 27, Laura Garner 36, Georgina Stebbings 110

Wolverhampton Wanderers (N)	0-2	Liverpool Marshall Feds (N1)
	Att: 45	Carla Lee 44, Chantelle Thompson 62

Nottingham Forest (N)	7-1	Leeds United (N1)
Kelly Darby 16, Amy Dicken 35, 48, Charlotte Griffin 46, Hazzana Parnell 50, Rebecca Kemp 70, Trina Greaves 79	Att: 94	Laura Porritt 59

PRELIMINARY ROUND: 24TH SEPTEMBER

Liverpool Marshall Feds (N1)	3-1	Steel City Wanderers (M1)
Sasha Rowe 28, Chantelle Thompson 36, Roisin Havelin 85	Att: 40	Lucy Ridley 53, *Claire Keats sent off 81*

Poole Town (SW1)	0-8	Crystal Palace (S)
	Att: 58	Gemma Bryan 18, 25, 30, 38, 45, Nikita Louise Whinnett 65, Ellie Stenning 80, Sandra Martin 89

Southampton Women (SW1)	2-0 (aet)	Actonians (SE1)
Own Goal 92, Jane Yeates 101	Att: 50	

The New Saints (M1)	2-5	Leicester City Women (N)
Kimberley Bebbington 58, Charlotte Canlett 61	Att: 55	Leigh Dugmore 16, Natalie Johnson 35, 72, Olivia Mitcham 52, Sophie Domingo 90

FIRST ROUND: 15TH OCTOBER

Charlton Athletic (S)	3-2	AFC Wimbledon (SE1)
Charlotte Lee 31, 61, Charlotte Gurr 90+8	Att: 88	Rebecca Sargeant 4, Katie Stanley 90+7

Crystal Palace (S)	1-2	Lewes (S)
Gemma Bryan 58	Att: 152	Amy Taylor 14, Avilla Bergin 32

Enfield Town (SE1)	0-2	Cambridge United (SE1)
Emma Thomas sent off 89	Att: 43	Laura Baker, Kelley Blanchflower

Sheffield United (M1)	1-2	Liverpool Marshall Feds (N1)
Own Goal 3	Att: 53	Laura Bartup 68, 87

Southampton Women (SW1)	1-3	Portsmouth (S)
Laura Vokes	Att: 108	Gemma Hillier 13, Shannon Albuery 24, Natasha Stephens 63

Stoke City (N)	2-2 (aet) (3-4p)	Blackburn Rovers (N)
Kate Asher 1, Emily Owen 67	Att: 130	Lydna Shepherd 58, Alexandra Taylor 78

Nottingham Forest (N)	5-0	West Bromwich Albion (N)
Nicola Emery 38, 90 Natasha Hudson 43, Trina Greaves 48, Samantha Conroy 71	Att: 124	

FIRST ROUND CONTINUED: 22ND OCTOBER

Derby County (N)	5-2 (aet)	Bradford City (N)
Sophia Bonser 90, Andrea Bell 90+6, 95, 104, Karagh Tait 116	Att: 106	Ellie Olds, Ellie White

Ipswich Town (SE1)	Aw/o	C&K Basildon (S) *
Zoe Cossey	Att: 46	

Loughborough Foxes (M1)	2-0	Middlesbrough (N)
Lindsey Tugby 20, Charlotte Cooper 43	Att: 60	

Stevenage (SE1)	0-2	Coventry United (S)
	Att: 45	Alison Hall 11, Helen Dermody 55

*Ipswich Town won 1-0 (Zoe Cossey) but were later disqualified for fielding an ineligible player. C&K Basildon handed walkover to 2nd Round.

FIRST ROUND CONTINUED: 29TH OCTOBER

Brighouse Town (N1)	5-1	Chester-le-Street Town (N1)
Jodie Redgrave 11, 50, 70, Aimi Beresford 36, Charlotte Proud 80	Att: 65	*Kimberley Wild sent off 39,* Nichole Goundry-Havery 76

Cardiff City (S)	3-1	Leyton Orient (SE1)
Ella Powell, Cori Williams (x2)	Att: 85	Leyre Bastyr 85

Guiseley Vixens (N)	3-2	Huddersfield Town (N)
Ebony Njie 67, Nikki Berko 72, Emily Scott 90	Att: 75	Katie Nutter 40, Sarah Danby 56

Leicester City Women (N)	3-0	Bolton Wanderers (N1)
Rosie Axten 9, 89, Olivia Mitcham 75	Att: 78	

Plymouth Argyle (SW1)	3-1	Chichester City (S)
Natasha Knapman 38, 65, Tori Marks 60	Att: 63	Jade Widdows

SECOND ROUND: 17TH DECEMBER

Cardiff City (S)	1-2	Plymouth Argyle (SW1)
Cori Williams	Att: 50	Rebecca Atkins 20, Natasha Knapman 68

Leicester City Women (N)	3-1	Loughborough Foxes (M1)
Sophie Domingo 16, Paige Stewart 59, Rosie Axten 79	Att: 95	Rebecca Knight 57

SECOND ROUND CONTINUED: 14TH JANUARY

C&K Basildon (S)	1-2 (aet)	Charlton Athletic (S)
Angela Addison	Att: 147	Charlotte Gurr 53, Kit Graham 111

Lewes (S)	5-1	Portsmouth (S)
Eilidh Currie (og) 19, Katie McIntyre 30, Sarah Kempson 31, Victoria Carleton 59, Georgia Bridges 83	Att: 196	Rachel Panting 57

Liverpool Marshall Feds (N1)	1-2	**Blackburn Rovers (N)**
Carla Lee 16	Att: 110	Kaylea Cunliffe 5, Alexandra Taylor 73

Nottingham Forest (N)	5-0	**Guiseley Vixens (N)**
Nicola Emery 8, 48, Charlotte Griffin 52, 66, Summer Holmes 63	Att: 73	

SECOND ROUND CONTINUED: 28TH JANUARY

Brighouse Town (N1)	3-2	**Derby County (N)**
Jodie Redgrave 47, 90, Aimi Beresford 87	Att: 92	Karagh Tait 25, Hannah Ward 30

Cambridge United (SE1)	0-5	**Coventry United (S)**
	Att: 70	Alison Hall 9, Jade Brook 50, 80, Natalie Haigh 59, Jessica Lundie 90

QUARTER-FINALS: 11TH FEBRUARY

Charlton Athletic (S)	1-2 (aet)	**Lewes (S)**
Kit Graham 38	Att: 242	Sarah Kempson 21, 110

QUARTER-FINALS CONTINUED: 18TH FEBRUARY

Brighouse Town (N1)	1-2	**Blackburn Rovers (N)**
Laura Doyle 83	Att: 107	Natasha Fenton 27, Ria Montgomery 88

Quarter-finals Continued: 25th February

Nottingham Forest (N)	(aet) (4-5p)	**Leicester City Women (N)**
Natasha Hudson 55	Att: 145	Ellie May 34

Plymouth Argyle (SW1)	0-3	Coventry United (S)
	Att: 55	Nikki Miles 18, 70, Amber Hughes 58

SEMI-FINALS: 11TH MARCH

Leicester City Women (N)	4-2	**Lewes (S)**
Leigh Dugmore 12, Holly Morgan 16, Sophie Domingo 46, 52	Att: 148	Amy Taylor 10, Sarah Kempson 90+4

SEMI-FINALS: 25TH MARCH

Blackburn Rovers (N)	2-2 (aet) (3-2p)	**Coventry United (S)**
Saffron Jordan 69, 90+1	Att: 197	Keeley Davies 41, Helen Dermody 50

FINAL: 29TH APRIL

Blackburn Rovers (N)   3-1   **Leicester City Women (N)**

Proact Stadium,
Chesterfield FC

Lynda Shepherd (pen) 33, Ellie Cook 74,   Sophie Domingo 14
Saffron Jordan 90

Att: 466

Blackburn Rovers: Danielle Hill, Chelsey Jukes, Lynda Shepherd, Alexandra Taylor, Kelsey Pearson, Jess Holbrook, Natasha Fenton, Saffron Jordan, Kayleigh McDonald, Ellie Cook, Kaylea Cunliffe (Hannah Walsh 68)

Manager: Gemma Donnelly

Leicester City Women: Charlotte Clarke, Ria Acton (Rachel Brown 79), Holly Morgan, Charlotte Greengrass, Hayley James, Nat Johnson (Paige Crossman 79), Nicole Nymoen (Ellie May 58), Paige Stewart, Leigh Dugmore, Sophie Domingo, Rosie Axten

Manager: Jonathan Morgan

Referee: Amy Fearn

WPL PLATE 2017/18

West Ham United of WPL Southern (Tier 3) won their first national Cup final as they saw off Luton Town from a division below. The Hammers had initially been expecting to play Fylde in the final, but the WPL Northern outfit were disqualified for fielding an ineligible player against Luton in the semi-finals, so Luton took their place. A brace from Ellie Zoepfl as well as goals from Amber Stobbs, Kelly Wealthall and Rosie Kmita saw the Hammers prevail as comfortable 5-0 winners.

The WPL Plate (renamed WNL Plate for 2018/19) is a secondary League Cup competition for teams in Tiers 3 and 4 of English football. The primary competition – the WPL Cup (now WNL Cup) – begins with a Determining Round. The winners of those one-off ties continue to compete in the Cup, but the losers drop into the Plate.

PRELIMINARY ROUND: 24TH SEPTEMBER

Chorley (N1)	2-1	Rotherham United (M1)
Madeline Cullin 30, Laura Walker 76	Att: 72	Catherine McDuff Viau

St Nicholas (SW1)	2-2 (aet) (4-2p)	Basingstoke Town (SW1)
Rhian Robbins 14, Kirsten Rendall 90+2	Att: 50	Helen Ogle 61, 72

Hull City (N1)	Hw/o	Leicester City Ladies (M1)

FIRST ROUND: 15TH OCTOBER

Norwich City (SE1)	5-0	Haringey Borough (SE1)
Natasha Snelling 13, Charlotte Broad 30, Aimee Durrant 56, 85, Laura Thacker 90+4	Att: 40	*Naomi Graham sent off*

FIRST ROUND CONTINUED: 22ND OCTOBER

Keynsham Town (SW1)	4-0	St Nicholas (SW1)
Katie Cook 6, 86, Carly Bryant 31, Asia Brown 81	Att: 45	

Barnsley (N1)	1-3	Chorley (N1)
Amy Woodruff	Att: 65	Laura Walker 52, 69, Megan Searson 88

Birmingham & West Mids (M1)	3-1	Sporting Khalsa (M1)
Charlotte Fisher 21, 72, 88	Att: 30	Lyndsey Glover

Cheltenham Town (SW1) 2-4 **Brislington (SW1)**

Jennifer Brown Wealls, Eleanor Marie Briscoe | Att: 63 | Jodie Arkell 8, 65, Chelsea Heal 29, Kim Maggs 34

Gillingham (S) 3-4 (aet) **Luton Town (SE1)**

Danielle Farmer 70, Kylie Manktelow 107, 110 | Att: 73 | Nicola Henman (x3), Jess McKay

Leeds United (N1) 3-2 **Solihull Moors (M1)**

Shelbey Morris, Rachel Stuart (x2) | Att: 79 | Tanya Dickinson 18, Abbie Taylor 80

Milton Keynes Dons (SE1) 2-0 **Denham United (SE1)**

Amelia Hazard, Kerry Newman | Att: 85

Southampton Saints (SW1) 3-0 **Larkhall Athletic (SW1)**

Nicole Matthews 34, Alisha Buckingham 41, Libby O'Dell 78 | Att: 15

Swindon Town (S) 7-1 **Maidenhead United (SW1)**

Annie Martin 36, 49, 90+2, Mia Mugford 44, 59, Emily Arrell 62, Natalie Jo Goodright 65 | Att: 47 | Lucy Casey 57

West Ham United (S) 3-1 **QPR (S)**

Chloe Burr 17, Amber Stobbs 44, Chenise Austin 56 | Att: 1,052 | Katie Knell 48

Wolverhampton Wanderers (N) 1-2 (aet) **Long Eaton United (M1)**

Billie Haynes 40 | Att: 50 | Viki Adam 35, Jade Arber 95

FIRST ROUND CONTINUED: 29TH OCTOBER

Fylde (N) 3-2 **Burton Albion (M1)**

Sophie Charlton 7, Lauren Davies 30, Hollie Kelsh 75 | Att: 53 | Own Goal 9, Sophie Cordon 50

Morecambe (N1) 1-5 **Hull City (N1)**

Melissa Brown | Att: 35 | Rachael Ackroyd, Katie Thompson (x2), Liverty Bott, Hope Knight, *Amy Halloran sent off*

Mossley Hill Athletic (N1) 2-3 **Crewe Alexandra (N1)**

Eve Davenport 55, Jodie Mortimer 73 | Att: 35 | Bethany Grice 8, Leanne Derry 19, Amanda Fallon 75

Newcastle United (N1)	2-0	Radcliffe Olympic (M1)
Stephanie Ord (x2)	Att: 30	

SECOND ROUND: 10TH DECEMBER

Hull City (N1)	1-0	Newcastle United (N1)
Rachael Ackroyd	Att: 20	

SECOND ROUND CONTINUED: 17TH DECEMBER

Birmingham & West Mids (M1)	3-1	Crewe Alexandra (N1)
Amy Eastwood, Charlotte Fisher, Harriet Shaw Roberts	Att: 25	Meg Booth 55

Long Eaton United (M1)	0-2	Chorley (N1)
	Att:44	Rachel Wood 24, Scarlett Smith 62

SECOND ROUND CONTINUED: 7TH JANUARY

Norwich City (SE1)	2-4	Milton Keynes Dons (SE1)
Chelsea Garrett 42, Jodie Drake 49	Att: 35	Amelia Hazard, Heather McDonnell, Sasha Newsome, Charly Wright

SECOND ROUND CONTINUED: 14TH JANUARY

Brislington (SW1)	0-6	West Ham United (S)
	Att: 63	Rosie Kmita 10, 26, 89, Molly Peters 60, Amber Stobbs 70, Kelly Wealthall 76

Fylde (N)	(aet) (4-3p) Att: 58	Leeds United (N1)

Luton Town (SE1)	3-1	Southampton Saints (SW1)
Natasha Fensome, Jess McKay (x2)	Att: 27	Krystal Whyte 60

Swindon Town (S)	1-10	Keynsham Town (SW1)
Emily Arrell 13	Att: 44	Justine Lorton 8, 45, Christina Vega Leandro 12, 82, Kerry Bartlett 20, 22, 24, 41, 43, Clarice White 62

QUARTER-FINALS: 11TH FEBRUARY

Birmingham & West Mids (M1)	1-5	Fylde (N)
Shannie Jennings	Att: 87	Sophie Charlton (x2), Olivia Fuller (x2), Laura Merrin

Hull City (N1)	4-0	Chorley (N1)
Joanne Symington, Hope Knight, Ellie Tanser, Rebecca Beech	Att: 60	

West Ham United (S)	7-0	Keynsham Town (SW1)
Kelly Wealthall 5, Leanne Mabey 18, 31, Amber Stobbs 34, 38, 79, Molly Peters 84	Att: 189	

QUARTER-FINALS CONTINUED: 25TH FEBRUARY

Luton Town (SE1)	3-2	Milton Keynes Dons (SE1)
Zara Carroll, Natasha Fensome, Nicola Henman	Att: 71	Vicky Holland, Alice Hughes

Semi-finals: 4th March

Hull City (N1)	0-3	West Ham United (S)
	Att: 80	Kelly Wealthall 60, 63, Andria Georgiou 73

SEMI-FINALS CONTINUED: 11TH MARCH

Luton Town (SE1)	1-2*	Fylde (N)
Nicola Henman	Att: 61	Olivia Wild 78, Alys Hinchcliffe 82

*FA expel Fylde from WPL Plate on 7th April due to fielding an ineligible player. Luton Town replace them in the final.

FINAL: 15TH APRIL

West Ham United (S)	5-0	Luton Town (SE1)
Amber Stobbs 25, Kelly Wealthall 29, Ellie Zoepfl 48, 73, Rosie Kmita 62	Keys Park, Hednesford Town FC Att: 262	Sophie Domingo 14

West Ham United: Cara Connaster, Chantelle Mackie (sub Chloe Burr 83), Hannah Wheeler, Chenise Austin, Jasmine Auguste, Leanne Mabey (sub Dayna Chong 66), Andria Georgiou, Amber Stobbs, Ellie Zoepfl, Kelly Wealthall, Rosie Kmita

Manager: Karen Ray

Luton Town: Kezia Hassall, Rachel Carter, Rachel Kosky, Lucy Webster, Erica Byron, Zara Carroll, Lisa Nixon, Nicola Henman, Dionne Manning, Jess McKay, Natasha Fensome

Manager: Nikki Baker

REGIONAL FA COUNTY CUP RESULTS 2017/18

Most of England's County FA's run a Cup competition for senior women's teams. The results for the 2017/18 competitions are listed here.

The Guernsey FA, Herefordshire FA, Huntingdonshire FA and Westmorland FA were not able to run a Cup competition for senior women's teams in 2017/18, in some cases this is because there were not enough teams in their geographical region.

BEDFORDSHIRE FA COUNTY CUP 2017/18

1st Round

15.10	Flitwick	0-4	Houghton Athletic
15.10	Shefford Town & Campton	0-6	Luton Town Development
15.10	Sharnbrook	5-1	Woburn & Wavendon (Lionesses) Blues
15.10	Bedford Development	1-3	Woburn & Wavendon (Lionesses) Clarets

Quarters

21.01	Houghton Athletic	P-P	Luton Town Development
21.01	Woburn & Wavendon (Lionesses) Clarets	P-P	Luton Town
21.01	AFC Dunstable	P-P	Sharnbrook
21.01	Bedford	H w/o	Sandy
28.01	Houghton Athletic	A-A	Luton Town Development
04.02	Houghton Athletic	1-0	Luton Town Development
28.01	Woburn & Wavendon (Lionesses) Clarets	0-17	Luton Town
28.01	AFC Dunstable	2-0	Sharnbrook

Semis

18.02	Bedford	4-0	Houghton Athletic
18.02	Luton Town	2-1	AFC Dunstable

Final

15.04	Bedford	3-1	Luton Town

BERKS & BUCKS FA SENIOR CUP 2017/18

1st Round

15.10	Newbury	0-1	Barton Rovers
15.10	Wargrave	3-1	Wokingham & Emmbrook
15.10	Wycombe Wanderers	4-1	Milton Keynes City
15.10	Ascot United	1-4	Woodley United

Quarters

19.11	Bye		Maidenhead United
19.11	Woodley United	3-0	Wycombe Wanderers
19.11	MK Dons	11-0	Wargrave
19.11	Barton Rovers	0-5	Chesham United

Semis

18.02	Chesham United	1-2	MK Dons
18.02	Maidenhead United	2-1	Woodley United
Final			
22.04	Maidenhead United	0-7	MK Dons

BIRMINGHAM FA COUNTY CUP 2017/18

1st Round

15.10	West Bromwich United	1-8	Kewford Eagles
15.10	Warwick	Aw/o	Walsall Phoenix
15.10	Birmingham Medsoc	1-2	Rubery Ravens
15.10	Alcester Town	Aw/o	Redditch Borough
15.10	Halas Hawks	Aw/o	Wolverhampton United
15.10	Alveston Open Age	Aw/o	Rugby Town
15.10	Coventry Development	Hw/o	Shipston Excelsior
15.10	Stourbridge	7-0	Sandwell
15.10	Solihull United	3-0	Coventrians
15.10	Leamington Hibernian	0-6	Coventry Sphinx
15.10	Redditch United	6-0	Solihull Sporting
15.10	Balls to Cancer	0-8	Gornal Open Age
15.10	Bilbrook	2-4	Starlands St Annes
22.10	Chelmsley Colts	1-5	St Johns

2nd Round

19.11	Starlands St Annes	4-5 (aet)	Wolverhampton United
19.11	St Johns	4-2	Rubery Ravens
19.11	Kewford Eagles	3-1	Redditch Borough
19.11	Rugby Town	9-1	Walsall Phoenix
19.11	Coventry Development	0-2	Coventry Sphinx
19.11	Stourbridge	0-2	Sutton Coldfield
19.11	Atherstone Rangers	4-1	Tamworth
19.11	Gornal Open Age	1-3	Solihull United
19.11	Redditch United	Hw/o	Solihull Moors
19.11	Bedworth United	2-4	Stockingford AA Pavilion
19.11	Coundon Court	1-7	Coventry United
19.11	Crusaders	1-3	West Bromwich Albion
19.11	Birmingham & West Midlands	9-0	Leafield Athletic
19.11	Leamington Lions	2-2	Knowle (Win 4-1 on pens)
19.11	Burton Albion	Hw/o	Kingshurst Sporting
05.12	Lye Town	1-8	Wolverhampton Wanderers

3rd Round

14.01	Wolverhampton United	8-2	Kewford Eagles
14.01	Coventry Sphinx	0-6	Birmingham & West Midlands
14.01	Wolverhampton Wanderers	5-0	Sutton Coldfield
14.01	Redditch United (Win 4-3 pens)	4-4	Rugby Town
14.01	Solihull United	1-2	West Bromwich Albion
14.01	Coventry United	12-0	Burton Albion

28.01	Atherstone Rangers (Win 4-3 pens)	6-6	Knowle
11.02	St Johns	Aw/o	Stockingford AA Pavilion

Quarters

18.02	Redditch United	7-2	Atherstone Rangers
18.02	Birmingham & West Midlands	Hw/o	Wolverhampton United
18.02	Wolverhampton Wanderers	1-3	Coventry United
18.02	West Bromwich Albion	9-1	Stockingford AA Pavilion

Semis

20.03	Birmingham & West Midlands	2-0	Redditch United
05.04	West Bromwich Albion	0-2	Coventry United

Final

03.05	Birmingham & West Midlands	0-15	Coventry United

CAMBRIDGESHIRE FA INVITATION CUP 2017/18

1st Round

20.01	Cambridge City	5-1	Peterborough ICA Sports
20.01	St Ives Town	4-1	Cambridge Rangers
20.01	Burwell Tigers	Aw/o	Wisbech St Mary
20.01	Fulbourn Institute Bluebirds	6-1	Park Ladies
20.01	Histon	4-2	Wisbech Town
20.01	Isleham United	1-6	March Town United

Quarters

18.02	Wisbech St Mary	0-12	Cambridge United
18.02	March Town United	0-2	St Ives Town
18.02	Cambridge City	7-0	Histon
25.02	Fulbourn Institute Bluebirds	0-3	Newmarket Town

Semis

18.03	Cambridge City	1-0	St Ives Town
18.03	Cambridge United	3-0	Newmarket Town

Final

10.05	Cambridge City	3-1	Cambridge United

CHESHIRE FA COUNTY CUP 2017/18

1st Round

19.11	Runcorn Linnets Open Age	6-1	Sandbach United
19.11	Chester FC	Hw/o	Manor Club JFC (Wallasey JFL) Torpedoes
19.11	Egerton	4-1	Sale United
19.11	West Kirby	6-0	Chester City
19.11	AFC Stockport	Hw/o	Macclesfield Town Angels

2nd **Round**

21.01	Egerton	2-1	Runcorn Linnets Open Age
28.01	Cammell Laird 1907 FC Open	9-1	AFC Stockport
28.01	West Kirby	1-5	Altrincham
28.01	Chester FC	5-0	Northwich Vixens
	Crewe Alexandra		Bye
	Stockport County		Bye

	Tranmere Rovers (Cheshire)		Bye
	Warrington Wolverines		Bye

Quarters

18.02	Stockport County	4-1	Warrington Wolverines
18.02	Altrincham	1-2	Crewe Alexandra
18.02	Cammell Laird 1907 FC Open	0-4	Tranmere Rovers (Cheshire)
18.02	Chester FC	2-1	Egerton

Semis

25.03	Crewe Alexandra	7-0	Chester FC
25.03	Stockport County	0-2	Tranmere Rovers (Cheshire)

Final

27.04	Crewe Alexandra	2-0	Tranmere Rovers (Cheshire)

CORNWALL FA COUNTY CUP 2017/18

1st Round

19.11	St Agnes	2-5	Helston Athletic
19.11	Mousehole	7-0	St Breward
19.11	St Teath	0-18	Callington Town
19.11	Charlestown	9-0	Newquay Celtic
19.11	Bude Town	4-0	Wadebridge Town
19.11	Illogan RBL	4-5 aet	Penryn

Quarters

25.02	Mousehole	6-0	Penryn
25.02	Bude Town	0-4	Calllington Town
25.02	Culdrose	Aw/o	Helston Athletic
25.02	Charlestown	11-0	Porthleven

Semis

18.03	Mousehole	1-11	Charlestown
18.03	Helston Athletic	3-7	Callington Town

Final

27.04	Callington Town (Won 6-4 pens)	4-4	Charlestown

CUMBERLAND FA COUNTY CUP 2017/18

1st Round

14.01	Seaton Juniors	10-1	Barrow Celtic

Quarters

18.02	Workington Reds	Hw/o	Seaton Juniors
18.02	Crown Newlaithes	9-0	Carlisle United Development
18.02	Vickerstown	0-4	Carlisle United
18.02	Penrith AFC	8-1	Penrith AFC Development

Semis

18.03	Workington Reds	1-2	Penrith AFC
05.04	Carlisle United	6-1	Crown Newlaithes

Final

11.05	Penrith AFC	0-1	Carlisle United

DERBYSHIRE FA COUNTY CUP 2017/18

1st Round

08.10	Derby Rovers	1-9	Belper Town	
08.10	Ilkeston Town	4-3	Buxton Juniors	
08.10	Mickleover Sports Club Juniors	2-1	Hasland Community	
08.10	Pride Park Juniors	10-0	Ashbourne	
08.10	Draycott Victoria	7-0	Hilton Harriers	
08.10	Chesterfield	4-0	Wirksworth Colts	
08.10	Matlock Town	0-5	GFC Alfreton Town	
15.10	Glossop North End AFC Juniors	1-4	Woodlands	

2nd **Round**

19.11	Woodlands	10-2	Belper Town
19.11	Ilkeston Town	0-2	Chesterfield FC
19.11	Mickleover Sports Club Juniors		Bye
19.11	Pride Park Juniors		Bye
19.11	Draycott Victoria		Bye
19.11	GFC Alfreton Town		Bye
19.11	Derby County Development		Bye
19.11	Long Eaton United		Bye

Quarters

28.01	Chesterfield FC	4-0	Mickleover Sports Club Juniors
28.01	Draycott Victoria	0-5	Derby County Development
28.01	GFC Alfreton Town	0-10	Woodlands
28.01	Long Eaton United	4-2	Pride Park Juniors

Semis

18.02	Long Eaton United	1-4	Woodlands
18.02	Chesterfield FC	0-4	Derby County Development

Final

22.04	Derby County Development	0-3	Woodlands

DEVON FA SENIOR CUP 2017/18

1st Round

15.10	Buckland Athletic	3-4 aet	Plymouth Argyle
15.10	Exeter City	Hw/o	Activate

Quarters

19.11	Exeter City	0-2	Torquay United
19.11	Marine Academy Plymouth	6-2	Bideford
19.11	Exeter & Tedburn Rangers	0-5	Plympton
26.11	Alphington	1-11	Plymouth Argyle

Semis

21.01	Plymouth Argyle	Hw/o	Marine Academy Plymouth
21.01	Torquay United	1-0	Plympton

Final

06.04	Plymouth Argyle	8-0	Torquay United

DORSET FA COUNTY CUP 2017/18

1st Round

19.11	Shaftesbury Town	1-3	Gillingham Town
19.11	Bridport Youth	Aw/o	Wool & Winfrith

Quarters

17.12	Gillingham Town	Aw/o	Dorchester Town
17.12	Blandford United Youth	1-2	Poole Town Reserves
17.12	Merley Cobham Sports Youth	Aw/o	Wareham Rangers
14.01	Wool & Winfrith	0-19	Poole Town

Semis

25.03	Poole Town Reserves	1-2	Dorchester Town
25.03	Wareham Rangers	1-12	Poole Town

Final

17.04	Dorchester Town	0-7	Poole Town

DURHAM FA COUNTY CUP 2017/18

Preliminary Round

19.11	Coxhoe United	3-6	Chester-le-Street SCFC
19.11	Chester-le-Street Waldridge Park (Won on pens)	1-1	Birtley Town
19.11	Chester-le-Street Amazons	1-4	Limley Ladies Pinks
19.11	South Shields Reserves	4-4	Lumley Ladies (Won 4-3 on pens)
19.11	Boldon CA Villa	3-0	Felling Magpies
19.11	Norton & Stockton Ancients	7-0	Washington Association
19.11	Hartlepool United Reserves (Won 4-3 on pens)	6-6	Gateshead Rutherford

1st Round

17.12	Chester-le-Street Waldridge Park	7-0	Washington Association Development
17.12	Lumley Ladies Pinks	0-2	Norton & Stockton Ancients Reserves
17.12	Chester-le-Street Town	3-1	South Shields
17.12	Gateshead Leam Rangers (Won 4-3 pens)	3-3	Bishop Auckland (DCWL)
17.12	Hartlepool United Reserves	1-7	Consett
17.12	Boldon CA Villa	0-7	Norton & Stockton Ancients
17.12	Darlington Spraire	3-1	Lumley
17.12	Chester-le-Street SCFC	0-8	Ryton & Crawcrook Albion Tynedale

2nd Round

21.01	Norton & Stockton Ancients Reserves	0-7	Chester-le-Street Town
21.01	Consett	8-0	Darlington Spraire
21.01	Ryton & Crawcrook Albion Tynedale	7-0	Gateshead Leam Rangers
21.01	Chester-le-Street Waldridge Park	0-15	Norton & Stockton Ancients

Semis

18.02	Chester-le-Street Town	7-0	Consett
18.02	Norton & Stockton Ancients	3-1	Ryton & Crawcrook Albion Tynedale

Final

03.05	Chester-le-Street Town	2-2 aet (4-5p)	Norton & Stockton Ancients

EAST RIDING FA COUNTY CUP 2017/18

1st Round

15.10	Mill Lane United	2-1	Hall Road Rangers
15.10	Bridlington Rovers	Aw/o	Malet Lambert YC
15.10	South Cave Sporting Club	2-6	AFC Preston
15.10	AFC Tickton	9-0	Hunmanby
15.10	East Yorkshire Carnegie	20-0	Hull University 1st
15.10	North Ferriby United Amateurs	1-3	Hull Kingston

Quarters

19.11	Mill Lane United	Aw/o	Hull City
19.11	AFC Tickton	1-4	East Yorkshire Carnegie
19.11	Hull Kingston	0-3	Malet Lambert YC
	AFC Preston		Bye

Semis

25.03	AFC Preston	4-2	Malet Lambert YC
25.03	Hull City	Hw/o	East Yorkshire Carnegie

Final

25.04	Hull City	w/o	AFC Preston **(AFC Preston awarded win)**

ESSEX FA COUNTY CUP 2017/18

Preliminary Round

10.09	Alresford Colne Rangers	0-7	Corringham Cosmos
10.09	Beacon Hill Rovers	3-9	Little Thurrock Dynamos

1st Round

17.09	Chelmsford City Reserves	Hw/o	Collier Row Athletic
17.09	Silver End United	1-5	Harlow Town
17.09	Corringham Cosmos	5-0	RayleighTown
17.09	Hutton	6-0	Collier Row Tigers
17.09	Chigwell	2-4	Frontiers
17.09	Lawford	10-0	Walden
17.09	Leigh Ramblers	Hw/o	Hullbridge Sports
17.09	Little Thurrock Dynamos	Hw/o	Wickford Town
17.09	Waltham Forest	Hw/o	Wickford Town Reserves
17.09	Hutton Reserves	1-2	Dagenham & Redbridge
17.09	Harlow Town Reserves	Hw/o	Eastern Avenue
17.09	Chelmsford City	5-2	Southend United Community Sports Club

2nd Round

15.10	Hutton	0-1	Little Thurrock Dynamos
15.10	Chelmsford City	0-9	Dagenham & Redbridge
15.10	Corringham Cosmos	8-0	Waltham Forest
15.10	Harlow Town	8-1	Harlow Town Reserves
15.10	Lawford	6-2	Leigh Ramblers
15.10	Chelmsford City	2-1	Frontiers

3rd Round

19.11	Little Thurrock Dynamos	3-0	Chelmsford City

432

19.11	Harlow Town	Hw/o	Lawford
19.11	Corringham Cosmos	6-1	Dagenham & Redbridge
Quarters			
21.01	Billericay Town	0-2	Brentwood Town
21.01	C&K Basildon	Hw/o	Colchester Town
21.01	Harlow Town	0-2	Writtle
21.01	Little Thurrock Dynamos	4-3	Corringham Cosmos
Semis			
18.02	Brentwood Town (Won 4-2pens)	2-2	Writtle
18.02	C&K Basildon	9-0	Little Thurrock Dynamos
Final			
29.03	Brentwood Town	0-7	C&K Basildon

GLOUCESTERSHIRE FA COUNTY CUP 2017/18

1st Round

15.10	St Nicholas	10-0	Bristol & West
15.10	Cheltenham Civil Service (Won 4-3 pens)	3-3 (aet)	Dursley Town
2nd Round			
19.11	Forest of Dean	5-4	AEK Boco
19.11	Cheltenham Civil Service	3-1	Chipping Sodbury Town
19.11	Oldland Abbotonians	3-6	St Nicholas
19.11	Abbeymead Rovers	1-1 (aet)	Cheltenham Town Development (Won 4-3 pens)
19.11	Frampton Rangers	0-2	Downend Flyers
19.11	St Nicholas Reserves	1-2	Almondsbury
19.11	Longlevens	1-1 (aet)	Bristol Ladies Union (Won 4-3 pens)
19.11	Forest Green Rovers	0-1	Cheltenham Town
Quarters			
18.02	Bristol Ladies Union	2-3	Almondsbury
18.02	Downend Flyers	0-2	Cheltenham Town
18.02	St Nicholas	Hw/o	Forest of Dean
18.02	Cheltenham Civil Service	3-1	Cheltenham Town Development
Semis			
18.03	Cheltenham Civil Service	Aw/o	Cheltenham Town
25.03	St Nicholas	4-2	Almondsbury
Final			
17.04	Cheltenham Town	0-1	St Nicholas

HAMPSHIRE FA COUNTY CUP 2017/18

1st Round

15.10	Alton	3-0	Shanklin
15.10	Eastleigh	8-0	Widbrook United
15.10	Moneyfields	6-1	Eversley & California
15.10	Southampton FC Women	2-1	Gosport Borough
15.10	AFC Portchester	2-11	Warsash Sports & Football Club
2nd Round			

19.11	Winchester City Flyers	0-7	Portsmouth
19.11	Team Solent	1-5	AFC Bournemouth CST
19.11	New Milton Town	3-4	Eastleigh
19.11	Fleet Town	Aw/o	Southampton Saints
19.11	Southampton FC Women	Hw/o	Mudeford Phoenix
19.11	Bournemouth Sports	Aw/o	Southampton Women
19.11	Alton	1-4	Warsash Wasps Sports & Football Club
26.11	Basingstoke Town	0-4	Moneyfields

Quarters

28.01	Southampton FC Women	4-1	Eastleigh
28.01	Warsash Wasps Sports & Football Club	0-10	Portsmouth
28.01	Moneyfields	0-2	Southampton Saints
28.01	AFC Bournemouth CST	0-3	Southampton Women

Semis

18.02	Southampton FC Women	0-4	Southampton Women*
18.02	Southampton Saints	0-3	Portsmouth

Final

28.03	Southampton FC	5-0	Portsmouth

*Southampton Women later expelled for fielding ineligible player. Southampton FC took their place in the final.

HERTFORDHIRE FA COUNTY CUP 2017/18

1st Round

15.10	BSC FC	1-3	Welwyn Pegasus (Adult) Sapphires
15.10	Wheathampstead Wanderers	Aw/o	Hemel Hempstead Town
15.10	Evergreen Eagles	Hw/o	Garston (Junior Section) U18
15.10	Garston (Senior Section) 2nd XI	1-14	Stevenage
15.10	BSC FC (Youth) U18	2-4	Hitchin Belles
15.10	Potters Bar United	2-1	Watton
15.10	Watford Development	0-3	Royston Town
15.10	Sherrardswood	6-3	Bedwell Rangers
15.10	Hoddesdon Town Owls	9-0	Welwyn Pegasus (Adult) Azures
15.10	Letchworth Garden City Eagles	0-4	Stevenage
15.10	Garston (Senior Section)	Hw/o	Hitchin Town

2nd **Round**

12.11	Welwyn Pegasus (Adult) Sapphires	2-3	Hemel Hempstead Town
12.11	Hitchin Belles	7-0	Potters Bar United
12.11	Hoddesdon Town Owls	5-3 aet	Stevenage Reserves
12.11	Hertford Town	2-3 aet	Colney Heath
12.11	Evergreen	Hw/o	Kings LangleyYouth U17 Belles
12.11	St Albans	4-2	Garston (Senior Section)
19.11	Evergeen Eagles	0-14	Stevenage
19.11	Royston Town	6-0	Sherrardswood

Quarters

03.12	Hitchin Belles	1-16	Royston Town
10.12	Evergreen	Aw/o	St Albans
07.01	Hemel Hempstead Town	0-3	Stevenage
07.01	Hoddesdon Town Owls (Won 3-1 on pens)	2-2	Colney Heath
Semis			
28.01	Stevenage	3-0	Royston Town
28.01	Hoddesdon Town Owls	5-2	St Albans
Final			
11.03	Stevenage	8-0	Hoddesdon Town Owls

ISLE OF MAN FA COUNTY CUP 2017/18

Semis			
20.01	Colby	2-4	Douglas Royal
20.01	Corinthians	4-0	Peel
Final			
28.01	Corinthians	2-1	Douglas Royal

JERSEY FA ZENITH CUP 2017/18

10.09	JTC Jersey Wanderers	2-3	St Lawrence
24.09	Grouville	1-6	JTC Jersey Wanderers
05.10	Grouville	1-0	St Peter
08.10	St Peter	1-5	St Lawrence
15.10	St Peter	0-5	JTC Jersey Wanderers
15.10	St Lawrence	2-1	Grouville

		P	W	D	L	Pts
1	St Lawrence	3	3	0	0	9
2	JTC Jersey Wanderers	3	2	0	1	6
3	Grouville	3	1	0	2	3
4	St Peter	3	0	0	3	0

KENT FA COUNTY CUP 2017/18

Preliminary Round			
17.09	Ashford	2-1	Maidstone United
17.09	Faversham Strike Force	3-2	Long Lane
17.09	Phoenix Sports	4-1	Cray Valley (PM)
17.09	Kent Football United	3-0	Glebe
24.09	Margate	1-8	Herne Bay
24.09	Meridian	8-0	Swale
24.09	Anchorians	1-7	Aylesford
24.09	Dartford	0-9	London Kent Football United
1st Round			
15.10	Meridian		Bye
15.10	Ashford		Bye
15.10	Aylesford		Bye
15.10	Kent Football United		Bye

15.10	London Kent Football United		Bye
15.10	Faversham Strike Force	2-3	Phoenix Sports
15.10	Herne Bay		Bye
Quarters			
19.11	Meridian	4-3	Phoenix Sports
19.11	Kent Football United	6-3	Aylesford
19.11	Herne Bay	0-8	Gillingham
26.11	London Kent Football United	8-2	Ashford
Semis			
21.01	Meridian	0-3	Kent Football United
21.01	London Kent Football United	2-1	Gillingham
Final			
26.03	Kent Football United (Won 4-2 pens)	2-2 (aet)	London Kent Football United

LANCASHIRE FA COUNTY CUP 2017/18

1st Round

17.09	Bolton Wanderers	4-2	Morecambe
17.09	Chorley	Hw/o	Haslingden
17.09	Fylde	10-0	Bury FC
17.09	Barrow Celtic Juniors Comets	0-16	Fleetwood Town Wrens
17.09	Sir Tom Finney FC	10-3	Wythenshawe Amateurs (Juniors)
24.09	Blackburn Community Sports Club	0-5	Blackburn Rovers
24.09	Bury FC (Youth) U18	0-11	Blackpool FC
24.09	Accrington Stanley CT	0-11	Burnley
Quarters			
08.10	Blackburn Rovers	2-1	Fylde
08.10	Sir Tom Finney FC	Aw/o	Fleetwood Town Wrens
15.10	Chorley	3-0	Blackpool FC
22.10	Burnley	0-4	Bolton Wanderers
Semis			
17.12	Blackburn Rovers	5-1	Bolton Wanderers
14.01	Fleetwood Town Wrens	0-6	Chorley
Final			
10.05	Blackburn Rovers	6-1	Chorley

LEICESTERSHIRE & RUTLAND FA COUNTY CUP 2017/18

1st Round

15.10	Loughborough Foxes Vixens	Hw/o	Cosby United Youth & Juniors
15.10	Heather St John's	1-8	Loughborough Students 1st XI
15.10	Leicester City Women Development	3-1	Leicester City Ladies
15.10	Loughborough Foxes	17-0	Castle Donington
15.10	AFC Leicester Girls & Ladies	Hw/o	Ketton
Quarters			
19.11	Leicester City Women Development	1-3	Loughborough Foxes
19.11	Leicester City Women	Hw/o	Desford
19.11	Loughborough Foxes Vixens	0-4	Oadby & Wigston
19.11	AFC Leicester Girls & Ladies (Won 6-5 on pens)	2-2	Loughborough Students 1st XI

436

28.01	Leicester City Women	3-0	Loughborough Foxes
28.01	AFC Leicester Girls & Ladies	1-0	Oadby & Wigston
Final			
10.04	Leicester City Women	15-0	AFC Leicester Girls & Ladies

LINCOLNSHIRE FA COUNTY CUP 2017/18

1st Round

19.11	Cleethorpes Town	4-1	HBW United
19.11	Lincoln Moorlands-Railway	7-1	Gainsborough Trinity
19.11	Sleaford Town	0-2	Hykeham Town
19.11	Appleby Frodingham JFC	0-3	Grimsby Borough

Quarters

21.01	Swineshead Institute	Aw/o	Boston United
21.01	Louth Old Boys	1-5	Cleethorpes Town
21.01	Hykeham Town	2-3 aet	Grimsby Borough
28.01	Nettleham	4-0	Lincoln Moorlands-Railway

Semis

18.02	Boston United	0-6	Nettleham
25.02	Cleethorpes Town	0-7	Grimsby Borough

Final

06.05	Nettleham	7-0	Grimsby Borough

LIVERPOOL COUNTY FA SENIOR CUP 2017/18

Quarters

19.11	City of Liverpool	2-14	Merseyrail
19.11	Mossley Hill Athletic	5-1	MSB Woolton

Semis

21.01	Liverpool Marshall Feds	12-0	Burscough Dynamo
28.01	Mossley Hill Athletic (Won 6-5 pens)	2-2	Merseyrail

Final

10.05	Liverpool Marshall Feds	1-0	Mossley Hill Athletic

LONDON FA CAPITAL CUP - INTERMEDIATE 2017/18

1st Round

15.10	Victoire	0-10	New London Lionesses
15.10	Tottenham Hotspur 3rd XI	3-2	Hackney
15.10	Godalming Town	4-2	QPR Development
15.10	Ashford Town (Middlesex)	4-3	Whyteleafe
15.10	Hampton & Richmond Borough	0-4	AFC Wimbledon Reserves
15.10	Crawley Wasps	0-2	Clapham United
15.10	Charlton Athletic Development	4-0	Denham United Reserves
29.10	University College London	5-1	Regents Park Rangers

2nd Round

19.11	Crystal Palace Reserves	3-2	Godalming Town

19.11	Colne Valley	3-1	Brentford
19.11	West Ham United Development	7-2	QPR Reserves
19.11	Kingstonian	0-1	Charlton Athletic Development
19.11	Ashford Town (Middlesex)	4-3	New London Lionesses
19.11	AFC Wimbledon Reserves	Hw/o	Northwood
19.11	Clapham United	4-6	Tottenham Hotspur 3rd XI
19.11	Hampstead	1-3	University College London
Quarters			
18.02	AFC Wimbledon Reserves (Won 3-2 on pens)	1-1	University College London
18.02	Ashford Town (Middlesex)	Aw/o	Colne Valley
18.02	Crystal Palace Reserves	1-2	Tottenham Hotspur 3rd XI
18.02	West Ham United Development	6-2	Charlton Athletic Development
Semis			
25.03	Colne Valley (Won 6-5 on pens)	4-4	Tottenham Hotspur 3rd XI
25.03	AFC Wimbledon Reserves	4-1	West Ham United Development
Final			
29.04	AFC Wimbledon Reserves	5-0	Colne Valley

MANCHESTER FA COUNTY CUP 2017/18

1st Round

24.09	Flixton Juniors	Hw/o	Droylsden Youth Centre OA
24.09	Manchester Rovers	0-5	Beechfield United
24.09	Curzon Ashton FC (Tameside)	9-3	Sale FC Summer League
24.09	Sale United	Aw/o	AFC Urmston Meadowside
24.09	Cadishead Rhinos FC Open Age	6-4	Moston Brook 5th XI
24.09	Manchester Stingers	19-0	Swinton
24.09	FC United of Manchester	3-1	Didsbury
24.09	Barrhill Women's Summer League	8-0	Reddish North End

2nd Round

	Beechfield United		Bye
	Manchester Stingers		Bye
15.10	West Didsbury & Chorlton	10-1	Flixton Juniors
	AFC Urmston Meadowside		Bye
	Barrhill Women's Summer League		Bye
	Cadishead Rhinos FC Open Aged		Bye
	Curzon Ashton FC (Tameside)		Bye
	FC United of Manchester		Bye
Quarters			
21.01	Beechfield United	0-8	FC United of Manchester
21.01	Manchester Stingers	Hw/o	Cadishead Rhinos FC Open Aged
21.01	Curzon Ashton FC (Tameside)	7-2	Barrhill Women's Summer League
04.02	AFC Urmston Meadowside	0-6	West Didsbury & Chorlton
Semis			
18.02	FC United of Manchester	3-0	West Didsbury & Chorlton
07.03	Manchester Stingers	3-2	Curzon Ashton FC (Tameside)
Final			
13.05	FC United of Manchester	2-0	Manchester Stingers

MIDDLESEX FA CAPITAL CUP – SENIOR SECTION 2017/18

1st Round

22.10	Haringey Borough	2-5	Enfield Town
22.10	Parkwood Rangers	2-7	Charlton Athletic
22.10	Actonians	0-2	Leyton Orient
22.10	QPR	1-0	AFC Phoenix
22.10	Carshalton Athletic	Hw/o	Camden Town
22.10	Crystal Palace	3-1	West Ham United

Quarters

19.11	Enfield Town	0-6	Charlton Athletic
19.11	Leyton Orient	4-1	Denham United
19.11	Fulham FC Foundation	0-1	QPR
19.11	Carshalton Athletic	0-5	Crystal Palace

Semis

18.02	QPR	0-2	Crystal Palace
25.02	Charlton Athletic	3-2	Leyton Orient

Final

06.05	Charlton Athletic	2-1	Crystal Palace

NORFOLK FA COUNTY CUP 2017/18

1st Round

15.10	Wymondham Town	3-1	Thorpe United

2nd Round

19.11	Stalham Town	0-8	Wymondham Town
19.11	Bure Valley Wildcats	2-1 aet	Freethorpe
19.11	North Walsham Youth	Hw/o	Tavern Old Boys
19.11	Sprowston	Hw/o	Gorleston Rangers
19.11	Toftwood United	Aw/o	Aylsham
19.11	King's Lynn Town	2-1	Norwich City
19.11	Gorleston	0-7	Acle United

Quarters

14.01	North Walsham Youth	1-3	King's Lynn Town
14.01	Sprowston	7-0	Bure Valley Wildcats
14.01	Aylsham	Aw/o	Acle United
14.01	Fakenham Town	0-15	Wymondham Town

Semis

18.03	Sprowston	0-7	Wymondham Town
25.03	King's Lynn	1-2	Acle United

Final

27.04	Acle United	2-3	Wymondham Town

NORTHAMPTONSHIRE FA COUNTY CUP 2017/18

1st Round

15.10	Rothwell Reserves	0-4	Rothwell
15.10	Blisworth	Hw/o	Corby Hellenic Fisher Youth
15.10	Roade	Hw/o	Spencer Community Trust JS

15.10	Northampton Town	5-0	Peterborough United
15.10	Corby Town	Hw/o	Crick Athletic Colts
15.10	Orton Rangers	Aw/o	Corby Stewart & Lloyds
15.10	Northampton Welland Valley	1-5	Peterborough United Reserves

2nd Round

19.11	Deanshanger Athletic	2-4	Moulton
19.11	Kettering Town	2-2	Thrapston Town (Won 5-4 on pens)
19.11	Corby Stewart & Lloyds	4-1	Woodford United
19.11	Peterborough United Reserves	3-1	Earls Barton United
19.11	Kettering FC Girls	1-2	Roade Ladies
19.11	Blisworth	1-7	Peterborough Northern Star
19.11	Rothwell	0-7	Northampton Town
26.11	Corby Town	Hw/o	Peterborough Northern Star Reserves

Quarters

28.01	Peterborough Northern Star	0-3	Thrapston Town
28.01	Peterborough United Reserves	1-12	Northampton Town
28.01	Corby Town	2-1	Moulton
04.02	Roade	4-0	Corby Stewart & Lloyds

Semis

11.02	Thrapston Town	2-3	Northampton Town
11.02	Roade	0-3	Corby Town

Final

29.04	Corby Town	0-4	Northampton Town

NORTH RIDING FA COUNTY CUP 2017/18

1st Round

21.01	Middlesbrough Reserves	Aw/o	York Railway Institute
21.01	Middlesbrough	Aw/o	Guisborough
28.01	Catterick Garrison Football Centre	Aw/o	Redcar Town

Quarters

18.02	York City	Hw/o	Brooklyn
18.02	York Railway Institute	3-3	Boro Rangers (Won 4-2 on pens)
18.02	Redcar Town	8-1	Guisborough
18.02	Poppleton	Hw/o	Cleveland

Semis

25.03	Poppleton	0-3	York City
25.03	Redcar Town	2-0	Boro Rangers

Final

08.04	York City	2-3	Redcar Town

NORTHUMBERLAND FA COUNTY CUP 2017/18

1st Round

15.10	Prudhoe Town	0-4	Cramlington United
15.10	Alnwick Town	Hw/o	Wallsend Boys' Club Reserves
15.10	Newbiggin Hall	Aw/o	Newcastle United

Quarters

19.11	Wallsend Boys' Club	0-5	Blyth Lions
19.11	Ashington Town	Aw/o	Newcastle United
19.11	Cramlington United	2-4	Alnwick Town
19.11	Bedlington	0-7	Newcastle United Reserves

Semis

18.02	Newcastle United Reserves	3-1	Alnwick Town
18.02	Newcastle United	9-0	Wallsend Boys' Club

Final

11.05	Newcastle United	2-0	Newcastle United Reserves

NOTTINGHAMSHIRE FA COUNTY CUP 2017/18

1st Round

22.10	Clifton All Whites	1-4	Market Warsop
22.10	Ollerton Town	2-3	Nottingham Forest
22.10	Radcliffe Olympic	3-1	Eastwood Community
22.10	Arnold Town	6-0	Rise Park
22.10	Mansfield Hosiery Mills	1-3	Nottingham Forest Reserves
22.10	Arnold Town Development	4-3	Eastwood Community Development
22.10	Bingham Town	2-5	Sherwood
01.11	Retford United	1-2	Teversal

Quarters

19.11	Nottingham Forest Reserves	0-11	Nottingham Forest
19.11	Arnold Town Development	2-5	Arnold Town
19.11	Teversal	0-8	Radcliffe Olympic
19.11	Sherwood	0-1	Market Warsop

Semis

18.02	Nottingham Forest	Hw/o	Arnold Town
18.02	Market Warsop	0-6	Radcliffe Olympic

Final

08.05	Radcliffe Olympic	1-2	Nottingham Forest

OXFORDSHIRE FA COUNTY CUP 2017/18

1st Round

22.10	Launton	1-3	Chinnor
22.10	Woodstock Town	0-5	Oxford City
22.10	Banbury United	Hw/o	Mansfield Road
22.10	Summertown Stars	0-8	Headington

Quarters

07.01	Chinnor Community Reds	Hw/o	Kidlington FC
07.01	Banbury United	1-3	Barton United
07.01	Chinnor	1-10	Oxford City
07.01	Headington	5-3	Carterton

Semis

18.02	Barton United	3-1	Headington
18.02	Chinnor Community Reds	0-19	Oxford City

Final

15.04	Barton United	0-9	Oxford City

SHEFFIELD & HALLAMSHIRE FA COUNTY CUP 2017/18

1st Round

15.10	Penistone Church	2-1	Handsworth
15.10	Sheffield United 2nd XI	2-3	Mexborough Athletic
15.10	Rovers Foundation	11-0	Swallownest Beighton
15.10	Millmoor Juniors	0-2	AFC Doncaster
15.10	Worsbrough Bridge Athletic	0-17	Huddersfield Town Development
15.10	Worksop Town JFC	3-1	Hemsworth Miners Welfare West H
15.10	Oughtibridge WMSC Development	2-6	Worksop Town
15.10	AFC Unity	0-14	Huddersfield Town Academy
15.10	Wakefield	Hw/o	Shaw Lane Aquaforce
15.10	Socrates (Adult)	2-4	Doncaster Belles
15.10	Dinnington Town	0-5	Oughtibridge WMSC

2nd **Round**

19.11	Sheffield Wednesday Development	4-1	Millmoor Juniors 2nd XI
19.11	Mexborough Athletic	1-8	Rovers Foundation
19.11	Sheffield Wednesday	2-6	Barnsley Reserves
19.11	Sheffield Wednesday Reserves	0-4	Penistone Church
19.11	Huddersfield Town Academy	2-4	AFC Doncaster
19.11	Doncaster Belles	5-1	Wickersley Youth
19.11	Wakefield	4-0	Worksop Town JFC
19.11	Worksop Town	2-8	Huddersfield Town Development
19.11	Oughtibridge WMSC	3-0	Hepworth United
26.11	Harworth Colliery	4-1	Dronfield Town Open Aged
26.11	Dearne & District	1-10	AFC Dronfield

3rd **Round**

17.12	AFC Doncaster	Aw/o	Huddersfield Town
17.12	Barnsley	Hw/o	AFC Dronfield
17.12	Doncaster Belles	1-2	Rotherham United
07.01	Rovers Foundation	18-2	Sheffield Wednesday Development
07.01	Oughtibridge WMSC	2-1	Sheffield United
07.01	Harworth Colliery	4-1	Steel City Wanderers
07.01	Wakefield	3-2	Barnsley Reserves
14.01	Penistone Church	1-5	Huddersfield Town Development

Quarters

21.01	Barnsley	Hw/o	Rovers Foundation
28.01	Rotherham United	1-6	Huddersfield Town Development
28.01	Huddersfield Town	8-0	Harworth Colliery
28.01	Oughtibridge WMSC	6-0	Wakefield

Semis

25.03	Huddersfield Town Development	0-1	Barnsley
25.03	Oughtibridge WMSC	1-2	Huddersfield Town

Final

15.05	Barnsley	0-3	Huddersfield Town

SHROPSHIRE FA COUNTY CUP 2017/18

1st Round

28.01	The New Saints	Hw/o	Shrewsbury Juniors

Quarters

21.01	Ellesmere Rangers	Hw/o	AFC Bridgnorth
11.02	Shifnal Town	1-2	The New Saints
11.02	The New Saints Reserves	0-2	AFC Telford United
11.02	Ludlow Town	Aw/o	Shrewsbury Town

Semis

11.03	Shrewsbury Town	2-1	AFC Telford
14.03	Ellesmere Rangers	0-9	The New Saints

Final

04.05	Shrewsbury Town	0-1	The New Saints

SOMERSET FA SENIOR CUP 2017/18

Quarters

15.10	Brislington	2-4	Larkhall Athletic
15.10	Frome Town	Aw/o	Keynsham Town

Semis

18.02	Larkhall Athletic	3-0	Bishops Lydeard
18.02	Hamilton	Aw/o	Keynsham Town

Final

03.05	Larkhall Athletic	0-3	Keynsham Town

STAFFORDSHIRE FA CHALLENGE CUP 2017/18

1st Round

15.10	Goldenhill Wanderers	0-3	Stoke City Development
15.10	Port Vale Open Age	2-1	Bradwell Belles
15.10	Pelsall Villa Colts	Hw/o	University of Wolverhampton
15.10	Shenstone Lionesses	Hw/o	Stone Dominoes
15.10	Wyrley Pumas	Hw/o	Pelsall Villa Colts Reserves
15.10	Abbey Hulton United	12-0	Goldenhill Wanderers Development
15.10	Stafford Town	2-7	Leek Town
29.10	Walsall	7-3	Walsall Wood Saints

2nd Round

19.11	Pelsall Villa Colts	2-5	Abbey Hulton United
19.11	Shenstone Lionesses	3-6	Wolverhampton Sporting Community
19.11	Sporting Khalsa Development	Hw/o	Walsall
19.11	Stoke City Development	4-0	Port Vale Open Age
19.11	Brereton Town	Aw/o	Stoke City
19.11	Florence	0-2	Wyrley Pumas
19.11	Leek Town	1-4	Sporting Khalsa
19.11	Wyrley	2-6	Stoke City Reserves

Quarters

17.12	Stoke City	2-1	Stoke City Reserves
17.12	Sporting Khalsa	18-0	Wyrley Pumas

07.01	Wolverhampton Sporting Community	4-0	Sporting Khalsa Development
14.01	Abbey Hulton United	1-5	Stoke City Development
Semis			
01.02	Stoke City Development	0-7	Stoke City
04.02	Sporting Khalsa	5-0	Wolverhampton Sporting Community
Final			
06.03	Sporting Khalsa	0-2	Stoke City

SUFFOLK FA COUNTY CUP 2017/18

1st Round

15.10	Lowestoft Town	Hw/o	Brandon Town Youth
15.10	AFC Sudbury (Sun)	Hw/o	Coplestonians
15.10	Ipswich Town	11-0	Walsham Le Willows
15.10	Beccles Town	1-13	Brantham Athletic (Sun)

2nd **Round**

19.11	Kirkley & Pakefield (Sun)	0-9	AFC Sudbury (Sun)
19.11	Ipswich Athletic Youth	0-14	Ipswich Town Development
19.11	Ipswich Wanderers	9-0	AFC Kesgrave
19.11	East Bergholt United	3-3	Brantham Athletic (Sun) (Won 4-3 on pens)
19.11	Leiston St Margarets	Hw/o	Lowestoft Town
19.11	Hadleigh United	Aw/o	Ipswich Town
19.11	Newmarket Town Reserves	0-12	Bungay Town
19.11	Bacton United 89	0-4	Newmarket Town

Quarters

18.02	Newmarket Town	3-3	Ipswich Wanderers (Won 6-5 on pens)
18.02	AFC Sudbury (Sun)	2-0	Ipswich Town Development
18.02	Ipswich Town	7-1	Bungay Town
18.02	Leiston St Margarets	5-2	Brantham Athletic (Sun)

Semis

| 25.03 | Leiston St Margarets | 0-5 | AFC Sudbury (Sun) |
| 25.03 | Ipswich Town | 7-0 | Ipswich Wanderers |

Final

| 07.05 | AFC Sudbury (Sun) | 1-5 | Ipswich Town |

SURREY FA CAPITAL CUP – JUNIOR SECTION 2017/18

1st Round

15.10	Abbey Rangers (Won 4-3 on pens)	2-2	Larkspur Rovers
15.10	Wandsworth Borough	0-10	AFC Phoenix Reserves
15.10	Carshalton Athletic Development	4-0	Sutton United Reserves
15.10	Guildford Saints	1-7	Milford & Witley
15.10	UCL Academicals London Academical	Hw/o	Wanderers
15.10	Royal Free Hospital School Med	0-2	Clapham United Reserves
15.10	Hampstead Development	1-3	Tower Hamlets
15.10	Tower Hamlets Reserves	Hw/o	Camden Town 2nd XI

15.10	Balham Panthers	6-0	Brentford Development
15.10	Harefield	Hw/o	London City (Middx)
15.10	Tooting & Mitcham	8-3	South London
15.10	South London Laces	3-2	Sutton United
15.10	Crystal Palace Development	Hw/o	Kent Football United
15.10	AFC Phoenix Development	0-6	Islington Borough
15.10	Alexandra Park	Hw/o	Tottenham Hotspur U18
15.10	Comets	Hw/o	Hampstead (Youth) U18
15.10	Denham United 3rd XI	4-0	Enfield Town Reserves
15.10	Tuff (Youth) U18	Aw/o	L.O.A.S.S. (Youth) U18
15.10	Peckham Town	7-0	Hackney Reserves
15.10	Mole Valley Girls U18	7-0	Crystal Palace (Youth) U18 Reds
15.10	Actonians Development	Hw/o	AFC Stoke Newington
15.10	Baldon Sports	1-1	Academy Dynamos (Won 4-2 on pens)

2nd Round

19.11	L.O.A.S.S. (Youth) U 18	0-4	Islington Borough
19.11	Beecholme Belles U18 Blues	1-3	Mole Valley U18
19.11	Alexandra Park	1-3	UCL Academicals London Academical
19.11	Carshalton Athletic Development	4-4	Crystal Palace Development (Won 7-6 on pens)
19.11	AFC Wimbledon Development	1-7	South London Laces
19.11	Woking	2-0	Milford & Witley
19.11	Abbey Rangers	Hw/o	Hampton & Richmond Borough Reserves
19.11	Tower Hamlets Reserves	Aw/o	Leyton Orient Development
19.11	Peckham Town	4-0	Tower Hamlets
19.11	Balham Panthers	1-3	Clapham United Reserves
19.11	Academy Dynamos	0-3	Comets
19.11	Actonians Development	0-3	Denham United 3rd XI
19.11	Wealdstone	2-0	Actonians Reserves
19.11	Harefield	0-4	Headstone Manor
19.11	Godalming Town Development	Hw/o	Westside
19.11	Tooting & Mitcham	0-2	AFC Phoenix Reserves

3rd Round

17.12	Mole Valley U18	2-1	Godalming Town Development
17.12	Wealdstone	0-5	South London Laces
17.12	Islington Borough	2-0	UCL Academicals London Academical
17.12	AFC Phoenix Reserves	4-2	Comets
28.01	Woking	0-2	Abbey Rangers
28.01	Headstone Manor	2-0	Denham United 3rd XI
28.01	Crystal Palace Development	1-3	Leyton Orient Development
11.02	Clapham United Reserves	1-6	Peckham Town

Quarters

18.02	Headstone Manor	P-P	Leyton Orient Development
18.02	Islington Borough	4-1	Peckham Town
18.02	Abbey Rangers	0-2	AFC Phoenix Reserves
25.02	South London Laces (Won 4-3 on pens)	2-2	Mole Valley U18

Semis

25.03	Islington Borough	1-2	AFC Phoenix Reserves

22.04	South London Laces	8-1	Headstone Manor

Final

29.04	AFC Phoenix Reserves	4-0	South London Laces

SUSSEX FA CHALLENGE CUP 2017/18

Quarters

17.12	Crawley Wasps	2-0	Chichester City Development
17.12	Worthing	2-3	Brighton & Hove Albion Development
17.12	Bexhill United	0-15	Lewes
07.01	Eastbourne	2-1	Eastbourne Town

Semis

24.01	Brighton & Hove Albion Development	1-4	Lewes
11.02	Eastbourne	0-2	Crawley Wasps

Final

22.03	Crawley Wasps	0-4	Lewes

WEST RIDING FA COUNTY CUP 2017/18

1st Round

15.10	Lower Hopton	5-3	Bradford Park Avenue
15.10	Ripon City	0-13	Leeds United
15.10	Harrogate Railway (Won 5-4 on pens)	3-3	Farsley Celtic Reserves
15.10	Tyersal	Hw/o	Amaranth Juniors
15.10	Brighouse Town	2-2	Bradford City (Won 4-2 on pens)
15.10	Ossett Albion	4-1	Clifton Rangers
15.10	Leeds United Reserves	7-0	Republica Internationale
15.10	Castleford White Rose	1-3	Altofts
15.10	Harrogate Town	12-2	OssettTown Juniors
15.10	Brighouse Athletic	0-6	Guiseley Vixens
22.10	Yorkshire Amateur	0-4	Farsley Celtic
29.10	Wetherby Athletic	2-3	Brayton Belles

2nd **Round**

19.11	Lower Hopton	3-5	Leeds United
19.11	Farsley Celtic	6-1	Harrogate Railway
19.11	Tyersal	0-5	Bradford City
19.11	Silsden AFC	1-2	Thackley AFC
19.11	Ilkley Town Juniors	Hw/o	Guiseley Vixens Reserves
19.11	Ossett Albion	0-5	Leeds United Reserves
19.11	Altofts	4-0	Brayton Belles
19.11	Harrogate Town	0-2	Guiseley Vixens

Quarters

17.12	Leeds United	1-1	Farsley Celtic (Won 6-5 on pens)
17.12	Bradford City	15-0	Thackley AFC
07.01	Ilkley Town Juniors	0-9	Leeds United Reserves
07.01	Altofts	Aw/o	Guiseley Vixens

Semis

14.03	Farsley Celtic	0-2	Bradford City

| 21.03 | Leeds United Reserves | 0-4 | GuiseleyVixens |

Final

| 02.05 | Bradford City | 1-3 | Guiseley Vixens |

WILTSHIRE FA COUNTY CUP 2017/18

1st Round

01.10	Trowbridge Town (Saturday)	2-0	Marlborough Town
01.10	FC Chippenham Youth	1-9	Swindon Town (Sun) Development
01.10	The Market Lavington & Easterton Unite	0-21	Wootton Bassett Town

Quarters

03.12	Trowbridge Town (Saturday)	2-1	Melksham Town
03.12	Wootton Bassett	6-2	Laverstock & Ford
03.12	Swindon Spitfires	6-1	Salisbury
03.12	Swindon Town (Sun) Development	6-0	Swindon Supermarine

Semis

| 11.03 | Swindon Spitfires | 0-7 | Wootton Bassett Town |
| 25.03 | Trowbridge Town (Saturday) | 2-4 | Swindon Town (Sun) Development |

Final

| 15.04 | Wootton Bassett Town | 2-0 | Swindon Town (Sun) Development |

WORCESTERSHIRE FA SUNDAY CUP 2017/18

1st Round

10.09	Worcester United	1-0	Wyre Forest Phoenix
17.09	Welland	9-3	Droitwich Spa Belles
17.09	Kingfisher	2-3	TDMS
17.09	Cookley Sports	10-0	Areley Kings
17.09	Kidderminster Harriers Reserves	3-3	Bartestree (Won 4-2 on pens)

Quarters

15.10	Worcester United	Aw/o	Kidderminster Harriers
15.10	Welland	2-4	Droitwich Spa
15.10	Nunnery Wood	1-4	TDMS
15.10	Cookley Sports	2-1	Bartestree

Semis

| 19.11 | Kidderminster Harriers | 5-0 | Droitwich Spa |
| 19.11 | TDMS | 1-1 | Cookley Sports (Won 4-3 on pens) |

Final

| 29.04 | Kidderminster Harriers | 3-1 | Cookley Sports |